THE ROUTLEDGE
HANDBOOK OF PHILOSOPHY
OF TEMPORAL EXPERIENCE

Experience is inescapably temporal. But how do we experience time? Temporal experience is a fundamental subject in philosophy – according to Husserl, the most important and difficult of all. Its puzzles and paradoxes were of critical interest from the Early Moderns through to the Post-Kantians. After a period of relative neglect, temporal experience is again at the forefront of debates across a wealth of areas, from philosophy of mind and psychology, to metaphysics and aesthetics.

The Routledge Handbook of Philosophy of Temporal Experience is an outstanding reference source to the key debates in this exciting subject area and represents the first collection of its kind. Comprising nearly 30 chapters by a team of international contributors, the *Handbook* is organized into seven clear parts:

- Ancient and early modern perspectives
- Nineteenth and early twentieth-century perspectives
- The structure of temporal experience
- Temporal experience and the philosophy of mind
- Temporal experience and metaphysics
- Empirical perspectives
- Aesthetics

Within each part, key topics concerning temporal experience are examined, including canonical figures such as Locke, Kant and Husserl; extensionalism, retentionalism and the specious present; interrelations between temporal experience and time, agency, dreaming, and the self; empirical theories of perceiving and attending to time; and temporal awareness in the arts including dance, music and film.

The Routledge Handbook of Philosophy of Temporal Experience is essential reading for students and researchers in philosophy of mind and psychology. It is also extremely useful for those in related fields such as metaphysics, phenomenology and aesthetics, as well as for psychologists and cognitive neuroscientists.

Ian Phillips is Associate Professor and Gabriele Taylor Fellow at St. Anne's College, Oxford University, UK, and a Visiting Research Scholar in the Program in Cognitive Science at Princeton University, USA. He is also an Editor for *Mind & Language* and a Consulting Editor for *Timing & Time Perception*.

ROUTLEDGE HANDBOOKS IN PHILOSOPHY

Routledge Handbooks in Philosophy are state-of-the-art surveys of emerging, newly refreshed, and important fields in philosophy, providing accessible yet thorough assessments of key problems, themes, thinkers, and recent developments in research.

All chapters for each volume are specially commissioned, and written by leading scholars in the field. Carefully edited and organized, *Routledge Handbooks in Philosophy* provide indispensable reference tools for students and researchers seeking a comprehensive overview of new and exciting topics in philosophy. They are also valuable teaching resources as accompaniments to textbooks, anthologies, and research-orientated publications.

Recently published:

The Routledge Handbook of Epistemic Injustice
Edited by Ian James Kidd, José Medina and Gaile Pohlhaus

The Routledge Handbook of Philosophy of Pain
Edited by Jennifer Corns

The Routledge Handbook of Brentano and the Brentano School
Edited by Uriah Kriegel

The Routledge Handbook of Collective Intentionality
Edited by Marija Jankovic and Kirk Ludwig

The Routledge Handbook of Libertarianism
Edited by Jason Brennan, Bas van der Vossen, and David Schmidtz

The Routledge Handbook of Metaethics
Edited by Tristram McPherson and David Plunkett

The Routledge Handbook of Philosophy of Memory
Edited by Sven Bernecker and Kourken Michaelian

THE ROUTLEDGE HANDBOOK OF PHILOSOPHY OF TEMPORAL EXPERIENCE

Edited by
Ian Phillips

LONDON AND NEW YORK

First published 2017
by Routledge

2 Park Square, Milton Park, Abingdon, Oxfordshire OX14 4RN
52 Vanderbilt Avenue, New York, NY 10017

Routledge is an imprint of the Taylor & Francis Group, an informa business

First issued in paperback 2019

British Library Cataloguing-in-Publication Data
A catalogue record for this book is available from the British Library

Library of Congress Cataloging-in-Publication Data
Names: Phillips, Ian, 1980- editor.
Title: The Routledge handbook of philosophy of temporal
      experience / edited by Ian Phillips.
Description: 1 [edition]. | New York : Routledge, 2017. | Series:
      Routledge handbooks in philosophy | Includes bibliographical
      references and index.
Identifiers: LCCN 2016052359| ISBN 9781138830745
      (hardback : alk. paper) | ISBN 9781315269641 (e-book)
Subjects: LCSH: Experience. | Time.
Classification: LCC B105.E9 R68 2017 | DDC 115—dc23
LC record available at https://lccn.loc.gov/2016052359

ISBN: 978-1-138-83074-5 (hbk)
ISBN: 978-0-367-37061-9 (pbk)

Typeset in Bembo
by Swales & Willis Ltd, Exeter, Devon, UK

CONTENTS

Contents

FIGURES

CONTRIBUTORS

Holly Andersen is an associate professor at Simon Fraser University in Burnaby, British Columbia, Canada. She works on areas including time consciousness and the relationship between temporal experience and time in physics, and on issues in philosophy of science related to causation, explanation and representation.

Aili Bresnahan is a former professional-level ballet dancer who is an assistant professor of Philosophy at the University of Dayton, USA. Her primary area of research specialization is in the philosophy of dance.

John B. Brough is Emeritus Professor of Philosophy at Georgetown University, USA. He has written essays on temporality, aesthetics, representation and imaging, and is the translator of *Husserliana Volume X* on time-consciousness and of *Husserliana Volume XXIII*, which collects Husserlian texts on memory, image-consciousness and phantasy. He is co-editor of *The Many Faces of Time*.

Scott W. Brown is Professor of Psychology at the University of Southern Maine, USA whose research concerns the role of attentional resources in time perception. His most recent papers involve the relation between timing and executive cognitive functions including memory updating, attentional switching and inhibitory control.

Philippe Chuard teaches philosophy at Southern Methodist University, USA. His work in the philosophy of perception (temporal experiences, non-conceptual content, phenomenal sorites) and epistemology (epistemic norms) has appeared in *Philosophers' Imprint*, *Noûs*, *Philosophical Studies*, *The Australasian Journal of Philosophy* and *The Journal of Consciousness Studies*. He is presently working on a book on the snapshot conception of temporal experiences.

Thomas Crowther is Associate Professor of Philosophy at the University of Warwick, UK. He is the author of several articles on the philosophy of mind and metaphysics. His research is mainly focused on perception and temporal ontology.

Barry Dainton is Professor of Philosophy at the University of Liverpool, UK. He works mainly in metaphysics and the philosophy of mind, and is the author of *Stream of Consciousness* (2nd edition, Routledge, 2006), *The Phenomenal Self* (Oxford University Press, 2008), *Time and Space* (2nd edition, Routledge, 2010) and *Self* (Penguin, 2014). He is also co-editor (with Howard Robinson) of *The Bloomsbury Companion to Analytic Philosophy* (2014).

Natalja Deng is Assistant Professor of Philosophy at Underwood International College, Yonsei University, Seoul, South Korea. She works mostly in metaphysics and philosophy of religion. She has held postdoctoral positions in Cambridge, Notre Dame, and Geneva.

Katherine Dunlop is Associate Professor of Philosophy at the University of Texas, USA. A main area of her research is Kant's theoretical philosophy. She is particularly interested in the relationship between Kant's account of our cognitive faculties and his views concerning mathematical and scientific knowledge.

Lorne Falkenstein is Professor of Philosophy at Western University in London, Canada. He works on issues surrounding theories of space, time, perception and mental representation in the early modern period and has published on Berkeley, Hume, Reid, Condillac and Kant. He is co-editor of *Essays and Treatises on Philosophical Subjects* (Broadview Press, 2013), a new edition of *Hume's An Enquiry Concerning Human Understanding* (Broadview Press, 2011) and other writings.

Akiko M. Frischhut is Assistant Professor of Philosophy at Akita International University, Japan. Previously, she was Postdoctoral Researcher at the University of Geneva, Switzerland. She works on metaphysics and the philosophy of mind, especially the nature and experience of time.

Geoffrey Gorham is Professor and Chair of Philosophy at Macalester College, USA and Resident Fellow of the Minnesota Center for Philosophy of Science, University of Minnesota, USA. He is co-editor of *The Language of Nature: Reassessing the Mathematization of Natural Philosophy in the Seventeenth Century* (University of Minnesota, 2016), and author of *Philosophy of Science: A Beginner's Guide* (Oneworld, 2009) as well as numerous articles on early modern philosophy and science.

Christoph Hoerl is Professor of Philosophy at the University of Warwick, UK. His research is mainly in the philosophy of mind, with a particular interest in philosophical questions about the nature of temporal experience, memory and the concepts in terms of which we think about time.

Alan Johnston is Professor of Psychology at the University of Nottingham, UK and Honorary Professor at University College London. He was previously Head of Psychology and Director of CoMPLEX at UCL. His work is focused on the perception of dynamic change from low-level temporal processing in vision to the encoding of facial action. He has published over 100 journal articles including three in *Nature* and six in *Current Biology*.

Mari Riess Jones is Professor Emerita from The Ohio State University, now currently affiliated with The University of California at Santa Barbara, USA. She has published on topics of attending and timing in psychology, developing a theory of dynamic attending.

Andrew Kania is Professor of Philosophy at Trinity University in San Antonio, USA. His principal research is in the philosophy of music, literature and film. He is the editor of *Memento*

(2009), in Routledge's series *Philosophers on Film*, and co-editor, with Theodore Gracyk, of *The Routledge Companion to Philosophy and Music* (2011).

Robin Le Poidevin is Professor of Metaphysics at the University of Leeds, UK. He was the 2007 Stanton Lecturer at Cambridge and the 2012 Richardson Fellow at Durham. Between 2010 and 2016 he was the editor of *Religious Studies*. He is co-editor of *The Routledge Companion to Metaphysics* (2009), and his publications include *Travels in Four Dimensions: The Enigmas of Space and Time* (Oxford University Press, 2003), and *The Images of Time: An Essay on Temporal Representation* (Oxford University Press, 2007).

Geoffrey Lee is Associate Professor of Philosophy at the University of California, Berkeley, USA. His research focuses on philosophy of mind and the foundations of cognitive science, including a special interest in the philosophical issues raised by temporal experience and temporal representation in the brain.

Carlos Montemayor is Associate Professor of Philosophy at San Francisco State University, USA. His research focuses on philosophy of mind and cognitive science. He is the author of *Minding Time: A Philosophical and Theoretical Approach to the Psychology of Time* (Brill, The Netherlands, 2013) and co-author (with Harry H. Haladjian) of *Consciousness, Attention, and Conscious Attention* (The MIT Press, 2015).

L. A. Paul is Eugene Falk Distinguished Professor of Philosophy at the University of North Carolina at Chapel Hill, USA and Professorial Fellow in the Arché Research Centre at the University of St Andrews, UK. Her research focuses on metaphysics, formal epistemology, philosophy of mind and philosophy of cognitive science. She is the author of *Transformative Experience* (Oxford University Press, 2014) and co-author (with Ned Hall) of *Causation: A User's Guide* (Oxford University Press, 2013).

Christopher Peacocke is the Johnsonian Professor of Philosophy at Columbia University, USA and a Fellow of the Institute of Philosophy, University of London, UK. He has interests across the philosophy of mind, metaphysics and epistemology. His books include *Being Known* (Oxford University Press, 1999), *Truly Understood* (Oxford University Press, 2008), and *The Mirror of the World* (Oxford University Press, 2014).

Michael Pelczar is Associate Professor of Philosophy at the National University of Singapore, specializing in metaphysics, philosophy of mind and philosophy of language. He is the author of *Sensorama: A Phenomenalist Analysis of Spacetime and Its Contents* (Oxford University Press, 2015).

Ian Phillips is Associate Professor of Philosophy and Gabriele Taylor Fellow at St. Anne's College, Oxford University, UK. From 2017 he will be a Visiting Research Scholar in the Program in Cognitive Science at Princeton University, USA. His work primarily focuses on topics at the intersection of philosophy of mind and cognitive science, most notably issues concerning temporal experience, the nature of perception and the science of consciousness.

Simon Prosser is Senior Lecturer in Philosophy at the University of St Andrews, UK. He is the author of *Experiencing Time* (Oxford University Press, 2016) and has published articles on a variety of issues in the philosophy of mind and metaphysics.

Oliver Rashbrook-Cooper is a lecturer in philosophy at Pembroke College, Oxford, UK. His primary area of research is philosophy of mind, with a particular focus on the unity of consciousness both at and over time.

Barbara M. Sattler works in the philosophy department at the University of St. Andrews, UK. Her main area of research is metaphysics and natural philosophy in the ancient Greek world, especially in the Presocratics, Plato and Aristotle, but she has also published papers in aesthetics. She is currently working on a book on ancient notions of time.

Matthew Soteriou is a professor of Philosophy at King's College London, UK. He is the author of *Disjunctivism* (Routledge, 2016), *The Mind's Construction: The Ontology of Mind and Mental Action* (Oxford University Press, 2013), and co-editor (with Lucy O'Brien) of *Mental Actions* (Oxford University Press, 2009).

Enrico Terrone is a postdoctoral research fellow at the University of Turin, Italy. He works on issues at the intersection of aesthetics, philosophy of mind and social ontology, especially issues concerning fiction and depiction. His primary area of research is philosophy of film.

ACKNOWLEDGEMENTS

My sincere thanks to all the contributors to this *Handbook* for their splendid (not to mention timely!) chapters. The field is richer for each and every one. Special thanks to Barry Dainton and Christoph Hoerl for their advice and enthusiasm about the project in its early stages. And, as in so many other things, to Hanna Pickard for her support and encouragement. I am also indebted to the exceptionally helpful and professional team at Routledge, in particular Tony Bruce, Adam Johnson and Rachel Singleton (of Swales & Willis), for all their patient assistance. I started work on the handbook whilst supported by a Leverhulme Trust Research Fellowship, which I gratefully acknowledge. I am also very grateful for the generous and friendly support of St. Anne's College where I have worked throughout the project.

INTRODUCTION

The significance of temporal experience

Ian Phillips

Experience is inescapably temporal. Not only is it of a restless world whose rhythms and ruptions our perceptual faculties have evolved to discern, it is also an occurrence which itself unfolds in time. These apparent platitudes set the stage for this handbook. For temporal experience is not merely pervasive: it is also puzzling in its own right – indeed many have wondered how it is even possible; probative of wider issues in metaphysics – not least concerning the nature of time itself; and provocative of a wide range of intriguing questions in other areas of philosophy – most notably in mind and aesthetics. It is also, of course, the focus of a great deal of work in the psychological sciences. Together with this introduction, the 27 contributions to this volume – all appearing in print for the first time – offer fresh and expert perspectives on diverse dimensions of temporal experience. Each testifies to the significance of temporal experience. The aim throughout has been not merely to present the contemporary debate but also to enrich it. Thus, for instance, the reader will find treatments of well-established topics and canonical figures intermingled with perspectives on less familiar issues and under-sung theorists. The primary (though far from exclusive) emphasis throughout is on our encounter with time in perception as opposed to memory. Memory deserves a handbook all of its own. It receives one in S. Bernecker and K. Michaelian (eds) *The Routledge Handbook of Philosophy of Memory*, forthcoming 2017. See also Phillips (forthcoming).

Part I: ancient and early modern perspectives

Parts I and II of the handbook explore historical approaches to temporal experience. We begin at the dawn of Western philosophy with early (pre-Platonic) Greek thought about time. Today we standardly think in terms of a single unified time (e.g. for us, "earlier than or simultaneous with" is a transitive and connected relation on the set of events). And whilst we recognize "several qualitatively different kinds of temporal experiences: simultaneity, successiveness, temporal order, duration, and temporal perspective" (Block and Zakay 2001: 59), we take such experiences all to present interrelated aspects of events locatable within this single time. However, as Barbara Sattler's fascinating chapter explores, for the early Greeks, such a unified conception was absent. Rather, the early Greek conception of time was fractionated, with temporal notions operating essentially in independence – each being "tied to different kinds of experiences". Arguably, this perspective has important implications for us as contemporary theorists. For it suggests, as Sattler puts it, that "our notion of time as unified is not something we gain directly from experience". In other words, however inevitable it may seem, we should be wary of taking our theoretical conception of time as the unadulterated deliverance of experience. This, of course, presses a central question of the handbook: how exactly do we experience time?

In Chapter 2, Geoffrey Gorham begins by charting thought about temporal experience from the Greeks (specifically, Aristotle) through to the Early Moderns. As he discusses, medieval philosophy largely follows the Aristotelian wisdom that time is inextricably tied both to motion and also to the mind. A conclusive break from this tradition does not occur until Descartes (1596–1650), who definitively rejects Aristotle's yoking of time to motion, and Newton (1643–1727), who famously declares: "Absolute, true, and mathematical time, of itself, and from its own nature, flows equably without relation to anything external" – not least the mind. Descartes and Newton, as well as Newton's great critic Leibniz, largely neglect our experience of time, however. Interest in temporal experience can be traced instead to the "decisive phenomenological turn . . . taken by the British empiricists Hobbes [1588–1679], Locke [1632–1704] and Berkeley [1685–1753]". As Gorham discusses in detail, these theorists not only turn our attention to our experiential relation to time, but each struggle to reconcile such experience with their favoured metaphysics: for Hobbes presentism, for Locke Newtonian absolutism and for Berkeley a radical solipsistic phenomenalism. As Part V of this volume explores, such struggles for reconciliation remain very much alive.

Chapters 3 and 4 turn to the more highly systematic treatments of time and temporal experience found in Hume (1711–1776) and Kant (1724–1804). In Chapter 3, Lorne Falkenstein discusses Hume's attempts to make sense of our experience of time – in particular Locke's vivid examples of flesh-cleaving cannon-bullets and rotating fiery coals – within his "atomist" framework on which our experience consists in a succession of simple and strictly durationless impressions. Here we find Hume grappling with an issue which runs throughout the volume, namely how successive experience can amount to experience of succession.

Many have thought that, for there to be any experience of succession, the elements experienced as successive would have to be presented *together* and so *simultaneously*. For example, James (1980: 628–629) notoriously declares, "A succession of feelings, in and of itself, is not a feeling of succession". He continues by quoting Volkmann with approval: "we come to this antithesis, that if A and B are to be represented *as occurring in succession* they must be *simultaneously represented*" (Volkmann 1875: §87). Following Miller (1984: 109), we can label this assumption the *Principle of Simultaneous Awareness* (PSA). (For recent discussion of the PSA, see Phillips 2010, Rashbrook-Cooper 2013a and Hoerl 2013b.) One familiar proposal is that to satisfy the PSA, the earlier element of the succession, A, must be presented in some form of memory alongside perceptual experience of the later element, B. Insofar as a theorist thinks of the resultant combination as a form of perceptual experience, this proposal is a version of what Dainton (2000, 2010) calls *retentionalism*: the view that our experiences of succession and change are themselves momentary (or extremely brief) but nonetheless have temporally extended contents. To anticipate later discussion, Dainton contrasts retentionalism with *cinematic* views which hold that neither our awareness itself nor its contents have temporal extension – and so sometimes deny that strictly speaking we experience succession at all, and with *extensionalist* views which hold that our experiences of succession and change are themselves extended in time and unfold alongside their contents.

Returning to Hume, Falkenstein discusses how Hume rejects Reid's distinctive attempt to conform to the PSA by appeal to memory. Instead, Falkenstein argues, Hume exploits his special non-cognitive notion of custom to distinguish between the perceptual situation of two individuals, both of whom are enjoying the same simple perception, but for only one of whom is that perception a part of a perception of succession. This leads Falkenstein to propose a "Humean" view of temporal experience which eschews James' "touted unity of consciousness" and holds that an "impression of succession" amounts to no more than our "feeling of confidence in the ability to recite the [relevant] succession of ideas without balking". (As Falkenstein notes, it is worth comparing and contrasting this perspective with that in Phillips 2010.)

In Chapter 4, Katherine Dunlop turns to the towering but obscure figure of Kant, leading us expertly through various interpretative approaches to his views about temporal experience in the *Critique*. Dunlop's primary focus is on the *Analogies of Experience* in which Kant argues that a necessary condition of cognizing temporal relations is that the events involved are subsumed under the concepts of cause and substance. Kant's argument here is apparently premised on the murky claim that time cannot be perceived in (or by) itself. As Dunlop discusses, on Guyer's important interpretation, Kant is here being driven by just the kinds of issues about unity discussed in relation to Hume and James. Thus, for Guyer, the "fundamental premise of Kant's transcendental theory of experience" (1987: 171) is the thesis that "each representation, insofar as it is contained in a single moment, can be nothing but absolute unity" (A99). Guyer reads this as claiming that each individual representation is completely independent from all others, and, since only one representation is ever present to us at a time, as implying (the apparently anti-realist view) that we are incapable of directly experiencing succession. Dunlop expresses simultaneous admiration and skepticism for this interpretation, noting, for one, the tension between Guyer's reading of the slogan that time cannot be perceived in (or by) itself, and Kant's earlier remarks about time in the *Aesthetic*, where Kant declares that time is an a priori intuition, and so apparently representable without concepts. How then to understand Kant's slogan? A promising possibility, suggests Dunlop, is that Kant is saying that temporal properties cannot be experienced apart from *spatial* properties.

Part II: nineteenth and early twentieth-century perspectives

In Part II we turn to the last heyday of theorizing about temporal experience – the late nineteenth and early twentieth century – and to four of its luminaries: Hodgson, Husserl, Bergson and Stern. (For discussion of debates about time-consciousness in the nineteenth century, see also Andersen and Grush 2009.) We begin in Chapter 5 with the now relatively obscure figure of Shadworth Hodgson (1832–1912). Although lately neglected, as Holly Andersen explains, Hodgson's work is pioneering and pivotal in the history of the philosophy of temporal experience. Looking backwards, Hodgson can be viewed as a great systematic philosopher in the tradition of Kant and Hume. Looking forward, he can be seen as the instigator of pragmatism, phenomenology and the "process"-oriented philosophies of Bergson and Whitehead. Indeed, as Andersen argues, he also has claim to being the "original neurophenomenologist".

In the preface to *The Principles of Psychology* (1890: vii), James recognizes Hodgson as due special gratitude for his inspirational writings (alongside Mill, Lotze, Renouvier and Wundt). And, partly channelled through James, Hodgson can be credited as the originator of ideas which remain at the core of modern thinking about temporal experience. James quotes extensively from Hodgson's *Philosophy of Reflection* in his famous chapter on the perception of time (James 1890: 607–8). And in the passages quoted we find Hodgson anticipating under the label of the "empirical present" the concept of the specious present made famous by James. Moreover, as Andersen brings out, Hodgson also augurs James in conceiving of experience "as a stream of consciousness consisting of many various currents, or a cable consisting of variously coloured strands, variously intertwined" (1898: 41). Andersen goes on to discuss how Hodgson clearly anticipates crucial features of Husserl's account (on which see Brough's Chapter 6), albeit with important differences. There are also striking affinities, I suggest, between Hodgson's insistence on the processive nature of experience, and the consequences for our thinking about the fine-grained structure of experience (see, especially 1898: chapter 2, §§5–6), and very recent work including O'Shaughnessy 2000, Soteriou 2007, Phillips 2011 and Crowther and Soteriou's Chapter 14. Andersen is thus surely right: Hodgson's *oeuvre* offers a "treasure trove of philo-sophical insights" for contemporary theorists of temporal experience.

In Chapter 6 we turn to Husserl (1859–1938) and his lifetime obsession with time-consciousness. As John Brough brings out, drawing on a profound knowledge of Husserl's corpus, Husserl starts out by seeking to avoid what he sees as two tempting mistakes which, combined, would imperil the very possibility of temporal experience. These mistakes are, on the one hand, the thought that we can *only* consciously experience what is present, and on the other, that we can *never* be consciously aware of the present since the present is an ephemeral instant, lost to the "past before consciousness can catch it". This leads Husserl to the view that we experience an extended, "living" present which contains the punctate now conceived of as the fountainhead of other modes of temporal appearance (varying degrees of just past, or soon to come). This yields Husserl's famous analysis of temporal awareness in terms of three inter-related aspects: primal impression, retention and protention. These ideas have strong affinities with Hodgson and James. They have also strongly influenced contemporary *retentionalist* views of temporal experience which echo not only Husserl's view that (as Brough puts it) "in a given moment of a temporally extended perception I can be presentationally aware of an entire tem-porally extended object", but also Husserl's intentionalism – his view that experience has an act–object structure, but *contra* the sense-datum theorist or naïve realist, that its objects need not exist in order for them to be the intended objects of experience. (On the connection between retentionalism and intentionalism see Hoerl's Chapter 13.)

Having set out these familiar ideas, Brough turns to an arguably more profound, and certainly more puzzling, dimension of Husserl's views. For Husserl insists that our experience is not only *of* time but is also "a temporal object itself" (1991: 239; cf. Phillips 2014a). Moreover, Husserl holds that in any act of awareness, say of a melody, it is not only the melody that we are aware of (though it is only the melody that we *perceive*). We are also aware of the unfolding experiential act which has the melody as its intentional object, as well as what Husserl calls the "absolute flow" which constitutes this awareness. Arguably, we can see Husserl here as grappling with the way in which experience's own temporal dimension, and our awareness of it, is explanatorily relevant to our experience of time – an idea downplayed by contemporary retentionalists but at the heart of rival extensionalist views. (For an excellent discussion of Husserl in connection with contem-porary theorizing, see Hoerl 2013a.) It is at this juncture that Husserl declares time-consciousness to be both the "most important" (1991: 346) but also the "most difficult of all phenomenological problems" (1991: 286).

In Chapters 7 and 8, Barry Dainton explores two other leading lights of turn of the century thinking about temporal experience: Bergson (1859–1941) and Stern (1871–1938). Dainton begins, in Chapter 7, with Bergson, once plausibly the most famous living philosopher yet whose influence has dramatically waned within analytical discourse. At the centre of Bergson's system, and Dainton's discussion, is Bergson's fundamental notion of *durée*. Bergson saw con-temporary physics as espousing a cinematic conception of the universe, one on which, as Dainton puts it, "the world ultimately consists of nothing more than a rapid succession of instantaneous momentary slices [or rather three-dimensional volumes]". Readers might here helpfully compare Kripke's *holographic hypothesis* – which clearly has Lewis' doctrine of *Humean Supervenience* in its intended ambit (see Kripke unpublished manuscript; Lewis 1986: xi). In Bergson's view such a conception, and likewise Humean and post-Humean atomism, cannot possibly accommodate the essential dynamism found in all experience. For Bergson, rather: "there is no feeling, no idea, no volition which is not underlying change every moment: if a mental state ceased to vary, its duration would cease to flow . . . we change without ceasing, and that the state itself is nothing but change" (1926 [1911]: 1–2). Again, readers might helpfully compare O'Shaughnessy's more focused suggestion that conscious experience is a process which is "occurrent to the core" (2000: 49). Bergson develops this thought by characterizing *durée* in terms of "qualitative multiplicity" or "heterogeneity": a form of diachronic unity in which each distinct moment of experience fuses with and penetrates the next. Dainton's discussion of these suggestive but obscure ideas leads him to ask whether Bergson is best understood as espousing a retentional or extensional model of consciousness. Dainton suggests that, in the end, Bergson's commitment to the seamless continuity of consciousness gives him grounds to adopt an extensionalist account.

Stern's contribution to the literature on temporal experience is limited to a single article, "Psychische Präsenzzeit" ("Mental Presence-Time") (2005 [1897]). Nonetheless, the article is important because it arguably offers the first clear articulation of an extensionalist view of temporal experience which (at least since Dainton 2000) stands as one of the major positions in the contemporary debate on temporal experience. Stern's intellectual predecessors such as Wundt, Brentano, Ward and Meinong took the view already mentioned that, for there to be an experience of succession, the elements experienced as successive would have to be presented together *and so simultaneously*. To accommodate this PSA, most took temporal experience to involve the simultaneous presentation of the present instant alongside "retentional" awareness of the immediate past. Stern rejects this retentionalist view as founded on mere "dogma" (2005: 313), declaring instead, that "mental events that play themselves out within a stretch of time can under circumstances form a unified and complex act of consciousness regardless of the non-simultaneity of individual parts" (2005: 315). Stern calls the stretches of time over which a complex but nonetheless unified act of consciousness can extend, its "presence-time", a notion closely related to that of the empirical or specious present. As Dainton sees it, discarding this dogma and so embracing an extensionalist view on which conscious experience can unfold alongside its objects, "brings the significant advantage that temporal consciousness need no longer be systematically misleading as to its own nature" (see further Dainton 2000, 2010; also, Phillips 2014a, 2014b).

As Dainton goes on to explore, Stern's article contains not just an articulation and defence of extensionalism but many other fascinating discussions, for instance of the ways in which anticipatory imagination and episodic memory are present within ordinary temporal experience – something Stern calls "projection"; of the different forms of perceptual memory; and whether and how "presence-times" can be measured empirically. It stands as testament to Stern's intellectual instincts that these issues have all since received significant attention within both psychology and philosophy.

Part III: the structure of temporal experience

Parts III and IV of the volume turn to the contemporary debate about temporal experience. Part III introduces and explores the central positions at the heart of that debate: cinematic or snapshot views, retentionalism and extensionalism. The reader should be warned, however, that whilst this way of framing the debate due to Dainton (2000, 2010) is both helpful and influential, its precise formulation and ultimate adequacy are much contested.

We begin in Chapter 9 with Philippe Chuard's vigorous defence of a snapshot view of temporal experience, a conception he regards as in the tradition of Locke, Reid and Hume (see Chapters 2 and 3). On Chuard's formulation, a snapshot view takes our streams of consciousness to reduce to a succession of very short, if not instantaneous, events none of which represents any temporal relations between non-simultaneous events. Chuard argues that perfunctory dismissals of this view are premature, and that the snapshot view has all the resources required to account for our phenomenology. (Chuard further calls into question the alleged explanatory merits of retentionalism and extensionalism.) The dialectic here is delicate. For many critics, the reason to reject the snapshot view is, as Dainton (2010) puts it, because the view lacks "any plausible account of how change and succession can feature in our immediate experience" and so "cannot be regarded as a promising form of realism". However, by "realism" Dainton means the view that "change, succession and persistence *can* be directly perceived or apprehended" (*ibid*; his emphasis). Yet it is not clear that Chuard wishes to offer a form of realism. As he writes: "the snapshot view isn't trying to explain how we do, in fact, have temporal experiences. We don't . . .". Nonetheless, Chuard does think the snapshot view can "account" for our phenomenology. It is just that it seeks to do so "without liberally assuming that [the phenomenological] appearances must be taken entirely at face value".

In Chapter 10, Oliver Rashbrook-Cooper turns to the debate between retentionalism (or what he calls "atomism") and extensionalism. For Rashbrook-Cooper, the critical distinction between these two positions is that for the atomist the temporal layout of experience itself has no explanatory role to play in accounting for our awareness of temporal features. In consequence, there is no reason why a very brief, or even instantaneous experience should not represent relations between non-simultaneous events which hold over a significantly longer period of time. In contrast, for the extensionalist, the temporal properties of experience *do* have an explanatory role to play in explaining our capacity to perceive temporal features. Thus, on some versions of extensionalism at least, our experience itself must have a temporal structure which corresponds to the temporal structure of its objects (e.g. Phillips 2014a, 2014b). Rashbrook-Cooper sides with extensionalism, arguing that only the extensionalist can simultaneously accommodate two fundamental and arguably intertwined features of temporal perceptual experience. These Rashbrook-Cooper labels (negative) Temporal Transparency and Temporal Presence. Negative Temporal Transparency is "the claim that one cannot distinguish between the temporal location of a perceptual experience and the apparent temporal location of its object" (cf. Soteriou 2013: 89–90). And Temporal Presence is the claim that perceptual experience "renders actions and *now*-judgements immediately appropriate" (cf. discussion in Crowther and Soteriou's Chapter 14, especially endnote 15).

In Chapter 11, Simon Prosser also grapples with the dispute between cinematic, retentionalist and extensionalist views. His perspective on these issues focuses specifically on the notion of the "specious present". As Prosser introduces it, this is the widely espoused doctrine, that "conscious experiences have temporally extended contents" or, put another way, "that the experienced present consists not of an instant, but of an extended interval of time". Prosser takes this idea to be a common commitment of both extensionalist and retentionalist views. As we have seen, it is a doctrine rejected by Chuard in Chapter 9. Prosser, however, sees no good argument for believing in the specious present so conceived. Instead, he finds in arguments for the specious present a tacit commitment to an "inner picture" model of perception. Prosser grants that, if experiences were like static pictures of a single moment in time, then they could not depict motion or change (an issue explored in detail in Chapter 24). Prosser, however, thinks that we have no good reason to accept any such model of perception and so no reason to think that just because an experience concerns only a single moment in time that it could not attribute motion or change to that point in time (cf. Johnston's discussion of motion perception in Chapter 21). In this way, Prosser develops a *dynamic snapshot theory* which unlike Chuard's "static" snapshot theory claims to account for the phenomenology of motion and change experience in a genuinely "realist" fashion.

In Chapter 12, Geoffrey Lee turns to another foundational issue concerning the nature of temporal experience, namely whether (and, if so, in what sense) there is such a thing as "subjective time". Lee approaches this issue by investigating whether there can be inter-subjective phenomenal variation in respect of what Lee terms "rate of temporal flow", despite there being no illusion. Such a possibility is, as Lee points out, not unintuitive. For example, when we try to imagine how a human being whose neuro-cognitive processes have been uniformly sped up (or a hummingbird or mayfly) might experience various events, there is a strong pull towards thinking that they would experience the events in much the same way that we would experience slower or longer-lived events. However, it is not obvious how to make sense of this intuition consistent with the absence of illusion. Lee discusses various tempting approaches here, including a simple account on which properties such as duration are experienced as relative to the rate of some internal process. As his probing discussion brings out, however, there are serious difficulties with such proposals and so a puzzle remains as to how to understand our experience of duration (and rate of change, etc.) in such a way which allows for inter-subjective phenomenal variation in the absence of illusion.

Part IV: temporal experience and the philosophy of mind

How do different perspectives on temporal experience interact with other debates in philosophy? One rich source of such interaction is in relation to issues in the philosophy of mind. This provides the unifying theme of Part IV of the handbook which continues many of the foundational discussion of Part III. In Part V, we turn to another rich seam of engagement, namely the relationship between temporal experience and views in metaphysics.

In Chapter 13, Christoph Hoerl argues that there is an intimate relationship between the two rival views which he sees as the most serious contenders for providing an adequate account of temporal experience – retentionalism and extensionalism – and the two rival views which dominate the recent literature in the philosophy of perception – representationalism and relationism (see Crane and French 2016 for a helpful overview). In particular, Hoerl suggests that retentionalist views can best be understood as the natural application of a more general representational account of perception to temporal experience, whereas extensionalist views are best understood as allied with relational accounts of perception. Hoerl goes on to make the fascinating suggestion that this pairing reveals an asymmetry, for extensionalists he argues are better equipped to meet a "meta-philosophical" constraint on philosophical approaches to temporal experience, viz. that they should explain why the temporal aspect of experience is of special importance when it comes to providing a proper account of our overall conscious perspective on the world. For Hoerl, this is because extensionalism, within the context of a relational approach to perception, uniquely captures the manifestly *occurrent* nature of conscious experience, or as O'Shaughnessy puts it, the fact that "even the unchanging perception of a fixed immobilized world conceals a processive continuity, that of the perceiving itself, which is occurrently renewed in each instant" (2000: 63).

The special relationship between consciousness and time emphasized and explored so vividly in O'Shaughnessy's work also provides the backdrop for Thomas Crowther and Matthew Soteriou's contribution in Chapter 14. Crowther and Soteriou's interest is in the contrasting relationships between temporal awareness in wakeful experience and in other states of consciousness. Their discussion begins with the contrast between temporal awareness in wakeful consciousness and such awareness in dreamless sleep. Drawing on O'Shaughnessy, they propose that those dreamlessly asleep lack a perspective which provides awareness of the present moment as "now", and moreover, which provides *successive* awareness of successively present moments as "now". On the other hand, the wakeful experiencer not only enjoys such a perspective but (at least characteristically) experiences successively present moments *as successive* and further occupies what Crowther and Soteriou call a "tensed temporal perspective" whose origin lies in their experience of the present moment and so which constitutes what they call an "experienced present" (cf. Hodgson's "empirical present" or James' "specious present"). What is not clear, however, is whether this privilege of wakeful consciousness is a privilege of conscious experience in general. In pursuit of this question, Crowther and Soteriou examine the temporal properties of experience in dreaming. Ultimately, they suggest that if we think of dreams as acts of conscious imagination, we must think that dreaming involves an experiential relation to time fundamentally different from that found in wakeful consciousness. In particular, they suggest that in dreaming one's experience cannot provide awareness of, or constitute a temporal perspective on, your actual past, present and future. Dreaming thus severs you from your present.

In Chapter 15, Carlos Montemayor offers an original perspective on traditional debates about temporal experience by drawing on empirical evidence concerning what he sees as two fundamental features of time perception: that it is *amodal* (in that it involves the cross-modal integration of sensorily specific signals, but is not itself dependent on, or associated with, any specific modality or stimulus) and that it is *action-guiding*. Montemayor argues against "atomist" (i.e. snapshot or retentional) models which operate under the simultaneity constraint that "Temporal order and duration must be represented at a moment in time" (essentially the PSA discussed above). Such models, he suggests, are incapable of explaining how an agent's temporally extended "actions and goals integrate time perception cross-modally" and so "cannot provide an adequate account of temporal experience". On the other hand, Montemayor does not entirely abandon retentionalism. Instead, he argues for a "Dual Model of temporal experience", a model that combines the advantages of both extensional and retentionalism. On this dual model, extensionalism is adopted as the correct account of temporal *consciousness*, but retentionalism is adopted as an appropriate account of early, non-conscious perceptual processing.

It is natural to suppose that, just as we can sometimes perceive the distance between two objects, so we can sometimes perceive the duration separating two events. In Chapter 16, Christopher Peacocke offers a framework which provides a unified understanding of these cases of perception. Peacocke's framework is founded on a general realism concerning magnitudes (Peacocke 2015). From such a perspective, the fact that two events are separated by a given duration can provide a partial explanation of an observer's perception of that duration. But what precisely is the nature of such perception? As emphasized by Burge (2010), mere sensitivity to a given magnitude does not suffice for representation of the relevant magnitude as such. A Kantian question thus arises: what are the minimal constitutive conditions for the perceptual representation of temporal magnitudes and relations as such? For Burge, perceptual representation arises through exercise of the perceptual constancies. However, in the case of time, Burge denies that temporal representation requires temporal constancies. Instead, temporal representation requires that our sensitivity to temporal properties is appropriately *coordinated* with perceptual representations which do directly implicate constancies. Peacocke concurs with Burge that a constancy criterion will not work for the temporal case. However, he provides a series of examples which cast doubt on Burge's alternative proposal. These motivate Peacocke's own account on which the attribution of temporal representational content is warranted only if such contents contribute non-redundantly to explanations of a creature's actions. For Peacocke, actions which require such explanations are those which require appeal to how a subject represents things as having been the case in the past together with identities between presently and previously encountered entities.

Peacocke's chapter ends with a discussion and robust defence of the phenomenal externalism implicit in his account. In particular, Peacocke rejects the suggestion made by Thompson (2010) and Chalmers (2012) that temporal and spatial magnitude terms are "Twin-Earthable", i.e. such as to allow for phenomenal and functional duplicates whose perceptual states represent different temporal and spatial magnitudes (e.g. since located on "Slowed" or "Doubled" Earths).

Part V: temporal experience and metaphysics

Part V turns to connections between our temporal experience and metaphysics. The most obvious and central of these being the relationship between our experience of time and time itself. In Chapter 17, Michael Pelczar discusses and defends a striking conception of this relationship: facts about time can be reductively analysed in terms of facts about conscious experience. Pelczar makes this claim by way of extending the kind of phenomenalist view systematically developed by Mill (1979 [1865]). On a Millian view, the physical world is conceived of as a tendency for the occurrence of specific patterns of conscious experiences, or as Pelczar puts it, as pure, phenomenological potential. Such potential can be expressed using "sensation conditionals". As Pelczar offers by way of illustration: "the fact that a tree has a certain shape and color" can be reduced to the fact that "if experiences with certain qualia were to occur, there would also occur experiences with certain phenomenal shapes and colors". Mill, however, declines to phenomenalize time. In Mill's view, time is special in that experiences *themselves* essentially have temporal features such as durations – whereas they do not have colours and shapes. As Mill puts it: "Sensations exist before and after one another. This is as much a primordial fact as sensation itself" (1979 [1865]: 198). Against this ubiquitous view, Pelczar argues that time is not in fact special: phenomenal duration no more entails objective duration than phenomenal shape requires objective shape. The upshot, according to Pelczar is that, *pace* Mill, "when it comes to amenability to phenomenalist reduction, time is in the same boat as shape or color". Pelczar's argument against time's specialness requires him to confront three putatively fundamental aspects of our temporal experience: its manifest phenomenal temporality (e.g. Phillips 2010, 2014a; Soteriou 2010, 2013; Rashbrook-Cooper 2013a, Chapter 10 this volume), its phenomenal continuity (e.g. Dainton 2000; Rashbrook-Cooper 2013b), and the way in which episodic memory involves memories of earlier experiences (e.g. Peacocke 1985; Martin 2001). Pelczar contends that, when properly understood, "none of these phenomena gives us a compelling reason to locate consciousness in time".

Chapters 18 and 19 move to more familiar issues concerning the relationship between temporal experience and the metaphysics of time, and to a familiar type of philosophical issue: an apparent clash between manifest and metaphysical-cum-scientific images. In Chapter 18, Natalja Deng discusses the bearing of temporal experience on what is conventionally known as the A- versus B-theory debate. This terminology comes from McTaggart (1908) and relates to two different ways in which we can describe events (or times). We can either describe them as standing in certain precedence relations to each other, as earlier than, later than or co-occurrent with one another. Events so ordered are ordered in what McTaggart calls the *B-series*. We can also describe events as being (more or less) past, present and (more or less) future. Here we can think of ourselves as ascribing events certain properties (e.g. the property of "pastness"). Or we can think of ourselves as claiming that the events stand in a certain B-series relation to "the present". Events so ordered are ordered in what McTaggart calls the *A-series*. As Deng presents it, the B-theory is the view that (a) all times and/or events exist, and (b) there is a complete tenseless description of reality – a description which mentions only tenseless facts concerning B-series precedence relations such as successiveness and simultaneity.

There are powerful arguments for endorsing the B-theory (e.g., as Deng notes, the A-theory is notoriously difficult to reconcile with the theory of relativity). Yet for many A-theorists the B-theory is simply incapable of accommodating the manifest fact that time passes. Although this argument need not appeal to experience, it is common for A-theorists to argue that our experience of time passing offers the basis for a powerful inference to the best explanation that time objectively passes. Deng discusses two responses to this argument. The first claims that our experience of passage is illusory and so does not require appeal to objective passage for its explanation (e.g. Paul 2010). The second, which Deng herself defends, denies that our experience is illusory and instead disputes the A-theorist's contention that we actually have experiences as of time passing. Crucially, what Deng denies here is not that we experience succession and change, and so passage in the B-theoretically acceptable sense of there being a succession of times. Rather Deng denies that we experience passage in any more "robust" sense which would serve the A-theorist's purposes. In defending this conclusion, Deng not only rejects the A-theorist's appeal to experience, but further raises a doubt about whether their idea of "robust passage" can even be made sense of.

In Chapter 19, Akiko M. Frischhut turns to a closely related issue, namely the relationship between temporal experience and the metaphysical view known as *presentism*. As Frischhut articulates the view, this is the thesis that all and only present things exist. Such a view might be thought to capture the folk wisdom that the dinosaurs have gone out of existence, and that future Martian outposts are not yet in existence. Frischhut's interest is in whether presentism is ultimately consistent with our perceptual experience of change and duration, and further with our (putative) experiences of time as passing. The answers to these questions of course depend on our preferred theory of perception in general, and of temporal perception in particular. In her systematic discussion, Frischhut first argues that because our experiences of worldly events must, due to light transmission and neural processing delays, lag behind the events themselves, presentists must reject direct realist views of perception according to which worldly objects and events are constituents of our experiences. Frischhut then considers the consistency of presentism and three leading theories of temporal experience: anti-realism (the view that, since our experience is confined to the instant, strictly speaking we do not experience change and passage), retentionalism and extensionalism. Frischhut concludes that the presentist faces severe challenges in combining their metaphysics with any of these theories (although in some cases the tension depends on what the presentist has to say about the independently vexing issue of cross-temporal relations). Frischhut's discussion reminds us of the struggles of Hobbes, Locke and Berkeley (emphasized in Gorham's Chapter 2) as each tried to reconcile their favoured metaphysics with our experience of time.

In Chapter 20, L. A. Paul turns to a different point of contact between temporal experience and metaphysics: the metaphysics of the self. Paul approaches these issues by way of an investigation of what she calls "subjective reality" and therein of our "subjective self". Paul thus sets aside questions of the nature and structure of objective reality, considered from an impersonal perspective, and focuses instead on the way in which reality and the self appear from the inside, from each self's own subjective perspective. Of critical interest here is the way in which the subjective self persists through time. As Gorham notes in Chapter 2, Descartes takes his own existence over time to be "so evident that [he] can see no way of making it any clearer" (1983, vol. 7: 29). But can we hope to say more about our grasp of our self-persistence? In Paul's view, we grasp our own persistence through time by mentally projecting ourselves into the past and future. This can be achieved both first- and third-personally. Drawing on empirical studies (e.g. Pronin and Ross 2006), Paul proposes that first-personal forms of such projection – projection *of* one's first-personal point of view *from* one's first-personal point of view – typically occur within temporally delimited windows. For Paul, such temporal projection provides for a distinctive understanding of oneself as an enduring entity. Paul here connects her discussion with theorizing about the nature of the specious present, proposing that the specious present should be thought of as the most basic "subjective temporal unit of agential experience for a self". She also suggests that temporal projection is what allows us to *empathize* with our future (and past) selves. However, as Paul develops this thought, it can only do this so long as the way in which I represent myself remains relatively unaltered. This means that at large distances as well as in cases which Paul has elsewhere theorized as involving transformative preference change (Paul 2014), it can cease to be possible to put oneself into the shoes of one's future (or past) self. In such contexts, there is a sense in which you are alienated from your future self: you fail to know who you will be.

Part VI: empirical perspectives

Temporal experience is, of course, not merely a philosophical preoccupation. Psychologists and neuroscientists have long been interested in the nature of our temporal awareness and its underlying mechanisms. Such work imposes important constraints on philosophical reflection. It also provides insights which philosophers might hope to exploit. For both these reasons, this handbook includes three chapters in which leading experts on the psychology of time perception survey different aspects of the field.

In Chapter 21, Alan Johnston examines how the brain encodes the timing of external events. As James (1890: 627f) argues against Helmholtz, whilst it may be tempting to suppose that the perceived time of events simply mirrors the timing of their neural representations, such a view is both conceptually and empirically problematic. In Johnston's view, to make progress we need instead to appeal to the critical concept of a neural channel or filter: a set of neurones specifically tuned (or differentially sensitive) to a class of stimuli, e.g. stimuli flickering at a given rate. Johnston reviews the state of the art concerning the nature and functioning of such filters. In doing so, he notes a wide range of potential implications for philosophical and theoretical issues about temporal experience. For example, Johnston notes that one consequence of the operation of temporal filters is that they integrate information over a period of time meaning that "the neural representation . . . of the external world is delayed by around 80ms relative to external events". As a result, Johnston concludes, we lack "direct access to the present in the external world" (cf. Frischhut's Chapter 19 in this volume). Johnston also notes that on one successful model of motion perception (Johnston *et al.* 1992, 1999), "motion is represented at a point and at an instant from a calculation made over a spatial region and an extended period of time". The attribution here of motion to a single point in space and time bears on debates about the specious present, arguably supporting Prosser's dynamic snapshot theory discussed in Chapter 11. Johnston also shines a light on a number of other important theoretical issues, for example, whether visual experience is continuous or comprised of a series of instants, and whether duration is encoded by a global, amodal cognitive clock (as in the classical models of Creelman 1962 and Treisman 1963 – see Wearden 2016 for an introduction and overview) or, as Johnston argues, rather by various content-sensitive and domain (e.g. modality or task) specific timing mechanisms.

In Chapter 22, Mari Riess Jones argues that human perception is fundamentally concerned with tracking events such as a baby's crying or a predator's approach as opposed to time per se. However, in contrast to Gibson's notorious paper, "Events Are Perceivable But Time Is Not"

(1975), Jones denies that an ecological emphasis on event perception implies that humans do not perceive time. Non-instantaneous events have temporal structures and rhythms, and, as Jones explores, such temporal features are richly exploited in service of event perception. In particular, perceivers are able to attune themselves to external temporal features via a process called *entrainment*. Entrainment – a term coined by Huygens in the seventeenth century following his observation of the mutual stabilization of the rhythms of two pendula – is a process whereby one process (e.g. internal cortical oscillations) is brought into synchrony with another (e.g. an external driving rhythm). Entrainment provides the basis for a model of timing which can be contrasted with traditional cognitive pacemaker models. In particular, Jones argues that traditional pacemaker models are too rigid to account for our adaptive, predictive and consequently fallible timing behaviours (cf. Johnston's critique of global clock models in Chapter 21). Jones goes on to discuss how the internal oscillations involved in the perception of complex events can be thought of as realizing a process of dynamic attending. Thus, a musical performance or speech act can act as a driving rhythm which voluntarily or involuntarily engages (via entrainment) an ongoing dynamic process of attending. In this way, event perception, time perception and attention (properly conceived of as an unfolding activity) are inextricably linked.

The relation between attention and time perception brings us to the final chapter of Part VI, in which Scott Brown considers cognitive influences on time perception, and in particular the role of executive attention in shaping temporal experience. Brown reviews studies by cognitive psychologists (including many from his own lab) which seek to systematize and understand phenomena enshrined in folk wisdom: how time drags when bored or waiting, or how it flies when distracted or having fun. Psychologists use a wide range of techniques to investigate the effects of expectancy and attention on temporal experience. One, already encountered in Jones' Chapter 22, exploits rhythmical and other musical structures to manipulate subjects' expectations. Another is the so-called oddball paradigm (Tse *et al.* 2004) in which a series of identical stimuli are presented successively, with an oddball (e.g. differently coloured) stimulus appearing at random points and thus capturing attention. Still another technique simply involves explicitly directing subjects to attend to the passage of time – even though it is not entirely clear what this involves (see Phillips 2012). These varied paradigms all support the notion that increased attention lengthens perceived duration. Conversely, evidence from dual-task paradigms in which a timing-task is combined with a distractor (e.g. visual search) task indicates that timing is disrupted when attention is withdrawn. Brown relates such findings to different models of timing – in particular, to traditional pacemaker-accumulator models combined with an attentional-gate (as in Zakay and Block 1996) – and to different theories of attention. Brown concludes his review of the evidence by suggesting that timing depends critically upon specific attentional resources, namely those associated with *executive* functions such as task-switching, memory updating and reasoning.

Part VII: temporal experience and aesthetics

Part VII of the volume turns to aesthetics, exploring some of the rich connections between traditional aesthetic theorizing and work on temporal experience. In Chapter 24, Robin Le Poidevin looks to the striking example of the Italian Futurists and their aspiration to capture the "dynamic sensation" on canvas in order to explore the question: can a static medium such as painting ever successfully depict our experience of motion? Le Poidevin's rich discussion carefully considers this issue from the perspective of different accounts of motion (on the one hand) and motion experience (on the other). Ultimately, he argues that by developing a suitably non-realist conception of depiction, the Futurists' ambition may be less hopeless than it might seem at first sight.

In Chapter 25, Enrico Terrone turns from painting to the paradigmatically temporal art of cinematography, or as Terrone suggests it might be better named, "chronography": the writing or recording of time. Drawing on a wealth of examples, Terrone subtly probes various tempting claims about cinematic depiction. For example: Does cinema conform to the "real-time principle" that, at least within scenes, the order and duration of depicted events are identical with the order and duration of their depiction? Or: Do spectators experience the events depicted in a film as occurring right now (as arguably we perceive worldly events, on which see Chapter 10)?

From cinema we turn, in Chapter 26, to dance, an art form relatively neglected by philosophy yet plausibly one of the earliest and most widespread expressions of human creativity – indeed arguably an art whose origins "lie deep in the evolutionary history of the animal kingdom" (Morriss-Kay 2010: 158). Drawing in part on her own experience as a professional-level ballet dancer, Aili Bresnahan offers us a rich analysis of a dancer's own embodied and inextricably spatio-temporal experience of dancing. She then begins the task of connecting this phenomenological analysis to extant theorizing about temporal experience, taking as her starting point James' celebrated discussion in *The Principles of Psychology* (1890), and in particular his articulation of the notion of the specious present. Drawing further on work by Damasio (1999) and Wittmann (2014), Bresnahan ultimately argues that an adequate account of a dancer's experience will have to involve elements of a retentional approach to temporal experience.

Finally, in Chapter 27, Andrew Kania offers us a lively survey of some of the many questions we can ask about music and temporal experience. For example: How, if at all, is temporal experience, and perhaps more specifically rhythmic experience, essential to, or paradigmatic of, musical works and their performances? In listening to recorded music, do we hear the original performance (now perhaps many years in the past), or perhaps only the sounds that were original produced, or neither of these? What about purely electronically created works for playback? How are we able to appreciate "formal" musical features which lie beyond the "specious present" and so, one might argue, outside our hearing? Finally, how does music's temporality contribute to its aesthetic value?

Throughout this final section, we find extensive interplay between traditional, broad-brush theorizing about temporal experience and the fine-grained aesthetic projects of providing proper theoretical accounts of particular art forms with all their many intricacies and idiosyncrasies. As Le Poidevin, Terrone, Bresnahan and Kania each bring out, philosophers – be they primarily aestheticians or philosophers of temporal experience – have much to gain from such interplay. Thus, in Le Poidevin's discussion thinking about the difficulties the Futurists face in depicting motion in light of standard views of motion of experience, spurs the development of an enriched conception of depiction. Or in the other direction, theorists endorsing or criticizing cinematic models of temporal experience would do well, I suggest, to think carefully about the issues Terrone discusses regarding how cinematic depiction actually functions. The extensive interplay just mentioned also reminds us of the way in which temporal experience suffuses our lives, once again underscoring its significance.

References

Andersen, H. and Grush, R. (2009) "A brief history of time-consciousness: Historical precursors to James and Husserl", *Journal of the History of Philosophy* 47(2): 277–307.

Bergson, H. (1926 [1911]) *Creative Evolution*, A. Mitchell (trans.), New York: Henry Holt.

Block, R. and Zakay, D. (2001) "Retrospective and prospective timing: Memory, attention, and consciousness", in C. Hoerl and T. McCormack (eds), *Time and Memory: Issues in Philosophy and Psychology*, Oxford, UK: Oxford University Press, pp. 59–76

Burge, T. (2010) *Origins of Objectivity*, Oxford, UK: Oxford University Press.

Chalmers, D. (2012) *Constructing the World*, Oxford, UK: Oxford University Press.

Crane, T. and French, C. (2016) "The problem of perception", in E. N. Zalta (ed.), *The Stanford Encyclopedia of Philosophy* (Winter 2016 ed.). Accessed 30 December 2016.

Creelman, C. (1962) "Human discrimination of auditory duration", *Journal of the Acoustical Society of America* 34(5): 582–593.

Dainton, B. (2000) (2nd edition 2006). *Stream of Consciousness: Unity and Continuity in Conscious Experience*, New York: Routledge.

Dainton, B. (2010) "Temporal consciousness", in E. N. Zalta (ed.), *The Stanford Encyclopedia of Philosophy*, available at http://plato.stanford.edu/entries/consciousness-temporal/. Accessed 30 December 2016.

Damasio, A. (1999) *The Feeling of What Happens: Body and Emotion in the Making of Consciousness*, San Diego, CA: Harcourt, Inc.

Descartes, R. (1983) *Oeuvres De Descartes*, 11 vols. C. Adam and P. Tannery (eds), Paris: J. Vrin.

Gibson, J. J. (1975) "Events are perceivable but time is not", in J. T. Fraser and N. Lawrence (eds), *The Study of Time II*, Berlin and Heidelberg, Germany: Springer, pp. 295–301.

Guyer, P. (1987) *Kant and the Claims of Knowledge*, Cambridge, UK: Cambridge University Press.

Hodgson, S. H. (1898) *The Metaphysic of Experience* (4 vols.), London: Longmans, Green and Co.

Hoerl, C. (2013a) "Husserl, the absolute flow, and temporal experience", *Philosophy and Phenomenological Research* 86(2): 376–411.

Hoerl, C. (2013b) "'A succession of feelings, in and of itself, is not a feeling of succession'", *Mind* 122(486): 373–417.

Husserl, E. (1991) *On the Phenomenology of Consciousness of Internal Time (1893–1917)*, (trans.) J. B. Brough, Dordrecht, The Netherlands: Kluwer Academic Publishers.

James, W. (1890) *The Principles of Psychology*, New York: Henry Holt.

Johnston, A., McOwan, P. and Benton, C. P. (1999) "Robust velocity computation from a biologically motivated model of motion perception", *Proceedings of the Royal Society of London B: Biological Sciences* 266(1418): 509–518.

Johnston, A., McOwan, P. and Buxton, H. (1992) "A computational model of the analysis of some first-order and second-order motion patterns by simple and complex cells", *Proceedings of the Royal Society of London B: Biological Sciences* 250(1329): 297–306.

Kripke, S. (1978) Time and identity, unpublished typescript.

Lewis, D. (1986) *Philosophical Papers Volume 2*, Oxford, UK: Oxford University Press.

Martin, M. G. F. (2001) "Out of the past: Episodic memory as retained acquaintance", in C. Hoerl and T. McCormack (eds), *Time and Memory*, Oxford, UK: Oxford University Press, pp. 257–284.

McTaggart, J. E. (1908) "The unreality of time", *Mind* 17(68): 457–474.

Mill, J. S. (1979 [1865]) *An Examination of Sir William Hamilton's Philosophy, and of the Principal Philosophical Questions Discussed in His Writings*, Toronto, ON: University of Toronto Press.

Miller, I. (1984) *Husserl, Perception and Temporal Awareness*, Cambridge, MA: MIT Press.

Morriss-Kay, G. M. (2010) "The evolution of human artistic creativity", *Journal of Anatomy* 216(2): 158–176.

O'Shaughnessy, B. (2000) *Consciousness and the World*, Oxford, UK: Clarendon Press.

Paul, L. A. (2010) "Temporal experience", *Journal of Philosophy* 107(7): 333–359.

Paul, L. A. (2014) *Transformative Experience*, Oxford, UK: Oxford University Press.

Peacocke, C. (1985) "Imagination, experience, and possibility", in J. Foster and H. Robinson (eds), *Essays on Berkeley: A Tercentennial Celebration*, Oxford, UK: Oxford University Press.

Peacocke, C. (2015) "Magnitudes: Metaphysics, explanation, and perception", in D. Moyal-Sharrock, V. Munz and A. Coliva (eds), *Mind, Language and Action: Proceedings of the 36th International Wittgenstein Symposium*, Berlin: de Gruyter.

Phillips, I. (2010) "Perceiving temporal properties", *European Journal of Philosophy* 18(2): 176–202.

Phillips, I. (2011) "Indiscriminability and experience of change", *The Philosophical Quarterly* 61(245): 808–827.

Phillips, I. (2012) "Attention to the passage of time", *Philosophical Perspectives* 26(1): 277–308.

Phillips, I. (2014a) "The temporal structure of experience", in V. Arstila and D. Lloyd (eds), *Subjective Time: The Philosophy, Psychology, and Neuroscience of Temporality*, Cambridge, MA: MIT Press.

Phillips, I. (2014b) "Experience of and in time", *Philosophy Compass* 9(2): 131–144.

Phillips, I. (forthcoming) "Time, consciousness and memory", in R. J. Gennaro (ed.), *The Routledge Handbook of Consciousness*, New York: Routledge.

Pronin, E. and Ross, L. (2006) "Temporal differences in trait self-ascription: When the self is seen as an other", *Journal of Personality and Social Psychology* 90(2): 197–209.

Rashbrook-Cooper, O. (2013a) "An appearance of succession requires a succession of appearances", *Philosophy and Phenomenological Research* 87(3): 584–610. Originally published under the name "Oliver Rashbrook".

Rashbrook-Cooper, O. (2013b) "Diachronic and synchronic unity", *Philosophical Studies* 164(2): 465–484. Originally published under the name "Oliver Rashbrook".

Soteriou, M. (2007) "Content and the stream of consciousness", *Philosophical Perspectives* 21(1): 543–568.

Soteriou, M. (2010) "Perceiving events", *Philosophical Explorations: An International Journal for the Philosophy of Mind and Action* 13(3): 223–241.

Soteriou, M. (2013) *The Mind's Construction*, Oxford, UK: Oxford University Press.

Stern, L. (2005 [1897]) "Mental presence-time", N. De Warren (trans.) in C Wolfe (ed.), *The New Yearbook for Phenomenology and Phenomenological Research*, London: College Publications, pp. 205–216.

Thompson, B. (2010) "The spatial content of experience", *Philosophy and Phenomenological Research* 81(1): 146–194.

Treisman, M. (1963) "Temporal discrimination and the indifference interval: Implications for a model of the 'internal clock'", *Psychological Monographs: General and Applied* 77(13): 1–31.

Tse, P. U., Intriligator, J., Rivest, J. and Cavanagh, P. (2004) "Attention and the subjective expansion of time", *Perception and Psychophysics* 66(7): 1171–1189.

Volkmann, W. (1875) *Lehrbuch der Psychologie vom Standpunkte des Realismus und nach genetischer Methode*, Cöthen, Germany: Verlag von Otto Schulze.

Wearden, J. (2016) *The Psychology of Time Perception*, Basingstoke, UK: Palgrave Macmillan.

Wittmann, M. (2014) "Embodied time: The experience of time, the body, and the self", in V. Arstila and D. Lloyd (eds), *Subjective Time: The Philosophy, Psychology, and Neuroscience of Temporality*, Cambridge, MA: MIT Press, pp. 507–524.

Zakay, D. and Block, R. A. (1996) "The role of attention in time estimation processes", in M. A. Pastor and J. Artieda (eds), *Time, Internal Clocks and Movement*, Amsterdam: Elsevier, pp. 143–164.

PART I

Ancient and early modern perspectives

1

HOW NATURAL IS A UNIFIED NOTION OF TIME?

Temporal experience in early Greek thought

Barbara M. Sattler

Introduction

Whatever our metaphysics of time, today we usually work with the assumption that we have one unified temporal framework which allows for situating all events, processes and happenings. What do I mean by this? Let us say that today there may be a battle in Syria, you are reading a philosophy paper, the Dalai Lama may be engaged in some meditation, and in the Austrian Alps the first avalanche of the season may come down – these things have nothing to do with each other, they are very different things, some of them are physical things, some mental, some occurrences in nature, others in the human world, and yet we would note down all these occurrences in the very same calendar; we could, for example, say of each event that it happened on Wednesday, 4 January 2017 (if that is when they happen). For us, all these things happen in the same time, we have a common framework for them all so that no matter which occurrences or processes we talk about, they can be put in a temporal relation to each other; they are either before, after, or simultaneous with each other.

For the early Greeks, by contrast, the very idea of such a unified notion of time would be foreign; instead they assume different temporal (and not necessarily comparable) structures belonging to different events. Not only do we not find a unified calendar throughout the ancient Greek world; more importantly, we also do not find a unified notion or idea of time before Plato. In this chapter, I want to show that such a unified framework is lacking in the very beginning of Western thinking and the effect this lack has on the quality of temporal experiences – it means that different temporal experiences are thus seen as experiences of genuinely different kinds.

With the exception of Anaximander and Empedocles, the philosophers before Plato hardly ever discuss temporal notions. For this reason and in order to make sure that we capture the earliest expressions of temporal notions, I will mainly discuss temporal ideas in non-philosophical authors before Plato. But these texts will not be looked at for merely historic reasons; rather they shall be shown to articulate an understanding of temporal structures that questions many of our modern temporal conceptions. A look at ancient notions of time suggests that our notion of time as unified is not something we gain directly from experience, but rather that such a unified conception is an interpretative or theoretical overlay.

Lack of unification

Today, we distinguish different aspects of temporal experience,[1] such as duration, sequence (i.e., the temporal order of before and after), those aspects that we express in terms of different tenses (recalling the past, facing the present and anticipating the future), and, perhaps, the passage of time.[2] But all these features are seen as different aspects of one unified time ("time" in the singular). If we look at the early ancient Greeks, by contrast, what we count as different aspects seem to be different types of experiences altogether. There are different kinds of temporal notions capturing different kinds of temporal experiences that are in the beginning not connected with each other: (1) there are notions of duration; (2) notions indicating sequence; (3) notions indicating measurable time; (4) notions linking time with agency; and (5) notions marked by tense.

Some of the literature on memory has pointed out the fragmented character of memory, that it contains gaps, as well as different and, in part, disjoint narratives[3] – features that also could be seen as suggesting that our conception of time as unified may not be something we can take for granted. We will see, however, that the disunity for the early Greeks is of a somewhat different kind – with them we are not dealing with gaps that are due to things being forgotten, some lack of memory; rather there are several temporal aspects that are not seen as belonging to the same kind of experience; furthermore, these disunities cannot simply to be brought into a linear succession, as, for example, John Campbell thinks is ultimately possible for all autobiographical memory.[4]

Let us have a closer look at the different kinds of temporal notions in early Greek thinking; due to constraints of space, I will only be able to give a very rough sketch and to point to a few examples for each notion.[5]

(1) *Chronos* is the most important notion of duration; scholars often understand it as *the* equivalent to our term "time" in such a way that other temporal notions could be subsumed under it. However, this is in fact only the case from Plato onwards. In the very beginning of Greek thinking, *chronos* indicates solely a particular time span – it is either qualified as a long or short time, or simply by itself understood as a long time. But *chronos* originally does not indicate a time that is measured with the help of any units; rather we are just experiencing something as lasting for some duration or as (too) long. Let me give you two of the earliest examples, from Homer's *Iliad* and *Odyssey*.

In *Iliad* Book III, the old leaders of the Trojans sit upon the wall and, when they see Helen coming upon the wall, they say to each other:

> There is no blame on Trojans and well-greaved Achaeans if for a long time (πολὺν χρόνον) they suffered hardship for such a woman; wondrously like is she to the immortal goddesses to look upon.
>
> *(lines 156–158)*

Chronos qualified by the adjective "long" is also what we find in *Odyssey* book V, where we hear that when Odysseus is sailing off from Calypso, he gets into a storm, his mast breaks and he is thrown into the sea:

> As for him, long time (πολὺν χρόνον) did the wave hold him in the depths, nor could he rise at once from beneath the onrush of the mighty wave, for the garments which beautiful Calypso had given him weighed him down.
>
> *(lines 319–321)*

In both passages, *chronos* is qualified as a long time; and both passages show that *chronos* is not only used to express a long duration, but, fairly typically for the early understanding of *chronos*, a particular long time, namely a negative time (the time Odysseus is under water, the time suffered in the case of the Trojans). There is a lot of waiting and wandering around in the *Iliad* and *Odyssey* and it is here especially where *chronos* comes in. This suggests that *chronos* is not simply understood as a neutral temporal framework (which embraces all events and lets us situate every process and event), but rather as expressing a specific emotional experience of duration. And *chronos* does not seem to be used to serve the interest of chronology. This does not mean that there cannot be a very sophisticated architecture of narrative time. For the *Iliad*, for example, Taplin has shown how the fourteen actually narrated days in the *Iliad* are marked by clear signs of closure and anticipation, and the role that the sequence of night, dawn, midday, etc. plays.[6] But if we attempt to reconstruct the exact sequence of events of the Trojan War with the help of the *Iliad*, we get entangled in inconsistencies.[7] There is no suggestion that *chronos* provides us with an overall framework or is an essential part of a chronology (as the different days and nights are). While we do find relations of order in the *Iliad* and *Odyssey* – with the unfolding of the narrative as well as with the sequence of night, dawn, midday, etc. – these definite relations are not explicitly linked to the experienced duration; there are no points that can serve as markers within *chronos* in its earliest occurrences.

This usage of *chronos* in Homer also suggests that our sense of duration need not be connected with measurability[8] in the sense that we can say at least roughly how long something lasted[9] – a connection, which, for example, Mayo assumes as naturally given.[10] According to Mayo, we "cannot endure through an interval of time without measuring it" (1950: 71).[11] By contrast, in Homer, we find the idea that a certain duration is just experienced as too long, or even endless seeming. It is not connected with the idea of measurability by the narrator, and we have no reason to assume that Odysseus had a sense of how much time had elapsed since he got under the wave.

(2) There are basic notions indicating sequence, like "before" and "after". These notions do not yet give us measurability, but are in some sense more basic: for it may be the case that we can tell whether one event X happened before or after another event Y (or simultaneously, for that matter), without thus necessarily knowing how much before or after they took place or how long either X or Y lasted; all we may be able to say is that X occurred before Y. Usually, earlier and later ordering is asymmetric, not reflexive, and transitive.[12]

In early Greek thinking, notions like "before" (*proteron*) and "after" (*hysteron*) are often expressed as adjectives, but never as adjectives qualifying *chronos*.[13] Rather they seem to qualify people or things, in the way properties do, so we find talk about "*andres proteroi*" ("former men", *Iliad* XXI.405) and "*anthrôpoi proteroi*" ("former human beings", *Iliad* V.637, XXIII.332 and *Theogony*, line 100). In translations, the adjective "former" or "old" is usually applied to times, but for Homer and Hesiod it is literally applied to human beings.

(3) There are a couple of temporal notions that express certain temporal units bound to natural processes and thus indicate what we can call measurable time; for example, *hêmera*, the day, *meis*, the month, or *eniautos*, the year. But it is only from the fifth century BCE onwards that *chronos* is seen as what is measured with the help of these temporal units. So in Sophocles' *Oedipus at Colonus* lines 607ff. we find the idea that "*chronos* brings forth countless nights and days". Here measurable time (expressed in terms of units of time like night and day) is connected with long time (*chronos*) by having *chronos* bring forth nights and days – presumably as its parts, so that we can say how much *chronos* has passed. But before the tragedians, these temporal units do not seem to measure

something else, time, as we would assume. For example, in Homer we find the expression "as the year rolled round, and the seasons came on" as a standard phrase expressing long time – "year" and "season" do not measure time; rather they themselves are what rolls around and comes on.

Moreover, these units are not always primarily used for exact quantitative measurement; rather they often also have a qualitative sense. Thus different days of the month can be seen as suitable or unsuitable for certain activities, for example, the twelfth day is good for weaving since then also the spider allegedly weaves its web.[14] A day is the unity that connects different experiences together[15] and can also be identified with the fate experienced.[16]

(4) There are temporal notions indicating agency, like *kairos*, which means the right or a critical time. *Kairos* as the appropriate or critical time has no connection with measurable time, and it is also not connected with the duration expressed by *chronos*. Its original meaning is "due measure", "proportion", "what is vital", which is then interpreted in a temporal sense to mean the critical time or opportunity to act.

Kairos is a notion that is of special importance in early medical writings: in the process of healing, certain times are especially critical for applying a treatment and for the success of the healing process. For example, in the treatise *Regimen in acute diseases*, a part of the Hippocratic corpus, we find a discussion of *kairos* as the right time to administer gruel (one of the main medical drugs, it seems, at that time). Unseasonable (that is, going against the *kairos*) administration of gruel or unseasonable feeding or fasting is understood to lead to attacks in the body.[17] And in the treatise *On Fracture*, *kairos* is the vital point of time in the healing of a fracture: it can be dangerous for the whole healing process or exactly the right time to apply some treatment.

Kairos is also prominently used in the context of Pindar's odes celebrating the winners of Olympic (and other Panhellenic) Games.[18] But it is not, as one might expect, the critical time the winner grasps in order to gain victory in the competition. Rather, it is a time for right action more generally: for example, in Pindar's *Olympian Ode* II, lines 54–56, we hear that Theron, ruler of Akragas and winner of the chariot race in the Olympic Games in 476 BCE, has "wealth embellished with virtue", which is what provides *kairos* for achievements. Wealth combined with virtue (*arête*) is what will lead to the right time for successful agency. What is characteristic of *kairos* is also that it has to be grasped quickly; otherwise the opportunity may be lost.

As the critical time to do something now that will have important consequences for later, *kairos* intimately ties the present to the future: I act now so as to bring about a certain effect in the future, for example, the healing of a patient. My intention for my action in this critical time can be seen as essentially future directed.[19]

(5) Finally, the experience we express with the help of tense is also not connected with the experience of *chronos*. While there seems to be a clear awareness of what we call the arrow of time early on, it is only with Plato that the direction of time is clearly coupled with *chronos*. And in early Greek thinking, we also find the possibility entertained that for moral or metaphysical reasons the normal direction of time might be reversed. For example, in Hesiod's *Works and Days*, we find the idea that acting in accordance with the seasons is the only way for us human beings to keep temporality as well as morality under control. Only this will ensure that babies will not be born grey. The threat of children being born with grey hair because of moral chaos shows how temporal order is seen as closely bound up with moral order: our immoral actions will turn the normal temporal structures upside down.

Comprehending how exactly tense is understood by the ancient Greeks is complicated by three factors:

(a) What we take as the grammatical tenses of the Greek verb can be as much an indication of aspect as of tense, and especially express aspect in the moods other than the indicative. The three basic stems of the Greek verb – present, aorist and perfect – correspond to three basic kinds of aspect – durative, punctual or completed, and resultant or stative. If we look, for example, at the verb form we classify as the past tense aorist in Greek, this verb form may simply express the punctual character of a happening, rather than the idea of a past event.[20]

(b) Furthermore, what we would call the present tense is not only understood as indicating the present moment (day, year, etc.). Rather, some philosophers relatively early on understand it also as indicating something outside of time, something like eternal truths.[21] The first hint in this direction we find in Parmenides' poem, which claims that what truly is "neither was nor will be, since it is now, all at once".[22] As a result past, present and future tense are not simply understood as referring to temporal dimensions on the same footing, on what we since McTaggart understand as the A-series. Rather, on this understanding of the present tense, it is opposed to past and future.

We may think that this understanding of the present is only to be found with some philosophers, but in fact Parmenides' understanding of the present as indicating eternity seems to take up Hesiod's account of the "race of the blessed" as those who always *are* (*aein eontôn*). And the present is also treated very differently than past and future when Homer and Hesiod take it as the point of view from which we look to past and future things. Today we usually talk about "past, present and future" (or the other way round) as a linear sequence that is independent of the person experiencing it. By contrast, Homer and Hesiod usually talk about the present first, then about the future and finally about past things: it is "things that are, shall be, and were".[23] True, this is a poetic formula for all things, present, future, past, and so may be seen simply as a different way of talking. But it is remarkable that the order given is not linear; rather the relation of the different dimensions is seen from the perspective of our experiences – it starts from where we are, here in the present moment, goes forward to the future things, and then backwards to the past ones.[24]

(c) Finally, words explicitly expressing "the future", and not just "future things", are only relatively late phenomena. In order to express the future time, we do find the term *chronos* specified by an adjective or participle of motion (for example, by *epherpôn*, which means creeping up, or *mellôn*, meaning that one is about to do something). But we only find these expressions centuries after Homer and Hesiod. Interestingly they all seem to be found first in Pindar in the first half of the fifth century BCE, so with a poet who is actually paid for writing odes praising past victories in sportive competitions. One way in which the future is understood in Pindar is as something that is already there and has now, in the present, come to us: "Approaching from far away, the future has arrived and made me ashamed of my deep debt" (*Olympian Ode* 10, 7).[25]

The understanding of temporal structures I have sketched so far concerns *early* Greek thinking. But this thinking develops soon afterwards: first the notion of *chronos* becomes the dominant temporal notion and is connected with the idea of measurement. Furthermore, there is increasing demand from the historians for a unified temporal framework.[26] And finally, with Plato, we do indeed get what we can understand as a unified account of time.[27] However, given the limits of space here, rather than looking at this process of unification, what I will do in the second part of this chapter is spell out what the lack of a unified notion of time in early Greek thinking means for human temporal experience.

Consequences for temporal experience

In contrast to us, the early Greeks were much more oriented towards the motions of the sun and stars, and their time was structured much more by these motions than by clocks.[28] There were certain kinds of clocks available, like sun-dials and water-clocks, but they did not structure the normal rhythm of the day (water-clocks, for example, were prominently used to make sure accuser and defender at trials got the same amount of speaking time). And the notion of hours became important only in the fourth century BCE.[29]

While these features do distinguish the way in which time shapes the daily rhythm of the early Greeks in contrast to our rhythm, these features are not necessarily an expression of a lack of a unified temporal framework. But what does give us a foretaste of the consequences for human experience of time, if a unified notion of time is missing, is a brief look at the lack of a unified calendar throughout the early Greek world, which has several philosophically interesting aspects: the early Greeks worked with local calendars, in which not only the beginning of the year, but also the beginning of the month differed from one city-state to the next. It was not meant to help dating events on a more than local level.[30] The Olympic Games were not used as a general dating system across the Greek world before the classical period.[31]

Furthermore, not only were the calendars not synchronised between different poleis, also within one polis more than one dating system may be used: if we look at the Athenian calendar, which is the best attested Greek calendar we have,[32] we see that the Athenians lived with at least two different calendars simultaneously, each used for different purposes: there was a calendar for the festivals which consisted of 12 months based on the cycle of the moon,[33] and a "political" calendar regulating the economic and administrative life, which consisted of 10 months and was based on the motions of the sun.[34] Originally these two calendars did not necessarily begin or end on the same days. And finally, for agricultural planning, the risings of stars were employed for fixing points in time.[35]

Moreover, originally, there seems to have been very little interest in the ordering of years. While our modern calendar allows for distinguishing each year by a serial number from all other years, accommodating any future or past date, the Attic calendar was not originally set up for such a sequential ordering of years and did not provide an easy way to do so. In Athens, the different years were identified by the names of the magistrates in power in a given year, which allows for ordering years back in time for a couple of generations, but it did not provide a means to date forward (in the way in which we talk about, say, "in 2050"). The year for the Greeks was first and foremost marked out by the alteration of summer and winter, not by absolute serial numbers; events were dated relative to other events. (Of course, also for us, the number we give to years is not absolute but refers to the years after the birth of Christ or the Hijri of Mohammed, or some other significant event. This significant event is, however, kept as a fixed point, with respect to which all years are determined; by contrast, with the early Greeks, some events used for local dating seem to have lost their relevance soon after the dating, and subsequently were not used any longer.)

Finally there is a lot of what we may call "manipulations" of the calendar: the duration of each month was not fixed in advance, but could vary. Furthermore, the coordination between the solar and the lunar year was initially done by inserting an additional month every now and then simply by repeating an existing month (as if we would say "between December and February we will have January twice"). While the astronomers suggested different cycles for inserting the additional months, it seems that the poleis did not adhere to a fixed pattern for these insertions.[36] And, in general, the calendar could be subject to political or military concerns, controlled by the magistrates.[37] Given these possibilities for ad hoc manipulations, in addition to the fact that one city-state would base its calendar on the successions of its main politicians, another one on the term of office of its main priestess, etc., we should not be surprised to see, for example, that Thucydides has to put some effort into telling his readers *when* the battles he describes in his book are happening.[38]

But, as mentioned already above, the lack of a unified calendar is at least to some degree an expression of a more basic lack in conceptual unity. One reason for this lack of a unified temporal framework is also one of the most important differences between early Greek conceptions of time and more modern ones: the fact that past, present and future were not seen as being on the same footing in a linear sequence. This is not a question of existence, as we find it in contemporary presentist discussions about the question of whether only the present or what is present exists[39] or also the past and future (or what is past and future). Rather, what we are facing with these early Greeks is the lack of thinking of past, present and future as constituting a linear order (a linear order presentists can also subscribe to).

For the early Greeks the present seems to indicate a point of view from which we look towards the past or the future. Contra presentists and growing block theorists the future also in some sense may be there already, but, in contrast to block universe theorists, the present is distinct vis-à-vis the past and the future, and in contrast to moving spotlight theorists we do not find any hint of the idea of the objective passage of the present.

Furthermore, for the early Greeks, present actions are seen as less directly prepared for by actions in the past so that I could say "I am doing X today so that I can do Y tomorrow and Z the day after tomorrow", since the idea that different days have different qualities in ways important for our actions and that we have to seize the right moment for an action is much more dominant. And the right moment cannot necessarily be brought about by us; rather we have to react to whatever the present moment may bring and cannot assume that our planning in the past will prepare us for an action now or in the future. One way the coming about of the right moment can be influenced to some degree, however, is by leading a virtuous life – we saw the idea that morality can either prepare the possibility for the right time to come about (as in Pindar), or that moral chaos can lead to temporal chaos in the sense that immoral behaviour can deform normal temporal structures (as in Hesiod).

Also the conceptualisation of the future is remarkably different: the future seems not to have been viewed as a predictable extension of our present on the calendar, given that we do not know in advance when exactly the current month will end, nor is it easy to specify years in advance. To some degree, future-directedness may be integrated with the present in the notion of *kairos*, the idea of a crucial time to act which will have important effects later on. But again this is not a future that is in any sense predictable or can be planned by us. In general, there seems to have been much less planning in the way we are used to, for which a unified and convenient calendar is an important precondition (and much less conceptual possibility to do so). Rather, the most important planning is independent of the succession of years according to serial numbers: it is either agricultural planning,[40] which is done in accordance with the seasons, or the planning of civic duties, which is also not tied to the progression of years, but to the repetition of the political cycle. While there certainly was some planning into the future, for example, for organising the Panhellenic games and other festivities, this form of planning could also basically work within a cyclical notion (of four years, in the case of the Olympic Games), and would hardly need to rely on the sequential ordering of years. In some sense, the future seems to have been treated more similarly to the past: for the agricultural calendar with the cyclical repetition of the seasons, the future does not seem to differ very much from the past, since if the harvest time is now in the future, it will soon be past and then future again. This treatment of the future may also be one reason why it is never expressed as a subject until the fifth century.[41]

Furthermore, the aspect of an action was sometimes more important than its exact temporal location. So at times it seems to have been more significant to express whether some process or state of affairs is finished or continuing, whether it is durative or point-like.

Finally, we saw that the different temporal notions are not necessarily related to each other – notions of succession, of duration, of measurable time and of agency describe independent temporal aspects tied to different kinds of experiences (as we would perhaps think of a business meeting and hiking on our own through the Scottish Highlands as unrelated experiences, even though we could, of course, still put them in the same calendar). Also in contemporary thought we sometimes use exact, discrete dating alongside inexact, analogue notions of duration or of past, present and future. But these inexact notions nevertheless are such that in principle they could be made more precise – if we talk about a time that is too long lasting because it is wasted, we are usually able to translate this easily into "I have wasted a whole day", or even "two wholly wasted hours".[42] So there is no problem for us to connect the duration that is lasting too long with a measuring framework (even if the measurement may not be very precise). By contrast, the early Greeks would not necessarily embed a time that lasts too long in their calendar. Such a time may not be related to the idea of measurability and there does not seem to be an expectation that all the different temporal phenomena are compatible by being situated in a common framework.[43]

And this is exactly one point where the early Greek conceptualisation of temporal structures may be philosophically fruitful for us: even if in scientific and historic contexts a unified temporal framework is essential, in other contexts assuming less of a unified understanding of all temporal occurrences may do more justice to the way we experience the world. We are used to being able to put everything into one calendar and to structuring our experiences to some degree according to this calendar (tomorrow I will do X from 9 am to 10 am, so that I am then prepared for doing Y from 10 am to noon, etc.). But some experiences clearly seem to have their own temporal structure, that we cannot know beforehand, and that we thus cannot integrate into our calendar plan in the same way, as when we meet a friend, or when we develop a thought – can we really say that developing this idea will take me one hour, so I block one hour of the day for that? And if we want to console somebody in her grief or attempt to get over something – do these actions not have their own temporal structures that we cannot anticipate in advance?[44]

Of course, we will be able to situate them in our calendar *afterwards*, but in the cases named there is no way to know their temporal structure (their duration, exact order and specific markers) in advance. Here our temporal experience may be formed almost exclusively by what is done, and not by a neutral temporal framework. Accordingly, we do more justice to these occurrences if we approach them by letting them unfold their own temporal structure; and we may get into problems if we start by assuming them to be compatible with our standard scheduling – the way we use our calendars for future happenings suggests that we could know or at least estimate their temporal duration within a neutral framework.

Furthermore, we all know the phenomenon that our experience of time depends on what is done during this time (time is experienced as short if lots of things happen, but as long if nothing is done during this time) and also on how involved we are, for example, whether we are agents of a certain event or not – we seem to preceive events as occurring closer in time when they are an action of ours and further apart if they are not.[45] The fact that our perception of temporal structures seems to depend on agency also shows that in a non-scientific context we are not simply starting from a neutral temporal framework in which everything gets objectively measured in its temporal duration. Implicitly, we are working with a much less unified understanding of time.

And the early Greeks show us that such a unified and neutral account is much less natural and obvious than we may typically assume.[46]

Notes

1 By "temporal experience" I want to understand not only our conscious (perceptual) experience of time and temporal phenomena, but also our psychological relation to time more generally.
2 See, for example, Le Poidevin 2000 and Pöppel 1978.
3 See Campbell 1997: 107.
4 Campbell 1997: 108 understands autobiographic memory as linearly structured since he sees it as based on our "conception of the self as spatiotemporally continuous".
5 For a fuller discussion see my book manuscript *Ancient Notions of Time* (in preparation).
6 See Taplin 1992, especially 14–26.
7 For example, in the case of the famous Pylaimenes inconsistency: King Pylaimenes is killed in book V of the *Iliad*, but reappears to mourn the death of his son Harpalion in book XIII.
8 We know, of course, that the Greeks were besieging Troy for nine years, but it is not *chronos* that is measured in years here.
9 By measure I do not simply mean that some period is taken to be too short or just right or too long (which presumably is a comparison with whatever we take the right time to be). Thus, I am not working with mere ordinal measurements where all that is preserved of the things to be measured is order but no concatenations can be taken into account, cf. Krantz *et al.* 2006: 2–3 and 11. Rather, I understand by measurement here that we are dealing with cases where we can also say that two days are twice as long as one day and that there may be so and so many days to a month or year.
10 Mayo 1950: 71–88.
11 For Mayo, the "sense of duration and the faculty of measuring length of time are the same thing" (1950: 71) – an assumption which seems doubtful if we look at the understanding of temporal experiences in early Greek times.
12 Cf. also Campbell 1997: 105.
13 We also find *hysteron* used as a temporal adverb, for example, in *Iliad* I, 27 or VII, 30.
14 See for example, Hesiod, *Works and Days*, lines 764 ff. and Onians 1954: 411–415.
15 Cf. Fränkel 1955.
16 Onians 1954: 413f. He describes such a day as not lasting just a day but "as a phase of fortune of greater or less duration".
17 Cf. especially, *Regimen in acute diseases* XX, XXXV, and XLI.
18 Cf. Theunissen 2000.
19 For a similar structure in modern debates on agency cf., for example, Andersen 2013: 472.
20 Cf. Kühner and Gerth 1898: §381.
21 This is a function of the present we are of course used to, for example, when we say "2 plus 2 *is* 4", but it is a function that is only developing in early Greek thinking.
22 Parmenides (2004 [1951], fragment 8, line 5). Cf. Owen 1966 for reading this as indicating eternity, and my defence of it in my *Natural Philosophy in Ancient Times*, which should also make it clear why I do not think Parmenides can be understood as a "block universe" theorist, as some people have claimed him to be.
23 Cf. *Iliad* I, 70 and *Theogony* 38. In Hesiod's *Theogony* 32–33, we find "what will be and what was before, and they commanded me to sing of the race of the blessed ones who always are". Here the present does not get the status of the point from which we look at past and future things. But, again, the present is not on the same footing as past and future; rather, it refers to everlastingness.
24 Interestingly, James 1890 in his account of the present uses a similar language: "the practically cognized present is no knife-edge, but a saddle-back, with a certain breath of its own on which we sit perched, and *from which we look in two directions into time*" (609, my italics). However, this does not prevent him from understanding time as a linear sequence (see, for example, 629).
25 Cf. also *Nemean Ode* 4, 43, *Olympian Ode* 8, 28 and Fränkel 1955.
26 Cf. also Williams 2002: 154 and chapter 3.
27 See my book manuscript *Ancient Notions of Time* (in preparation).
28 This orientation was of course the case in most later times and changed only relatively late in history.

29 Cf. Bickermann 1968: 15.

30 While we are used to the differences between the Gregorian and other calendars, like the Jewish or Islamic ones, we also have a clear mode of converting one into the other. With the ancient Greeks, by contrast, this was much more difficult, since in each local calendar a lot was done on an ad hoc basis.

31 Hippias of Elis is reported to have compiled the first victor lists around 400 BCE, see Christesen 2007: 2 and 47–48. But even from the classical period onwards, these lists seem to have been used mainly by chronographers and historians, while, according to Christesen 11, "individual communities continued to maintain their own eponym systems".

32 Cf. Bickermann 1968: 34. Unfortunately, our testimony for the Athenian calendar is mainly from the fifth century onwards, so from a time that only partly overlaps with the time I am mainly focusing on (and presumably after important reforms in the official calendar under Kleisthenes in the late sixth century).

33 Even though the purpose of this calendar was mainly religious in the fifth century, it is usually called the "civil calendar" in the literature. Because some effort was made to connect it also with the solar year, it is sometimes called a luni-solar calendar; for both points, see Pritchett and Neugebauer 1947: 5.

34 This second calendar is called the "prytany calendar" or "senatorial calendar" see Pritchett and Neugebauer, 35. See Meritt 1928: 123ff. for the relationship between prytany (senatorial) and civil years.

35 As we find it, for example, in Hesiod's *Works and Days*.

36 See Bickermann 1968: 28–30 and 35. In Athens, only the civil calendar was tempered with, while the prytany calendar seems to have been free from intercalation, see Bickermann (1968: 37) and Meritt (1928: 71).

37 For example, Thucydides, *The Peloponnesian War* V, 54 reports on the attempt of the Argives to manipulate the calendar in such a way as to get a few more days of fighting before the holy month would start when battles were forbidden; cf. Pritchett and Neugebauer 1947: 4–5.

38 See Thucydides, beginning of book II, where he dates the beginning of the Peloponnesian war by referring to the dating system of the three most important poleis, to the priesthood at Argos, the *ephor* at Sparta and the *archon* at Athens, as well as to the "16th month after the battle of Poteidea" and the opening of spring.

39 Or whether everything that is, is present.

40 One of the central points of Hesiod's *Works and Days*.

41 Developmental literature on time suggests that reasoning about the future requires abilities in addition to those about the past so that, at least in early child development, understanding of past and future are not simply on the same footing (see McCormack and Hanley 2011, especially 303 and 311). Reasoning about past events only requires retrieving a sequence from memory and then reasoning about it, while reasoning about future events in addition requires the mental construction of a novel series of events.

42 And we may use relative dating in identifying a past event as having occurred before the fall of the Berlin Wall or as having taken place on the day of the Brexit referendum. But, again, we usually assume that we can translate this into a dating relative to the birth of Christ, etc.

43 Research on temporal notions in other cultures has also pointed out that our Western understanding of time is "neither natural nor intuitive but is the result of a gradual, constructive process" (so Friedman 1990: 103). Perhaps the most interesting understanding of time for us that Friedman discusses is that of the Mursi in Ethiopia, for whom our exact position in a lunar cycle is not a question of exact measurement but of social consensus (1990: 105).

44 Hallowell (1937: 656–657) has pointed out that when he was doing research with the Saultaux of Canada, it was hard to arrange a particular time in the day to meet a person, because common reference points of time were lacking; social occasions simply start when people are ready.

45 See Haggard *et al.* 2002.

46 I want to thank Michael Della Rocca, Stephen Halliwell, John Kennedy and Ian Phillips for helpful comments on the chapter.

References

Andersen, H. (2013) "The representation of time in agency", in H. Dyke and A. Bardon (eds), *A Companion to the Philosophy of Time*, Oxford, UK: Wiley-Blackwell.

Bickermann, E. (1968) *Chronology of the Ancient World*, London: Thames & Hudson.

Campbell, J. (1997) "The structure of time in autobiographical memory", *European Journal of Philosophy* 5(2): 105–118.

Christesen, P. (2007) *Olympic Victor Lists and Ancient Greek History*, Cambridge, UK: Cambridge University Press.

Fränkel, H. (1955) "Die Zeitauffassung in der frühgriechischen Literatur", in F. Tietze (ed.), *Wege und Formen frühgriechischen Denkens*, Munich, Germany: Beck, pp. 1–22.

Friedman, W. (1990) *About Time: Inventing the Fourth Dimension*, Cambridge, MA: MIT Press.

Haggard, P., Clark, S. and Kalogeras, J. (2002) "Voluntary action and conscious awareness", *Nature Neuroscience* 5(4): 382–385.

Hallowell, I. (1937) "Temporal orientation in Western civilization and in a pre-literate society", *American Anthropologist* 39(4): 647–670.

Hesiod (2007) *Theogony. Works and Days, Testimonia*, ed. and trans. in Glenn W. Most, Cambridge, MA: Harvard University Press.

Hippocrates (1959) *Regimen in Acute Diseases*, trans. W. H. S. Jones, Cambridge, MA: Harvard University Press.

Hippocrates (1960) *On Fracture*, trans. E. T. Withington, Cambridge, MA: Harvard University Press.

Homer (1919) *The Odyssey*, trans. A. T. Murray, Cambridge, MA: Harvard University Press.

Homer (1924 and 1925) *The Iliad*, trans. A. T. Murray, Cambridge, MA: Harvard University Press, volumes I and II.

James, W. (1890) *The Principles of Psychology*, New York: Henry Holt and Company.

Krantz, D., Luce, D., Suppes, P. and Tversky, A. (2006) *Foundations of Measurement*, San Diego, CA: Academic Press.

Kühner, R. and Gerth, B. (1898) *Ausführliche Grammatik der Griechischen Sprache, Zweiter Teil: Satzlehre, vol. 1*, Hannover, Germany: Verlag Hahnsche Buchhandlung.

Le Poidevin, R. (2000) "The experience and perception of time", *Stanford Encyclopedia of Philosophy* (Summer 2015 Edition), E. N. Zalta (ed.), https://plato.stanford.edu/archives/sum2015/entries/time-experience/.

Mayo, B. (1950) "Is there a sense of duration?" *Mind* 59(233): 71–78.

McCormack, T. and Hanley, M. (2011) "Children's reasoning about the temporal order of past and future events", *Cognitive Development* 26(4): 299–314.

Meritt, B. D. (1928) *The Athenian Calendar in the Fifth Century*, Cambridge, MA: Harvard University Press.

Onians, R. B. (1954) *The Origins of European Thought: About the Body, the Mind, the Soul, the World, Time and Fate*, Cambridge, UK: Cambridge University Press.

Owen, G. E. L. (1966) "Plato and Parmenides on the timeless present", *Monist* 50(3): 317–340.

Parmenides (2004 [1951]) *Fragmente*, in H. Diels and W. Kranz (eds.), *Fragmente der Vorsokratiker*, vol. 1, Berlin: Weidmann'sche Verlagsbuchhandlung.

Pindar (1997) *Olympian Odes, Pythian Odes*, Cambridge, MA: Harvard University Press.

Pöppel, E. (1978) "Time perception", in R. Held, H. W. Leibowitz and H.-L. Teuber (eds), *Handbook of Sensory Physiology, Vol. VIII: Perception*, Berlin: Springer-Verlag.

Pritchett, W. K. and Neugebauer, O. (1947) *The Calendars of Athens*, Cambridge, MA: Harvard University Press.

Sattler, B. (submitted for publication) *Natural Philosophy in Ancient Times: Logical, Methodological, and Mathematical Foundations for the Theory of Motion*, book manuscript.

Sattler, B. (in preparation) *Ancient Notions of Time*, book manuscript.

Sophocles (1964) *Oedipus at Colonus*, in M. Griffith, G. Most, D. Grene and R. Lattimore (eds and trans.), *Sophocles I*, Chicago, IL: University of Chicago Press.

Taplin, O. (1992) *Homeric Soundings: The Shaping of the Iliad*, Oxford, UK: Clarendon Press.

Theunissen, M. (2000) *Pindar. Menschenlos und Wende der Zeit*, Munich, Germany: Beck.

Thucydides (1919 and 1921) *History of the Peloponnesian War*, trans. C. F. Smith, Cambridge, MA: Harvard University Press, vol. I and III.

Williams, B. (2002) *Truth and Truthfulness: An Essay in Genealogy*, Princeton, NJ: Princeton University Press.

2

TIME AND TEMPORAL EXPERIENCE IN THE SEVENTEENTH CENTURY

Geoffrey Gorham

Introduction

The major philosophers of the early seventeenth century were engaged primarily with the metaphysics of time rather than the content of our temporal experience. This ontological orientation was inherited from the long scholastic tradition whose touchstone was the authoritative Aristotelian formula: "time is the number of movement with respect to the before and after" (220a 24; *ACM* I: 373). The scholastics were interested in the precise connection between time and motion, as well as between time and the mind since Aristotle also thought it worth asking whether there would be time without souls: "if there cannot be someone to count there cannot be anything that can be counted either, so that evidently there cannot be number" (223a 23–25; *ACM* I: 377). Seventeenth-century philosophers, especially those devoted to some version of the new science, generally worked against this tradition to separate time from motion and the mind. The apotheosis of this trend is Newton's absolute time, which "without reference to anything external, flows uniformly" (Principia: 408). But even those who defended a version of the traditional view, such as Leibniz, said very little about the phenomenology of time. The experience of time was relevant only because it secured the successive structure of duration and, for certain authors, the abstract or "imaginary" status of time. However, a decisive phenomenological turn was taken by the British empiricists Hobbes, Locke and Berkeley, who prioritized the *origin* of our idea of time over its ontological status. Although their accounts of temporal experience are diverse, incomplete and problematic, they set the stage for the more systematic and influential treatments of Hume and Kant.

Scholastic background

The most prominent medieval philosophers tended to follow Aristotle's view that time is conceptually and metaphysically tied to motion. Aristotle himself stops short of reducing time to any particular movement: "it is of movement qua movement that time is the number . . . the number of continuous movement, not any particular kind of it" (223a 33; *ACM* I: 377).[1] But later medieval authors typically pinned time to the continuous "first motion" of the heavens or outermost celestial sphere. Thus, in order to preserve the unity of time among all the diverse movements in the world, Averroes stipulates that time is properly the measure of "first motion".[2] In the *Summa Theologica* Aquinas argues that there is no time without motion since "in a thing bereft of movement, which is always the same, there is no before or after" (*ST*: Part 1a, quest. 10, art. 1), and in his *Commentary on Aristotle's Physics* he asserts "time is consequent upon the quantity of only the first motion" (SCAP: Bk. IV, lec. 17, sec. 576; 258). Indeed, it was not uncommon for Aristotelians to assert that "if the first heaven were to stop rotating, a falling stone would stop falling" (Duhem 1985: 297).[3]

In the wake of Copernicus and Galileo, "celestial reductionism" about time waned as the celestial spheres themselves were dissolved (Ariotti 1973). Furthermore, a number of anti-Aristotelian theological condemnations encouraged philosophers to entertain time (and space) independently of motion (and body). For example, in 1277, Bishop Tempier of Paris formally condemned the proposition: "if heaven stood still fire would not burn flax because [in that event] time would not exist" (Proposition 79 in Duhem 1985: 299). So influential late scholastic authors like Francisco Suarez were prepared to admit an "imaginary" time prior to the creation of the world which is not merely a figment of our imagination. However, Suarez is at pains to emphasize that imaginary space and time are mere conceptual tools or *beings of reason*: "We conceive of this imaginary space as having dimensions. But so conceived this space is a mere being of reason, a negation or privation . . . this is also true in the example of imaginary succession, which we conceive apart from real time" (MD: Disp 54, Sec. 4, 7). Suarez and the other main scholastics continued to hold that "time is . . . is not really distinct from motion" (MD: Disp. 50, Sec. 9, 1).[4]

The mainstream scholastics generally did not dwell on the subjective experience of time, including the time we imagine apart from motion, other than to observe that it is intrinsically *successive* (as opposed to the *permanent* duration of God and angels) and not merely a construct or figment of our imagination. The exception is St. Augustine, who devotes an entire chapter of his *Confessions* to the enigma of time. While holding that "neither the past nor future but only the present truly is" (11.14), Augustine is led to wonder how there nevertheless can be pasts and futures of longer and shorter durations. His answer is that a long past must somehow be a present "long memory" and a long future must be a present "long anticipation" (11.28). Augustine doesn't explain how a mental state without duration in its own right can nevertheless represent various durations; indeed, this is a puzzle about temporal experience that remains with us to this day.

Descartes and Newton

While a number of Renaissance thinkers, with allegiances to Plato rather than Aristotle, explored the distinction between time and change, the clearest break with Aristotle was initiated by Descartes.[5] He insists that "the duration which we find to be involved in movement is certainly no different from the duration involved in things which do not move" (AT 8A: 27; CSM 1: 212). It is true that in order to measure this duration generally "we compare their duration with the greatest and most regular motions, which give rise to years and days, and call this duration time" (Ibid.). But we must not conflate duration itself, which is intrinsic to all things, with its temporal measure, which is an intellectual abstraction: "when time is distinguished from duration taken in the general sense and called the measure of movement, it is simply a mode of thought" (Ibid.). Descartes went so far as to bring finite minds and God, traditionally assumed to have a non-successive mode of being, into time. Thus he explains to Burman that in finite minds "thought is extended and divisible with respect to its duration", and adds, "It is just the same with God: we can divide his duration into an infinite number of parts, even though God himself is not therefore divisible" (AT 5: 148; CSMK: 335).[6] But although his world is thoroughly saturated by time, Descartes offers hardly any analysis of the content of our experience of time and duration. Even the crucial "clear and distinct" perception of our own existence over time is left unanalysed: "the fact that it is the same I who am doubting and understanding and willing is so evident that I can see no way of making it any clearer" (AT 7: 29; CSM 2: 19). He indicates that we derive the idea of duration from our own experience – "I perceive that I now exist and remember that I existed for some time; moreover I have various thoughts which I can count; it is in these ways that I acquire the ideas of duration and number" (AT 7: 44–5; CSM 2: 30–l) – but he says little about the character of this experience.

Although Descartes breaks with the Aristotelian tradition by extending successive duration to all things, movable or not, he does not give duration an absolute existence apart from things themselves. Rather, "since a substance cannot cease to endure without also ceasing to be, the distinction between a substance and its duration is merely a conceptual one" (AT 8A: 39; CSM 1: 214). And hence he dismisses Henry More's postulation of "intermundane" duration: "it involves a contradiction to conceive of any duration intervening between the destruction of an earlier world and the creation of a new one" (AT 5: 343; CSMK 3: 373). The decisive final step of separating time from other created things was taken by Newton. In the unpublished manuscript *De Gravitatione* Newton finds it impossible to conceive an end of time, even if the world itself were destroyed: "we cannot think that there would be no duration, even though it would be possible to suppose that nothingness (*nihil*) endures" (DG: 22). And in the first edition of the *Principia* (1687), space and time each have their "own nature without reference to anything external" (*Principia*: 408). Specifically about time, he says: "Absolute, true, and mathematical time, of itself, and from its own nature, flows equably without relation to anything external" (Ibid.). Absolute time is not perceived directly, only its measure, "relative, apparent, and common time" such as "an hour, a day, a month, a year" (Ibid.). But, like the scholastics and Descartes, Newton says nothing about the structure and content of temporal perception, except that we can never be sure it perfectly tracks time itself: "it may be that there is no such thing as an equable motion, whereby time may be accurately measured" (Ibid.).

The neglect of temporal experience is not restricted to absolutists. Leibniz famously rejected the Newtonian view that space and time are "anything absolute". On the contrary, he maintained against the Newtonian Samuel Clarke: "I hold space to be something purely relative, as time is – that is, I hold it to be an order of coexistences as time is an order of successions" (L: 682). Leibniz's idealism applies to space and time considered abstractly, i.e. by the mind and independently of concretely extended and enduring bodies. But Leibniz offered no detailed account of temporal experience either of abstract time or concrete duration. Even more fundamentally, Leibniz conceived of concretely extended/enduring substances as merely "well-founded appearances" of aggregates of un-extended monads. But the states of these monads themselves unfold according to an internal "law of the series" which "involves all of the future states of that which we conceive to be the same – that is the very fact I say which constitutes the enduring substance" (L: 535). Leibniz characterizes the monadic relations as "perceptions" analogous to mental experiences (L: 608) including a sort of memory: "An immaterial being or spirit cannot 'be stripped of all' perception of its past experience. It retains impressions of everything which has previously happened to it" (NE: 239). However, besides suggesting that such perceptions come in degrees, are subject to memory and are comparable to visual perspective, Leibniz says hardly anything about the experiential aspect of the successive perception that gives rise to monadic time.[7]

The Experiential Turn: Hobbes, Locke and Berkeley

We have so far seen that, with rare exceptions, mainstream medieval and seventeenth-century philosophy devote little attention to the nature of temporal experience, focusing instead on time's metaphysical relation to motion and the mind. The sense in which time is (or is not) "imaginary" and/or "abstracted" from enduring things, is a core issue for Descartes and his scholastic precursors; but the investigation of this issue is strictly logical or conceptual rather than phenomenological. So despite their very different conclusions about the reality of time, Suarez, Descartes, Newton and Leibniz all share a concern with ontology rather than experience. The situation is different among the strongly empiricist philosophies of space and time developed in the latter half of the seventeenth century, especially in Britain.

Since Thomas Hobbes treats time as analogous to space, I begin with his famous account of imaginary space. As an avowed empiricist and materialist, Hobbes traces the origin of all ideas to motions in the body produced by sense experience. All such ideas are images or "phantasms". To account for the phantasm of space – which unlike body isn't directly observable – Hobbes relies on a remarkable thought experiment. In the text *Anti-White* he invites us to consider what would pass in the mind of a man left alone after all other bodies are annihilated: "there remain in the mind their images, i.e. the shapes or spaces in which they had appeared" (AW III.1: 40). The post-apocalyptic man would imagine "a space extending from him in all directions as far as he pleased" and so derive the abstract notion of "imaginary space", which Hobbes defines as "the image of any body merely insofar as it is body" (Ibid.). Later in *De Corpore*, he repeats the thought experiment and arrives at the definition of space as "the phantasm of a thing existing simply insofar as it exists" (OL i: 83; EW i: 94). Hobbes offers a parallel account of imaginary time. The remembered motion of a body is the cause of imaginary time just as its remembered magnitude is the cause of imaginary space: "just as a body leaves a phantasm of its magnitude in the mind so also a moved body leaves also a phantasm of its motion" (OL i: 83; EW i: 94). Time is thus defined as "the phantasm of before and after in motion" (OL i: 84; EW i: 94).

So Hobbesian time is fundamentally experiential – the present memory of a previous motion.[8] Like Augustine, he embraces a presentist reconstruction of the past and future. For he conceives of memory as a "sixth sense, but internal not external"; not a thought of something past – since "sensation is only of what is present" – but rather a taking notice about certain conceptions "that we have had the same conception before" (EL 1.3.6). When people speak of the "times of their predecessors", they cannot mean that these times exist "any where else but in the memories of those that remember them" (OL i: 84; EW i: 94–5). Similarly, "this word *future* is a name but no future thing has yet any being . . . nevertheless, since our thought is used to conjoin things past with things present the name *future* serves to signify such conjoining" (OL i: 15; EW i: 17). But Hobbes faces even more difficulty than Augustine in adhering to a strict presentism. Most importantly, motion depends on time for Hobbes – "whatever is moved is moved in time" (OL i: 176; EW i: 204) – and imaginary time is produced by motion just as imaginary space is produced by body: "just as a body leaves a phantasm of its magnitude in the mind so also a moved body leaves also a phantasm of its motion" (OL i: 83; EW i: 94). So, if only the present were real, there would be no real motion and hence no cause of our idea of time. But there is no indication Hobbes embraced such a strong form of idealism.[9]

Locke is also concerned, first and foremost, with our experience of time. In part, this derives from his overarching empiricist project: to explain the origin of our ideas in the two great "fountains" of experience: sensation of external things and reflection on the operation of our own minds (Essay II i 2; 104). But he is also concerned to refute – and indirectly defend his friend the "incomparable Mr Newton" (Essay Epistle; 10) – the Aristotelian view that time and motion are mutually defined, i.e. that "motion and duration were the measure of one another" (Essay II xiv 19; 188). Because men have commonly used heavenly bodies to measure time, "they were apt to confound time and motion" (Ibid.); any regular, periodic phenomena – such as the freezing of lakes, the blooming of plants, or seasonal diseases – "would not fail to measure out the succession of course of succession, and distinguish the distances of time" (Essay II xiv 20; 189). He also points out that ordinary clocks require space just as much as motion, in order to measure time; but no one defines time as the measure of space (Essay II xiv 22; 190). And he insists we can perfectly well conceive duration prior to the beginning of motion (Essay II xiv 26; 193).

In common with the scholastics and Descartes, succession is the crucial element in temporal concepts for Locke: we get the idea of duration from "the fleeting and perpetually perishing parts of succession" (Essay II xiv 1; 181). However, somewhat surprisingly, our idea of succession is in turn derived not from *sensation* of external changes but from *reflection* on the constant "train of ideas" in the understanding: "reflection on these several ideas one after another is that which furnishes us with the idea of succession" (Essay II xiv 3; 182). The idea of space, by contrast, comes directly from the sensations of sight and touch (Essay II xiii 2). This has been fixed on by some recent commentators as suggesting an idealist, perhaps proto-Kantian, theory of time as inner sense.[10] However, in noting the origin of our idea of time in reflection, Locke seems concerned merely to underscore the anti-Aristotelian divorce of time from motion, rather than evince any theoretical commitment to the subjectivity of our temporal notions. Locke does not rule out sensation as a cause of the idea of succession. Indeed, he explicitly includes it (along with existence, power, etc.) among the ideas received by sensation and reflection: "There is another idea which though suggested by our senses, is more commonly offered us by what passes in our own mind and that is the idea of succession" (Essay II vii 9; 131). Outside of the chapter on duration, motion is much more often classified as an idea of sense than an idea of reflection.[11] And in the chapter on duration itself, after remarking on the "constant succession" of fresh ideas received by a waking person, he indicates that his primary aim is not to rule out motion as a cause of the idea of succession, but rather to exclude motion from the content of that idea. "Whether these several ideas in a man's mind be made by certain motions, I will not here dispute. But this I am sure they include no idea of motion in their appearance" (Essay II xiv 16; 186). He does go on to say about duration, "of which motion no otherwise gives us any perception than as it causes in our mind a constant succession of ideas" (Ibid.). This remark is hardly controversial: how else would motion be perceived? In any case, he returns to his main thesis: "we should as well have the idea of duration, were there no sense of motion at all" (Essay II xiv 16; 187).

Consider one of Locke's main thought experiments in support of the reflective origin of temporal ideas. A man becalmed at sea would not perceive the real motion of the sun, sea or ship. So such motions would not give rise to the idea of succession or, consequently, the idea of duration. Fortunately, "he will perceive the various ideas of his own thoughts in his own mind, appearing one after another, and thereby observe and find succession, where he could find no motion" (Essay II xiv 6; 184). But the example seems merely to establish that the perception of external motion or change is not the *only* source for the idea of succession and duration, rather than the much stronger theoretical doctrine that our temporal concepts all derive from reflection. For this reason, the argument has seemed rather "silly" to a recent proponent of the subjectivist reading, Gideon Yaffe (2011: 393). To avoid attributing a silly argument to Locke, Yaffe develops an elaborate distinction between the merely "halting" (discrete) ideas of sensation and the both halting and "smooth" (successive) ideas of reflection. Essentially, the idea is that sensation at most represents the distinct locations of a moving object; reflection includes also the successive order of the locations.[12] Yaffe admits that the evidence for this reconstruction is at best "indirect" (2011: 401). I would like to propose a simpler reconstruction, aimed at a much more modest conclusion and supported by sensible (not silly) arguments.

If we keep in mind that Locke's primary interest is undermining the traditional conceptual link between motion and time, the various thought experiments he offers seem less silly.

Like the becalmed sailor, they all involve scenarios in which a person would experience succession and duration but not motion (because it is too slow or too fast). In these cases, it does seem plausible that our sense of time passing is grounded on our awareness of our own passing thoughts. In the midst of these examples, he does insist that we cannot perceive the succession in motion "without a constant succession of varying ideas arising in us" (Essay II xiv 7; 184). But, as already noted, the sensory origin of succession does not seem to violate this condition. Understood as reinforcing the conceptual distinction between motion and duration, Locke's arguments against the sensory origin of succession in ch. xiv mirror the overall strategy of the previous chapter "On Space". That chapter is largely concerned to refute the Cartesian identification of body and space. To this end, he provides various arguments for the possibility of a vacuum, emphasizing that since "the question here being whether the idea of space or extension be the same as the idea of body, it is not necessary to prove the real existence of a vacuum, but the idea of it" (Essay II xiii 23; 178). In this way, these arguments parallel the arguments of ch. xiv that ideas of succession and duration "include no idea of motion in their appearance" (Essay II xiv 16; 186). The two chapters are thus intended to make conceptual room for the absolute space and time of Newton, typical work of the philosophical under-labourer "clearing the ground a little and removing some of the rubbish that lies in the way of knowledge" (Essay Epistle; 10).

Despite his openness to a variety of sources, internal and external, for our temporal ideas, Locke has good reason to suppose that reflection is in fact their primary origin. Properly conceived, duration "is to be considered as going on in one constant, equal uniform course" (Essay xiv 21; 190). Locke frequently draws attention to the "constant" and "regular" rising and passing of ideas in the mind of man which he cannot hinder "though he may commonly choose whether he will heedfully consider them" (Essay II xiv 15; 186). While he concedes that this train of ideas may be "sometimes faster and sometimes slower", he suspects that "it varies not very much in a waking man" (Essay II xiv 9; 184). In contrast, the various motions we perceive begin and end irregularly. And Locke is sceptical that we can be sure of the true periodicity of even the most regular motions, like the stars and pendulums. "Seeming equality" is the most we can have, "of which seeming equality we have no other measure but such as the train of our own ideas have lodged in our memories" (Essay II xiv 21; 190). Reflection on the train of our own ideas is therefore our best and last hope for a constant and regular measure of duration. Thus, in a summary lesson on the too-slow/too-fast cases, Locke concludes "the constant and regular succession of ideas in a waking man is as it were the measure and standard of all other successions" (Essay II xiv 12; 185). So while Locke is firmly realist about the ontology of duration itself, he is ultimately a kind of idealist about the succession we experience and measure. This is one consequence of his attempt to reconcile his own hard-fought empiricism and his admiration for the incomparable Mr Newton.[13]

Berkeley follows Locke in deriving our idea of time from our idea of succession and our idea of succession, in turn, from reflection on the train of ideas within our own minds. Despite this shared epistemic starting point, their ontologies of time seem to diverge radically. Locke admits an objective measure of time independent of the train of our ideas; but, in addition, we must "carefully distinguish between duration itself and the measures we make use of to judge its length" (Essay II xiv 21; 190). Berkeley, of course, rejects the Newtonian conception of duration itself "considered as going on in one constant, equal, uniform course" (Ibid.); but he also seems to reject the distinction between objective measures of time and the subjective flow of our ideas: "A succession of ideas I take to *constitute* time, and not be only the sensible measure thereof" (J: 293). His fervent opposition to absolutism leads him to an extreme temporal solipsism: time is nothing more than the succession I experience in my own ideas; and if there are other successions of ideas, then there are *other times*.

In his first major philosophical work, the *Principles of Human Knowledge* (1710), Berkeley attacks the Newtonian/Lockean notion of time which as a typical "abstract idea" of which he says "I have no notion at all" (P 98; 83). Rather than a bare "continuation of existence or duration in the abstract", time is "nothing abstracted from the succession of ideas in our minds" (Ibid.). This proper conception of time seems to be arrived at by reflection and memory, rather than sensation, since it is a perceived relation among ideas. Thus, Berkeley says the duration of a finite spirit is "estimated by the number of ideas or actions succeeding each other in that same spirit or mind" (P 98; 83; see also D 1; 190).[14] So I am familiar with duration simply by perceiving and quantifying the continuous train of ideas in my mind. Insisting on the strict subjectivity of time enables Berkeley to avoid what he takes to be the twin absurdities that someone "passes away innumerable ages without a thought or else that he is annihilated every moment of his life". The former (Lockean) absurdity is avoided because there is no time without thoughts; the latter (Cartesian) absurdity is avoided because as the succession of my ideas, time is accidental rather than the very "continuation of existence" itself (recall that for Descartes a substance and its duration in being are merely two ways of conceiving the same thing).

Earlier and later in his philosophical career, Berkeley seems even more inclined to temporal subjectivism. Time is a major preoccupation in his notebooks, where Berkeley observes "the same το νυν [now] not common to all intelligences" (N 9; 9) and suggests that "the age of a fly for ought that we know may be as long as that of a man" (N 48; 12). Much later, in a 1630 letter to Johnson, he indicates that we are "confounded and perplexed about time" in part because we suppose that "the time in one mind is to be measured by the succession of ideas in another" (J 293).[15] As in the *Principles*, Berkeley takes his temporal subjectivism to vindicate the doctrine of the always-thinking soul. It dispenses with the counter-example of deep sleep: "Certainly the mind always & constantly thinks . . . in sleep and trances the mind exists not there is no time no succession of ideas" (N 651; 79; cf. P 98; 83). We never sleep deeply; rather time stops. The same solution is applied to the problem of the general resurrection. If no time passes of which we are unaware, then the resurrection can be universal, "simultaneous" and instantaneous: "No broken intervals of death or annihilation. Those intervals are nothing. Each person's time being measured to him by his own Ideas" (N 590; 73).[16]

But this advantage is more than offset by serious problems. If time cannot pass while I am asleep or dead, then likewise there was no time before I was born (Tipton 1974: 280; Hestevold 1990: 187). Berkeley might bite this bullet, attributing pre-birth time to the perceptions of God or other finite beings. But in that case, it seems events like "the Great Depression" cannot mean the same for my grandmother and myself. For her, it denotes a succession of ideas originating in the 1930s. For me, it picks out (at best) a jumble of recent ideas derived from books, movies and stories. A more serious problem concerns the *coordination* of shared events. If I nap while my room-mate studies, I will observe the sun to have set, and the clock to have advanced, instantaneously while he observes the same events to have taken hours. It does not seem possible to assimilate such dis-coordination to the familiar experience of the same event seeming longer or shorter to different perceivers (a phenomenon Locke and Berkeley both emphasize). In these cases, we synchronize our subjective temporal experiences by consciously pegging them to motions or changes we take to be regular and independent of our ideas – typically clocks and heavenly motions. But Berkeley's temporal solipsism eschews any time apart from subjective successions.[17]

The problem of coordination is what motivates Locke to extend the idea of time beyond its origin in reflection to the common objects of sense:

Having thus got the idea of duration, the next thing natural for the mind to do is to get some measure of this common duration . . . without which a great part of our knowledge would be confused and a great part of our history be rendered very useless.

(Essay II xiv 17; 187)

Berkeley too should want a common measure of time. Even if any time is strictly a succession of ideas in a thinking being – and hence no mind persists without thinking – Berkeley's commitments in natural philosophy seem to require an objective and coordinated (if not absolute) time. In the notebooks, he endorses the view that motion and velocity are "proportional to space described in a given time" (N: 129–130). And in *De Motu*, he says that "motion never meets our senses apart from corporeal mass, space and time" (DM 43; 42). If time were entirely subjective, then these commitments would entail that motion is likewise subjective. But in the *Principles of Human Knowledge*, he argues that the distinction between motion and rest is not a matter of subjective viewpoint: "we are capable of mistaking a thing to be in motion which is not" (P 115; 92).[18] And in *De Motu* he endorses the "primary law of nature" that a body "persists exactly in a state of motion" if unaffected by external forces, without any indication that this inertial velocity holds only for minds undergoing a constant succession of ideas (DM 51; 44). While he is convinced that the "famous theorems of mechanical philosophy by which the secrets of nature are unlocked" do not require absolute time and space (DM 66; 49), he seems equally convinced that they hold independently of this or that mind. And this requires a common standard of time if not an absolute flow of time.

Berkeley himself insists that "time, place and motion" considered concretely are known by everybody: "bid your servant to meet you at such a time, in such a place, he shall never stray to deliberate on the meaning of those words" (P 97; 83). While this remark is commonly, and rightly, read as a validation of ordinary language and common sense,[19] I think it also applies to the somewhat less concrete time of natural philosophy. The constant velocity or acceleration of a moving body is determined by our most regular common measures, a pendulum in Berkeley's day. Despite insisting that regular motion is not the only measure of time, Locke acknowledges that "men have of late made use of the pendulum as a more steady and regular motion". He nevertheless observes that "if anyone should be asked how he certainly knows that two successive swings of a pendulum are equal it would be very hard to satisfie himself" since unlike measures of extension "no two portions of succession can be brought together" (Essay II xiv 21; 190). Locke concludes that we can never be sure our best clocks' infallibly track duration itself. For Berkeley, the worry is not the accuracy of temporal measures relative to absolute time but their coordination with the subjective successions of ideas. If the duration of free fall is measured as accelerating, perhaps this is only because the clock itself is accelerating, but this goes unnoticed because the succession in my ideas is likewise accelerating. We certainly measure the lives of (most) men to be longer than the lives of (most) flies; but despite this "the age of a fly for ought that we know may be as long as that of a man" (N 48; 12).

The solution, I think, is not to measure the laws of nature against subjective temporal succession, but rather to identify an objective passage of time with the unfolding laws of nature themselves. By observation, we learn that there are "general laws which run through the whole chain of natural effects", i.e. "regular constant methods of working observed by the Divine agent" (P 62; 67–8). This "consistent uniform working" is a consequence of God's benevolence (P 32; 54), though Berkeley acknowledges (with Locke) that we cannot know certainly that the "Author of Nature always operates uniformly" (P 107; 88; *Essay* IV iii 29; 560). Berkeley identifies Newton's *Principia* as the "best key" to the laws of nature (P 110; 89). Among the general rules Newton derives from the laws of nature is that cycloidal pendulums are isochronous, i.e. their successive swings have the same period or duration despite different amplitudes (*Principia*: 553). So Berkeley can take the objective regularity of certain temporal processes like the pendulum to follow directly from God's constant "method of working". In this way, the regular passage of time is independent of any finite succession of ideas in the same sense as any other law-governed phenomenon, such as the motion of the earth around the sun (P 58; 65–6; Cf. D 253).[20]

The conception of objective time I am attributing to Berkeley is similar to the causal theory of time in the sense that it derives the temporal order and the regularity of certain clocks from natural laws. In this respect, it is noteworthy that Berkeley's favourite illustration of God's wise and good decision to work through natural mechanical laws is the clock. God could miraculously display the time of day in bodies and motions inscrutable to us; but it is better that He ground these motions in the predictable workings of mechanical clocks so that we know how to correct any "disorder in these movements" (P 62; 68). And the like may be said of "all the clockwork of Nature" (P 60; 67). Of course, Berkeley, does not allow causal connections among natural events (since they are passive ideas produced by God). But he does admit the "order and connexion" among our ideas of nature is "like to that of cause and effect" (P 64; 68). It is better conceived as the relation between sign and signified, as the fire I approach forewarns me of pain (P 64; 69). On this conception, time is simply the most regular and predictable pattern of motions which enables us to measure and anticipate our own ideas and coordinate them with the ideas of others.[21]

Conclusion

The major task of seventeenth-century philosophy of time was to reconcile our concept of time with emerging scientific programmes of Galileo, Descartes and Newton. For Descartes, this meant shearing time from its traditional connection to motion; for Newton, it meant attributing to time an existence and metric absolutely independent of bodies and change. But for the empiricist philosophers of Britain, the legitimacy of our temporal ideas required also an account of their origin in experience. Their common prioritization of temporal experience accompanied radically different ontologies of time: Augustinian presentism (Hobbes); Newtonian absolutism (Locke); temporal solipsism (Berkeley). Their challenge then, as now, was how to coordinate the manifest image of our temporal experience with the scientific image of an impersonal, law-governed world of bodies in motion. The challenge was taken up, with results still reverberating, by Hume and Kant.[22]

Abbreviations

ACM = Aristotle (1971) *Complete Works*. 2. vols. Jonathan Barnes (ed.), Princeton, NJ: Princeton University Press. Cited by Bekker number and page number.

AG = Leibniz. *Philosophical Essays*. R. Ariew and D. Garber (eds), Indianapolis, IN: Hackett, 1989.

AT = Descartes, R. (1983) *Oeuvres De Descartes*, 11 vols. C. Adam and P. Tannery (eds), Paris: J. Vrin. Cited by volume and page number.

AW = Hobbes, T. (1976) *Thomas White's De Mundo Examined*. H. Jones (ed.), London: Bradford University Press. Cited by chapter and page number.

C = Hobbes, T. (1994) *Leviathan with Selected Variants from the Latin Edition of 1668*, E. Curley (ed.), Indianapolis, IN: Hackett. Cited by page number.

CSM = Descartes R. (1988) *The Philosophical Writings Of Descartes*. 2 vols., John Cottingham, Robert Stoothoff, and Dugald Murdoch (eds), Cambridge, UK: Cambridge University Press. Cited by volume and page number

CSMK = Descartes R. (1991) *The Philosophical Writings of Descartes: The Correspondence*, John Cottingham, Robert Stoothoff, Dugald Murdoch, and Anthony Kenny (eds), Cambridge, UK: Cambridge University Press. Cited by page number.

D = Berkeley, G. (1948) *Three Dialogues between Hylas and Philonous*. In W, vol. 2. Cited by dialogue and page number.

DG = Newton, Isaac. (2004) *De Gravitatione et aequipondio fluidorum*. In *Newton: Philosophical Writings*. A. Janiak and C. Johnson (eds), Cambridge, UK: Cambridge University Press. Cited by page number.

DM = Berkeley, G. (1948) *De Motu*, In W, vol. 4. Cited by section number and page number.

EL = Hobbes, T. (1928) *Elements of Law*, F. Tonnies (ed.), Cambridge, UK: Cambridge University Press. Cited by part, chapter and paragraph.

Essay = John Locke, *An Essay Concerning Human Understanding*. Ed. P. H. Nidditch, Oxford, UK: Oxford University Press, 1975. Cited by book, chapter, section and page numbers.

EW = Hobbes, T. (1839–45) *English Works*. 11 vols., edited by W. Molesworth. London, 1839–1845. Cited by volume and page number.

J = Berkeley, G. (1948) *Philosophical Correspondence with Samuel Johnson*. In W, vol. 2. Cited by page number.

L = Leibniz, G. (1989) *Philosophical Papers and Letters*. L. E. Loemker (ed.), Dordrecht, The Netherlands: Kluwer. Cited by page number.

MD = Suarez, F. (1866) *Disputationes Metaphysicae*. In *Opera Omnia*. Edited by Carolo Berton. Paris: Vives. Cited by disputation, section and paragraph.

N = Berkeley, G. (1948) *Private Notebooks*. In W, vol. 1. Cited by editorial numbering and page number.

NE = Leibniz, G. (1996) *New Essays on the Human Understanding*. P. Remnant and J. Bennett (eds), Cambridge, UK: University of Cambridge Press. Cited by section number.

OL = Hobbes, T. (1845) *Opera philosophica quae latine scripsit omnia*. 5 vols. W. Molesworth (ed.), London. Cited by volume and page number.

P = Berkeley, G. (1948) *Principles of Human Knowledge*. In W, vol. 2. Cited by section number and page number.

Principia = Newton, I. (1999) *The Principia: Mathematical Principles of Natural Philosophy*. I. B. Cohen, A. Whitman, and J. Budenz (eds), Berkeley, CA: University of California Press, 1999. Cited by page number.

ST = Aquinas, St. Thomas. (1952) *Summa Theologica*. Translated by Fathers of the English Dominican Province (ed.). In *Great Books of the Western World*, vols. 19 and 20. Chicago, IL: Encyclopedia Britannica.

SCAP = Aquinas, St. Thomas. (1999) *Commentary on Aristotle's Physics*. R. Blackwell (ed.), South Bend, IN: St. Augustine's Press.

W = Berkeley, G. (1948–57) *The Works of George Berkeley*. 9 vols. A. A. Luce and T. E. Jessop (eds), London: Thomas Nelson. Cited by volume and page numbers.

Notes

1 Though in *On Generation and Corruption* he says that time is the number "of the circular movement" (337b 25; *ACM* I: 552).

2 *Aristotelis de Physico Auditu* IV (Frankfurt: Minerva, 1962), t.c. 132, fol. 203.

3 Even Suarez asserts that "absolutely speaking [. . .] the first motion (*motu primi mobilis*) is, simply speaking, time" (MD: Disp. 50, Sec. 11, 5).

4 See Daniel 1981 and Bexley 2012.

5 See Gorham 2012.

6 See further Gorham 2007, 2008.

7 Though see Rutherford 1998, ch. 8 and Arthur 2014, ch. 14 for plausible reconstructions of the perceptual ground of Leibnizian time.

8 Leibniz himself invokes Hobbes's doctrine in support of his own (L: 583).

9 See further Gorham 2014.

10 Dunlop 2009; Yaffe 2011.

11 For example: Essay II ix 9; 146; II i 1; 104.

12 Cf. Katherine Dunlop, who also takes Locke to be relying on reflection because the sensation of motion is not adequate to represent succession: "outer sensory representation is temporally ordered only insofar as it is also represented as 'inner', as contents of the mind" (2009: 4).

13 See further Gorham and Slowik 2014.

14 For a more detailed defense of the reflective origin of the Berkelean idea of succession, see Hynes 2005: 341.

15 Armstrong makes the interesting observation that succession must at least be unified across a given mind's sensory ideas, for example, across the sight and touch of motion: otherwise "it would become completely impossible to make any sort of correlation between the deliverances of the two senses" (1960: 83).

16 Better: all the times of the resurrected will be "coordinated" (presumably in the presence of God). As Hestevold observes, these times will still be strictly distinct successions (Hestevold 1990: 188).
17 See, further, Tipton 1974: 274; Pitcher 1977: 208–210; Furlong 1982: 153–154.
18 On Berkeley's views on apparent vs. real motion, see, further, Downing 2005.
19 Tipton 1974: 282; Furlong 1982: 150; Hestevold 1990: 182–183; Hynes 2005: 343.
20 Hestevold (1990: 185) suggests that time arises from God's conception of finite events and ideas "as successive", rather than from the laws of nature themselves, but does not explain how a mind lacking succession conceives ideas *as successive*. Hynes (2005: 339) hints at a law-grounded account of objective time for Berkeley; but he goes on to develop a corpuscular theory of time emphasizing Berkeley's philosophy of mathematics.
21 This account may also help Berkeley explain the sense in which time (a few days) passed between the initial creation and the arrival of sentient beings, a problem Philonous famously struggles with in Day Three of the *Dialogues* (D: 250–256). For an interesting recent discussion of this problem, focusing on time, see Hestevold (1990: 188–189).
22 Earlier versions of this material were presented to the Eastern Division meeting of the American Philosophical Association in Philadelphia, PA, the Locke Workshop in London, ON, and the Midwest Conference on British Studies, Ames, IA. I am grateful to audiences at these meetings and particularly to Martha Bolton who commented on the APA presentation.

References

Ariotti, P. (1973) "Toward absolute time: The undermining and refutation of the Aristotelian conception of time in the sixteenth and seventeenth centuries", *Annals of Science* 30(4): 31–50.
Armstrong, D. M. (1960) *Berkeley's Theory of Vision*, Melbourne, Australia: Melbourne University Press.
Arthur, R. (2014) *Leibniz*, Cambridge, UK: Polity Press.
Bexley, E. (2012) "Quasi-absolute time in Francisco Suárez's *Metaphysical Disputations*", *Intellectual History Review* 22(1): 5–22.
Daniel, S. (1981) "Seventeenth century scholastic treatments of time", *Journal of the History of Ideas* 42: 587–606.
Downing, L. (2005) "Berkeley's natural philosophy and philosophy of science", in K. Winkler (ed.), *The Cambridge Companion to Berkeley*, Cambridge, UK: Cambridge University Press.
Duhem, P. (1985) *Theories of Infinity, Place, Time, Void and the Plurality of Worlds*, Chicago, IL: University of Chicago Press.
Dunlop. K. (2009) "Unity of time's measure: Kant's reply to Locke", *Philosophical Imprints* 9: 1–31.
Furlong, E. J. (1982) "On being 'embrangled by time'", in C. M. Turbyane (ed.), *Berkeley: Critical and Interpretive Essays*, Minneapolis, MN: University of Minnesota Press.
Gorham, G. (2007) "Descartes on time and duration", *Early Science and Medicine* 12(1): 28–54.
Gorham, G. (2008) "Descartes on God's relation to time", *Religious Studies* 44(4): 1–19.
Gorham, G. (2012) "'The twin brother of space': Spatial analogy in the emergence of absolute time", *Intellectual History Review* 22(1): 1–17.
Gorham, G. (2014) "Hobbes on the reality of time", *Hobbes Studies* 27(1): 80–103.
Gorham, G. and Slowik, E. (2014) "Newton and Locke on absolute time and its sensible measure", in Z. Biener and E. Schliesser (eds), *Newton and Empiricism*, Oxford, UK: Oxford University Press.
Hestevold, H. S. (1990) "Berkeley's theory of time", *History of Philosophy Quarterly* 7: 179–192.
Hynes, D. (2005) "Berkeley's corpuscular philosophy of time", *History of Philosophy Quarterly* 22(4): 339–356.
Pitcher, G. (1977) *Berkeley*, London: Routledge & Kegan Paul.
Rutherford, D. (1998) *Leibniz and the Rational Order of Nature*, Cambridge, UK: Cambridge University Press.
Tipton, I. C. (1974) *Berkeley: The Philosophy of Immaterialism*, London: Methuen & Co.
Yaffe, G. (2011) "Locke on consciousness, personal identity and the idea of duration", *Noûs* 45(3): 387–408.

Further reading

E. Grant, *Much Ado about Nothing: Theories of Space and Vacuum from the Middle Ages to the Scientific Revolution* (Cambridge, UK: Cambridge University Press, 1981) offers a thorough account of the medieval and early modern ontological debates about space, most of which apply, mutatis mutandis, to time.

C. Leijenhorst, *The Mechanisation of Aristotelianism: The Late Aristotelianism of Thomas Hobbes's Natural Philosophy* (Leiden, The Netherlands: Brill, 2002) presents an insightful reconstruction of Hobbes' influential metaphysics and natural philosophy, including his theories of space and time.

J. Gibson, *Locke's Theory of Knowledge and Its Historical Relations* (Cambridge, UK: Cambridge University Press, 1960) is an historically sensitive discussion of Locke's epistemology which gives considerable attention to his views of space and time.

Michael Ayers, *Locke: Epistemology & Ontology*, London: Routledge, 1990) is a nearly exhaustive critical analysis of Locke's non-political philosophy, with detailed discussion of time.

A. C. Grayling's, *Berkeley: The Central Arguments* (LaSalle, PA: Open Court, 1986) stands out among the many introductions to Berkeley's philosophy for its incisive analysis and engaging style.

3

HUME ON TEMPORAL EXPERIENCE

Lorne Falkenstein

It is one thing to give an empiricist account of temporal experience. It is another to give a sensationist account. An empiricist can see more than a sensationist, who reduces sensory experience to the experience of sensations. In book 1, part 2, section 3 of his *Treatise of Human Nature*, David Hume offered an empiricist account of time as a manner of appearance of sensations.

The Lockean background

Hume considered his views on space and time to comprise a two-part "system". According to the first, our perceptions of space and time consist of unextended parts. According to the second, there must be something else to these parts to make them real. From this, Hume inferred that our ideas of space and time must be "those of the manner or order, in which objects exist", and that it is impossible to conceive "a time, when there was no succession or change in any real existence".[1]

Hume argued for the first part of this system over the first two sections of *Treatise* 1.2. However, when he turned to the second part in *Treatise* 1.3, he made a new beginning. He did not derive either the claim that time is a manner of existence or the claim that each part of time must be filled with a perceptibly different thing from the indivisibility of temporal parts. Instead, he appealed to phenomenological considerations cited on John Locke's authority.

(Hume did appeal to indivisibility at a later point (T 1.2.3.12–17). But this passage focuses on space. It concludes with the remark that "the same reasoning" will apply to time. But Hume wanted to infer that the perception of an unchanging object cannot make us aware of the passage of time (T 1.2.3.7–8), whereas he thought that the parts of space may be qualitatively identical (T 1.2.3.5, T 1.2.5.8). What he said about space cannot justify the stronger thesis concerning time.)

Locke had maintained that while our idea of time is drawn from experience, it is not drawn from experience of the motions of bodies, as implied by the Aristotelian view that time is the measure of motion. It is instead drawn from experience of the succession of ideas in our minds.[2] To establish that the latter can occur without the former and that the experience of time is dependent on the latter, Locke appealed to two examples: sitting on the deck of a ship on a becalmed sea out of sight of land on a cloudless day (E 2.14.6), and observing anything that moves in a circle so quickly as to seem a circle (E 2.14.8). In the first case, motion is too

42

slow, in the second, too fast to notice. In the first case, time is still perceived to pass as long as there is a succession of ideas in the observer's mind; in the second, it is not because there is no such succession.

That there really are motions too slow or too fast to be experienced is demonstrated by appeal to what we do sense and to background commitments. Slowly moving objects do not produce different ideas before a number of other ideas have occurred, giving the impression that they are not moving at all for that period. When we eventually notice a change in their position, we are not tempted by the alternative that they moved by a sudden jump, but suppose that they must have moved too slowly to catch our notice (E 2.14.11). Locke addressed motions too fast to be perceived with the disturbing example of a "cannon bullet" that rips through the walls of a house, taking the occupant's leg with it in the process. The occupant experiences the impact on the first wall, the leg and the second wall as occurring at the same moment. But metaphysics again intervenes to lead us to infer that the cannon ball cannot have occupied all of these places at once, but must have moved from one to the next (E 2.14.10). The case implies that time passes even when there is no succession in our ideas. It is just not experienced to pass.

Locke further maintained that, during waking hours, the speed with which ideas succeed in the mind "varies not very much" (E 2.14.9). Where external stimuli change too slowly, thought supplies a train of ideas at the normal rate (E 2.14.6 and 9); where they change too quickly their effects are assimilated (E 2.14.8).

Locke never explained exactly how "*Reflection* on these Appearances of several *Ideas*, one after another, in our Minds . . . furnishes us with the *Idea* of *Succession*" (E 2.14.3). If the earlier ideas no longer exist, the later do not exist yet, and the act of reflection is confined to a present moment, then denominating any of them "earlier" or "later memories" of "past" ideas begs the question of the origin of temporal ideas.[3] Locke may not have been aware of the problem. More charitably, he might have thought that since a succession of ideas does give rise to an idea of succession, the difficulties explaining how need not detain us. Thomas Reid charged him with taking reflection on the succession of our ideas to extend beyond the present moment and so confusing reflection with memory (Reid 1785: 325–326).

A further complication arises with the idea of duration. Succession is a relation, but Locke's discussion of duration does not occur in the later part of *Essay* 2 devoted to the discussion of ideas of relation (E 2.25–28). It instead occurs in the earlier part devoted to ideas of "simple modes" (E 2.13–21). Locke did not reduce duration to succession. He maintained that reflection on the succession of our ideas reveals that there is a certain "distance" between the ideas. It is the experience of this "distance" that properly serves as the foundation for the idea of duration.

> *Reflection* on these appearances of several *Ideas* one after another in our Minds, is that which Furnishes us with the *Idea* of *Succession*: And the Distance between any parts of that Succession, or between the Appearance of any two *Ideas* in our Minds, is that we call Duration.
>
> *(E 2.14.3)*

Locke's employment of words notwithstanding, he most likely did not mean to say that successive ideas are separated from one another by an intervening distance. His point was more likely that any idea takes up a distance between those on either side. While he maintained that a single idea "seems . . . to have no Distance" to someone capable of keeping it in mind "without Variation and the Succession of others" (E 2.14.4), this could not be because the idea in fact takes up no distance. Locke's point may have been that we only become aware of this distance through attending to the succession of three ideas necessary to mark its ends. When focusing just on one idea to the exclusion of the terminal ideas, the distance vanishes for lack of definition like the blackness between two stars that becomes blindness in their absence. Reid, citing Richard Price, missed this subtlety when he charged Locke with neglecting to consider that succession presupposes duration because a succession of durationless elements would vanish in an instant.[4]

Hume's Lockean arguments

Like Locke, Hume claimed that our idea of time is based on experience of the succession of our perceptions (T 1.2.3.6). But whereas Locke had been concerned to establish that the idea of time need not arise from sensation of the motion of external objects, Hume was concerned to establish that we cannot experience time "either alone, or attended with a steady unchangeable object" (T 1.2.3.7). To this end, he appealed to two phenomena Locke had invoked at *Essay* 2.14.4. "A man in a sound sleep, or strongly occupy'd with one thought, is insensible of time; and according as his perceptions succeed each other with greater or less rapidity, the same duration appears longer or shorter to his imagination" (T 1.2.3.7). But the claim that we do not experience time in sound sleep only establishes that when we are unconscious we really are unconscious whereas the claim that "the same" duration appears longer or shorter depending on the rapidity of the succession of perceptions presupposes some other way of measuring the sameness of duration.

Hume also appealed to Locke's example of rotating bodies, where "'tis impossible for our perceptions to succeed each other with the same rapidity, that motion may be communicated to external objects" (T 1.2.3.7). Like the "cannon bullet" case, this case implies that bodies move, and so time passes even when there is no succession in our ideas. It further implies that perceptions endure relative to this background passage of time and "succeed each other with greater or less rapidity" because they have different durations. These implications could not have been welcome to Hume, but they had both been features of Locke's account, and Hume did say that the "greater or less rapidity" with which our "perceptions succeed each other" has "certain bounds . . . beyond which no influence of external objects on the senses is ever able to hasten or retard our thought". He also said that where there is no succession in perceptions, there is no perception of time "even tho' there be a real succession in the objects" (T 1.2.3.7).

Despite all these problems, there is a profound point about the nature of our experience of time to be gathered from what Hume chose to take from Locke.

> It has been remark'd by a [fn: Mr. *Locke*] great philosopher, that our perceptions have certain bounds in this particular, which are fix'd by the original nature and constitution of the mind, and beyond which no influence of external objects on the senses is ever able to hasten or retard our thought.
>
> *(T 1.2.3.7)*

The bounds to the rapidity with which our perceptions succeed each other are not due to the "influence of external objects on the senses" but to "the original nature and constitution of the mind". This is not something Locke said in so many words, though it might be read into what he did say (E 2.14.8–11). Hume would not have meant it in so many words, either. He would later make a number of sceptical observations about the existence of external objects as well as minds. But that does not detract from what is said here. The influence of external objects on the senses, should there be any, is to produce impressions. The mind is who knows what. A contrast between "the influence of external objects on the senses" and "the original nature and constitution of the mind" is still a contrast between what produces impressions and something else. Something else prevents whatever causes our impressions from hastening or retarding our thought beyond certain bounds. The scepticism about minds that emerges over ensuing parts of the *Treatise* means that this factor will not turn out to be a feature of the mind. But neither is it due to the simple impressions themselves, which for Hume are not temporally extended and so capable of occurring in arbitrarily close succession. It is most austerely described as an empirically observed aspect of the experience of time itself. Experiences like those with the whirling coal reveal that it is not possible for further perceptions to be disposed between any two given perceptions, and so for there to be an arbitrarily numerous collection of perceptions succeeding upon one another between given limits. There is a perception immediately before and immediately after any given perception, and these perceptions are so disposed that a continual passage from one to the next is found to exceed any given bound. Since these features of temporal experience cannot be accounted for by unextended perceptions, they must be due to something else. Something makes it possible for some perceptions to endure, by consisting of otherwise identical, simple parts disposed immediately after one another, and so defines what it means for perceptions to succeed more rapidly or more slowly and for there to be bounds beyond which their succession cannot be hastened or retarded. This thing also sets limits to the divisibility of those that endure. There is therefore something more to the experience of time than the experience of a succession of durationless perceptions. There is experience of a structure that imposes constraints on the character of this succession.

(George (2006) has argued that Hume considered simple impressions to have a minimal size (30 seconds of arc in the case of vision), but no "extension", because at the time only what has more than one part was called "extended". But Hume invoked the claim that the parts of space and time must have some quality to make them real when inferring the second part of his system from the first (T 1.2.4.2). If the parts have size, then there is already something real to them and they do not also need quality. This scuttles the second part of the system so clearly that it is unlikely Hume would have countenanced it.)

(It may seem counterintuitive that a sound that has no duration should still be heard, but for Hume it will if it is loud enough. Its quality makes it real, and its being located in time makes it a real thing that exists in a certain manner. See T 1.2.3.15.)

Hume said something similar about space. "A blue and a red point may certainly lie contiguous without any penetration or annihilation" (T 1.2.4.6). This is proven by our ability to see a blue point lying contiguous to a red point. For the two points to be contiguous is for there to be no gap or intervening colour point between them. Yet, though contiguous, the two points do not touch in the sense of sharing a point in common. For point-entities to share a point in common is for one to penetrate or annihilate the other. Since both points are visible, neither point has annihilated the other. Yet, since nothing is visible between them, they are contiguous. This must mean that the one is immediately adjacent to the other, without touching the other at a point, and yet without leaving an intermediate gap. This is only possible in a space that does not contain further places between any two given places and so prevents there always being a gap between any two coloured points that do not touch at a point.

The absence of a further location between any two given locations is not the only empirically observable feature of the space and time in which perceptions are disposed. In an earlier passage, Hume observed that "repeating" an idea causes:

> [t]he compound idea of extension, arising from its repetition, always to augment, and become double, triple, quadruple, &c. till at last it swells up to a considerable bulk, greater or smaller, in proportion as I repeat more or less the same idea.
>
> (*T* 1.2.2)

Were this augmentation due to the ideas themselves, they must have some minimal extension to be doubled and tripled. But then they would not be unextended, as Hume wished to claim that they are (T 1.2.3.12–14). The only way that "repeating" extensionless ideas can augment an extension is if something prevents denser manners of disposition or succession, even though the simple perceptions are unextended and so would allow it. (This is not to say that preventing a denser manner of disposition would produce a speckled or flickering compound. For the compound to be speckled or flickering, there would have to be unoccupied locations between the occupied ones and the thesis is that the space in which perceptions are disposed and the time over which they appear are discrete and so do not contain these further locations.)

Hume considered unboundedness to be a further, *perceptually* evident feature of space and by implication time: "and were I to carry on the addition *in infinitum*, I clearly perceive, that the idea of extension must also become infinite" (T 1.2.2.2). "I clearly perceive" is an exaggeration. But Hume would have at least wanted to claim it is perceptually evident that only a finite number of perceptions can be packed between the bounds set by birth and death, or the edges of the visual field.

At T 1.2.4.2, Hume described the ideas of space and time as those of "the manner or order in which objects exist". This brings up further structural features. The idea of space is said at T 1.2.3.6 to be received "from the disposition of visible and tangible objects" whereas that of time is said to be formed "from the succession of ideas and impressions". In vision and touch, simple sensations are discretely and unboundedly disposed over a precise number of dimensions – two for vision, three for touch (Hume 1997: 256). Dimensionality is not due to simple visual or tangible impressions, which have no sides or dimensions. It is instead a feature of their manner of disposition.

In contrast, time has a special relation to existence. Because the idea of time arises from the experience of succession, and succession is coming to be and passing away, time is the order in which perceptions come to be and pass away. But just as simple impressions contain nothing that would prevent them from being disposed arbitrarily closely to one another, so they contain nothing to prevent their being disposed contemporaneously. And in fact they often are. Hume said that an unchangeable object produces "none but co-existent impressions" (T 1.2.3.8), implying that different impressions do coexist. But he was also insistent that the parts of time cannot coexist (T 1.2.2.4, 1.2.3.8). Moments in time cannot therefore be identified with simple perceptions, which are as capable of coexisting as of occurring in succession. Neither can they be identified with compound impressions, without begging the question of what distinguishes a spatial compound from a temporal one. Antisymmetry governs only the parts of time, not the perceptions in time.

Time is a discrete and unbounded successive series of moments, distinct from simple perceptions, at which collections of simple perceptions appear. Metaphysically, for the moments of time to be successive means they form a series, that only one member of the series is the present moment, and that each is present in turn. There is no rate at which the alteration of presence occurs (so, no meta-time over which time passes). But it does occur and so marks the rate at which all other changes occur. Phenomenologically, as musicians speak of themselves marking (not making) time by playing music, so the parts of time are marked (not made) by the coming to be and passing away of perceptions, with the present moment being marked whenever an impression comes to be or passes away.

Compound impressions

Locke accepted that ideas have duration and that time can pass and be thought to pass even when there is no succession in ideas, though it is not experienced to pass in that case. What has just been said explains how Hume could employ Locke's arguments without accepting Locke's views on the duration of simple ideas or imperiling his rejection of the infinite divisibility of time. But it leaves the question of whether Hume could also sustain the tenets that "the indivisible moments of time must be filled with some real object or existence" (T 1.2.3.17) and that the idea of duration "can never in any propriety or exactness be apply'd to [objects, which are perfectly unchangeable]". The question comes to a head at *Treatise* 1.2.3.9–10, where Hume asked whether time can be conceived apart from conceiving a succession of perceptions. He answered this question in the negative, on the grounds that the original impressions from which (according to Hume) all our ideas must be copied contain no distinct impression of time apart from the impressions of successive objects. But the devil is in the details.

> The idea of time is not deriv'd from a particular impression mix'd up with others, and plainly distinguishable from them; but arises altogether from the manner, in which impressions appear to the mind, without making one of the number. Five notes play'd on a flute give us the impression and idea of time; tho' time be not a sixth impression, which presents itself to the hearing or any other of the senses. Nor is it a sixth impression, which the mind by reflection finds in itself. These five sounds making their appearance in this particular manner, excite no emotion in the mind, nor produce an affection of any kind . . . nor can the mind, by revolving over a thousand times all its ideas of sensation, ever extract from them any new original idea . . . But here it only takes notice of the *manner*, in which the different sounds make their appearance.
>
> *(T 1.2.3.10)*

Time is not a sixth impression in addition to the five flute note impressions. But neither is it any one of the flute note impressions. Neither is it anything that can be subsequently derived from the five flute note impressions by "reflection", whether understood in Humean terms, as an "impression of reflection" or passion, or in Lockean terms, as the product of a process performed on ideas. Time is already experienced with the five flute note impressions. But it is not experienced with any one of them, if we follow Hume in supposing that they have no duration (T 1.2.3.14–17). It is only experienced in the compound impression of two or more.

This compound impression could just as well contain a number of simple ideas or a mixture of simple impressions and simple ideas. (Even when the perceptions are ideas, they still appear and disappear in turn, producing a compound *impression* of the temporal succession of *perceptions*.) But it also presents those simple perceptions in a manner characterized by the structural features discussed earlier. For both manner of appearance and content, all ideas are copied from impressions, the simple ideas from prior simple impressions and the manner of appearance from prior compound impressions.

Hume did deny that we have any experience of time on its own. The impression of time is not separable from that of the notes. Since "Every thing, that is different, [is] distinguishable; and every thing, that is distinguishable, may be separated", as Hume had reiterated as a part of this very discussion, it follows that the compound impression of time could not even be different from the compound impression of five flute notes. But this compound impression still has distinct aspects or "circumstances of resemblance" to other compounds that can be identified by way of a "distinction of reason" (T 1.1.7.7n.5, T 1.1.7.18). As a distinct aspect of the compound impression of the flute notes, time is neither one of the notes, nor something that only subsequently arises from them. It is their manner of occurrence. The flute notes appear and disappear in succession. They cannot be without coming to be and passing away in this particular manner, and this particular manner cannot be without them being there to mark it. Imagination can separate the five notes from one another. It can also "afterwards consider [the manner of their disposition] without considering these particular sounds, but may conjoin it with other objects" (T 1.2.3.10). But any note or collection of notes must be imagined to appear and disappear in some manner, and any similar manner must be punctuated by some ideas.

"The ideas of some objects it certainly must have", Hume wrote, "nor is it possible for it without these ideas ever to arrive at any conception of time", and that much can be granted to him. Where there are no ideas conceived to appear, there can be no conception of any manner of appearance. But Hume failed to explain why the ideas must be different from one another, or disposed at every available location, and so failed to explain why one note held for five beats, or two identical notes separated by three beats of silence, would not give us an impression of the same duration as five different notes.

At T 1.2.3.8, Hume claimed that "an unchangeable object, since it produces none but co-existent impressions, produces none that can give us an idea of time". This begs the question. A reason needs to be given why an unchangeable object could not produce a succession of identical impressions, and none ever was.

T 1.2.3.8 gives a reason for rejecting its own premise: that no two parts of time are co-existent. The phenomenal temporal order is punctuated by the appearance of perceptions, so that what is earlier is what appeared, and what is present is what appears. Think of looking at a mountain while hearing music play. As one note, P, ceases to be perceived, so one part of time, T_P, passes, to be followed by another, T_Q. By definition, an "unchangeable object" would not be destroyed at T_P, but would continue to exist at T_Q, be it as a succession of identical impressions or an enduring impression divisible into successive parts (the distinction is moot), incidentally nullifying the contortions of T 1.2.5.29.

(The alternative that the unchangeable object might occupy its own, indivisible part, T_U, of a different time line (Baxter 2008: 36–43) is not an option, given Hume's claim that "each of [time's] parts succeeds another, and that none of them, however contiguous, can ever be co-existent" (T 1.2.2.4). If T_U were a different part of time from T_P or T_Q, it could not coexist with either of them, since only one part can ever exist.)[5]

Succession of perceptions vs. perception of succession

Like Locke's, Hume's view that the idea of time arises from the experience of succession raises a difficult question about the nature of that experience. It is natural to think that there can be no knowledge of a relation, like succession, unless all its terms are apprehended and compared, and that this requires a "unity of consciousness". A succession of impressions is not enough. An impression of succession is required.[6]

If this is what is needed, then it is hard to see how Hume could provide it.[7] Hume thought that only one part of time ever exists and that this part is unextended. Of course, earlier parts might be remembered, but Hume's account of memory is not particularly helpful. Hume was not Reid, whose position on this matter merits contrast with Hume's.

Reid maintained that memory acquaints us with the past members of a succession. But his position on how it does so was highly idiosyncratic. Though he denied that sensation or consciousness can give us the idea of succession (1785: 325–326), he also denied that to remember is to presently perceive an image or copy of a past perception (1785: 338–356). For Reid, the act of remembering occurs in the present moment, but the direct object of this act is the past object. To remember is to directly apprehend the no longer existent object (this is not the block universe), not a presently existing image of that object.

Suppose that once, and only once, I smelled a tuberose in a certain room where it grew in a pot, and gave a very grateful perfume. Next day I relate what I saw and smelled. When I attend as carefully as I can to what passes in my mind in this case, it appears evident, that the very thing I saw yesterday, and the fragrance I smelled, are now the immediate objects of my mind when I remember it . . .

Philosophers indeed tell me, that the immediate object of my memory . . . in this case, is not the past sensation, but an idea of it, an image, phantasm, or species of the odour I smelled: that this idea presently exists in my mind or in my sensorium; and the mind contemplating this present idea, finds it a representation of what is past . . . Upon the strictest attention, memory appears to me to have things that are past, and not present ideas, for its object.

(Reid 1764: 44–46)

Reid believed that the non-existence of an object is no impediment to directly conceiving it – *it*; not some mental image of it (1785: 362–365, 376–381, 390–395). The non-existence of a *past* object is therefore no impediment to directly conceiving it either. Reid was not a "common sense champion of phenomeno-temporal antirealism".[8] Though he thought that change, succession and persistence can only be apprehended with the aid of memory, he also maintained that they are directly apprehended. For Reid, from our vantage point in the present, we apprehend the past as it was and no longer is. We see it off in a distance in the past, just as we see what is off in the distance in space (Reid was a direct realist about this as well). We do not experience a "memory image" that is "far less vivid, far less detailed, than the corresponding perceptual experiences".[9] Perception is conception with belief in present existence, memory conception with belief in past existence. The only difference is in the belief that attends the conception, and the beliefs can be equally strong. The clarity, distinctness and other qualities of the conception of the past object, and the strength of the belief in its past existence, may change with circumstances such as the passing of time since the initial perception (1785: 305, 341–342, 361, 369–374). But it does so gradually and in different ways with different circumstances, so that there is no sharp dividing line between what is remembered with all the clarity and vivacity and certainty of a perception and what is only remembered with doubt, difficulty and lack of clarity. There need be no other difference between memory and perception than that the object of the one is, and is believed to be, past; the object of the other, present. The distinction between sensation and perception is merely verbal, not phenomenological (1785: 326–327).[10]

But this was not Hume's account. Hume's account was the one Reid rejected, that to remember is to presently experience a copy of a past impression (T 1.1.3.1). Whatever might be said for or against this account, it is of no use in the present context, because to experience a present copy of a past impression simultaneously with some other present perception is not to experience a succession of perceptions. The status of the copy as a copy of what is past, and the nature of the experience of succession is left unexplained.

However, Hume had a way of accounting for access to information about the past that does not rely on memory. At T 1.3.8.13, he remarked that the past can have a non-cognitive influence on present thoughts, "the mind makes the transition [between perception of cause and belief in effect] without the assistance of the memory. The custom operates before we have time for reflection".

This allows for an account that does not demand a unity of consciousness. Rather than grasp all the parts at once, compare them and find a relation of succession between them, we are changed by past experience, which endows us with the ability to subsequently review the events in their original order as the occasion requires, and the ability to imagine other objects in that same sequence. These abilities to repeat the sequence are what distinguishes a being who has an apprehension of the sequence from one who does not.[11]

When I am asked, "how many notes did you hear?" or "for how many beats did it last?", I am at first baffled. Time being a manner of appearance rather than a manner of disposition, I have no instantaneous memory that displays the answer, the way a memory of five dots on the face of a die displays five dots. Instead, I replay the sequence of notes in my mind, tapping a different finger after each one. Or I make marks on paper and then count them. Performing these processes puts me in a position to provide some number, which is not the same thing as grasping all the notes in a unity of consciousness. Something similar happens if I am asked to say which note or which word of a verse occurs between which others. I need to map the temporal relations onto space by reciting them in order as I draw symbols for the notes or words and then contemplate the spatial relations between the symbols. Such unity of consciousness as I achieve is of spatial relations between signs, not temporal relations of signata.

The most difficult cases for this account are posed by phenomena like the perception of motion or the hearing of the syllables of a word. As classically claimed by Broad (1923: 351), there is a difference between seeing a second hand moving and seeing that an hour hand has moved. Accounting for the former seems to demand some sort of unified consciousness of the very recent past and the present precluded by Hume's insistence that the present is unextended, that the past no longer exists and that the past is not directly conceived in present memory. But as compelling as Broad's distinction may be, Hume could make a respectable case for rejecting it. A bird soars past me against a featureless background. A person stands before me against the same background as I rotate my eyes and head to one side. Or I hold a magnifying glass at arm's length and raise it, along with my eyes and head, while looking through it at the person's inverted image. The bird is perceived to move across my visual field. But my visual field is perceived to turn past the motionless person. And the image seen through the magnifying glass is perceived to race in the direction the glass is moving at twice its speed while the glass appears stationary (Welsh 1986: 24.21). That such different experiences should result from such similar sequences of retinal excitation suggests that the experiences are not as direct as they seem to be. Some background operation is involved, opening the door to the kind of account Hume would need to provide – an account like Berkeley's account of visual depth perception. Perhaps perceiving motion is just a more effortless, rapid or pre-cognitive form of perceiving that something has moved, drawing on proprioception or habituation.

Someone struggling to learn a language appreciates how a succession of syllables or words can only be grasped after repetition has ingrained a habit, so that hearing the first syllable raises a limited number of expectations, further narrowed by hearing the next syllable, and ultimately only confirmed by the remainder. Hence the difficulty of understanding those with foreign accents, and the shock and confusion we experience when hearing those who do not respect the common idiom in the sequence of their words. The novelties force us to rewind and replay to figure out the meaning, and this opens the possibility that the meaning is never grasped by way of a unity of consciousness of the successive words or symbols, but only by having pre-conceptions narrowed and confirmed over the course of time. It is so long since we learned to see that we are no longer judges of whether something similar happens with moving bodies.

We think that having an impression or an idea of succession consists in grasping a relation between the successive elements. But it takes time to hear *do, re, me, fa, so*; and it also takes time to remember that I heard them that way because at no point am I able to recall all five notes at once. My memory instead takes the form of reciting these five notes in the order they were first apprehended. I am only ever conscious of them sequentially and of a potential to start myself on a course that will lead me to imagine the rest in sequence – a sequence that I can't see in advance, but can only grasp incrementally as I recite it yet again. The touted unity of consciousness of the five notes may not exist. The "impression of succession" that is something more than a "succession of impressions" may just be the feeling of confidence in the ability to recite the succession of ideas without balking.

Hume did not make the various observations I have just made. But he did appeal to the mechanisms I have appealed to – habituation, the formation of expectations and the projection of feelings – when accounting for such related phenomena as causal inference, the understanding of abstract terms and the attribution of necessitating power to causes. They can serve as a Humean way of defending Hume's account of temporal experience as having experiences over time rather than having experiences of time.

Having developed this intriguing approach, Hume muddied it by going on to insist that the temporally disposed perceptions must all be different from one another and that no gaps could occur in the sequence. These are claims for which he had no good argument. Perhaps he thought that a succession of identical perceptions or a succession of gaps would be too hard to notice or measure when most of the members of the succession no longer exist. He is so far from having given any good reason for his position that even this is speculation. Aside from that extravagance, he offered a bold and plausible account of temporal awareness.[12]

Notes

1 Hume 1739–40: 1.2.4.1–2 and 1.2.3.13–14. T in subsequent references. Cited using the numbering of the critical edition.
2 Locke 1706: 2.14.6, 16, 22. E in subsequent references.
3 For further discussion, see Bardon 2007: 48–49 and Yaffe 2011: 399. Drawing on the closing sentences of *Essay* 2.14.3, Yaffe proposes an ingenious solution, which involves assimilating two different sorts of ideas and appealing to a Cartesian notion of self-consciousness. See also Chapter 2: 34 of this volume.
4 1785: 325 and 327–328. Cf. Price 1758: 30–31.
5 Baxter's argument neglects antisymmetry, instead defining coexistence purely negatively, so that being coexistent has no more to do with being earlier or later in time than being red or blue. On Baxter's account, a simple impression may "coexist" with a succession of others without detriment to its simplicity. This would mean that for any given simple impression, there will always be a possibility that a succession of arbitrarily many other impressions may "coexist" with that impression. A more robust notion of coexistence is needed to save Hume's position on infinite divisibility from this consequence.
6 For expressions of this view, see Bardon 2007: 56; Dainton 2011: 389; Yaffe 2011: 399 and, classically, James 1890: 628. Hoerl 2013 provides further history and discussion.
7 For a particularly eloquent statement of this objection, see Bardon 2007: 56–58.
8 Dainton 2014: 2.3.
9 Dainton 2011: 388–389.
10 Reid resists classification on the spectrum of positions on temporal consciousness identified by Dainton 2014: 1.1–1.2. He was not an antirealist, because he believed the past is directly apprehended. He was not a retentionalist, because he denied that memory retains representations of past events. He was not an extensionalist, because he confined acts of consciousness to the present moment.
11 See Phillips 2010: 192–195 and 198 for a more recent ability-based account of temporal awareness that involves some of the elements presented here but that differs in taking the very recent past to have an equally important, constitutive (as opposed to a merely causal) role to play in determining the content of current experience.
12 Thanks to Ian Phillips and Maité Cruz-Tleugabulova for comments on earlier drafts.

References

Eighteenth-century texts are cited from original edition page photographs accessed through *Eighteenth Century Collections Online* compared to modern critical editions where the reproduction is poor.

Bardon, A. (2007) "Empiricism, time-awareness, and Hume's manners of disposition", *Journal of Scottish Philosophy* 5(1): 47–63.

Baxter, D. (2008) *Hume's Difficulty*, New York: Routledge.

Broad, C. D. (1923) *Scientific Thought*, London: Routledge and Kegan Paul.

Dainton, B. (2011) "Time, passage, and immediate experience", in C. Callender (ed.), *The Oxford Handbook of Philosophy of Time*, Oxford, UK: Oxford University Press, pp. 382–418.

Dainton, B. (2014) "Temporal consciousness", in E. N. Zalta (ed.), *The Stanford Encyclopedia of Philosophy*, available at http://plato.stanford.edu/archives/spr2014/entries/consciousness-temporal/. Accessed 15 May 2016.

George, R. (2006) "James Jurin awakens Hume from his dogmatic slumber. With a short tract on visual acuity", *Hume Studies* 32(1): 141–166.

Hoerl, C. (2013) "'A succession of feelings, in and of itself, is not a feeling of succession'", *Mind* 121(486): 373–417.

Hume, D. (1739–40) *A Treatise of Human Nature*, London: John Noon; critical edition (2007) Norton, D. F. and Norton, M. J. (eds), Oxford, UK: Clarendon Press.

Hume, D. (1997) Letter to Hugh Blair of 4 July 1762, in T. Reid *An Inquiry into the Human Mind*, D. Brookes (ed.), Edinburgh, UK: Edinburgh University Press.

James, W. (1890) *Principles of Psychology*, vol. 1, New York: Henry Holt.

Locke, J. (1706) *An Essay Concerning Human Understanding* (5th edition) London: Awnsham and John Churchill and Samuel Manship; critical edition (1975) Nidditch, P. H. (ed.), Oxford, UK: Clarendon Press.

Phillips, I. (2010) "Perceiving temporal properties", *European Journal of Philosophy* 18(2): 176–202.

Price, R. (1758) *A Review of the Principal Questions and Difficulties in Morals*, London: A. Millar.

Reid, T. (1764) *An Inquiry into the Human Mind*, Edinburgh, UK: A. Millar, and A. Kincaid & John Bell.

Reid, T. (1785) *Essays on the Intellectual Powers of Man*, Edinburgh, UK: John Bell.

Welsh, R. B. (1986) "Adaptation to the loss of visual position constancy", in K. Boff, L. Kaufman and J. P. Thomas (eds), *Handbook of Perception and Human Performance*, vol. 1, New York: Wiley.

Yaffe, G. (2011) "Locke on consciousness, personal identity and the idea of duration", *Noûs* 45(3): 387–408.

Further reading

L. Falkenstein, "Hume on the idea of a vacuum", *Hume Studies* 39 (2013): 131–168 argues that Hume's rejection of ideas of empty space was likewise inconsistent with his account of space as a manner of disposition.

D. A. Larivière and T. M. Lennon, "The history and significance of Hume's burning coal example", *Journal of Philosophical Research* 27 (2002): 511–526, argues that Hume drew his example and his morals from Bayle rather than Locke, but does not explain why he would not have said so.

D. Baxter has continued to press his opposed account in contributions to D. F. Norton and J. Taylor (ed.), *The Cambridge Companion to Hume*, 2nd edition (Cambridge, UK: Cambridge University Press, 2009) and P. Russell (ed.), *The Oxford Handbook of Hume* (Oxford, UK: Oxford University Press, 2016).

4

TEMPORAL EXPERIENCE IN KANT'S *CRITIQUE OF PURE REASON*

Katherine Dunlop

As a designation for a subject of philosophical inquiry, "temporal experience" is suggestively ambiguous. It can refer to the informing of experience by temporality (the "temporality of experience"): in what manner, and to what extent, experience is temporally structured. Or it can pertain to how temporal features are experienced (the "experience of temporality"): whether experience portrays them correctly, which capacities are used to represent them, and so forth. In the *Critique of Pure Reason*, Kant offers answers to both kinds of question as he describes the mind's contributions to experience.

The divisions of the *Critique* follow the distinction between the sensible and rational faculties (sensibility and understanding). The forms according to which these faculties operate are the most important of the mind's contributions to experience. In the "Transcendental Aesthetic", which sets out the necessary conditions on sensible representation, Kant argues that time is a form of sensibility. The "Transcendental Analytic" concerns the forms of the understanding,[1] which include substance and causality. Each faculty's forms are represented a priori within the faculty, and Kant's distinctive methodology is to justify (the application of) such representations by showing their application to be presupposed by, or otherwise required for, other, less exotic, cognitive phenomena. In the "Analogies of Experience" section, Kant argues that the application of the concepts of substance and causality is necessary for "perceiving" (B225; A192/B237) or "cognizing" (A211/B258) temporal relations between physical events.

Generally speaking, the role in representing time that Kant gives to the understanding in the Transcendental Analytic raises questions about how to understand the doctrines of the Transcendental Aesthetic. For in the Aesthetic, Kant not only argues that certain features of the representation of time show it to be non-conceptual in the sense that concepts are not sufficient to express its content; he seems also to explain the origin of the representation of time without reference to the understanding and its forms, implying that concepts are not necessary (to represent time) either. In this chapter, I consider specifically how these puzzles are raised by the Analogies of Experience, which not only purport to show the necessity of using concepts to represent temporal relations, but assume as a premise that time cannot be perceived in itself.[2] A main goal is to understand the meaning of Kant's denial of time's perceivability; a secondary one is to explain how it is compatible with the Aesthetic's doctrines.

Coming to terms with the main interpretative approaches to the Analogies will take us further into the Transcendental Analytic, so by the end of the chapter, we will have considered the most important remarks about temporal experience in the *Critique*. These approaches differ on some basic matters: for instance, whether Kant thinks we passively apprehend (are given) the temporal ordering of our own mental states, or must instead work it out by applying a priori concepts. For the most part, such disputes will not be adjudicated here; I hope only to show how both sides can find support for their answers in the *Critique* and its historical context.

The Transcendental Aesthetic

The first pair of arguments concerning time in the Transcendental Aesthetic purport to show that time is represented a priori. First, Kant argues that the representation of time could not be empirical because it is already presupposed by the representation of things as existing simultaneously or successively. In the critical literature on the parallel argument concerning space, it has been objected that the argument shows the representation of space to be a priori only in a trivial sense, on which the representation of spatially related things presupposes the representation of space just in the way that the representation of things as related in respect of any property presupposes the representation of that property. Kant's argument has been defended by construing it as an attack on relationalist, empiricist views (such as Leibniz's), on which the representation of space is formed by abstracting an ordering from experience of particular things. In particular, Kant has been credited with the point that representation of spatial relationships uniquely presupposes a spatial framework. This is in contrast to qualities such as colour or brightness. Orderings with respect to such qualities can be set out as spatial arrays and thereby give rise to a representation of space, but they can also be represented without the apparatus of places contained in a space. In the case of space itself, there is no such "independently available" basis from which the ordering could be derived (see Warren 1998). Similarly, temporal relationships contrast with other one-dimensional orderings, in that the latter can but need not be represented as temporal series.[3] So on a charitable reading of Kant's conclusion, time is a priori in the substantive sense that an encompassing temporal framework is presupposed by the representation of particular relations (as temporal) and could not be abstracted from such representation.

The second argument for the apriority of time asserts that time is "necessary" in the sense that it cannot be "removed" with regard to "appearances in general, though one can very well take the appearances away from time" (A31/B46). This argument is presumably intended to rule out the possibility, left open by the first argument, that representation of time and representation of appearances mutually depend on one another.

Next, Kant argues from certain features that time manifests in experience to the conclusion that the representation of time is an intuition. Kant defines intuition as "that through which [cognition] relates immediately to [objects]" (A19/B33), in contrast to concepts, whose relation to objects is mediated by intuition (A68/B93). He also claims that intuition is "singular" representation, whereas a concept relates to its object "by means of a mark, which can be common to several things" (A320/B377). Kant makes clear that we (humans) have intuition only through the sensible faculty, insofar as we are affected by objects. Since we are passively given particulars through it, intuition as Kant conceives it overlaps with perception (as ordinarily understood); but since intuition can be a priori, while perception is always empirical, Kant's notion is broader.

The general doctrine that whatever "can only be given [as] a single object" is represented intuitively is applied to the case of time. Kant argues that the representation of time designates a single individual (and is therefore not a "general concept") because "different times are only parts of one and the same time" (A31/B47). The priority of time over particular instances of succession asserted in the first arguments concerning time can be understood phenomenologically, as the point that particular temporal intervals (those delimited by the succession of particular events) are given only within an encompassing temporal framework. In phenomenological terms, what is now further asserted is that this framework is always experienced as the same. The claim that we experience time as single and unitary has been widely accepted, even by those who challenge the parallel view concerning space.[4]

Kant also claims that time is represented as "infinite" in the sense that determinate portions of time are represented only by limiting the single, given whole. This can be taken to mean merely that time has the topological property of boundlessness, rather than the metrical property of having infinite extent. It furnishes another argument that time is given intuitively, from the general principle that if the parts of a representation can be given only by limiting the whole (which must therefore be given antecedently to them), that representation is given intuitively rather than through concepts (A32/B48).

From the claim that the representation of time is an a priori intuition, Kant draws the further conclusion that "time is nothing other than the form of inner sense, i.e., of the intuition of our self and of our inner state" (A33/B49).[5] This yields a characterization of the contents that are passively given within the form of time: one's own mental states. The view that time is the format in which mental states are experienced derives from Locke. Kant acknowledges the oddity of supposing that the mind is sensibly, i.e. passively, related to its own states (B153); but this view has the advantage that it can explain how time is represented, if it is not represented either by abstracting from experience of particular events (as on Leibniz's view), or by somehow grasping Newton's absolute time (which Kant derides as a "self-subsisting non-entity", A39/B56).

By "nothing other than the form of inner sense", Kant means, first, that time is not "a determination of outer appearances" (Ibid.). It seems strange to deny that time pertains to things that appear in space, such as bodies, since such things obviously undergo change, such as motion. But Kant can explain how these outer appearances come to be represented as in time. As the form of inner sense, time is "the a priori formal condition of all appearances in general". It conditions even the appearance of objects in space because "all representations, whether or not they have outer things as their object, nevertheless as determinations of the mind belong to the inner state" and are thus subject to "the formal condition of inner intuition", namely time (A34/B50). This view may seem to displace, rather than dispel, the strangeness, for time now pertains to things that appear in space only on the condition that those things are represented by a subject. But on Kant's (idealist) view, this condition is trivial to satisfy, since things that appear must appear to some subject. More importantly for Kant's account of temporal experience, to represent an appearance in "inner sense" could just be to situate it in a temporal order, without also representing it *as* a "determination of the mind". Representation in inner sense, that is, need not include any reflexive element marking it as my representation, or indeed as representation. (So we need not construe physical things as mental in order to represent them as temporal.) Such a view is clearly articulated in Norman Kemp Smith's classic commentary:[6]

> [Kant] would seem to mean that . . . in the process of "setting" representations of outer sense in space [the mind is] constrained to arrange the given representations likewise in time. No new content, additional to that of outer sense, is thereby generated [nor is the content of the representations of outer sense modified], but what previously as object of outer sense existed merely in space is now also subjected to conditions of time.
>
> *(Kemp Smith 1999: 294)*

Notice that Kant here gives conditions on time's pertaining to things, not on our knowledge of their temporal determinations. The view that cognition of outer things' temporal relations derives from the (introspectible) temporal ordering of inner states will be discussed in the following section.

We thus find in Kant the view that all representations which "as determinations of the mind belong to the inner state" are ordered in time, indeed in a single temporal sequence. This is a strong position on the temporality of experience. Before moving on, we should note that Kant countenances a kind of conscious thought that is not subject to this constraint. Kant claims that "in the original synthetic unity of apperception", I think "only *that* I am" rather than intuiting myself "as I appear to myself" (B157, emphasis original). In a footnote to the Preface to the *Critique*'s second edition, Kant makes clear that "in the representation *I am*, which accompanies all my judgments and actions of my understanding", I have an "*intellectual consciousness* of my existence" which is not "bound to a condition of time", unlike the inner intuition "in which alone my existence can be determined" (B*xln*.). But he also claims that "inner experience" requires "determination" (in inner intuition) of my existence (Ibid.); and at A354, he makes explicit that the "formal proposition of apperception . . . on which every experience depends" is "of course obviously not an experience". So despite the atemporality of intellectual self-consciousness, all experience remains temporal for Kant.

The claim that time is only the form of inner sense also means that time is nothing "in itself", or in abstraction from our way of intuiting ourselves (A34–5/B51). Thus time is "ideal": it pertains only to appearances, not to things as they are in themselves. Although this chapter is not about Kant's metaphysics, his idealism about time will be relevant to our discussion in two ways. First, it may lead us to think of experience's temporality as a kind of misrepresentation, and thereby misunderstand Kant's position on the accuracy or veridicality of experience. For instance, Andrew Brook sees it as fundamental to Kant's idealism that we "are aware of objects [only] as they appear to us after the mind has engaged in various appearance-doctoring activities", in consequence of which temporal position and order are properties "that we *represent* [things] as having, not properties they have", so far as we can know (2013, 121). But Kant insists that time has "empirical reality" as a condition of experience (A37/B54), meaning that it is "objectively valid" with regard to "all objects that may ever be given to our senses" (A35/B52). He makes explicit that that which appears in intuition is not "mere illusion", because "in the appearance the objects, indeed even characteristics that we attribute to them, are always . . . really given" (B69). As difficult as it may be to see how Kant is entitled to his "empirical realism", it is clear that he does not intend a global skepticism about experience's temporal features. The second way in which Kant's idealism about time will come under discussion is that we will be concerned to determine what role, if any, it plays in the arguments of the Analogies.

The Transcendental Analytic (I): Analogies of Experience

The First Analogy of Experience argues that the application of the concept of substance is necessary for perceiving persistence (which is necessary for perceiving change), the Second Analogy argues that the application of the concept of causality is necessary for perceiving succession, and the Third Analogy argues that substances must be conceived as mutually interacting in order to cognize simultaneity. The Second Analogy is the longest and involves the First and Third (as well as the preceding "Anticipations of Perception"). It has received the most attention from commentators and will be our focus here.

The three Analogies are prefaced by a "general principle" which states, in the *Critique*'s first edition, that all appearances "stand a priori under rules" that determine their relations "in *one* time" (A176, emphasis original). While some commentators take all three Analogies to concern the representation of all events and states within one, unitary temporal system,[7] others take the Second Analogy to establish conditions just on representing particular events and states as successive. In the second edition, Kant reformulated his general principle as "Experience is possible only through the representation of a necessary connection of perceptions" (B218). (Kant retained, however, the immediately following claim that experience is made possible by "three rules of temporal relations" that determine how each appearance exists "with regard to the unity of all time" (A177/B219).)

In the *Critique*'s second edition, Kant also inserted a proof of the (restated) general principle. A key claim of the proof is that for objects to be cognized through sense-experience, the appearances that are represented must be not only contingently juxtaposed, as they are "in apprehension", but connected with the necessity that comes from following a rule. (Kant's notion of apprehension will be discussed further, but in short, he conceives it as the first stage of the process that guarantees the objective reference of perceptions. Representations said to be "in apprehension" are considered as inwardly intuited "modifications of the mind" (A97), without regard to their reference.) In the second edition's Transcendental Deduction, Kant already contrasted "empirical consciousness of the manifold [of intuition] as simultaneous or successive", which is contingent (because it "depends on circumstances"), with the "necessary relation of the manifold" to "the one *I think*" that is instituted by the understanding's rule-governed synthesis; while the former "has merely subjectively validity", the latter constitutes relation to an object (B139–140). What becomes clear in the Analogies is that there is a specifically *temporal* objective ordering to contrast with the subjective ordering of empirical consciousness. As Eric Watkins explains, the distinction between objective and subjective time-orders, together with the claim that time cannot be perceived of itself (which appears here as a premise in the proof), raises an epistemological problem: It is not "trivial" to determine, e.g. relations of simultaneity (say by observing that two objects now exist next to one another), precisely because objective temporal relations "cannot be perceived directly but rather can be presented only through the subjective temporal order of apprehension" (2005, 188–189).

In making the temporal order of empirical consciousness proprietary to it and denying the perceivability of time in itself, Kant may appear to deny that our experience of the objective world conveys any of its temporal structure. But the best way to see what Kant is committed to is to consider how these premises function in his arguments. I will first explain how claims weaker than the ones he seems to express may suffice for his purposes. I will then show that even if the unperceivability claim is taken literally, some formal aspects of temporality could still manifest in experience. Discussion of this second point will involve some consideration of what the Analogies are meant to achieve.

In the Second Analogy, Kant famously uses the example of perceiving a house to illustrate the subjective temporal ordering of empirical consciousness.

> [t]he representation of [the manifold of appearance] in apprehension is always successive. Thus, e.g., the apprehension of the manifold in the appearance of a house that stands before me is successive. Now the question is whether the manifold of this house itself is also successive, which certainly no one will concede.
>
> *(A190/B235)*

This paragraph begins "The apprehension of the manifold of appearance is always successive" (A189/B234). The claim that apprehension is always successive is easily taken to mean that we are only ever conscious of one representational content (item or feature) at a time. But since that typically strikes commentators as false, many prefer to interpret the claim differently.[8] Still others point out that Kant does not need to claim *all* empirical consciousness stands in a temporal ordering (which we now learn to be successive) different from the objective world's. He needs only to claim that, as James Van Cleve puts it, "sometimes the apprehension of an enduring state of affairs is successive, i.e., consists in a temporal series of diverse representations" (1973: 75).[9]

Kant claims in the Second Analogy that the determination of appearances' positions in time cannot be "borrowed from" the appearances' "relation to absolute time (for that is not an object of perception)" (A200/B245). In expositions of the argument, Kant's point is usually taken to be that in perception, events are not given with "time stamps" that specify their time of occurrence.[10] This way of narrowing down to what is required for Kant's argument weighs against one natural reading of the claim that time cannot be perceived by itself: as just pointing out that this form cannot be perceived separately from the contents that occupy it.[11] For if we did perceive time, but always only as occupied by appearances, it is likely that we would also perceive appearances' relations to time. This consideration is not decisive, since we could in fact be given both time and appearances, without also perceiving how the appearances are positioned in time. (As a crude illustration, we might think of seeing an object against the background of a large building while being unable, for lack of the relevant distance cues, to determine how far apart the two are. But whatever the unperceivability of time amounts to, it is more radical than this, for Kant argues in the First Analogy that time itself cannot be the unchanging "backdrop" against which change is perceived.) The important point here is that being unable thus to perceive the relations of events to time does not entail an inability to perceive time. In particular, it does not preclude perceiving the uniqueness or boundlessness of time (the features that are supposed to evince the intuitive origin of the representation of time). So if the unperceivability claim is restricted to the relations of events to time, it does not contradict the doctrine of the Transcendental Aesthetic.

Even if Kant is taken to deny the perceivability of time, full stop, there are ways of understanding this claim that have little bearing on the experience of temporality. Kant claims specifically that time *in itself* cannot be perceived (see Note 2), and some interpreters take this to assert the ideality of time. For instance, Arthur Melnick claims that "the reason [Kant] holds that time itself cannot be perceived" is (at least "roughly") that "time itself as an object does not exist" (2004a: 105).[12] Such a reading leaves open that time relativized to our faculties, i.e. time as a form of intuition, could be perceived in some way. I will not pursue this approach, because I do not think it fits the Analogies very well. The Analogies mainly concern appearances' positions in time. Pointing out that time pertains only to appearances would serve at most to frame or motivate the questions they address, not to answer those questions. But the claim that time cannot be perceived appears to be an indispensable premise in Kant's arguments.

Kant also claims (at A200/B245, quoted above, and A215/B262) that *absolute* time is not an object of perception, and it is plausible to suppose that he refers specifically to time conceived as prior to particular temporal relations, as it is by Newton.[13] In the Transcendental Aesthetic, Kant claims that the Newtonian view allows, while the Leibnizian view precludes, the application of mathematics in "the field of appearances" (A40/B57). Kant seems thereby to endorse the Newtonian conception with regard to appearances, although he also claims we "become very confused" if these concepts of space and time are to apply outside this context, to things as they exist in themselves (A40/B56). If time, as it applies to appearances, is absolute in Newton's sense, then it is impossible in principle to perceive it. In the *Principia*, Newton distinguishes absolute time, whose nature is to "flow uniformly", from relative time, which is "any sensible and external measure of duration" (specifically by means of motion) (Newton 1999: 408). Any "part" or interval of time that can be marked off by a sensible physical process is, accordingly, a relative time. The relative times marked off by a given process may be aliquot parts of absolute time, but only in the special case of a process that shares the uniformity of absolute time's flow.[14] (To be clear, on the Leibnizian alternative there is no such bar to perceiving the elements that comprise time as a whole. Kant takes the Leibnizians to hold that time is a "relation of appearances ([as] successive to one another) that [is] abstracted from experience" (op. cit.), so on this view we have experience of instances of succession, from which we abstract an overall temporal ordering.) If Kant is denying the perceivability of Newtonian absolute time, he can allow that we have some experience of temporality, namely of the sensible processes that mark off relative times.

I think Kant does regard absolute time as unperceivable, but that is not his point in the Analogies of Experience. The problem with this understanding of the unperceivability claim is that the most natural way of relating Newton's absolute/relative distinction to Kant's objective and subjective temporal orderings seriously dims the Second Analogy's prospects for success, as I will now explain.

On the Newtonian view, it is a problem to determine which of our "sensible and external measures" (periodic processes, such as rotations, revolutions and pendulum swings) most closely matches absolute time's uniform flow.[15] In contrast, the Second Analogy does not specifically concern the *rates* at which things succeed. But it does seem to address a problem of determining which sequences of apprehended representations (all of which are successive) correspond to successions in the outer world. The argument's opening lines appear to raise this problem: "The apprehension of the manifold of appearance is always successive. Whether [the parts of the manifold] also succeed in the object is a second point for reflection, which is not contained in the first" (A188–9/B234).[16] Similarly, Kant claims that the successiveness of our apprehension of the house's manifold raises the question "whether this manifold in the house itself is also successive". And he indicates that his transcendental idealism makes it possible "to assess from the succession of representations how the manifold is combined in the object" (A190/B235). We can see how determining which sequences of apprehended representations correspond to objective change would serve Kant's ultimate objective, if, namely, he argues that the method or means of determination ensures the applicability of the concept of cause.

Now, the claim that certain sequences of apprehended representations are irreversible – those which represent objective change – figures prominently in the Second Analogy.[17] If we suppose Kant's objective is to explain how perception of objective change can be distinguished from that of unchanging objects, then the importance of the notion of irreversibility is clear: it just is the criterion for perception of objective change.

Although it is appealingly straightforward, this interpretation of the Second Analogy is now widely rejected, because (as prominent twentieth-century commentators pointed out)[18] it makes the argument into a *non sequitur*. For Kant, showing the applicability of the concept of cause requires showing that every occurrence is subject to a rule by which it is "determined through the preceding state" (A195/B240).[19] So the strategy I have outlined involves an inference to the necessity of an order of objective states of affairs, from the necessity of an order (i.e. the irreversibility) of perceptions. But, it is objected, the order of perceptions is necessary only given the order of states, and more importantly, in the context of a theory about how states give rise to perceptions (according to which perceptions of successively ordered states will have the same successive order). Since the order of perceptions is made necessary by the theory, its necessity can only be conceptual. This is not a sufficient basis for concluding that states of affairs follow one another with causal necessity.

So far I have argued against the view that the Second Analogy addresses the epistemological problem arising from Newton's distinction between absolute time and its sensible measures, specifically by supplying the means to determine when a succession (of representations) in the subjective ordering of apprehension corresponds to an objective change. In this chapter's final section, I will offer another interpretation of the unperceivability claim (on which it does not specifically concern Newton's absolute time), and return to the claim that apprehension is always successive. But I wish first to raise the question of whether succession is given on Kant's view, either subjectively, as an ordering of (inwardly intuited) inner states, or objectively, as an ordering of perceived states of affairs. The extent to which this interpretative question is subject to dispute can be seen by comparing two readings of the Second Analogy, both of which deny that the ordering of inner states is the basis from which the objective temporal ordering is inferred. The first reading takes succession to be given objectively, while the second (which will be especially important for us) denies that succession is given even subjectively.

Interpretations of the first sort have been offered by commentators including Henry Allison, Lewis White Beck, Graham Bird and Béatrice Longuenesse. Allison maintains that rather than moving "from the irreversibility of perceptions in a putative instance of event perception" to the causal necessity of the states perceived, Kant takes for granted that certain sequences of perceptions represent objective successions, and concludes that in these cases "I am constrained to regard the order of my perceptions as determined or irreversible". Kant's objective is then to specify the condition under which sequences of perception can be "thought as" irreversible: it is the application of the concept of causality (2004: 250–256). Similarly, Beck maintains that on Kant's view we can "immediately" recognize "the difference between seeing successive and seeing coexistent states of an object", while insisting that such immediate recognition involves the application of concepts and "adherence to rules" (1978: 139). On this reading, irreversibility and the application of the concept of cause are not criteria by which objective and subjective successions are distinguished, but rather make possible and explain our ability to recognize changes as objective.

Generally speaking, these commentators look beyond the text of the Second Analogy to support their interpretation. For some (notably Bird), it is associated with understanding Kant's "appearances" as ordinary objects, rather than phenomenalistic constructs. Others point out that Kant can safely assume we can distinguish subjective from objective succession because this is presupposed by Hume's account of causation, the ostensible target of Kant's argument.

The second interpretation's main proponent is Paul Guyer.[20] Guyer claims "the real argument of" the Analogies depends on a "fundamental premise" which also underlies Kant's so-called "Refutation of Idealism", namely that "even merely subjective sequences of representation are not directly given in passive apprehension alone". On this reading, although the Analogies seem to comprise "a self-contained theory" of the necessary conditions for judging objective temporal relations, their conclusions are proved only by means of "the further argument that even the mere ability to make determinate judgments about temporal relations of representations in the self also presupposes the ability to make such judgments about the objective world" (1987: 207–208).

Guyer's interpretation is a suitable "leading thread" for our discussion. Not only is it a model of rigorous engagement with Kant's text, but it exhibits a concern with temporal cognition running through the entire Transcendental Analytic. I will close this section by indicating why Guyer takes further argument to be necessary; the following section will consider how the argument is articulated later in the *Critique* and where Guyer finds its key premise.

According to Guyer, this further argument is required to answer the objection that cognizing objective temporal relations requires "knowledge of *some* determinate relations among states of objects", but not specifically causal relations. To order two states of affairs, the objection runs, we need only regard them as "opposite or incompatible", from which it follows that "they cannot exist at the same time", so one of the states must succeed the other (1987: 252–253). On Kant's behalf, Guyer replies that from the incompatibility of two states of affairs, A and B, we can infer only that *some* succession has occurred, not whether it was the succession from A to B or that from B to A. According to Guyer, this point has been overlooked because it has been assumed that in reflecting on any pair of perceptions, we can determine which one is present (and so conclude that whichever state the present perception represents must have succeeded the other state). But in fact:

> [i]t *is not actually given which is the present perception and which is the prior one.* For all that can be given in one moment is a *present representation* of the contents of two (or more) possible perceptions, but not both the present *and the past representation itself. Which* is the present representation and which the past is something *which itself* must be judged.
>
> *(1987: 254)*

Guyer maintains that judgments about the ordering of representations (inner states) must be based on causal laws governing the represented states of affairs, so that the application of the concept of cause is indeed crucial for cognition of temporal relations.

The Transcendental Analytic (II): Refutation of Idealism and Transcendental Deduction

On Guyer's interpretation, judgments about the temporal ordering of representations must be based on causal laws that govern enduring objects, paradigmatically bodies, rather than the (fleeting) representations themselves. That the judgments should depend (epistemically) on such unlike subject-matter is already surprising. And the laws are "inductively confirmed" in the course of experience, so they appear to presuppose the subjective temporal order that they puta-tively determine. I will now explain what motivates these features of Guyer's interpretation: the first reads the Refutation of Idealism into the preceding Analogies, while the second has to do with the resolution of an important ambiguity.

The Refutation of Idealism begins with the premise "I am conscious of my existence as deter-mined in time", and concludes that my existence in time can be determined "only by means of the existence of actual things that I perceive outside me", i.e. perceive in space (B275).[21] (This conclusion and Kant's other claims about the dependence of temporal on spatial cognition do not militate against the view that the succession of inner states is simply given in apprehension, because the representation of succession can have spatial cognition as its necessary condition without being mediated by it.) The Refutation may seem to demand more prominence in this chapter, but I introduce it only now for two reasons. First, the temporally ordered conscious thought (of one's own existence) that it concerns appears to be a special case. Presumably we can be conscious of the temporally determined existence of other appearances besides ourselves.[22]

The second reason for not giving the Refutation more attention is its obscurity. In the criti-cal literature, there is less agreement about the Refutation's goal and strategy, and more doubt about its success, than in the case of the Analogies of Experience. Even Guyer, who places the Refutation in the "absolutely central role" of "completing" the argument for the categories' objective validity (1987: 279), does not think Kant clearly states either the argument or "the exact metaphysical import of [its] conclusion" (1987: 284).

One point disputed by commentators is which epistemic state is invoked in the first premise (and shown to presuppose the existence of actual things in space): mere consciousness, or rather empirical knowledge, of one's temporally determined existence.[23] Guyer holds that Kant must be adducing conditions on knowledge. Because Kant accepts "an empiricist model for the knowledge of particular causal laws", his

[a]rgument would certainly imply a vicious circle if [the Refutation was] meant to describe the psychological process [of generating consciousness of subjective time-order] . . . Causal laws would have to be learned from particular experiences but, in order to individuate and order those experiences themselves, would also have to be known already. If, however, Kant's argument does not describe the generation of particular occurrences of belief about [the self] but rather the perhaps ideal conditions under which such beliefs, however they actually arise, may be confirmed or [justified as part of] a system of empirical knowledge . . . then it involves no circularity.

(1987: 315)

Since, according to Guyer, the Second Analogy also shows that judgments about subjective temporal order must be based on causal laws, there too the laws are necessary conditions for the "*justification, verification,* or *confirmation* of the judgments", not "psychological preconditions" of the judgments' occurrence (1987: 246). Since the laws can be learned without the judgments' having achieved this epistemological status, the threat of circularity is avoided. What Guyer offers on Kant's behalf is in this respect a theory of empirical self-knowledge rather than temporal experience per se. But as we will shortly see, it depends on a premise about temporal experience in the strict sense.

I will now consider how Guyer traces the argument concerning time-determination back to the Transcendental Deduction (where Kant purports to show that the possibility of experience presupposes the applicability of the categories in general, before arguing, as in the Analogies of Experience, that certain aspects of experience depend on particular categories). Here Guyer's interpretation makes clear how Kant's views can bear on present-day discussion. We will then see how the argument extends beyond the Analogies and Refutation, and return to the interpretation of Kant's unperceivability claim.

According to Guyer, the claim that the subjective ordering of representations is not "passively given in apprehension", which functions as a premise in the Second Analogy and the Refutation, itself follows from the thesis that "each representation, insofar as it is contained in a single moment, can be nothing but absolute unity", which appears at the beginning of the first edition's Transcendental Deduction (A99). Accordingly, the latter claim for Guyer is the "fundamental premise of Kant's transcendental theory of experience" (1987: 171). It implies, in the first place, that every representation is a new existence, with no ontological link to past or future representations (1987: 302). Now, one can know at any particular time that "any particular succession has occurred" only on the basis of the "single representational state available at that time" (1987: 171–172). But since this state lacks all connection with preceding and succeeding representations, it can represent their multiplicity (or manifoldness) only in virtue of an interpretation placed on it. Kant can then fulfil the aim of the Transcendental Deduction, namely showing that a priori knowledge of the categories' applicability is a condition of empirical self-knowledge, by showing that the categories must be applied in order to justify taking the current state as a member of a series. In particular, the concepts of substance and cause are employed as they occur in the causal law that determines the order of representations in the series.

The view Guyer finds in the Transcendental Deduction is prominent in contemporary discussions of temporal experience. For Guyer, the claim that each representation as contained in a moment is "absolute unity" implies that "no more than one representation ever is present to us; the manifold of successive representations [and thus the succession of representations] is not in fact before one's mind . . . in the way in which a dozen eggs can be before one's eyes" (1987: 302). The view that temporal succession cannot be directly experienced, because it is never contained in the single moment to which present experience is restricted, has been called the "paradox of temporal awareness", and is the basis of diverse theories of how moments separated in time can be compresent "before the mind".

Much as I want to defend the continuing relevance of Kant's view, I have reservations about Guyer's reading of the passage at A99. The claim about the "absolute unity" of a representation at a moment is stated as a condition affecting the synthesis of apprehension. Between the Transcendental Deduction and the Analogies, Kant suggests two further conditions on this synthesis. That it takes place successively is implied by Kant's claim that appearances, as intuitions, must be cognized through "successive synthesis (from part to part) in apprehension" (B204). And at A167/B209, Kant claims that apprehension by means of "mere sensation" "fills only an instant (if I do not take into consideration the succession of many sensations)". So there is good reason to hold that each exercise or iteration of (the synthesis of) apprehension is momentary or "fleeting", and accordingly restricted to the "absolute unity" available at that moment. But it is not clear that these constraints on how apprehension takes place must also constrain how representations are present to or come before the mind (as Guyer supposes). Admittedly, at B202 Kant glosses "apprehended" as "taken up into empirical consciousness", which does suggest that we become conscious of representations in just the manner in which they undergo apprehension. But the synthesis of apprehension is merely the first stage of this taking-up. It is characterized in the Transcendental Deduction as the first moment of a "three-fold synthesis" that makes all cognition possible (A97),[24] and the very fact that it is required for a manifold "to become unity of intuition" (A99) indicates that the representations on which it operates are not themselves intuited (as states of the mind).[25] Kant describes the synthesis of apprehension more precisely as "aimed directly at the intuition" (A99), and we could reasonably suppose that it is constrained on the one hand by the formal structure (successiveness) of its end product, and on the other by the atomic character of the raw material on which it operates. There would then be no need to posit a kind of representation that is successive and yet discretized into unitary moments.

A less controversial, yet equally important, feature of Guyer's interpretation is his emphasis on changes Kant made to the *Critique*'s second edition that assert the dependence of temporal cognition on spatial cognition. We will end with these revisions, because they give us a way to understand Kant's claim that time itself cannot be perceived.

Guyer speculates that Kant became dissatisfied with the Refutation of Idealism "even before the revisions [to the *Critique*] of 1787 were ready for the press" (1987: 284), and that the "General Note" appended to the chapter containing the Refutation is intended to remedy its defects.[26] In particular, the Note provides more explanation (than the Refutation) of why perception of objects in space should be necessary for cognizing temporally determined existence. The Note claims that "something that persists in intuition" (which is identified as a necessary condition in the Refutation's second premise) can only be spatial "since space alone persistently determines, while time, and thus everything that is in inner sense, constantly flows" (B291).

The Note argues, further, that alteration can be intuited (or even thought) only through "motion, as alteration in space"; to represent inner alteration, in particular, "we must be able to grasp time, as the form of inner sense, figuratively through a line, and grasp the inner alteration through the drawing of this line (motion)" (B291). Kant makes very similar claims in the second edition version of the Transcendental Deduction. He argues there that to represent time, we must draw "a straight line (which is to be the external figurative representation of time)" and attend "merely to the action of the synthesis of the manifold through which we successively determine the inner sense", and goes on to describe this action as a sort of motion (B154).

The passage at B154 is important for understanding the respective roles of the sensible and rational faculties in temporal cognition, because Kant describes this determination of inner sense as an action of the understanding. What matters more for our purposes is how these passages let us make clear sense of Kant's claim that time cannot be perceived in or by itself. I submit that at least part of their import is that temporal properties cannot be experienced separately from spatial ones.

We sought to understand the claim as it functions in the Analogies. If it serves to remind us that temporal properties are always experienced in the context of spatiality, then it may begin the argument by prompting us to reflect on how temporal representation is possible in this context, and thus indirectly point to the conditions Kant adduces on representing persistence, succession and simultaneity. It is not hard to see how these conditions could require spatial representation for their satisfaction. (Indeed, in the General Note, Kant gives only the briefest of arguments that spatial representation is required for cognizing persistence and alteration.) While taking the unperceivability claim to concern spatial representation is congenial to Guyer's interpretation, it also fits the view held by Allison, Beck and others. For whether judgments about the order of inner states are justified on the basis of laws governing physical events, or subjective succession is given together with physical changes that are recognized as objective, temporal experience is inextricably linked with spatial experience.

Finally, on this interpretation, the unperceivability of time by itself is no bar to representing the singularity and boundlessness of time (which mark it as intuitively represented). The spatial representation which we are now supposing to be necessary (for perceiving time) could even be a means for grasping these features. If we take seriously Kant's view that the successiveness which characterizes both alterations and time's own structure can be represented only in terms of motion, then the singularity and boundlessness of the space in which this motion occurs may make evident these features of time.

Notes

1 Kant identifies the subject-matter of "Transcendental Logic" (which includes the "Transcendental Analytic") as a form of thinking (A51/B75) and "the form of the understanding" (A56/B80). Cf. A125.
2 Kant claims variously that time cannot be perceived "itself" [*selbst*] (B219, B257), "in itself" [*an sich*] (B207), or "by itself" *für sich* (B225). I regard these differences as mere stylistic variants.
3 This point may have force against Hume's view, in particular. Hume claims the idea of time is derived from the succession of ideas and impressions (*Treatise* I.2.3.6–7); what makes a sequence (of representations) a succession, in his view, may well be the increasing "faintness" of persisting ideas corresponding to impressions that precede in the sequence. Then the temporality of sequences would be represented by abstracting an ordering of comparative faintness. See Rosenberg (2005: 71) and Guyer (1987: 306).
4 In his influential "Spaces and times" (1962), Anthony Quinton argues that "we can at least conceive circumstances in which we should have good reason to say that we knew of real things located in two quite distinct spaces" (1962: 147), but the same does not hold for time, because "it seems unintelligible to speak of a collection of events as constituting the experience of one person unless its members form a single temporal sequence" (1962: 146).
5 The argument for this further conclusion is suppressed in the case of time, but explicit in the case of space: B40–41.
6 A more recent *locus* for such an interpretation is Patricia Kitcher's *Kant's Thinker* (2011). If inner sense had a reflexive element, it would presumably suffice to explain the "mineness" of representations, but Kitcher maintains it is not adequate for this purpose (2011: 146).
7 Melnick (1973) and Walsh (1967) are prominent examples of such interpretations.
8 For instance, as we will see below, it can be taken to describe the process ("synthesis") of apprehension rather than the conscious representation it produces.
9 Others who make this point are Broad (1926: 192), Walsh (1967: 378) and Melnick (1973: 85).
10 Examples are Walsh (1967: 376), Guyer (1987: 170) and Bird (2006: 457).
11 Furthermore, this reading of the unperceivability claim is in tension with Kant's assertion in the Transcendental Aesthetic that "one can very well take appearances away from time", although "in regard to appearances in general one cannot remove time" (A31/B46).

12 Henry Allison also appears to read the claim this way (1971: 373).

13 Here the priority of time with respect to particular temporal relations should be understood either as epistemological or with respect to determining states of motion, but *not* as the claim that time exists independently as a "thing in itself", to keep this interpretation of the unperceivability claim distinct from the interpretation just considered.

14 Newton draws a parallel distinction with respect to space and claims explicitly that "sensible measures" of space are required precisely because the "parts of space cannot be seen and distinguished from one another by our senses" (1999: 410).

15 Newton points out that this problem confronts astronomers, who "correct the inequality" of the days as measured by sundials "in order to measure celestial motions on the basis of a truer time" (1999: 410). On the relevance of this passage to Kant's account of temporal representation, see Dunlop 2009.

16 In the *Critique*'s second edition, Kant inserted a summary "proof" of the Second Analogy's principle before these lines.

17 Since we are concerned with how temporality is experienced, it is appropriate to specify the notion of reversibility at issue. To reverse a sequence of representations cannot be to experience those very same (token) representations in a different order, for the mind cannot have these (numerically identical) determinations at other times. So it must be to experience type-identical representations (in a different order). Reversal cannot be a matter of generating type-identical representations in a different order *in imagination*, for every sequence of representations, whether or not it represents objective change, is in this sense reversible (as Kant acknowledges at A201/B246). Kant says that what is determined is the order of the perceptions "in apprehension" (A192/B237), or as they are taken up into empirical consciousness. If the perceptions represent an objective change, then a reversal in this sense would be tantamount to perceiving some different event.

18 A. O. Lovejoy in 1906, and P. F. Strawson in 1966, labelled the argument a *non sequitur*.

19 Kant speaks of "appearances" as determined according to such a rule, but in this context "appearances" are clearly objective states, explicitly distinguished from "the representations of apprehension" (A191–193/B236–238).

20 Views similar to Guyer's are defended by Hoke Robinson.

21 Kant intends to refute "empirical idealism", in contrast to his own "transcendental" idealism, on which objects appearing in space (and time) have "empirical reality". This point is briefly discussed in the "Transcendental Aesthetic" section of this chapter.

22 Moreover, the Refutation is placed after a "Postulate" that connects actuality (likewise existence) with "the material conditions of experience (of sensation)" (B266; cf. B272–273); Kant also designates sensation as that through which "reality" and "being" are represented (A143/B182). He holds one can have temporally ordered thought that does not represent its subject-matter either through sensation, or as existing (or actual or real). An example would be mathematical cognition, which is constrained by the forms of intuition (hence by time), and is of mere "forms of objects" rather than actual things (B146).

23 See Allison 2004: 289.

24 Guyer sets little store by the distinctions between the moments of the threefold synthesis (1987: 456 n.4).

25 Patricia Kitcher explicitly draws this conclusion: "if conscious perception requires a synthesis, then the representations that are available to be synthesized can only be unconscious" (2013: 17).

26 Kant writes that the Note is important not only for "confirming" the Refutation "but, even more", for setting limits on "self-cognition from mere inner consciousness and the determination of our nature without the assistance of outer empirical intuitions" (B293). This is compatible with Guyer's reading, since Kant might think these limits are set precisely by completing the argument of the Refutation.

References

Kant's *Critique of Pure Reason* is cited, following standard practice, according to the pagination of the "A" (1781) and "B" (1787) editions. I have followed the translation by Paul Guyer and Allen Wood (Cambridge, UK: Cambridge University Press, 1999).

Allison, H. (1971) "Kant's non-sequitur. An examination of the Lovejoy–Strawson critique of the second analogy", *Kant-Studien* 62: 367–377.

Allison, H. (2004) *Kant's Transcendental Idealism*, New Haven, CT: Yale University Press.

Beck, L. W. (1978) "On 'just seeing' the ship move", in *Essays on Kant and Hume*, New Haven, CT: Yale University Press.

Bird, G. (2006) *The Revolutionary Kant*, LaSalle, IL: Open Court.

Broad, C. D. (1926) *Kant's First and Second Analogies of Experience*, Proceedings of the Aristotelian Society (n.s.) 26: 189–210.

Brook, A. (2013) "Kant and time-order idealism", in *A Companion to the Philosophy of Time*, Bardon, A., and Dyke, H. (eds), Chichester, UK: Wiley-Blackwell.

Dunlop, K. (2009) "The unity of time's measure", *Philosopher's Imprint* 9: 1–31.

Guyer, P. (1987) *Kant and the Claims of Knowledge*, Cambridge, UK: Cambridge University Press.

Kemp Smith, N. (1999) *A Commentary to Kant's "Critique of Pure Reason"*, 2nd ed., Amherst, NY: Humanity Books.

Kitcher, P. (2011) *Kant's Thinker*. Oxford, UK: Oxford University Press.

Kitcher, P. (2013) "Kant's unconscious given", in *Kant's Philosophy of the Unconscious*, Giordanetti, P., Pozzo, R. and Sgarbi, M. (eds), Berlin: De Gruyter.

Melnick, A. (1973) *Kant's Analogies of Experience*, Chicago, IL: University of Chicago Press.

Melnick, A. (2004a) "Kant's proofs of substance and causation", in Melnick 2004b.

Melnick, A. (2004b) *Themes in Kant's Metaphysics and Ethics*, Washington, DC: Catholic University of America Press.

Newton, I. (1999) *The Principia: Mathematical Principles of Natural Philosophy*, Cohen, I. B. and Whitman, A. (eds), Berkeley and Los Angeles, CA: University of California Press.

Quinton, A. M. (1962) "Spaces and times", *Philosophy* 37(140): 130–147.

Rosenberg, J. F. (2005) *Accessing Kant*, Oxford, UK: Clarendon Press.

Van Cleve, J. (1973) "Four recent interpretations of Kant's second analogy", *Kant-Studien* 64: 71–87.

Walsh, W. H. (1967) "Kant on the perception of time", *The Monist* 51(3): 376–396.

Warren, D. (1998) "Kant and the apriority of space", *Philosophical Review* 107(2): 179–224.

Watkins, E. (2005) *Kant and the Metaphysics of Causality*, Cambridge, UK: Cambridge University Press.

PART II

Nineteenth and early twentieth-century perspectives

5

THE HODGSONIAN ACCOUNT OF TEMPORAL EXPERIENCE

Holly Andersen

Introduction

Shadworth Hollway Hodgson may have been the first philosopher to develop an account of the temporal structure of experience and to explicitly relate the temporal characteristics of consciousness to the body and brain. His account of temporal experience is historically significant in its own right. His development of what is essentially a form of phenomenological analysis both predates and influenced that of Husserl (Andersen and Grush 2009). Hodgson's views were deeply influential on William James, who widely cites him in *The Principles of Psychology* (1950). His work is also philosophically significant in that he offers something genuinely new with respect to contemporary philosophical discussions of time consciousness and its relationship to the brain. His work is rich territory to mine for insights to be applied to contemporary issues related to experience, temporality, and especially neurophenomenology.

Hodgson's trailblazing work involves analysis of the present moment in experience as the keystone element in a much larger project concerning experience, consciousness, knowledge, and action. While Hodgson's views on the character of the present moment in experience are distinctive, they are only the first part of a massive project in philosophical thought. His four-volume lifework, *Metaphysic of Experience* (1898) ("ME" throughout this chapter), lays out a sophisticated and complete system for philosophy, in terms of its proposed scope of inquiry, its method for analysis, its orientation towards its subject matter, and the substantive views of experience and knowledge that emerge from this method. It is intended to unify and complete projects started by Kant and the British Empiricists but which remained, according to Hodgson, unfinished. Space restrictions prevent a full exploration of Hodgson's idiosyncratic notions of experience, knowledge, and consciousness. My focus will be on laying out the key features of Hodgson's account of the experience of the present moment that stands as a potential alternative to that of Husserl's well-known account. My synopsis is intended to pull out philosophically useful material that can be applied to contemporary discussions, in particular to neurophenomenology.

I'll begin with a brief overview of the motivation for Hodgson's work, in terms of its relationship to early modern rationalism, empiricism, and idealism, since that motivates much of his proto-phenomenological method. Then, I'll discuss a series of key ideas that are distinctive to Hodgson's account of temporal experience, and compare some of these features to Husserl's account.

Motivating his methodology

Hodgson wants to answer the question of how we have knowledge of the world and how such knowledge is related to experience. While this is a common enough theme, his take on it is unique: experience *is* what is present, and the totality of what is, *is* experience, in a metaphysically fundamental way. His emphasis on the present moment as central to empiricism is novel in this historical discussion. The unification of rationalist, empiricist, and idealist thought that he purports to offer turns completely on the temporal character of experience.

He opens his discussion of experience with a long discussion of philosophical methodology. How ought we to proceed in using philosophical inquiry to get genuine knowledge? He identifies each of empiricism, rationalism, and idealism as having gotten something right in its philosophical methodology, while also going astray in various regards.

Empiricism is right to emphasize that experience must be the ultimate source of knowledge. Thinkers like Hume, however, took common-sense experience as providing the materials from which knowledge could be drawn. But, according to Hodgson, this presupposed certain common-sense assumptions, such as the positing of an objective existence outside of consciousness. Instead, we have to *establish* such a claim, not assume it a priori, and in order to establish it, we must take a subjective orientation, as Hodgson calls it, as the basis for philosophical investigation, not an objective one like common-sense offers. Rationalism, such as that offered in Descartes' *Meditations*, has the correct subjective orientation. But thinkers like Descartes found errors in the common-sense understanding of the world and spuriously assumed that experience must always err. Idealists have come closer but still failed to understand the full extent of the relationship between knowledge and experience by introducing noumena.

The result Hodgson reaches is a view of philosophy as reasoning based on experience that is an early version of phenomenology of consciousness and, in particular, of the present moment in experience as all that is genuinely available for analysis. The proper approach to philosophical analysis focuses on what Hodgson calls the empirical present moment.

> [w]hatever we are actually experiencing is always the content of a present moment of experience, which may be called the empirical present, in order to distinguish it from an abstract mathematical moment of time, which, like a mathematical point of space, has in itself no content at all. We have no actual experience which is not included in the content of the empirical present moment . . . The term *actual* expresses the reality of the present content, when and while it is present in consciousness.
>
> *(ME, 35)*

What is actually real must be actually in experience, and everything that has ever been real has been so because it was a present moment in experience. The core of the real just is the contents of current consciousness, and whatever else can be shown to exist based on those current and changing contents of consciousness.

After detailed preparations for the analysis, the actual empirical moment Hodgson considers is given in a single sentence:

> Let me suppose, then, that I am seated writing in my study, and that some one in the room strikes the note C on a pianoforte behind me. The sound enters the field of consciousness, and takes its place there as part of the content of my immediate experience.
>
> *(ME, 46)*

While Hodgson eventually adds to his scenario – another note, D, follows after C – he relies on little experiential material in order to perform the analysis. He brackets all questions of history and genesis, as he puts it, in order to consider the contents of experience free of questions about what brought about or sustains those parts of experience.

Hodgson claims that analysis of this single moment enables it to highlight universal and genuinely "metaphysic" features of that experience. He draws a parallel with geometry:

> First, however, I must remark that the instance now examined, and every part of it, which may be examined separately, may be considered as a representative case, standing for all empirical present moments of experience, or for their parts; just as a triangle drawn on paper stands as a representative for all possible triangles.
>
> *(ME, 43–44)*

His method should be verifiable by readers' putting themselves into the same scenario. "It is an analysis, not an argument; and its proof lies in accuracy of observation, not in cogency of inference" (ME, 46).

Hodgson's analysis is intended to have the double feature of illustrating how the method of analysis is supposed to proceed, while also beginning the task of coming up with the actual results of such an analysis. His analysis asks, of what do we actually gain knowledge through experience once we succeed in avoiding undue assumptions? The effect of the analysis is less like building an edifice, adding one utterly sure foundational block at a time, than it is like starting with a massive block of common-sense experience and cutting away portions of it, the unjustified assumptions, to reveal the genuine content and structure of experience in the present.

Key features of a Hodgsonian account of temporal experience

This section lays out key elements of Hodgson's view, drawing both from the method for performing the analysis and the results of that analysis. It is helpful to see how all these features contribute to the overall coherence of his account before each element is elaborated in the following two sections. Hodgson is refining a view of the empiric present moment that he originally introduced in *Time and Space* (1865), which was the first time the experienced present was clearly defined as extending over some relevant duration.

1   Experience only is the present, and the present is experience. Experience and the present moment of experience are metaphysically coeval, and can be used interchangeably. Temporal experience of the present is not a special species of experience; all experience is fundamentally temporal and always *is* the present.

2   The ultimate structure of experience is process-contents. The processual aspects of time cannot be fundamentally separated from their contents. There is no content-free structure of the present moment or flow to bare time, nor is timeless or atemporal content genuinely possible.

3   There is a threshold in experience, above which process-contents abruptly appear and then away from which they flow. The genesis and sustaining conditions of our experience should be bracketed at first, but are already contained in the succession of process-contents in experience by dint of this threshold. By standing at the edge of the threshold, watching the ever-new process-contents rise above it, the analysis moves past the bracketing by revealing in conscious experience that which is outside of and gives rise to conscious experience.

4   The way process-contents fade from immediacy into the past is called retention. There are no fixed boundaries to retention as process-contents trail off to memory proper. Process-contents may enter experience together but leave the present differentially.

5   The fontal character of experience involves process-contents continually rising above the threshold, retaining their ordering as they flow away from that threshold. It is how experience can serve as the basis for all knowledge.

6   All experience is reflective in character. No matter how thinly one slices experience in analyzing it, the result is always reflective of other parts of experience. Process-contents are in experience as soon as they cross the threshold, but must be slightly past the threshold to be part of reflective experience. This means that experience that is fully reflectively available is always just past the leading edge of the threshold.

7   The present moves in two distinguishable ways, depending on the perspective from which it is considered. One perspective considers the threshold and the present just after the threshold, such that process-contents move through the present and into the past. The other perspective follows a given process-content as it rises above the threshold, is reflectively full in experience, and fades into retention, where the present moment moves forward from that process-content into the future.

8   There are two temporal arrows, with opposing directionalities. One is the order of real conditions in the world, including brain conditions, that points from past to future. The other is the order of knowledge, which points from the present as most surely known, towards the past, as content is progressively less surely known. These two arrows yield the same ordering of events but in reverse. They are united at the threshold in experience.

The empirical present in experience

This section will explain points 1 through 4 from the previous section. These points jointly elaborate what Hodgson calls the empirical present moment.

1   The central tenet of his new empiricism is point 1, that experience and the present moment are the same.

> Not only, therefore, is an empirical present moment the only thing which it is possible to analyse as it actually occurs, but it is the only thing which ever exists as an immediate experience of ours. When we say that experience consists of a succession of empirical present moments, we are expressing an inference drawn from the content of the empirical moment actually present at the time of speaking . . . Indeed it is only from the analysis of an empirical present, that the meaning of the term *present*, as distinguished from past or future, can itself be ascertained.
>
> *(ME, 35–36)*

There is a tendency in contemporary discussions to treat temporal experience as a particular subspecies of experience, individuated by its object of awareness. There is visual experience, for instance, and experience of the present moment, which could be compared as each a subspecies of some more generic notion of experience. On the Hodgsonian view given here, though, experience just is temporal experience, or put another way, just is the present moment. There is no non-temporal experience, either as atemporal content or as contentless structure into which temporal content could be placed.

2   Experience is inextricably temporal, and, as we see in point 2, he places Time and Feeling, process and content respectively, as the fundamental units of experience.

The lowest conceivable empirical moment of experience contains both time and feeling, and the lowest empirical moment in experience as it actually comes to us contains both sequence in time and difference in feeling . . . We see, then, that time and feeling together are experience. They are elements of experience in inseparable relation with each other; and this is at once the simplest and most general of all the facts of experience, upon which the general conception of Relation is founded.

(ME, 64–65)

He uses the term of art 'process-contents' to refer to experience and its contents in a way that indicates we can distinguish in analysis between experience as temporally structured and experience as contentful, but also that these are two facets of one underlying unity, separable *only* in analysis.

Experience in its simplest form, and in the simplest possible instance of it, is both process and content; and it should be expressly noted, that, according to the analysis here given, duration is common to both aspects of it, common to it both as a process and as content; the duration element in every content being that which adds its aspect as a process to its aspect as a content.

(ME, 61–62)

Process-contents as a term reminds the reader that there is no non-temporal content, and there is no content-free process of experience.

In several places, he relies on an analogy between the process-contents of experience and the intertwined parts of a rope.

The common-sense experience or empirical present analyzed is, as it were, a transverse section or segment, taken out of what may be figured as a stream of consciousness consisting of many various currents, or a cable consisting of variously coloured strands, variously intertwined.

(ME, 41)

While process-contents can be distinguished by their content as they exist together in a given empirical moment, such content still figures in that moment holistically. This does not mean, he says, that the contents in consciousness lie next to one another separately, in the way that parts of a rope sit next to one another and each comprise some percentage of the total volume of the rope in any section.

We have now to analyse this same experience as a process, or in other words, the *fact that* the experience takes place . . . Its experience is an event in time having duration. One and the same duration of time is an element in the content of the experience analysed, in the one way of taking it, and is the foundation of the other way of taking it, namely, as a process of experiencing . . . But, as it is, the process-content analysed is experienced as a distinct but unsevered portion of a larger process, which is partly simultaneous and partly antecedent. It is, as it were, the end-portion of a thread, in a rope consisting of many threads.

(ME, 54)

Hodgson uses this underlying unity of experience as process-contents as a kind of epistemic lever by which to close any gap between what genuinely exists in reality and that which can be the content of experience. He will ultimately pronounce the content of experience and what exists as same in extent, differing only in the aspect under which we consider them.

3   The notion of process-contents rejects the idea that there is a fixed structure of the present in experience, through which content then flows. This is often how Husserl's tripartite account of time consciousness is understood (see Brough, Chapter 6 in this volume, and the next section below). Hodgson argues that, just like there is no rope without the strands that are woven together, there is no bare present to be filled by separate content.

> Consequently we are compelled by the facts of perception to conceive, that the duration of every content of consciousness, simple or complex, passes away into memory along with its content, and is no fixed form or measure, filled by a fleeting content, which for a brief moment, the empirical present, is arrested and retained therein; or in other words, is no form or measure, existing separably from, or prior to, its content, feeling, and into which feelings must be brought in order to their being perceived. Duration and content are inseparable, arising together in consciousness, and together passing away into memory.
>
> *(ME, 133–134)*

Hodgson started his analysis by bracketing the possible causes or conditions for experience, in order to analyze experience without assumptions about how it came to be. Quite early on in his analysis, however, he returns to those ideas that he earlier bracketed, such as the existence of an external world. Knowledge of the existence of a world external to experience cannot be assumed prior to analyzing experience, he emphasized, but very little analysis is required to show that such knowledge is already contained in experience. The process-contents arise freshly in an ongoing fountain, and they rise, he notes, above some threshold. The threshold just is that which marks the boundary of experience that is crossed by new process-contents. Consciousness, here taken to be equivalent to experience, includes within it the notion of that which is external to consciousness. Thus Hodgson recognizes the existence of the world that is external to consciousness, but not as a posit or assumption. It is uncovered as already contained in and justified with surety by the very notion of consciousness.

> The supposition of a reality which is not consciousness is thus introduced by the figurative expression, a *threshold* of consciousness, which is an image drawn from space, involving the ideas, (1) of a boundary between consciousness and non-consciousness, and, (2) that the appearance of consciousness above the boundary line is in some way due to something real in the region of non-consciousness below the boundary . . . A state or process which is both consciousness and non-consciousness, as a supposed state of consciousness below the threshold must be, is impossible. The term *consciousness* in its widest sense implicitly contains *above the threshold* as part of its own meaning.
>
> *(ME, 55–56)*

The existence of a threshold in the present moment, such that the crossing of this threshold just is a process-content coming into the empirical present moment, is sufficient to take us back out of the bracketing. It establishes the first clear and assumption-free evidence in experience for something external to experience, namely, what will eventually be shown to be the external world.

In consequence of real conditions that lie below the threshold of conscious-ness . . . states of consciousness appear above the threshold, and from the instant of arising recede into the past, since their contents have duration, and the ever-arising new content is that portion of the whole which is nearest in time to the ever advancing present instant, which is the instant of origin of every successively arising empirical portion or content.

(ME, 66)

"Real conditioning", another term of art, refers to the processes on which experience depends. He insists that real conditioning is not what had, at that point, traditionally gone under the name of causality. Neither is his view that consciousness supervenes on physical processes: the relationship between consciousness and real conditions is not the same as supervenience, even though it is suggestively similar. He also hasn't yet reached the place in the analysis where we could call the real conditions that are external to consciousness "physical" without making an illegitimate assumption. But he is progres-sively showing how broad metaphysical conclusions can be derived from this simplest of empirical present moments under analysis. Hodgson spends a substantial portion of volume 2 of ME on real conditioning as key to understanding the relationship between natural science and philosophy.

4   The term "retention" is introduced to characterize the portion of the empirical present moment that leads to the past. The threshold forms the leading edge towards the future, but what is the character of the trailing edge? Hodgson says that there is no determinate boundary for the empirical present moment, such that new content pushes the old out beyond the threshold of the past, neither do the contents of consciousness fade in synchrony through retention into what he calls memory proper. This is not merely the weak claim that, when comparing distinct empirical present moments, they have different durations. Hodgson is making the stronger claim that even for a given empirical present moment, there is no definitive boundary to where it ends. The present itself is comprised of different contents in an intriguing way, such that two contents in consciousness at the same time might each leave retention and become part of memory proper at two different instants. A knock at the door and a C note played on a piano might both occur simultaneously, yet leave conscious-ness differently, such that a single empirical present moment might be identified where the knock is already in memory while the tone lingers in retention.

Any content during that time of its remaining in consciousness belongs to what I have called an empirical present moment. Some content the empirical present moment must always have, since otherwise it would not be a moment of experi-ence at all. But inasmuch as different contents have different durations, and many different contents may be simultaneously present in consciousness, at least for some part of their durations, it follows that consciousness or experience does not occur in portions of uniform or fixed duration . . . The concrete content of consciousness consists of many different strains or features, not all beginning or ceasing together; so that, while we must always speak generally of the whole content, whatever it may be, as composing an empirical present moment, it is impossible to lay down any fixed duration applicable to the whole, as that in which its limit consists.

(ME, 36–37)

Retention is the way in which process-contents that are just past linger in the empirical present moment somewhat before fully leaving the empirical present.

> Now retention, or memory in its lowest terms, is a character which certainly cannot be said to be discriminated, or perceived as such, in the experience, though it is actually involved in the perceived element of duration.
>
> *(ME, 59)*

Retention is distinguished from memory proper because the process-contents in retention are still part of the present, and are part of it with a just-past character. This gives us a sense of how the empirical present moment is structured, even while recognizing that it can be identified as a separate structure only in analysis. The leading or forward edge is sharp; it is the threshold across which new process-contents continually flow. Newer process-contents displace those just prior to them, while retaining the order in which they crossed the threshold as they move through the empirical present. The trailing edge is ragged and changing, because process-contents that crossed the threshold together may yet leave retention at different instants.

Two motions of the present, two directions of time

5   The fontal character of knowledge and the way in which process-contents maintain their ordering as they pass through and out of consciousness, is crucial for any knowledge based on experience. There must be genuine content arising above the threshold to provide substantive knowledge, but in addition, it must remain in the order in which it first crossed the threshold for those contents to undergird knowledge. Without both of these two features, knowledge would be impossible. The first was well-discussed before Hodgson, but the role of the second had not yet been appreciated.

Consider the very first appearance of content above the threshold. A given new process-content appears above the threshold, which means it enters the front edge of the empirical present moment. It comes from not-consciousness, which is just part of saying that it carries no mark of having been formed by, influenced by, constructed by, or otherwise being merely dependent on pure consciousness itself. Hodgson calls this the fontal character of experience. It is helpful to think of the threshold like a line above which bubbles a spring or fountain of process-contents. The source is hidden from view, but there is clearly something that wells above the threshold itself. One can imagine Hodgson and Hume together considering this very threshold as new content emerges so ongoingly and yet so substantively, both marveling that new content just keeps coming, even though the future out of which it comes is utterly opaque, and that it somehow does constitute meaningful experience once it has crossed that threshold into experience. Hume might focus more on the way in which we cannot, from this present, say anything utterly sure about what *will* appear in the future; but Hodgson is focused on the present contents and how they do just keep appearing.

This threshold provides the ordering of process-contents by lining them up, as it were, as they go over. This ordering in turn gives us the coherence of events at longer time scales than can fit into an empirical present moment.

> A present instant of consciousness defined merely by its place in time is always present; a present instant of consciousness defined as the beginning of a particular content of consciousness recedes along with that particular content into the past. Accordingly, as each new content arises and recedes into the past, it retains, or tends to retain, in the fading vista, the same place in the sequence, in which it originally arose.
>
> *(ME, 66–67)*

6   Experience that is fully across the threshold becomes reflective (see also Hodgson 1878). Hodgson relies on a conception of reflection to flesh out the character of the central part of the empirical present moment, that which is after the leading edge of the threshold and before the trailing edge of retention. Process-contents cannot be apprehended in the very instant at which they appear, but instead must be separated from the threshold above which they rise by at least some small margin in order for the content to be fully in experience. There must be space in which to reflect on the content, according to Hodgson, and that space means that there is some new as-yet-unreflected content between it and the very edge of the threshold. The empirical present moment is comprised of immediate reflection, in the sense of looking back, upon the just-past contents that have now already crossed the threshold but have not yet faded into the past. Reflection thus metaphorically positions the subject performing the analysis at the threshold itself, looking towards retention, able to "see" process-contents after they have risen fully above the threshold.

7   This vantage point from which the empirical present is considered highlights two distinguishable directions in which the present can be said to be moving. One is the movement of a process-content through consciousness, if we track it from the instant it appears above the threshold till the last of its contents have faded from retention. The other is the movement of the present that goes forward as the crest of a wave of the ongoing fountain of new process-contents.

> Even in the simplest case of perception, a single sound for instance, the moment of its appearing above the threshold of consciousness is also the moment of its beginning to recede into the past, so as to take its place in the panorama of empirical experience. One and the same process-content begins and continues for a time in consciousness, seeming, to us who think about it, to bear the present moment along with it as it advances, and so constituting what may be most properly called the empirical present; while at the same time since it is consciousness, and consciousness involves memory in the sense of retention, the mathematically present instance, at which we imagine ourselves, or any percipient, to be placed, when perceiving an empirical present, is always an instant of retrospection upon the consciousness process of that which that empirical present consists. We thus have an apparent movement in two opposite directions at once, involved in one and the same process of consciousness, and that in all cases.
>
> *(ME, 84–85)*

8   Each of these directions of motion is associated with an arrow of time, or an ordering of process-contents. One ordering is given by real conditions in the objective world, an ordering of contents in terms of chains of causally linked events in a world that is external to experience. That direction moves into the future from the present. The second ordering is given by the order in which process-contents cross the threshold and retreat into the past. The arrow points from present towards the past, an ordering of process-contents in terms of their distance from the vantage of the threshold. Closer process-contents are surer than those in the far past. The order of *real conditions* is from past to the present as pushing into the future, with the tip of the arrow at the threshold. The order of *knowledge* is from the present to the past, with the tail of the arrow at the threshold.

> To a Subject, therefore, standing at that rudimentary stage, both the receding order of the process-contents (in which it is seen at any present moment, and seen in retrospect), and the advancing order (in which it seems to bear the present

moment along with it), are as yet one and the same; the former being what he will afterward call the order of knowledge (*cognoscendi*), and the latter the order of existence of real genesis and history (*existendi*) . . . This union of differences (implicit to him but explicit to us) which are really present in one and the same process, though recognized only at a later stage, is only possible because the process is one of consciousness; which, being both a knowing and an existent, has the psychological moment of its real genesis (or appearance above the threshold) coincident with the moment of reflective perception, in which it is a part of knowing.

(ME, 85–86)

The instant of crossing the threshold is, in the order of real conditioning, or, of events in the external world including the cerebral activity sustaining consciousness, the forward edge that pushes from the past into the future as chains of events unfurl. That very same threshold is the moment of the present in experience, where Hodgson imagines the percipient to be viewing the ordering of process-contents facing towards the past, such that the newest contents are the first, or closest, in the order of knowledge. Considering the order of real events, the present moment is moving along from the past towards the future. Considering the order of process-contents in experience, the present moment is unfurling from the present towards the past. The directions meet at the present.

[c]onsciousness as an existent, or what is the same thing, as the consciousness of a real Subject or Percipient, is always moving forwards, with the rest of the real existents, in the order of real genesis and history, and always consists, as a knowing, in reflection upon itself, that is, upon its own past contents, from every successive present moment actually reached in that forward movement, this reflective perception constituting what we call the order of knowledge.

(ME, 91)

This offers an exciting unification of the Subject as an experiencing knower with the Subject as a real part of the existing world, along with all the non-knowing parts of that world. The empirical present gets pushed along a timeline towards the future along with other events, while also facing backwards to reflect on what has just transpired. These two directions of motion provide the means to integrate our subjective experience with the genuine existence of an objective world of which we are also a part.

Comparison with Husserl

Husserl is good counterpoint for a comparison with Hodgson on the experience of the present moment. Contemporary discussions of the experience of time largely draw on Husserl, especially for projects like neurophenomenology (e.g., Varela 1999; Lutz and Thompson 2003; Thompson *et al.* 2005). Hodgson's work strikingly prefigures many key parts of Husserl, both in methodology and in the details about the character of temporal experience. Yet they also differ in stark and surprising ways. Most notably, Hodgson moves from a phenomenological bracketing of the external world and what causes our experience, to connect our experience to what he calls neuronal processes. While there isn't space for detailed discussion here, Hodgson offers an early neurophenomenological account that is surprisingly detailed given that it dates from the late nineteenth century.

Readers unfamiliar with Husserl's phenomenology of inner time consciousness can find more in Brough (Chapter 6 in this volume). Briefly, Husserl offers a tripartite fixed structure of the present moment through which contents flow. The forward-directed edge is called protention, the central part is called primal impression, and the trailing edge is called retention. Hodgson's version is similar with respect to retention, but differs markedly in several ways: his notions of threshold and reflection in the empirical present do not correspond in any neat way to protention and primal impression; and Hodgson rejects a fixed structure of the present through which content flows, emphasizing the inseparable character of process-contents.

With respect to method, Hodgson's bracketing of the questions of real conditions and genesis may differ in small details from the phenomenological approach of Husserl, but only in small details. Husserl brackets the external world, setting those questions aside and not returning to them. Yet Hodgson moves past the bracketing and re-introduces the world outside of experience, even the brain processes that sustain experience, in a very non-Husserlian way. This makes his account more amenable to direct application in neurophenomenology than Husserl's. Hodgson's threshold is explicitly tied to neuronal activity, even though the precise nature of that activity is not specified. His method of connecting underlying brain activity and events in the external world to the ongoing content of experience arguably makes Hodgson the original neurophenomenologist.

In addition to similarities in methodology, both thinkers offer a very similar notion of retention as a way of characterizing just-past contents of experience that are not yet in memory. In both cases, the phenomenon of retention is illuminated by contrasting it with memory proper, which requires recollection to bring the contents back into current experience. That they use such similar terminology to mark this phenomenon is also remarkable.

There are a number of such commonalities between their works that may stem from genuinely direct influence. The question of whether Husserl was familiar with the work of Hodgson was first raised by Spicker (1973). Spicker provides a very detailed comparison of several main points of comparison between Husserl and Hodgson, noting repeatedly that Hodgson anticipates Husserl in numerous ways. Spicker offers a timeline by which to track a multitude of possible pathways from Hodgson to Husserl. Some of these are indirect, where Hodgson's influence on Husserl was filtered through the lens of William James's writings (see also, Andersen 2014). Some were more direct, where Husserl had access to and clearly read at least some of Hodgson's work. Scholars at the Husserl archives continue to translate Husserl's dense shorthand into German, such that potentially decisive evidence about specific passages of Hodgson's that Husserl drew on, or which he read during the critical time period during which he was writing his lecture notes developing his own account of time consciousness, may be forthcoming in yet-untranslated material.

Even with these commonalities in their views, both thinkers still diverge on central ideas. A major point of difference lies in the present as a structure. Husserl is often taken to provide a structure for the present moment in experience, through which content continuously flows (e.g., Dainton 2006). Hodgson straightforwardly rejects this idea. Once one gets to this fundamental metaphysical level of analysis for experience, there are only process-contents, which cannot have their duration or place in the present moment separated from their content. The present moment itself has no fixed permanent structure, or a fixed duration, because it lacks a fixed or unified trailing edge in retention.

There are also clear differences between Hodgson's notions of threshold and reflection, and Husserl's protention and primal impression. The phenomenon of protention cannot find a space in Hodgson. It would require current process-contents to shape or influence those about to cross or just crossing the threshold, a possibility for which Hodgson does not allow. The threshold is a stark boundary, and the way process-contents just keep coming over the threshold does not correspond to protention in Husserl's sense.

The Husserlian phenomenon of primal impression is also awkward to translate into Hodgson's view. Husserl has no equivalent to the threshold. The primal impression might be best understood as process-contents that are crossing or have only just barely crossed the threshold, such that they are not yet in reflective consciousness. However, the primal impression already has its content in a certain way, whereas Hodgsonian content just crossing the threshold is not yet reflected in experience. One might think that when a process-content has crossed the threshold of consciousness fully, such that it is now reflected in experience, it would be equivalent to the primal impression. But this would misconstrue Hodgson's emphasis on the way in which different process-contents traverse the present moment in experience, namely, that they can do so differentially.

Husserl's work has been the almost exclusive focus for neurophenomenologists. Part of what is potentially so useful about a Hodgsonian account of neurophenomenology is the place his thought occupies in the overall canon of philosophy. Hodgson is, I would argue, the last of the classic British Empiricists, and explicitly situates his own work as the conclusion of a trajectory of thought that begins in the early modern period. Husserl's work, while worthwhile, is harder to incorporate directly into much of the existing philosophical discussion of knowledge, experience, and scientifically informed philosophy of mind (see, for instance, Smith 2013 for concerns about neurophenomenology from the phenomenological perspective). Husserl struck out on a new path with his development of phenomenology, one that was followed up by thinkers like Heidegger and Merleau-Ponty, but which involved fewer direct discussions with the philosophical literature growing under the twentieth-century tradition of analytic philosophy. Accordingly, most authors working to bring together time consciousness and brain processes draw only on Husserl's work, and draw only on the first portions of his work, offering the tripartite structure as sufficient for their purposes. Hodgson's work offers an account of the empirical present moment that is recognizably phenomenological in many regards, but also begins to draw connections to neuronal processes, and which is clearly situated in a philosophical tradition stemming back to the early modern period and continuing through the twentieth century.

Conclusion

Hodgson developed a novel philosophical method and account of the fundamentally temporal character of experience that differs in significant ways from any other existing account of temporal experience (even, arguably, from any other account of experience broadly construed). His work is both historically significant and philosophically useful in contemporary discussions. Hodgson's *Metaphysic of Experience* comes just at the close of a long-standing British tradition of a certain style of empiricist thought. It also stands just before the beginning of a new distinctive style of British empiricism that emerged with Russell, Whitehead, and others. It is likely that Hodgson's work is part of the tradition being rejected by these new empiricists, who are sometimes characterized by contrast with the phenomenological tradition in terms of the analytic-continental divide. Hodgson's work straddles these two traditions before the split by standing at the culmination of the earlier trajectory of British empiricism. The Hodgsonian account of temporal experience offers a new version of phenomenology that is the completion of a familiar form of British empiricism, explicitly developed in responses to figures such as Descartes, Hume, and Kant. While Hodgson had an enormous influence in late nineteenth-century English philosophy, his voice is rarely heard today, and is ripe for re-evaluation and re-incorporation. His *Metaphysic of Experience* is a treasure trove of philosophical insights for application to numerous contemporary discussions.

Acknowledgements

Much thanks to Endre Begby and Kathleen Creel for discussions of and feedback on this work. Thanks also to the SFU 2015 Philosophy of Time seminar for their helpful discussions on Hodgson's work. I am grateful for the opportunity to live and work on unceded Coast Salish territories.

References

Andersen, H. (2014) "The development of the 'specious present' and James' views on temporal experience", in D. Lloyd and V. Arstila (eds), *Subjective Time: The Philosophy, Psychology, and Neuroscience of Temporality*, Cambridge, MA: MIT Press, pp. 25–42.

Andersen, H. and Grush, R. (2009) "A brief history of time-consciousness: Historical precursors to James and Husserl", *Journal of the History of Philosophy* 47(2): 277–307.

Dainton, B. (2006) *Stream of Consciousness: Unity and Continuity in Conscious Experience*, London: Routledge.

Hodgson, S. H. (1865) *Time and Space: A Metaphysical Essay*, London: Longmans, Green and Co.

Hodgson, S. H. (1878) *Philosophy of Reflection*, 2 vols, London: Longmans, Green and Co.

Hodgson, S. H. (1898) *The Metaphysic of Experience*, 4 vols, London: Longmans, Green and Co.

James, W. (1950) *The Principles of Psychology*, 2 vols, New York: Henry Holt and Co. Reprint.

Lutz, A. and Thompson, E. (2003) "Neurophenomenology integrating subjective experience and brain dynamics in the neuroscience of consciousness", *Journal of Consciousness Studies* 10(9–10): 31–52.

Smith, D. W. (2013) "Phenomenology", in E. N. Zalta (ed.), *The Stanford Encyclopedia of Philosophy*, available at: http://plato.stanford.edu/archives/win2013/entries/phenomenology/. Accessed 6 September 2016.

Spicker, S. F. (1973) "The fundamental constituents of consciousness: Process-contents and the Erlebnisstrom", *Man and World* 6(1): 26–43.

Thompson, E., Lutz, A. and Cosmelli, D. (2005) "Neurophenomenology: An introduction for neuro-philosophers", in A. Brook and K. Akins (eds), *Cognition and the Brain: The Philosophy and Neuroscience Movement*, Cambridge, UK: Cambridge University Press, pp. 40–97.

Varela, F. J. (1999) "Present-time consciousness", *Journal of Consciousness Studies*, 6(2–3): 111–140.

6

THE WONDER OF
TIME-CONSCIOUSNESS

John B. Brough

Edmund Husserl's analysis of temporal experience represents a body of work that any philosopher seeking to understand time and our awareness of it should take into account. Husserl began to investigate temporal experience at the start of the twentieth century. By the time of his death in 1938, he had produced hundreds of pages of notes, sketches, and lecture manuscripts that collectively amount to the most extensive reflection on the subject in the literature. What he said about temporal experience influenced later figures in the phenomenological movement, and more recently has drawn attention from some writers in the analytic tradition as well. The aim of this chapter is to give a sense of the scope of Husserl's investigations, the positions they involve, and the questions they pose.

Husserl describes time-consciousness as a "wonder" (Husserl 1991: 290),[1] as "rich in mystery" (1991: 286), and as the "most important" (1991: 346) but also the "most difficult of all phenomenological problems" (1991: 286). Its wonder and its difficulty arise from the ways it goes about its business. Its importance lies in the fundamental role it plays in every aspect of conscious life. Its mysteries, and the difficulties in unraveling them, derive from its seeming obviousness and maddening elusiveness. Husserl and Augustine are of one mind in holding that nothing is more familiar and yet more resistant to understanding than temporal experience.

The awareness of time, Husserl claims, is a cardinal instance of "intentional" experience. Husserl is an "intentionalist" in the sense that he maintains that conscious experiences, such as perception, memory, or phantasy, are directed toward or "intend" objects. Thus one hears a melody, recalls watching the Concorde take off years ago, or expects to see a friend walk into the room. Husserl's version of intentionalism distinguishes between act and object. Intentional acts are precisely conscious experiences directed toward objects. The relation between intending act and intended object, however, is not a real relationship. The act does not intend its object by being caused by its object, which would entail that the object actually existed. One can be directed intentionally toward nonexistent or absent objects, as in memory or phantasy, or in thinking about "ideal" objects such as the Pythagorean Theorem. The intentional relation, in Husserl's view, is a cognitive relation in the broadest sense.

The temporal object

Time-consciousness is a foundational form of intentionality, entwined with every other form and instance of conscious life. Since intentionality is a matter of an act intending an object,

Husserl's investigation of temporal awareness includes both the intending temporal experience and its correlate, the intended temporal object, the "objective sense" and "descriptive content" (2001: 9) of the experience.

Time and the experience of time are complex phenomena. Husserl respects their complexity by refusing to force them into simple formulae. This is the case in part because there is no pure experience of time, as if one could be conscious of time apart from temporal objects. Time is not experienced in the way in which, say, a flowering tree is perceived. I can see the tree in the garden; I cannot "see" time. It is neither the sort of thing that could be to the left or right of the tree, nor is it an ordinary quality, like the color of the tree's blossoms. Even to look at the movement of the hands of a clock or to hear its ticking is not to see or hear time. Such objects, however, no matter how different they may otherwise be, have in common that they exist in time. Their time shows itself in certain formal features that they possess and in certain ways in which they appear. Perhaps the closest one can come to a concise formulation of time in Husserlian terms is to say very generally and with more than a hint of circularity that time as the objective correlate of temporal awareness is that set of features and modes of appearance that mark an object as being in time, or even, as in the case of something like the "timeless" Pythagorean Theorem, as not being in time. The temporal object, of course, has a "material" dimension that determines the distinct sort of thing that it is. A tree, for example, short of petrification, is not a rock. Both tree and rock, however, are temporal objects; but it is not the tree's arboreality that, by itself, makes it a temporal object, any more than it is the rockiness of the rock that makes *it* a temporal object. They are temporal objects because they are perceived as existing and enduring in time.

Duration

Duration is a feature of all temporal objects. Enduring objects also succeed one another, and some of them, such as melodies and events generally, embody succession. The enduring object "spreads itself out" in time, "exists in time and continuously lasts throughout time" (1991: 267). As enduring, it appears as a unity and as identical across the stretch of time it occupies. The Eiffel Tower, for example, appears as one identical thing in each time-point of its duration. Even the melodies I hear and the events I see, which, in contrast to static material objects such as the Eiffel Tower, are not wholly present in each time-point, may be said to endure and enjoy a certain identity for as long as they continue to unfold in their changes and variations. A performance on the vault in a gymnastics competition would be a case in point.

While duration is an essential characteristic of the temporal object, it is "not a property in the true sense" (1991: 269). The properties of a temporal object – say, the Eiffel Tower's shape and color – endure, but duration itself does not endure. Enduring things or events and their properties fill out an extent of time with their contents, which is precisely their duration (1991: 279). The object can remain constant throughout its duration or can change. If a red house is painted blue, the house will continue to endure, although one of its enduring properties will have ceased and been replaced by a new property. At some point, the house itself may be destroyed, in which case it and all of its properties will cease to endure. However, it is only the particular house's duration that ends. Duration as a *form* of temporal objects, which the house shared with other objects for a while, no more ends than time does. When multiple objects have the same duration, they are simultaneous.

Once finished, the duration of a temporal object is fixed in perpetuity. I cannot expand it or contract it. An enduring object's position in relation to other objects is fixed as well. "No event", Husserl writes, "can leap out of its temporal position or its determinate temporal extent. They belong to its essence" (2001: 134). This is the case in the sense that a temporal object, whether an event or a physical thing, must exist at a particular point in time and across a particular extent of time. The Colossus at Rhodes has its place in time and its finite duration there. The Great War and World War II have their temporal locations and durations as well. This presumes that there is a single time embracing all temporal objects posited as real. This time would include both what Husserl calls "immanent" unities, such as intentional acts, and their intentional correlates, which are commonly, although certainly not always, "transcendent" objects in the world. An act of perception, for example, is immanent in the sense of being a conscious experience, while its object is transcendent. Husserl sometimes indicates that each of these sorts of entities has its own time – "immanent time" or the time of consciousness, on the one hand, and "world" or "transcendent" time, on the other. Husserl's settled position, however, seems to be that, despite their fundamental dimensional difference, transcendent objects and immanent unities, such as acts, share a common time. "The time of the perception and the time of the perceived are identically the same" (1991: 74). This does not mean that Husserl subscribes to what Itzchak Miller calls the "Principle of Presentational Concurrence", which "rules out the possibility of my being *presented* at t with [for example] a temporally extended tone-quality" (Miller 1984: 110, 107). On the contrary, as we shall see later, Husserl maintains that in a given moment of a temporally extended perception, I can be presentationally aware of an entire temporally extended object or of a portion of one. This occurs, however, within the context of a perceptual act that is extended in time and directed toward a perceptual object that is also extended in time. From that perspective, the act of perceiving as a whole and the object it perceives occupy the same stretch of time and have the same duration, at least for as long as the perception lasts. One might observe here that a star I am now seeing, given the finite velocity of light, may have ceased existing before my present act of seeing it. From Husserl's point of view, however, the act of seeing is, phenomenologically, a perceptual act that may properly be said to perceive the star's light, which exists at the same time as the act perceiving it. (Husserl does not claim, in the case of material things and qualities, that *esse est percipi*. Such things can go on existing after my perception has ceased, or, for that matter, after anyone's perception has ceased.)

Husserl claims, then, that perception, understood as the consciousness of an object as actually present to the perceiver "in person", is possible only if it exists at the same time as its object. This stands in sharp contrast to memory, in which the time of the act of remembering is precisely not identical with the time of the remembered object. This points to another and broader sense of Husserl's claim about the oneness of time: that there is a single time embracing all temporal objects, whether immanent or transcendent, in which they can have varying durations and enjoy relations of succession and coexistence. The synchrony of the perceiving act and its object and the asynchrony of memory and what it remembers can occur only in a common time, making it possible for these disparate relationships to establish and display themselves. We will return to the theme of immanence and transcendence in a later section.

The temporal modes of appearance

The features of temporal objects we have discussed to this point are revealed in time-consciousness but not produced by it. The Eiffel Tower does not depend on my consciousness for its existence or duration. The Tower began to exist long before I first saw it, and presumably will endure long after I am no longer able to see it. Similarly, the succession of sounds when my telephone rings is simply given to me. Features such as duration and succession, Husserl claims, represent "time in itself", time as the "objective form" (Husserl 2001: 181) of temporal objects, the "fixed" element in temporal objectivity. This "time in itself" is obviously not something unknown and unknowable. My temporal experience is precisely my awareness of it, not in isolation from temporal objects, but as filled with them. In my experiencing of time itself, it becomes time for me (2001: 194), that is, it appears to me from the perspective of my "actual now" (2001: 194). Experienced in relation to the subject, the temporal object "'is presently occurring' or has occurred or . . . will occur" (2001: 182). Temporal objects and the stretches of time they fill therefore appear to me in temporal modes – specifically, as now, past, and future. We are conscious of time only in such modes. "The consciousness of time is the consciousness of the succession of points, each of which can only be intended as actual now or as a now that has been or is future" (2001: 36).

The modes of now, past, and future in which temporal objects appear are not themselves objects, parts, or properties of things, any more than the spatial perspectives in which the Eiffel Tower appears are parts or properties of the Tower. Now, past, and future are also not time-points, and therefore do not combine to form durations or successions. The duration of the Eiffel Tower is the objective extent of time the Tower's existence occupies, which stands in an unchanging relationship to other objects and events. In contrast, now, past, and future, as ways in which the object and the time-points it occupies appear, shift continuously. What I experience as future in one moment appears as now in the next, and what has just appeared as now is experienced as sinking further and further into the past, preserving in ever-changing temporal modes its temporal extension and its unchanging relationships to other objects. What appears remains stable and fixed, while its ways of appearing are in ceaseless flux.

Husserl notes that one might be tempted to understand past and future as the "two counter-directions of earlier in time – later in time" that belong to the fixed positions of temporal objects and the time-points making them up. Past and future, however, as modes of givenness of enduring objects, "are entirely different concepts" (2001: 146). The difference does not simply lie in the presence or absence of change. Objects and events certainly do change in time, but Husserl maintains that these changes, which have their fixed temporal locations, should not be confused "with the 'flow' of the modes of givenness in which everything temporal 'appears' to the subject. The appearing of a change is a continuous 'flow', but the objective change is a fixed existent . . . a fixed event in time" (2001: 183). The fixed objective change is given in the ever-changing "subjective" flow of temporal modes.

Now, past, and future, as modes of appearance, cannot exist independently of the objects appearing in them. They are never empty. They also cannot exist apart from one another. Thus the now "is a relative concept and refers to a past, just as 'past' refers to the 'now'" (1991: 70). Husserl also characterizes present, past, and future as "orientation forms" (2001: 36), with the now as the hub of orientation. Thus "the consciousness of time is the consciousness of the succession of points, each of which can be intended as actual now or as now that has been or is future" (2001: 36). The duration and its time-points remain the same regardless of the orientation modes in which they appear, which are always changing. It is in these terms that one can make sense of Husserl's statement that "time is fixed, and yet time flows" (1991: 67).

In the consciousness of time, therefore, we always and necessarily have "two kinds of things: the being itself and the changing . . . modes of givenness of this . . . being" (1991: 183). These two are inseparable in temporal experience and together form the intentional correlate of our awareness of time.

The "now"

Among the temporal modes of appearance, the "now" holds a special position: It is the "original or ground form" (1991: 142) of which all the other modes are modifications. Although now, past, and future are mutually related and oriented with respect to one another, the now is the privileged point of orientation. Temporal objects appear as past or future in relation to what appears as now. Furthermore, the now is a single form of appearing, while "'just past' and 'just coming' are 'universal titles' for a continuum of forms" (2001: 142). As I listen to a melody, for example, only one note will appear as now. The other notes will appear in varying degrees of the just past and the just coming, thus forming a continuum of ways of appearing. With each successive moment of hearing the melody, a new part of the melody in a new time-point will appear as now, and all of the previous points will appear as further past.

This suggests another aspect of the now's primacy: The now is the source of the new. The temporal modes of appearing, the "running-off modes" (*Ablaufsmodi*), as Husserl sometimes calls them, "have a *beginning*, a *source-point*, so to speak", which is the mode "with which the object begins to exist, and it is characterized as now" (1991: 375). But the now is not only the source-point of new temporal objects and new phases of objects, it is also "the source-point of all temporal positions" (1991: 74). When a new object or phase of an object is experienced as now, it emerges as planted in a specific point in time. Once planted, nothing can uproot it. It will recede from the now in continuously changing modes of the past, but never relinquish its position. The now is therefore "a continuous moment of individuation" (1991: 68), for an object is individuated when it makes its appearance at a certain point in time, and this first occurs in the now. Finally, the now, like the time-points experienced in it, is broadly hospitable. Multiple objects, transcendent and immanent, can appear together as present, and then, in the process of running off, appear together in modes of the past.

Husserl's analysis of temporal modes enables him to avoid two prejudices. The first is the "prejudice of the now": the view that one can be conscious only of what is present. The second might be called "the prejudice of anything but the now", according to which one can never be aware of the present because it becomes past before consciousness can catch it. Husserl claims, to the contrary, that we are aware of the now, but never aware of only the now. During the perception of a melody, what I experience appears to me as now, but also in part as just past and to come. The now has a "temporal fringe" (Husserl borrows James's term; 1991: 172), a "horizon" of past and future, which together with the now forms an extended present, a "rough now" embracing a "finer now" (1991: 42) that "is always and essentially the border-point" between what is immediately past and future (1991: 72). It is in this extended or "living" present that things happen. The melody would never make its appearance as a melody rather than as a series of disconnected tonal moments – which, indeed, could not even be experienced as disconnected – if I were not aware of the tones that immediately preceded the tone I am now hearing. If these twin prejudices were correct, we would have no experience of what is now as now, and therefore no experience of past and future, of what is not now. We would have no temporal experience at all.

These last remarks bring us to the second major aspect of Husserl's account of temporal experience.

The structure of time-consciousness

What Husserl says about temporal objects and the modalities in which they appear represents one side of his account of temporal experience. The other side is his investigation of the intentional structure that makes possible the awareness of temporal objects. Husserl's analysis here is rich and instructive, and sometimes daunting.

There are experiences whose time-constituting function is obvious. In ordinary memory, I am aware of something as past and in expectation of something as future. Husserl's initial efforts to penetrate the mystery of temporal experience, however, focused on perception, for it is in perception that time-consciousness is at work preeminently and originally. In perceiving, I first experience temporally extended objects, and memory and expectation presuppose as essential to their sense that something has already been perceived or will be perceived.

Perception presents its object as now. The perceived object, however, is extended in time, which means that if it is to be perceived in its temporality, it cannot be experienced simply as now. Perception must be aware, in each of its phases, not only of the object's now-moment, but also of a limited stretch of its past and future. To perceive a temporal object – a melody, for example – perception in each of its phases must reach out beyond the part of the melody appearing as now and grasp its elapsed and coming moments. By letting us escape the now, time-consciousness opens the doors to temporality. Given that now, past, and future exist only in relation to one another, if consciousness did not transcend the now, there would be no awareness of temporal modes of appearance, including the now, and therefore no aware-ness of temporal objects. A condition of temporal experience, then, is that each of its phases transcends the now and intends what is no longer and what is not yet. Each "perceptual phase has intentional reference to an extended section of the temporal object and not merely to a now-point given in it and simultaneous with it" (1991: 239).

Reaching out beyond the now means that what has elapsed is preserved along with what appears as now. Preservation alone, however, is not enough to account for temporal experi-ence. It must be coupled with modification; specifically, the elapsed portions of the melody must appear, not as now, but as just past in varying degrees. If they were preserved without modifica-tion, they would fuse with the melody's now-point into a single instantaneous burst of sound. No temporally extended melody would appear. What is just coming must also be intended in modi-fied form, that is, as future. Preserving a temporal object involves an awareness of flowing away, but always in union with an awareness of flowing toward, an awareness of what is just coming. It is difficult, if not impossible, to imagine what the experience of temporality would be without such future directedness. Openness to the future does not seem to be an optional element in the structure of time-consciousness. It is the ground of our perpetual awareness that experience is not finished, that more is to come. Furthermore, it is sewn into experience in such a way that what is perceived as now is experienced as the actual presence of what was intended as future a moment before, and what is past is experienced as what had been future, became now, and is now elapsed.

Each actual phase belonging to a perception is therefore conscious of the temporal object as in part now, in part past, and in part future. Perception's consciousness of past and future, however, differs fundamentally from the consciousness of past and future in ordinary memory and expectation. Ordinary memory is an independent act that is not part of a perception but presumes a perception's prior constitution. A personal memory of something as past is the memory of something I once perceived. I remember it by recalling the perception in which it was originally given. The past that memory represents is ordinarily not part of the living present but lies further back in the past. It is possible, however, to remember the immediately perceived past in the sense that, while the perception is still living, I can return to its initial moments and run through them once again in memory. In this case, I recall the earlier phases of the percep-tion while the perception is still in the process of developing. What is unique about personal memory, then, is not that its object belongs to the distant past, but that it is conscious of its object by returning to the perception in which the object was originally given.

Husserl makes a further point about memory, which will no doubt strike some as controversial. He rejects, after initially flirting with it, what he calls the "image theory" of memory; that is, the view that the direct and immediate object of an episode of memory is an image present in the mind. While it is true that the remembered object is not there "in person", not actually present, Husserl claims that it is the past perceived object *itself* that is remembered, not an image or picture of it (1991: 190). If I recall my mother, I am conscious of my mother herself, not of a mental snapshot depicting her. It is "as if" I were perceiving her. "*Memory* is not image-consciousness, but something totally different", Husserl concludes (1991: 328). While this is not the place to explore the difference, it can be remarked that Husserl's rejection of the image theory of memory enables him to avoid much of the troublesome baggage the theory brings with it, particularly the issue of the supposed resemblance of a present memorial image to a past object or event assumed to be inaccessible in itself.

Memory can retrieve the past and expectation can anticipate the future, but in their case past and future are only re-presented, seen "as if through a veil" (1991: 50), as quasi-present (1991: 301). In perception, however, the just past phases and the immediately approaching phases of the temporal object are perceived, presented rather than re-presented, not as now, of course, but rather in modes of the immediate past and future. Perception of a temporal object is therefore perception throughout and not an experience that is only in smallest part perception and in larger parts ordinary memory and expectation. If that were the case, we could never be said actually to hear a melody or see a train pass by. More than that, since neither the melody nor the passing train would be perceived in their temporal extension, they could not become objects of ordinary memory, since memory depends on its object's having been perceived beforehand.

Husserl calls the three forms of presentational temporal awareness belonging to each phase of perception "primal impression", "retention", and "protention". They are dependent moments of the perceptual phase, not independent acts. They form the generative core of temporal experience in the sense that through them the phases of temporal objects first appear in temporal modes. Thus primal impression is the consciousness of something as now. It enjoys a certain primacy among the three originating moments, just as the now, which primal impression first constitutes, has priority among the modes of temporal appearance. Furthermore, since the now is the temporal mode in which the new appears, primal impression as the source of the now is also the intentional moment in which the new displays itself. Retention, on the other hand, is the consciousness of the just elapsed phases of the object and is the origin of the sense of the past. It is only in retention that we can be said actually to perceive what is past, to "see" it as it sinks away. Protention as the consciousness of what is just coming constitutes our original sense of the future. Compared to retention, which is the awareness of what has already appeared as now and is therefore fixed, protention is open and undecided, though its content is ordinarily determined by what one is perceiving at the moment. Its openness to the future is again "perceptual", not re-presentational. Protention's perceptual character shows itself in the fact that we can be genuinely surprised or, perhaps better, startled when something altogether unanticipated happens, as when a scream suddenly interrupts a performance in a concert hall.

The schematic interpretation

Early in the twentieth century, Husserl turned to what he called the "schema of apprehension and contents of apprehension" to explain how primal impression, retention, and protention make us aware of the temporal object. Generally, the schematic interpretation maintains that perception occurs when sensory contents are animated by an appropriate apprehension. The contents themselves are neutral with respect to objective reference, which accrues to them only through the intentional apprehension. The sensory content red, which Husserl takes to be immanent to consciousness, is not in itself the quality of any particular thing. Whether it is taken to be the color of a flag or of a ship's funnel depends on the apprehension animating it. Similarly, in the case of the perception of a temporally extended object such as a melody, a particular tone in itself is temporally neutral and only appears as past, present, or to come thanks to a temporal apprehension. A tone therefore appears as now when it is animated by a now-apprehension and as past when it is animated by a past-apprehension. Primal impression, retention, and protention, as the fundamental modes of time-consciousness, thus occur when temporally neutral contents are animated by temporal apprehensions.

The schematic interpretation threatens to fill consciousness to the bursting point with contents and apprehensions. Since each phase of the perception intends one phase of the object as now and several elapsed phases as just past in various degrees and still other phases as yet to come, each perceptual phase on the schematic account would have to contain multiple contents and multiple apprehensions corresponding to the multiple phases of the temporal object. When a given perceptual phase ceases to be actual and is replaced by a new perceptual phase, the new phase will contain a new "continuum" of contents and a new "continuum" of apprehensions, making possible a new primal impression of a new phase of the appearing object and new retentions and new protentions of the object's just past and future phases. Since the perception is a continuum of phases, each containing contents and temporal apprehensions, Husserl described perception in a text from 1905, when he adhered to the schematic view, as a "continuum of these continua" (1991: 239).

Not long after embracing the schematic interpretation, however, Husserl abandoned it, at least as far as time-consciousness is concerned. For one thing, it treated consciousness as a kind of bag containing the various ingredients needed to account for temporal experience, a conception that Husserl came to see as a falsifying "materialization" of consciousness (1991: 337). More significantly, the interpretation assumes that the contents in any given phase of perception are neutral with respect to time and that they become bearers of temporality only through intentional apprehensions. This, however, cannot be the case, for the contents filling the actual phase of perception are not, in fact, temporally neutral. They share the actuality of the perceptual phase they occupy. They exist now, and no apprehension can magically transform them into the past or into presentations of the past. As now, the contents "*are not able to switch their temporal function*: the now cannot stand before me as not now" (1991: 334; emphasis in original). The schematic interpretation does not deny that the contents of which I am currently aware as now will recede and be experienced as just past, or that other contents will be experienced as just coming. The interpretation's failure lies in its inability to explain these phenomena and our awareness of them on the basis of present contents held in the actual moment of perceptual experience. One can indeed be conscious of a content that *was* now as past, but not, as the schematic view would have it, of a content that *is* now as past. The latter content is actually present, and pasting labels on it proclaiming its purported pastness will not change its status.

A new approach

Soon after his criticism of the schematic interpretation, Husserl introduced a distinction between three dimensions or levels involved in time-consciousness:

1   the things of empirical experience in objective time . . .;

2   the constituting multiplicities of appearance . . . the immanent unities in pre-empirical time;

3   the absolute time-constituting flow of consciousness.

(1991: 77)

With the introduction of this division and particularly of the notion of "the absolute time-constituting flow of consciousness", Husserl's interpretation of temporal experience takes a new, fruitful, and sometimes perplexing turn. Husserl's earlier investigations of temporal experience were largely confined to objects (on level one above) intended in perceptual acts or acts founded on perception (the "immanent unities" on level two). With the discovery of the absolute flow (level three), he plunges into what he later called "the phenomenological depths" (2006: 407). He continues to investigate the features and appearances of temporal objects, but he now focuses particularly on the consciousness of "the immanent unities in pre-empirical time", such as sensory contents and acts of perception, memory, wishing, judging, and so on. I will limit my discussion here to acts. Acts of consciousness are temporal unities extended in time just as much as the "things of empirical experience" they intend. "It belongs to the essence of the perception of a temporal object", Husserl claims, "that it is a temporal object itself. Under all circumstances it has a temporal extension" (1991: 239). Built into Husserl's statement is the further claim that I am aware of my temporally extended acts when I have them, and that this awareness occurs thanks to the absolute flow, which Husserl also refers to as "internal consciousness" and as "the original consciousness that constitutes immanent temporal objectivity" (2001: 281).

The absolute flow accomplishes something else as well. It is conscious of itself in its flowing. "There is one, unique flow of consciousness" in which both immanent temporal unities and:

> [t]he unity of the flow of consciousness itself become constituted at once. As shocking (when not initially even absurd) as it may seem to say that the flow of consciousness constitutes its own unity, it is nonetheless the case that it does. And that can be made intelligible on the basis of the flow's essential constitution.
>
> *(1991: 84)*

Not everyone will agree that, short of explicit reflection, I am conscious of my intentional acts or of the continuity and unity of my conscious life. It may be that I simply hear the melody and am not aware at all of my experience of hearing it. I will not attempt to settle that issue here. For our purposes, it is sufficient to say that Husserl takes it to be the case that I do experience my mental acts while I am having them and that I do possess a sense of the ongoing identity of my conscious life.

An obvious objection at this point is that if the continual awareness I have of my acts of consciousness is ordinary reflection or is of essentially the same sort as the perception I have of a melody, then I will be caught in an infinite regress. The act of perceiving the original act of perception would itself have to be perceived, and so on *ad infinitum*. Husserl attempts to dodge this objection by claiming that the absolute flow "experiences" (*erlebt*; 1991: 301) the immanent temporal unity, and that experiencing (*erleben*) is not an act that makes an object of what it intends. It is simply the flow's non-objectifying, pre-reflective awareness of its acts and of itself. In hearing a melody, therefore, only the melody is perceived; the act intending it and the flow constituting the act are experienced. Husserl's tripartite distinction among the dimensions of time-consciousness is a concise way of capturing this and all that is involved in our experience of temporal objects and of ourselves as beings living across time.

The double intentionality of the absolute flow

What, then, is the intentional structure – the "essential constitution" – through which the flow is conscious of immanent temporal unities and of itself in its flowing? Husserl locates it in what he calls the flow's "double intentionality" (1991: 85ff). The two directions of intentionality here are "inseparably united . . . requiring one another like two sides of the same thing [and] are interwoven with each other in the one, unique flow of consciousness" (1991: 87).

Husserl calls the intentionality that intends or constitutes temporal unities in immanent time "transverse intentionality" (*Querintentionalität*; 1991: 85). The other intentionality, which he describes as "horizontal" (*Längsintentionalität*; 1991: 86), runs lengthwise along the flow, relating its phases to one another intentionally and constituting its self-awareness, but never in separation from what is intended in immanent time. Husserl holds that the immanent time of the acts intended in transverse intentionality is "an objective time, a genuine time in which there is duration and the alteration of what endures" (1991: 87). It is in immanent time that acts begin and end, co-exist and succeed one another. Horizontal intentionality, on the other hand, is conscious of the succession of phases of the absolute flow in their flowing. It discloses a "quasi-temporality" rather than a genuine temporality, "a prephenomenal, preimmanent temporality" that "becomes constituted intentionally as the form of the time-constituting consciousness and in it itself" (1991: 88). Husserl's choice of "preimmanent" and "prephenomenal" to describe the constituting flow and its "temporality" in distinction from the acts the flow constitutes and their temporality suggests the limits of language here. As he writes at one point: "For all of this, we have no names". Even "flow" is a metaphor (1991: 382).

The assertion that the flow's two intentionalities are inseparable and work hand-in-glove in constituting immanent temporal unities and the flow's self-appearance, does not explain the nature of their cooperation. Several interpretations are possible at this point, and it is here that time-consciousness earns its reputation as "the most difficult of all phenomenological problems". I will examine two of these interpretations. The first effectively identifies the absolute flow with the stream of acts. The virtue of this approach is that it avoids any hint of an act/object distinction within consciousness itself that would mirror the distinction between, for example, a perception and its object in the world. The duplication of such a distinction within consciousness, aside from leading to an infinite regress, would seem to be experientially implausible. This interpretation would still leave room for the act's self-awareness, but the self-awareness would be a "feature of the act itself" (Zahavi 1999: 70) and not something accomplished by a flow distinct from the act or the flow of acts. The act brings about its own self-awareness, and the self-manifestation of the flow would be no more than the ongoing self-manifestation of the acts (Zahavi 1999: 80). This interpretation has the difficulty that it assumes present acts retain just past acts. Many conscious experiences happen simultaneously within the living present, and it is difficult to understand how a mix of present acts could retain a multiplicity of just past acts or act-phases. Could a phase of perception or of phantasy retain a phase of an act of judging? Furthermore, it is not clear how the self-manifestation of particular acts could assume the absolute flow's apparent role as the source of our experience of the continuity and identity of ourselves over time.

Another interpretation, which admittedly lacks the virtue of economy, takes Husserl's distinction between the unities in pre-empirical time and the absolute flow to mean that there is a distinction within consciousness itself between the "level" of acts and the absolute flow constituting them. To refer to the absolute flow as a "level" should not be construed to mean that it could be separated from the immanent acts it constitutes or that it "perceives" them as objects. Husserl's point, on this interpretation, is that consciousness is a unity with constituting and constituted dimensions that are distinct but inseparable. There is no flow without the acts it experiences, and there are no acts without the flow that experiences them. They form a single consciousness with two interlocking intentionalities.

According to this interpretation,[2] the absolute flow has phases, one of which will be actual, while others will have elapsed or have not yet occurred. Primal impression, retention, and protention, which Husserl had originally developed as intentional moments of acts, are now taken to belong to each phase of the absolute flow that constitutes the acts. The primal impressional moment of the actual phase of the flow is conscious of the now-phase of the act, and, through it, conscious of the now-phase of the act's object. Hence one would be aware pre-reflectively of the perceiving of a phase of a melody as now. The actual phase of the flow also has a retentional moment that retains the preceding phase of the flow and, in retaining that phase, also retains the elapsed phase's primal impression and the phase of the act the primal impression originally intended, only now that act-phase is experienced as just past. When the actually present phase of the flow elapses and gives way to a new phase, the new phase will have a fresh primal impressional moment intending a new phase of the perception of the melody as now. Since this new phase of the flow will also have a retentional moment, it will retain the flow's just elapsed phase and through it the elapsed phase of the act of hearing the melody. "What is brought to appearance in the actual momentary phase of the flow of consciousness – specifically in its series of retentional moments – are the past phases of the flow of consciousness" (1991: 87–88). By retaining its elapsed phases, the flow is at once aware of itself and of its acts and of what those acts intend. The wonder of temporal experience is that it binds together intentionally the fundamental components of our conscious lives – objects, acts, and the absolute flow itself, the ground of our sense of continuity and identity.

Notes

1 All citations are to Husserl's texts unless otherwise indicated. Translations of Husserl's texts are mine.
2 I offer a defense of this view in "Notes on the absolute time-constituting flow of consciousness". See the entry under J. Brough in "Further reading" at the end of this chapter.

References

Husserl, E. (1991) *On the Phenomenology of the Consciousness of Internal Time (1893–1917)*, trans. J. Brough, Dordrecht, The Netherlands: Kluwer.

Husserl, E. (2001) *Die Bernauer Manuskripte über das Zeitbewusstsein (1917–1918)*, Husserliana XXXIII, Dordrecht, The Netherlands: Kluwer.

Husserl, E. (2006) *Späte Texte über Zeitkonstitution (1929–1934)*, Husserliana Materialen VIII, Dordrecht, The Netherlands: Springer.

Miller, I. (1984) *Husserl, Perception, and Temporal Awareness*, Cambridge, MA: The MIT Press.

Zahavi, D. (1999) *Self-Awareness and Alterity*, Evanston, IL: Northwestern University Press.

Further reading

J. Brough, "Notes on the absolute time-constituting flow of consciousness", in D. Lohmar and I. Yamaguchi (eds.), *On Time: New Contributions to the Husserlian Phenomenology of Time* (Dordrecht, The Netherlands: Springer, 2010): 21–49. This essay considers two competing interpretations of Husserl's notion of the absolute flow of time-consciousness.

C. Hoerl, "Husserl, the absolute flow, and temporal experience", *Philosophy and Phenomenological Research*, Vol. LXXXVI No. 2 (2013): 376–409. Examines Husserl's position from the perspective of contemporary representationalist theory.

T. Kortooms, *Phenomenology of Time: Edmund Husserl's Analysis of Time-Consciousness* (Dordrecht, The Netherlands: Kluwer, 2002). A helpful study of Husserl's evolving thought about time-consciousness over three decades.

Martin, M. G. F., "Out of the past: Episodic recall as retained acquaintance", in C. Hoerl and T. McCormack (eds.), *Time and Memory* (Oxford, UK: Clarendon Press, 2001): 257–284. A recent account of memory that has affinities with Husserl's position on the subject.

J. Mensch, *Husserl's Account of Our Consciousness of Time* (Milwaukee, WI: Marquette University Press, 2010). Another overview of Husserl's phenomenology of temporality, with particular attention to his late manuscripts.

R. Sokolowski, *Husserlian Meditations* (Evanston, IL: Northwestern University Press, 1974). A refreshingly clear presentation of the core of Husserl's position.

7

BERGSON ON TEMPORAL EXPERIENCE AND *DURÉE RÉELLE*

Barry Dainton

Henri Bergson (1859–1941) introduced his concept of *durée* or "duration" (also *durée pure*, or *durée réelle*) in his first book, *Essai sur les données immédiates de la conscience* (English translation *Time and Free Will: An Essay on the Immediate Data of Consciousness*) in 1889. As a first approximation, *durée* just is experienced change and succession as we find it in our immediate experience – though (as we shall see) it has other distinctive features as well. The concept of *durée* remained at the centre of Bergson's philosophy, as this was elaborated in subsequent major works: *Matière et Mémoire* (1896) (*Matter and Memory*), *L'Évolution Créatrice* (1907) (*Creative Evolution*), *Durée et Simultanéité* (1922) (*Duration and Simultaneity*) and *La Pensée et le Mouvant* (1934) (*The Creative Mind: An Introduction to Metaphysics*).

Bergson's writings – and the opposition to the purely mechanistic world-view of modern science developed in them – granted him world-wide popularity in the first decades of the twentieth century of a sort that is only rarely achieved by philosophers. The French themselves spoke of "le boom Bergson" after the publication of *L'Évolution Créatrice*, and his lectures in Manhattan in 1913 caused a traffic jam on Broadway – one of the first ever recorded.[1] Bergson was awarded the Nobel Prize for Literature in 1927 "in recognition of his rich and vitalizing ideas and the brilliant skill with which they have been presented".

Durée: a first look

In a letter to Harald Høffding written in March 1915, Bergson observed that any account of his work will be a distortion if it does not:

> [c]easelessly return to what I consider the very centre of the doctrine: the intuition of duration. The representation of a multiplicity of 'reciprocal penetration', quite different from numerical multiplicity – the representation of a heterogeneous, qualitative, creative duration – was my point of departure and the point to which I have constantly returned.
>
> *(Bergson 2002: 366–367)*

But while an understanding of *durée* may be the key to understanding Bergson's metaphysical position, it is also a non-trivial task. William Barnard, in a recent commentary, attempts to summarize the core elements of it thus:

[d]*urée* is Bergson's term for the dynamic, ever-changing nature of consciousness, a consciousness expressed and manifested in-and-through-as *time*. From Bergson's perspective, *durée* is an indivisible fusion of manyness and oneness; it is the ongoing, dynamic, temporal flux of awareness; it is a flowing that is ever new and always unpredictable; it is the continual, seamless, interconnected, immeasurable movement of our awareness, manifesting simultaneously, as both knower and what is known.

(2011: 6–7)

If this weren't enough to be digesting, there is a further complication. In his earlier work, particularly the 1889 *Essai*, Bergson confined *durée* – and its flowing and distinctively unified character – to consciousness alone; he explicitly contrasted the dynamic character of experience with the static character of the physical realm. In his later work, beginning with the 1896 *Matière et Mémoire*, he abandoned the earlier dualism in favour of a form of panpsychist monism. For the later Bergson, *durée* is the building block (and driving force) of everything in the entire universe: it may be a feature of conscious experience, but every other part of concrete reality has it too. Although this expansion of the domain of *durée* has significant ramifications – or so I will be suggesting – let's start with Bergson's views concerning the distinctive features of our ordinary temporal experience.

The cinematic universe

What initially led Bergson to *durée* was the firm conviction – which formed very early in his career – that for all their successes, the physical sciences of his day were defective by virtue of the way they treated *time*. During the 1880s Minkowski's Einstein-inspired four-dimensional block universe was still some decades away, but in Bergson's eyes at least, classical physicists were nonetheless guilty of regarding time as essentially space-like in nature. For Bergson and other nineteenth-century French "temporalists", the defining feature of time – and so reality itself, which they viewed as inherently temporal – included *passage* and the *openness of the future*.[2] Reality consists of an irreducible continuous flow in which what is present sinks into the past as new presents are created and added to the sum total of reality. This passage-process is doubly creative: not only are new presents generated, the process which brings them into being is not entirely deterministic: genuine novelty is possible, so quite what the future will bring will only be revealed by its arrival.[3]

Some of the basic ways in which classical physics treats time – ways Bergson thought to be irredeemably flawed – are shown in Figure 7.1. The diagram illustrates the way in which the motion of an object through space is represented in physics. The object's movement is represented by a continuous series of spatio-temporal correspondences, two of which are labelled: at the temporal instant t_1 the object is at spatial location p_1, and at time t_2 it is at p_2. In a three-dimensional space, these spatial locations will be represented by triples of real numbers, indicating a precise location in the relevant frame of reference.

In effect, by construing motion in this manner, physics adopts what Bergson calls a *cinematic* conception of the physical universe: the world ultimately consists of nothing more than a rapid succession of instantaneous momentary slices. In the real world, the static states are momentary three-dimensional volumes of space, but the essentials remain the same. Since each of these states is strictly durationless and any movement takes some amount of time – involving as it does a change of position *over* time – their contents considered, in and of themselves, are necessarily completely motionless.

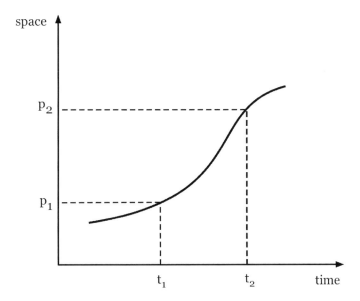

Figure 7.1 How classical physics treats time

When Bergson compared his direct experience of movement and succession with the cinematic conception of reality offered by physics, he could see no way to reconcile the two.

> But how can we help seeing that the essence of duration is to flow, and that the fixed placed side by side with the fixed will never constitute anything which has duration? It is not the "states", simple snapshots we have taken once again along the course of change, that are real; on the contrary, it is flux, the continuity of transition, it is change itself that is real. This change is indivisible, it is even substantial.
>
> *(2007 [1946]: 6)*

Think of what it is like to observe a pendulum smoothly swinging back and forth. We see something that is *intrinsically dynamic*: the pendulum's movements, at least as they feature in our sensory experience, are not decomposable into a series of static motionless snapshots. Similarly, when we hear a sequence of notes unfolding as part of a melody, we not only hear each note seamlessly flowing into the next, but the individual notes are themselves inherently dynamic: we hear each *enduring* even if only briefly (if the note in question is itself of short duration). Here again it seems implausible to hold that our auditory experience consists of nothing more than a series of durationless snapshots.[4] Indeed, it is far from clear that we can make any real sense of a strictly durationless auditory sensation or content. So far as Bergson was concerned, *all* forms of experience have some finite duration, and even in the briefest of experiences there is directly experienced passage or transition.

It might be tempting to think that true continuity *can* in fact be generated by the cinematic model. From the perspective of mathematical physics, both space and time are infinitely divisible into dimensionless geometrical points. If between any two points, no matter how close together, there is always a further point lying between them, there are no *gaps* in space or time (or motion) thus construed. But Bergson argued that it is this property of the mathematical continuum which makes it entirely unsuited to serving as a model for experiential continuity. In the latter case, not only is there nothing corresponding to durationless points or instants, each phase of a stream of consciousness is *experientially connected* to the next. In the mathematical continuum – as modelled by the real number line – no point ever makes immediate contact with another: for precisely the reason that between any two points there is an infinite number of other points. If duration were structured in this way it would "disappear in a dust of moments not one of which has duration, each one being instantaneous" (2007 [1946]: 156).[5]

Multiplicities

Although Bergson believed, *contra* Kant, that it was possible for us to attain knowledge of the real – of both the "inner" world of experience and "outer" world of physical reality – he did not believe it was easy. He held that our perceptual and cognitive faculties had been moulded over enormous periods of time by the exigencies of evolution via natural selection, and this makes for particular difficulties when it comes to discovering the true character of our own consciousness via introspection. Although, in a sense, nothing is closer to us than our own experience, our instinctive patterns of thought are better adapted to dealing with the external spatial world of material three-dimensional bodies. To arrive at a remotely adequate understanding of inner reality – that of *durée réelle* – we have to struggle to overcome our natural "spatializing" tendencies.[6]

In Bergson's eyes, the associationist movement in psychology was guilty of having succumbed to space-dominated ways of conceiving time. Physical atomists hoped to explain the enormous range and variety to be found in the macroscopic physical world by appealing to a few basic types of micro-entities and their laws of motion and combination. Psychological atomists hoped to do much the same thing for the mind. Post-Humean associationists such as Condillac, Herbart and Mach, adopted an essentially Humean view; they held that our streams of consciousness are composites of phenomenal atoms. Each of these atoms is an entirely autonomous self-contained entity and is capable of existing – intrinsically unchanged – in very different experiential configurations. Different associationists gave different accounts of the psychological laws governing these atomic constituents, but the underlying ontology was otherwise very similar.

Bergson concedes that this way of thinking is very natural and appealing, and it has the further advantage of making it possible to formulate theories in geometrical and arithmetical terms. However, he also insists that it is a mistake to extend these modes of conceptualization to the world of experience, for in this domain careful introspection reveals that there are no repeatable, readily countable or accurately quantifiable phenomena. Shifts in tone and intensity in felt emotions will obviously be difficult to quantify in a meaningful way, but Bergson suggests we tend to overlook the subtle alterations in our sensory experience that each new moment brings.

> Change is far more radical than we are at first inclined to suppose.
>
> For I speak of each of my states as if it formed a block and were a separate whole. I say indeed that I change, but the change seems to me to reside in the passage from one state to the next: of each state, taken separately, I am apt to think that it remains the same during all the time that it prevails. Nevertheless, a slight effort of attention would reveal to me that there is no feeling, no idea, no volition which is not underlying change every moment: if a mental state ceased to vary, its duration would cease to flow . . . The truth is that we change without ceasing, and that the state itself is nothing but change.
>
> *(1983 [1911]: 1–2)*

To mark the distinction between the kinds of complex one finds in the material world, and the kind of complex one finds in consciousness, in chapter 2 of his *Essai* Bergson distinguished "quantitative multiplicity" from "qualitative multiplicity". A typical example of a quantitative multiplicity would be a collection of discrete physical objects. Bergson suggests that "externality is the distinguishing mark of things which occupy space, while states of consciousness are not essentially external to one another" (2002 [1910]: 59) – experiences can only seem external to one another when we overlook their temporal features. If we succeed in appreciating their true character, it will be clear that the successive parts of our experience are *not* separate from one another at all.

> Pure duration is the form which the succession of our conscious states assumes when our ego lets itself *live*, when it refrains from separating its present state from its former states . . .We can thus conceive of succession without distinction, and think of it as a mutual penetration, an interconnexion and organization of elements, each of which represents the whole, and cannot be distinguished or isolated from it except by abstract thought. Such is the account of duration which would be given by a being who was ever the same and every changing, and who had no idea of space.
>
> *(2002 [1910] [1889]: 100–101)*

On hearing a melody, for example, such a being would be aware of each tone as "melting into" and "permeating" the next. This sort of immediate connectedness is the distinguishing feature of qualitative multiplicities. In a qualitative multiplicity, there is "succession without mutual externality", whereas in a quantitative multiplicity there is "mutual externality without succession" (Ibid.: 108).

Bergson uses formulations such as these to bring the distinctive character of the unity of consciousness into clearer view. Since our ordinary experiences invariably occur within deeply unified wholes, it is easy to overlook just how pervasive (and noteworthy) conscious unity is. Consider, for example, how your current bodily sensations are experienced together with your conscious thoughts and mental images, how your visual and auditory experiences are also unified with one another, despite being so different in character – of how *all* your experiences are experienced together, from one moment to the next. This form of togetherness – or "mutual penetration" – does not involve the (sub-)merging or fusing of sensory qualities. Sounds remain distinct from colours, despite being experienced together, as Bergson emphasized by characterizing *durée* as a "qualitative *heterogeneity*". The same holds over time: when we hear a succession of tones, or the syllables which make up a word, we hear each flowing into the next, but there is no qualitative fusing of sounds.

Durée: Retentional or Extensional?

How do episodes of experienced change or succession relate to ordinary objective time? On this issue different theorists adopt very different positions. One option is the *Retentional* view, which was dominant in nineteenth-century psychological circles, and influentially introduced into philosophical debates by Brentano and Husserl. Proponents of this doctrine hold that our direct experiences of change consist of episodes of consciousness that are in fact momentary (or close to it).[7] These durationless episodes possess contents which appear dynamic and to extend through a brief interval of time, even though in reality they do not. The competing *Extensional* view, explicitly propounded by William Stern (1897; see also Chapter 8, this volume) – albeit not under that name – is very different. Extensional theorists hold that the episodes of experience which house our immediate experiences of change and succession are *not* momentary, but themselves unfold over periods of (objective) time, in much the way they appear to.

Was Bergson committed to an Extensional or a Retentional conception of temporal experience – or to an entirely different sort of view? Is it possible to ascertain? In contrast with Stern, in the *Essai* (and elsewhere in his writings for that matter) Bergson does not explicitly contrast his own account of temporal experience with competing accounts in either the philosophical or psychological literature. While this does complicate the task of situating his position on the theoretical landscape, a plausible answer is not too difficult to discern.

It would certainly not be impossible for a reader of the *Essai* to draw the conclusion that Bergson was in the Retentionalist camp. Not only does he make it clear that *durée* is confined to the mental realm, Bergson repeatedly ascribes the unity characteristic of *durée* to an act of "mental synthesis" and at one point describes synthesis as "a psychic and therefore unextended process" (2002 [1910] [1889]: 111). However, since he could here be intending only to suggest that the act of synthesis lacks *spatial* extension, it would be a mistake to conclude that Bergson was here suggesting that *durée* was confined to momentary (or very brief) conscious states. In any event, the doctrines and claims Bergson will go on to make in subsequent writings makes a Retentional interpretation of his position difficult to sustain.

One of Bergson's main goals in *Matter and Memory* (1990 [1896]) is to clarify the relationship between the physical and the mental. At the start of the book, he announces that he will be defending a form of dualism, but by the end of the book it is clear that his dualism is quite unlike Cartesian dualism. There remain differences between matter and consciousness, but these are only of degree, not in fundamental character. Bergson's metaphysical position is in fact profoundly monistic: mental and physical things are both conscious to some (very different) degrees. This is because both are temporal, and (real) temporality requires consciousness:

> [w]e cannot speak of a reality that endures without inserting consciousness into it . . . it is impossible to distinguish between the duration, however short it may be, that separates two instants and a memory that connects them, because duration is essentially a continuation of what no longer exists into what does exist. This is real time, perceived and lived. This is also any conceived time, because we cannot conceive a time without imagining it as perceived and lived. Duration therefore implies consciousness: and we place consciousness at the heart of things for the very reason that we credit them with a time that endures.
>
> *(1965 [1922]: 48–49)*

In adopting a form of panpsychism, Bergson may have adopted a conception of the intrinsic nature of matter that few physicists – then or now – would themselves be tempted to adopt, but he had no wish to reject other scientific orthodoxies of his day.[8] He fully accepted that the physical world was composed of unimaginably small particles, and that space was flooded with electromagnetic radiation of differing wavelengths and frequencies. He also accepted the consequence: there is a vast disparity in the temporal scales of ordinary human life and that of the micro-world. A one-second experience of red, say, corresponds to about 400 billion electromagnetic oscillations of red light. Bergson's solution – in bare outline at least – is straightforward: there are different *scales* of *durée*. The temporal extension of the *durée* of elementary physical events is of the order of billionths or trillionths of a second: very very brief but (importantly) *not* instantaneous. In comparison, the *durée* we are acquainted with in our everyday experience – whether it be a tenth of a second, half a second or a couple of seconds – is comparatively enormous.[9] Intriguingly, Bergson suggests that the different durations of *durée* are associated with different degrees of a distinctive kind of mental *density* or *concentration*, in virtue of which matter is a "more relaxed" more "distended" – more spatial – form of consciousness when compared to our own.

For present purposes, however, the key point to note is that in making these claims, Bergson is clearly assuming that these different scales of *durée* all unfold together in the objective time-system that physical events occur within. The instances of *durée* enduring only billionths or trillionths of a second (or less), which are to be found at the atomic and sub-atomic levels, flow synchronously with the instances of *durée* which exist at the macro-level. All forms of *durée* extend through greater or smaller intervals of objective time. Given this, it is difficult to see how Bergson could be working within anything other than Extensional framework, rather than the Retentional one, even if he does not explicitly mark the distinction himself. Despite their other doctrinal differences, Retentional theorists hold that *all* directly experienced changes and successions occur within conscious episodes which do *not* extend through time.[10]

According to the metaphysical position known as "Presentism", the present moment has a particularly privileged ontological status: times and events that are *not* present simply do not exist. Since Extensionalists hold that our experiences of succession occur within episodes of experience that are themselves extended through intervals of time – and so not confined to momentary presents – their view does not sit easily with Presentism. In this connection, it is interesting to note that Bergson himself was certainly *not* a Presentist. He spends a good deal of effort in Part 3 of *Matter and Memory* attempting to overcome resistance to the idea that the past is fully real, and argues that when we see things as they are "there will be no longer any more reason to say that the past effaces itself as soon as perceived, than there is to suppose that material objects cease to exist when we cease to perceive them" (1990 [1896]: 142). Also pointing in this direction is Bergson's claim that the (objective) temporal extension of *durée* is variable.

> My present, at this moment, is the sentence I am pronouncing. But it is so because I want to limit the field of my attention to my sentence. This attention is something that can be made longer or shorter, like the interval between two points of a compass . . . an attention which could be extended indefinitely would embrace, along with the preceding sentence, all the anterior phases of the lecture and the events which preceded the lecture, and as large a portion of what we call our past as desired. The distinction we make between our present and past is therefore, if not arbitrary, at least relative to the extent of the field which our attention to life can embrace.
>
> *(1946 [1934]: 177–178)*

It would only be possible to extend our experienced presents far into the past if the past is itself real.

Transitions, overlaps and intelligibility

Our immediate experience of change may occur within episodes of *durée*, but it would be wrong to assume that Bergson supposed individual instances of *durée* are isolated, self-contained and experientially encapsulated with respect to one another. If this were the case, there would be discontinuities in our experience, as one *durée* ends and another begins. But Bergson frequently emphasizes the *seamless continuity* of experience. Writing to William James, Bergson observes:

[w]hen I wrote my essay on Les Données de La Conscience . . . I was led, through an analysis of the idea of time, to a certain conception of psychological life which is entirely compatible with yours (except perhaps that I see places of flight in the resting places themselves.

(Pearson and Mullarkey 2002: 357)

Elsewhere he tells us "I believe that our whole psychological existence is just like this single sentence, continued since the first awakening of consciousness, interspersed with commas, but never broken by full stops" (1920: 70).

The accounts typically given by Retentionalists and Extensionalists of the internal structure of streams of consciousness are very different. The vertical columns in Figure 7.2 represent – in a simplified schematic form – the durationless episodes of change-filled experience posited by Retentional theorists. Two such episodes are depicted. E_A on the left consists of a very brief auditory experience of a C-tone; this is accompanied by representations (or "retentions") of a B-tone and an A-tone. The asterisks indicate that the B-tone is experienced as having occurred in the very recent past, and the A-tone is experienced as having occurred in the slightly less recent past. Although objectively speaking C, B* and A** occur simultaneously, they appear to their subject to be occurring successively. Similarly, *mutatis mutandis*, for D, C* and B** in E_B.

The account usually provided by Extensional theorists, again in simplified, schematic form is depicted in Figure 7.3. Here E1 is a unified conscious episode consisting of an A-tone being experienced as being succeeded by a B-tone. The experiencing of the succession A-B is itself extended over an interval of objective time – and contrary to what is the case in the Retentional model, the experiencing of the B-tone does *not* occur simultaneously (objectively speaking) with the experiencing of the A-tone. E2 consists of the directly experienced succession B-C, and here too we are dealing with a unified experiential succession which is itself extended over a short interval of time. Although there is an experiencing of the B-tone in both E1 and E2, the B-tone is *not* experienced twice-over (which would be phenomenologically unrealistic, given that we are assuming the subject experiences A-B-C-D, hearing each tone only once). This is simply because E1 and E2 overlap: they each possess the same token

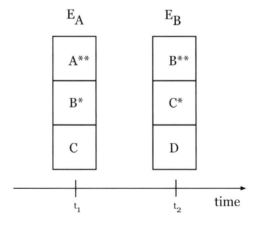

Figure 7.2   Durationless episodes of change-filled experience posited by Retentional theorists

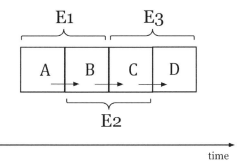

Figure 7.3   The temporally dispersed overlap structure provided by Extensional theorists

experience of the B-tone as a proper parts. The same holds, *mutatis mutandis,* for the C-tone which occurs in both E2 and E3.

Extensionalists maintain that this temporally dispersed overlap structure is better equipped to accommodate the seamless continuity of experience than the Retentionalist alternative. As could be seen from Figure 7.2, although there are directly apprehended successions *within* each of E_A and E_B, there is no experiential bridge *between* the two; in effect, each is an entirely discrete episode of experience. In sharp contrast, as can be seen from Figure 7.3, there are no such ruptures of experiential continuity to be found in the Extensional model. A is experienced as flowing into B, B is experienced as flowing into C, and C into D. Anyone who is committed – as Bergson undoubtedly was – to the thesis that consciousness *is* seamlessly continuous has reason to take the Extensional account of stream-structure very seriously.[11]

Interestingly, William James construed Bergson in precisely this fashion. In *The Pluralistic Universe* (1909) James devotes his sixth lecture to expounding some of the core features of Bergson's philosophy. After observing that for "conceptual logic, the same is nothing but the same", James goes on to remark that this isn't always the case for concrete experience, and supplies a concrete example of what he has in mind.

> Take its continuity as an example. Terms like A and C appear to be connected by intermediaries, by B for example . . . Imagine a heavy log which takes two men to carry it. First A and B take it. Then C takes hold and A drops off; then D takes hold and B drops off, so that C and D now bear it; and so on. The log meanwhile never drops, and keeps its sameness throughout the journey. Even so it is with all our experiences. Their changes are not complete annihilations followed by complete creations of something absolutely novel. There is partial decay and partial growth, and all the while a nucleus of relative constancy from which what decays drops off, and which takes into itself whatever is grafted on, until at length something wholly different has taken its place . . . such a universe is continuous. Its members interdigitate with their next neighbors in manifold directions, and there are no clean cuts between them anywhere.
>
> *(1909: 257–258)*

If we construe (A-B), (B-C), (C-D) to be partially overlapping episodes of *durée* – as James presumably intended – then we have precisely the sort of overlap structure depicted in Figure 7.2.

Was James guilty of misrepresenting Bergson's views? There is no reason to think so. After reading drafts of *The Pluralistic Universe* in July 1908, Bergson told James:

Never have I been examined, understood, penetrated in such a manner. Never, moreover, have I been so conscious of the sympathy and the sort of "pre-established harmony" which attunes your thought and mine. Let me tell you, moreover, that you have not limited yourself to analyzing my ideas; you have transfigured them, without every disfiguring them in any way. In reading your expositions of my theses, I thought of those superb reproductions that the great masters made of sometimes quite ordinary paintings.

(Pearson and Mullarkey 2002: 363)

James' chapter is entitled "Bergson's critique of intellectualism", and over the course of it he rejoices in the liberating effect reading Bergson has had: James no longer feels obliged to let mere logic and the law of identity constrain his thought. If experience *shows* that a certain structure or fact is possible, then it is, even if logic suggests otherwise. James admits to having struggled for years trying to make sense of the "compounding" of consciousness, the problem of understanding how seemingly discrete centres of consciousness of the sort that we possess could be made up of large numbers of smaller and simpler centres of consciousnesses – of the sort that individual neurons, or elementary particles, might possess[12] Finding himself increasingly drawn to a form of panpsychism James had reason to think consciousness must compound, but could see no way to characterize the process in a non-contradictory way. Having read and learned from Bergson, he no longer believes that an ineliminable contradiction need be of concern: reality can still *be* a certain way, even if we cannot make intellectual or conceptual sense of how this is possible.

It is clear from their correspondence that Bergson greatly appreciated the praise James generously showered upon him. However, it may well be that Bergson's views in general, and his views on temporal experience in particular, have suffered – in the eyes and minds of some if not all – by being associated with James' rejection of so-called intellectualism in his later works, and so too the Extensional model of temporal experience. James' problem of understanding how consciousness could compound in the way he believed it must is very difficult indeed. The problem may well be insoluble; it may well be impossible for consciousness to be structured in this manner. But even if this turns out to be the case, it does not mean that the *temporal* structures we have been discussing latterly are equally problematic or difficult to comprehend.

Let's return to the example of the overlapping episodes of *durée* (B–C) and (C–D), where B, C and D are brief auditory tones. James claims that, if an experience C is co-conscious with both an earlier experience B and a later experience D, this involves a "violation" of our logical axioms. It is far from clear that this is necessarily the case. It certainly *would* be the case if the intrinsic properties of the C–tone in (C–D) were different from those of the C–tone in (B–C), for under these conditions it would be incoherent to hold that numerically the same tone exists in both experiential episodes. But although some accounts of diachronic phenomenal unity might well entail that this qualitative variation occurs, other accounts may well *not* have this consequence.[13] In which case, this form of overlap looks unproblematic – or at least, unproblematic for this reason. Whether or not the overlap structure the Extensional model posits in order to accommodate the continuity of consciousness really *is* contradictory or incoherent is still very much an open question.

Conclusions

If Bergson were committed to an Extensional conception of temporal experience, he – along with William Stern – was among the earliest philosophers to adopt this view. Indeed, since

Bergson's *Essai* predates Stern's essay "Psychische Präsenzzeit" by a decade, Bergson has a claim to be the very first proponent of this approach.[14] That said, if both Bergson and Stern undeniably deserve to figure prominently in the history of late nineteenth- and early twentieth-century debates on temporal experience, they did not exist in isolation, and a fair assessment of their originality and intellectual boldness would need to take into proper account their historical context, in all its complexity. That is a task for another occasion, but one does not need to look very far to find evidence that others were already thinking along similar lines.

In his article, Stern himself tells us that Friedrich Schumann had "for many years" been arguing in lectures that "we can apprehend a complex of contents of consciousness even in its totality when the individual parts of consciousness are not simultaneous, but rather exist only in successively in consciousness" (2005 [1897]: 315).[15] As for Bergson, along with many of his French contemporaries, he was significantly influenced by Renouvier, who also argued for the metaphysical primacy of time and process.

> The world is one immense pulsation composed of an unassignable (though always determinate) number of elementary pulsations, of which the harmony – whether less or more comprehensive, whether blind or conscious – after being established and developed in many kinds and degrees, finds its consummation in the production of autonomous beings, in who it, appearing at first merely as spontaneity, tends finally to become voluntary and free.
>
> *(Renouvier 1864: 43–44)*

While it is true, as Lovejoy remarks (1912a: 23), that these lines could easily pass for an excerpt from Bergson's *L'Évolution Créatrice*, their respective positions on temporal experience were in reality quite different. For Bergson, the continuity of experience is a primitive and irreducible feature of consciousness; for Renouvier it was merely an appearance. In the latter's *Troisième Essai* (1864) he argues that macro-scale temporal phenomena are constituted from series of elementary durations that are far too brief to be separately perceivable and that are separated by very brief temporal gaps (or "intermittences"). Since this atomistic view of the structure of our streams of consciousness is not easily reconcilable with our ability to directly apprehend change and succession, it is phenomenologically problematic. Bergson's emphasis on the seamless continuity of consciousness might well, in part, be a response to problems deriving from Renouvier's doctrine: what would bind the envisaged fragmented pulses into a single stream of consciousness, or a single universe?[16]

One final observation. In their enlightening "A brief history of time-consciousness: Historical precursors to James and Husserl" (2009), Andersen and Grush set out to correct the widespread assumption that in chapter 15 of the *Principles of Psychology* (1890), James was largely responding to work done by experimental psychologists in Germany over the previous three decades. They argue that the standard picture is incomplete, because it omits "a clearly discernible line of philosophical debate about the temporality of experience which began with Thomas Reid, ran through a number of nineteenth century Anglophone philosophers" – including Dugald Stewart, Thomas Brown, William Hamilton, Robert Kelly and Shadworth Hodgson – who also exerted a powerful influence on James. This may well be true. But as should also by now be clear, so far as James' views concerning the nature of time are concerned, the standard picture is incomplete in another way. Lovejoy (1912a) expounds and criticizes the work of four French temporalists, Renouvier, Bergson, Pillon and James. With respect to the inclusion of the latter, he offers the following explanation:

In view of the title borne by this article, the reader will perhaps ask what William James is doing in this company. We all, certainly, like to think of him as characteristically American; and we are not unjustified in doing so. But though his personality and his style were singularly American, he none the less truly belongs, as a technical metaphysician, to the apostolic succession of French temporalism. At the beginning of his career he was decisively influenced by Renouvier . . . To Renouvier he seems unquestionably to have owed his initial conversion to conscious and explicit pluralism and temporalism.

(1912a: 17)

The influence on James of a number of nineteenth-century French thinkers was not insignificant either, then, and it was not restricted to Bergson.[17]

Notes

1 For more on Bergson's early twentieth-century renown, and his 1922 debate with another Nobel Prize winner – Einstein – see Canales (2015).
2 I take the term "temporalists" from Lovejoy (1912a). Lovejoy's series of articles on temporalism sheds much illumination on the philosophical context from which Bergson emerged (1912a, 1912b, 1912c).
3 Or as Bergson puts it in the opening chapter of *Creative Evolution*: "The universe endures. The more we study the nature of time, the more we shall comprehend that duration means invention, the creation of forms, the continual elaboration of the absolutely new" (1983 [1907]: 11).
4 When Bergson tells us that motion is "indivisible", he generally means *irreducible*.
5 The adequacy or otherwise of cinematic views of reality remains a controversial issue. According to David Lewis, "All there is to the world is a vast mosaic of local matters of fact" (1986: xi). Since for Lewis "local matters of fact" depend solely on the properties of *spacetime points*, Lewis' mosaic-metaphysics is a version of the cinematic view. For more on the debates concerning the adequacy of Lewis' position, see Butterfield (2004) and Arntzenius (2012, chapter 2).
6 Bergson's view that arriving at an accurate understanding of the character of our experience is both crucially important and very difficult, may be why Husserl is reported to have told a gathering of phenomenologists at Göttingen Circle in 1911 "we are the true Bergsonians", see Spiegelberg (1965: 399).
7 Retentional theorists who are sceptical as to whether any form of consciousness can be strictly *durationless* hold instead that our perceptions of change occur within conscious episodes that are very brief – so brief they do not feature experiences which seemingly possess any temporal extension. This complication will not be relevant in what follows.
8 William James, on the other hand, was very impressed, as he told Bergson in a letter he wrote to him on 14 December 1902: "[Matter and memory] is a work of exquisite genius. It makes a sort of Copernican revolution as much as Berkeley's Principles or Kant's Critique did, and will probably, as it gets better and better known, open a new era of philosophical discussion. It fills my mind with all sorts of new questions and hypotheses, and brings the old into a most agreeable liquefaction" (James 1920: 180).
9 As Čapek remarks, in the course of his useful discussion, "If we consider, for instance, the number of times one molecule clashes with others within one second according to the kinetic theory of gases, we can appreciate the more how far below the temporal threshold of consciousness the corresponding temporal intervals separating two successive changes lie. For this reason the *microcosmos* can be appropriately characterized as *microchronos*" (1971: 198).
10 There is one consideration which could be taken to point in precisely the opposite direction. When attempting to characterize *durée*, Bergson often suggests that *memory* is involved. In the passage from *Duration and Simultaneity* quoted above he tells us that even in the briefest of physical events there will be "a memory that connects" their earlier and later phases. This is not the place for a full account of Bergson's complex views relating to memory. A case can be made, however, for holding that in these contexts Bergson's "memory" is simply the unifying relation which connects the earlier and later phases of a single episode of *durée*. For more on this, see Barnard (2011, chapter 17) on "primal memory".
11 To put the point in Bergsonian terms, the Extensional model is fully compatible with streams of consciousness being entirely free from "full-stops" for hours at a time; the Retentional model is not.

12 The compounding of consciousness also poses a problem for those absolute idealists who hold all human centres' consciousness are in fact parts of an all-encompassing consciousness, despite being seemingly entirely separate from one another. It was this version of the compounding problem that James focused on in *The Pluralistic Universe* (James 1909).

13 For one such, see Dainton (*Stream of Consciousness*, 2006, chapters 7 and 9, and in particular §9.6).

14 We might credit James with being the first to defend explicitly the overlap model of stream-structure. It should be noted that this model also features in the opening section of chapter 15 of *Principles of Psychology*, "The perception of time", but in these earlier writings James was generally inclined to endorse the then-dominant Retentional paradigm.

15 See Schumann (1898).

16 In a similar vein, the strenuous efforts Bergson undertakes to establish the inapplicability of numerical measures to aspects of consciousness may well not be entirely unconnected with Renouvier's thesis that *everything* has a definite number. Renouvier himself, it should be noted, was not oblivious to the possibility that his temporal atomism could result in a fragmented universe. In 1887 he wrote to James, "I have come during these last years . . . to draw from a deepened reflection on the requirements of idealism, this conclusion: there is a universal consciousness, without which the relations of *space, time* and *cause* would lack unity, order and control, and would prevent individual consciousnesses, with their private spatial, temporal and causal modifications, from establishing communication and agreement with one another" (Perry 1935: 701).

17 In James' review of Renouvier's *Les Principes de la Nature*, he remarked "to put the matter ultra-simply . . . the philosophy of the future will have to be either of Renouvier or of Hegel" (1893: 213). Renouvier's influence on James from 1868 onwards, particularly with regard to the freedom of the will, is well-documented, e.g. Myers 1986: 46–47.

References

Andersen, H. and Grush, R. (2009) "A brief history of time-consciousness: Historical precursors to James and Husserl", *Journal of the History of Philosophy* 47(2): 277–307.

Arntzenius, F. (2012) *Space, Time and Stuff*, Oxford, UK: Oxford University Press.

Barnard, W. (2011) *Living Consciousness: The Metaphysical Vision of Henri Bergson*, Albany, NY: SUNY.

Bergson, H. (1920) *Mind-Energy*, trans. H. Wildon Carr, London: Hold and Company.

Bergson, H. (1965) *Duration and Simultaneity* (*Durée et Simultanéité* 1922), trans. L. Jacobson, New York: Bobbs Merill.

Bergson, H. (1983 [1911] [1907]) *Creative Evolution* (*L'Évolution créatrice*, 1907), trans. A. Mitchel, Henry Holt and Company, New York: University Press of America.

Bergson, H. (1990) *Matter and Memory* (*Matière et Mémoire*, 1896), trans. N. M. Paul and W. S. Palmer, New York: Zone Books.

Bergson, H. (2002 [1910] [1889]) *Time and Free Will: An Essay on the Immediate Data of Consciousness* (*Essai sur les données immédiates de la conscience*, 1889), trans. F. L. Pogson, London: Allen & Unwin.

Bergson, H. (2007 [1946] [1934]) *The Creative Mind: An Introduction to Metaphysics* (*La Pensée et le Mouvant*, 1934), trans. M. L. Andison, New York: The Philosophical Library.

Butterfield, J. (2004) "On the persistence of homogeneous matter", available at https://arxiv.org/pdf/physics/0406021.pdf. Accessed 10 January 2017.

Canales, J. (2015) *The Physicist and the Philosopher: Einstein, Bergson, and the Debate that Changed Our Understanding of Time*, Princeton, NJ: Princeton University Press.

Čapek, M. (1971) *Bergson and Modern Physics*, Dordrecht, The Netherlands: Nijhoff.

Dainton, B. (2000/2006) *Stream of Consciousness*, London: Routledge.

James, H. J. (1920) *The Letters of William James*, Volume 2, Boston, MA: Atlantic Monthly Press.

James, W. (1890) *The Principles of Psychology*, New York: Holt.

James, W. (1893) "Review. *Les Principes de la Nature* by Charles Renouvier", *Philosophical Review*, 2(2): 212–218.

James, W. (1909) *A Pluralistic Universe*, New York: Longmans, Green & Co.

Lewis, D. (1986) *Philosophical Papers Volume 2*, Oxford, UK: Oxford University Press.

Lovejoy, A. (1912a) "The problem of time in recent French philosophy I", *The Philosophical Review*, 21(1): 11–31.

Lovejoy, A. (1912b) "The problem of time in recent French philosophy II", *The Philosophical Review*, 21(3): 322–343.

Lovejoy, A. (1912c) "The problem of time in recent French philosophy III", *The Philosophical Review*, 21(5): 527–545.

Myers, G. E. (1986) *William James: His Life and Thought*, New Haven, CT: Yale University Press, pp. 46–47.

Pearson, K. A. and J. Mullarkey (eds) (2002) *Bergson: Key Writings*, London: Continuum.

Perry, R. B. (1935) *The Thought and Character of William James*, Vol. I, Oxford, UK: Oxford University Press.

Renouvier, C. B. (1864) *Troisième Essai de Critique Générale: Principes de la Nature*, Paris: Ladrange.

Schumann, F. (1898) "Zur Psychologie der Zeitanschauung", in *Zeitschrift für Psychologie und Physiologie der Sinnesorgane*, XVII: 106–148.

Spiegelberg, H. (1965) *The Phenomenological Movement: A Historical Introduction* Vol. II, The Hague, The Netherlands: Martinus Nijhoff.

Stern, L. (1897/2005) "Mental presence-time", trans. N. De Warren, in C. Wolfe (ed.), *The New Yearbook for Phenomenology and Phenomenological Research*, London: College Publications.

Further reading

Barnard, W. (2011) *Living Consciousness: The Metaphysical Vision of Henri Bergson*, Albany, NY: SUNY.

Bergson, H. (2002) *Bergson: Key Writings*, edited by K. A. Pearson and J. Mullarkey, London: Continuum.

Canales, J. (2015) *The Physicist and the Philosopher: Einstein, Bergson, and the Debate that Changed Our Understanding of Time*, Princeton, NJ: Princeton University Press.

Čapek, M. (1971) *Bergson and Modern Physics*, Dordrecht, The Netherlands: Nijhoff.

Dainton, B. (2010) "Temporal consciousness", in E. N. Zalta (ed.), *The Stanford Encyclopedia of Philosophy*, http://plato.stanford.edu/entries/consciousness-temporal/. Accessed 10 January 2017.

Dainton, B. (2016) "Some cosmological implications of temporal experience", in Y. Dolev and M. Roubach (eds), *Cosmological and Psychological Time*, Boston Studies in the Philosophy and History of Science 285, pp. 75–106, Springer International, London/Dordrecht.

Guerlach, S. (2006) *Thinking in Time: An Introduction to Henri Bergson*, Ithaca, NY: Cornell University Press.

Lawlor, L. and Leonard, V. (2016) "Henri Bergson", in E. N. Zalta (ed.), *The Stanford Encyclopedia of Philosophy*, http://plato.stanford.edu/entries/bergson/. Accessed 10 January 2017.

8

WILLIAM STERN'S "PSYCHISCHE PRÄSENZZEIT"

Barry Dainton

The relationship between consciousness and time was a source of fascination and puzzlement among both philosophers and psychologists in the final decades of the nineteenth century. German psychologists played a prominent role in these debates, and William Stern (1871–1938) was one such. Stern was a student of Ebbinghaus and spent the bulk of his career as Professor of Psychology, first at Breslau, then at Hamburg. In his early years, he was a leading figure in differential psychology and, among other things, invented the IQ test. He published just one article on temporal experience, "Psychische Präsenzzeit" (or "Mental presence-time") in 1897.[1]

Despite being discussed by Husserl – albeit in a cursory manner – until very recently Stern's bold and innovative work on this topic has been largely overlooked.[2] What makes his work of particular interest is that he was one of the very earliest developers and defenders of what I have elsewhere called the *Extensional* approach to temporal experience.[3] Extensionalists hold that we directly experience change, persistence and succession. They are not – of course – alone in this; many other philosophers and psychologists would say the same. What is distinctive about the Extensionalist's position is the stance they take on *how* temporally extended phenomena are experienced.

According to a number of influential nineteenth-century figures – including Wundt, Brentano, Ward and Meinong – our direct experiences of change occur within episodes of consciousness that are themselves momentary. On this (then) dominant view, our streams of consciousness consist of dense successions of states, each of which consists of (i) an instantaneous phase of presently occurring experience and (ii) a collection of distinctively vivid representations – "immediate memories" or "retentions" – of recently elapsed experiential phases. According to proponents of this *Retentionalist* view (as we can call it), the simultaneous presence in consciousness of these two ingredients gives rise to our direct (seeming) experiences of change. So for Retentionalists, when we hear one brief musical note follow another, or see someone's hand going up, or a bird swooping down from the sky, the contents of our experience have (apparent) temporal extension, but our experiences themselves do not. In contrast, Extensionalists hold that our experiences of change are themselves extended through (brief intervals of) time in just the way one might naively suppose them to be.[4]

Given the intellectual milieu from which he emerged, Stern was fully familiar with the Retentionalist approach, and the motivations and assumptions upon which it was based. He diverged from his contemporaries in finding these less than compelling.

Presence-time

Stern begins "Mental presence-time" by observing that psychology, like other sciences, has to work with complex unities, and he suggests a criterion for genuine as opposed to fictitious conscious unity: it exists when mental contents are immediately apprehended as belonging or occurring together. He goes on to note that recent psychological theorizing has generally been working on the assumption – sometimes implicit, sometimes explicit – that phenomenal unity is constrained in a particular way: only contents that are *instantaneous* and *simultaneous* can be apprehended together. Stern proposes that we jettison this constraint on unity:

> That only those contents can belong to a whole of consciousness that exist together and are simultaneously present at any given time and, therefore, that an ideal cross-section at any given moment in the life of the soul would have to contain every element belonging to that whole of consciousness is a dogma, which, in a more or less veiled form, determines numerous psychological reflections. I consider this dogma, at least in this generalized form, to be false. I believe that there are instances when an apprehension first comes into being on the basis of temporally extended content of consciousness, in such a manner that every part of this content exists in an insoluble connection with every other part. It is only in this and through this connection that the characteristic resulting act can be produced without, however it being the case that every part has to exist simultaneously, or as an after-duration. Indeed, under certain circumstances "non-simultaneity" can be the necessary pre-condition for a resulting apprehension. In these instances, a momentary "cross-section through the life of the soul" is revealed to be an artificial unity, comparable, for example, to the way in which an individual point on the surface-section of a microscope slide often does not allow us to recognize correctly what . . . we have in view. It appears to me unjustified to take apart such a distinctive content of consciousness and dissect it into artificial elements simply because it is not completed in a moment.
>
> *(2005 [1897]: 313)*

When referring to "wholes of consciousness", Stern intends to refer to instances of directly experienced succession and persistence. For the Retentional theorists from whom Stern is here distancing himself, our experiences of succession and persistence are invariably contained in momentary cross-sections of our streams of consciousness. This doctrine is itself a consequence, or so Stern maintains, of an unwarranted assumption – a "dogma" – that only contents which exist simultaneously, and at a given moment of time, can be experienced as unified.

If we *do* abandon the instantaneity/simultaneity constraint on experienced unity, then our direct experiences of change, persistence and succession need not be confined to momentary states of consciousness. Contents which appear to be successive can really be successive (as Extensionalists maintain), rather than existing simultaneously (as with the Retentional model). Similarly, episodes of consciousness which *seem* to persist through intervals of ordinary objective time can really do so. Abandoning the dogma brings the significant advantage that temporal consciousness need no longer be systematically misleading as to its own nature.

Throughout the nineteenth century, the beginning of wisdom for German psychologists working on temporal experience was the distinction between a succession of experiences (or representations) and an experience (or representation) of succession. They appreciated the fact that a succession of durationless sensations does not by itself constitute an experience *of* succession. The experiencing of a succession of musical notes (for example) as a succession requires successive notes to be apprehended *together*, as following on from one another. Stern was as aware of the rationale for this distinction as anyone, and he was not proposing that it was ill-founded. He was simply proposing that the unified experiential wholes within which succession is directly apprehended can *themselves* be extended in time, rather than momentary.

> I therefore put forth the following principle: mental events that play themselves out within a stretch of time can under circumstances form a unified and complex act of consciousness regardless of the non-simultaneity of individual parts. That stretch of time over which a mental act can be extended I call its presence-time.
>
> *(2005 [1897]: 315)*

So Stern's presence-times are both temporally extended and experientially *unified* conscious episodes. Figure 8.1 is a depiction of a single presence-time, consisting of a rapid succession of brief auditory tones, 1–2–3–4. As indicated by the small arrows, each tone is experienced as flowing into its immediate successor; but the entire sequence also constitutes a unified experiential whole, as indicated by the upper arrow.

Describing this case, Stern claims that we don't hear the four tones occurring simultaneously, neither when we hear the final tone do we hear the three earlier ones persisting on – as the Retentionalists would have us believe. Rather,

> [t]he four parts are in consciousness one after the other in succession; yet, nevertheless, they exist within one and the same act of apprehension, within a presence-time. We do not hear the four tones at once nor do we, while hearing the fourth tone, also have the entire group of tones in consciousness on the basis of a continued presence of tones 1, 2 and 3. Rather, the four tones constitute a successive unity with a common effect in the form of apprehension.
>
> *(2005 [1897]: 319)*

Wundt held that complexes of sensory contents could only be apprehended directly if they exist in a conscious whole simultaneously. Stern rejects this: "As a whole, yes; as simultaneous, no" (2005 [1897]: 319).

This simple auditory example provides a useful illustration of the structure of presence-times, but as Stern makes clear, he does not intend his account to be confined to the auditory sphere. Presence-times house all forms of directly experienced change: perceived movements, mental images, thoughts and bodily sensations.

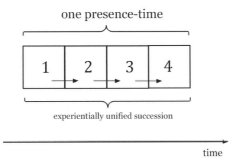

Figure 8.1 Depiction of a single presence-time

On seeing what is depicted in Figure 8.1, some proponents of the "dogma" Stern wants to reject might discern a difficulty of principle. Stern accepts that the successive phases in the tone-sequence 1–2–3–4 have to be experienced as unified in order to be experienced as a succession. If we posit a unifying awareness that is itself extended through time, this awareness will itself consist of a succession of phases – let's label them A1, A2, A3 and A4. A question now arises: what unifies A1, A2, A3 and A4? Unless *something* unifies them, aren't we left with a succession of discrete awarenesses, and no awareness of succession? Moreover, since the same problem will arise for any temporally extended form of consciousness, it looks as though we have no option but to insist that the experiential unity must derive from a form of consciousness that is *not* temporally extended.

However, as will now be clear, the Extensionalist has a swift reply to this line of argument. From Stern's vantage point, anyone arguing along these lines is simply revealing their commitment to the assumption "that only those contents can belong to a whole of consciousness that exist together and are simultaneously present at any given time". If we reject this assumption, there is no obstacle to accepting that 1–2–3–4 can form a *successive unity*, a unity that unfolds over the successive phases of an interval of ordinary objective time. Presence-times are perfectly equipped to contain unities of precisely this kind.

Presence and the present

What becomes of *the present* if we adopt the Extensional model? Is the concept entirely ill-adapted to the characterization of experience? Stern argues that this need not be the case. What we can do is define the present "as the totality of temporal and spatial relations that can become the object of a direct perception" (2005 [1897]: 325). Since we directly perceive events spanning brief intervals, the present thus construed is a positive and finite stretch of time (even if brief). A presence-time can also possess earlier and later phases, just as an experienced region of space has a "right" and a "left", a "near" and a "far". When we do construe "the present" in this way, Stern suggests that the neighbouring notes in a melody "are all present for us, yet nevertheless they are present to us in succession. A sustained tone is present to us and yet is not instantaneous" (Ibid.). There is nothing incoherent here provided we follow Stern and take "present to us" to mean "exist within the same presence-time".

Accepting that the psychological present has genuine temporal extension helps with otherwise intractable problems. In 1894, William James gave the Presidential Address to the meeting of the American Psychological Association in Philadelphia. His paper was "The knowing of things together" (James 1895). Here James claims that all forms of consciousness – even the most primitive – involve the experience of passage or transition:

> The smallest effective pulse of consciousness, whatever else it may be consciousness of, is also consciousness of passing time. The tiniest feeling that we can possibly have involves for future reflection two sub-feelings, one earlier and the other later, and a sense of their continuous procession.
>
> *(James 1895: 111)*

In a rejoinder published a year later, the psychologist Charles Strong subjects James to withering criticism. For Strong, to claim that these earlier and later feelings could possibly be experienced together – or constitute a successive unity – is simply absurd, "radically inconsistent" (Strong 1896: 155). Strong's reasoning is straightforward:

Later states can have no direct and intuitive dealings with earlier states, for the simple reason that the two do not exist at once. When the earlier state is present the later state is non-existent. Our apparently direct consciousness of the immediate past is an illusion . . . Earlier and later states cannot be bound up into a successive unity because they do not exist together, and because they are past and gone when the perception of succession arises. When this perception arises, the relation is perceived between images existing in consciousness simultaneously. It therefore implies only a simultaneous unity of consciousness; not a successive unity, which, to tell the truth, is a monstrosity, a contradiction in terms.

(Ibid.: 155–156)

Strong is clearly assuming that (a) only the present is real, and (b) the present is strictly duration-less. If this applies both to time and temporal experience, then James' position does look to be problematic: non-existent experiences are not in a position to co-exist with – or be experienced together with – experiences which do exist.[5]

However, the claim that the sequence of tones in a melody – or any other sort of experiences – can be both present and successive is only incoherent if the "present" in question is duration-less. If we adopt Stern's proposal, this is simply not the case. Successive tones in a melody can be experienced *as* successive in a presence-time which both extends a short distance through (objective) time and consists of a unified conscious whole.[6]

Motivations

Establishing that the Extensional model of temporal experience is coherent – or at least not obviously incoherent – is one thing; establishing its superiority over the Retentional alternative is quite another. What reasons are there for preferring it? Stern provides several.

Consider the contents that will fill your consciousness while you hear a multi-syllable word such as "theatre" if the Retentional account is true. You will first hear "th". This will vanish from your consciousness to be replaced by your hearing the "ea" sound; but the latter will not occur by itself: it will be accompanied by the Retentional reproduction (or primary memory) of the preceding "th". Last comes your experiencing of "tre". Again, this won't occur by itself: it will be accompanied by simultaneous re-presentations of both "ea" and "th". Does this complex sequence of presentations and re-presentations correspond remotely to what it's actually like to hear "theatre" pronounced? Is the initial "th" sound echoed and repeated in this sort of way? Stern suggests not, claiming – not implausibly – that it does considerable violence to the actual facts of experience.

This point aside, if the Retentional model is to be viable, an account of retentions is obviously required. When you hear the final syllable of "theatre", in precisely what way are "th" and "ea" also present (simultaneously) in your consciousness? More precisely, what property does "th" possess which makes it seem *earlier* than "ea"? With regard to this issue, different Retentional theorists have different stories to tell. For Herbart, earlier and later retentions have different intensities. Lotze posited "temporal signs", a distinctive kind of qualitative feature which determines apparent temporal order. Brentano appealed (at different periods) to temporal judgements and temporal modes of presentation. These differing theories are all confronted with a serious challenge.

Consider again the succession of the four tones 1–2–3–4 we encountered earlier. We are trying to account for the *immediate experience* of change and succession. The most obvious way for the Retentionalist to supply this is by holding that in this sort of case retentions are ordinary forms of perceptual experience. But this is obviously problematic. If this *were* the case, then when tone 1 is heard, it will be accompanied by reproductions (or re-presentations) of the 2-tone, the 3-tone and the 4-tone that are qualitatively indistinguishable from the originals. Since these sounds will all seem to be occurring simultaneously, the result will be a (decidedly unlovely) chord. So retentions cannot be anything closely resembling ordinary forms of experience. Hence when the 4-tone occurs, it will be accompanied by representations of 1-tone, 2-tone and 3-tone which are qualitatively quite different from the original sounds. The trouble now is that whatever account we do give of the nature of retentions, it's not obvious that we'll be able to account for the immediate experience of change, for the simple reason that immediate experience has dropped out of the picture. Here is Stern making the point:

> [f]or those who cannot and do not want to give up simultaneity, there is only one consequence: a direct apprehension of time as such must be repudiated entirely. What can be grasped as self-contained contents of consciousness in a moment are merely symbols of temporal relations and not an actual perception of time relations.
>
> *(2005 [1897]: 321)*

While there is more to be said on this topic, Stern is right about one thing: the Extensional approach accommodates the direct apprehension of temporal relations in a simpler and more direct manner than the Retentional alternatives he considers.

Projection

The directly experienced flows of sensory experience which constitute the bulk of typical presence-times are centrally important to our experience of temporality, but there are other important aspects of temporal experience to be reckoned with. Stern devotes the third section of his paper – "Projection in presence-time" – to showing how the theory can accommodate at least some of these.

We are all familiar with the way depictions on a map can represent spatial phenomena that are far larger than anything we could normally perceive visually, e.g. the Pacific Ocean, or the solar system or a galaxy. Stern suggests that there are temporal analogues: forms of consciousness which exist within presence-times and which represent, in compressed or condensed form, events which in reality unfold over hours, days or years, rather than seconds or fractions of seconds. When listening to a familiar piece of music, for example, while the notes unfold, we often have an awareness – in our acoustic imaginations, difficult to describe but nonetheless real – of the way the piece is going to develop, of the notes which are still to come. These anticipated/imagined notes have their own temporal features and order, but they unfold with great rapidity. Stern provides other examples:

> In the course of delivering a lecture, while I am speaking a word, the next words are already – and more importantly, even the next chain of thoughts (admittedly, not in their linguistic formulation) – present in the correct sequence in my consciousness. Moreover, the intellectual side of volitional acts does not only consist, as is often portrayed, in that I represent to myself the result and final goal of the act. Rather, while and insofar as I actually exercise an act of volition, the entire course of action is present to me, not, however, as a timeless content of representation, but as a compressed content.
>
> Not only future events, but also past events can be projected into presence-time, for example, when the entire course of the day is briefly passed in review in our

minds during the evening, for when we "bring to mind by making present again" (an extremely characteristic expression!) earlier experiences (e.g. the course of a discussion or a journey). Perhaps, there also belongs here the often-reported phenomenon that in instances of a sudden threat to life, years and even decades of our life flashes by in our mind in a matter of seconds.

(2005 [1897]: 329)

We need not be awake to encounter temporal compression. Stern suggests that the most dramatic instances of temporal projection probably occur while we are dreaming. In a dream, we can seem to have lived through long stretches of time in (objectively) just a few minutes.

Since Tulving's work in the 1980s, psychologists have used the expression "mental time travel" to refer to our impressive – but also effortless seeming – ability to situate ourselves at will at different locations in the past and future, and work is being done to isolate the various cognitive capacities which underpin it.[7] Although Stern confined himself to noting its existence and importance, he also points to some of its more subtle phenomenological features, and emphasizes that mental time travel takes place within the dynamic, flowing confines of presence-times.

Primary memory

Stern may have rejected the Retentionalist doctrine that memories – perhaps of a very special kind – underpin our immediate experience of duration, but he nonetheless appreciated that memory plays an important role in temporal phenomenology, and what he has to say about this is of interest.

Memory comes in a variety of forms. Most of us can remember a great many experiences from our earlier lives – e.g. some of our doings on our twenty-first birthday, or on last summer's holiday. This *episodic memory* gives us the ability to re-create past experiences from our earlier lives in our sensory imaginations. So-called *semantic memory* is quite different and consists of our general knowledge of the world, and is expressible in propositional form (e.g. "Paris is the capital of France", "Water is H_2O"). Different again are the various forms of vivid, but rapidly decaying, *short-term* memory which give us a distinctive mode of access to the very recent past. Anyone who has searched frantically for a pen to write down a telephone number or address – perhaps while replaying the original auditory or visual experience in their imaginations – has encountered one of the characteristic properties of this form of memory.[8] In his *Principles of Psychology* (1890), James labels this short-term storage facility "primary memory", and Stern adopts the same terminology:

> When remembering what has just immediately elapsed, the distinctive liveliness and intuitive presence of memory representations has been observed by many researchers in addition to the striking certainty of judgments of memory. These observations occasioned the acceptance of a qualitatively different form of memory from that of authentic memory. . . . in the case of primary memory, there is a continuation of the original representation, whereas in the case of authentic memory, there is the re-appearance of the corresponding representation.
>
> *(2005 [1897]: 333)*

Stern's discussion then takes an original and interesting turn. He argues that although primary memory is its own "authentic type of perception", it is ultimately dependent on the distinctive features of presence-time.

Let's suppose you are listening to a succession of rapid C-tones, played on a harpsichord. The tones are all qualitatively indistinguishable from one another, and this is something that is immediately apparent to you – if the tones were different (if say, you were listening to the rising scale C-D-E-F-G) this too would be immediately obvious. It is only because successive C-tones occur together within single presence-times that it is possible for you to be quite certain that they are in fact identical, or so Stern argues. Contents that occur together within unified conscious states have an epistemically privileged status: they can be directly compared with one another, in a way that is simply not possible for contents that are not so related.[9]

The sequence of C-tones that you are currently perceiving is also registering, or so we can suppose, in your primary memory. As a consequence, your auditory experience is accompanied by vivid recollections of earlier C-tones in your acoustic imagination. Since these recollections are primary memories, you have no doubt whatsoever that they are accurately reflecting your recent auditory experience. But what allows you to be confident of this? From where does this subjective certainty derive? Stern suggests that experiential contents of *all* kinds can be directly compared within presence-times, and it is this which makes primary memory possible: "With authentic [long-term] memory, identity is inferred, whereas with primary memory identity is experienced immediately and perceived as a result of direct successive comparison" (2005 [1897]: 335). It is only because we can introspect the successive phases of our unfolding perceptual experiences, along with their accompanying primary memories, that we can directly apprehend whether the contents of our experience are changing (or not), and that our primary memories are accurately reflecting our perceptions.

While this line of argument certainly requires further development, it is potentially significant. If Stern is right, appealing to primary memories to explain our experience of change, succession and persistence – as some Retentional theorists are wont to do – is fundamentally misguided. The very existence of retentions, in this guise at least, presupposes the direct apprehension of duration and succession in presence-times.

Measurements

In the final part of his paper, Stern moves on to consider whether "quantitative determinations" of presence-times are possible. Can the objective duration of presence-times be measured experimentally? Stern does not rule this out entirely, but he points out that there are several obstacles to be overcome.

Although presence-times possess a specific finite duration, their temporal boundaries are not clearly indicated; there is a continual passage of phenomenal content through presence-times, and nothing discernible in experience marks where one presence-time ends and the next begins. In the absence of any obvious boundaries, subjects will inevitably find it more difficult than would otherwise be the case to estimate the duration of presence-times.[10]

The situation is further complicated by the phenomenon (discussed above) of *projection* in presence-time. Over a period of just a few seconds, a subject might be mentally creating (or re-creating) events which correspond to objective days or weeks or years, and this increases the odds of subjects overestimating the durations of presence-times. Stern suggests that James was guilty of precisely this when he reached the verdict in the *Principles* that the nucleus of the specious present is typically around a dozen seconds. In reality, it is considerably less: "as soon as the perspective foreshortening is missing, only the content of a few seconds can come together into a whole of consciousness" (2005 [1897]: 339).

Stern also thinks it unlikely that a general (or universal) value for presence-time exists. Its duration may well vary, from subject to subject and from time to time, depending on the type of content, the degree to which a subject is attending to it and the "intensity of the psychological energy". Even if it's possible for the objective durations of presence-times to range from a fraction of a second to several seconds, it is generally *not* found inhabiting these extreme values.

He concludes his discussion, somewhat opaquely, by proposing two guiding principles for future research. The first is that "for every temporally extended act of consciousness there exists an optimal value of presence time . . . the time that is required for an impression to attain its complete mental unfolding and effectiveness, and which is apprehended subjectively as immediately befitting it"; and second "that optimal value is largely dependent on the contents of acts of consciousness" (2005 [1897]: 341). As Stern's subsequent discussion makes clear, these optimal time values are related to temporal patterns, or gestalts:

> If I hold a pocket-watch to my ear (with a ticking interval of 0.2 seconds), I involuntarily perceive a group of ticks, each of which is the object of a thoroughly unified act of consciousness. (The impression is extremely striking: here is perhaps an observation in which unity without simultaneity – the stretch-like character of presence-time – appears most compelling). This observation reveals to me that with the passive reception of an impression a group or more groups of up to four sounds are formed automatically. I am also able to make out other groupings of up to 2, 6, or 8 sounds; but always, an act of volition is here definitely required . . . In these instances the optimal value is around 0.8 seconds, which comes close to the adequate rhythms [discussed earlier].
>
> *(Ibid.: 346–347)*

The study of temporal "grouping" in music, speech perception and action has subsequently proved a fruitful one for psychologists interested in time-perception. A number of distinct temporal intervals, ranging from milliseconds to several seconds, have been found to have cognitive and phenomenological significance. For a useful introduction to the literature on these findings, see Wittmann (2011).

Stream-structure

We have been focusing thus far on individual presence-times and have neglected an important issue: how do presence-times combine to form continuous streams of consciousness? In his otherwise very useful discussion of Stern's article, Romand (2011, §3.2) suggests Stern held that (i) a stream of consciousness consists of a series of discrete, non-overlapping presence-times, and (ii) that this account of stream-structure is fully capable of capturing all the continuity we find in our actual streams of consciousness. This is questionable on both counts.

Consider a sequence of tones C-D-E-F that is of sufficiently long duration to be divided between two entirely distinct presence-times [C-D], [E-F]. On the view Romand suggests Stern held, although C is experienced as flowing into D, and D is experienced as flowing into F, there is no direct experiential continuity between the D-tone and the E-tone. This is phenomenologically suspect: don't we hear *each* tone flowing into the next? If presence-times *do* overlap, the continuity problem is solved, as shown in Figure 8.2. Here the succession C-D is located in the initial presence-time PT-1, the succession D-E is located in presence-time PT-2, and E-F is found in PT-3. Each actually experienced transition is accommodated. Moreover, by virtue of the fact that the "D" in PT-1 is numerically identical with the "D" in PT-2, there is no phenomenologically unrealistic repetitions of tones – each of C-D-E-F is heard just once.

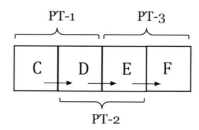

Figure 8.2 Overlapping presence-times

It is true, as Romand relates, that Stern does not give us much guidance on the way he envis-aged different presence-times fitting together to produce entire streams of consciousness. But he is not entirely silent, and the little he does say is suggestive. In a footnote at the end of §2, Stern observes:

> Strong is correct when he says that the present is nothing comparable to a point of rest, but rather something continually in flux, one should, nevertheless, not designate it as a "moving point". It is rather an uninterrupted displacement of existing short stretches of time.

> *(2005 [1897]: 325)*

Since Stern does not expand further, we cannot be certain of what he had in mind, but we can make some reasonable surmises. Presumably, when referring to "short stretches of time", he means intervals of presence-time (since it makes little sense to suppose intervals of time per se could move). Given this, it seems far from inconceivable that an "uninterrupted displacement" of a presence-time along the temporal axis would result in the sort of overlap structures depicted in Figure 8.3.

More concretely, we can suppose that a first presence-time contains the auditory succession C-D, a slightly later one D-E, and a still later one E-F. Provided the overlaps between successive presence-times involves part-sharing – and there is no reason to think it wouldn't or couldn't – the resulting structure would be identical to that depicted in Figure 8.2. In which case, the structure of our streams of consciousness envisaged by Stern would be precisely the same as the structure proposed by later Extensional theorists.[11]

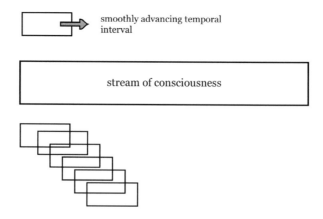

Figure 8.3 Uninterrupted displacement of a presence-time along the temporal axis

Notes

1 Stern's article first appeared in *Zeitschrift für Psychologie und Physiologie der Sinnesorgane*, XIII (1897), 325–359. An English translation by De Warren was published in 2005.

2 Husserl outlines Stern's views on his 1905 lectures on time consciousness (1991: 22). Stern is also discussed in Gallagher (1998: 32–42) and De Warren (2005).

3 See, for example, Dainton (2000, 2008).

4 For a more detailed overview of these competing approaches see Dainton (2010) and the chapters in Part III of this volume.

5 Strong accepts that James is right about one thing. If in reality our consciousness is confined to dura-tionless phases, it certainly doesn't seem that way: we seem to be directly aware of change and succession over short periods (half a second, say). This illusion is created, suggests Strong, by the representations of just-past experiences which do coexist with our present (momentary) experiences.

6 Stern himself observes: "The assumption of a successive unity appears to Strong as a monstrosity and as self-contradictory. But why? It comes down to how one defines 'unity'" (2005 [1897]: 330–331). If, like Strong, we stipulate that experiential unity is confined to instantaneous cross-sections of our streams of consciousness, then a successive unity is indeed impossible. But if we reject this constraint, as Stern recommends, it isn't.

7 The term mental time travel (also known as "chronosthesia") was introduced in Tulving (1983). For a review of recent work, see Suddenorf *et al.* (2009).

8 Work on short-term memory dates back to Ebbinghaus' (1913 [1885]) research into the accuracy with which short sequences of random letters of the alphabet can be recalled: very accurately for the first few seconds, far less so after longer intervals. More recent research has led psychologists to distinguish visual, auditory and tactile forms of short-term sensory memory (typically half a second or less), and *working memory* (a duration of 10–15 seconds). For an overview, see Cowan (2008).

9 "We are therefore able to perceive directly either the difference or the correspondence between two successively given tones, just as we are able to perceive either the difference or correspondence between two neighboring colored surfaces; in each of these cases, we have no need to assume artificially that comparison only comes into being on the basis of a memory-image of the first tone existing next to the second tone. Instead, the entire unfolding content of consciousness within presence-time becomes the appropriate foundation for the resulting apprehension of either identity or difference" (2005 [1897]: 331).

10 For more on the importance of boundaries (or the lack thereof), see Rashbrook-Cooper (2016).

11 See, for example, Dainton (2000, 2008) and Pelczar (2015).

Bibliography

Cowan, N. (2008) "What are the differences between long-term, short-term, and working memory?" *Progress in Brain Research* 169: 323–338.

Dainton, B. (2000) *Stream of Consciousness*, London: Routledge.

Dainton, B. (2008) "Sensing change", *Philosophical Issues* 18(1): 362–384.

Dainton, B. (2010) "Temporal consciousness", in E. N. Zalta (ed.), *The Stanford Encyclopedia of Philosophy*, available at http://plato.stanford.edu/entries/consciousness-temporal/. Accessed 10 January 2017.

De Warren, N. (2005) "The significance of Stern's 'Präsenzzeit' for Husserl's phenomenology of inner time-consciousness", *The New Yearbook for Phenomenology and Phenomenological Philosophy V*, London: College Publications, pp. 81–122.

Ebbinghaus, H. (1913 [1885]) *Memory: A Contribution to Experimental Psychology*, trans. H. Ruger and C. Bussenius, New York: Dover.

Gallagher, S. (1998) *The Inordinance of Time*, Evanston, IL: Northwestern University Press.

Husserl, E. (1991) *On the Phenomenology of the Internal Consciousness of Time*, trans. J. B. Brough, Dordrecht, The Netherlands: Kluwer.

James, W. (1890) *The Principles of Psychology*, New York: Holt.

James, W. (1895) "The knowing of things together", *Psychological Review* 2(2): 105–124.

Lamiell, J. T. (2010) *William Stern (1871–1938): A Brief Introduction to His Life and Works*, Lengerich, Germany: Pabst.

Pelczar, M. (2015) *Sensorama*, Oxford, UK: Oxford University Press.

Rashbrook-Cooper, O. (2016) "The stream of consciousness: A philosophical account", in B. Mölder, V. Arstila and P. Øhrstrøm (eds), *Philosophy and Psychology of Time*, Dordrecht, The Netherlands: Springer.

Romand, D. (2011) "William Stern on the 'psychical time of presence': Historical and theoretical study of a cognitive model of time perception and autonoetic consciousness", *Journal für Philosophie & Psychiatrie*, July Supplement, available at http://www.jfpp.org/87.html. Accessed 10 January 2017.

Stern, W. L. (2005 [1897]) "Mental presence-time", trans. N. De Warren, in C. Wolfe (ed.), *The New Yearbook for Phenomenology and Phenomenological Research V*, London: College Publications, pp. 310–359.

Strong, C. A. (1896) "Consciousness and time", *Psychological Review* 3(2): 149–157.

Suddenorf, T., Addis, D. R. and Corballis, M. C. (2009) "Mental time travel and the shaping of the human mind", *Philosophical Transactions of the Royal Society London B Biological Sciences* 364(1521): 1317–1324.

Tulving, E. (1983) *Elements of Episodic Memory*, Oxford, UK: Oxford University Press.

Wittmann, M. (2011) "Moments in time", *Frontiers in Integrative Neuroscience* 5(66): 1–9.

PART III

The structure of temporal experience

9

THE SNAPSHOT CONCEPTION OF TEMPORAL EXPERIENCES

Philippe Chuard

Temporal experiences, I assume, are perceptual experiences of temporal relations between perceived events, such as the *succession* and *order* of notes in a melody, the *duration* of an awkward silence, a sudden *change* in facial expression, etc. Like other experiences, temporal experiences themselves instantiate temporal properties: occupying a certain interval, occurring before or after other experiences, etc. One question is how our sensory experiences make us perceptually aware – if at all – of temporal relations between perceived events. Another is whether their own temporal features affect how these experiences present or represent such temporal relations. Most accounts combine some metaphysical view of the temporal ontology of conscious experiences with an explanation of how temporal relations between worldly events can be represented perceptually.

The so-called "snapshot conception" I'll describe is no exception:

> The snapshot conception:
> SM: our streams of consciousness only contain short-lived experiential events, arranged in succession.
> SC: no temporal relation between non-simultaneous perceived events figure in the content of any such short-lived experiential event.

The metaphysical thesis (SM) has it that, insofar as the occurrence of perceptual experiences in time is concerned, all there really is reduces to very short (perhaps even instantaneous) slices, temporal parts or "snapshots", and temporally ordered successions thereof. The representational thesis (SC) adds a negative answer to whether the contents of these slices include temporal relations between non-simultaneous events.

This combination may sound radical, yet it isn't so radical as to imply that we can't perceive temporally extended events: we do, of course, by successively experiencing enough successive temporal parts of those events. Neither does it rule out the seemingly continuous and dynamic phenomenology we can introspect when hearing melodies or seeing changing facial expressions. But the phenomenology typically associated with such putative temporal experiences is best accounted for as owing to the *pace* of successive experiential slices, their temporal arrangement, successive contents and phenomenology, or so the snapshot theorist insists.

Most disagree. For extensionalists,[1] our perceptual experiences are not only extended in time (*contra* SM), but can represent extended events *and* the temporal relations (succession, order, duration, change) between some of their temporal parts (*contra* SC). Extensionalists might admit that extended experiences are composed of successive slices, yet argue that it is whole experiences which, in virtue of their temporal extension, make us aware perceptually of temporal relations in the world.

Retentionalists,[2] in contrast, deny that perceptual experiences need be extended temporally, or involve successive temporal parts – *pace* SM and the extensionalist. Against SC, retentionalists claim, there can be experiences – possibly instantaneous or short-lived ones – the content of which simultaneously represents an extended event with some of the temporal relations between its distinct temporal parts (without representing the latter *as* simultaneous: Lee 2014a: 6; 2014c: 149, 154). This representational claim does almost all the work for retentionalists: importantly, the extended content in question is that of a sensory experience *alone*, not of a momentary experience fused with memories of previous experiences (Lee 2014a: 3, 6; 2014c: 153).[3]

If the snapshot conception enjoyed some popularity in the days of Locke (1690), Hume (1739) and Reid (1855), it hasn't garnered much good press since. Usually dismissed, often perfunctorily, in the fashion of James's (1952) formula to the effect that successions of experiences aren't experiences of succession,[4] it's deemed "incompatible with obvious phenomenological data" (Lee 2014c: 150) or "implausible in the extreme" (Dainton 2008b: 621).

My aim is to sketch *some* of the considerations which can serve to support the snapshot conception, and to explain why skeptical concerns like those just alluded to are misguided. The line of argument is abductive and purports to suggest that the snapshot view constitutes a viable account of temporal experiences and their phenomenology, one perhaps superior to its rivals.

Perduring experiences

The first consideration concerns the ontology of perceptual experiences, which seem best thought of as *events*: particulars happening at or over a time.[5] And if events extend or persist through time, it seems uncontroversial that they *perdure*: unfolding through some interval *t* by being composed of distinct *temporal parts* located at shorter intervals or instants comprised in *t*.[6] Hence, perceptual experiences too, as events that can extend temporally, are composed by their successive temporal parts – just like the events they are experiences of.

What might temporal parts of experiences be? It helps to consider the typically "experiential" properties of experiences: their phenomenal character and "intentional" properties – whether the latter are representational contents or relations between subjects and features of their environment. A proper *temporal part e* of an experience *E* must meet at least three conditions, I propose: (i) *e* occurs *only* during some interval or instant *t* which is properly encompassed by the longer interval *E* occupies; (ii) *e* and *E* occur in the same stream of consciousness of the same subject; (iii) the experiential properties *e* instantiates at *t* are shared by *E* at *t* – they qualitatively overlap in this respect.[7]

Considerations like these remain entirely compatible with all theories of temporal experiences on the table, to be clear. The snapshot theorist takes experiences to *reduce* to successions of their temporal parts. But extensionalists can allow the whole extended experiences they posit to be made up of such temporal parts, *provided* these wholes satisfy whatever further requirements extensionalists impose so as to be distinct from what composes them. In turn, if the retentionalists' experiences are instantaneous, they still have temporal parts, though improper ones. And a retentionalist like Lee grants that experiences can last as long as the neural processes realizing them (Lee 2014a: 4–5), in which case, such experiences can have proper temporal parts in exactly the sense cashed out – even if successive temporal parts perfectly share the very same experiential properties. Lee also acknowledges that, when it comes to perception of longer events, one may enjoy a succession of experiences, each representing a temporally extended subpart of the whole event (Lee 2014a: 5; 2014c: 163–165).

Causation and perceptual contents

The second consideration revolves around the assumption that the physical and physiological processes underlying perception, from the stimulation of a sensory organ by a stimulus, through-out various stages of processing in the relevant areas of the sensory cortex, all the way to the generation of a conscious perceptual experience of the initial stimulus (when things go well), are essentially causal. Succinctly: perceptual experiences have distal causes in the environment, including some of the very events they present or represent.[8] And causal processes take time: the complex of physiological processes underlying the stimulation of a sensory organ all the way to a conscious experience must be temporally extended through distinct temporal parts, some of which may correspond to stages of processing in distinct cortical areas, for instance.

This means, first, that there must be a "temporal gap" – an interval between distal stimulation and the resulting experience – and, second, that such interval may be *relatively constant* through-out successive stimulation. That is, at least relative to a particular perceptual context (including specific environmental conditions and setting) in connection with a given sensory modality, stimuli of a similar type (e.g. colors of a similar intensity) are likely to be processed for a similar duration within a certain temporal window.[9] After all, owing to their similarity, stimulus fea-tures can be processed by the same mechanisms in roughly the same way, so that the processing behind our experiences of similar features can be expected to take roughly the same time. *More or less*: all this allows for small but significant variations in the time it takes to process less similar stimuli, or the same stimuli in different circumstances.[10] These caveats are consistent, however, with there being little variation in processing time when it comes to one kind of case highly relevant to our concerns: successive stimulation by the very same stimuli over a short time span, as with putative temporal experiences involving change, succession, and order.[11]

Imagine hearing, say, a brief progression of three similar notes or sounds – s_1, s_2, and s_3 – lasting not more than two seconds altogether. The whole progression is temporally extended and, as such, is composed of successive temporal parts, each shorter than two seconds, some of which correspond to single notes in the progression: s_1, s_2, and s_3. Suppose you perceive the whole progression, hearing all three notes. The causal assumption implies that some of the successive temporal parts composing the progression are causally responsible for bringing about experiences of themselves – thus, with the notes, s_1 might cause an experience e_1, s_2 causes e_2, and in turn s_3, e_3. These temporal parts of the progression, the notes, not only are similar in pitch, but occur in the same perceptual context, *albeit* at slightly different times. Presumably, then, most such temporal parts of the progression which causally stimulate your ears are processed via the same mechanisms in roughly the same conditions: mechanisms which take more or less the same time to process each successive temporal part of the progression in bringing about experiences e_1, e_2, and e_3. In which case, the resulting experiences will likely succeed one another (with some over-lap, perhaps), since they occur at roughly the same temporal distance from their source. Hence, experiencing a progression of notes involves a temporally extended conscious event, with dis-tinct temporal parts, some of which represent – and are caused by – distinct temporal parts of the stimulus. In short, applying the causal assumption to such a case (with some simplification, admittedly), the picture obtained of sensory stimulation and the production of experiences in a short time span looks something like this (Figure 9.1):[12]

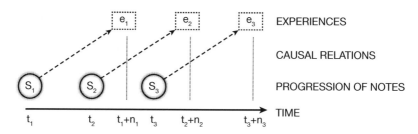

Figure 9.1 Sensory stimulation and the production of experience

The picture suggests a rough match between the order of experiential states produced and that of successive temporal parts of the stimulus perceived – what Lee calls "topological mirroring" (2014a: 8). It needn't suggest a more perfect match: for instance, enough tiny variations in processing time may well add up to a relative mismatch in duration between an extended stimulus and the succession of experiential states it generates.

Again, note how unremarkable this conclusion is. Of course, it coheres very nicely with the snapshot theorist's contention that experiences reduce to successions of short-lived experiential states, each of which represents at most one temporal part of an extended stimulus. Yet it remains entirely friendly to the extensionalists' posit of temporally extended whole experiences composed of distinct temporal parts. And it raises no real trouble for retentionalists, more interestingly, *provided* they grant (as Lee does) that we enjoy successions of experiences – whilst insisting, I take it, that each experience in the succession represents more than just one single temporal part of the overall stimulus (one note, say), but other temporally contiguous temporal parts as well (e.g., several notes), which all figure in the temporally extended content of each successive experiential state.[13]

So construed, then, our two starting points that (a) there are successive temporal parts of longer stretches of experience, which (b) are causally connected to the temporal parts of events they represent, remain perfectly neutral with respect to all three theories of temporal experience.

Phenomenological explanations in time

In light of the constraints imposed by (a) and (b), the snapshot view can be seen to not only provide a viable characterization of the phenomenology typically associated with temporal experiences, but one that is simpler, and at least as explanatorily powerful as its rivals – or so the abductive argument for the snapshot view hopes to establish.

First, a word about perceptual content: though (a) and (b) do not entail Reid's contention that the senses "are confined to the present moment of time" (1855, essay 3, chapter 5), their combination intimates, according to the snapshot theorist, that insofar as sensory experiences go, our streams of consciousness are made up essentially of successive short-lived experiential states, each representing a particular temporal part of a perceived event (the one causally responsible for such an experiential state, when things go well) and *nothing more*. After all, the fast and relatively constant processing at play in perceptual mechanisms would suggest that, once one temporal part of an event is processed, it's the next temporal part's turn to be processed and then experienced, and so on. For instance, if experience e_2 represents sound s_2 at the end of the causal chain from s_2 to e_2, e_2 is unlikely to represent a later sound s_3 as well, if s_3 is not yet done being processed. And e_2 won't represent an earlier sound s_1 either, since experience e_1 (which represented s_1) is gone when e_2 occurs: the subject may well have memories of e_1 concurrent with e_2, but there's no reason to think the experience itself persists. Of course, earlier processing might causally affect later processing and influence how later experiences represent what they do, but this needn't mean that earlier stimuli actually show up in experiences of later stimuli, given the temporal constraints on causal processing. In short, at least in those cases where successive processing *is* constant, successive temporal parts of experience each represent just one temporal part of a perceived event, the snapshot theorist has it.

Phenomenologically, (a) and (b) help make sense of Locke's observation that when seeing motion, for instance, one may introspect "a constant train of successive ideas" (1690, chapter 14, §6). It's here that the snapshot view resorts to cinematic metaphors: not by assuming some sort of projector, let alone some "Cartesian" spectator, but only in the sense that the *pace* of successions of experiential states (the "snapshots" in question) is crucial in accounting for their phenomenology, *provided* such pace falls within certain limits.[14] On this view, the temporal arrangement and speed with which successive snapshots replace one another – a function of the number of snapshots produced by our brains over short intervals – are central to the dynamic aspects of our streams of consciousness: that in virtue of which one experiences a "seamless" and constant transition of contents, when seeing a passing car or hearing a melody.[15]

In addition to each snapshot with its own phenomenal character and content, the snapshot theorist's explanation relies heavily on certain relations between the contents of adjacent experiential states as they are temporally arranged. As when, for instance, tiny representational differences between subsequent contents lead to gradual and typically coherent transitions. When things go well, that is, it's not as if an urban scene in daylight is immediately replaced by a moon-lit horizon on the ocean, itself followed by a group of cows grazing in a pasture. Instead, the background of successive snapshots remains relatively stable throughout. And a moving object, for instance, can keep appearing across successive snapshots with its relative location shifting ever so slightly from one snapshot to the next, rather than suddenly jumping from one side of the road and mysteriously reappearing on the other side. In other words, small and gradual successive representational differences, and the appropriate pace of their transitions, can be responsible for a significant amount of what it's like to have such experiences, the snapshot theorist maintains.

Memories, too, play a role: not in accounting for the dynamic phenomenology of sequences of snapshots, but our cognitive access to it – and more importantly, our access to the successive temporal parts of perceived events, and some of their relations. That you remember where the car was only a fraction of a second ago isn't insignificant: if you didn't, your mental life might seem quite different. And different kinds of memories may be in play: short-term episodic memories, as well as rapidly decaying iconic memories associated with the apparent persistence of objects, for instance.[16]

The snapshot view also acknowledges the possibility of small gaps, and small jumps in content, between adjacent snapshots. Many such gaps and jumps, the hypothesis goes, might simply be too small, or happen too fast, to be noticed: our perceptual, cognitive, mnemonic, and introspective capacities are likely to be limited, and many such gaps and jumps could just fall below what one can detect and discriminate. Bigger gaps and jumps above such detection thresholds are possible too, of course, yet their absence suffices to explain why we usually experience successive events without any apparent discontinuity.

Thus, the snapshot theorist argues, the phenomenology we seem to introspect when enjoying successive experiential states not only *supervenes upon*, but *reduces* to, those features of successions of snapshots just listed: the experiential properties of snapshots, their temporal arrangement, the gradual transitions in their successive contents, our memories of previous experiences, and inability to detect small gaps and jumps, all contribute to determining what it's like to enjoy the sort of phenomenology associated with putative temporal experiences. Phenomenological differences within and between such experiences, the argument goes, necessarily come with differences in such respects.[17]

The explanatory argument then proceeds, first, by insisting that such resources suffice to account for the phenomenology of experiences of melodies or passing cars: our streams of consciousness consist in just one experiential state after another, at such a pace that an experiential state is immediately replaced by another, usually with very similar content, so as to give the impression that such experiences "flow into" one another, the snapshot theorist claims. *Ditto* with the appearance of continuity and unity accompanying such experiences: the seemingly uninterrupted flow of successive contents, together with their representational overlap, are such that there's no reason to suspect successive snapshots are disunified.[18]

As for *perception* of temporal relations between events, none figure in the content of any experiential state in any succession thereof, strictly speaking. The snapshot theorist can admit that such successions, caused as they are by the successive temporal parts of extended events, can in some sense "track" these events, if only by successively representing their successive temporal parts. In this respect, successive snapshots could even be said to indirectly carry information, perhaps implicitly, about temporal relations between events. That is, when one experiences a temporal part of an event immediately followed by another experience of the next temporal part, one might naturally believe the latter succeeds the former. Memories of successions of experiential states help in this regard, and they may well represent the successive contents of experiences and the temporal relations between them. Finally, the snapshot theorist certainly shouldn't deny that perceptual *judgments*, themselves causally based upon successions of experiential states, can be about distinct perceived events and their temporal relations. But the contents of beliefs, judgments, memories, and other cognitive states, ought not be conflated with those of sensory experiences proper, the snapshot theorist warns.[19] Perhaps, some might decide that talk of "perception" of temporal relations could simply be used to stand for such judgments, for instance, or the process leading to them. Still, James had a point: successions of experiences aren't really experiences of succession, not by a mere stroke of the pen, in any case. Just like a sequence of individual sentences, each describing a single note in a melody, with the sentences arranged in the order in which the notes occur, doesn't make for an explicit description of the temporal relations between those notes: at least, if the analogy holds, not without some substantive explanation of how the contents of successive snapshots can somehow fuse to form an informationally richer whole content.

To be clear, the snapshot view isn't trying to explain how we do, in fact, have temporal experiences. We don't, the snapshot theorist surmises. Rather, the view aims to explain what it's like to go through successions of very short conscious experiential states, to then point out how the phenomenology thus accounted for seems indiscriminable from the sort of phenomenology associated with the temporal experiences we allegedly enjoy. Thus, the snapshot view doesn't reject the phenomenological appearances, quite the contrary. It aims to explain them without liberally assuming that such appearances must be taken entirely at face value, as revealing the metaphysical structure of our streams of consciousness.

The second step in the explanatory argument highlights the fact that the snapshot view offers a simpler account of the sort of phenomenology under consideration, at least in using resources which rival accounts already accept anyway. Like the fact that our streams of consciousness consist of successions of temporal parts, each of which causally traces back to successive temporal parts of the events perceived. Or the fact that we have memories of our just past experiences, which aren't completely idle explanatorily. And the fact that our discriminatory capacities are limited, that such limitations may even extend to introspection of what goes on in our streams of consciousness.

And yet, advocates of extensionalism and retentionalism argue, the snapshot conception is patently ill-suited to account for our temporal experiences and their phenomenology. Something altogether different is needed. The last part of the abductive argument aims to show why it's far from clear what exactly such additional resources are supposed to achieve.

The explanatory argument: extensionalism

What needs explanation for an extensionalist like Dainton (2000, 2008a, 2010, 2014a, 2014b)[20] is how the phenomenology of temporal experiences is *unified* and seems *continuous* in such a way that each experience has a "dynamic content which appears to extend a short way through time" (Dainton 2014a: 178) and "seamlessly flows into the next" (Dainton 2014a: 184).

The mereological structure of experience is key: each temporal part of a longer experience is unified with adjacent temporal parts in an overlapping structure of larger, more encompassing, temporal parts. For instance, in a succession of experiences, e_1, e_2, e_3, e_4, etc., a subject might first experience e_1 and e_2 as a unified whole, followed by e_2 unified with e_3, leading into the next larger temporal part e_3–e_4, etc. (Dainton 2014a: 179). The overlap between such larger temporal parts is meant, it appears, to account for both the *dynamic* nature of temporal experiences – longer temporal parts *succeed* and partially overlap one another: first the e_1–e_2 pair, then e_2–e_3, followed by e_3–e_4, etc. – and apparent *continuity*:

> We see the ice skater glide from X to Y and then from Y to Z. The seamlessly flowing character of the whole experience is explained by the fact that the second half of the first episode is numerically identical with the first half of the second episode. Overlap by part-sharing supplies a single but effective underpinning for sensible continuity.
>
> *(Dainton 2014a: 184)*

Such overlap, Dainton insists, also helps explain why there is no "stuttering" (Dainton 2014a: 180), as when, say, the very same note might be experienced twice over, had it figured in the respective contents of two successive experiences. This counterintuitive consequence is avoided, according to Dainton, since, in the longer overlapping temporal parts the extensionalist posits, a single temporal part (e.g., e_2) remains "numerically identical" to itself, and experienced just once.

Further details could be added to this brief sketch of Dainton's approach, but the essential ingredients are all here. So, can this theoretical apparatus really explain the phenomena the snapshot conception allegedly cannot, and does it do any better? There are several reasons to be skeptical. First, the mereological structure Dainton resorts to does little to differentiate his extensionalism from the snapshot theory.[21] Given mereological universalism (i.e., any collection of parts can form a whole), for one thing, longer overlapping temporal parts such as e_1–e_2, e_2–e_3, etc., can be had for free, and the snapshot view treats them simply as shorter successions of experiential parts. Similarly with the dynamic aspects of this structure: the snapshot theorist, too, can say that, at t_2, experiential state e_2 is part of a shorter succession, the pair e_1–e_2, then becomes part of another extended succession at t_3, the pair e_2–e_3, and so on. No additional commitment is needed to this effect. Presumably, Dainton might retort, this isn't quite enough to rescue the snapshot view from the charge of being "static" or "frozen" (Dainton 2014a: 177). But then, how exactly does it suffice to render the extensionalist account an appropriately dynamic one – merely, it seems, by adding a little more structure to successions of experiential states?

If this mereological structure itself isn't enough, the heart of the extensionalist explanation must lie somewhere else, presumably in what grounds such a structure. There is, for Dainton, a basic phenomenal relation of "flowing into" which binds adjacent temporal parts of experience into phenomenologically unified wholes – a sort of phenomenal glue, along the lines of Dainton's earlier focus on the primitive relation of co-consciousness (Dainton 2000, 2010). That is, temporal part e_1 might be phenomenally linked by the "flowing into" relation to e_2, itself connected with e_3 in the same manner, etc. Leaving aside questions about the exact nature of this relation, how can positing such a relation help the extensionalist with the dynamic nature of successive experiences? After all, snapshot theorists posit several relations between adjacent experiential states, e.g., the fact that e_2 succeeds e_1 without any noticeable gap, that e_2's content largely overlaps e_1's, etc. These relations can serve to ground the same overlapping mereological structure as the extensionalist's: so why can't they help turn the snapshot theory into a dynamic account, if something similar supposedly works for the extensionalist? Presumably, there is something special about the "flowing into" relation in virtue of which it suffices to explain the phenomenology of temporal experiences where other relations fail.

Does it really suffice, though? Consider a succession of experiential states which might seem highly discontinuous: first, you experience the layout of my office (e_1), immediately followed by the sight of the crowd in a stadium (e_2), after which a uniform yellow surface is instantly presented (e_3), and then a kitten asleep on a sofa (e_4), all experienced within two or three seconds. For the snapshot view, such a succession should appear *discontinuous*, precisely because the snapshots' respective contents, with little representational overlap, fail to constitute a gradual and coherent progression. For the extensionalist, in contrast, it seems there's nothing barring e_1, e_2, e_3, e_4, from being connected by the "flowing into" relation, at least in principle, thereby unifying these experiential parts into some dynamic and seamlessly continuous whole. If, on the other hand, the "flowing into" relation only links adjacent experiences under certain conditions which aren't met in this case, what are these conditions? Can they explain the difference between such a succession and the clearly continuous succession of experiences of ice skaters gliding on a pond? In the latter, the similarities and overlap in content between adjacent experiential states, their succession constituting a gradual and coherent progression with no gaps or jumps, might offer a plausible candidate for the relevant conditions. If so, the extensionalist would have little to add to what is doing most of the explanatory work for the snapshot view. In any case, the account remains incomplete: we're owed some explanation of what conditions need to hold for the "flowing into" relation to be instantiated, and it'd better not resemble too closely those relations between successive experiential states the snapshot theorist highlights.

Finally, extensionalism faces a *missing content* difficulty: since the view asserts that temporal relations between separate events can be perceptually represented in experience (Dainton 2014a: 178), how exactly does such a content arise? A stream of consciousness crucially involves successive experiential states, say e_1–e_2, where e_1 might represent temporal part x of an extended event and e_2 represents its successive part y, and the pair are phenomenally unified so that e_1 flows into e_2. Very well, but how does all this explain how the pair doesn't just represent first x, and then y, but also their temporal relations – that one succeeds the other? The details of that part of the extensionalist account seem to be missing.

The explanatory argument continued: retentionalism

The focus, for retentionalists like Lee (2014a, 2014c), is largely on the role *temporally extended contents* must play. In this light, retentionalism can be developed in a manner that is consistent with our streams of consciousness consisting of successions of experiences, each of which has a temporally extended content, which might overlap: "Since the content of atomic experiences covers a temporally extended portion of what is happening in the world, a single event may appear in the content of a series of consecutive experiences in the stream, not just a single experience" (Lee 2014c: 155). Here, the retentionalist needn't overly worry about the "stuttering" concerns Dainton (e.g., 2014a: 180–183) raises, if the temporally extended contents of successive experiences can represent "consecutive events as occurring at different times" (Lee 2014c: 155), provided relative temporal locations (or differences therein) are updated from one content to the next, as the successive experiences unfold.[22]

On the other hand, retentionalists thereby face the further costs of having to posit the additional processing mechanisms needed for our perceptual systems to produce these temporally extended sensory contents, including extended contents which align perfectly in temporal information with the contents of adjacent experiences. In particular, the *temporal updating* required to avoid "stuttering" must presumably involve some machinery to guarantee that the same event be represented at different relative temporal locations through the extended contents of successive experiences – machinery which, for instance, the snapshot theory has no need for, at least not at the level of conscious sensory experiences.

Another difficulty relates to the retentionalist's insistence that temporally extended contents be contents of *perceptual experiences* proper, and not just of *memories* of successive experiences – a significant feature of the account, differentiating it from those rivals resorting to compounds of momentary experiences merged with memories of previous experiences (Lee 2014a: 3, 6; 2014c: 153). Suppose, plausibly enough, that short-term memory essentially involves mechanisms by which, at the very least, such memories are (a) causally dependent upon earlier perceptual experiences, and (b) imbued with a content partially overlapping that of experiences they causally depend on.[23] For the retentionalist, one might enjoy a single experience of some present event y as succeeding an earlier event x, followed by another single experience of some now present event z as succeeding y. The representation of y in the second experience is supposed to be purely perceptual, for retentionalists, and not that of a memory of the first experience. But why not?

After all, such content presumably depends on the content of the previous experience of y: at least, the temporal updating of the representation of y in the second experience must causally depend on the representation of y in the first experience. And it overlaps with its contents too: both experiences represent y more or less in the same manner, except for the change in relative temporal location, and the temporal relations between x, y, and z. In which case, the content in question would naturally fit one relatively standard way of thinking of perceptual memory. Retentionalists, it seems, cannot just declare such contents to be simply perceptual: they either owe a plausible account of perceptual memory which avoids this consequence and helps explain what makes the relevant contents genuinely perceptual, or need to say why those contents don't fall under the conditions determining mnemonic contents. One might also ask why it matters in the end, if the contents in question really are perceptual rather than mnemonic, given the causal and functional (perhaps even phenomenal) similarities between them.[24] If it doesn't really matter, however, the contrast between retentionalism and the snapshot theory, in this respect, may not be so stark as it initially seemed.

The snapshot view has a history of hastily pronounced demise, and if the remarks sketched above are any indication, such pronouncements remain premature – informed, as they often seem to be, by a failure to appreciate all the resources the snapshot theorist has at its disposal. Not only that, but rival accounts have their own blindspots to address, if only to properly demarcate themselves from the snapshot theorist's framework. Much work remains to be done, in any case, to fully develop – and vindicate – a snapshot conception. But at least, if the characterization it promises of the phenomenology of our streams of sensory consciousness is indeed more viable than it has seemed, this suggests a path for a more deflationary theory – less demanding, metaphysically and perhaps even physiologically – of how our sensory experiences convey information about the temporal dimensions of events.

Notes

1 Including Dainton (2000, 2008a, 2010, 2014a, 2014b), Phillips (2010, 2014a, 2014b) and Hoerl (2013).
2 I borrow Dainton's (2010) terminology rather than Lee's, since (a) retentionalism can be cleared of any essential reliance upon memory, as Lee (2014a: 3) and Phillips (2010: 193–195) observe; (b) I prefer to reserve the term "atomism" used by Lee (2014a, 2014c) for another somewhat orthogonal thesis concerning the mereology of experience – see Lee (2014b).
3 Tye (2003), Grush (2007, 2008) and Pelczar (2010a, 2010b) are retentionalists in this sense too, I take it.
4 For instance, Dainton (2000: 114, 129, 132–133; 2008a: 369–371), Tye (2003: 86–88).
5 Contrast Byrne (2009: §2).
6 Despite the ongoing controversy regarding the perdurance of continuants and material objects, almost all participants in these disputes appear to share the assumption that events perdure. See Sider (2001), Hawley (2002), Haslanger (2003) and Hawthorne (2006) on perdurance; and Steward (2000) and Simons (2003) on events.
7 So defined, temporal parts are experiential states or slices with distinctive experiential properties, but needn't be "experiences" themselves, depending on what the latter term is taken to mean – see Grube (2014) for an argument that they aren't.
8 This assumption, note, need only rest on our limited familiarity with the processes at play in the perceptual brain – not on any grand causal theory of mind, let alone a commitment to physicalism.
9 For instance, there is evidence of *visual asynchrony* between different perceivable features. Moutoussis and Zeki (1997) report a processing gap of 100 ms between color and motion when, at certain alternation rates, subjects are presented with objects the color of which changes from red to green as the moving objects reverse direction: color is processed at a higher speed so that subjects mistakenly pair as simultaneous the direction of motion of one stimulus with the color of the subsequent stimulus (i.e., the same object moving in the reverse direction). See Arnold (2010), Eagleman (2010), Moutoussis (2014) and Holcombe (2015) for discussion. There's also evidence that the brightness of a flash can affect processing time: Holcombe (2009, 2015), Eagleman (2010). Not to mention differences in processing times across different modalities (see Holcombe 2009) or even within the same modality (as in the cutaneous rabbit illusion: cf. Geldard and Sherrick 1972; Dennett and Kinsbourne 1992).
10 Perceptual attention, for instance, including the effects of different external attentional cues in otherwise similar settings, can affect judgments of simultaneity and order – as with the phenomenon of "prior entry": see Spence and Parise (2010).
11 The constancy of successive processing time still holds, note, even on Eagleman's (2010) "delayed perception" model, according to which the brain waits (for about 80 ms, Eagleman estimates) for the slower processed stimulus feature (motion) to be bound with the faster processed one (color), but the delay remains constant throughout the successive presentations of those stimuli. For a critical discussion, see Holcombe (2015).
12 Such a picture only aims to portray what happens when things go well. It is silent on what happens when the causal processes underlying neural mechanisms misfire or give way to various mismatches. Neither does it have much to say about stimuli differences (including differences in temporal location) that are either too small, or occur too fast, and thus fall below various detection thresholds.
13 Thus, a temporal part of an extended stimulus might figure in the content of more than one experience in a succession thereof, so that a given temporal part of a stimulus holds multiple causal relations with successive experiences. I lack the space to discuss Lee's "trace" argument for retentionalism, to the effect that temporal information be "represented *all at once*" (Lee 2014a: 13) to "causally impact post-perceptual processing" and be "integrated in the right way" (Lee 2014a: 15). Suffice it to note that, when it comes to how sensory information pertinent to temporal relations can impact upon thought and action, everyone can agree that the relevant information has to be "simultaneously present" in some sense at some point (Ibid.): the question is where that point lies – somewhere in the middle of perceptual processing, or at the interface between perception, memory, and cognition. Even if the first option were granted, the conclusion of the "trace argument" adds a level of complexity to the picture of perceptual processing in Figure 9.1, but needn't be inconsistent with it.

14 That is, the pace isn't so fast as to seem blurry, or so slow as to appear gappy, or even frozen: see Kelly (2005b: 223) for a discussion of Locke and Hume on this point – compare Kelly (2005a).
15 Contrast Dainton (2014a: 177).
16 On the latter, see Coltheart (1980) and Pashler (1998), for a start. On the role of memory, see Le Poidevin (2007: 81, 91, 104–107).
17 See also Chuard (2011) and Grube (2014).
18 Dainton (2000, 2010, 2014a, 2014b) focuses on such phenomenological features of temporal experiences.
19 Compare Le Poidevin (2007: 98–99).
20 I ignore alternative versions of extensionalism – Phillips (2010, 2014a, 2014b) or Hoerl (2013) – owing to the lack of space, and focus on Dainton's more recent defense of his extensionalism: for discussion of some of his earlier arguments (Dainton, 2000, 2008a), see Chuard (2011) and Grube (2014).
21 Contrast Phillips's (2014a: §7.8) embrace of a more holistic explanation, where parts are mere abstractions from a whole. Dainton (2000: chapter 8) seems somewhat reticent to go along with such holism – rightly to my mind (Chuard 2011: §3.5).
22 Compare Grush (2007).
23 Compare Le Poidevin (2007: 58).
24 Compare Phillips (2010: §§6, 9).

References

Arnold, D. (2010) "Relative timing and perceptual asynchrony", in R. Nijhawan and B. Khurana (eds), *Space & Time in Perception & Action*, Cambridge, UK: Cambridge University Press.
Byrne, A. (2009) "Experience and content", *The Philosophical Quarterly* 59(236): 429–451.
Chuard, P. (2011) "Temporal experiences and their parts", *Philosophers' Imprint* 11(11): 1–28.
Coltheart, M. (1980) "Iconic memory and visible persistence", *Perception and Psychophysics* 27(3): 183–228.
Dainton, B. (2000) *The Stream of Consciousness*, London: Routledge.
Dainton, B. (2008a) "Sensing change", *Philosophical Issues* 18(1): 362–384.
Dainton, B. (2008b) "The experience of time and change", *Philosophy Compass* 3(4): 619–638.
Dainton, B. (2010) "Temporal consciousness", in E. N. Zalta (ed.), *The Stanford Encyclopedia of Philosophy*, available at http://plato.stanford.edu/entries/consciousness-temporal/. Accessed 6 June 2004.
Dainton, B. (2014a) "Flow, repetitions, and symmetries: Replies to Lee and Pelczar", in Oaklander, N. (ed.), *Debates in the Metaphysics of Time*, London: Continuum.
Dainton, B. (2014b) "The phenomenal continuum", in Lloyd, D. and Arstila, V. (eds), *Subjective Time: The Philosophy, Psychology, and Neuroscience of Temporality*, Cambridge, MA: MIT Press.
Dennett, D. and Kinsbourne, M. (1992) "Time and the observer: The where and when of consciousness in the brain", *Behavioral and Brain Sciences* 15: 183–247.
Eagleman, D. (2010) "How does the timing of neural signals map onto the timing of perception", in R. Nijhawan and B. Khurana (eds), *Space & Time in Perception & Action*, Cambridge, UK: Cambridge University Press.
Geldard, F. and Sherrick, C. (1972) "The cutaneous 'rabbit': A perceptual illusion", *Science* 178(4507): 178–179.
Grube, E. (2014) "Atomism and the contents of experience", *Journal of Consciousness Studies* 21(7–8): 13–33.
Grush, R. (2007) "Time and experience", in T. Müller (ed.), *Philosophie Der Zeit*, Frankfurt, Germany: Klosterman.
Grush, R. (2008) "Temporal representation and dynamics", *New Ideas in Psychology* 26(2): 146–157.
Haslanger, S. (2003) "Persistence through time", in M. Loux and D. Zimmerman (eds), *The Oxford Handbook of Metaphysics*, Oxford, UK: Oxford University Press.
Hawley, K. (2002) *How Things Persist*, Oxford, UK: Oxford University Press.
Hawthorne, J. (2006) "Three-dimensionalism", in *Metaphysical Essays*, Oxford, UK: Oxford University Press.
Hoerl, C. (2013) "'A succession of feelings, in and of itself, is not a feeling of succession'", *Mind* 122(486): 373–417.
Holcombe, A. (2009) "Seeing slow and seeing fast: Two limits on perception", *Trends in Cognitive Science* 13(5): 216–21.
Holcombe, A. (2015) "The temporal organization of perception", in J. Wagemans (ed.), *Oxford Handbook of Perceptual Organization*, Oxford, UK: Oxford University Press.
Hume, D. (1739) *A Treatise of Human Nature*, P. Nidditch (ed.), 1978, Oxford, UK: Oxford University Press.

James, W. (1890/1952) *The Principles of Psychology*, New York: Dover.

Kelly, S. (2005a) "The puzzle of temporal experience", in Brook, A. and Akins, K. (eds), *Cognition and Neuroscience*, Cambridge, UK: Cambridge University Press.

Kelly, S. (2005b) "Temporal awareness", in Thomason, A. and Smith, D. W. (eds), *Phenomenology and Philosophy of Mind*, Oxford, UK: Oxford University Press.

Le Poidevin, R. (2007) *The Images of Time: An Essay on Temporal Representation*, Oxford, UK: Oxford University Press.

Lee, G. (2014a) "Temporal experience and the temporal structure of experience", *Philosophers' Imprint* 14(3): 1–21.

Lee, G. (2014b) "Experiences and their parts", in Bennett, D. and Hill, C. (eds), *Sensory Integration and the Unity of Consciousness*, Cambridge, MA: MIT Press.

Lee, G. (2014c) "Extensionalism, atomism, and continuity", in Oaklander, N. (ed.), *Debates in the Metaphysics of Time*, London: Continuum.

Locke, J. (1690) *An Essay Concerning Human Understanding*, P. Nidditch (ed.), 1975, Oxford, UK: Oxford University Press.

Moutoussis, K. (2014) "Perceptual asynchrony in vision", in Lloyd, D. and Arstila, V. (eds), *Subjective Time: The Philosophy, Psychology, and Neuroscience of Temporality*, Cambridge, MA: MIT Press.

Moutoussis, K. and Zeki, S. (1997) "A direct demonstration of perceptual asynchrony in vision", *Proceedings of the Royal Society B: Biological Sciences* 264(1380): 393–399.

Pashler, H. (1998) *The Psychology of Attention*, Cambridge, MA: MIT Press.

Pelczar, M. (2010a) "Must an appearance of succession involve a succession of appearances?" *Philosophy and Phenomenological Research* 131(1): 49–63.

Pelczar, M. (2010b) "Presentism, eternalism, and phenomenal change", *Synthese* 176(2): 275–290.

Phillips, I. (2010) "Perceiving temporal properties", *The European Journal of Philosophy* 18(2): 176–202.

Phillips, I. (2014a) "The temporal structure of experience", in Lloyd, D. and Arstila, V. (eds), *Subjective Time: The Philosophy, Psychology, and Neuroscience of Temporality*, Cambridge, MA: MIT Press.

Phillips, I. (2014b) "Experience of and in time", *Philosophy Compass* 9(2): 131–144.

Reid, T. (1855) *Essays on the Intellectual Powers of Man*, Boston, MA: Derby.

Sider, T. (2001) *Four-Dimensionalism: An Ontology of Persistence and Time*, Oxford, UK: Oxford University Press.

Simons, P. (2003) "Events", in Loux, M. and Zimmerman, D. (eds), *The Oxford Handbook of Metaphysics*, Oxford, UK: Oxford University Press.

Spence, C. and Parise, C. (2010) "Prior entry: A review", *Consciousness and Cognition* 19(1): 364–379.

Steward, H. (2000) *The Ontology of Mind: Events, Processes, and States*, Oxford, UK: Oxford University Press.

Tye, M. (2003) *Consciousness and Persons*, Cambridge, MA: MIT Press.

10

ATOMISM, EXTENSIONALISM AND TEMPORAL PRESENCE

Oliver Rashbrook-Cooper

Introduction

This chapter concerns the debate between Atomism and Extensionalism. Historically, the Atomist Theory of temporal experience was characterised by the claim that experiences of temporally extended items are strictly instantaneous (Broad 1923; Husserl 1991). More recent formulations of the Atomist Theory eschew, or at least remain neutral about, commitment to strictly instantaneous experiences (Tye 2003; Le Poidevin 2007; Lee 2014). What these different varieties of Atomism have in common is the thought that the temporal properties of experience have no role to play in explaining how we come to be aware of items and their temporal properties.

Proponents of the Extensionalist Theory of temporal experience, by contrast, claim that experiences of items exhibiting certain temporal properties (for example, duration and succession) must themselves exhibit those properties (Foster 1982; Dainton 2006; Hoerl 2013; Phillips 2014; Soteriou 2013). Extensionalists hold that the temporal properties of experience have an explanatory role to play in accounting for how it is that we are able to perceive items possessed of temporal properties as such. This contrast between Atomism and Extensionalism is represented in Figure 10.1.

In this chapter, I argue that we should adopt the Extensionalist Theory of temporal experience. I argue that the Atomist Theory cannot simultaneously account for two important

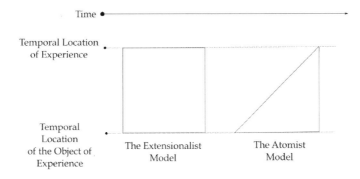

Figure 10.1 Contrast between Atomism and Extensionalism

features of perceptual experience: Temporal Presence, and negative Temporal Transparency. The Extensionalist Theory, by contrast, is able to explain both of these phenomena. We can begin by considering negative Temporal Transparency.

Negative Temporal Transparency

Temporal Transparency is distinct from a more wide-ranging pair of claims about the "transparency" of experience that we can call "General Transparency". General Transparency consists of the following two claims: when we introspect, we find the worldly objects of perceptual awareness and their properties (positive claim), and not anything that is merely a property of experience itself (negative claim).

"Temporal Transparency" likewise consists of two claims about perceptual experience: one positive and one negative. The idea is nicely expressed by Soteriou in the following:

> Introspectively, it doesn't seem to one as though one can mark out the temporal location of one's perceptual experience as distinct from the temporal location of whatever it is that one seems to be perceptually aware of. Furthermore, it seems to one as though the temporal location of one's experience depends on, and is determined by, the temporal location of whatever it is that one's experience is an experience of.
>
> *(Soteriou 2013: 89–90)*

The negative feature of Temporal Transparency is the claim that one cannot distinguish between the temporal location of a perceptual experience and the apparent temporal location of its object.[1] The positive feature is that one's experience seems to "depend upon, and be determined by" the temporal location of its object. Temporal Transparency is a phenomenal feature of experience – a feature that captures something important about what it is like to perceptually experience temporal items.

My argument depends only upon the negative Temporal Transparency claim, so we can put the positive transparency claim to one side in what follows. Henceforth, I refer only to *negative* Temporal Transparency when I refer to Temporal Transparency. We can now consider the second phenomenal feature: Temporal Presence.

Temporal Presence

In his *Theory of Knowledge* manuscript, Russell distinguishes between two senses of "present" – one of which he calls the "temporal" sense of "present":

> Whatever I experience is, in one sense, "present" to me at the time when I experience it, but in the temporal sense it need not be present – for example – if it is something remembered.
>
> *(Russell 1992: 38)*

Here Russell is attempting to articulate something distinctive about the way that we are acquainted with objects in perception and sensation. The objects of perception and sensation seem to be "temporally present" to us in a way that they are not in other kinds of experience – for instance, memory and imagination.[2, 3]

We need to be careful, in setting up these issues, to distinguish between different kinds of imagination and memory. We can distinguish between propositional and sensory imagining/ remembering. Propositional imagining and remembering is imagining/remembering that *p*. There need not be any mental imagery associated with propositional imagining/remembering – for instance if I remember that Henry VIII was born in 1491, or imagine that he was born in 1500.

It is also possible for us to engage in sensory imagining/remembering. In these cases, we do exploit our grasp of what it was or might be like to experience the item in question. Items that are remembered or imagined in this manner are present to the mind in a way that more closely resembles perceptual experience than propositional imagining/remembering, but they nevertheless do not seem to be temporally present.[4]

We should agree with Russell that there is a distinctive way in which items feature as "temporally present" in perceptual experience for the following reasons. First, it is generally the case that perceptual experience of an object renders actions involving that object immediately appropriate in a way that imagination and memory do not. Second, if we are confronted in perception with an event/process, we tend to judge on the basis of that perceptual experience that the event or process is happening *now* – we don't do this on the basis of mere imagination/memory of an event/process.

Temporal Transparency and Temporal Presence

Perceptual experience, then, is such that:

(a)   One cannot distinguish between the temporal location of one's perceptual experience and the apparent temporal location of its object (Temporal Transparency).
(b)   It renders actions and *now*-judgements immediately appropriate (Temporal Presence).

There is reason to think that there is an important connection between these two features of perceptual experience. Those varieties of experience that do not exhibit Temporal Presence also do not exhibit Temporal Transparency. To demonstrate this, we can turn again to the cases of imagination and memory in order to see how we are able to discern a difference between the temporal location of the experience and its object(s).

This is perhaps clearest in the case of episodic recollection, in which we recall one of our past experiences – for instance, walking down the main street of a particular city for the first time. In this case, we are aware that the act of recollection is not taking place at the same time as the recollected event. We take the recollected event to have occurred before the act of recollection. The experience is not temporally transparent, and neither does it exhibit Temporal Presence.

Likewise, imagination is not temporally transparent. Of course, there is such a thing as imagining what it would be like for a tarantula to be crawling across my hand *right now*. This kind of imagining differs from merely imagining what it would be like for a tarantula to crawl across my hand in general, and from imagining what it would be like for a tarantula to crawl across my hand in this very room. When I imagine the tarantula to be crawling across my hand *right now*, I am imagining the tarantula is *temporally present* to me.

However, even if I imagine the tarantula is crawling across my hand *right now*, I needn't take the imagined tarantula to be *genuinely* temporally present to me. This helps to illustrate the connection between Temporal Presence and Temporal Transparency. I don't take the tarantula to be temporally present because the imagined tarantula doesn't seem to have any temporal location at all. It would not make sense for me to ascribe to the imagined tarantula a location in the objective temporal order of things.

In these varieties of experience, there is a distinction to be drawn between the temporal location of experience and the apparent temporal location of its object. In the case of perceptual experience, however, there is no such distinction to be drawn. When we introspect our perceptual experience, we do not find any objects of experience that seem to (a) occupy a temporal location earlier than the location of perceptual experience (as in the memory case), or (b) possess no temporal location (as in the imagination case).

There thus seems to be an important connection between Temporal Transparency and Temporal Presence. Below, I argue that both of these features of perceptual experience are best explained by the Extensionalist account of temporal experience, according to which the temporal location of experience and the apparent temporal location of its object(s) are identical (see "Extensionalism"). First, however, I want to set out the case against the Atomist account. In order to do this, we must introduce a third phenomenal feature of temporal experience: the Continuity of Consciousness.

The Continuity of Consciousness

"Continuity" can be illustrated by considering what it is like to experience a C-major scale played very quickly. When we experience the scale, we experience every note in the scale as following on from the note that immediately preceded it. According to the Atomist, accounting for this specific example requires the positing of a particular arrangement of atomic experiences.

In order to account for Continuity, it is necessary for the Atomist to insist that our streams of consciousness consist of a series of atomic experiences whose contents temporally overlap (represented in Figure 10.2 below). If the contents of atomic experiences were not to overlap in this way, the Atomist Theory would not be consistent with Continuity. To see this, consider Figure 10.3. There, a series of atomic experiences whose contents don't overlap are represented. This means that not all of the notes that constitute the chromatic scale are experienced together with the notes that preceded them. Note G would thus not be perceptually experienced as following on from note F. This is inconsistent with the Continuity of Consciousness.

While it appears unavoidable that the Atomist posits that the stream of consciousness has the kind of structure set out in Figure 10.2, it is this very structure that ultimately proves problematic for the account. A consequence of the required overlap of atomic experiences is that the Atomist is committed to the thought that we remain in perceptual contact with temporally short-lived items for a duration greater than the duration occupied by such items. It is this feature that will ultimately prove problematic for the Atomist when attempting to account for both Temporal Transparency and Temporal Presence.

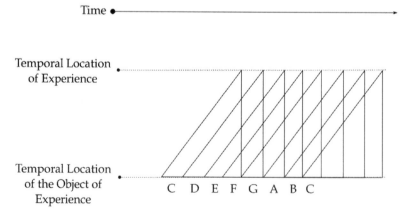

Figure 10.2 Series of atomic experiences whose contents temporally overlap

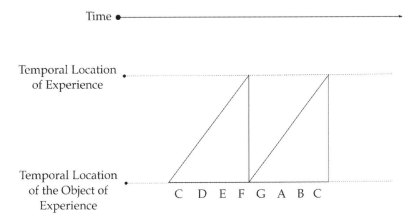

Figure 10.3 Series of atomic experiences whose contents do not overlap

Atomism: Specious Present Theory and Memory Theory

We can begin by considering two different varieties of Atomism: Specious Present Theory, and Memory Theory. According to the Specious Present Theory, everything that features in a single atomic experience is experienced as temporally present. According to the Memory Theorist, only a "snapshot", without discernable earlier and later temporal parts, is experienced as temporally present. For items to be "temporally present" in the sense I am interested in here, is simply for them to bear the above-discussed connections to action and judgement. To keep the discussion manageable, I remain neutral about what is involved in items featuring in experience in this way.[5]

We can begin by considering the Specious Present Theory,[6] according to which everything featuring in an atomic experience is experienced as temporally present. Figure 10.4 illustrates the Atomist model of the stream of consciousness. From this diagram, it is clear that the Atomist account proposes that the duration for which a subject experiences a brief item – in this case, a brief flash of light – is greater than that item's own duration.

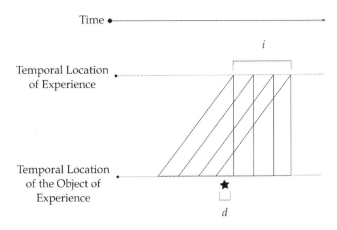

Figure 10.4 Atomist model of the stream of consciousness

This feature of the Specious Present Theory is problematic, as it means that (a) our judgements about what is going on now will be systematically misleading, and (b) the relationship between the temporal content of perceptual experience and judgement will go awry.

As is clear from Figure 10.4, the flash is perceptually represented over interval i (though of course it is not represented as occupying interval i). Assuming that the objects of perceptual experience are always experienced as temporally present, this means that the flash is experienced as temporally present over the course of interval i.

Over the interval i, perceptual experience will thus incline one towards judging "the flash is occurring now". However, given that the flash has a much shorter duration than i, this judgement, at some point over the interval i, will inevitably come out false.[7] What this illustrates is that, if the Specious Present Theory version of Atomism is adopted, perceptual experience will be misleading as a basis for judgements concerning brief items that are going on now – perceptual experience will incline one towards making false judgements of this kind.

While this first problem concerns the relationship between judgement based upon perceptual experience and reality, the second problem for the Specious Present Theory concerns the relationship between perceptual experience and judgement. In the model of experience represented in Figure 10.4, the flash is represented as possessed of duration d. This duration is shorter than the duration occupied by interval i – the interval for which the flash is perceptually represented.

If perceptual experience represents the flash as possessed of duration d, then this content ought to explain certain things about the judgements I might make about the flash, and actions involving the flash that I might attempt to perform. In particular, I ought to be disposed to attempt to act directly upon that item only for duration d. I also ought to be disposed to judge that the item is possessed of duration d. Most crucially, however, if perceptual experience represents the item as possessed of duration d, I should only be inclined to judge that the item is going on now for a maximum interval of duration d.

This principle certainly seems to be true when we consider the relationship between beliefs about duration and judgements about what is going on now. If I am told that some event that I know will last five seconds has just this instant begun to occur, I will only be inclined to judge "the event is going on now" for a maximum of five seconds. In this case of belief, the represented duration of an event determines the interval for which I will be inclined to judge "the event is going on now". If we conceive of perceptual experiences as possessed of representational content that pertains to duration, then we can reasonably expect this same principle to apply – namely, that a perceptual representation of an event with duration d will incline me to judge "the event is going on now" for an interval of duration d.

However, adopting the Specious Present Theory version of Atomism means that, in the case of perceptual experience, the relationship between represented duration and judgement about what is going on now goes awry. If I perceptually represent an item as possessed of duration d, I should only be inclined to judge that the item is going on now for a maximum of duration d. On the Atomist model, however, I will be inclined to make this judgement for an interval greater than d.

The Atomist picture of the stream of consciousness is thus doubly problematic if one adopts the Specious Present Theory. It presents a problematic picture of not just the relationship between judgement and reality, but also between perceptual experience and judgement. Given the problems faced by the Specious Present Theory, an Atomist might be inclined instead to adopt the Memory Theory.

According to the Memory Theory,[8] only a snapshot of what is perceptually presented to a subject in a single Atomistic experience is temporally present. This proposal raises the question of the status of the remainder of the snapshot – if it is not experienced as temporally present, how is it experienced? The Memory Theorist proposes that at least part of the remainder is experienced as *past* (see, for instance, Le Poidevin 2007 and Husserl 1991).

The Memory Theory doesn't entail that items with duration *d* are experienced as temporally present for interval *i*. Rather, on this view, items are experienced as temporally present only for a moment, and they are then experienced as increasingly *past*. The Memory Theory thus avoids the problematic results about Temporal Presence that faced the Specious Present Theory.

The problem facing the Memory Theory, however, is that it is inconsistent with Temporal Transparency. As noted earlier, when we introspect, we are not able to discern any difference between the temporal location of perceptual experience and the apparent temporal location of the object of experience. The Memory Theory, however, entails that such a difference should be discernable, for some of the objects of perceptual experience will be given as *past*.

When I introspect perceptual experience, the target of my introspection is my *present* perceptual experience. If the content of perceptual experience is as the Memory Theorist proposes, it should sometimes seem to me that I am *now* aware of an item that seems to be located in the past.[9] When I introspect, I should be able to discern items experienced as occupying temporal locations earlier or later than "now", i.e. earlier or later than the time at which I experience them. However, as we have seen in the discussion of Temporal Transparency, such a distinction is not available in the case of perceptual experience.

The Memory Theory, while avoiding the problems concerning Temporal Presence that trouble the Specious Present Theory, is ultimately itself unsatisfying, as it is inconsistent with the Temporal Transparency of temporal experience. Given that both varieties of Atomist Theory face difficulties in accounting for the phenomenal features of temporal experience, we have reason to adopt the Extensionalist Theory. In the remainder of the chapter, I set out an Extensionalist account.

Extensionalism

The root of the problems facing the Atomist Theory in both its Specious Present Theory and Memory Theory incarnations is its commitment to the thought that the temporal extent of experience and the apparent temporal extent of its object are not identical. The Extensionalist Theory, by contrast, rejects this and is consistent with the claim that the temporal extent of experience and the apparent temporal extent of its object are one and the same. This enables the Extensionalist Theory to explain both Temporal Transparency and Temporal Presence without running into the problems that faced the Atomist. We can begin by considering Temporal Presence.

Recall that we have introduced Temporal Presence in terms of (a) appropriateness of certain actions and *now*-judgements, and (b) a contrast with imagination and memory. In order to provide an account of Temporal Presence, then, all that is required is that we provide an explanation of (a) why certain actions and *now*-judgements are appropriate, and (b) why objects *don't* seem temporally present in cases of imagination and memory.

One temptation at this point might be to think of an account of Temporal Presence as requiring us to specify some extra ingredient that features in perceptual experience/sensation. For example, if we were to think, as Russell does, that both imagination and perception/sensation involve some form of acquaintance with objects, then it might seem that in order to account for Temporal Presence we need to specify the additional feature of sensational/perceptual acquaintance that explains why we act and judge on their basis in the way that we do.[10]

However, accounting for Temporal Presence doesn't require that we adopt this strategy. In order to explain why it is appropriate for us to perform certain actions and to form *now*-judgements upon the basis of perceptual experience, we need only appeal to the fact that the apparent temporal location of the object of experience is, in general, a reliable guide to the *actual* location of the object of experience. And we can explain why objects don't seem temporally present in the cases of imagination and memory by appeal to the additional complexity of imagination/memory relative to perception.

In his discussion of "unarticulated constituents", Perry notes that, in certain cases, the subject of an experience need not be (and indeed usually is not) explicitly represented in that experience. Consider the perceptual experience of left and right. The objects of perception can be represented egocentrically as to the left or to the right. In having such experiences, I learn about how objects in the environment are situated relative to me. However, as Perry notes, there are cases in which "I am not in the field of vision: no component of my visual experience is a perception of me" (1992: 137). This raises the question: How then can this experience provide me with information about how objects are related to me?

Perry suggests that the reason explicit representation of the self isn't required in spatial vision is that "the eyes that see and the torso or legs that move are parts of the same more or less integrated body" (Ibid.: 151). This general feature of a subject's situation renders explicit representation of the subject redundant. Again, in Perry's words, the perceptual experience "need only have the burden of registering differences in [the] environment, and not the burden of identifying the person about whose relation to the environment perception gives information with the person whose action it guides" (Ibid.).

The lesson here is that, in order for a perceptual experience of something to the left or right to guide action and judgement for a particular subject, all that is required is that the subject *has* that experience. No additional feature of experience need be built into the perceptual relation in order to explain why it is appropriate for *this* subject, as opposed to any other, to have their action and judgement guided by the experience.

An analogous explanation applies in the case of temporal location. To see this, note first that the temporal location of the subject having the perceptual experience is, as a matter of fact, the same as the temporal location as the subject who is acting and judging upon its basis. Second, note that, in general, the speed at which information from objects reaches our sensory organs (in the case of vision, the speed of light, and audition, the speed of sound) is in general sufficiently high so as to guarantee the presence of the object in our environment.

If I stand in perceptual relation to some object, then that object will in general feature in my immediate environment and so be available for immediate action. While the temporal locations of experience and object are not strictly speaking identical, due to the time lag generated by the speed of light/sound, these lags are normally sufficiently miniscule that perceptual experience remains a good guide to the object of perception featuring in our environment.

These general features of a subject's situation can explain why it is appropriate for us to act immediately upon the basis of perceptual experience, and also why it is appropriate for us to judge, when perceiving an event or process, that the event is going on now. "Now" represents a time concurrent with the temporal location of the judgement in question – and the temporal location of an experience-based judgement about what is going on now will in general be the same (for the reasons given above) as the temporal location of the object of experience.

The objects of experience thus need not be experienced as possessing presentness,[11] nor be experienced *as* concurrent with our experience of them,[12] in order to explain why it is appropriate for us to perform actions and make *now*-judgements upon their basis.[13] Note that the above explanatory strategy is unavailable to the Atomist, for whom the temporal location of experience and the apparent temporal location of its object must always come apart, due to the fact that the temporal extent of the latter always exceeds that of the former. Note also that the

Extensionalist is not vulnerable to the objection raised to the Specious Present Theory above as the Extensionalist is not committed to the idea that we remain in perceptual contact with items for an interval greater than that of the items' own duration.

Before turning to a discussion of imagination and memory, we can briefly consider how the Extensionalist is able to explain Temporal Transparency. Above, we saw that the Memory Theory is inconsistent with Temporal Transparency because it proposes that the objects of perceptual experience are given as *past*. This rendered a distinction between the temporal location of experience and the apparent temporal location of its object discernible, and thus rendered the Theory inconsistent with Temporal Transparency.

The Extensionalist Theory, by contrast, has a simple explanation of Temporal Transparency. On the Extensionalist Theory, no temporal part of an experienced event or process is experienced as either earlier or later than one's experience of it. This serves to explain why there is no discernible difference between the temporal location of experience and the apparent temporal location of its object.

Imagination and memory

Thus far, I have suggested that the Extensionalist need not claim that the objects of perceptual experience are experienced as *now* or as *present* in order to accommodate the idea that experience exhibits Temporal Presence. I have also suggested that in order to explain Temporal Transparency the Extensionalist can simply propose that items are not experienced as occurring either earlier or later than our experience of them. This strategy is, however, vulnerable to a challenge based upon the nature of imaginative experience.

As noted earlier, imaginative experience doesn't involve items being experienced as in any particular temporal relation to the subject. Accordingly, the objects of imagination are not experienced as occurring either earlier or later than our experience of them. Therefore, one might wonder whether the Extensionalist can account for the Temporal Transparency of perceptual experience by simply claiming that items are not experienced as occurring either earlier or later than our experience of them – for they are not experienced in this way in imaginative experience either. One might also wonder why the objects of imagination aren't experienced as temporally present, given that imaginative experience also doesn't involve its objects being experienced as *now* or as *present*.

In this final section, I address this challenge as well as completing the account of Temporal Presence by setting out an explanation of why the structure of imagination and memory are such that they exhibit neither Temporal Presence nor Temporal Transparency.

I noted earlier that the objects of imagination and memory are not experienced as temporally present, and neither are imagination or memory temporally transparent. In order to account for this difference, I propose that we adopt the account of imagination and memory found in, for instance, Vendler 1984, Peacocke 1985 and Martin 2001, according to which we imagine objects by representing a perceptual experience of the object.

This proposal enables us to respect the way in which these experiences are phenomenally similar to their perceptual counterparts, while also accounting for their differences. Most important for our purposes is seeing how adopting this strategy will help to explain the lack of Temporal Presence and Temporal Transparency.

In thinking of imagination and memory as taking the form "representation of perceptual experience of object", we need not claim that the subject has anything other than the intention to imagine the object itself and, relatedly, we need not claim that the subject is able to attend to the phenomenal character of the imagined experience without attending to the imagined object. Neither need we think that in representing a perceptual experience of an object we need imagine a subject having that experience. The claim is that, in Vendler's words:

> The *materia ex qua* of all imagination is imagined experience: sights and sounds – not as physical things, but as pure perceptions – and other sensations, feelings and sentiments . . . These are the atoms out of which the world of the imagination, subjective and objective, is constructed.
>
> *(1984: 51)*

We have seen that perceptual experience doesn't allow for a distinction to be drawn between the temporal location of experience and object – it doesn't allow for this distinction because the temporal location of experience and the apparent temporal location of the object are as a matter of fact the same. Imagination and memory, by contrast, do make available a distinction between the temporal location of experience and object.

Let us focus first upon the case of imagination. Let's say I imagine what it would be like if a spider were crawling across my hand. In this case I will typically imagine seeing and/or feeling the spider crawl across my hand – I will thus be representing a visual and/or tactual experience of a spider crawling across my hand. As discussed earlier, in imagining this I need not be imagining that the spider be crawling across my hand at any particular time – this kind of imaginative experience need not assign any kind of temporal location to the crawling incident.

Insofar as I am representing a perceptual experience, it isn't possible for me to distinguish between the temporal locations of the represented experience or the object of that represented experience. This is because, as we have seen, the Temporal Transparency claim is distinctive of perceptual experience. It also isn't possible for me to distinguish between the temporal location of the representation of the perceptual experience and my own temporal location – these are of necessity the same. The available distinction in temporal location is thus between the temporal locations of me and my act of representation on the one hand, and the experience and its object on the other.

In imagining or remembering an object or event, I have suggested that I am representing a perceptual experience of the object or event. In representing a perceptual experience of that object or event, I am representing a perspective upon that object or event. Martin expresses this point about a spatial perspective as follows:

> When one visualizes a red light as to the left, it need not be that one visualizes it as actually to the left of where one is . . . rather one visualizes it as to the left of the point of view within the imagined situation. We can think of the perspectival elements of the visualizing as aspects of the imagined visual experience . . . Perspective in vision determines the actual orientation of objects relative to the subject, but does not do so in visualizing.
>
> *(Martin 2001: 273)*

Imagining or remembering a visual experience of an object as to the left makes available a distinction between the spatial perspective within the imagined experience and the spatial perspective of the person doing the imagining. Analogously, in the case of Temporal Presence, the imagined object is temporally present as regards the imagined experiential perspective, but we are able to distinguish between the imagined experiential perspective and our own current temporal perspective.

The structure of imaginative experience thus makes available a distinction between (a) the temporal location from which I represent the object of imagination, and (b) the temporal location of the object of imagination. It does this by making available a distinction between my actual experiential perspective and the imagined experiential perspective. It is this feature of the model of imagination and memory that can render the objects of imagination present to mind in a way that is more akin to perception than pure thought without rendering them *temporally* present. This distinction also serves to explain why imaginative experience is not temporally transparent – because our actual and imagined experiential perspectives are discernibly distinct.

This account of the structure of imagining explains why the objects of imagination aren't taken to be temporally present. Thinking of the imagination in this way explains why its objects lack the phenomenal immediacy of perceptual experience – we are not directly acquainted with the objects of imagination as we are in perception. I have also suggested that sensory imagination and memory share a similar structure: they both involve representing a perceptual experience of an item. This proposal clearly raises the question of what distinguishes these two varieties of experience, and of what might be involved in our grasp of the fact that the remembered items are given as past.

However, attempting to account for this difference between sensory memory and imagination is too great a task to carry out in this chapter. My proposal is rather that by thinking of memory as involving representation of experiences we can at least explain why the objects of memory are not taken to be temporally present. Adding the extra ingredient that explains why these objects are taken to be past is then a matter for another time.

Conclusion

I hope to have shown that Extensionalism is the most promising account of two important aspects of the phenomenology of temporal experience: Temporal Presence and Temporal Transparency. Atomism is unable to adequately account for both of these simultaneously. Adopting the Specious Present Theory variety of Atomism generates problems when we consider the relationship between judgement, experience and reality. Adopting the Memory Theory variety renders the Atomist account inconsistent with Temporal Transparency.

I hope also to have shown that providing an explanation of the Temporal Presence of items in perceptual experience need not involve appeal to our experiencing things *as present* or *as happening now*. While it might initially appear tempting to invoke such contents in order to give an account of the contrast between imagination, memory and perception, the phenomenon of Temporal Presence does not point to the complexity of the perceptual relation, but rather to the complex structure of our acts of imagination and memory.

Notes

1 This claim is consistent with two different views. First, one might think that we have *no* access to the temporal location of our perceptual experiences at all. Second, one might think that we have such access, but that we always find that the temporal locations of experience and object are one and the same. One might be inclined to adopt the first view if it seems implausible that when we introspect we find, as well as the objects and properties we are perceptually presented with, some additional things: "experiences". However, even if one were inclined towards this way of thinking, it is nevertheless plausible that we are able to discern the times at which we are perceptually presented with objects. Further, it is equally plausible that we are unable to distinguish between the time at which we are perceptually presented with an object and the apparent temporal location of that object. This claim is all that the argument against Atomism that I provide depends upon and is a claim that one could agree with even if convinced that we don't find "experiences" when we introspect.

2 Russell also entertains the proposal that the objects of imagination are not temporally present: "It may be that ... in imagination the object is given without any temporal relation to the subject" (1992: 56). I defend this view in this chapter.

3 In what follows, I refer only to perception, but my remarks are intended to also apply to cases of sensation (experiences of pain, for example).

4 Henceforth, references to imagining/remembering will be references to this second, sensory, variety of imagining/remembering.

5 Typical accounts of what it is for an item to be temporally present in experience involve appeal to the thought that items are experienced as possessing *presentness* (e.g. Broad 1923), or are experienced as *now*, i.e. as simultaneous with experience (e.g. Husserl 1991).

6 Proponents of the Specious Present Theory include Broad (1923) and Tye (2003).

7 It is important to distinguish here between two varieties of "now"-judgement. The first variety of "now"-judgement picks out an interval of time within which the judgement falls – an interval that can sometimes be extremely long (e.g. "Now the crust of the earth has cooled, it is possible for complex life to flourish"). The second variety picks out an interval of time concurrent with the judgement. This second variety of "now"-judgement is the kind of judgement that we would express via an utterance of "The race is starting *now!*" – where we intend that only "*now!*" picks out the relevant portion of time in question. It is the second variety of "now"-judgement that I have in mind in the following discussion.

One important role played by perceptual experience is that of supplying us with the basis of knowledge about the fine-grained temporal location of events – the kind of knowledge expressed by judgements of this second variety. On the basis of perceptual experience, we can come to know of an event not merely that it occurs within a window of time within which the judgement falls, but that it occurs concurrently with one's "now"-judgement.

8 The Memory Theory is so-called because it involves the thought that our awareness of temporally extended items involves at least some of their temporal parts being given as *past* – in being given as past, our awareness of such items thus shares something in common with memory. Proponents of the Memory Theory include Husserl (1991) and Le Poidevin (2007).

9 A parallel argument can be run for the idea that objects can be experienced as *future*.

10 As Russell notes in this connection: "If . . . imagination involves no time-relation of subject and object, then it is a simpler relation than sensation, being, in fact, merely *acquaintance with particulars*" (Russell 1992: 63). The thought here is that to explain temporal presence, we need to explain the additional complexity of the perceptual relation relative to imagination.

11 See, for instance, Craig 2000 and Smith 1994.

12 See, for instance, Husserl 1991 and Williams 1994.

13 For a similar proposal, see Hoerl 2009. Sympathy for this idea can also be found in Le Poidevin 2015: "To perceive something as present is simply to perceive it: we do not need to postulate some extra item in our experience that is 'the experience of presentness'".

References

Broad, C. D. (1923) *Scientific Thought*, London: Routledge & Kegan Paul.

Craig, W. (2000) *The Tensed Theory of Time: A Critical Examination*, Dordrecht, The Netherlands: Kluwer Academic Publishers.

Dainton, B. (2006) *Stream of Consciousness: Unity and Continuity in Conscious Experience*. 2nd ed., London: Routledge.

Foster, J. (1982) *The Case for Idealism*, London: Routledge & Kegan Paul.

Hoerl, C. (2009) "Time and tense in perceptual experience", *Philosophers' Imprint* 9(12): 1–18.

Hoerl, C. (2013) "'A succession of feelings, in and of itself, is not a feeling of succession'", *Mind* 122(486): 373–417.

Husserl, E. (1991) *On the Phenomenology of the Consciousness of Internal Time (1893–1917)*, J. B. Brough (trans), Dordrecht, The Netherlands: Kluwer Academic Publishers.

Le Poidevin, R. (2007). *The Images of Time: An Essay on Temporal Representation*, Oxford, UK: Oxford University Press.

Le Poidevin, R. (2015) "The experience and perception of time", in E. N. Zalta (ed.), *The Stanford Encyclopedia of Philosophy* (Summer 2015 Edition), available at http://plato.stanford.edu/archives/sum2015/entries/time-experience/. Accessed 1 January 2016.

Lee, G. (2014) "Temporal experience and the temporal structure of experience", *Philosophers' Imprint* 14(3): 1–21.

Martin, M. G. F. (2001) "Out of the past: Episodic recall as retained acquaintance", in C. Hoerl and T. McCormack (eds), *Time and Memory*, Oxford, UK: Oxford University Press, pp. 257–284.

Peacocke, C. A. B. (1985) "Experience, imagination, and possibility", in J. Foster and H. Robinson (eds), *Essays on Berkeley: A Tercentennial Celebration*, Oxford, UK: Oxford University Press, pp. 19–35.

Perry, J. (1992) "Thought without representation", in J. Perry (ed.), *The Problem of the Essential Indexical and Other Essays*, New York: Oxford University Press, pp. 205–226.

Phillips, I. (2014) "The temporal structure of experience", in D. Lloyd and V. Arstila (eds), *Subjective Time*, Cambridge, MA: MIT Press, pp. 139–158.

Russell, B. (1992) *Theory of Knowledge: The 1913 Manuscript*, London: Routledge.

Smith, Q. (1994) "The phenomenology of A-time", in N. Oaklander and Q. Smith (eds), *The New Theory of Time*, New Haven, CT: Yale University Press, pp. 351–359.

Soteriou, M. (2013) *The Mind's Construction: The Ontology of Mind and Mental Action*, Oxford, UK: Oxford University Press.

Tye, M. (2003) *Consciousness and Persons*, Cambridge, MA: MIT Press.

Vendler, Z. (1984) *The Matter of Minds*, Oxford, UK: Clarendon Press.

Williams, C. (1994) "The phenomenology of B-time", in N. Oaklander and Q. Smith (eds), *The New Theory of Time*, New Haven, CT: Yale University Press, pp. 360–372.

11

RETHINKING THE SPECIOUS PRESENT

Simon Prosser

Introduction

In this chapter I shall argue that despite its current popularity the doctrine of the *specious present*, or at least every current version of it, should be rejected.[1] In its place I propose two different accounts, which deal with experiences of two different kinds of change. The first is what I shall call the *dynamic snapshot theory*, which accounts for the way we experience continuous changes such as motion and other motion-like phenomena. The second account deals with the way we experience discontinuous changes, those for which there is no finite rate of change. In defending both accounts, but especially the latter, I shall argue that much of the current debate implicitly presupposes a problematic Cartesian view about the nature of conscious experience. If this view is rejected – as I think it should be – then a different kind of account emerges that avoids commitment both to the specious present and to its main current rival, the cinematic view.

The current orthodoxy

A significant majority of philosophers writing about temporal experience today accept one or another version of the doctrine of the specious present, according to which conscious experiences have temporally extended contents. That is to say, they hold that the experienced present consists not of an instant, but of an extended interval of time. The duration of this interval is usually taken to be small: around half a second, say. There are also those who, following James (1890), use the phrase "specious present" to denote a temporal interval of several seconds. In such cases, however, it usually turns out that what they have in mind is a kind of "psychological present" associated with short-term memory. I have nothing to say about the latter notion of the specious present; I shall be concerned only with the former. The question before us is whether, or in what sense, conscious perceptual experiences – experiences with a phenomenology, or "something that it is like" (in Nagel's (1974) sense) – have a short but temporally extended content.

There are two main versions of the doctrine which, following Dainton (2008, 2010), I shall call the *retentional* and *extensional* models. Suppose the duration of the specious present is *n* seconds. According to the retentional model (Broad 1938; Lee 2014), there is no reason to expect that the experience itself should occur over a period of *n* seconds; the experience need not be, and typically is not, extended to the same degree as its content. Traditionally, the experience itself was assumed to take place instantaneously; however, Geoffrey Lee (2014) has made a strong case for the view that the experience itself may take some time to occur. Crucially, however, even on Lee's "extended atomism" version of retentionalism, it is not the case that an experience of the short sequence A–B–C involves the subject experiencing A, then experiencing B, then experiencing C. Instead, there is a single experience of the sequence A–B–C. According to the extensional model (Foster 1979, 1982: chapter 16, 1991: 246–250; Dainton 2000, 2001, 2008; Hoerl 2009, 2013; Phillips 2010, 2011, 2014; Rashbrook 2013), by contrast, the temporal structure of the experience matches the temporal structure of its content. Thus if the content of the experience is an interval of time *n* seconds long, then the experience itself lasts *n* seconds. Moreover, most extensionalists also assume that the internal structure of the experience matches the structure of the experienced events; if the content of the specious present is the sequence A–B–C, then the subject experiences A, then experiences B, then experiences C.

The most discussed competitor to the doctrine of the specious present is the *cinematic* model (defended by Chuard 2011. The name is used in Dainton 2010 and elsewhere.) According to the cinematic model, experience consists of a series of "static snapshot" experiences, the content of which is a single instant of time. Change, on this view, is experienced only indirectly, through the combination of a current experience with a very recent memory.

Arguments for the specious present

The literature on temporal experience contains surprisingly few direct arguments in favour of the specious present. The most common type of argument appeals to the fact that we can perceive change. As C. D. Broad observed, there is at least a strong prima facie case for thinking that we do perceive certain kinds of change, such as motion, rather than inferring them from a combination of immediate experience and episodic memory:

> We do not merely notice that something *has* moved or otherwise changed; we also often see something *moving* or *changing*. This happens if we look at the second-hand of a watch or look at a flickering flame. These are experiences of a quite unique kind; we could no more describe what we sense in them to a man who had never had such experiences than we could describe a red colour to a man born blind. It is also clear that to see a second-hand *moving* is a quite different thing from "seeing" that an hour-hand *has* moved. In the one case we are concerned with something that happens within a single sensible field; in the other we are concerned with a comparison between the contents of two different sensible fields.
>
> *(Broad 1923: 351)*

It does indeed seem that motion perception has a robust phenomenology; it involves a phenomenological element that is quite unlike anything that can be encountered in the perception of a static scene. Many philosophers have dismissed the cinematic model, with its "static snapshot" content, as incapable of accounting for this phenomenology, and have assumed that it can only be accounted for by some version of the doctrine of the specious present. The idea seems to be that because a single specious present would contain the moving object at different positions at different times, motion would be part of the content of the experience.

Sometimes a more direct argument is given. This usually takes something like the following form. Motion, and indeed change of any other kind, essentially takes time. An experience whose content consisted in the state of the world at an instant could only have in its content that which could occur within the instant. It thus could not include anything essentially extended in time. Therefore, given that motion essentially takes time but can be perceived, the content of an experience cannot be an instant.[2]

Similar arguments can be given by appealing to anything perceptible but essentially extended in time. Consider sounds, for example. There are differing views about what one is aware of when one hears a sound. Suppose, for present purposes, that when one hears a sound, the object of one's experience is an objective entity such as a *process* or *event* – the fingernails scraping across the blackboard, the wind moving through the trees, the vibration of the violin string, and so on.[3] It seems plausible that a process essentially takes time; there is no such thing as an instantaneous process. In that case, it might be argued, since the object of auditory experience is essentially temporally extended, auditory experience cannot have an instantaneous content.

Arguments of this kind are not sound; they fail because they mistakenly assume that an experience with an instantaneous content can have, in its content, only that which could occur instantaneously. This is simply false, for extended processes nevertheless have instantaneous parts, even if the nature of such parts depends on what occurs at other times. All that can be concluded from such arguments is that the surrounding temporal context must be detected by the system that produces the experience. Rather than continue to address this point in the abstract, however, I shall illustrate it by sketching a theory, which I shall call the *dynamic snapshot theory*, that allows for motion to be perceived without recourse to the specious present.

One small concession must be made. Perception has a finite resolution, and this affects the degree to which experience can be said to have precisely one time as its content. By analogy, consider spatial perception. All else being equal, below a certain size, it is impossible to tell which of two very small objects is the smallest; all extremely small objects will look the same, at least insofar as they reflect or produce the same amount of light. This means that using vision alone it would be impossible to detect the difference between a point-sized object and a small but slightly extended one. Something similar is true of temporal experience: below a certain temporal extension, one cannot detect differences.[4] It does not follow from this, however, that experience has a temporally extended content in any interesting sense. It follows only that it is indeterminate, to a small degree, which moment in time is the content of the experience. If the doctrine of the specious present is to account for the experience of change, then it requires instead a duration long enough to include different, temporally discriminable states.

The dynamic snapshot theory

Suppose that having a perceptual experience were like being aware of a kind of internal picture. If that picture were a snapshot of a single instant, it would contain no motion. Objects would be depicted as occupying a single location in space; there would be no way to tell which objects were moving, or in what way. A photograph taken with an exposure time greater than zero would show objects as slightly blurred due to their motion, but if the picture really depicted a single instant then there would be no clues of this sort. In order to judge that there was motion, one would have to compare the picture with another picture taken at a different time, showing the objects in different places.

But conscious experience is not at all like an awareness of an inner picture. To think of experience in that way would be to fall into a problematic Cartesian view of the conscious mind. I shall say more about this in the final section, but for now note the obvious difficulty with the "inner picture" model: if perception of the external world involved awareness of an inner picture, an account would have to be given of this "awareness". But this could not be accounted for in the same way as perceptual awareness of the external world, for an infinite regress of inner pictures would threaten. If it worked in some other way, however, then it is unclear why that account would not already explain awareness of the external world, removing the need for the inner picture.

We can make better sense of experience by thinking in terms of the *content* of the experience. The content of an experience is what the experience is *of*. When you see a tree next to a hill, the content of your experience is that there is a tree next to a hill (along with your own perspective on the scene and whatever further details are perceived). Sometimes philosophers claim that experiences have *representational* contents. The main point of this is to allow that the experience could be falsidical; it could have the content that there is a tree next to a hill, even if this were not the case. But for present purposes, we can side-step the debate over whether experiences are representational by focusing on the veridical case and using the word "content" as neutral with regard to the notion of representation (different theories of perception, such as naïve realism and intentionalism, will still say different things about falsidical cases).

Now, the "inner picture" model makes it tempting to think that if the content of an experience concerned only a single time, it could not include motion. But, as Broad notes in the passage quoted above, "we also often see something *moving* or *changing*". "Moving" is a state that something can be in at an instant, even though it can only be in that state by virtue of being in other places at other times. So the motion of an object, including its direction and rate, could be part of the content of an experience, even if the content of that experience concerned only what was the case at one specific time. Suppose that a perceived object, O, were moving with velocity *v*, where *v* is a vector (that is, it encodes both the rate and direction of motion). Then the content of the experience could be: O is moving with velocity *v*. A corresponding claim could be made for any other case in which there was an ongoing process whose state could be specified by a vector at a single time, even if the existence of the state at that time was metaphysically dependent on what was the case at other times. Cognitive scientists sometimes refer to all such continuous perceptible changes, such as the steady dimming of a light, the shifting of a colour hue or the rise and fall in the pitch or volume of a sound, as "motion" (see Rensink 2002). I shall refer to them as *continuous* changes, or sometimes as *motion-like* changes.[5]

It would, of course, take time for the brain to *detect* motion, for example by comparing patterns of retinal stimulation at different times. But it clearly does not follow from this that the resulting experience must have a temporally extended content. The necessary properties of the stimulus can differ from those of the resulting experience.

I shall call the theory outlined above the *dynamic snapshot theory*.[6] It is a "snapshot" theory because it accounts for the experience of motion without appeal to a specious present, but it is very different from the cinematic or "static snapshot" theory. I agree with those who hold that the latter theory cannot adequately account for the phenomenology of motion experience, or the experience of other motion-like changes.

The dynamic snapshot theory gains some plausibility from various empirical sources. Perhaps one part of the intuition that snapshot experiences can only be static is connected with the idea that for there to be an experience of change, the content of one's experience must itself change over time. But this appears to be false; there are many examples of motion illusions in which motion is experienced despite the fact that no part of the content of the experience changes (apart from the time itself). The best-known example is the waterfall illusion (Wohlgemuth 1911) in which, after a period of looking at steady motion such as motion of the water in a waterfall, when the subject looks at a stationary scene, the scene appears to move in the opposite direction to the motion that had been perceived. Yet subjects report that the positions of objects in the scene do not appear to change. There are many similar phenomena: see, for example, the "fine grain motion illusion" (Exner 1875; Thorson *et al.* 1969), in which motion is experienced between points that are indistinguishably close together, or the phenomenon in which motion is observed in a two-frame sequence where one frame is below the threshold for pattern detection (Morgan and Cleary 1992). In all such cases, motion is experienced even though relevant aspects of the content of the experience remain constant. If experience were anything like an encounter with an inner picture, such cases ought not to be possible.

The standard explanation for the waterfall illusion appeals to neural adaptation that leads to a shift in the base activation level in populations of neurons that are associated with motion detection in early visual processing (see Anstis *et al.* 1998). Due to this shift, the adapted neurons indicate motion in the absence of a moving stimulus. The suggestion is then that the brain processes information in a variety of different streams, each of which computes something different. The content of conscious experience comprises various different contents thus computed. Sometimes, due to neural adaptation, those processes produce the result that an object is moving, despite there being no variation over time in its independently computed location.

Whether or not this is the correct explanation for the waterfall illusion, the very possibility of such an explanation illustrates the possibility that computational processes in the visual system could yield the content that the object *is moving* (with velocity *v*) at a specific time.

According to the dynamic snapshot theory, what is experienced as happening at *t* is in no part constituted by what is experienced as happening at other times close to *t*. This conflicts with what is said by certain other theories (e.g. the extensional account defended by Phillips (2010, 2011, 2014), if I understand it correctly). But it does not follow that the dynamic snapshot theory entails the possibility of a subject who experiences motion at *t* and has no experience as of any other times close to *t*. For all the dynamic snapshot theory says, there might be other reasons for denying such a possibility (see Prosser 2016: 148–154 for related discussion).

Discontinuous changes

Although the dynamic snapshot theory gives a straightforward account of the experience of motion and other continuous changes, it cannot explain the experience of discontinuous changes. These are changes such that there is one state of affairs up to and including time *t*, but a different state of affairs at all times thereafter, and hence no finite rate of change between the states. An example would be a light that illuminated or changed colour instantly, or at least quickly enough that the human visual system would not distinguish the change from one that was genuinely instantaneous. Suppose the light were red at all times up to and including *t*, and green at all times thereafter. There would be no time at which the change was taking place; the light would always be determinately one colour or the other, and would never be in a state of transition between the two. (Perhaps no real light changes colour instantaneously. But there are real lights that change colour sufficiently quickly to be indistinguishable, to our limited visual systems, from a genuinely instantaneous change. See Prosser 2016: 128–129 for further discussion of this issue.) Consequently, if the content of experience included only a single instant of time, it would be impossible for the change of colour to be part of the content of any experience. Yet there does seem to be some sense in which we can see a light instantly change colour.

One option at this point would be to regard discontinuous change as a counterexample to the dynamic snapshot theory and consequently to reject it. I believe, however, that a good case can be made for giving two different accounts, one for the experience of continuous changes – the dynamic snapshot theory – and a different account for the experience of discontinuous changes. It seems plausible that the human brain should detect different kinds of changes in different ways. Given the finite nature of human beings, those systems that detect the rate of a continuous change must have a threshold beyond which the rate is too quick for the brain to measure. It follows that discontinuous changes cannot be detected in the same way. But it is nonetheless useful to be able to perceive rates of change in those cases in which the rate falls within the measurable range. Many organisms may also have a need to detect discontinuous changes. Consequently, it should not seem surprising if different kinds of change are detected using different systems. I shall suggest below that the empirical evidence weighs in favour of this. Finally, there is arguably a significant phenomenological difference between experiences of continuous and discontinuous changes. When one perceives a continuous change such as motion, there is a robust phenomenology associated with the change, as illustrated by Broad's comments about the second hand of the watch. It is robust enough to be straightforwardly attended to. But the phenomenology of discontinuous change seems far more elusive; by the time there is anything to notice, the change, and the experience of it, has already taken place.

I shall develop a tentative model of discontinuous change perception that will initially appear to resemble the cinematic model. In the next section, however, I shall argue that the cinematic, retentional and extensional models can only be distinguished from one another if a problematic Cartesian assumption is made concerning the nature of conscious experience. If that assumption is rejected, as I think it should be, then we arrive at a better theory according to which the question of whether experience has a temporally extended content should be rejected rather than answered.

Consider how the human visual system could detect discontinuous changes (I shall concentrate on visual examples, but there is no obvious reason why a broadly similar story could not be told for other sensory modalities). One very simple model would say that all of the perceived information in a scene is retained in some kind of short-term memory and compared with the scene a moment later. This would require a lot of memory capacity and a lot of information processing. The result would be that any change in the visible properties of a scene should be noticed. But this is not the case. Studies of *change blindness* (Rensink *et al.* 1997; Simons and Levin 1997) show that when a change is sufficiently slow or is masked by a flicker in all or a large part of the scene, the subject may fail to notice even quite a large change. Consequently, most cognitive scientists have rejected the simple model just outlined (see Rensink 2002: 260–264 for further details of empirical evidence against the model).

Instead, the following model has become fairly widely accepted among empirical scientists working on change detection (see Rensink 2002 and O'Regan 2002). Among other things, the early stages of visual processing detect visual *transients*, rapid changes in the luminance or colour of the retinal image. At the stage of processing at which transients are detected, no details of the change itself have yet been computed. The function of the detection of the transient appears to be to automatically draw the subject's visual attention to the location of the transient. Ordinarily, where there is no attention, experiential information is not retained. One function of attention, however, is to cause information concerning the attended location to be briefly retained in a short-term memory buffer. This in turn makes it possible to compare the current scene with what went immediately before in the region in which the transient was detected. Consequently, when a transient draws attention to a location, the subject typically notices what has changed at that location. At unattended locations, however, a change may be missed, because information about the preceding state at that location is discarded before the subject can become aware that anything has changed. When changes are slow, no transient is produced; and when there is a flicker, the visual system is swamped with transients, making it relatively unlikely that attention will be directed to the location at which the change occurs. This is thought to be why change blindness occurs.

This empirical model of change detection fits well with the phenomenology of discontinuous change. My hypothesis is that when a transient is detected, this produces an element of experience with a content something like "a change has just occurred here" or perhaps "a change is occurring here", where "here" refers to the perceived location of the transient. This helps explain the familiar experience of noticing a brief change in peripheral vision without being able to say exactly what changed.[7] It also, I suggest, accounts for the fact that when one does notice a discontinuous change, there is something phenomenological associated with the change, but something rather less robust than the phenomenology of continuous changes. This is associated with a feeling that the perceived object was in a different state a moment before (a state which one may be able to recall).

Given the appeal to a short-term memory that is compared with current experience, the account of the experience of discontinuous change suggested here does have a certain amount in common with the cinematic model. Note that the memory in question is unlikely to be long-term episodic memory; the case is not like Broad's example of seeing that the hour hand has moved by remembering that it was in a different place at an earlier time. In the model under discussion, it is not supposed that there is any kind of conscious inference involved. The short-term memory buffer in which the earlier state of the object is stored presumably allows a more direct kind of comparison. I shall now argue, however, that the distinction between the cinematic, extensional and retentional models should itself be rejected, and the theory just proposed should be reconstrued accordingly.

Rejecting Cartesian *qualia*

Do the cinematic, retentional and extensional models differ empirically? If they did, then it would be an empirical question which, if any, was correct. But it is not clear that they do differ empirically. At any rate, each seems committed to the following claims about the information processing involved when someone perceives a change and reports on it. For simplicity, consider a simple discontinuous change, as described above: an object is red at all times up to and including *t*, and green at all times thereafter. Each theory must acknowledge that first, information must be received to the effect that the object is red, and that this information must still be present in the brain when it subsequently detects that the object is green. These two pieces of information then interact to produce a verbal report to the effect that the object changed from red to green. According to the cinematic model, the information is retained as a short-term memory, which is compared with current experience. According to the retentional model, the information that the object was red at times up to *t* is retained and combined with the information that the object was green thereafter to produce an experience whose content is that the object changed from red to green. The experience of the change then produces the verbal report. Finally, the extensional theory holds that the object is experienced as red, then experienced as green, and the temporally extended experience that encompasses both states is an experience of the object changing from red to green.[8] Again, this temporally extended experience somehow leads to the verbal report, though in order to do so some trace of the "red" experience must be retained for long enough to influence the report.[9]

So, on the face of it, all three theories tell much the same story about information processing; they all agree that information about the "red" state of the object must be retained and combined with information about the "green" state in order to produce the verbal report that the object changed from red to green. At any rate, I shall take it as a working hypothesis that all of these theories tell the same story about the way information is processed during the perception of discontinuous change. If this turns out to be incorrect, then it should be possible, in principle, to rule out at least one theory on empirical grounds. But let us suppose that this is not so; the theories are empirically equivalent. The difference between them, then, seems to consist entirely in what they say about conscious experiences. Given a flow diagram of the information process-ing that is involved in experiencing discontinuous change, the difference between the theories will amount to differences in which parts of the diagram should be designated as constituting (or causing) conscious experiences and which should be designated as memories.[10] To put this another way, the difference will consist in where the *qualia* appear in the diagram.

This assumes that there are such things are qualia. Daniel Dennett (1988, 1991) has argued, however, that qualia, as commonly construed, are a myth (he does not, of course, deny that there are conscious experiences in some broad sense, or that there is "something that it is like" to have a conscious mind). The notion of qualia to which Dennett is opposed says that qualia are ineffable, intrinsic, private and directly or immediately apprehensible. This, for Dennett, is associated with the notion of the mind as a *Cartesian theatre*, where the qualia are like actors on a stage, appearing before an audience (the "self"), such that the qualia enter and leave the stage at a definite time, and there are definite facts about such matters as what counts as the cessation of the conscious experience and the beginning of the reaction to it.

I shall not rehearse Dennett's arguments here. But if his characterization of the problematic assumption is even roughly right (and we need not accept every detail of his description of the putative qualia to think so), then it is not clear that the distinction between the three main models of temporal experience can be sustained. Let us start by considering the difference between the cinematic and retentional models. Suppose that a change from A to B is experienced. The former theory says that change is experienced because a current perception of A is combined with a very recent short-term memory of B; the latter says that change is experienced because a single experience has the content that A is followed by B. Provided we restrict attention to discontinuous changes, is there any way that introspection could tell us which of these theories was correct? How would we know what to look for? It does not seem at all clear that we have any capacity to distinguish, introspectively, between the different models. Indeed, if both mod-els agree on all matters of information processing, as I suggested above, then both models should predict exactly the same verbal reports of conscious experiences. If we then compare either of these two models with the extensional model, we find exactly the same situation: introspection cannot, and should not, be able to settle which model is correct.[11]

It will nevertheless seem to many people that there has to be an answer. The three models disagree concerning *when* the various experiences occur, or when a given experience begins and ends. According to the cinematic and extensional models, the subject experiences A, then experiences B. But according to the cinematic model this consists in a sequence of independent snapshot experiences, whereas according to the extensional model it is a single experience that takes time to occur. According to the retentional model, A and B both belong to the content of a single experience, with no sense to be made of the claim that the experience of A precedes the experience of B.

All of this makes sense only if it is assumed that a conscious experience begins and ends at a precise, determinate moment in time – that incoming information crosses a "finish line" at some determinate point and thereby enters consciousness, and then exits at a similarly determinate moment. This is very much the notion of the Cartesian theatre; a given actor (i.e. a quale) is either on the stage or is not, and must enter and leave the stage at determinate moments in time. If one accepts this, then one must hold that one of the three theories of temporal experience is correct. But why must we accept it? Presumably, it is part of an implicit theory that has qualia as part of its ontology. If we reject the theory, we may also reject the ontology. I suggest that we have no good reason to accept this theory. It entails that there are facts about matters about which we have no reason to believe that there are facts. The three models do not differ in what they say about information processing, or in what they say about introspection (or so I am assuming). So there is no observation, of any kind, that could determine which was correct.

Most philosophers these days hold that we should not, in general, reject ontological claims for purely verificationist reasons. It is not always the case that if we cannot detect the difference empirically, then it is meaningless to suppose that there is a difference. But conscious experience may be an exception to this. Qualia are supposed to be properties of experiences whose whole essence is to determine "what it is like" for the subject who has the experience. But can there be facts about what it is like that transcend one's ability to introspect, even in principle? The issue is not whether introspection is an infallible guide to conscious experience. Clearly it is not; there are many examples that show subjects can make mistaken judgements about their conscious experiences. But to say that introspective error is possible is one thing; it is quite another thing to claim that there could be intelligible differences in the way we model conscious experiences, such as those described above, such that it would be impossible in principle for introspection ever to discern which model was correct. When it comes to conscious experience, if we cannot tell the difference, even in principle, then we should be deeply suspicious of the claim that there really is a difference.

Perhaps there could be some kind of a priori argument that would show one theory to account for experience better than another. Perhaps one or more of the models could be shown to be internally inconsistent or problematic in some other way. I cannot rule this out. But the anti-Cartesian considerations described above suggest that we should consider another possibility: that the issue over which the cinematic theorists, retentional theorists and extensional theorists are disagreeing is entirely chimerical. If we relax the assumption that there is a definite moment at which information "enters" or "leaves" consciousness, or that a conscious experience starts and ends at determinate moments in time, then we can describe temporal experience in a different way. Perhaps we might think of the question of when information enters consciousness as comparable to the question of when exactly some information has been received by a large organization such as the BBC. The information might reach different parts of the organization at different times, with no principled reason to pick one of them as more important than the others. Following this line of thought, we might eschew the notion of *an* experience and say instead, for example, that there are long periods during which a subject is experiencing the world, and that during such a period – a period that does not start at a precise, determinate instant – the subject becomes aware that A is followed by B, which is followed, by C, and so on. There is indeed something that it is like for the subject during that episode of conscious experience, but what it is like is perhaps exhausted by what the subject experiences (the various events and the sequence in which they occur). There need be nothing more to say than that.

Notes

1 A more detailed account of the ideas presented in this chapter can be found in Prosser 2016: chapter 5.
2 A clear example of this kind of argument is given by Grush (2007: 1), but similar arguments are encountered frequently.
3 See Casati and Dokic 1994, Pasnau 2007 and O'Callaghan 2007 for theories of sound broadly of this kind.
4 For vision, the threshold for detecting distinct stimuli is 20 ms, for audition it is 2–3 ms, and for touch it is 10 ms (see Ruhnau 1995). See also Pockett 2003. In all sensory modalities, there is the same threshold for the discrimination of temporal order: around 20–40 ms (Hirsh and Sherrick 1961; Pöppel 1997).
5 What about sounds? If the perceived object of auditory experience is an event or a process, as suggested above, could this be represented by a vector? I see no reason why not, though I have space only for a very limited explanation here. At any given moment, the auditory signal can be represented by a frequency spectrum, representing the intensity at different wavelengths of sound at a given time.

This corresponds to the frequency distribution of a perceived physical vibration (the sound source) at that time, and this could be represented by a vector.

6 Something similar is briefly outlined by Robin Le Poidevin (2007: 88–92), who also makes a similar appeal to the waterfall illusion (see below). While writing this chapter, subsequent to completing Prosser 2016 (in which I also used the name "dynamic snapshot theory"), I discovered that Valtteri Arstila (2016) has also used the same name for a similar view (Arstila's ambitions for the dynamic snapshot theory appear to be a little more extensive than mine, but he does not distinguish sharply between continuous and discontinuous change, so I'm not certain of his view regarding the latter. Arstila also has an interesting take on the much-discussed "postdiction" phenomena.) I have also heard Bradford Skow suggest something similar to the dynamic snapshot theory in a talk in June 2015.

7 There is good independent evidence that change detection (i.e. detecting *that there was* a change) is distinct from change identification (i.e. identifying *what* changed). See, for example, Turatto and Bridgeman 2005, especially p. 596.

8 It is not clear to me what makes it the case that the temporal stages of the experience are parts of a unified experience, on the extensional model, or how this would account for the phenomenology. See Prosser 2016: 143–148 for details.

9 Lee (2014) raises a similar point as an objection to the extensional model; see his discussion of the "trace integration" argument.

10 See Prosser 2016: 156–157 for diagrams of this kind.

11 Phillips (2014) does suggest that introspection favours extensionalism, but his argument for this interpolates from long-term to short-term experience in a way that strikes me as problematic. See Prosser 2016: 143–146 for discussion. However, Phillips (2010) does also briefly express some doubts, not entirely dissimilar to those expressed here, about how much of a difference there really is between the main competing theories.

References

Anstis, S., Verstraten, A. J., and Mather, G. (1998) "The motion aftereffect", *Trends in Cognitive Sciences* 2(3): 111–117.

Arstila, V. (2016) "The time of experience and the experience of time", in B. Mölder, V. Arstila and P. Øhrstrøm (eds), *Philosophy and Psychology of Time*, vol. 9 of the series *Studies in Brain and Mind*, Dordrecht, The Netherlands: Springer.

Broad, C. D. (1923) *Scientific Thought*, London: Kegan Paul.

Broad, C. D. (1938) *An Examination of McTaggart's Philosophy (Volume II, Part 1)*, Cambridge, UK: Cambridge University Press.

Casati, R., and Dokic, J. (1994) *La Philosophie du Son*, Nîmes, France: Chambon.

Chuard, P. (2011) "Temporal experiences and their parts", *The Philosophers' Imprint* 11(11): 1–28.

Dainton, B. (2000) *Stream of Consciousness: Unity and Continuity in Conscious Experience*, London: Routledge.

Dainton, B. (2001) *Time and Space*, Durham, UK: Acumen. Second edition 2010.

Dainton, B. (2008) "Sensing change", *Philosophical Issues* 18(1): 362–384.

Dainton, B. (2010) "Temporal consciousness", in E. N. Zalta (ed.), *The Stanford Encyclopedia of Philosophy* (Fall 2010 edition). Available at http://plato.stanford.edu/archives/fall2010/entries/consciousness-temporal/. Accessed 1 December 2015.

Dennett, D. C. (1988) "Quining qualia", in A. Marcel and E. Bisiach (eds), *Consciousness in Contemporary Science*, Oxford, UK: Oxford University Press.

Dennett, D. C. (1991) *Consciousness Explained*, London: Penguin.

Exner, S. (1875) Experimentelle Untersuching an der einfachsten psychischen Process, *Pflügers Archiv* 11: 403–432.

Foster, J. (1979). "In *self*-defence", in G. F. Macdonald (ed.), *The Problem of Pure Consciousness*, London: Macmillan.

Foster, J. (1982) *The Case for Idealism*, London: Routledge and Kegan Paul.

Foster, J. (1991) *The Immaterial Self*, London: Routledge.

Grush, R. (2007) "Time and experience", in T. Müller (ed.), *The Philosophy of Time*, Frankfurt, Germany: Klosterman.

Hirsh, I. J. and Sherrick, C. E. (1961) "Perceived order in different sense modalities", *Journal of Experimental Psychology* 62(5): 423–432.

Hoerl, C. (2009) "Time and tense in perceptual experience", *Philosophers' Imprint* 9(12): 1–18.

Hoerl, C. (2013) "'A succession of feelings, in and of itself, is not a feeling of succession'", *Mind* 122(486): 373–417.

James, W. (1890) *The Principles of Psychology*, New York: Henry Holt. Reprinted Cambridge, MA: Harvard University Press, 1983.

Le Poidevin, R. (2007) *The Images of Time*, Oxford, UK: Oxford University Press.

Lee, G. (2014) "Temporal experience and the temporal structure of experience", *The Philosopher's Imprint* 14(3): 1–21.

Morgan, M. J. and Cleary, R. (1992) "Effects of contrast substitutions upon motion detection in spatially random patterns", *Vision Research* 32(4): 639–643.

Nagel, T. (1974) "What is it like to be a bat?" *The Philosophical Review* 83(4): 435–450.

O'Callaghan, C. (2007) *Sounds*, Oxford, UK: Oxford University Press.

O'Regan, J. K. (2002) "Change blindness", *Encyclopedia of Cognitive Science*, Oxford, UK: Wiley.

Pasnau, R. (2007) "The event of color", *Philosophical Studies* 142(3): 353–369.

Phillips, I. (2010) "Perceiving temporal properties", *European Journal of Philosophy* 18(2): 176–202.

Phillips, I. (2011) "Indiscriminability and experience of change", *The Philosophical Quarterly* 61(245): 808–827.

Phillips, I. (2014) "The temporal structure of experience", in D. Lloyd and V. Arstila (eds.), *Subjective Time: The Philosophy, Psychology, and Neuroscience of Temporality*, Cambridge, MA: MIT Press, pp. 139–158.

Pockett, S. (2003) "How long is 'now'? Phenomenology and the specious present", *Phenomenology and the Cognitive Sciences* 2(1): 55–68.

Pöppel, E. (1997) "A hierarchical model of temporal perception", *Trends in Cognitive Sciences* 1(2): 56–61.

Prosser, S. (2016) *Experiencing Time*, Oxford, UK: Oxford University Press.

Rashbrook, O. (2013) "An appearance of succession requires a succession of appearances", *Philosophy and Phenomenological Research* 87: 584–610.

Rensink, R. A. (2002) "Change detection", *Annual Review of Psychology* 53(1): 245–277.

Rensink, R. A., O'Regan, J. K. and Clark, J. J. (1997) "To see or not to see: The need for attention to perceive changes in scenes", *Psychological Science* 8(5): 368–373.

Ruhnau, E. (1995) "Time-gestalt and the observer", in T. Metzinger (ed.), *Conscious Experience*, Paderborn, Germany: Ferdinand Schöningh/Imprint Academic, pp. 165–184.

Simons, D. J. and Levin, D. T. (1997) "Change blindness", *Trends in Cognitive Science* 1(7): 261–267.

Thorson, J., Lange, G. D. and Biederman-Thorson, M. (1969) "Objective measure of the dynamics of a visual movement illusion", *Science* 164: 1087–1088.

Turatto, M. and Bridgeman, B. (2005) "Change perception using visual transients: Object substitution and deletion", *Experimental Brain Research* 167(4): 595–608.

Wohlgemuth, A. (1911) *On the After-Effect of Seen Movement: Volume 1*, Cambridge, UK: Cambridge University Press.

12

MAKING SENSE OF SUBJECTIVE TIME

Geoffrey Lee

Introduction: subjective time

In what sense, if any, is there such a thing as "subjective time", as distinct from the objective temporal relations between physical events? With most perceptible features, like color, taste, smell, shape, distance, lighting, etc., it is widely accepted that experience is not simply a direct confrontation with an objective feature; in particular, we need a distinction between the objective feature, and the *way we experience it*. One way of understanding the question about subjective time is this: is there a "way we experience" duration, and if so, how should it be characterized? This chapter is an overview of some of the problems we encounter trying to answer this question. The overall message is that although there are strong arguments for believing in subjective features of duration experience in a fairly strong sense, there are pitfalls to avoid in thinking about them, and serious problems understanding how they are individuated.

A classic entry point for thinking about the idea of a "subjective aspect" of experience, is through the notion of *inter-subjective phenomenal variation*, of which we can distinguish weak and strong varieties. We have weak inter-subjective variation in experience of a feature if it is possible for different subjects to have different experiences of that feature of an object or event in a given context. Weak variation is pretty uncontroversial, because most philosophers and psychologists accept the possibility of *perceptual illusion*. So in the case of duration, we might both hear the same sound, but have different experiences of its duration, because one of us is suffering from a perceptual illusion of its duration. Such duration illusions are widely documented in the empirical literature (see Eagleman (2008) and Grondin (2010) for reviews). This at least forces us to distinguish between objective duration and *apparent* objective duration, and gives us one important sense in which there is "subjective time".

More controversial is the possibility of *strong inter-subjective variation*: variation between subjects in the experience of a stimulus feature, despite the normal functioning of the subjects' perceptual systems, and despite the subjects' experiences *not* being illusory. For example, some have argued that strong variation in color experience is possible[1]: your color qualia might be inverted (or otherwise variant) with respect to mine, despite both our visual systems functioning normally, delivering us accurate information about the surfaces of objects.

Such variation is at least prima facie conceivable for duration experience. For example, it's conceivable that other well-functioning creatures could be living in an experiential world that is analogous to a time-lapse video or a slow-motion replay. Consider the hummingbird: perhaps their experience of a 500 msc flash is comparable to a human's experience of a 2 second flash, and, more generally, they experience changes as occurring more slowly than we do by some determinate factor. But does this really make sense? What would it consist in, and what would show that it is possible?

The image of "slow-motion" experience suggests a very specific picture of what strong variation in duration experience would consist in. It suggests that there is a parameter, something like "rate of flow", that measures how fast events pass through the stream of consciousness for a given subject, which could vary between us and, say, a hummingbird. One main goal of this chapter is to explain why we should be wary of this picture. It embodies a number of substantive assumptions about duration experience which I want to tease out, and which are not necessarily required for thinking that duration experience has strongly variable subjective features. But first, a little more clarificatory setup is in order.

It's important to note how varied duration experience is: in particular, we experience duration at different temporal scales, and in different sensory modalities.[2] At small temporal scales (less than about 1–2 seconds), our experience of duration is analogous to our perceptual experience of visual features like shape, color, lighting, or features of sounds like pitch and timbre, in that it feels like an immediate perceptual confrontation with a feature of a currently perceived event. Beyond this scale, duration experience is in an interesting category that straddles memory and perception. Consider the example of reflecting on how long you have been reading this chapter. This involves a memory of an event – your starting to read the chapter. But it is also quasi-perceptual, in the sense that it involves a perceptual tracking mechanism (a mental timing device) that delivers awareness of information *about the present*: namely, how present events are temporally related to a past event.

For each of these wide-ranging forms of duration experience, I'll assume that there is "something it's like" to have the experience, so we can talk about the features of experience that constitute this "duration phenomenology", which I'll call "experiential duration properties", or ED properties. Different accounts of the metaphysics of such phenomenal properties (and there's a whole zoo of these) can be applied here. In particular, they might consist of relations of acquaintance or representation to objective duration properties,[3] or they might have a more contingent relationship to external stimulus features, being more like internal subjective signs of external temporal properties. These distinctions will become relevant later in the chapter. What will now be important is the (more metaphysically neutral) claim that there exists a space (or spaces) of such ED properties, a *duration quality space*, structured by *similarity relations*, the kind of similarity relations we have (perhaps highly fallible) access to, when we make temporal similarity judgments based on experience.

What makes it at least *conceivable* that there is strong inter-subjective variation for duration is that we can imagine subjects having dispositions to have experience with systematically different ED properties in response to the same stimuli: that is, they have different *psychometric mappings* from physical durations into a duration quality space. (A psychometric mapping is a function telling us what the probable psychological or behavioral response is to a certain stimulus; of course, because perception is noisy, there will typically be variation in the response a particular stimulus causes; and the mapping may only be valid in a limited range of contexts.) For example, the hummingbird's psychometric mapping might map an objective duration onto a different duration experience from the human mapping.

Actually, as mentioned, what we tend to imagine here is something much more specific, something more like *time flowing at different rates for different subjects*. It is as if the stream of consciousness is a liquid that can flow at different speeds in different subjects at different times.

I'll now turn to the task of articulating the assumptions suggested by such a picture. I'll argue that contemplating the ways in which they might fail reveals a wider range of ways in which there could be strong inter-subjective variation in duration experience than mere variation in "rate of flow" (if that is even a well-defined quantity).

Rates of flow

What would it take for differences in dispositions to have duration experience to be capturable be a single, variable, *quantity*, the "rate of flow"? First, it requires that all the duration experiences of different individuals, and also of a single individual, be drawn from a single quality space. Call this *comparability*. If comparability fails, then some duration experiences across or even within individuals are in *alien* quality spaces, much as human color experience and bat echolocation experience may be alien. Comparability is non-obvious; for example, different creatures might measure time using very different timing mechanisms, and code it in different ways on totally different hardware. If there are such differences, is it clear that our experiences are comparable with theirs? (Compare how, if we found such differences in the detection and coding of surface reflectance features, we wouldn't assume comparable *color* experience.) Even *intra*-subjective comparability is not totally obvious; for example, maybe visual and auditory duration form different spaces, or duration experiences at different scales form different spaces.

Notice that if comparability fails, then this gives us a (less obvious) way in which strong variation could obtain. We just need to assume that if a creature's temporal experiences form an alien quality space, this doesn't mean that their experience is illusory or that they aren't optimally functioning. But that seems reasonable, since the mere fact that they have alien experiences doesn't set up any relevant asymmetry between us and them.

Even if we assume comparability, we may not have *unitarity*. This is the assumption that there is a single psychometric function modeling a single subject's experiences across modalities, at different scales and domains. Strict unitarity is actually quite unrealistic – as any psychophysicist will tell you. The issue is controversial, but much research suggests that human cognitive timing doesn't use a single internal clock, but rather a variety of devices in different scales and domains with at least slightly different psychometric characteristics (Buhusi and Meck 2005; Johnston *et al.* 2006). In terms of the metaphor of "flow", it is more like there are many inter-connected streams running noisily and unevenly at approximately the same speed, rather than one single smooth stream; therefore there can be no single precise value for the "rate of flow" (let's be careful though: the stream metaphor is inept in certain other ways I'll bring out below).

Note that we are very familiar with experiences where unitarity fails (although they may involve illusions). For example, consider "time flying when you're having fun". This is a case where mechanisms keeping track of the passage of time at the level of minutes/hours function differently, changing the psychometric relation for temporal experience at the minute/hour scale; nonetheless the psychometric function for *millisecond* timing typically remains normal: it is not as if having fun makes the world look to run in "fast-motion".

Assuming comparability and unitarity, we have a single psychometric function from objective durations to subjective durations modeling a subject's dispositions to have duration experience, and different subjects' experiential dispositions will be relatable as a transformation of this function. What form does this function take? To answer this question, we first need to know what kind of structure the quality space of ED properties has. Duration experience allows individuals to discriminate *metric* relations between durations, such as "d_1 is equally similar to d_2 and d_3", not just order relations on durations (d_1 is greater than d_2 and smaller than d_3). This gives us a reason for thinking that duration quality space has a *metric structure*. Duration quality space is, plausibly, also *one-dimensional* – there is only one dimension of similarity on which we compare durations (unlike, say colors or spatial locations). Thus, a duration quality space will have the same 1-d metric structure as the space of durations itself (or an initial segment of that space, as some durations are too long to perceive).

What shape does the psychometric function from objective duration into this space take? The idea of "rate of temporal flow" as a quantity measurable by a single number suggests a linear function that is origin-crossing, i.e., it has the form $S = cD$, where S is a variable for ED properties, D is objective duration, and c is the rate of flow, corresponding to the gradient or steepness of the function. I'll call this assumption *linearity*.

Even if human temporal experience is actually (approximately) linear, the existence of *non-linear* temporal experience either in humans or other organisms is pretty clearly possible, and wouldn't even be particularly strange. Non-linear psychometric functions are pretty much the norm when it comes to the experience of other stimulus features like loudness, brightness, etc. And we can at least conceive of non-linear functions for duration experience. For example, a hypothetical creature might have timers that represent *log* duration, and which realize temporal experience in such a way that it has a log psychometric function (indeed, psychologists take seriously the idea that some of our timers might be non-linear (Crystal 2001)), including the idea that they use log timing (Gibbon and Church 1981). It is hard to be more specific about what exactly the functional/physical conditions are under which experience would involve non-linear timing, such as log timing (in fact, I think the difficulties here run deep (see Lee 2016)). Nonetheless, in so far as we think that our observations of the functional/physical structure of perceptual processing in other cases (loudness, brightness, heaviness, color, etc.), give us evidence for believing they are governed by a non-linear psychometric function, it is hard to see why we couldn't have similar reason for thinking that duration experience is non-linear.

Assuming that's right, would there be any reason for thinking that such a subject's (non-linear) experiential responses would be illusory or that they would not be optimally functioning? Take the case of *log* coding of duration. Would this entail sub-optimal functioning? In other cases, the rationale for such coding is that it allows us to represent differences in a quantity over a wide range of scales using a single representational parameter. As it happens, we have evolved separate representational systems for time at different scales (from milliseconds to years), and so we probably don't need to use the trick of log coding. But there is no reason why a less sophisticated cognitive system couldn't employ this trick for duration, or, indeed, why we couldn't. So optimal functioning is clearly compatible with log timing. Would it involve some kind of massive illusion? The trouble with saying this is that it commits you to saying human experience is massively illusory all over the place: most perceptual representations involve non-linear coding of stimulus features, but we still think of them as providing accurate information, and therefore as "veridical" in the most important sense (this issue clearly deserves much more extensive discussion).

In sum, it seems to be possible for linearity to fail, so that temporal experiential dispositions are given by a more complex psychometric function than the linear function presupposed by the "rate of flow" picture. Moreover, if it's true that such non-linear experiences need not involve illusion or non-optimal functioning, this provides us with another non-obvious way for strong variation to be realized.

Let's call the combination of comparability, unitarity, and linearity "the simple flow view"; it entails that "rate of flow" is a well-defined inter-personal quantity. A further important clarification: on the simple flow view, "rate of flow" is just a number describing our *dispositions* to experience external stimuli; it need not be understood as measuring something more *intrinsic*, like *how much experience* flows by each second. Thus, even if we accept the view, there is *still* something potentially misleading about the "flowing water" analogy. Whether there is some such intrinsic measure of "how much" experience we have over time is a further interesting question, which is important for certain practical issues about experience (e.g., more pain is worse than less pain) (see Lee (draft manuscript 2013) for more detailed discussion).

Having noted this, let's return to our discussion of strong variation. We have seen in this section that one way of arguing for strong variation is by challenging elements of the simple flow view: comparability, unitarity, and linearity. But we can also argue for strong variation in a way that is compatible with the simple flow view – this is the topic of the next section.

The possibility of strong variation on the simple flow view

Assuming the simple flow view, the kind of "strong phenomenal variation" we are interested in can be described as follows: can there be a possible individual whose "rate of temporal flow" is uniformly faster or slower than ours, in the sense that the psychometric function describing their disposition to have duration experiences is a linear transformation of ours, or more specifically, it is the same function multiplied by a constant factor?

What physical/functional differences would there be between us and such an individual? Because their experiences differ from ours only in that their "absolute value" is multiplied by a constant (unlike an individual whose psychometric function is a non-linear transformation of ours), you might think that they will be disposed to make the same temporal judgments as us. For example, if a two-second stimulus seems to us equally similar to a one-second and three-second stimulus, this will be true for them too, even if all the stimuli appear to them to last, say, twice as long (in a phenomenal sense). However, characteristic functional differences (including differences in judgments) may nonetheless exist, for example, those having to do with differences in *range of sensitivity* (which temporal stimuli they can perceive at all), and the *variance* of their responses to a particular temporal stimulus (i.e., how *reliably* they perceive durations, rates of change within some range). For example, a hummingbird might be able to visually perceive changes that are too rapid for human vision, and be more reliable at perceiving fine-grained temporal detail.

To clarify, I think it is helpful to see that there are possible cases where conditions obtain that are plausibly *sufficient* (but not necessary) for a difference in "rate of flow". In particular, we can consider a case where an individual has a cognitive system almost exactly like a normal human's, except that their neural processing operates faster or slower than ours by some constant factor: the signaling speed between neurons and the firing rates of neurons, and any other processes relevant for cognition all happen at a uniformly faster or slower rate.[4]

For example, consider an individual whose processing speeds are five times faster than ours. Then the temporal resolution and range of sensitivity of their cognitive timers would all be shifted by a factor of five. More generally, their response to a stimulus with certain temporal features would be isomorphic to our response to a version of the stimulus stretched out in time by factor of five. For example, if we enjoy listening to music with a tempo range of 70 bpm to 200 bpm, they would enjoy listening to music with a tempo range between 350 bpm and 1000 bpm. If we find speech to be intelligible when the syllables are pronounced at a certain rate, they would find it intelligible at a rate scaled from ours by a factor of five. And so on.

I think such an exact functional correspondence between our reactions to stimuli (including all internal processing) and their reactions to rescaled versions of the same stimuli, makes it plausible that there is also an experiential correspondence here: that is, their experiential psychometric function for duration is simply a rescaled version of ours. More specifically, the only difference between our neuro-cognitive reaction to a *n* second stimulus and their reaction to a rescaled *n*/5 second version of the same stimulus is the period of time over which the neuro-cognitive response unfolds: their response is a temporally rescaled version of our response. It is only if the temporal scale of the response is experientially relevant that our experiences of these counterpart stimuli could be different. In other words, not only is there an exact correspondence in the causal structure of neural events occurring in response to the counterpart stimuli, every other physical aspect of the response is the same, except for temporal scale. This is why there is a very strong argument for saying that there is experiential sameness here (i.e., our experiences are exactly like those they would have of a temporally rescaled stimulus).

I would give the following supplementary argument to back this up. We argued above that a subject with a non-linear psychometric function for time is surely possible, and moreover we can imagine a functional organization that we might take as evidence for such experiential dispositions. But if there are physical/functional differences between us and another subject that are sufficient for our psychometric functions to be related by a *non*-linear transformation, it would be surprising if there were not also physical/functional differences that are sufficient for our functions to be related by a simpler *linear* transformation; and the differences described seem like a very plausible candidate for this.

What we have here is an argument that certain conditions are sufficient for an individual's duration psychometric function to be a rescaled version of ours. Let's note a couple of things about this. First, if linearity and unitarity fail to be true of us, this doesn't really spoil the argument. If in fact our experiential dispositions can only be accurately captured with a bunch of different functions for different ranges, domains, sensory modalities, contexts, etc., then that will be true of our rescaled duplicate. And if these functions are non-linear, that will be true of our duplicate. So what we really have here is an argument for a sufficient condition for a relationship between subjects of *psychometric rescaling*.

Finally, let us note that given the evident symmetry between us and such a "rescaled" subject, it would be very implausible to claim that their perceptual system is functioning any better or worse than ours, or that it is producing mental representations that are any more or less accurate than ours. So if such a subject could exist, they are clearly an instance of strong variability in duration phenomenology.

More could be said about these arguments in favor of strong variability, but I now want to switch tacks, looking at some problems that arise when we try to make sense of what such properties consist in. As we will see, there are serious difficulties giving a clear account of the conditions of individuation for these subjective properties; so although there are good arguments that they exist, their existence is not straightforwardly philosophically unproblematic.

Problems individuating experiential duration properties

Let's now assume that ED properties are individuated in a way that allows for strong interpersonal variation. We gave a sufficient condition for psychometric rescaling in terms of processing speeds. However, that does not tell us what the necessary and sufficient conditions are for a subject to have a certain ED property. For example, what are the exact conditions under which the kind of duration experience you typically have in response to a 2 msc auditory stimulus occurs? There are a number of serious problems that arise when we try to answer this question.

One approach here that will tempt many is a representational (or more generally "relational") one. The idea is that the character of a subject's experience is constituted by the properties of the stimulus that it represents[5] (or to which it enables some other intentional relation like "acquaintance"[6]). If such a general approach to individuating phenomenal properties is correct, then we can distinguish ED properties from others in terms of which property or properties they represent.

Suppose we want a representational account that allows for strong inter-subjective variation in duration phenomenology. Then duration experience can't simply consist in experiential representation of objective duration. If it did, then phenomenally different experiences had by different subjects in response to the same stimulus duration would represent different objective durations, and therefore could not all be veridical. Rather, such a representationist is likely to appeal to the representation of *relative* duration. Compare size perception: an object might in some sense look larger to a small rodent than it does to a fully grown adult; nonetheless they might both be veridically perceiving its size. The obvious way to resolve the superficial contradiction here is to say that they perceive its size only relative to *their* size (or some more specific aspect of it like eye-height). Similarly, a representationist might say that stimulus duration is represented by an ED property only relative to a bodily temporal parameter, such as the rate of some internal process in the brain involved in time perception. If the relevant process is running faster in me than in you, then having veridical experiences of the same duration will require it to look longer to me.[7]

This might seem like an attractive approach, giving us a neat account of the metaphysics of ED properties that allow for strong variation. But it raises two difficult questions. First, how exactly should we understand the sense in which objective duration is *relativized* to the rate of an internal process? Second, what is the relevant internal process?

On the first question, I want to distinguish two different versions of the "relative duration view" and argue that they are both problematic, to the detriment of a representational approach.

On one version, there is an internal process that provides a *particular* duration relative to which everything is measured, such as the duration of one click of an internal clock. This duration provides a *unit*, so there will be some specific number of units associated with each ED property, and a shift to a different "rate of temporal flow" will correspond to a change in units. On this view, it is literally the case that each time you experience a duration, there is a certain number of "mental seconds" that it is experienced as having.

This view is quite implausible, however. It is phenomenologically implausible, as there is nothing in experience indicating that one duration has a special privileged status, or that there is a number associated with each duration experience. Peacocke (1992: 68–69) is surely right in holding that our experiences of temporal and spatial quantities are "unit-free". But perhaps more significantly, there is no reason to think of the states of internal timers that are used to track time and which underpin these experiences as using a unit-relative representational system. For example, one kind of timer that might be used by cognitive systems is an accumulator. To give an example, imagine a tank of water filling up at a uniform rate in response to the onset of a stimulus, and stopping at the termination of the stimulus. The height of water in the tank represents the duration of the stimulus. There are no units in which time is measured here. It is represented by a physical quantity – height of water – that does not itself intrinsically involve a unit: we could measure it in cm, meters, or whatever we like; moreover, there is no segmentation between different water heights indicating temporal units (e.g., there are no lines notched up the side of the tank). I believe that in the case of more realistic representational systems (such as ramping or decaying neural firing rates representing the passage of time), there will similarly be a physical quantity (e.g., firing rate) representing duration that doesn't inherently involve a unit of representation (although the point certainly deserves longer discussion to account for different kinds of timing mechanisms and representational systems[8]).

In response, we might try to find an alternate way of understanding relativization that doesn't require units. This can be done. Imagine again using a tank filling with water to measure duration. Everything is relative to the rate of filling of the tank. If we sped this up, then different durations would be represented by different heights (or the device would start misrepresenting). The amount of "tank time" indicated by water height is *proportional* to filling speed, so the "relative" temporal quantity represented can be thought of as [duration of stimulus * tank filling speed]. Since both components of this are unit-free physical quantities, the overall quantity is unit-free. So in this way, we can relativize our representation of duration to tank filling speed (or, more realistically, the rate of some internal neural process) without understanding the situation as involving units of measure.

This way of understanding relativization has the advantage of being unit-free, but unfortunately it has a serious problem too. It boils down to this: the relative quantity "duration of stimulus * tank filling speed" is really the same quantity as "height of water in the tank" (e.g., imagine this relative to units like seconds and meters: seconds * (meters/second) = meters). Or to give a more realistic example, the quantity "duration of stimulus * decay rate of neural decay timer" is really the same as "firing rate of neural timer" (here I'm imagining a timer that uses a firing rate inversely proportional to elapsed duration to measure duration). In trying to relativize the represented objective temporal quantity to the rate of an internal process, we end up with a view on which the system is representing its own internal state rather than the state of the stimulus! Perhaps a little more charitably, we could think of the proposal as saying that the system is representing the stimulus's disposition to produce a certain internal state in the system (water height/firing rate), one that correlates with a certain objective duration. Still, this is an odd way of looking at it: what is really going on is that the system is going into a certain internal state whose role it is to represent the objective duration of the stimulus. It's true that had the normal operating speed of the timer been different, it would have represented a different objective duration. In that way, the water height/neural firing rate representation is "relative to the speed of the timer". Still, attempting to construe this as the representation of a relative quantity tends to lead to this odd result.

Of course, anti-representationists (such as myself) will take this as grist for their mill; representationists will have to find a way to circumvent or deflate these problems (one option is to deny that strong variation is possible, and thus undercut the motivation for relativization in the first place. But of course, that will be unattractive without a response to the considerations of rates of flow and the possibility of strong variation on the simple flow view discussed earlier).[9] Here is not the place to try to adjudicate the big theoretical question of whether representationism in general is true, however. I rest content by pointing out that clarifying in a plausible way what "relativization" is, is problematic.

Another problem with relativization is identifying the relevant internal process whose rate is being used to measure time. There are two versions of this problem. On the representational view currently under discussion, we want to identify a represent*ed* internal quantity. But even if we reject the representational view, we may well think that there is some set of internal states that are necessary and sufficient for different kinds of duration experience, or some internal process whose rate determines the "rate of flow" of a subject's experience, and want to know what these physical quantities or processes are. There are very similar problems that arise identifying the "individuating quantity" in either case, so I will discuss them in the same breath.

I want to distinguish three closely related problems that arise with individuation: the *localization problem*, the *abstraction problem*, and the *mapping problem* (see Prosser 2016, chapter 4, for a related discussion). It should be noted at the outset that similar problems are likely to arise for the individuation of *any* phenomenal properties (see, in particular, Papineau 1993: §§4.8–4.10, 2002, chapter 7), although I think the issues play out in a particularly interesting way in this case.

The localization problem is this: even if we identify relatively local neural populations whose features code the duration properties represented in experience, it is implausible that the phenomenology of duration is determined solely by such localized properties; context matters too. For example, replacing a neural timer involved in auditory perception with a faster one that has a higher resolution (e.g., more "ticks" per second), and uses the same states to code different durations (e.g., the representation caused by ten ticks now denotes a different duration), won't necessarily "speed up time" or otherwise change the experience the subject has of a certain objective duration, because the timer may be integrated with surrounding neural processing in a way that is exactly the same as in the old system. Plausibly, these contextual factors are phenomenally relevant too.[10] But if duration phenomenology is partly grounded in such contextual features of local timers, what exactly are they? That's the localization problem.

A good way to see the abstraction problem is through the lens of comparability: the assumption that all duration experiences are drawn from a single quality space. If comparability is true, then the individuating quantity will have to be a physical quantity that is present whenever there are experiences of duration, in *absolutely any context*: it will be there for every kind of human temporal experience, as well as in temporal experiences of every possible subject, including non-human cognitive systems. This immediately rules out a lot of natural candidates: for example, you might picture time being measured against the rate of an internal clock. But if ED properties are individuated by a specific kind of clock mechanism, then such a mechanism will have to be in place for them to be instantiated. That means that if non-human creatures use a different mechanism to keep track of time, they can't have temporal experiences like ours – we will have a failure of comparability. This leads to the abstraction problem: if ED properties can be shared by a wide variety of creatures using different systems to track and code time, then they must be individuated sufficiently abstractly to allow for this.

The mapping problem is a way of illustrating through example the myriad problems with individuation (in a sense then, it is not a separate problem, but a way of dramatizing these problems). Suppose we encounter a creature that has conscious experience, but whose temporal processing is different from ours in a highly *non*-systematic way. Perhaps they are able to perceptually experience a broader range of durations than us, and their perceptual systems operate at a broader range of speeds and temporal resolutions. For example, suppose they have something like vision and audition; but their visual processing is adapted to pick up changes at a longer temporal scale than ours, and in general operates more slowly; but their auditory processing is significantly faster and has a higher temporal resolution than ours, and is adapted to pick up changes at finer temporal grain. Moreover, the temporal coding schemes and detection mechanisms these systems use are at least somewhat different from ours. The question is: how do their experiences map onto ours? For example, how do we figure out what it is like for them to experience a 500 msc stimulus under normal conditions? Which of our experiences is this phenomenally comparable to?

In the case where an organism has processing exactly like ours but uniformly faster or slower, there was a principled reason why one mapping could be taken to be correct. But in a case like this – where their processing is in one way faster, and in another way slower, and there are other differences too – it is hard to see how there could be one mapping that is more natural than others. The physical state they go into when they experience, say, a 500 msc stimulus is similar to each of a *range* of states we go into when experiencing a *range* of different stimulus durations, but not most similar to any one of those states. But *all we have to go on in figuring out phenomenal similarity here is similarity in physical/functional states*: so, viewed from an external perspective, nothing can tell us what the right mapping is.

What to make of this? There are various responses (I can't attempt to adjudicate between them here). First, we could conclude that it is simply *indeterminate* how to map their experiences onto ours (Papineau 1993, 2002). Second, we could hold that there is a single mapping that preserves phenomenal character, it is just that it is inscrutable from a third-person perspective, and would seem arbitrary if we knew what it was. This option can be glossed in a more deflationary way, on which it really *is* arbitrary what the mapping is (this is similar to the first response), or in an inflationary way, on which the mapping does correspond to a deep "joint in nature", albeit one that is inscrutable from an objective perspective (see Lee forthcoming). Third, we could conclude that comparability fails, holding that their temporal experiences form an alien quality space, despite also being experiences *of* duration (the fact that this option is considerably less attractive for time than for "secondary" qualities like color is an important reason why this case is independently interesting). Finally, (and more obscurely), we might be tempted by the "Frege-Schlick" view, on which one cannot meaningfully compare phenomenology across organisms (Stalnaker 1999; Shoemaker 2006), and so the mapping problem is based on a false presupposition. All of these options (which are unattractively counterintuitive in different ways) deserve extensive further discussion.

Finally, it is worth noting that there is a related *intra*-personal mapping puzzle. In particular, the kinds of physical/functional differences between individuals that lead to inter-personal phenomenal mapping puzzles might in principle also exist in different sensory modalities within a single individual. Specifically, if temporal processing is modality-specific, then quite different physical/functional states might underlie temporal experience in different modalities. For example, it is well known that human vision and audition have very different temporal resolution (audition is finer-grained).[11] Considering the inter-subjective case, theorists have been tempted to conclude that an organism with higher temporal resolution perception than a human may be living in a "slow-motion" world (see e.g., Healy *et al.* 2013). But should such theorists therefore conclude that time passes at quite different rates in human audition and vision? More generally, is it an epistemic possibility that unitarity or comparability fail in a significant way across modalities within a single organism?

It might seem like the answer is "obviously not" – we can tell introspectively that auditory and visual temporal phenomenology are congruent: they involve very similar experiences of the same objective temporal phenomena. Therefore, there is no intra-subjective mapping problem here. Or to put it another way, if auditory duration and visual duration are massively different, then we are subject to massive systematic introspective illusion – but such illusions seem inconceivable (although see Lee (2016), for doubts about the significance of this intuition).

Things are not so simple, however. One might worry that for *any* proposal for what the individuating quantity is, we can set up a case where it is multiply realized in different sensory modalities, in such a way that they involve quite different psychometric functions for duration experience (we have a large failure of unitarity). Nonetheless, if the modalities are wired together so that the subject can make accurate inter-modal comparisons of (objective) duration, they wouldn't notice any inter-modal discrepancy in phenomenology (here I'm assuming that introspection of phenomenology works through the redeployment of objective perceptual judgments). If we assume that systematic introspective illusions are always impossible, we can use this setup to rule out *any* candidate for the individuating property. We might start wondering if any satisfactory account can be given of what it is. I think this issue raises serious, possibly intractable, problems that deserve more extensive discussion (see Lee 2016).

To sum up: there are a number of serious problems we face attempting to individuate ED properties. First, if we think that they involve the representation of (or some mental relation to) *relative* duration properties, then we must say in what sense we have "relativization" here;

we saw that both unit-relative and unit-free answers to this question have problems. Second, if an internal neuro-functional quantity individuates duration experience (either because it is represented as the quantity against which external duration is measured, or because it directly constitutes duration phenomenology), then we want to know what it is: this is the individuation problem. This leads to the localization, abstraction and mapping problems just described. My goal here is not to solve the problems; I simply want to raise them as a way of highlighting how hard the individuation problem is.

Concluding remarks

We have seen that there are strong motivations for believing in the possibility of strong phenomenal variation for duration experience, some of which involve questioning the assumptions of a picture of temporal experience I precisified as "the simple flow view", on which experience has a well-defined "rate of flow". Nonetheless, there are some serious difficulties understanding how such variable phenomenal features are individuated. Future work in this area ought to address these problems, which will require confronting difficult questions (some of which I raised here) about the ways in which timing devices in the brain represent time, and how these representational states relate to the conscious experience of time. Our understanding of the underlying neuro-functional mechanisms here is still extremely rudimentary, and no doubt further developments on the empirical side will inform our philosophical accounts of subjective time. This is an area with much interesting philosophical work waiting to be accomplished.[12]

Notes

1 See Shoemaker (1982), Block (1990), Nida-Rümelin (1996).
2 For reviews see Buonomano and Karmarker (2002), Buhusi and Meck (2005), Grondin (2010), Merchant *et al.* (2013), and the papers in Merchant and De Lafuente (2014).
3 For the representational view, see, e.g., Dretske (1997), Tye (2000); for the acquaintance view, see, e.g., Campbell (2002). Phillips (2013) theorizes temporal awareness from an acquaintance perspective; Tye (2003) defends his representational view specifically for temporal awareness.
4 Prosser (2016, chapter 4) considers a similar example.
5 See, e.g., Dretske (1997), Tye (2000).
6 See, e.g., Campbell (2002).
7 Thompson (2010) discusses a version of the relativizing response for space, and Phillips (2013) defends a version of the view for duration experience.
8 For theoretical accounts of the representational properties of different timing systems, see Gallistel (1990), Montemayor (2012).
9 Another option is to consider relational properties other than relative duration, e.g., Prosser (2016, chapter 4) argues that duration experiences represent relational functional properties.
10 Although see discussion of the intra-subjective mapping problem for considerations that somewhat problematize this intuition.
11 This formulation is an oversimplification, because there is no such thing as "the" resolution of vision; rather different visual processes have different resolution (Holcombe 2009).
12 Thanks to Ian Phillips for comments on an earlier draft.

References

Block, N. (1990) "Inverted earth", *Philosophical Perspectives* 4: 53–79.
Buhusi, C. V. and Meck, W. H. (2005) "What makes us tick? Functional and neural mechanisms of interval timing", *Nature Reviews Neuroscience* 6(10): 755–765.
Buonomano, D. and Karmarker, U. (2002) "How do we tell time?" *The Neuroscientist* 8(1): 42–51.
Campbell, J. (2002) *Reference and Consciousness*, Oxford, UK: Oxford University Press.

Crystal, J. D. (2001) "Nonlinear time perception", *Behavioural Processes* 55(1): 35–49.

Dretske, F. I. (1997) *Naturalizing the Mind*, Cambridge, MA: MIT Press.

Eagleman, D. M. (2008) "Human time perception and its illusions", *Current Opinion in Neurobiology* 18(2): 131–136.

Gallistel, C. R. (1990) *The Organization of Learning*, Cambridge, MA: The MIT Press.

Gibbon, J. and Church, R. M. (1981) "Time left: Linear versus logarithmic subjective time", *Journal of Experimental Psychology: Animal Behavior Processes* 7(2): 87–108.

Grondin, S. (2010) "Timing and time perception: A review of recent behavioral and neuroscience findings and theoretical directions", *Attention, Perception and Psychophysics* 72(3): 561–582.

Healy, K., McNally, L., Ruxton, G. D., Cooper, N. and Jackson, A. L. (2013) "Metabolic rate and body size are linked with perception of temporal information", *Animal Behaviour* 86(4): 685–696.

Holcombe, A. O. (2009) "Seeing slow and seeing fast: two limits on perception", *Trends in Cognitive Sciences* 13(5): 216–221.

Johnson, A., Arnold, D. H. and Nishida, S. (2006) "Spatially localized distortions of event time", *Current Biology* 16(5): 472–479.

Lee, G. (2016) "Does experience have phenomenal properties?" *Philosophical Topics* 44(2): 197–226.

Lee, G. (forthcoming) "Alien subjectivity and the importance of consciousness", in *A Festschrift for Ned Block*, edited by Pautz, A. and Stoljar, D., Cambridge, MA: MIT Press.

Lee, G. (draft manuscript 2013) "Subjective duration", available at http://philpapers.org/rec/LEESD. Accessed 7 January 2017.

Merchant, H. and De Lafuente, V. (eds) (2014) *Neurobiology of Interval Timing*, New York: Springer.

Merchant, H., Harrington, D. L. and Meck, W. H. (2013) "Neural basis of the perception and estimation of time", *Annual Review of Neuroscience* 36: 313–336.

Montemayor, C. (2012) *Minding Time: A Philosophical and Theoretical Approach to the Psychology of Time*, vol. 5, Leiden, The Netherlands: Brill.

Nida-Rümelin, M. (1996) "Pseudonormal vision", *Philosophical Studies* 82(2): 145–157.

Papineau, D. (1993) *Philosophical Naturalism*, Oxford, UK: Blackwell.

Papineau, D. (2002) *Thinking about Consciousness*, Oxford, UK: Clarendon Press.

Peacocke, C. (1992) *A Study of Concepts*, Cambridge, MA: The MIT Press.

Phillips, I. (2013) "Perceiving the passing of time", in *Proceedings of the Aristotelian Society* 113(3/3): 225–252, Oxford University Press.

Prosser, S. (2016) *Experiencing Time*, Oxford, UK: Oxford University Press.

Shoemaker, S. (1982) "The inverted spectrum", *The Journal of Philosophy* 79(7): 357–381.

Shoemaker, S. (2006) "The Frege-Schlick view", in J. Thomson and A. Byrne (eds), *Content and Modality: Themes from the Philosophy of Robert Stalnaker*, Oxford, UK: Clarendon Press.

Stalnaker, R. (1999) "Comparing qualia across persons", *Philosophical Topics* 26(1/2): 385–405.

Thompson, B. (2010) "The spatial content of experience", *Philosophy and Phenomenological Research* 81(1): 146–184.

Tye, M. (2000) *Consciousness, Color and Content*, Cambridge, MA: MIT Press.

Tye, M. (2003) *Consciousness and Persons: Unity and Identity*, Cambridge, MA: MIT Press.

PART IV

Temporal experience and the philosophy of mind

13

TEMPORAL EXPERIENCE AND THE PHILOSOPHY OF PERCEPTION

Christoph Hoerl

As attested to by the multifarious contributions to this handbook, temporal experience has become a particularly vibrant research area in recent philosophy. The growth (or rather resurgence) of interest in this topic is arguably fuelled, in part, by the hope of correcting a distorted picture of the nature of conscious experience that results from focusing only on experiences of static states of affairs, as much existing work on consciousness in effect does.[1] There is a growing consensus that getting it right about the nature of conscious experience requires giving an account of its temporal dimension; ignoring that temporal dimension means missing out on some of the most fundamental features of consciousness. In this respect, recent work on temporal experience can be seen to be animated by an intuition that can already be found in Husserl, who calls the analysis of time-consciousness "the most difficult of all phenomenological problems" (1893–1917: 286), but also "perhaps the most important in the whole of phenomenology" (Ibid.: 346).

Interestingly, if this intuition is along the right lines, it also, in turn, imposes something like a meta-philosophical constraint on philosophical approaches to temporal experience. The kind of explanatory account of our perceptual abilities they provide should also, at the same time, deliver an answer to the question as to *why* the temporal dimension of consciousness is of special relevance when it comes to accounting for its nature. Part of my aim in this chapter, ultimately, is to suggest that some approaches to temporal experience may fare better in meeting this meta-philosophical constraint than others.

However, my main focus will be on a second way in which work on temporal experience intersects with wider debates about the nature of conscious perceptual experience. Much of the current debate about temporal experience in philosophy is framed in terms of a debate between three specific main positions, sometimes referred to as the *extensional model* (or *extensionalism*), the *retentional model* (or *retentionalism*) and the *cinematic model*. It is typically assumed that the differences between these three models are obvious. Yet, on closer inspection, it turns out to be quite difficult to make out what exactly distinguishes the cinematic model from the retentional model, on the one hand, and from the extensional model, on the other. In what follows, I will criticise some existing ways in which the models are sometimes demarcated from one another (e.g. in terms of the notion of "diachronic unity", or of a distinction between "memory" and "retention"), before suggesting that the differences between them become clearer if they are construed as embodying contrasting pictures of the very nature of perceptual experience.

Models of temporal experience: picturing the differences

An initial, crude, characterization of the three main models of temporal experience might run as follows. As the name indicates, the cinematic model takes our perceptual system to operate in a way that is akin to the way a cinematic camera works: Just as a movie consists of a rapid succession of "still" images, perceptual consciousness consists of a succession of momentary experiences, none of which is itself an experience of succession. In other words, we cannot, strictly speaking, *perceive* instances of succession and change in the way we can perceive colours for example. Rather, our awareness of succession and change has to be explained in some other way. Or so defenders of the cinematic model think. Both retentionalists and extensionalists, by contrast, do think that there are instances of succession and change that we can directly perceive. Retentionalists explain how this is possible by appealing to the idea that, whilst perceptual experiences are realized at a moment in time, they encompass not just what happens at that moment, but also a short stretch of what is by then already in the past. (A portion of the past is itself "retained" within the very experience – hence the name.) Extensionalists, by contrast, deny that there can be any such thing as a perceptual awareness of the past, just as defenders of the cinematic model do; yet, they hold that experience itself unfolds over time, with individual experiences extending through a period of clock time, and that this can explain our ability to perceive succession and change.

On the face of it, this seems to give us three fairly clearly demarcated theoretical positions, which Barry Dainton's entry on temporal consciousness in the *Stanford Encyclopedia of Philosophy* (Dainton 2010) illustrates with the diagrams reproduced in Figure 13.1. Yet, one only has to take a closer look at the three diagrams to realize that matters may not be quite so straightforward.[2]

Take, for instance, the difference between the cinematic model and the retentional model, as illustrated here. As already indicated, according to the cinematic model, all that happens over time, in as far as perceptual experience is concerned, is that we have a succession of individual momentary experiences, each of which is an experience of what is the case at the moment we

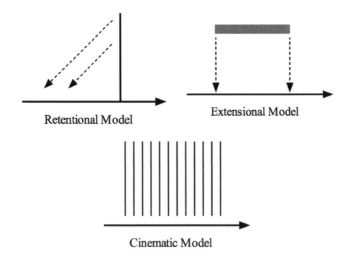

Figure 13.1   The three main conceptions of temporal consciousness (reproduced with permission from Dainton 2010)

have the experience.[3] Something like this succession of individual experiences, I take it, is what the vertical lines in the diagram illustrating the cinematic model represent. But whilst defenders of the cinematic model will want to insist that, perceptually speaking, all we are ever aware of is how things are at a moment in time, they can of course allow that we also have ways of becoming aware of things that go on over a period of time. For instance, at each moment in time, we are not just aware, through perceptual experience, of how things are at that moment in time. We are also at the same time aware, through memory, of how things were prior to that time, and can therefore have an awareness, for example, of change and succession. In other words, to each of the vertical lines in the diagram in Figure 13.1 depicting the cinematic model, another arrow pointing backwards could be added to represent the awareness the subject has at that time, through memory, of how things were before. But that would of course yield a diagram that looks just like the diagram that is supposed to illustrate the retentional model. (The fact that that diagram only contains one vertical line is simply because, in contrast to the other two diagrams, it is drawn in a way that singles out only what happens at one moment in time. More such vertical lines – with corresponding backward-pointing arrows – could be added to make it a more complete picture.) Thus, whilst the diagrams depicting the retentional model and the cinematic model look quite different, it in fact turns out that the differences are mainly due to what appear to be relatively arbitrary-looking choices about what is included and what is left out in each of them.

Now let us also consider the way the extensionalist model and the cinematic model, respectively, are illustrated in Figure 13.1. One thing the diagrams might be taken to suggest is that the distinction between the two models turns on a continuity vs. discreteness contrast – that the extensionalist model thinks of experience as a continuous process, whereas the momentary experiences the cinematic model conceives of are separated by gaps. Again, though, it is not obvious that this is the crucial contrast. The essence of the cinematic view – that experience, strictly speaking, is only ever of momentary states of affairs – seems compatible with the possibility of gapless transitions between individual such momentary experiences; conversely, versions of extensionalism are conceivable on which temporal experience is quantized, with each extended experience being made up of a sequence of experiential phases with brief periods of unawareness between them.[4] Perhaps the only obvious difference between the two models captured by the diagrams is that the extensionalist thinks of what goes on over an extended period of time as "one experience", whereas the defender of the cinematic model will insist that it is actually a succession of discrete "momentary" experiences. As we will see, though, it is quite difficult to pin down what the substance of the disagreement, thus put, is supposed to be.

Clearly, highlighting these issues would be of little interest if they concerned merely the fact that diagrams are of limited help when it comes to explaining the differences between the three models of temporal experience. I think a case can be made, though, that they trace back to some substantive questions regarding the demarcation between those models themselves. In what follows, I want to make a case for the following two claims in particular, that: (1) the challenge of demarcating retentionalism from the cinematic model ultimately resides in the question as to what distinguishes retentionalism from one particular version of the cinematic model already alluded to, which I will call the *memory theory*; and (2) the challenge of demarcating extensionalism from the cinematic model ultimately resides in the question as to what distinguishes extensionalism from another version of the cinematic model, which I will refer to as the *resemblance theory*. I will then go on to argue that, in each case, one way of responding to the relevant challenge is by conceiving of the respective theories as embodying a different understanding of the very nature of perceptual experience.

The cinematic model, part 1: the contrast with retentionalism

Probably the most prominent proponent of a cinematic model of temporal experience is Thomas Reid, who writes:

> It may here be observed, that if we speak strictly and philosophically, no kind of succession can be an object either of the senses, or of consciousness; because the operations of both are confined to the present point of time, and there can be no succession in a point of time; and on that account the motion of a body, which is a successive change of place, could not be observed by the senses alone without the aid of memory.
>
> *(Reid 1785: 270)*

As he goes on to explain in more detail:

> We see the present place of the body; we remember the successive advance it made to that place. The first can then only give us a conception of motion, when joined to the last.
>
> *(Reid 1785: 271)*

Reid is here putting forward what I will call the *memory theory* version of a cinematic model of temporal experience, according to which our awareness of temporally extended goings-on (at least if it is to be awareness of them *as such*) has to involve a combination of perceptual experience and memory.

A view of essentially this kind was also what Husserl (1893–1917) ascribed to Brentano, and in response to which Husserl developed his own retentional model of temporal experience. A key impetus behind Husserl's work on time-consciousness is his realization that the memory theory faces several deep problems, which his retentionalism seeks to overcome. Where Husserl agrees with the memory theory is in the thought that an awareness of temporal goings-on must involve a past-directed element alongside an awareness of the present. Yet, to mention just one problem with the memory theory, it is unable to explain the apparent phenomenological difference between two quite different ways in which succession and change can figure in our awareness, as exemplified by the contrasting experiences we have when we look at the hour hand and the second hand of a clock, respectively. Both hands are in fact moving (supposing all is working properly), and in the case of the second hand, we are *aware of it moving* when we look at it. In the case of the hour hand, by contrast, we can at best become *aware that it has moved*; we cannot discern its movement just by looking at it.[5] Thus, it seems we need an account of two separate ways in which present experience can interact with past-directed awareness to yield awareness of succession and change, but the memory theory provides for only one.

Husserl thinks the right way to respond to problems with the memory theory such as this is by postulating a second form of past-directed awareness distinct from memory, which he calls *retention*. The direct perceptual experience of succession and change is different from cases in which we have to draw on memory by virtue of the fact that, in the former case, an element of past-directed awareness is built into the very perceptual experience itself. In retention, we are directly aware of a portion of the past itself, as part of our current experience, in contrast to the more indirect awareness we have of the past when we recollect past experiences. Or so Husserl thinks.

Thus, going by Husserl, it looks as though the difference between the cinematic model (at least in the guise of the memory theory) and the retentional model turns crucially on the difference between memory and retention. Yet, how much of a genuine explanation of the difference does this give us? As Dainton asks:

> To what extent is the explanation merely verbal rather than real? Husserl is *stipulating* that retentions have precisely the properties they need to have for his purposes . . . Husserl tells us what retention is not, and what it does, but provides no explanation of how it accomplishes this . . . Husserl gives us a "new word", but nothing more.
>
> *(Dainton 2000: 155f.)*[6]

Husserl wants to explain how his account is different from the memory theory by appealing to the distinction between retention and memory, and in particular the idea that retentions are part of the same "act of consciousness" as our perceptual awareness of the present, whereas recollection and perception each constitute a separate act of consciousness. Yet, this can easily look like a mere *re-description* of the complaint that the memory theory fails to account for our apparent ability to become directly aware of instances of succession and change within perceptual experience itself. For a genuinely explanatory alternative account of temporal experience, more seems required.

The cinematic model, part 2: the contrast with extensionalism

Viewed at some level of abstraction, problems remarkably similar to the problems with Husserl's attempt to distance his own retentionalism from the cinematic model of temporal experience also plague some existing attempts to demarcate extensionalism from the cinematic model. Recall that one of the few things the diagrams illustrating the cinematic and the extensionalist model in the *Stanford Encyclopedia of Philosophy* seem to show (see Figure 13.1) is that the extensionalist will think of what goes on over an extended period of time as "one extended experience", whereas the defender of the cinematic model will insist that it is actually a succession of discrete "momentary" experiences. Just as with Husserl, it thus appears that the crucial issue at stake is whether something other than our awareness of what is present at one moment in time can form part of one and the same experience – that something other being, for Husserl, an awareness of what is just-past, and for the extensionalist, an awareness, at other moments in time, of what is present then.

Once again, though, it is hard to get a handle on what exactly the substance of the debate is supposed to be, if it is framed in terms of this issue. In the context of the debate between extensionalism and the cinematic model, this issue is often conceived of in terms of the question as to whether there can be a relation of "diachronic unity" between non-contemporaneous experiences (see, e.g. Chuard's (2011) discussion of Dainton (2000)). Yet, just as with Husserl's notion of retention, the notion of diachronic unity is hardly free of obscurities.[7] Moreover, it is once again easy to get the feeling that the appeal to the notion of "diachronic unity" simply amounts to another way of describing the distinction the extensionalist wants to draw between the idea of one temporally extended experience and the idea of a mere succession of discrete experiences, rather than explaining what makes for that difference.[8]

That there should be any difficulty in distinguishing between the cinematic model and extensionalism might perhaps at first seem surprising, given what has been said so far about the cinematic model. Note that, unlike with retentionalism, it seems that there isn't even a prima facie problem distinguishing between extensionalism and the memory theory. Awareness of succession and change, according to the extensionalist, does not require any backward-looking element at all – whether conceived of as retention or memory. As our temporally extended experiences unfold, she will say, all we are perceptually aware of are events as and when they happen. But if extensionalism is so obviously different from the memory theory, how can there nevertheless be a problem demarcating it from the cinematic model of temporal experience?

The reason why it can be difficult to get clear about the difference between extensionalism and the cinematic model, I want to suggest, is that, apart from taking the form of a memory theory, the latter can also come in another guise. Consider, for instance, the following passage from Philippe Chuard, in which he tries to argue that the cinematic view – which he refers to as "atomism" – can account for the seeming continuity of conscious experience.

> Consider a succession of instantaneous sensory experiences of the sort atomists countenance. It's possible, if atomism is true, that small gaps separate adjacent experiences in the succession – short intervals where no sensory experience occurs, so that the succession is really discontinuous. Atomists can perfectly acknowledge that it seems as though there aren't any such gaps – the succession seems smooth and continuous. One putative explanation for this is that the gaps are simply too short to be noticed: they fall below some relevant threshold for accessibility.
>
> *(Chuard 2011: 11)*

I take it that the explanatory question Chuard is trying to get at goes something like this. According to the cinematic model, the experiential process itself consists of "a succession of instantaneous sensory experiences" with gaps between them (or so we are to assume). Yet, when we look at an apple rolling across a table, for instance, we do not have an impression of seeing the apple first in one place and then, after an experiential gap, seeing it in another place. We seem to see it the whole time, and see it rolling continuously during that time. How can these two facts be reconciled with one another?

Chuard's answer is that the gaps in experience are too small to be noticed. Thus, the transitions between individual experiences, and therefore also the transitions of the apple from one position to another, seem continuous. We have reconciled the experience of continuity with the de facto discontinuous nature of the experiential process.

Note that the crucial idea that does the work here is that of an apparent *resemblance*, due to limitations in our introspective capacities, between our stream of experiences and the putative object of awareness – the movement of the apple. Because of these limitations in our introspective capacities, the succession of our own experiences resembles a smooth succession more than the discontinuous one it actually is, and this, it seems, is also what is supposed to explain how we can be aware of the rolling apple in the seemingly continuous way we are – even though the movement of the apple itself is not, strictly speaking, an object of perceptual experience, because all we have is a mere succession of discrete experiences of it occupying a succession of different places.

I will refer to the general type of approach to temporal experience at issue here, which is a version of the cinematic model separate from the memory theory, as the *resemblance theory* of temporal experience. On this theory, whilst the stream of consciousness is made up of the kind of succession of momentary perceptual experiences envisaged by the cinematic model, none of which are themselves experiences of succession or change, we can nevertheless become aware of succession and change in the seemingly direct way we do because the stream of such experiences is itself successive, and changes over time in a way that resembles and reflects the changes in the objects we perceive.

It is this particular version of the cinematic model, the resemblance theory of temporal experience, which it can look difficult to demarcate extensionalism from. If extensionalism is to be genuinely different from the cinematic model of temporal experience, we need an answer to the question as to just how it differs from the resemblance theory. Similarly, as I have argued, we need an answer to the question as to how retentionalism differs from the memory theory of temporal experience in order to be clear about how retentionalism differs from the cinematic model. To some extent, existing debates between proponents of the respective models already implicitly acknowledge these points, in so far as they turn on questions about the unity of experience over time, or alleged differences between retention and memory. As I have also sought to bring out, however, framing the differences between the three models in this way runs into danger of making the disputes between them look like mere verbal ones. In the next section, I will try a different tack.

An alternative attempt at demarcation

"No kind of succession can be an object either of the senses, or of consciousness; because the operations of both are confined to the present point in time" (Reid 1785: 270). This, we saw, is how Reid motivates his endorsement of the cinematic model of temporal experience. But why exactly does Reid think that the operation of the senses "is confined to the present point in time", and how exactly is that claim meant to bear on whether we can perceive succession? I think it is plausible that an important background assumption in play in Reid's argument is the particular view of the nature of perception he holds.

Reid's view of the nature of perceptual experience is plausibly interpreted as a version of what Bill Brewer terms the "object view" of perception. According to this view, as Brewer explains, "the most basic characterization of perceptual experience is to be given by citing and/or describing certain *direct objects* with which the subject is *acquainted* in such experience" (Brewer 2011: 16). On such a view, the relevant direct objects – on some versions, mind-independent physical entities; on others, mind-dependent entities such as sense-data – are themselves constituents of the experience, and they are what account for the specific nature of individual experiences.[9] The acquaintance relation, by contrast, in virtue of which the relevant objects figure in our experience, is in an important sense an entirely generic relation. There is a basic, binary, distinction to be drawn between standing, or not standing, in such a relation to a given object. But beyond that, for any object to which we do stand in such a relation, we stand to it in the same relation.

This type of approach to the nature of perceptual experience is also sometimes referred to as *the relational view of experience*.[10] Such a relational view does indeed seem to be committed to the idea that perceptual experience is "confined to the present point in time", both in the sense that we can only be perceptually aware of events that presently impinge upon our senses, and in the sense that we can't experience those events as anything other than present.[11] There is an intuitive sense in which past events are simply no longer around to figure as constituents of our experience in the way envisaged by the relational view. For us to continue to experience events after they have ceased to impinge on our senses, and to experience them as something other than present, our perceptual system itself would have to modify the way in which they are experienced from how they were experienced when we first encountered them in experience, which is at odds with the idea that its sole role is to put us in a relation of acquaintance with objects of experience, and that it is these objects that account for the specific nature of individual experiences. If perceptual experience is a matter of standing in a generic relation of awareness or acquaintance to items that serve as the objects of experience, any past such items are ones we have already stood in such a relation to in the past, when they were present, and we now stand in that relation to present such items instead.[12]

For the same reason, I believe, a retentionalist account of temporal experience has to involve an approach to the nature of perceptual experience that differs from the relational or object view. The main such alternative in the literature is now typically referred to as *the representational view of experience*. Brewer also calls this the "content view". According to it, "perceptual experience is most fundamentally to be characterized by its *representational content*, roughly, by the way it represents things as being around the perceiver" (Brewer 2011: 54). Perceptual experience, on this view, is a matter of the perceiver being in a certain kind of representational state, where this is to be conceived of as a state with a content in the sense of a set of veridicality or accuracy conditions. The work of the perceptual system, essentially, is to put the subject into a state of this kind.

Adopting such a view of perception, it becomes possible to see how perceptual experience can encompass a past-directed element as envisaged by the Husserlian notion of retention. Even though past events can no longer be the objects of sensory experience as conceived of by Reid, the subject can of course now still be in a state with a representational content in which these events figure as just-past.

What I am suggesting, then, is that the retentionalist's opposition to the cinematic model (at least as it is found in thinkers such as Reid) is at least in part a matter of the retentionalist rejecting the general approach to perceptual experience that informs that model and adopting a representational view of experience, which takes as basic the idea of perceptual experiences as having a content in the sense of veridicality or accuracy conditions. More to the point, the veridicality or accuracy conditions of perceptual experience, as the retentionalist conceives of them, always include conditions that range over what has just been as well as what is present. That, the retentionalist will say, is what is required for it to be possible for instances of succession and change to figure in perceptual experience.

This gives us a way of understanding the dialectic between the cinematic model and retentionalism that does not turn on the kinds of difficult-to-make-precise claims about differences between retention and memory that feature heavily in the existing literature on retentionalism.[13] What, then, of the other demarcation problem, that of explaining what the difference consists in between extensionalism and the cinematic model? I have said that the extensionalist, if she is to clarify how her position is genuinely different from the cinematic model, needs to distance herself specifically from the latter in the guise of the resemblance theory of temporal experience. In fact, such a need plausibly also arises for another reason, which is the frequent accusation extensionalists face that they are committing a vehicle/content confusion.

The "vehicle/content" terminology (in the relevant sense) is again one that belongs specifically to one of the two general approaches to perceptual experience that I distinguished above, viz. the representational view of experience. As we saw, perceptual experience, according to this view, is a matter of the subject being in a certain state with a representational content in the sense of veridicality or accuracy conditions. The distinction between vehicle and content, in this context, is typically used to emphasise the distinction between the properties of the state that does the representing – the vehicle – and the properties (of the objects that are being perceived) that are being represented by the state – its content. According to the representationalist, the latter properties are fixed by (some of) the former, but it is nevertheless important not to confuse the two.

To commit a vehicle/content confusion is to assume, simply because of a failure to distinguish between vehicle and content, that what determines which properties a mental state or event represents is that the mental state or event itself possesses the same properties. This latter assumption is of course one that is implicit in the resemblance theory, according to which we become aware of change in the world, because it produces in us a succession of experiences that is itself changing. The idea, in other words, is that the mechanism by which the content of temporal experience is fixed is resemblance: experience is accurate in so far as it itself, as an occurrence with a certain sort of temporal structure, resembles the temporal structure of the occurrences it is an experience of.

The idea that extensionalists endorse a version of the resemblance theory, and are committing a version of the vehicle/content confusion in doing so, is expressed by Michael Tye as follows:

> Granted, I experience the red flash as being before the green one. But it need not be true that my experience or awareness of the red flash is before my experience or awareness of the green one. If I utter the sentence
>
> The green flash is after the red flash,
>
> I represent the red flash as being before the green one; but my representation of the red flash is not before my representation of the green flash. In general, represented order has no obvious link with the order of representations. Why suppose that there is such a link for experiential representations?
>
> *(Tye 2003: 90)*

One strategy the extensionalist might use to respond to this passage is to treat the question at the end as a genuine rather than a rhetorical one, and offer reasons as to why temporal experience should be considered a special case, in the sense that there are special grounds for thinking that what fixes the temporal structure of what is experienced is the temporal structure of the experience itself.[14]

In as far as it would saddle the extensionalist with an endorsement of the resemblance theory, though, this strategy also carries a significant cost. For, as I have argued, the resemblance theory can also be interpreted as a version of the cinematic view of temporal experience, and it is at least not obvious what sort of genuine alternative to the cinematic view an extensionalist of the sort we are considering at the moment is proposing. Even more to the point, the resemblance theory of temporal experience appears explanatorily vacuous. As with resemblance theories of experience in general, it faces the obvious problem that it seems to presuppose what it is trying to explain. In assuming that a resemblance between temporal features of our own experience and temporal features of the world can be made to do explanatory work in accounting for our awareness of the latter, it seems to take our ability to become aware of the former for granted. For the succession of our own experiences to explain our awareness of temporally extended goings-on, it seems, we would have to have a way of becoming introspectively aware of that succession as such, i.e. not just successively becoming aware of each experience in turn, but becoming aware of their succeeding each other. And it is not at all clear that it is any easier to account for our introspective awareness of temporal features of our own stream of experiences than it is to account for our awareness of temporal features of the world presented in experience. In fact, we have made no progress in explaining how an awareness of succession is possible.[15]

I think a better strategy for the extensionalist to use in order to respond to the charge of committing a vehicle/content confusion – which will at the same time serve to distinguish her view from the resemblance theory – is to reject the representationalist assumptions on which, e.g. Tye's argument quoted above is based. The charge of a vehicle/content confusion only makes sense against the background assumption of a representational view of the nature of perception. If, by contrast, we see the extensionalist as being motivated by a relational view of experience, it can be sidestepped altogether. On the relational view of experience, there is no representational vehicle the subject instantiates, the particular properties of which fix the contents of her experience. This of course does not mean that questions about the temporal properties of experience don't also arise for the relational view of experience, but they do not involve the idea of two things, the temporal properties of which can either match each other or not, as envisaged by the picture of experiences as involving both a vehicle and a content. The question for the relationalist on her view, rather, is whether the relation of acquaintance in which we stand to objects of experience is most fundamentally a relation in which we stand to objects at a time, or must most fundamentally be seen as something that itself unfolds over intervals of time. As I have suggested, an extensionalist motivated by the relational view of perception will argue that we need to think the latter because we can perceive instances of succession. As the relation of acquaintance is a generic one in which we simply either do or do not stand to items, perceiving instances of succession must involve standing in such a relation to a succession of such items over time, as they succeed each other. Experiencing goes on over time, on this view, and this is how the items that can figure in experience include not just individual entities that succeed each other, but the very instance of succession in which they partake. Yet, the only sense in which this makes experience temporally structured is that such different entities can figure in it in turn.

This, then, would be a way for the extensionalist to respond to the charge of committing a vehicle/content confusion that would, at the same time, serve as a way of demarcating her view from the cinematic model in the guise of the resemblance theory of temporal experience. If what I said before about the retentional model is along the right lines, it would of course imply that the debate between retentionalists and extensionalists, too, should be seen as being informed by a different view of the nature of perceptual experience on each side – the representational view and the relational view of perception, respectively. In concluding, I will briefly look at whether our discussion might also be able to contribute something to deciding between them.

Concluding remarks

I have argued that viewing debates between different approaches to temporal experience as turning on contrasting views of the very nature of perceptual experience that those approaches embody, might help us to come to a better understanding of what the differences between them consist in.

One part of my argument in which this thought has played a crucial role was in the claim that the "cinematic model of temporal experience" can actually take two quite different forms. Defenders of the cinematic model are, in effect, pulled in two different directions, each implicitly motivated by a different view of the nature of perception. In its memory theory guise, it can be seen to be motivated by a relational view of experience, which views perception as a particularly direct form of contact in which we can stand to things in the world around us when they are temporally present. In its resemblance theory guise, it can be seen to be motivated by the idea that experiences constitute a representation of what they are experiences of, with the added thought that, at least in the case of experiential representations of temporal properties, the mechanism of representation is resemblance.

What I also hope to have shown is that, once the two different versions of the cinematic view are clearly distinguished from one another, it becomes obvious that neither of them constitutes a viable theory of temporal experience – the memory theory flies in the face of phenomenology, and the resemblance theory is explanatorily vacuous.

This leaves the retentional model and the extensional model as the two main contenders, which I have suggested are again best seen as embodying a representational and a relational view of experience, respectively, to demarcate them from the versions of the cinematic model they would otherwise be hard to distinguish from. How should we decide between them? At this point, I wish to come back to an issue I raised at the beginning of this chapter. There, I said that there is something like a meta-philosophical intuition that might be seen to be driving the recent resurgence of interest in the topic of temporal experience: that we leave out something central to the nature of conscious perceptual experience itself if we ignore its temporal dimension. If what I have been saying in this chapter is right, I now want to suggest, the retentionalist might be seen to face more of a difficulty when it comes to accounting for this intuition than does the extensionalist.

The retentional model, I have suggested, is best seen as applying a representational view of experience to account for experiences of change and succession. At its most basic, what that means is that the retentional model allows temporal properties to figure in the representational content of experience alongside other properties. If that is all there is to the retentional model, though, then it is a legitimate question to ask why temporal experience should be accorded any special sort of status when it comes to giving an account of the nature of conscious perceptual experience. If experience is construed as a matter of being in a state with a certain representational content in the sense of veridicality or accuracy conditions, why think that, amongst those veridicality or accuracy conditions, those that concern temporal properties are somehow special?

If we adopt the extensionalist model of experience, by contrast, it perhaps becomes somewhat easier to see why considerations about temporal experience might be thought to be able to contribute something quite distinctive to our overall account of the nature of perceptual experience. I have suggested that the extensionalist model is best interpreted as an attempt to account for temporal experiences within the framework of a relational view of perception. The distinctive contribution it can be seen to be making to such a view is that it shows that the relation of acquaintance is not just one in which we stand to objects of awareness at a time, but also one which displays an essential on-going aspect – that somehow, within the general framework of a relational view of experience, we have to account for the idea of experiences as most fundamentally things that unfold through a period of clock time. As Brian O'Shaughnessy says: "Even the unchanging perception of a fixed immobilized world conceals a processive continuity, that of the perceiving itself, which is occurrently renewed in each instant . . . And this is how it is with experience as such" (O'Shaughnessy 2000: 63).[16]

Notes

1 Even this last claim is perhaps not strong enough, because experiences of static, i.e. unchanging, scenes, too, have a temporal dimension to them, in so far as we experience them as unchanging *over a period of time*.

2 I do not mean the following remarks as a criticism of Dainton. I can't think of any *better* way of illustrating the three models either. My point, in some sense, is that besides serving as illustrations of the three models, what the diagrams in Figure 13.1 also illustrate is the difficulty in getting a clear fix on where exactly the differences between them lie.

3 I will speak in this way even though I think one should allow for a version of the cinematic model on which perceptual experience has something akin to a shutter speed. That is to say, the "moment" taken in by each individual experience in fact consists of a very brief interval (because the physical phenomena that allow us to perceive, e.g. sounds or colours need some time to register on our senses). Just as with the images composing a film, however, this does not mean that those experiences themselves convey any temporal information.

4 Whilst this may be an unconventional way of thinking about the extensional model, it may in fact be more in line with perceptual psychology. See, e.g. Busch and VanRullen (2014).

5 Plumer (1985: 27f.), who endorses the cinematic model, somewhat heroically maintains that there is no such contrast, saying: "[Broad] claims we cannot see either the minute- or the hour-hand moving . . . I suspect he did not look at them very long (who does?)". Note that the term "see" here is somewhat

misleading. Plumer's official position is that there is no contrast because "no matter what hand you are looking at, at an instant you are *seeing* the hand where it is at an instant and *remembering* it where it has been for however long you looked" (Ibid.: 28).

6   The reference to a "new word" is intended to echo one of Husserl's own criticisms of Brentano.

7   On appeals to the notion of "unity" in debates about temporal experience more generally, see also Hoerl (2013: sec. 6).

8   On this, see also Phillips (2014: 149f.). Instead of appealing to the notion of unity, Phillips proposes that what makes extensionalism distinctive is the idea that "there are certain durations of experience that are *explanatorily* or *metaphysically* prior to their temporal subparts" (Ibid., see also Soteriou (2007), for related ideas). The characterization of extensionalism that I outline below is intended to be compatible with the thought that it is committed to an idea along those lines. My own focus is on other issues regarding the dialectic between extensionalism and its rivals.

9   Reid is typically interpreted as a direct realist, i.e. as holding that it is mind-independent objects that figure in experience in this way, though matters are complicated by the fact that he also assigns "sensations" a crucial role in perception.

10 See, e.g. Campbell (2011). The term "relational view" is typically reserved for a view on which perceptual experience is most basically conceived of as a relation specifically to mind-independent entities. Brewer's term "object view", by contrast, is meant to be neutral on the question as to whether the relevant entities are mind-dependent or mind-independent. The latter question is also tangential to my concerns.

11 The finite speed of, e.g. sound or light, does of course imply that, strictly speaking, events that figure in perceptual experience in fact happened some time ago – some of them even a considerable amount of time ago. The point here is that those events are, at any rate, not experienced *as past*. For present purposes, we can remain neutral as to whether this implies that our experiences of them are therefore in some respect illusory, or whether experience should actually be seen as being neutral about the timing of distal events (in contrast to the timing of those events being registered).

12 Recent defences of the object or relational view often stress that the relation in question should be conceived of as a *three-place* relation between the perceiver, the scene perceived and a "standpoint" from which the perceiver perceives the scene (Campbell 2011). This standpoint is supposed to be what accounts for the obvious differences there can be, for instance, between experiences of the same object seen from different spatial viewpoints. Against this background, a version of the relational view might be thought conceivable which allows for the idea that events can be experienced "as past" as well as "as present", where the difference between the two lies with one's *temporal* point of view on them. Some of the remarks above are meant to indicate what seem to me to be important disanalogies between time and space that cast doubt on the viability of such a position, though this is an issue that deserves a more detailed treatment.

13 It can also explain what unites Husserl's retentionalism with the views of authors such as Grush (2006) and Lee (2014b), who relate their theories to Husserl's, but who also significantly diverge from Husserl on some of the details.

14 For a related debate as to whether "time is special", see Phillips (2014) and Lee (2014a).

15 Compare here also Ruth Millikan's critical discussion of what she calls the "passive picture theory" of perception, and her charge that it produces "a façade of understanding that overlooks the need to give any account *at all* of the way the inner understander works, any *account* of the mechanics of inner representation" (2000: 112).

16 Thanks to Elliot Carter, Ian Phillips and members of the Warwick Mind and Action Research Centre for helpful comments.

References

Brewer, B. (2011) *Perception and Its Objects*, Oxford, UK: Oxford University Press.

Busch, N. A. and VanRullen, R. (2014) "Is visual perception like a continuous flow or a series of snapshots?" in V. Arstila and D. Lloyd (eds), *Subjective Time: The Philosophy, Psychology, and Neuroscience of Temporality*, Cambridge, MA: MIT Press.

Campbell, J. (2011) "Consciousness and reference", in B. McLaughlin, A. Beckermann and S. Walter (eds), *The Oxford Handbook of Philosophy of Mind*, Oxford, UK: Oxford University Press.

Chuard, P. (2011) "Temporal experiences and their parts", *Philosophers' Imprint* 11(11): 1–28.

Dainton, B. (2000) *Stream of Consciousness: Unity and Continuity in Conscious Experience*, London: Routledge.

Dainton, B. (2010) "Temporal consciousness", in E. N. Zalta (ed.), *The Stanford Encyclopedia of Philosophy*, available at http://plato.stanford.edu/entries/consciousness-temporal/. Accessed 1 September 2016.

Grush, R. (2006) "How to, and how not to, bridge computational cognitive neuroscience and Husserlian phenomenology of time consciousness", *Synthese* 153(3): 417–450.

Hoerl, C. (2013) "'A succession of feelings, in and of itself, is not a feeling of succession'", *Mind* 122(486): 373–417.

Husserl, E. G. (1893–1917) *On the Phenomenology of Consciousness of Internal Time (1893–1917)*, J. B. Brough, trans., Dordrecht, The Netherlands: Kluwer Academic Publishers.

Lee, G. (2014a) "Extensionalism, atomism and continuity", in L. N. Oaklander (ed.), *Debates in the Metaphysics of Time*, London: Bloomsbury.

Lee, G. (2014b) "Temporal experience and the temporal structure of experience", *Philosophers' Imprint* 14(3): 1–21.

Millikan, R. G. (2000) *On Clear and Confused Ideas: An Essay about Substance Concepts*, Cambridge, UK: Cambridge University Press.

O'Shaughnessy, B. (2000) *Consciousness and the World*, Oxford, UK: Clarendon Press.

Phillips, I. (2014) "The temporal structure of experience", in V. Arstila and D. Lloyd (eds), *Subjective Time: The Philosophy, Psychology, and Neuroscience of Temporality*, Cambridge, MA: MIT Press.

Plumer, G. (1985) "The myth of the specious present", *Mind* 94(373): 19–35.

Reid, T. (1785) "Essays on the intellectual powers of man", in D. Brookes and K. Haakonssen (eds), *The Edinburgh Edition of Thomas Reid*, 2002 ed., Edinburgh, UK: Edinburgh University Press.

Soteriou, M. (2007) "Content and the stream of consciousness", *Philosophical Perspectives* 21(1): 543–568.

Tye, M. (2003) *Consciousness and Persons: Unity and Identity*, Cambridge, MA: MIT Press.

14

TIME IN THE DREAM

Thomas Crowther and Matthew Soteriou

It is a natural thought, testified to in different ways by the contributions to this handbook, that there are philosophically significant connections between experience and temporal awareness. In this chapter, we aim to elucidate aspects of these connections by reflection on the distinctive temporal properties of experience in different states of consciousness. We take it that experiences are those mental occurrences that constitute the stream of consciousness over time. Our focus here is the form of temporal awareness one has in virtue of such occurrences in the stream of consciousness.

The character of any such discussion will clearly be determined by what experience is taken to be. For the purposes of discussion in what follows we assume the following:

(a) Experience is "occurrent". Experience occupies time by occurring rather than obtaining.[1]
(b) Experience is phenomenally conscious occurrence. Where experience occurs, there is "something it is like" for the subject of experience, in virtue of experience so occurring.

Two questions about experience and temporal awareness guide discussion in this chapter:

1 What are the distinctive temporal properties of experiences *simpliciter*? What is the distinctive kind of temporal awareness that obtains in virtue of a subject's having any experience at all?
2 Experience occurs in a range of different states of consciousness. What is distinctive of temporal awareness in dreams, by contrast with temporal awareness in the wakeful condition?

The discussion of the temporal properties of experience offered by Brian O'Shaughnessy (2000) is unusual in the literature on temporal awareness in that it directly engages with these questions. What follows here builds answers to these questions that develop ideas we take to be at work in O'Shaughnessy's account.

The temporal properties of experience in general

Let us begin with the first question. We assume that subjects who are asleep and in dreamless sleep do not undergo experience. Therefore, one way to approach the question of what is distinctive of the temporal awareness that characterises experience is to assess what must be missing, with respect to temporal awareness, in the dreamless sleeper, by contrast with the wakeful experiencer.[2] It is natural to think that one who is dreamlessly asleep lacks a "temporal point of view", or a "temporal perspective" in some sense. But what precisely does such lack amount to?

One suggestion is that what is missing by way of such a temporal perspective is that one who is dreamlessly asleep cannot be in psychological states with a temporal representational content, that is, a content that must be specified in temporal terms. This suggestion, though, is clearly false. When one falls asleep, for example, one may have many beliefs with a temporal content, including the belief that the year of Aristotle's death is 322 BC. On awakening from dreamless sleep, one does not need to reacquire such a belief. Such beliefs are states that persist throughout the time one was asleep. So it cannot be that what the sleeper who is dreamlessly asleep must lack is a psychological state with any temporal content.

In this example, the temporal content of belief is tenseless. Perhaps what is missing in dreamless sleep is the capacity for belief or representation with any tensed content. But this suggestion does not appear to be correct. For example, one may fall dreamlessly asleep believing that Aristotle died in Chalcis. That is a belief that represents it as true that Aristotle's death occurred some time in the past, and occurred in Chalcis, and is true if and only if Aristotle's death did occur in the past, and in Chalcis. For it to be true that one believes this proposition the following day, at some time after one has woken, does not require that one has reacquired that belief. It can persist across the time that one was in dreamless sleep.

Similarly, dreamless sleepers appear to be capable of belief with representational content that must be characterised in terms of the temporal indexical "now". As one falls asleep, for example, one believes that it is now 2017. On waking, one does not need to reacquire this belief. It persisted as one slept. And so also, falling asleep after lunch, one may believe that it is now Sunday. One's absence of confusion about one's temporal location, on awakening half an hour later, after a period of dreamless sleep, suggests that one's belief that it is now Sunday was available on awakening, and had persisted throughout the interval of time one slept.

But though dreamless sleepers may be capable of belief with a content that includes the notion of "now" where the referent of "now" is a relatively long interval of time such as a year or a day, what does not seem possible is that a dreamless sleeper has a belief about some much shorter interval of time during the period she is dreamlessly asleep as "now". This is one part of what O'Shaughnessy suggests in the following:

> If [a dreamless sleeper] fell asleep at 6.00 a.m., and awoke at 6.10 a.m., he cannot at 6.05 a.m. entertain a belief about the instant 6.05 a.m. singled out as "now". He can at 6.05 a.m. entertain a belief about 6.05 a.m., but he cannot at 6.05 a.m. entertain a belief about the instant 6.05 a.m. singled out purely as "now". And he cannot do so, because he cannot do what an experiencer can do: pick out the present as "now"; and that because a non-experiencer is not conscious of "now", nor therefore of a continuity of "now"s, which is to say of "the passage of time".

(2000: 51)

There are different suggestions here. The first is that those who lack experience are not capable of a temporally indexical mode of awareness of the present moment. The thought seems to be this. Suppose one is expecting an important phone call at 6.05 am, but one falls dreamlessly asleep at 6.00 am. During the dreamless sleep that commences, one might retain the belief that at 6.05 am the phone will ring. If one does retain that belief, then when it is 6.05 am one will thereby have a belief that is about the moment that is present, 6.05 am. But in so believing, the suggestion goes, one would not have a belief about the present moment *as* "now". That requires the believer to be "conscious of 'now'". The suggestion is that what experience provides by way of temporal awareness is such consciousness of "the now". The occurrence of experience constitutes an "experience of the now" or "experience of the present moment". Nothing further at this stage need be assumed about the temporal character of "the now". In particular, it need not be assumed that the notion of a "now" or "the present moment" must be understood in terms of the notion of the "mathematical present" or what E. R. Clay (1882: 168) describes pejoratively as the notion of the present "which philosophy denotes by the name Present", that is, as something that lacks temporal extension at all.[3]

A second idea is that dreamless sleepers are not merely incapable of being aware of present moments as now. They lack a distinctive kind of awareness of time *over* the intervals of time during which they are dreamlessly asleep.

Take the subject who is dreamlessly asleep from 6.00 am to 6.10 am. It has been suggested that such a subject is incapable of being aware, at 6.05 am, of that moment of time as "now". But so also is such a sleeper incapable of successive awareness of moments of time as "now" during that interval of time, as each of those moments becomes successively present. Compare here the character of the temporal awareness of the wakeful experiencer over that interval of time. A subject who has experience during 6.00 am to 6.10 am has the capacity to be aware of certain shorter sub-intervals of that period of time as "now". But what one who has experience also appears capable of here is successive awareness of sub-intervals of time from 6.00 to 6.10 as "now" as each becomes present. An experiencer can be aware of the present moment as "now" at one moment, followed by the awareness of the present moment as "now" at the next moment, followed by awareness of the present moment as "now" over the next moment.

This characteristic lack of temporal awareness over an interval of dreamless sleep appears to reflect the ontology of experience and the way in which experience occupies intervals of time. Experience occupies time by occurring or unfolding "processively" over an interval.[4] On the processive occupation of an interval of time, O'Shaughnessy (2000) writes:

> Processes "go on" or "continue" occurrently in time, each new instant realizing more of the same as what has gone on so far . . . [their mode of persistence over time is] temporally repeated sameness.
>
> *(2000: 44)*

Of the processive constitution of experience, he notes:

> Yet even when experience is not changing in type or content, it still changes in another respect: it is constantly *renewed*, a new sector of itself is there and then *taking place*.
>
> *(2000: 42)*[5]

Hence, what it is for experience to occur processively over an interval of time is for there to be a succession of experience-phases over that period of time, with each phase of the succession that comes into existence "realizing more of the same" or "renewing" what has come previously. In turn, the character of the temporal awareness that a subject has over the interval of time is that of renewal. A subject who has experience during a minimal sub-interval is in a position to be aware of the present moment as "now" during that time, and this capacity to be aware of the present moment as "now" is renewed successively as experience unfolds in a succession over time.

However, the idea of successive experience of the present moment of time over an interval of time and the successive temporal awareness of the present as "now" that this makes possible is not sufficient to elucidate the temporal awareness that is characteristic of experience in general. William James (1950 [1890]: 628) famously remarks that: "A succession of feelings, in and of itself, is not a feeling of succession".[6] Successive experience (or a succession of experiences) of successive sub-intervals of time over an interval of time is not necessarily experience of change or succession.

But the experience of change or succession in the objects of experience is, at the very least, a near-necessary feature of temporal awareness in wakeful experience. Much of our everyday experience presents us with change and temporal succession in our perceptible environment: leaves visibly stirring in the trees outside the window, fingers visibly moving on the keyboard and the succession that's audible in the piece of music one is listening to.

There is some room for debate about whether the experience of change and succession is a necessary feature of experience, whenever experience occurs. Here we note just that there are no very clear cases of experience over an interval in which it is not possible to discern succession or change in the objects of experience over that interval. Even in cases in which experience occurs in conditions of complete darkness, silence and immobility, experiencers in such conditions are characteristically proprioceptive aware of their breathing and other internal bodily goings on, as well as the occurrence of imaginative processes of different kinds. Such awareness can also be taken to accompany the perceptual awareness of an array of unchanging material objects over an interval of time.[7]

The experience of change and succession that marks much of our experienced life has distinctive temporal characteristics. The objects of such experience are not instantaneous, but have temporal duration. The stirring of the leaves on the tree and the audible succession of the piece of music are things that unfold processively over intervals of time.[8] Not only do the objects of experience unfold processively; in the experience of change and succession that is distinctive of experience, such temporally extended objects of experience are presented to experiencers *as* temporally extended over intervals of time. And finally, and most notably, in cases of experience of change and succession, such as that which is involved in listening to a piece of music that extends over a few minutes, a subject who experiences such change or succession occurring at the present moment of time is characteristically aware, at that moment, of a temporally extended object of experience as temporally extended over an interval of time which is longer than the present moment.[9]

This suggests that a distinctive feature of experience over an interval is not just that over that time there is successive experience of moments of time but that such successive moments of time are experienced *as* successive. To illustrate, consider our visual experience of concrete material objects. Our visual experience of concrete material objects presents those objects as having spatial parts which are not currently visible (the back surface which faces away from the viewer). There is an analogue of this in our experience of the temporal objects of experience in experience of change and succession.[10] Suppose that over the course of twenty seconds you watch someone walk slowly from one end of the garden to the other. During the final three seconds, you experience that person walking the final few paces of his traversal of the garden. That you experience someone as walking the final few paces of a traversal of the garden during those seconds is for the walk to be presented to you during those moments as something which has earlier stages. The respect in which the walk is presented to you during that moment as something that has earlier stages does not involve one's making a judgement that what one sees now has been going earlier. Rather, what goes on during the final three seconds one watches the walk is visually experienced as having earlier parts. This is the minimal respect in which the experience of change and succession appears to involve experience of successive moments over time *as* successive.

Our purpose here is not to explain why experience in the wakeful condition has such features. But some of the remarks that O'Shaughnessy (2000) makes are useful in clarifying the minimal commitments involved in the idea that in experience one has successive experience of the present moment, and experiences these successive moments as successive. According to O'Shaughnessy (2000), the fact that the objects of experience at an instant in time have temporal duration and can be experienced as having temporal duration shows the role for some kind of basic notion of short-term memory that makes such representation of temporal objects possible. He says that "The present experience must unite with and depend upon past experience. This means that the past must in some sense be 'co-present' with the present, and such a co-presence is a mode of remembering" (2000: 56). He describes this as a "developmentally early form of memory" (2000: 56). And in characterising this, he adds: "What in effect we are concerned with is the tendency on the part of experience and its given objects to unite across time to form determinate wholes. It is not unlike the property of momentum in a moving object" (2000: 56).[11]

The proposals outlined so far are not yet sufficient to characterise the temporal awareness that is distinctive of experience in the wakeful condition. For the temporal objects of experience to be presented as having immediately preceding phases is not for the objects of experience to be presented to one in some tensed way, as having past stages, or as being present. Though the proposals offered so far require the experiencer to stand in certain relations to the past – the suggestion is that the experience of change and succession as temporally extended requires previous phases of experience to determine the present temporal characteristics of the objects of experience – this does not entail that the experiencer must be psychologically oriented to the past, or the immediate past, in a way that constitutes a "tensed temporal perspective" on the past, in a sense to be presently explained.

This suggests that the proposals outlined so far are not yet sufficient to characterise the temporal awareness that is distinctive of experience in the wakeful condition. For, normally, wakefully conscious experiencers are psychologically oriented to the past in a way that constitutes such a tensed temporal perspective on the past. Most relevantly to our current concerns, they are normally psychologically oriented in this way to their *immediate* past. This is particularly well illustrated in cases of wakeful experience that involves conscious intentional action. Here, a tensed psychological orientation towards what one was doing in one's immediate past seems to be required for an awareness of what one is doing at the present moment, at least where one experiences that moment *as* present. Suppose one writes a paragraph longhand over a minute. Then it seems that halfway through that minute one must be psychologically oriented to the fact that moments ago one was writing a sentence. In such cases, the absence of an orientation towards what one was doing in one's immediate past would seem to undermine the idea that one is aware of one's writing as unfolding in the present. Given that wakefully conscious intentional action brings with it the awareness of what one is doing at the present moment, then wakefully conscious intentional action seems to bring with it a tensed temporal orientation to the past.[12]

Cases of wakefully conscious intentional action also illustrate the idea that wakeful experiences normally involve psychological orientation towards the immediate future, in a way that constitutes a tensed temporal orientation to the immediate future. As one writes longhand over the course of a minute, one characteristically anticipates what one will be doing over the next few seconds, as one writes. When one is halfway through the writing of a paragraph at some moment, one anticipates what is to come. The idea that one fails to have such attitudes that orient one towards one's immediate future, similarly to the case involving one's attitudes to the past, seems to jeopardise the idea that one experiences one's writing a paragraph as present. And given the connections between conscious intentional action and such awareness of what one is doing, this seems to threaten the very idea that one intentionally writes a paragraph over that time. In general, experience in the wakeful condition appears to involve expectations and anticipations about what will occur in one's immediate future. These attitudes appear central to the generation of successful action and to the ongoing management of actions already under way.[13]

One explanation of these features of our experienced life locates the phenomena not in the requirements for intentional action as such but in general features of temporal awareness in wakeful experience. In debates about the nature of time and the semantics of temporal language, it is a familiar idea that the notion of tensed language and tensed content manifests one basic sense in which a subject has a perspective on time.[14] Setting aside issues about tensed language and thought, what these observations about the psychological orientation to their immediate past and immediate future suggests is that wakefully conscious experiencers occupy a tensed temporal perspective.[15]

For reasons related to earlier discussion, it is clear that some form of tensed perspective is available to the non-experiencer. One may wake up believing that one's fiftieth birthday lies in the future as well as believing that Aristotle's death occurred in the past. Several things are different about the temporal perspective of the non-experiencer by contrast with that occupied by one who has experience, however. What is not available to the non-experiencer is a tensed temporal perspective the point of origin of which is experience that affords awareness of "now". In virtue of the fact that it serves as the point of origin for such a perspective, we can think of the wakefully conscious subject's experience as an experienced *present*. The wakefully conscious experiencer is psychologically oriented to the future from an experienced present and also oriented to the past from an experienced present. Also, unlike the dreamless sleeper, the wakefully conscious experiencer can have "short-range" as well as "long-range" attitudes to the past and future. Wakeful experiencers are oriented to their immediate past and future. Those lacking experience are not.

The idea that wakeful experience involves a tensed temporal perspective suggests a number of further ideas about temporal awareness in the condition. First, the idea of such a tensed perspective seems to be one in which the subject's psychological orientation is to past, present and future or not at all. It cannot be that subjects have experience in which they are oriented to their immediate past in this way, but do not have an experience of the present moment as present, or that they experience the present but are not psychologically oriented towards their future. That would undermine the idea that the experience of the present moment was a mode of awareness of the present *as* the present.

These claims about tensed awareness are suggested in different places in O'Shaughnessy's discussion. For example, after reflection on the way that the occurrence of intentional action in experience appears to involve anticipation of the immediate future, he writes:

> One might easily suppose that the great temporal novelty ushered into being by experience is the "co-presence" in the experiential instant of *present and future*: orientation to both dimensions of time at each point in experience. However, this would be an error. The great temporal novelty is the irreducible "co-presence" of the *other two* temporal dimensions in the experiential instant: it is the meeting of the past and/or future in the present.
>
> *(2000: 55)*

A consequence of this is that:

> Close up the past, wall off the future, and you cover over the present too. For there is simply no such thing as "the solipsistic fruits of the instant".
>
> *(2000: 62)*

The notion of a tensed temporal perspective with an origin in the experienced present might also be taken to support a further kind of claim about the character of the experienced present. The temporal present is what temporally intervenes between past and future. So, it is natural to think that the experienced present, in the context of such proposals about tensed temporal perspective, is the moment which temporally intervenes between the future as the experiencer is psychologically oriented to it, and the past as the experiencer is psychologically oriented to it. But the notion of the moment of time that temporally intervenes between the immediate future as one anticipates it, and the immediate past as one remembers it, does not, it seems, determine a notion of the experienced present as the notion of a "mathematical present" or the present as a moment that lacks temporal extension. If one is writing a paragraph of prose longhand at some moment of time, there is experienced movement that falls between the immediate future one is oriented to in anticipation and the immediate past one is oriented to through memory. But such experienced movement is not durationless. It has temporal extension. So the experienced present that it occupies appears not to be a durationless instant, but an instant understood as a temporally extended interval of time of some short duration.[16]

In this section, we have begun developing some suggestions about the temporal properties of experience in general. In summary:

1   Dreamless sleepers lack awareness of the present moment as "now" because they lack experience of the present moment.
2   Over the intervals of time they are dreamlessly asleep, dreamless sleepers lack successive awareness of successively present moments of time as "now", because they lack experience over that interval.
3   Wakeful experiencers characteristically experience change and succession in the objects of experience. Hence such subjects must experience successively present moments as successive.
4   Wakeful experiencers occupy a "tensed temporal perspective" with a point of origin in the experience of the present moment (which is thereby an "experienced present").

For these claims to constitute a satisfactory answer to question 1 (posed at the start of the chapter), they must be true of all experiences. But are they? Experience occurs in dreaming. Are these proposals true of experience in the dream? If they are not, how does that impact on our suggestions about question 1? And how should the distinctive temporal properties of experience in the dream, by contrast with those that occur during wakefulness, be explained?

The temporal properties of experience in dreaming

It should be noted at the outset that there are very few philosophical claims about dreams that are entirely free from controversy. Our question about temporal awareness in dreams assumes that dreams are, or involve, conscious experiences that we have during sleep; and that is an assumption that some philosophers have questioned.[17] Even among those who accept the assumption, it is difficult to identify anything like a consensus on the question of the nature and constitution of dreams;[18] and arguably, philosophical disagreement on this topic is exacerbated by the distinctive methodological challenges that are associated with the empirical enterprise of attempting to access and conduct a scientific study of the *sleeping* mind.[19] However, while we don't propose to settle here which of the extant accounts of dreaming is correct, our guiding assumption in what follows is that progress can be made in addressing our question about temporal awareness in dreams by drawing out the implications for temporal awareness of different hypotheses about the constitution of dreams. Moreover, we suggest that the exercise of drawing out such implications can, in turn, help illuminate what is at stake in these disagreements about the constitution of dreams.

Among those philosophers who accept the common sense view that our dreams do involve conscious experiences, one central area of dispute turns on the question of whether it is appropriate to categorise our dream experiences as perceptual experiences that are akin to waking hallucinations. Many of those who deny this, propose instead that our dream experiences should, rather, be regarded as acts of imagination.[20] An associated dispute turns on the question of whether we should regard dreaming and waking states as *constitutively* different.[21] These disagreements are sometimes presented in the philosophical literature in the following terms. Those who propose that our dream experiences are akin to waking hallucinations, as opposed to acts of imagination, deny that dream states and waking states are constitutively different; whereas those who propose that our dream experiences are acts of imagination affirm a constitutive difference.[22]

There are various qualms one might have about this way of characterising what's in dispute about the constitution of dreams. First, given that one can imagine things when one is awake, it isn't clear in what sense one establishes a "constitutive" difference between waking states and dream states by way of the proposal that our dream experiences are acts of imagination. Second, it is not clear that it is in any case correct to assume that waking hallucinations do not involve acts of imagination; so the question of whether dream experiences are akin to waking hallucinations, as opposed to acts of imagination, may be thought to be ill-posed. Moreover, matters are further complicated by the fact that waking hallucinations can occur amidst a syndrome of other features which might together be thought to constitute an altered state of consciousness. Although a subject suffering from such a syndrome may be awake and not asleep, and hence not dreaming, it is not obvious that we should rule out the proposal that there is a *constitutive* difference between her *altered* state of consciousness and the state of consciousness of a subject in the "normal" wakeful condition.

So, for example, J. Allan Hobson (1999) proposes that our dreams are comprised, in part, of the kinds of hallucinations that subjects can have when awake. However, his view accommodates the idea that there are significant differences between dreams and normal waking experience, for he proposes that our dreams are akin to waking psychosis, and in particular, delirium. In making the comparison with delirium, Hobson notes a syndrome of features associated with delirium, which he claims are also present in core, paradigmatic instances of dreaming. As well as visual and motoric hallucination, this syndrome includes disorientation (with respect to persons, places and times), recent memory loss, confabulation and delusion. Does Hobson's proposal about the nature and constitution of dreams commit him to the claim that there is no constitutive difference between dream states and "normal" waking states? That question is no more straightforward to answer than is the corresponding question of whether there is a constitutive difference between psychotic episodes of delirium and normal waking experience.

In what follows, we will be suggesting that despite such qualms, the question of whether our dreams are acts of imagination does indeed connect with a substantive disagreement as to whether dream states and waking states are constitutively different; and that the nature of this disagreement can be clarified by drawing out the implications that the imagination model of dreaming has for an account of the form of temporal awareness which is available to a subject as she dreams.

An account of the constitution of dreams of the sort that Hobson proposes has the resources to accommodate and explain profound effects on the quality of a dreaming subject's temporal awareness – in particular, on the dreamer's diminished ability to orient herself temporally, both with respect to her past and future. However, the variety of degradation in temporal awareness that it envisages does not amount to a form of temporal awareness that is inconsistent with being awake, as the comparison with delirium makes clear.[23] By contrast, there are reasons for thinking that the imagination model of dreaming countenances a form of temporal awareness that is inconsistent with being awake. It therefore suggests a view according to which dream states and waking states are constitutively different in the following special respect. The stream of consciousness of the dreaming subject cannot occur in the wakeful condition, and the stream of consciousness of the awake subject cannot constitute a dream.

The latter claim is one that O'Shaughnessy attempts to argue for. He asserts that "There is no possible world in which the dream is the stream of consciousness of a conscious [i.e. awake] being" (2002: 412). Part of his argument for this assertion rests on the claim that dreaming involves a relation to time that is inconsistent with wakeful consciousness (2000: 92). And his argument for that claim in turn depends on the assumption that our dreams are imaginings. To see how the imagination model of dreaming might lead to the proposal that dreaming involves a relation to time that is inconsistent with wakeful consciousness, we first need to note some distinctive features of the representation of time in imagination. Those features can be highlighted by considering some comparable features of the representation of space in imagination.

When a subject sensorily imagines a scene, she typically imagines a spatial point of view on objects within the imagined scene. For example, in visualising an array of objects, some objects may be imagined as being to the left and others to the right, *from an imagined point of view*. In saying that the spatial point of view, and not just the array of objects, is itself imagined, we mean the following. The centre of origin of the spatial point of view from which objects are visualised to the left and right is not determined by the actual spatial location and orientation of the subject who is visualising.[24]

For example, suppose you are lying in bed on your back with your head facing towards the ceiling, and suppose that, so situated, you close your eyes and visualise a stormy seascape. You do not thereby imagine the stormy sea as occupying a spatial location relative to your actual location, i.e. somewhere above the spatial location that is actually occupied by your bed. If you happen to move your head as you visualise that scene, you do not thereby imagine a change in the spatial location of the scene you visualise. As you visualise, any change in your actual spatial location is consistent with no change in the imagined spatial location of scene you imagine, and consistent with no change in the spatial location of the origin of the imagined point of view from which aspects of the scene are imagined as being to the left and right.

Suppose that as you visualise this scene, you imagine saying to a companion, "we should be able to see the lighthouse from here". Your imagined use of the indexical "here" does not pick out any spatial location that is relative to the actual spatial location you occupy as you imagine (i.e. your bedroom). Now suppose that you stop visualising a seascape and instead start visualising a mountain range. In such a case, there may be nothing to determine the actual, or represented, spatial relations between these imagined scenes, i.e. the sea and the mountain range. At least not if that question is not settled by your intentions in so imagining.

Corresponding points apply to the temporal perspectives that we imagine when we engage in acts of sensory imagination. For instance, when you visualise a friend walking towards you, there is a respect in which the successive temporal parts of her approach are each imagined as being temporally present, e.g. now she is walking towards the zebra crossing, now she stops at the zebra crossing, now she is crossing the road, and so on. But the temporal location of your act of imagining does not determine a represented temporal location of the event you imagine. That is to say, when you imagine your friend walking towards you, you needn't thereby be imagining that her approach occurs at the actual time of your act of imagining. You could be imagining a future encounter, or you could be imagining the past encounter you hoped for, and indeed the question of the time of the imagined event could be left entirely open.

Suppose you imagine steeling yourself to make some momentous revelation to your approaching friend, and in doing so you imagine saying to yourself "it's now or never". That imagined use of a temporal indexical "now" need not pick out the actual time of your act of imagining. And since the temporal location of your imagined present is not determined by the actual temporal location of your act of imagining, your imagined past needn't be earlier than the actual time of your act of imagining, and your imagined future needn't be later than the actual time of your act of imagining.

Now suppose that you stop imagining your friend walking towards you and you start imagining a clown cycling on a pier. In such a case, there may be nothing to determine the actual or represented temporal relations between these imagined events, i.e. your friend's approach and the event of a clown cycling. At least not if that question is not settled by your intentions in so imagining. The temporal location and temporal order of your acts of imagination do not in themselves determine the represented temporal location and temporal order of the events you imagine. In consequence, the temporal location and temporal order of these acts of imagination does not in itself determine the temporal relations between each imagined present.

Given these points, we can note the following. In the case of a subject who is awake and imagining, we can mark a distinction between (a) the imagined temporal perspective that she has on events she imagines, and (b) the actual temporal perspective that she has on her acts of imagination. And we can note that the actual temporal order of her acts of imagining constitutively determines (b), but they need not determine (a). We said that the temporal location and temporal order of a subject's acts of imagining do not in themselves determine the represented temporal location and temporal order of the events she imagines. That is to say, the fact that one act of imagining an event occurs prior to a subsequent act of imagining an event does not in itself determine the represented temporal order of these imagined events. In consequence, the temporal order of these acts of imagination doesn't in itself determine, at any given time, which of these imagined events is in the imagined past or the imagined future. So the temporal order of the subject's acts of imagining does not in itself determine the imagined temporal perspective that she has on these imagined events. By contrast, the temporal order of her acts of imagination does determine, at any given time, her actual temporal perspective on those acts. That is to say, it does determine which of these acts of imagining are presented to her actual temporal perspective as present, past or future. In consequence, the awake subject can be aware of what she is now imagining (where "now" picks out the actual time of the act of imagination), what she has just been imagining, and what she intends to imagine subsequently.

With these points in mind, let us now consider the proposal that our dreams are acts of imagination. The particular version of the imagination model of dreaming we shall consider is this. All of the events that you dream of, including your dreamt actions, judgements, choices, and so on, are imagined events. To dream you are φ-ing is to imagine yourself φ-ing. But as you dream, you are not in a position to tell that all of these dreamt events and actions are merely imagined. According to this proposal, your dreamt temporal perspective is an imagined temporal perspective. But as you dream, you are not in a position to know that all dreamt events are merely imagined, and so you are not in a position to know that the temporal perspective of your dream is merely imagined. What implications would the truth of this proposal have for a subject's temporal awareness during dreams?

We noted that when you are awake and imagining a clown cycling on a pier, you need not be thereby representing that imagined event as occurring at the actual time of your act of imagining (just as you need not be thereby representing the event to occur at a spatial location specifiable egocentrically relative to the actual spatial location that you occupy when imagining). So if the above imagination model of dreaming is correct, then, likewise, when dreaming such an event, there may be no reason to think that you are thereby representing the dreamt event as occurring at the actual time of your dream (just as there may be no reason to think that the dreamt event is represented as occupying a spatial location that is to be specified egocentrically relative to your actual spatial location, e.g. from the actual spatial location that you occupy in your bedroom when dreaming). If, when awake, you imagine a clown starting a race by shouting "now", there need be no reason to think that your imagined utterance of the indexical "now" picks out the actual time of your act of imagining. So likewise, if you dream you are shouting "now", there may be no reason to think that this dreamt use of the indexical "now" picks out the actual time of your dream.

Let us suppose that any dreamt use of the temporal indexical "now" is an imagined use of that indexical, and let us suppose that as you dream you are not in a position to know that any such use of an indexical is merely imagined. The consequence, we suggest, would be this. When you dream that you are referring to the present, there is no guarantee that you are thereby referring to the time of your dream. So if, while you are dreaming, any use of a temporal indexical is a merely dreamt use of that temporal indexical, then as you dream you aren't in a position to pick out the temporal location of your dream using the temporal indexical "now". In consequence, there is a respect in which you are cut off from your actual present when you dream. Contrast this with your situation when you are awake and imagining. When you wakefully imagine, you are able to deploy a temporal indexical that falls outside the scope of your imagining, e.g. *now* I am imagining a clown shouting "now". In this case, the former temporal indexical picks out the actual time of your imagining – your *actual* present – even if the latter does not.

We noted earlier that the actual temporal order of a subject's acts of imagining doesn't constitutively determine the imagined temporal perspective that the subject has on events she imagines. So on the hypothesis that our dreams are comprised of acts of imagining, we should likewise expect that the actual temporal order of the acts of imagining that comprise a subject's dream experience doesn't constitutively determine the dreamt temporal perspective that the dreaming subject has on dreamt events. The temporal location and temporal order of the subject's acts of imagining doesn't in itself determine the represented temporal location and temporal order of the events she thereby dreams of. The fact that one act of imagining occurs prior to a subsequent act of imagining does not in itself determine the represented temporal order of the events she dreams of. In consequence, the temporal order of acts of imagining that comprise her dream experience doesn't in itself determine, at any given time, which of the events she has dreamt of is in the dreamt past or the dreamt future. For that reason, the temporal order of the acts of imagining that make up her dream experience doesn't in itself determine any temporal relations between the dreamt present/past/future at one time, and the dreamt present/past/future at subsequent or earlier times. Indeed, the temporal order of these acts of imagining does not in itself determine that these dreamt events can be ordered in a common time.

So a further consequence of the imagination model of dreaming that we can note is this. If, when dreaming, you are not in a position to tell that your dreamt temporal perspective is merely imagined, then the actual temporal order of your dream experience won't be sufficient to constitute an *actual* temporal perspective, i.e. a temporal perspective on your *actual* present, your *actual* past and your *actual* future. Your ignorance of the fact that your dreamt temporal perspective is merely imagined, will result in your failure to access a temporal perspective that isn't your imagined temporal perspective. Which is to say, you will thereby lack a temporal perspective on your *actual* present, past and future.[25]

In summary, we suggest that if the version of the imagination model of dreaming that we are considering is correct, then your temporal awareness as you dream will be distinctive in the following respects:

1   As you dream, you cannot refer to your actual present as "now". In that respect, when you dream, you are cut off from your actual present, i.e. actual time at which you dream.
2   When you dream, you do not have access to a temporal perspective on your *actual* past and your *actual* future.

We noted earlier that O'Shaughnessy suggests dreaming involves a relation to time that is inconsistent with wakeful consciousness; and that his argument for that claim depends on the assumption that our dreams are imaginings. O'Shaughnessy makes a number of remarks that indicate that he endorses claim 2 above. He claims that "Consciousness [i.e. waking consciousness] necessitates a certain simultaneous orientation towards past, present, and future. Significantly this is absent in the experience of the dream" (2000: 89–90). And he remarks:

> The dream present is a sort of Time Island. First in its failure to have internal or constitutive connections with its own past; second in having neither an actively projected nor merely expected future . . . Such a relation to time is inconsistent with [wakeful] consciousness.
>
> *(2000: 92)*

However, it seems that O'Shaughnessy doesn't endorse claim 1 above, i.e. the claim that as you dream, you cannot refer to your actual present as "now". O'Shaughnessy suggests that dreamers do have a consciousness of a present instant as the instant "now". He writes:

> "At a certain moment in the dream I became conscious of the presence of my grandfather", a dream report goes; and if the report is veridical, if that really happened during the night, dream experience at a certain moment was that "now grandfather is here", which singles out an instant of time via the use of "now", implying a consciousness at that time of that instant as "now".
>
> *(2000: 51)*

For the reasons we gave earlier, if the imagination model dreaming is assumed, one might question whether the subject's dreamt use of the temporal indexical "now" really does succeed in picking out the actual instant of time at which she dreams, or indeed any instant of time at all. Just as one might question whether the dreamt use of the indexical "here" picks out the actual spatial location of the dreamer, or indeed any spatial location at all.

In any case though, we suggest that if the imagination model of dreaming is correct, and if the imagination model of dreaming implies either claim 2, or both claims 1 and 2, a case can be made for O'Shaughnessy's proposal that our dreams involve a form of temporal awareness that is inconsistent with being awake. This in turn may give grounds for accepting that dream states and waking states are *constitutively* different in the following special respect: the stream of consciousness of the dreaming subject cannot occur in the wakeful condition, and the stream of consciousness of the awake subject cannot constitute a dream.

It should be said that we haven't given any arguments for thinking that the imagination model of dreaming that we have been considering is correct; and we don't have the space here to consider and address the various concerns one might have about its tenability. But we shall make some brief remarks on one possible source of concern, namely the concern that it is incompatible with the existence of so-called lucid dreaming, i.e. dreams in which the dreaming subject seems to be aware that she is dreaming, and seems to be able to exercise some level of control over her dream.[26]

One option for those advocating some version of an imagination model of dreaming is to say that during lucid dreams, the dreaming subject becomes aware that the events she is imagining are not real and that she may subsequently be able to exercise some level of control over her imaginings. That proposal might grant that during a lucid dream, the dreaming subject can have conscious thoughts about her dream that are not merely imagined, and it might also grant that during a lucid dream, the dreaming subject can engage in intentional agential mental acts that are not merely imagined. In granting those points, the advocate of the imagination model might allow that in the case of a lucid dream, the dreaming subject's ability to refer to her actual present as "now" is re-instated, and so too is her access to a temporal perspective on her actual past and her actual future.

Would that concession mean abandoning the proposal that dreaming involves a relation to time that is inconsistent with wakeful consciousness? It may rather result in the need to qualify the general proposal, to the following: *non-lucid* dreaming involves a relation to time that is inconsistent with wakeful consciousness. The stream of consciousness of the *non-lucidly* dreaming subject cannot occur in the wakeful condition, and the stream of consciousness of the awake subject cannot constitute a *non-lucid* dream. This qualification may in turn reflect the need to mark distinctions between different states of consciousness during sleep.

Conclusion

At the beginning of this chapter we raised the following question: What are the distinctive temporal properties of experiences *simpliciter*, i.e. what is the distinctive kind of temporal awareness that obtains in virtue of a subject's having any experience at all? A natural way of answering this question is to seek to identify features of temporal awareness that are common to experience in the wakeful condition and experience in non-wakeful states of consciousness. So how should this question be answered if the kind of imagination model of non-lucid dreaming that we have been considering is correct? Here are some temporal features that dream experience shares with experience in the wakeful condition, according to the imagination model of dreaming.

1   Dream experience is ontologically akin to wakeful experience, for dream experience is successive and occupies time processively.
2   The objects of dream experience have temporal extension and are experienced as such.
3   Dream experience involves a tensed temporal perspective, and there is a respect in which the origin of this tensed temporal perspective is an "experienced present".

However, according to the imagination model of dreaming, in the case of the non-lucid dream, the experienced present is an *imagined* present – an imagined present that need not pick out the actual time of the occurrence of the dream experience. That is to say, in the case of non-lucid dream experience, the point of origin of the subject's tensed temporal perspective need not be the actual present moment at which the dream experience occurs. So unlike the wakeful experiencer, the subject of a non-lucid dream may lack awareness of the actual present moment as "now". In consequence, she may lack successive awareness of such successively present moments as "now".

An outcome is that this view of dreaming suggests a respect in which dream experience reproduces, or imitates, the form of temporal awareness that is possessed during wakeful consciousness, *but without instantiating it*. It grants that the dreaming subject dreams that she has the form of temporal awareness that obtains during wakeful consciousness. But, according to this view of dreaming, to dream is to imagine. And to imagine having that distinctive form of temporal awareness isn't thereby to possess it. What this view of temporal awareness in dreams thereby accommodates is the idea that the dreaming subject seems, but merely seems, to be wakefully conscious. More specifically, it suggests a view on which the dreaming subject seems to be awake in a way that necessitates not being awake. This is precisely the view of dreaming that O'Shaughnessy recommends. He characterises dream experience as "purely and essentially an as-if [wakeful] consciousness that of necessity is not [wakeful] consciousness" (2002: 428).

Here we have not attempted to offer anything like a defence of this imagination model of dreaming, and there are many questions that can be asked of this view of dreaming that we haven't tried to address. The tenability of the view depends upon the idea that during a non-lucid dream the dreaming subject is not in a position to tell that the events that she dreams of are merely imagined. That hypothesis figured prominently in the suggestion that during a non-lucid dream the dreaming subject is not in a position to know her dreamt temporal perspective is merely imagined, she is not in a position to know that any dreamt use of a temporal indexical is merely imagined, which in turn prevents her from being able to deploy a temporal indexical which is outside the scope of her imagining. An obvious question to ask of that proposal is whether some explanation can be given of this hypothesised epistemic privation.

O'Shaughnessy (2000) suggests an answer. He proposes that the explanation is to be found in the fact that dreamers lack the "mental activeness" that is a distinguishing and fundamental mark of the wakeful condition.[27] According to O'Shaughnessy, the subject's "mental will" is not operative when she dreams, and, in consequence, the dreaming subject lacks the kind of practical self-knowledge that accompanies exercises of her mental agency – the kind of practical self-knowledge that would disclose to her that she is merely imagining. If O'Shaughnessy is right, then what this suggests is a basic connection between the notion of temporal awareness in the wakeful condition and the obtaining of some form of "mental activeness" in that condition. A development of this suggestion may promise to further illuminate both the notion of temporal awareness and an understanding of the state of wakeful consciousness.

Notes

1 See O'Shaughnessy 2000, chapter 1; Soteriou 2013, chapters 2 and 6.
2 This is the method pursued by O'Shaughnessy in O'Shaughnessy 2000, chapter 1, part 3.
3 *The Alternative: A Study in Psychology* was originally published anonymously in 1882. The name "E. R. Clay" is William James's invention (see James (1950 [1890]: 609ff.) and is the name that has been used in the literature to refer to the author of this work. The author was in fact E. Robert Kelly, a retired Boston cigar manufacturer. See Andersen (2014: §2.3) for discussion. In this chapter, we use the name by which the author of this work has been referred to in the literature since James's discussion. Thanks to Ian Phillips for pointing this out.
4 For more on the distinctive mode of persistence of process and the idea of experience as process, see Soteriou (forthcoming) and see Crowther (forthcoming a) for discussion of contrasts between the persistence of processes and of concrete material objects, and the analogy between process and space-filling stuff.
5 Granting that experience unfolds over time processively, there remain further questions about the relation between experience as *process* and experiential *events*. O'Shaughnessy (2000: 42) says: "Experiences are events (glimpsing, picture-painting) or processes (walking, picture-painting), and each momentary new element of any given experience is a further happening or *occurrence*". Of the relation between

experiential processes and events he writes: "[Process is] the very stuff of phenomenal matter of events the same in kind as itself" (2000: 44). On this approach, when a process of Φing (e.g. skidding) terminates, then an event, a Φ (e.g. a skid) has occurred. For the development of a temporal ontology along these lines, see Crowther (2011).

6 For development, see James (1950 [1890]: 628–629).

7 For discussion that develops this type of response to the idea that some experiences do not have change or succession as their objects, see James (1950 [1890]: chapter XV, 619–627); O'Shaughnessy (2000: chapter 1, §6, 60–63). Aspects of this response appear to be anticipated in Aristotle's discussion of time and change at *Physics* IV.11, 219a1–219a10 (Aristotle 1984), and also in (Locke 1975 [1689]: II.XIV, particularly §6 and §16).

8 Some change or succession is instantaneous (crossing the finishing line, reaching the summit). But one could not experience such change without experiencing temporally extended changes as temporally extended over intervals (running a race, climbing up a mountain). Thanks to Hemdat Lerman for pressing us to clarify this.

9 For interesting characterisation of these distinctive temporal characteristics, see E. R. Clay (1882), Book I, chapter XIV, §§XCVI–XCIX.

10 For discussion of this analogy, including some of its limits, see Soteriou (2013: chapter 5, esp. 5.3).

11 Compare here the discussion in Phillips (2010: §6).

12 A familiar suggestion is that there is a connection between intentional action and the agent's possession of non-observational and non-inferential knowledge or awareness of what she is doing. Much discussion explores the idea that the guarantee of awareness of action of such kind follows from the role of the agent as the author of her own intentional actions. The source of much contemporary discussion is Anscombe (1957). For further treatments, see Velleman (1989), Moran (2001), O'Shaughnessy (2000: chapters 3 and 5), O'Shaughnessy (2008: volume 2, chapter 16), and the essays in Roessler and Eilan (2003).

13 This appears to hold of the perceptual activities, such as watching and looking, that are a near constant feature of waking experience, as well as of bodily activities such as walking to the kitchen to get a drink. Thanks to Hemdat Lerman for emphasising this point.

14 See the essays in Higginbotham (2009) and Ludlow (1999).

15 Christoph Hoerl (1998, 2009) offers arguments against a number of different manifestations of the idea that temporal experience is tensed, which should be distinguished from the claims made here. Hoerl (1998) argues that it is not possible to explain our grasp of tensed temporal concepts in terms of temporal experiences. We do not here advance any such claim about our grasp of tensed temporal concepts. Hoerl (2009: §5) argues that it is not the case that parts of the specious present can be presented to the experiencer as past or future. We do not advance such a claim here, and we agree with Hoerl (2009) that this claim is not correct. Hoerl (2009: §5) considers the suggestion that perceptual experience presents one with change and succession as occurring in the present. He suggests it might be thought necessary to take experience of change and succession as occurring in the present in order to explain "why I act when I do" (Hoerl 2009: 14). On our view, what is problematic with taking experience to lack tensed features is not the timing of action, so much as the very possibility of intentional action. On the view we suggest, the awareness of some moment as present is to be explained in terms of the subject's being simultaneously cognitively oriented to the immediate future and the immediate past. For experience to lack a tensed element is for such simultaneous psychological orientation to be absent. But intentional action surely cannot occur at all if the subject is not so psychologically oriented.

16 This suggests a point of contact between the present proposal and aspects of the notion of the so-called "specious present" as it figures in the discussion by E. R. Clay (1882) and James (1950 [1890]). See, for example, E. R. Clay (1882: Book I, chapter XIV, §CIV), and James (1950 [1890]: volume 1, chapters XV and XVI). Reasons of space prevent these points of contact being pursued further here.

17 E.g. see Malcolm (1956, 1959) and Dennett (1976).

18 For an introduction to these disputes, see Windt (2016).

19 For an introduction to the history of sleep research, see Kroker (2007) and Windt (2015: chapters 2 and 3).

20 E.g. see O'Shaughnessy (2002), Sosa (2005, 2007), Ichikawa (2008, 2009), and Crowther (forthcoming b). McGinn (2005) argues that dreamt scenes are imagined scenes, but he also holds that dreaming subjects form genuine beliefs (and not merely imagined beliefs) about these scenes as they dream. Windt (2015) argues that dream experience may be *sui generis*, and so we should not assume that dream experience falls into either the category of perceptual experience or the category of imagination.

21 The assertion of a constitutive difference between waking states and dream states may be understood as the claim that each of these states of consciousness is comprised of different constituent mental states/events, and/or the claim that these states of consciousness differ in their fundamental natures. Those who make a case for a constitutive difference between dreaming and waking states include O'Shaughnessy (2000), Sosa (2005, 2007) and Crowther (forthcoming b).

22 E.g. Sosa (2005, 2007) presents his imagination model of dreaming to commit to the claim that waking states and dream states are constitutively different.

23 In particular, we take it that the variety of degradation in temporal awareness that accompanies delirium in the wakeful condition is not inconsistent with the idea that the subject of delirium experiences successively present moments as successive, and the idea that she occupies a tensed temporal perspective with a point of origin in the experience of the present moment.

24 Martin (2002) uses such considerations to argue for a thesis about sensory imagination that he labels the "dependency thesis". This is the thesis that to sensorily imagine an *F* is to imagine an experience of an *F*. This is a view of sensory imagination that is endorsed by Peacocke (1985) and Vendler (1984). In this chapter, we remain neutral on the question of whether the considerations about sensory imagination that we invoke commit one to the dependency thesis. For further discussion of this issue, see Soteriou (2013, chapter 7).

25 According to the proposal being considered here, the dreaming subject's failure to access a temporal perspective that isn't her imagined temporal perspective is a consequence of her not being in a position to tell that her dreamt temporal perspective is merely imagined. So what ultimately explains her failure to access a temporal perspective that isn't her imagined temporal perspective, will be whatever explains her ignorance of the fact that what she is imagining is merely imagined. We do not have the space here to consider and assess how one might explain such ignorance, but in the final section of the chapter we briefly mention O'Shaughnessy's proposal about this. Thanks to Ian Phillips for pressing for clarification on this issue.

26 For discussion of lucid dreaming, see e.g. LaBerge (2007) and Windt (2015) chapter 3, §2.

27 See, in particular, O'Shaughnessy (2000: chapter 2, §7, chapter 2, conclusion, and chapter 5). He says, for example: "Consciousness necessitates a simultaneous orientation towards past, present and future. Significantly this is absent in the experience of the dream . . . Why? My suspicion is, that the inactiveness of the mind of the dreamer is a determinant" (2000: 89–90).

References

Andersen, H. (2014) "The development of the 'specious present' and James's views on temporal experience", in V. Arstila and D. Lloyd (eds), *Subjective Time: The Philosophy, Psychology, and Neuroscience of Temporality*, Cambridge, MA: MIT Press.

Anscombe, G. E. M. (1957) *Intention*, Oxford, UK: Blackwell.

Aristotle (1984) *The Complete Works of Aristotle; Revised Oxford Translation*, in Barnes, J. (ed.), Bollingen Series, Princeton, NJ: Princeton University Press.

Clay, E. R. (1882) *The Alternative: A Study in Psychology*, London, Macmillan.

Crowther, T. (2011) "The matter of events", *The Review of Metaphysics* 65(September): 3–39.

Crowther, T. (forthcoming, a) "Processes as continuants and process as stuff", in R. Stout (ed.), *Process, Action and Experience*, Oxford, UK: Oxford University Press.

Crowther, T. (forthcoming, b) "Experience, dreaming and the phenomenology of wakeful consciousness", in F. Dorsch, F. Macpherson and M. Nida-Rumelin (eds), *Phenomenal Presence*, Oxford, UK: Oxford University Press.

Dennett, D. C. (1976) "Are dreams experiences?" *The Philosophical Review* 85(2): 151–171.

Higginbotham, J. (2009) *Tense, Aspect and Indexicality*, Oxford, UK: Oxford University Press.

Hobson, J. A. (1999) *Dreaming as Delirium. How the Brain Goes Out of Its Mind*, Cambridge, MA: MIT Press.

Hoerl, C. (1998) "The perception of time and the notion of a point of view", *European Journal of Philosophy* 6 (2): 156–171.

Hoerl, C. (2009) "Time and tense in perceptual experience", *Philosopher's Imprint* 9(12): 1–18.

Ichikawa, J. (2008) "Scepticism and the imagination model of dreaming", *The Philosophical Quarterly* 58(232): 519–527.

Ichikawa, J. (2009) "Dreaming and imagination", *Mind and Language* 24(1): 103–121.

James, W. (1950 [1890]) *The Principles of Psychology, Volume One*, New York: Dover Publications.

Kroker, K. (2007) *The Sleep of Others and the Transformations of Sleep Research*, Toronto, ON: University of Toronto Press.

LaBerge, S. (2007) "Lucid dreaming", in D. Barrett and P. McNamara (eds), *The New Science of Dreaming*, vol. 2, Westport, CT: Praeger, pp. 307–328.

Locke, J. (1975 [1689]) *An Essay Concerning Human Understanding*. Edited with an introduction by P. H. Nidditch, Oxford, UK: Clarendon Press.

Ludlow, P. (1999) *Semantics, Tense and Time: An Essay in the Metaphysics of Natural Language*, Cambridge, MA: Bradford/MIT Press.

Malcolm, N. (1956) "Dreaming and skepticism", *The Philosophical Review* 65(1): 14–37.

Malcolm, N. (1959) *Dreaming*, London: Routledge & Kegan Paul.

Martin, M. G. F. (2002) "The transparency of experience", *Mind and Language* 17(4): 376–425.

McGinn, C. (2005) *Mindsight: Image, Dream, Meaning*, Cambridge, MA: Harvard University Press.

Moran, R. (2001) *Authority and Estrangement*, Princeton, NJ: Princeton University Press.

O'Shaughnessy, B. (2000) *Consciousness and the World*, Oxford, UK: Oxford University Press.

O'Shaughnessy, B. (2002) "Dreaming", *Inquiry* 45(4): 399–432.

Peacocke, C. (1985) "Imagination, experience and possibility", in J. Foster and H. Robinson (eds), *Essays on Berkeley*, Oxford, UK: Clarendon Press, pp. 19–35.

Phillips, I. (2010) "Perceiving temporal properties", *European Journal of Philosophy* 18(2): 176–202.

Roessler, J. and Eilan, N. (eds) (2003) *Agency and Self-Awareness*, Oxford, UK: Oxford University Press.

Sosa, E. (2005) "Dreams and philosophy", *Proceedings and Addresses of the American Philosophical Association*, 79(2): 7–18.

Sosa, E. (2007) *A Virtue Epistemology: Apt Belief and Reflective Knowledge*, vol. I, Oxford, UK: Clarendon Press.

Soteriou, M. (2013) *The Mind's Construction*, Oxford, UK: Oxford University Press.

Soteriou, M. (forthcoming) "Experience, process, continuity and boundary", in R. Stout (ed.), *Process, Action and Experience*, Oxford, UK: Oxford University Press.

Velleman, J. D. (1989) *Practical Reflection*, Princeton, NJ: Princeton University Press.

Vendler, Z. (1984) *The Matter of Minds*, Oxford, UK: Oxford University Press.

Windt, J. (2015) *Dreaming: A Conceptual Framework for Philosophy of Mind and Empirical Research*, Cambridge, MA: MIT Press.

Windt, J. (2016) "Dreams and dreaming", in E. N. Zalta (ed.), *The Stanford Encyclopedia of Philosophy* (Spring 2016 edition), available at http://plato.stanford.edu/archives/spr2016/entries/dreams-dreaming/. Accessed 12 October 2016.

15

TIME PERCEPTION AND AGENCY

A Dual Model

Carlos Montemayor

Extant models of temporal experience focus on different aspects of time perception. Some models emphasize the constraints required for temporal representations to have accuracy conditions, while others highlight the subjectively experienced unity of temporal consciousness. In this chapter, I propose an empirically grounded Dual Model of temporal experience that incorporates the advantages of these extant philosophical views on time perception and temporal consciousness. This Dual Model, however, is not entirely conciliatory, and favors the Extensional view as the best account of conscious temporal experience. A key aspect of this proposal is that agency effects on time perception play a central role in the explanation of temporal consciousness.

The intricacies of time perception

Suppose you are playing table tennis. You are really focused on the game and your movements are surprisingly fast, accurate, and spontaneous. The sounds, relevant external objects, and coordinated body movements are all part of the integral synchrony of the game, as the ball bounces back and forth. Hitting the ball at a certain angle, with a specific orientation and force, aims at disorienting your opponent. Calculating when the ball will hit on your side of the table involves simultaneity and duration judgments concerning how long the ball will take to bounce on the other side of the table and how quickly your opponent will react to it. Timing is obviously of the essence in successfully playing this game.

A few aspects about this case seem intuitively obvious. First, perceptual representations of time must have accuracy conditions. Representations about the timing of your body's movements, the ball's trajectory and your opponent's likely move must correspond to the objective spatiotemporal structure of these events.[1] Second, time perception requires cognitive integration. Auditory, visual, and proprioceptive neural signals must be properly integrated, in such a way that the events that constitute the game are adequately perceived as the game unfolds. The bouncing sound of the ball must be correctly integrated with the visual sensation of the ball, as well as with your movements as you decide how to hit the ball. Third, based on the previous considerations, time perception is amodal – it does not necessarily depend on a single sense modality or specific sensorial stimuli. In fact, one can perceive duration independently of any specific sensorial stimuli, for instance, by estimating or reproducing an interval simply by counting seconds. These three aspects seem to characterize all cases of time perception in humans, and possibly in most species capable of perceiving time.

It is tempting to think that a Direct Representation model can explain these three aspects of time perception, roughly as follows. Time perception encodes the temporal structure of external events by seeking to accurately represent simultaneity and duration.[2] Temporal representations guide actions that are accurate and reliable, such as those involved in table tennis, in virtue of the amodal integration of the contents of these representations with the actual temporal structure of events. How exactly these constraints are implemented is a matter for empirical investigation. The point is that these requirements must be met: actual simultaneity and duration are the satisfaction conditions of perceived simultaneity and duration.

A crucial question, which has been central in recent philosophical debates, is whether this model of time perception is capable of explaining how we consciously experience time. It would be ideal to provide an account of perceived duration based exclusively on accuracy conditions that could also account for the experience of time, which seems to be unified and extended, rather than discretely parsed in terms of momentary judgments about simultaneity and duration. Before considering specific issues concerning conscious awareness and time perception, however, it is useful to clarify the implications of the Direct Representation model. According to this model, temporal representations are reliable in virtue of the amodal integration of the contents of these representations, which correspond to the actual timing of events. Thus, this model is committed to the following constraints on time perception:

- *Recalibration*: Cross-modal temporal information recalibrates within-sense temporal information in typical instances of time perception.
- *Accuracy*: Perceived simultaneity and duration must satisfy the accuracy conditions that are determined by external events.

An intuitive interpretation of the Direct Representation model proposes that accuracy is the main constraint: Recalibration must guarantee accuracy, and recalibration is not functional or explanatory independently of accuracy, which states the main goal of time perception. Using the previous illustration, when you are planning to react to the ball bouncing from the table, you need to amodally – cross-modally – represent the ball's sound and its position in coordination with your plans and reactions. It is not crucial *how exactly* information is integrated. What is fundamental is that the relevant contents of temporal representations accurately correlate with the relevant temporal structure of external events. Two further constraints have appeared to many as necessary to explain how accuracy determines recalibration:

- *Simultaneity1*: For perceived duration to be reliable, events that occur at the same time must be represented as co-occurring when recalibrated.
- *Simultaneity2*: Temporal order and duration must be represented at a moment in time.

Simultaneity has two aspects according to Direct Representation, one related to accuracy (Simultaneity1) and the other related to time perception more generally (Simultaneity2). Simultaneity1 provides intuitive plausibility to accuracy by explicitly establishing a structural correlation between the contents of represented simultaneity and actual simultaneity, thereby grounding an order relation for duration between non-simultaneous events. This way of modeling time perception is not only intuitive, but it also seems to be necessitated by considerations concerning the basic structure of any temporal representation because duration and temporal order seem to depend on asymmetrically organizing co-occurring events. First, co-occurring events must be related by simultaneity and then duration imposes an order relation on different simultaneity frames or windows, similarly to the way a film works (i.e., as in the "Cinematic" view of time perception). Duration actually imposes a *measure*, since it establishes a metric for intervals that goes beyond a mere ordering. It is important, therefore, to provide compelling reasons to abandon this intuitive model.

Simultaneity relates to time perception more generally – the second aspect of Direct Representation – by establishing simultaneity as a constraint on any experience of time: duration and temporal order are represented at a moment in time. The Direct Representation model can explain experiences of time in this way, by appealing to representations of simultaneity and duration, which are integrated in accordance with Simultaneity (1 and 2).[3] Henceforth, I shall refer to Simultaneity 1 and 2 simply as "Simultaneity".

In what follows, I provide compelling reasons to adopt a different model of temporal consciousness, one in which recalibration grounds accuracy. Although most of the reasons I will provide are based on ample scientific evidence, I will also present intuitive reasons for this alternative model. More specifically, at very early stages of simultaneity and temporal order perception, the relation between contents and accuracy conditions is more direct and unconscious. As cross-modal simultaneity is cognitively integrated with representations for action and motor control, recalibration becomes fundamental, and this accuracy relation is much less direct. We are never consciously aware of any of this recalibration-integration process. In fact, the evidence shows that two of the fundamental aspects of time perception described above pull in opposite directions – one towards cognitive integration and the other towards sense-specific accuracy. Recalibration, given the evidence, must be redefined as follows:

Recalibration(AA) – asynchrony and agency: Cross-modal temporal information recalibrates *asynchronous*, within-sense temporal information, in order to guide motor control and intentional action.

Can Recalibration(AA) be a readjustment of asynchronous information that happens at a moment in time, rather than an interval of time? If so, momentary representations of intervals of time and what happens within them could be the basis of a Retentional account of Recalibration(AA). I shall argue against this possibility, on empirical and theoretical grounds.

Briefly stated, my objection is that Retentional recalibration is incompatible with agency. An assumption of this objection is that only agents can perceive their environment, and since Retentional recalibration cannot explain how the agent's non-momentary actions and goals integrate time perception cross-modally, it cannot provide an adequate account of temporal experience. A problem with this claim is that it seems too strong because one could easily imagine an agent (say an artificially intelligent agent) that recalibrates information for action according to certain programmed goals in the way that the Retentional view prescribes. But whether or not such computational agency should be considered genuine agency is at the very least controversial. Programmed motivations and goals do not meet the intentional requirements to count as genuine motivations and goals. So although neurobiological truths may not suffice to account for time perception, they may suffice once agency is properly considered. I shall argue that considerations about agency favor the Extensional rather than the Retentional view (Dainton 2000). Time perception is not merely momentary *detection* of motion, causality, or duration. It is fundamentally perceptual *integration* based on agency.

A further qualification is that since attention is involved in time perception and attention is also a characteristic of agents with intentions and goals (see Wu 2011), the type of effects intentions have on time perception should manifest in behavioral performance.[4] The evidence indeed confirms this. Since Recalibration(AA) is incompatible with Simultaneity, the evidence I review in the next section shows that Simultaneity is not an adequate constraint for a model of conscious time perception for which agency is fundamental. There are temporal distortions concerning simultaneity and also systematic distortions concerning duration, which are part of the normal recalibration of information in time perception. These influences of automatic and voluntary agency in temporal recalibration strongly favor the Extensionalist view, as I argue in the section after next.

Evidence on the intricacies of time perception

The scientific evidence on time perception robustly and systematically shows that one should avoid assuming direct objective-subjective mappings for simultaneity in modeling interval timing. It is worth emphasizing that the relevant experimental evidence exclusively concerns perceptual representations of simultaneity and duration – and their accuracy conditions – rather than neural events or vehicles of representations. I first review this evidence and then show that the findings on interval timing or perceived duration also make accuracy problematic.

The evidence regarding simultaneity representations in humans reveals that such representations are integrated in complex ways. For instance, representations involving implicit simultaneity judgments vary depending on their cognitive integration with other implicit representations, such as representations of agency and causality (Eagleman and Holcombe 2002; Haggard *et al.* 2002; Stetson *et al.* 2006). Since causality and agency influence simultaneity perception, Recalibration(AA) receives support from these findings, rather than the unqualified recalibration, even if one focuses exclusively on simultaneity.

The critical findings against accuracy show that simultaneity windows correspond to events that occur at different brief durations, representing them as if they were simultaneous (there is no direct within modality or cross-modal direct mapping within "the moment" in which two events are simultaneous). Critically, simultaneity representations vary depending on the perceptual modality, with each modality having a different window – a brief amount of time in which contents represented within it are represented as simultaneous even though they are actually asynchronous (Pöppel 1988, 1997; Van Wassenhove 2009; Wittmann 2011).[5] Cross-modal simultaneity also differs from within modality simultaneity, and has unique characteristics (Vatakis and Spence 2007). Even within a specific modality, such as the visual system, one finds distinct windows for processing temporal order (Holcombe 2009). There is also evidence that the consciously experienced present has a larger window of integration than the cross-modal simultaneity window (Montemayor 2013; Montemayor and Wittmann 2014). All these representations of simultaneity – within, across modalities, and in working memory – involve brief intervals of time, so none of them maps neatly to actual simultaneity.

Representations concerning temporal order and duration present similar challenges. Judgments for duration, for example, vary depending on whether one is exclusively attending to an elapsed duration task or to two tasks, a timing and a non-timing task, with the dual task *shortening* perceived duration (Zakay *et al.* 1983; Brown 1985, 1997). The effects of attention, voluntary and involuntary, very likely interact with implicitly represented causality and agency, which are also known to affect simultaneity perception. This interdependence between represented agency and attention suggests that the same underlying mechanisms may be driving distortions in perceived duration and in simultaneity judgments, providing further support for Recalibration(AA).

The effects of agency and causality are fundamental to studying the mechanisms underlying the cross-modal window of simultaneity. For instance, with respect to the cross-modal integration of representations for action, Parsons *et al.* write: "While it is clear that it would be useful to calibrate the timing of motor acts and sensory feedback, the mechanism by which this is accomplished is not well understood" (2013: 46). They proceed to explore the available options and argue in favor of a causally based mechanism for calibration, proposed by Eagleman and Holcombe (2002) and Stetson *et al.* (2006) among others. Parsons *et al.* (2013) further argue that instead of a single centralized clock for interval timing, there are multiple coexisting timelines in the brain. It is important to note, however, that such timelines would need to be cognitively integrated in order to produce reliable simultaneity and duration judgments for intentional action and motor control, and the evidence suggests that representations of causality and agency play a critical role in cross-modal integration. In fact, *all models* for recalibration require cognitive integration with either causality or agency.

The interdependence between interval timing and the mechanism for cross-modal simultaneity is manifest in the contraction of the perceived duration of events associated with voluntary action. The "intentional binding" hypothesis (Haggard *et al.* 2002) postulates a module that binds intentional actions to the events they cause, contracting their duration in order to create a coherent experience of agency. Notice that this module would work independently of the sense-specific simultaneity windows and only interact with the cross-modal simultaneity window when agency is implicitly represented. Presumably, these implicit representations of agency occur beyond the consciously experienced sense of agency, which suggests that already at the unconscious motor control level Simultaneity is not determining recalibration, confirming Recalibration(AA). This mechanism for contraction must also interact systematically with attention-related contractions of duration, such as those involved in dual tasks.

An interesting question is how complex these representations of agency need to be in order to influence simultaneity and duration judgments. A strictly implicit representation of intentional action with no conscious awareness would be consistent with the view that the conscious experience of time is represented differently from time estimation and simultaneity judgments for motor control (Montemayor 2013). Implicit representations of intentional action involve attention and could be attributed to species that estimate time for navigation and planning. Such implicit representations of agency involve episodic and semantic memory, as research on corvids demonstrates. In particular, corvids are capable of long-term intentional planning and reward postponement (Clayton *et al.* 2006; Cheke and Clayton 2012), and seem to be capable of representing their intentions in a way that implies representing the past and the future (Clayton and Dickinson 1998; Clayton *et al.* 2003a, 2003b).

If implicit temporal representations comply with Recalibration(AA), and if voluntary attention in duration judgments operates independently of this more automatic and implicit system, then two consequences seem to follow, both of which favor the Dual Model defended below. First, Recalibration(AA) seems to be a necessary component of time perception at all levels of cognitive integration associated with *agency* (the level of cognitive integration required for integrated action, access to information, thought, and memory). The second consequence is that conscious time perception must be cognitively integrated with voluntary attention, emotions, and a wider range of cognitive contents. These two information-processing systems for time perception may systematically interact, as the research on duration-contraction suggests, but more evidence is needed to elucidate how exactly they interact.

An alternative way of understanding the contractions of simultaneity judgments dependent on representations of agency is by emphasizing the role of causality, rather than intentional action. The causal approach predicts that causally related events will be judged as closer in time and space than those that are not causally related. This causal account also predicts that intentional action would produce contraction because causality is necessarily involved in intentional action. In this sense, the mechanism for cross-modal simultaneity would rely on causality judgments, rather than on a module for intentional binding and an internal clock (a view defended by Wenke and Haggard 2009). This issue remains controversial. What is crucial, however, is that Recalibration(AA) involves more than the simple recalibration of asynchrony, and requires implicit representations of either agency or causality. It is more natural to assume that the intentional binding hypothesis is right because actions associated with intentions are more tightly connected to voluntary attention than mere perceived causality and thus this hypothesis seems to be the best explanation of contraction effects.

Yet another finding against Simultaneity is that the cross-modal window of simultaneity is biased towards events occurring at identical locations by representing them as more likely simultaneous (Zampini *et al.* 2005). Since the mechanism for intentional binding seems to operate independently of spatial location, then the integration of cross-modal simultaneity would depend on two sub-systems, one biased towards spatial location and the other biased towards intentional action and causality, disconfirming the Direct Representation model even further.

Regarding evolution, human intentional action may occur automatically and implicitly (Hommel 2010) or through effortful conscious attention (Kahneman 1973). The findings on intentional binding suggest that different species may represent simultaneity differently – some would involve agency, most likely implicitly, and some species closer to humans perhaps even consciously, although it is highly unlikely that robust forms of self-awareness are involved in intentional binding. Presumably, other species would just calculate simultaneity and duration at the motor control level, without any representation of agency or the involvement of voluntary attention or intentional action, and with a higher reliance on causality. These implications for evolution remain speculative, but all the available evidence indicates that recalibration is needed, and that agency plays a fundamental role in human time perception.

Conclusions about evolution are easier to draw from the evidence on interval timing. Complex and reliable behavior based on interval-timing skills has been experimentally confirmed, with various degrees of sophistication, across species. Accurate temporal representations allow for optimal responses to complex stimuli involving: (a) comparisons of intervals, (b) addition and subtraction of intervals, (c) spatial calculations and (d) representations of rate and probability (Gallistel 1990; Mazur 1991, 2000). The species capable of representing time to optimize behavior range from invertebrates such as honey bees (Renner 1960) and bumble bees (Boisvert and Sherry 2006), to a wide variety of vertebrates such as goldfish (Drew *et al.* 2005), rats (Calvert *et al.* 2010), starlings (Brunner *et al.* 1992) and pigeons (Cheng and Roberts 1991; Mazur 1991), as well as primate species (Platt and Ghazanfar 2010).

Although there are important similarities concerning interval timing between humans and other species, such as rats (Balci *et al.* 2009), there are also critical differences. For instance, some findings suggest that interval timing (i.e., timing that resembles estimating an interval with a stopwatch) may occur in invertebrates (Boisvert and Sherry 2006), but interval timing may be very rare in invertebrate species (Craig *et al.* 2014). This difference could depend on the less automatic nature of short-scale interval timing (seconds to a few minutes), which requires a central nervous system and a more effortful kind of attention, signaling a difference between the evolutionary ancient circadian system and the more recent interval system (Agostino *et al.* 2011; Montemayor 2013). Unlike circadian rhythms, which are ubiquitous in nature, interval timing may not be ubiquitous even among vertebrates (Craig *et al.* 2014). The evidence on the circadian and interval systems, therefore, raises intriguing possibilities for how Recalibration(AA) operates across species.

Based on these evolutionary considerations, it seems that attention to perceptually represented magnitudes for motor control and navigation (e.g., duration, distance, or rate) differs from conscious attention to the duration of sensations and emotions, including experienced effort. Accordingly, attention to magnitudes and implicit agency would occur unconsciously, for instance in cross-modal coordination. Unconscious forms of attention may not only be involved in these motoric representations, but they may also be indispensable to execute them, as voluntary conscious control would be too demanding and distracting. However, attending to the intensity and duration of an experience, for instance of pain, seems necessarily to involve conscious attention. One way of characterizing this distinction between conscious and unconscious duration judgments is in terms of the distinction between *decision* utility and *experienced* utility (Kahneman 2000).[6] This distinction is fully compatible with a Dual Model, but not with a Direct Representation model.

In sum, the available findings falsify a Direct Representation model. Moreover, the effects of agency on time perception show that recalibration incorporates non-environmental features into time perception. Collectively, these findings suggest that Extensionalism – the view that our conscious experience of time is itself temporally extended – is correct because alternative views are inadequate to account for the evidence on agency recalibration. Crucially, agency effects seem incompatible with Simultaneity. The Dual Model and Extensionalism about temporal experience best fit the evidence.

Direct Representation is more accurate at the unconscious, low-sensorial level. In terms of modeling time perception, this means that direct mappings stop early on, and then integration takes over. In terms of the theories discussed in the next section, Atomism stops, and then Extensionalism takes over. This suggests that the transition from modal mappings to amodal time perception depends on an agency-formatted representation. Its role is not to momentarily project and compute information, but to integrate information narratively (through agency) and in time, according to intentions and goals. Haggard is right in claiming that intentions shape time (with contraction effects) in order to create a coherent experience of agency. Assuming that this occurs in an extended period of time, rather than as a sum of memory-like retentions, is a much more natural explanation of these effects. What matters in cross-modal time perception is the articulation of goals and intentions, linked with attention routines, as they unfold in time. Agency, automatic or effortful, determines how cross-modal temporal information is structured, not Simultaneity.

Two models of time perception

If what I have said so far is correct, then extant models of temporal experience (conscious time perception) focus on partial aspects of information processing that occur at different levels of cognitive integration. Some models emphasize the constraints required for temporal representations to map directly to objective time, while others highlight the subjectively experienced unity of temporal consciousness and agency. These two incompatible views describe different levels of representation, with very different purposes, and may therefore be compatible if one assumes a more comprehensive model: a Dual Model.

Direct Representation is in principle compatible with all extant models of temporal experience. The Cinematic and Retentional models emphasize structural relations for mapping actual and subjective simultaneity, duration, and temporal order. If direct mappings are necessary, then conscious experiences must be structured independently of any information regarding agency, in accordance with Direct Representation. Thus, Cinematic and Retentional views entail Direct Representation. There are good reasons to endorse both Direct Representation and Extensionalism (such as intersubjective accuracy, which I address in the conclusion), also independently of agency. I shall instead propose that agency is central to motivate Extensionalism and that this means abandoning an unqualified endorsement of Direct Representation. Thus, the version of Extensionalism I propose is different from extant views.

For non-Extensionalist views, the subjective experience of continuity or temporal extension must be illusory, not a necessary aspect of time perception. To avoid terminological confusion, I shall call the view that conscious experiences are never temporally extended "Atomism" and I will remain neutral with respect to whether or not such a view is Cinematic or Retentional. The view that denies Atomism by claiming that experiences are always temporally extended is Extensionalism. An argument against the structural commitments of Extensionalism, and in favor of Atomism, is as follows:

Atomism

1 Extensionalism requires some kind of extended parthood relation as the main structural relation among experiences in time, which are experienced as successive.
2 There is no extended parthood relation that could structure temporal perception, which depends exclusively on the temporal relations of simultaneity and temporal order.[7]
3 Since there is no such extended parthood relation, experiences must be atomic in the sense that they never elapse over time.
4 Atomism is true.

Although there are crucial differences between Retentional and Cinematic versions of Atomism, which make them incompatible views, they both accept some version of Direct Representation, and could be based on this argument. Atomism is also committed to the existence of temporal experiences, which must be explained on their own and not be reduced to the mere detection of features, based on the comparison of a multitude of simultaneous snapshots, which need not be experienced. According to Atomism, temporal experiences are irreducible to the detection of features, but such experiences can never be extended, which makes Atomism compatible with Simultaneity. An important intuition the argument for Atomism captures is that the parthood relation is arbitrary and thus unnecessary. Introducing agency, however, makes the need for extended experiences justified and not ad hoc.

As explained in the previous section, the evidence favors Extensionalism because of agency effects. Direct mappings, however, do play a fundamental role in time perception for motor control, which occurs unconsciously. But this statement must be qualified with two caveats. First, direct mappings occur at a very low level of information processing because implicit, automatic agency seems to be constitutive of cross-modal motor control. Second, the voluntary and conscious experience of time is influenced by much more information related to agency, such as autobiographical memory and experienced emotions. This is why in the version of Extensionalism I propose, attention to perceptually represented magnitudes for motor control and navigation (e.g., duration or rate) differs from conscious attention to the duration of sensations and emotions. The first type of attention is more perceptually encapsulated and constitutive of perceptual scenes than the other.

Although Extensionalism is compatible with Recalibration(AA), it makes a largely negative point. One version of Extensionalism is based on an argument by elimination, to the effect that since direct mapping relations cannot account for the continuity of temporal experience, some kind of parthood relation must be postulated. As mentioned, an advantage of the kind of Extensionalism I propose is that introducing this relation is no longer arbitrary.

Extensionalism

1 Our experience of time cannot be structured merely by direct mappings for simultaneity and temporal order relations because it is essentially defined by how succession is continuously experienced.

2   Atomism assumes that Simultaneity is the main relation for unifying experiences.
3   Atomism cannot account for the experience of succession.
4   Atomism is false.

Since each view entails the falsehood of the other, there seems to be a stalemate between Atomism and Extensionalism. But although the intuitions in favor of both views seem basically correct, they are relevant for different levels of cognitive integration. The intuitions that favor Atomism are correct at the very early perceptual level, while the intuitions driving Extensionalism are correct at the phenomenally conscious level, which includes emotions, agency, and memory.[8] Mappings for simultaneity and temporal order are necessary but not sufficient to explain temporal experience. A further step of cognitive integration that involves agency is needed, and representations of emotions and memory are implicitly encoded in such reframing of information.

Unlike the stalemate one confronts by reasoning based on intuition alone, a close look at the evidence suggests a superficial truce between Extensionalism and Atomism. It is superficial because Atomism is a view about temporal experience, and, therefore, a Dual Model denies its explicit purpose. The evidence indicates that a more comprehensive model of time perception is required: a Dual Model of temporal experience and implicit time perception.

Overcoming incompatible and partial models: a third option

Based on previous considerations, a Dual Model of time perception must be favored. Dual models have been proposed in other areas of psychology, such as reasoning and decision-making. Unlike those models, the main contrast of the Dual Model of time perception is not based on idealized solutions to decisions or problems and actual forms of reasoning, but on *cognitive integration*.

A problem for the Dual Model is that it seems puzzling that important aspects of time perception, such as those associated with accuracy, are unconscious. But one only needs to draw the well-confirmed distinction between motor control and conscious experience to eliminate this problem. Motor control and automatic attention are associated with implicit forms of agency, and only voluntary and effortful forms of attention may be associated with the richest forms of temporal experience. Thus, the distinction between consciousness and attention provides independent (and considerable) support to the Dual Model (see Montemayor and Haladjian 2015).

Another potential problem for the Dual Model is that it is easy to understand the representations and accuracy conditions of Atomism, but the agency-based representations that justify Extensionalism seem more problematic. To clarify, I do not think there is anything to subjective duration above and beyond represented duration, but I do think that only the Extensional model can account for subjective duration because other components that elapse in time, such as agency and the operation of attention, influence how representations of duration are structured. For instance, we are aware of these representations of duration, as when one consciously estimates or counts time, but not of recalibration processes.

The distinction between non-phenomenally conscious representations of time and conscious temporal experience, given the current findings in cognitive science, should not be surprising. Consider the case of color. Until scientific evidence showed how color is processed at early stages, and how drastically different such early processing is from what we consciously experience as color, it was difficult to imagine that conscious experience could be processed independently from signal detection. Conscious time perception is even more independent from early processing because of its amodal nature, so it must be treated as a unique form of perception in which agency plays a more fundamental role.

Evolution also supports the Dual Model. There are multiple simultaneity windows and two mechanisms for duration perception, one associated with the ancient circadian system and another one associated with the more recent interval system, which depends on perceptual attention. The effects of agency on time perception are likely dependent on the interaction between different forms of attention and these mechanisms, although this issue needs to be explored in more detail. Time perception is as complicated, or perhaps even more complicated, than modally specific perception. In visual perception, for example, it is standard to distinguish conscious and unconscious forms of perception. It is also standard to distinguish different forms of attention (e.g., spatial, feature, and object based).[9] It is not surprising that time perception requires similar distinctions.

Conclusion

Consider again the table tennis example. You and your opponent succeed in tasks with non-trivial objective constraints, so agency effects cannot be distorting mappings for temporal accuracy too much. Coordinated action can involve more people and become more skilled and complex. But this does not mean that Direct Representation is correct. We do not perceive contents at a time that we project to represented durations, only to then coordinate that information with our movements and plans. On the contrary, we perceive our movements, intentional actions, and projected expectations. This is part of what makes time so intimately related to subjectivity. Although more work needs to be done with respect to the problems facing models of time perception, the Dual Model seems to be the most promising and well supported. Dual models seem counterintuitive for a number of reasons and they also seem to go against Occam's Razor. But these reasons can be efficiently disqualified by the evidence and also by the conviction that only agents can be perceivers.

Notes

1 In this chapter, I shall assume representationism about perception – the view that perception consists in representing the environment – as opposed to a direct realist view – the thesis that one is in an unmediated relation to the environment when one perceives it. The problems I present here are relevant to both views and although some of these problems seem more difficult for direct realism (particularly issues concerning recalibration) I will not argue in favor or against direct realism. The Dual Model is clearly compatible with representationism, and for this reason, I assume such view, for the sake of clarity. Whether the Dual Model is compatible with direct realism is an issue I will not address here.

2 This is not a claim about vehicles, but about the contents of representations. Given the anatomy of the brain and the distribution of sensorial detectors across the human body, it is trivially true that vehicles will have differences in transmission times that cannot be accounted for by simply considering actual simultaneity and duration. Rather, it is the contents of temporal representations "X is simultaneous with Y" or "X happened two seconds before Y" that must accurately represent the structure of events. I am grateful to Ian Phillips for helping me clarify this issue.

3 Some authors have proposed forceful arguments against Simultaneity as a constraint on temporal experiences, e.g., Dainton (2000, 2010) and Phillips (2010); for criticism see Chuard (2011) and Lee (2014). So-called "Retentionalist" and "Cinematic" views favor some version of Simultaneity2.

4 See Phillips (2012) for a review of relevant findings on the effects of voluntary attention on time perception.

5 These contents are generally referred to as "objective" and "subjective" Simultaneity. Within each simultaneity window, modal or cross-modal, asynchronous contents are not only judged and represented as occurring within a brief interval, but also perceived as simultaneous (i.e., no temporal order or duration between these contents can be discriminated).

6 This distinction was introduced to interpret the findings on "duration neglect", which demonstrated that subjects judge the unpleasantness of pain in terms of its experienced intensity according to a "peak-end" rule, instead of judging such unpleasantness according to the actual duration of the painful experience.

These findings show that the hypothesis, assumed in utility theory, that all moments must be weighed equally (decision utility) is false in cases of *experienced* utility.

7 See Philippe Chuard (2011) for a defense of this claim.

8 The effects of emotion in time perception (particularly duration estimation) are well documented. In humans, evidence shows that there is a systematic lengthening of duration-effect in time-estimation tasks when subjects are presented with facial expressions that trigger some types of negative emotion arousal (Droit-Volet *et al.* 2013). On one theory, emotional arousal in the brain causes the interval timing-clock to speed up its rate, generating the lengthening effect (Droit-Volet and Meck 2007). But these responses do not seem to depend on voluntary attention and may even be independent from any representation of agency. In fact, findings suggest that voluntary conscious attention compensates the lengthening effect in the opposite direction, thereby eliminating the lengthening distortion (Droit-Volet *et al.* 2015). More research in this area is needed to fully understand this phenomenon of compensation by conscious attention, but clearly recalibration is much more complex than previously thought.

9 See Haladjian and Montemayor (2014) for a review of issues concerning the evolution of different forms of attention.

References

Agostino, P. V., Golombek, D. A. and Meck, W. H. (2011) "Unwinding the molecular basis of interval and circadian timing", *Frontiers in Integrative Neuroscience* 5(64): 1–11.

Balci, F., Freestone, D. and Gallistel, C. R. (2009) "Risk assessment in man and mouse", *Proceedings of the National Academy of Science* 106(7): 2459–2463.

Boisvert, M. J. and Sherry, D. F. (2006) "Interval timing by an invertebrate, the bumble bee *Bombus impatiens*", *Current Biology* 16(19): 1636–1640.

Brown, S. W. (1985) "Time perception and attention: The effects of prospective versus retrospective paradigms and task demands on perceived duration", *Perception and Psychophysics* 38(2): 115–124.

Brown, S. W. (1997) "Attentional resources in timing: Interference effects in concurrent temporal and nontemporal working memory tasks", *Perception and Psychophysics* 59(7): 1118–1140.

Brunner, D., Kacelnik, A. and Gibbon, J. (1992) "Optimal foraging and timing processes in the starling (*Starling vulgaris*): Effect of inter-capture interval", *Animal Behavior* 44(4): 597–613.

Calvert, A. L., Green, L. and Myerson, J. (2010) "Delay discounting of qualitatively different reinforcers in rats", *Journal of the Experimental Analysis of Behavior* 93(2): 171–184.

Cheke, L. C. and Clayton, N. S. (2012) "Eurasian jays (Garrulus glandarius) overcome their current desires to anticipate two distinct future needs and plan for them appropriately", *Biology Letters* 8(2): 171–175.

Cheng, K. and Roberts, W. (1991) "Three psychophysical principles of timing in pigeons", *Learning and Motivation* 22: 112–128.

Chuard, P. (2011) "Temporal experiences and their parts", *Philosopher's Imprint* 11(11): 1–28.

Clayton, N. S. and Dickinson, A. (1998) "Episodic-like memory during cache recovery by scrub-jays", *Nature* 395(6699): 272–274.

Clayton, N. S., Bussey, T. J. and Dickinson, A. (2003a) "Can animals recall the past and plan for the future?" *Nature Reviews Neurosciences* 4(8): 685–691.

Clayton, N. S., Yu, K. S. and Dickinson, A. (2003b) "Interacting cache memories: Evidence of flexible memory use by scrub jays", *Journal of Experimental Psychology: Animal Behavior Processes* 29(1): 14–22.

Clayton, N. S., Emery, N. J. and Dickinson, A. (2006) "The prospective cognition of food caching and recovery by western scrub-jays (*Aphelocoma californica*)", *Comparative Cognition & Behavior Reviews* 1(1): 1–11.

Craig D. P. A., Varnon, C. A., Sokolowski, M. B. C., Wells, H. and Abramson, C. I. (2014) "An assessment of fixed interval timing in free-flying honey bees (*apis mellifera ligustica*): An analysis of individual performance", *PLoS ONE* 9(7): e101262.

Dainton, B. (2000) *Stream of Consciousness: Unity and Continuity in Conscious Experience*, New York: Routledge.

Dainton, B. (2010) "Temporal consciousness", in E. N. Zalta (ed.), *The Stanford Encyclopedia of Philosophy*, available at http://plato.stanford.edu/entries/consciousness-temporal/. Accessed 20 June 2016.

Drew, M. R., Zupan, B., Cooke, A., Couvillon, P. A. and Balsam, P. D. (2005) "Temporal control of conditioned responding in goldfish", *Journal of Experimental Psychology: Animal Behavior Processes* 31(1): 31–39.

Droit-Volet, S. and Meck, W. H. (2007) "How emotions colour our time perception", *Trends in Cognitive Sciences* 11(12): 504–513.

Droit-Volet, S., Fayolle, S., Lamotte, M. and Gil, S. (2013) "Time, emotion and the embodiment of timing", *Timing and Time Perception* 1(1): 99–126.

Droit-Volet, S., Lamotte, M., and Izaute, M. (2015) "The conscious awareness of time distortions regulates the effect of emotion on the perception of time", *Consciousness and Cognition*, 38: *155–164*.

Eagleman, D. M. and Holcombe, A. O. (2002) "Causality and the perception of time", *Trends in Cognitive Sciences (regular ed.)* 6(8): 323–325.

Gallistel, C. R. (1990) *The Organization of Learning*, Cambridge, MA: MIT Press.

Haggard, P., Clark, S. and Kalogeras, J. (2002) "Voluntary action and conscious awareness", *Nature Neuroscience* 5(4): 382–385.

Haladjian, H. H. and Montemayor, C. (2014) "On the evolution of conscious attention", *Psychonomic Bulletin and Review* 22(3): 595–613.

Holcombe, A. O. (2009) "Seeing slow and seeing fast: two limits on perception", *Trends in Cognitive Sciences* 13(5): 216–221.

Hommel, B. (2010) "Grounding attention in action control: The intentional control of selection", in B. Bruya (ed.), *Effortless Attention: A New Perspective in the Cognitive Science of Attention and Action*, Cambridge, MA: MIT Press, pp. 121–140.

Kahneman, D. (1973) *Attention and Effort*, Englewood Cliffs, NJ: Prentice-Hall.

Kahneman, D. (2000) "Experienced utility and objective happiness: A moment-based approach" in D. Kahneman and A. Tversky (eds), *Choices, Values, and Frames*, New York: Cambridge University Press, pp. 673–692.

Lee, G. (2014) "Extensionalism, atomism, and continuity", in L. N. Oaklander (ed.), *Debates in the Metaphysics of Time*, New York: Bloomsbury, pp. 149–174.

Mazur, J. E. (1991) "Choice with probabilistic reinforcement: Effects of delay and conditioned reinforcers", *Journal of the Experimental Analysis of Behavior* 55(1): 63–77.

Mazur, J. E. (2000) "Tradeoffs among delay, rate, and amount of reinforcement", *Behavioural Processes* 49(1): 1–10.

Montemayor, C. (2013) *Minding Time: A Philosophical and Theoretical Approach to the Psychology of Time*, Leiden, The Netherlands: Brill.

Montemayor, C. and Haladjian, H. H. (2015) *Consciousness, Attention, and Conscious Attention*, Cambridge, MA: MIT Press.

Montemayor, C. and Wittmann, M. (2014) "The varieties of presence: Hierarchical levels of temporal integration", *Timing and Time Perception* 2(3): 325–338.

Parsons, B. D., Novich, S. D. and Eagleman, D. M. (2013) "Motor-sensory recalibration modulates perceived simultaneity of cross-modal events at different distances", *Frontiers in Psychology* 4(46): 1–11.

Phillips, I. (2010) "Perceiving temporal properties", *European Journal of Philosophy* 18(2): 176–202.

Phillips, I. (2012) "Attention to the passage of time", *Philosophical Perspectives* 26(1): 277–308.

Platt, M. L. and Ghazanfar, A. A. (2010) *Primate Neuroethology*, Oxford, UK: Oxford University Press.

Pöppel, E. (1988) *Mindworks: Time and Conscious Experience*, New York: Harcourt Brace Jovanovich.

Pöppel, E. (1997) "A hierarchical model of temporal perception", *Trends in Cognitive Science* 1(2): 56–61.

Renner, M. (1960) "Contribution of the honey bee to the study of time sense and astronomical orientation", *Cold Spring Harbor Symposium on Quantitative Biology* 25: 361–367.

Stetson, C., Cui, X., Montague, P. R. and Eagleman, D. M. (2006) "Motor-sensory recalibration leads to an illusory reversal of action and sensation", *Neuron* 51(5): 651–659.

Van Wassenhove, V. (2009) "Minding time: An amodal representational space for time perception", *Philosophical Transactions of the Royal Society B* 364(1525): 1815–1830.

Vatakis, A. and Spence, C. (2007) "Crossmodal binding: Evaluating the 'unity assumption' using audiovisual speech stimuli", *Perception & Psychophysics* 69(5): 744–756.

Wenke, D. and Haggard, P. (2009) "How voluntary actions modulate time perception", *Experimental Brain Research*, 196(3): 311–318.

Wittmann, M. (2011) "Moments in time", *Frontiers in Integrative Neuroscience* 5(66): 1–9.

Wu, W. (2011) "What is conscious attention?" *Philosophy and Phenomenological Research* 82(1): 93–120.

Zakay, D., Nitzan, D. and Glicksohn, J. (1983) "The influence of task difficulty and external tempo on subjective time estimation", *Perception & Psychophysics* 34: 451–456.

Zampini, M., Guest, S., Shore, D. I. and Spence, C. (2005) "Audio-visual simultaneity judgments", *Perception & Psychophysics* 67(3): 531–544.

16

TEMPORAL PERCEPTION, MAGNITUDES AND PHENOMENAL EXTERNALISM

Christopher Peacocke

What are temporal magnitudes? What is it to perceive them? And what are the consequences of plausible answers to these two questions? These three questions set my agenda.

Durations treated realistically

Consider truths about the length of a wall, or the velocity of a planet, or the mass of a rock. Under a general realism about the ontology of magnitudes, such truths about the possession of particular magnitudes by particular objects and events cannot be reduced to truths not involving an ontology of magnitudes. Such truths about the magnitudes of objects and events are not reducible to facts about the results of the application of measuring procedures. Neither are they reducible to truths about systems of magnitude-free relations to some chosen entities as units. The fact that an entity, or an n-tuple of entities, has a particular magnitude of a certain type can causally explain other facts. It can itself potentially be explained by other facts. For the purposes of this chapter, I will take for granted a background realism about magnitudes that endorses all these claims. For the positive case for this kind of realism about magnitudes, see Peacocke (2015).

Under this realistic conception, particular magnitudes of a given kind – particular distances, masses, accelerations, areas – are in themselves unit-free. They can be assigned numerical measures once a unit has been selected. But these numerical measures are a means of picking out a magnitude whose nature does not involve numbers at all.

I propose that all these claims flowing from a realistic conception of magnitudes apply equally to duration and to other temporal magnitudes. My starting point in this chapter is that duration and other temporal magnitudes should be regarded as on a par with other physical magnitudes in accordance with this realistic treatment.

These claims of realism and irreducibility of the ontology of magnitudes do not imply absolutism about magnitudes. For a huge range of magnitude-types, real and irreducible magnitudes of those types are relative to a frame of reference. We know from the special theory of relativity that this applies to durations. Such relativity is entirely consistent with the fact that two events' being separated by a certain duration, in a given frame, is causally explanatory of other events and states of affairs. Neither does this realism about magnitudes mean that they exist in splendid isolation from other magnitudes. Magnitudes of a given type can be real and irreducible, even if they have fundamental and even individuative connections with magnitudes of other types.

One of the things that can be explained by two events being separated by a certain duration, in a given frame of reference, is the perception, by a person at rest in that frame, that they are separated by that duration, relative to that frame. The duration between two events can sometimes be perceived, as the distance between two objects can sometimes be perceived. In both the temporal and the spatial cases, the perception of the magnitude is unit-free, just as the magnitude itself is unit-free. We do not perceive the length of time since the person left the room in seconds or minutes, any more than we perceive the width of the desk in inches or centimetres. In the spatial case, we specify how the world seems to be to a perceiving subject in part by specifying how the space around the subject has to be filled in for her spatial experience to be veridical. This is what I called scenario content (Peacocke 1992). In the temporal case, we specify how the world seems to be to a perceiving subject in part by specifying how the recent past has to be filled out with events, at certain durations from the present, for her temporal experience to be veridical. Just as spatial magnitudes feature in the scenario-like content of perception, so temporal magnitudes should be included correspondingly in the representational content of perception. The notion of scenario content should be expanded accordingly and given a temporal dimension. My question now is: If we conceive of durations as real magnitudes that are on occasion perceptible as such, then what is the nature of such perception? What makes an event an event of temporal perception?

What is perception of temporal magnitudes?

For an organism to be sensitive to a magnitude of a given type, to be in states causally explained by some object or event having that magnitude, is not yet for the organism to represent that magnitude as such. Sensitivity is not representation. The point is developed forcefully by Tyler Burge (2010, Part III).

In the case of genuine representation of spatial properties and relations in perception, Burge says that what makes the difference between representation of such a property or relation, as opposed to mere sensitivity to it, are the perceptual constancies. Varying proximal states, themselves caused by the same constant property, cause the same objective representational state representing that property, within a wide range of normal background circumstances. For example, different projected retinal sizes or shapes cause perceptual representation of the same objective size of object as distance from the object varies, or angle with respect to the object varies. Conversely, the same retinal size on two different occasions will cause states with representational contents concerning different objective sizes, when appropriate, and in a range of normal conditions. There are analogues of this for colour constancy and so forth.

This constancy criterion does not carry over to provide a constitutive account of the representation of temporal properties and relations. The general problem is that in the spatial case, the very characterization of constancy involves either variation in three-dimensional conditions producing the same two-dimensional pattern of proximal stimulation, or else (as in colour constancy) involves multiple environmental conditions, instantiated in normal circumstances, producing the same proximal stimulation property (retinal colour in the visual case). Conversely, one and the same objective length, for example, produces many different sizes of retinal image at various distances of that length from the perceiver. The retinal image of the length varies also with the orientation of the perceiver. But neither of these kinds of variation in three-dimensional relations, nor of varying normal environmental conditions producing the proximal stimulus state, applies to the case of duration and to other temporal properties and relations. Consider as an example the perception of the whole duration of a temporally extended event, such as the sounding of a fire alarm bell. We can take the proximal stimulus event to be that of the series of sound waves hitting the ear drum, from the initial striking, up to their later cessation, just after the bell stops ringing. In normal circumstances, extended proximal events of this kind *will* be reliably correlated (and explained by) the objective complete duration of the ringing of the alarm bell. In ordinary circumstances, there is no highly variable environmental feature or dimension such that a wide range of different such features or dimensions will produce the same extended event of pressure on the eardrum. The correlation, in normal circumstances, between objective duration of the bell ringing and the duration of the stimulation of the eardrum is uniform. Our perceptual systems are not in fact adapted, and do not need to be adapted, to circumstances in which there is no uniform correlation between the length of the objective event and the length of the auditory stimulation. This is a sharp contrast with the variability of projected retinal shape produced, according to the angle of the perceiver, of a given objective shape.

It is true that there is a limited subclass of cases in which the objective duration of some external event is not reliably correlated with the length of the proximal stimulus. There is in fact no reliable correlation in the special case in which the duration is an event of lateral motion across the visual field. The so-called Kappa effect is that the perceived duration between two events increases with the objective distance between those events, even when the corresponding retinal separation of those events is the same (Cohen *et al.* 1953). But there remains a reliable correlation when we are concerned with the perception of the duration of an event at a single location over time, and in many cases other than lateral motion. We have an obligation to explain philosophically why there is genuine temporal representation in the case of duration perception when there is reliable distal/proximal correlation. The Kappa effect is also not something that at all fits a model of constancy in which varying proximal stimulation is consistent with generally correct objective representation. On the contrary, the dilation effect of perceiving durations between distant events as longer means that some perceptions of durations between spatially separated events must be non-veridical, rather than correct.

So does the inapplicability of the constancy criterion to a range of temporal examples mean that the distinction between representation of a property and mere sensitivity to it collapses in the temporal case? That does not seem plausible, for the notion of representation has real work to do everywhere. But what then is that work, if constancy is no longer the test of it in the temporal case?

Here we have to address two questions.

Question 1: What is the nature, philosophically, of the distinction between mere sensitivity to temporal distinctions and representation of temporal distinctions, as temporal distinctions? This we can call "the constitutive question of the representation of time".

Question 2: Whatever is the correct answer to Question 1, the constitutive question, what then unifies that answer with the constancy answer that is so plausible in such cases as spatial perception and colour perception? What makes all these kinds of cases genuinely representational? This is an equally pressing question, which we can call "the question of representational unification".

Burge's own proposal about temporal representation in *Origins of Objectivity* is as follows:

> I believe that, at least in actual animal life, the functioning of temporal sensitivity in perception (and hence representational agency) is necessary and sufficient for temporal representation. A functioning psychological coordination of perception of *other matters* with temporal sensitivity is both necessary and sufficient for temporal representation in perception . . . First, sufficiency. Suppose that an animal tracks a moving particular. The tracking relies on sensitivity to temporal order. The particular is represented as the same through the motion. The coordination of later perceptions with earlier

215

perceptions in representing the particular depends on sensitivity to temporal order. Then temporal sensitivity is incorporated into perceptual representation of movement. One represents the particular's being in one position as temporally after its being in an earlier position . . . Or a single diachronic perception contains a representation of temporally ordered change. Such perceptions are further coordinated with actional representations guided by perceptual memory . . . Incorporation of sensitivity to temporal order in perception of change or movement is probably the simplest sort of temporal representation in perception. Similar points apply to sensitivity to temporal intervals.

(Burge 2010: 521)

So Burge's proposal is that in the temporal case, it makes a difference if the sensitivity to temporal distinctions is coordinated with genuine perceptual representation of other matters. Earlier in the book, he also wrote, "A perceptual system achieves objectification by – and I am inclined to believe *only by* – exercising *perceptual constancies*" (2010: 408).

Here is a series of three examples that suggest temporal sensitivity, even when coordinated with the genuine representation of other matters, does not suffice for temporal representation:

1   Consider the nectar-feeding amakihi bird in Hawaii (Gallistel 1990: 292). The amakihi avoids flowers it has recently visited, because the nectar will not be replenished for a certain period of time. But it must also not leave a revisit too late, or else some other bird will consume the nectar. It has to be sensitive to a certain magnitude of duration to return to the flower at the optimal interval. This seems to involve only a sensitivity to duration, not a representation of it as a duration. But this sensitivity can certainly be coordinated with a functioning perceptual representation of other matters. The creature that is sensitive to duration may have perceptual constancies for objective shape and shade, and representations of shape and shade may influence its actions. But adding a sensitivity to duration that is integrated with these spatial representational capacities in coordinated action is not enough to ground the claim that the organism represents temporal duration. Saying that there is representation of duration simply on these grounds would make the notion of representation add nothing in the temporal case that is not already explained by temporal sensitivity to a duration. It would be a violation of a content-theoretic version of Lloyd Morgan's (1904) famous canon.[1]

There is a way of making this vivid that can be helpful in thinking about the distinction between mere sensitivity and representation. All that is necessary to explain the actions of the amakihi bird is that after the relevant duration has elapsed, some system in the bird generates the means-end command, "To obtain food, go to such-and-such location". The time at which this means-end command appears in the bird's systems is sensitive to the duration that has elapsed since the bird's last visit to the flower; but duration does not enter the content of the command. Neither does the past tense enter the content of the command. The bird's actions are entirely explained by the presence of that command whose content is duration-free and entirely in the present tense. The philosophical question becomes: What is it that can be explained only by the presence of a notion of duration and of the past in the content itself?

This point illustrated by the amakihi bird should, incidentally, make us suitably demanding when presented with a claim that a creature has episodic memory of a past event. It is not sufficient to establish the claim of episodic memory that the creature's actions are sensitive to how long ago a particular event occurred in the creature's history. If such sensitivity can be explained purely by present tense representations that arise after the corresponding duration, further evidence is necessary to establish the existence of episodic memories with a past-tense content.

2   We can make a similar case about organisms which are sensitive in their actions to which stage they have reached in some endogenously generated cycle, what Gallistel (1990: 240) calls "phase sense". Bees will reappear at a feeding site 24 hours after the last of several daily feedings, even in circumstances of constant light. They will also reappear at a local feeding site in a contained space 24 hours after the last feeding, even when the container is flown from its home site in Paris to New York (Gallistel 1990: 255, citing work of Renner (1960)). This kind of temporal sensitivity to the stage of an endogenously generated cycle could clearly be present in an organism with rich spatial representational capacities and constancies. But again, being sensitive to phase is to be distinguished from representing temporal phase. Mere sensitivity seems to explain everything that needs to be explained here. Again, we can put the issue in terms of what needs to be in the content of the creature's representational states and what does not. The actions of the bees are fully explained by the generation, at a certain stage of the endogenously generated cycle, of the instruction "Get food now", and by the sensitivity of the time at which that command appears to the passage of a certain duration. Duration and the past do not need to be in the content of the representation.

3   Consider the case of fireflies that emit flashes of light, and whose conspecifics are sensitive to such flashes:

> Normally the flying male crisscrosses an area and rhythmically emits his species-specific flash pattern. In the simplest case this pattern is characterized by flashes of fixed duration emitted at fixed intervals. Stationary females, located in the underbrush, on bushes, or in trees, respond with simple flash answers whose latency is stereotyped, determined by their conspecific male's flash. Upon receiving an answer the male hovers in flight and orients his lantern toward the female, often dimming his lantern to locate the female more precisely. Eventually the male lands near the female and proceeds to her on foot.
>
> *(Copeland 1978: 341)*

> At dusk males can be seen flashing about 1 meter above the ground. Each flash lasts approximately 0.5 seconds at 20 degrees centigrade (flash timing is temperature sensitive) and is emitted during a short swoop that makes an upward arc of light. Flashes are repeated about every 7 seconds. Stationary females answer each flash with a 0.5-second flash of about 3 seconds latency.
>
> *(Copeland 1978: 341)*

Now, I do not know whether fireflies exhibit spatial constancies in their perceptual systems. But again, we can conceive of a creature that makes and is sensitive to flash patterns, and also uses a perceptual system with spatial constancies to recognize and steer towards a female of the same species. This creature would exhibit temporal sensitivities, in a way that is coordinated with genuine perception of other matters, viz. spatial properties and relations. I do not think this would suffice for this creature to represent temporal matters, as opposed to merely being sensitive to them. It is compatible with this description of the creature that it has no capacity for temporal representation beyond the sensitivity described, and no capacity to represent the past. Its actions are entirely explained by the temporal pattern of its reception of light stimulation. At no point in the explanation of this creature's actions do we need to appeal to anything beyond that. To put the point again in terms of content: the fireflies need to have something that represents the command "Fly towards that light" that is sensitive to number of flashes, and to duration between the flashes. But duration, and the past tense, does not need to enter the content of these instructions or commands.

In these three examples, the mere sensitivity to temporal durations, or phase stages, or flash patterns, stands in sharp contrast to what we need to invoke in explaining the actions of a creature with objective spatial representations. Those actions do not involve merely a sensitivity to retinal or proximal stimulation patterns. Explanation of such spatial actions involves sensitivity to the spatial representational content of the creature's perceptual states.

The attribution of temporal representational content is correspondingly well-founded only if there are actions not fully explained by temporal features of proximal states, including properties of the time at which a command appears, but are explained by states of the creature whose content involves duration and the past. Our next task is to say what capacities could be explained only by such temporal contents. Equivalently, our task is to say what it is to grasp such temporal contents.

When you are functioning properly, in normal circumstances, you have some conception of the layout of the world around you at any given time and have various experiences at that time. As time passes, some of this conception is retained and is given a suitably adjusted temporal and spatial labelling. The conception needs to be given the right past-tense labelling, as time passes. If you have moved, the indexical spatial content in the conception needs to be adjusted too. If you have turned rightwards, then the earlier perception of the tree in blossom straight ahead of you needs to be adjusted to a representation of the tree in blossom to your left. Similar remarks apply to distance. The earlier perceptual demonstrative "that tree" generates a corresponding memory demonstrative of the same tree, and so forth.

Such a process of preservation of a conception has three crucial and interrelated components.

First, there is some kind of preservation, as just illustrated, of a conception. It may be tempting to call this "objectivity preservation", but that may be too strong. The conception can certainly contain elements concerning the subject's own experiences and other subjective states, so it is probably better to call what is in question "representational preservation".

Second, the later representation is sensitive to time itself. When all is working properly, the representation is given a past-tense label that is sensitive to how much time has passed. We are capable of thinking of a duration of a certain (unit-free) length, and, again when all is working properly, the adjusted representation represents the world as being a certain way that same unit-free length of time ago.

For the third component, which is arguably implicit in the first two, consider the subject's total representational conception at the later time, a total conception that concerns the state of the world both past and present. This total representational conception is one that registers certain identities between objects, events or places that are represented as being a certain way at the earlier time and objects, events or places that are given to the subject at the later time. If you have moved a certain distance from the tree in blossom, that tree that you represent as having been in blossom earlier is also represented by you as having a certain distance from your present position. If your left ankle hurt earlier, that ankle is, in your total representational system, represented as being one of the same ankles you have now, and so forth.

So we are concerned here with temporally sensitive representational preservation that registers identities over time. I will label this, with capitals "Representational Preservation" for brevity, the capitalized label being understood to cover all three components we just identified.[2]

I propose the hypothesis that Representational Preservation is what distinguishes the representation of time and temporal distinctions, as opposed to a mere sensitivity to time and to temporal distinctions. When there is Representational Preservation, we have representation of objective temporal relations, durations and properties. In a case of genuine perception of the duration of an event, that duration is fitted into the perceiving subject's local history of the world built up by the operation of Representational Preservation. There is of course no one type of action we should expect when there is perception of duration – any more than there is one type of action to be expected in the case of genuine perception of spatial extent. Any actions produced will depend on the appetites and projects of the agent. But when the duration of the ringing of the bell is perceived, a subject may be in a position to know what else was happening when the ringing began, whether someone would have had time to exit the building while the ringing continued, whether some other event occurred before or during the ringing, and so on. These are all species of objective temporal information of potential practical relevance.

To say there is representation of objective temporal conditions is not to say that the subject who is representing temporal matters has a conception of objectivity, is capable of representing the notion of objectivity. That would be a more sophisticated capacity, not required for minimal temporal representation. As in the spatial case, so also in the temporal case: we should always distinguish representing objective states of affairs from representing them as objective, which requires a notion of mind-independence. Both are distinct from the more primitive capacity of being merely sensitive to temporal states of affairs.

There is no Representational Preservation in the capacities we considered in the amakihi bird, nor in the bees whose actions are sensitive to the stage of an endogenously generated cycle, nor in the fireflies with their sequences of flashes. In all of these cases, there is indeed an explanatory and counterfactual sensitivity to temporal distinctions. If a certain duration has not yet been reached since the amakihi bird last visited the flower, it will not return. This conditional is projectible to counterfactual situations that could easily have obtained. A similar point applies to the bees and the phase of their cycle that needs to be reached before they return to a food source. It is equally true that in the actual world and worlds that could easily have been actual, the fireflies will not respond to a non-standard number of flashes, or to flashing that is not at the regular interval. These cases illustrate the point that reliable counterfactual sensitivity can be present without any Representational Preservation.

What then are the kinds of actions that can be explained by the possession of temporal representation and which cannot be explained by mere temporal sensitivity? Obviously, the requirement cannot be that present actions can explain what happened in the past. But it can be the case that present actions are rationally explained by what a subject represents as being the case in the past, together with the identities over time registered by the subject. Past states of affairs have significance for present action because of registered identities over time, or chains of identities over time.

Consider an everyday case. You discover that your wallet is not in your pocket. You remember where you were the last time you used it and retrace your steps back to that location in searching for it. These actions are explained not only by what you represent as being the case in the past, but also by various identities over time that you register as holding. These identities include the identity of various places and objects that you now encounter with those you remember as encountering since you last saw your wallet. Your actions in searching for the wallet, the particular route you take, cannot at all be explained by a mere sensitivity to temporal properties and distinctions. How you represent the world as having been around you when you last saw your wallet is an essential part of the explanation, and so too is your route since that last sighting of your wallet. If those past-tense representational states were to have different contents, you would take or could have taken a different route now, and different actions of yours would be explained. Your searching actions cannot be explained merely by simple conformity to an imperative "Go to such-and-such location to obtain your wallet". If such a practical maxim is eventually derived by the subject, it is derived in part from representational states with past-tense content.

We can ask what would need to be added to the capacities and states of the amakihi bird to make it genuinely represent the past, and not, like that bird, to be merely sensitive to durations.

Suppose we imagine a creature that needs to feed by consuming some organism, again at fixed intervals, but that the organism that it needs to consume moves around and has to be located. The feeding creature needs to have information over what sort of distance it needs to look for its food source, needs to preserve a representation of where the source was last time it visited, in what direction it was then moving, a representation whose content may vary from occasion to occasion. It needs to register identities between directions it perceives now and the direction in which its prey was moving earlier. Even if there remains a fixed interval at which the food becomes available from the source, with this modification it becomes much more plausible that the feeding creature is operating with past-tense representations that explain its actions. The creature's mental states with durational contents and identities over time form an essential component of the explanation of the creature's representation of the likely current location of its prey, and hence of the creature's actions.

Under this treatment, the answer to Question 2, the question of representational unification, is that both temporal and spatial perception contribute non-redundantly to the explanation of a creature's actions. Perceptual constancies are a sufficient condition, but not a necessary condition, for such a non-redundant contribution to the explanation of action.

In emphasizing the importance of the registration of identities over time in a creature's past-tense representations, there is a point of contact, but only of limited agreement, with Kant. Kant in various ways emphasized the importance of the identity of substances over time in our thought. From the above discussion, it should be clear that the conditions for the registration of identities over time can be met by the registration of identity of places over time, something much weaker than the identity of substance. But the enterprise in which I have been engaging is certainly Kantian in goal and spirit, if not in its conclusions. There is a common concern with the minimal constitutive conditions for the representation of temporal properties, relations and magnitudes.

It is also a consequence of the fulfilment of the Representational Preservation condition that a creature that meets it will be able to use the same kinds of reasoning about how things are in the world at past times as it uses in the present tense about the world as it is around it now.

The capacities mentioned in Representational Preservation are those present when all is functioning properly. Subjects may not be functioning properly when ill, when taking drugs that affect the perception of time, when in some sudden life-threatening situation, or when suffering from damage that affects their ability to order remembered events (or even to remember at all). Subjects in one or another of these suboptimal conditions are still capable of representing, and misrepresenting, temporal properties, relations and magnitudes, but only because there is some applicable notion of what is proper perceptual functioning for them.

Under the hypothesis that Representational Preservation is what matters for temporal representation, it is one thing for a subject to be able to represent particular past states of affairs, events and objects, and another for the subject to represent causal relations between earlier and later events. Under the hypothesis that Representational Preservation is what matters, a subject can represent particular earlier events and objects, and leave it open which, if any, of them cause, or have properties which causally explain, later events and states of affairs. The temporal sensitivity involved in Representation Preservation, and the role of Representational Preservation in the explanation of action, already supply a foundation for representation of temporal relations and for thought about particular past events and times. Once Representational Preservation is in place, a subject can speculate about, and work out, which if any of the earlier events and objects has properties that cause the properties, or existence, of later events and states of affairs. But the subject does not need to exercise or rely on the notion of causation to grasp genuine temporal priority of particular events, or to represent particular past times, and perhaps does not even need to possess a notion of causation to do so. This is, evidently, a non-Kantian feature of the account.

Temporal perception and phenomenal externalism

I have been presuming that the perception of magnitudes contributes to the phenomenal character of perception. If this presumption is correct, then the account so far is a version of what has come to be called phenomenal externalism. It has some immediate attractions. In treating magnitudes themselves as perceptible, it meshes straightforwardly with such ordinary attributions as "she heard the rumbling last for a certain length of time". We can form beliefs, and sometimes gain knowledge, about the magnitudes themselves by taking particular perceptual experiences of magnitudes at face value. Magnitudes themselves are cognitively accessible in perception itself.

The account also dovetails with the externalist character of what is explained in action-explanation (Peacocke 1993). Perception of a magnitude explains actions under relational characterizations, in relation to the very magnitude perceived. Asked how long the rumbling lasted, our subject may answer "From now . . . to now", where the perception explains the magnitude of the duration between the two utterances of "now".

But for all these attractions, this form of phenomenal externalism is controversial. In particular, it contrasts strongly with the functionalism about spatiotemporal notions, and more generally the internalism about perceptual content, endorsed in important and interesting discussions by Brad Thompson (2010) and David Chalmers (2012).

Here I outline the components of an externalist, anti-functionalist view of perceptual content involving magnitudes by addressing the considerations that have been offered in support of the Chalmers-Thompson functionalism. On the Chalmers-Thompson view, spatial and temporal expressions are "Twin-Earthable":

> [l]et us say that two possible speakers are *twins* if they are functional and phenomenal duplicates of each other: that is their cognitive systems have the same functional organization and are in the same functional states, and they have the same conscious experiences . . . We can then say that an expression *E* is Twin-Earthable if there can be a non-deferential utterance of *E* for which there is a possible corresponding utterance by twin speaker with a different extension.
>
> *(Chalmers 2012: 317)*

The Chalmers-Thompson view is that spatial and temporal magnitude expressions are Twin-Earthable, because, they say, two twins may be functional and phenomenal duplicates, but their spatial and temporal expressions refer to different magnitudes because different magnitudes may produce the same functional and phenomenal states in the twins.

I dispute the thesis of the Twin-Earthability of the spatial and temporal magnitude terms. An initial argument offered for Twin-Earthability is that it is not coherent to suppose that our experiences and judgments of magnitudes are massively illusory, throughout time in the actual world (for the spatial case of this argument, see Chalmers 2012: 326). I agree. But this verdict of incoherence would also be delivered by the view that perceptual experience has contents concerning the magnitudes themselves, together with the thesis that which magnitudes those experiences have as their content is determined by which magnitudes normally cause them, when the conditions for genuine representation, and not mere sensitivity, are fulfilled.[3]

Alternatively, we are asked to consider Doubled Earth, on which everything is doubled in length from actual Earth, or Slowed Earth, on which everything happens at half the speed on actual Earth. The functionalist view is that experiences of subjects on Earth, Doubled Earth or Slowed Earth can all be veridical. The phenomenal externalism I endorse agrees. It does not, however, agree that the experiences on Earth, Doubled Earth and Slowed Earth are phenomenally identical. They have different magnitudes in their content. The subjects on Earth, Doubled Earth and Slowed Earth are also not functional duplicates if our functionalism is of the "long-arm" variety that takes into account functional relations beyond the boundary of the body (cp. Harman 1982: 247). The experiences in the three kinds of world produce actions in relation to correspondingly different magnitudes in the environment. The fact that one could trick a subject, at least temporarily, in carefully designed circumstances, by moving her from one kind of environment to another does not establish that the phenomenal (subjective) contents are the same across the cases. Perceptual content is grounded in the relations to a baseline normal environment in which the subject is functioning properly. On the position which I am opposing to the Chalmers-Thompson view, the subjects on Earth, Doubled Earth and Slowed Earth are not twins under the definition, and spatiotemporal magnitude expressions are not Twin-Earthable.

The phenomenal externalist will sharply distinguish between Twin-Earthability and relativity to a frame of reference. Spatiotemporal magnitudes are always nontrivially relative to a frame of reference. A subject can perceive a temporal or a spatial magnitude as it really is, relative to the frame of reference in which the subject is at rest. The fact that the magnitude between the two events will be different in a frame in which the subject is not at rest does not imply the Twin-Earthability of magnitude expressions and concepts. In the temporal case, if a subject travelling with a clock in rapid motion relative to the Earth perceives his clock correctly, his phenomenal experience of that same clock will not be the same as those on Earth not in such rapid motion.[4] I doubt that there is any notion of phenomenal duplication on which the fast traveller's temporal experience of the clock must be a duplicate of those on Earth. Experience of a duration is always as of an objective duration, relative to the frame of reference centred on the subject.

It is sometimes objected to phenomenal externalism that it is committed to implausible verdicts on "El Greco" examples. These are examples, originally suggested by Hurley (1998) in which everything in some part of the universe is stretched two to one in the vertical direction.

> Bodies that seem rigid within the environment will be nonrigid by standards outside the environment, in that they change their shape when they rotate. And beings in that world will typically say "That is a square" when confronted by what outsiders would call a rectangle that is twice as high as it is tall.
>
> *(Chalmers 2012: 330)*

Chalmers wonders what an externalist would say of the experiences of twin subjects in an El Greco case: "will one have an experience as of a rectangle, despite insisting that she is confronted by a square?" (2012: 331, note 10). Externalism about phenomenal content is consistent with pervasive illusions. Suppose the objects around subjects in the special part of the universe really are stretched in one direction, say by special forces, but they still look square. If perceivers discover this fact, they will come to realize that when they reach to touch the top and bottom of a seemingly square object, their hands are actually twice as far apart as when they pick it up from the sides. Even in the actual world, there is what is called the vertical-horizontal illusion. Vertical lines seem to humans to be 6 to 8 per cent longer than lines that are actually of the same length, but have a horizontal orientation (Rock 1973: 96–98). So even in the actual world, some things that look square in normal circumstances are not so. The externalist can consistently admit extensive and pervasive illusions, as long as these illusions gain their status as such from their relations to a base of cases in which subjects are perceiving correctly. The Muller–Lyer illusion is pervasive in the actual world, but it is not a counterexample to externalism about phenomenal content.

I do think that we can make sense of the inverted spectrum and of Ned Block's inverted Earth (1990). A functional account of colour terms and concepts is highly plausible in these cases. So what is different, on my view, about the spatiotemporal cases? A crucial difference is that there is no difficulty in imagining inverted spectrum cases from the inside. We have a notion of phenomenal similarity, of looking the same way, on which we can clearly make sense of the possibility that everything that is actually green looks the way things that are actually red look. Imaginability is indeed not always a guide to genuine possibility, but it matters here that what is imagined is something in the imagined experience of the inverted state of affairs, not just something merely suppositionally imagined. (For the distinction, see Peacocke 1985.) Similarly, we have no difficulty in imagining that our colour experience is the same, but the reflectance properties of objects that cause those experiences are different from those which cause them in the actual world. For the temporal case to be like the colour case, it would have to be that there is a constant phenomenal temporal property common to an alleged pair of twins, one on Earth and the other a subject travelling very fast, subject to time dilation. There would also have to be a constant phenomenal temporal property common to an alleged pair of twins, one on Earth and the other on Slow Earth. I surmise that there is no such phenomenal property.[5]

Notes

1 "In no case is an animal activity to be interpreted in terms of higher psychological processes, if it can be fairly interpreted in terms of processes which stand lower in the scale of psychological evolution and development. To this, however, it should be added, lest the range of the principle be misunderstood, that the canon by no means excludes the interpretation of a particular activity in terms of the higher processes, if we already have independent evidence of the occurrence of these higher processes in the animal under observation" (Lloyd Morgan 1904: 59).
2 There are obvious connections here with the notion of perspectival sensitivity in Peacocke (1983).
3 Chalmers (2012: 331, footnote 10) notes the availability of this response and relies on the El Greco cases in rejoinder, on which see below.
4 The phenomenon of time dilation in special relativity. See, for instance, Young and Freedman (2004: 1410).
5 This chapter draws on material presented to my seminars at Columbia University and UCL in 2013–15, and in talks to Susanna Schellenberg's Marc Sanders Seminar at Rutgers, to a Seminar in Fribourg, Switzerland and to a joint NYU-Institut Jean Nicod Conference in Paris, all in 2015. I benefited from the discussions at all these occasions, and I have also learned from several conversations on these topics with Tyler Burge, David Chalmers and Susanna Schellenberg. I thank Ian Phillips for his important editorial advice, both presentational and substantive. This short chapter should be taken as a position paper on its topic: there are multiple issues in this territory that need a much longer treatment.

References

Block, N. (1990) "Inverted earth", *Philosophical Perspectives* 4: 53–79.
Burge, T. (2010) *Origins of Objectivity*, Oxford, UK: Oxford University Press.
Chalmers, D. (2012) *Constructing the World*, Oxford, UK: Oxford University Press.
Cohen, J., Hansel, C. and Sylvester, J. (1953) "A new phenomenon in time judgment", *Nature* 172: 901.
Copeland, J. (1978) "Communication systems of fireflies", *American Scientist* 66(3): 340–346.
Gallistel, C. (1990) *The Organization of Learning*, Cambridge, MA: MIT Press.
Harman, G. (1982) "Conceptual role semantics", *Notre Dame Journal of Formal Logic* 23(2): 242–256.
Hurley, S. (1998) *Consciousness in Action*, Cambridge, MA: Harvard University Press.
Lloyd Morgan, C. (1904) *An Introduction to Comparative Psychology*, 2nd ed., New York: Charles Scribner's Sons.
Peacocke, C. (1983) *Sense and Content: Experience, Thought, and Their Relations*, Oxford, UK: Oxford University Press.

Peacocke, C. (1985) "Imagination, possibility and experience", in J. Foster and H. Robinson (eds), *Essays on Berkeley*, Oxford, UK: Oxford University Press.

Peacocke, C. (1992) *A Study of Concepts*, Cambridge, MA: MIT Press.

Peacocke, C. (1993) "Externalist explanation", *Proceedings of the Aristotelian Society* XCIII: 203–230.

Peacocke, C. (2015) "Magnitudes: Metaphysics, explanation, and perception", in D. Moyal-Sharrock, V. Munz and A. Coliva (eds), *Mind, Language and Action: Proceedings of the 36th International Wittgenstein Symposium*, Berlin: de Gruyter.

Renner, M. (1960) "Contribution of the honey bee to the study of time-sense and astronomical orientation", *Cold Spring Harbor Symposium on Quantitative Biology* 25: 361–367.

Rock, I. (1973) *Orientation and Form*, New York: Academic Press.

Thompson, B. (2010) "The spatial content of experience", *Philosophy and Phenomenological Research* 81(1): 146–194.

Young, H. and Freedman, R. (2004) *University Physics with Modern Physics 11th Edition*, San Francisco, CA: Pearson Addison Wesley.

PART V

Temporal experience and metaphysics

.

17

WHAT IS TIME?

Michael Pelczar

This question elicits many responses, but a successful analysis of time has never been one of them. I argue that it is premature to rule out the possibility of such an analysis. We might be able to give a successful analysis of time, in terms of conscious experience.

Introduction

The headline question is, on the face of it, a request for a definition of time. Today, few philosophers take it that way. Instead, they take it as an invitation to answer any of a variety of other questions, such as: Are the past and future real? How does time differ from space? In what sense, if any, does time pass? Is an object wholly present at each moment of its existence? How is change possible? Does time require change? Is time absolute, or relational? What is the metaphysical significance of tense?

David Chalmers (1996) distinguishes the hard problem of consciousness from the easy problems of consciousness. A similar distinction applies here. The easy problems of time are the ones posed by questions like those collected in the foregoing paragraph. The hard problem of time is that of saying what time is.[1]

As with consciousness, the easy problems of time are "easy" only relative to the hard problem. The fact remains that solutions to the former can never add up to a solution to the latter. Answering the easy questions might constrain the project of finding out what time is, as answering the question whether rainbows touch the ground might constrain the project of figuring out what rainbows are. But if we want to find out what time, or a rainbow, is, we need to go beyond the easy questions.

Eliminativism about time

The analogy between the philosophy of consciousness and the philosophy of time doesn't end there. Confronted with the question "What is consciousness?" or "What is time?" some philosophers offer answers, while others offer resistance. The most common form of resistance to the consciousness question is anti-reductionism. Anti-reductionists refuse to offer any solution to the hard problem of consciousness, on the grounds that consciousness is a fundamental feature of the world, resistant to analysis in terms of anything more basic. Explicit avowals of anti-reductionism about time are less common, but that probably just reflects the fact that anti-reductionism about time is so widespread that people feel no need to avow it.

A different way to resist the consciousness question is by denying that consciousness exists. This is eliminativism about consciousness. In the philosophy of time, there is a long tradition of eliminativism, the latest manifestation of which is an argument that takes its cue from developments near the forefront of modern science:[2]

1   Our best scientific theories represent our world as one in which there is no such thing as time.
2   If our best scientific theories represent our world as one in which there is no such thing as time, then there is no such thing as time.
3   So, there is no such thing as time.

The first premise hinges on speculative scientific theories, or contentious interpretations of well-established theories. That, however, isn't the main problem with the argument. The main problem is this: given a choice between (a) understanding our best science as a machine for generating predictions, rather than a way of representing the world, and (b) denying that you were alive two minutes ago, which do you choose? If you have a Moorean bone in your body, you choose (a). But then you also reject 1, if the alternative is to accept 3.[3]

Perhaps the most obvious objection to temporal eliminativism is also, prima facie, the most damning. When I look inward, I find conscious experiences changing over time; or, so it seems. For example, I find an experience as of a traffic light changing from red to green. Maybe my experience is illusory. Maybe there is no physical light and no physical change. But doesn't the conscious experience itself change? In order to have an experience as of a light changing from red to green, mustn't I *first* have an experience as of a red light *and then* an experience as of a green light? Isn't change – and, therefore, time – an essential feature of my *experience*, regardless of how things stand in the external world?

We return to this question below. Now let's look at some theories that acknowledge the reality of time, but try to reduce it to something more basic.

Mainstream analyses of time

Reductive theories of consciousness attempt to reduce facts about consciousness to facts about an ostensibly more basic level of reality (e.g. physical or functional facts). Similarly, reductive theories of time attempt to reduce facts about time to facts about something ostensibly more basic (e.g. causal or entropic facts).

Any reductive theory entails a supervenience claim, to the effect that the facts being reduced supervene on the proposed reduction base, and a major threat to reductive theories of consciousness are prima facie modal counterexamples to the supervenience claims they entail (possible worlds that duplicate ours physically or functionally, but not phenomenologically). Reductive theories of time entail analogous supervenience claims and face an analogous threat.[4]

According to Michael Tooley (1997), our world comprises a (large) number of durationless events standing in various causal relations. In Tooley's view, the temporal order of these events supervenes on their causal order, i.e. on which events cause, or are caused by, which others.[5]

However, we can conceive of a world, *W*, in which events instantiate the same pattern of causal relations as the events in our world, but in which all events are simultaneous. (Maybe *W* is a momentary three-dimensional array of objects, wherein the states of various objects depend on the states of various other objects, via forces that propagate with infinite velocity.) Since the temporal order of events in W is different from the temporal order of actual events, W is a prima facie counterexample to Tooley's theory.[6]

According to Julian Barbour (2009), our world comprises a (large) number of intrinsically timeless spatial configurations of objects, where these configurations are uniquely ordered by a timeless version of the least-action principle. In Barbour's view, the temporal order of events supervenes on the least-action ordering of the configurations in which they occur.[7]

However, if our universe is governed by the least-action principle, so is a time-reversed counterpart of our universe, U, that comprises the same configurations as our world (assuming, with Barbour, that the configurations are intrinsically timeless). So, there isn't a unique least-action ordering of the configurations that comprise our universe. To get the uniqueness that Barbour's account requires, we'd have to add a further constraint. But what constraint might that be? Invoking a further natural regularity (e.g. an entropy gradient) won't help, since we can also imagine that regularity being temporally reversed in U without violating the least-action principle. U is therefore a prima facie counterexample to Barbour's theory.

A phenomenological analysis

If finding a good analysis of time is as hard as the foregoing discussion suggests, why not acquiesce to anti-reductionism and conclude that time is just part of the ontological bedrock?

Let me answer that question with another one.

What if there's a world-view in which time *does* have a good analysis? An analysis that illuminates not only the nature of time, but also the relationship of our own experience to it? If such a world-view exists, the fact that time reduces to something more basic in it is an intriguing point in its favour. So, even if you don't think an analysis of time would be valuable for its own sake, you might still like to know whether, and on what terms, such an analysis is possible.

I suggest that we can give a reductive analysis of time, as part of a more general reduction of facts about spacetime and its contents to facts about conscious experience.

The world-view in which this reduction is possible is a kind of phenomenalism. Phenomenalism has been unfashionable for a long time, but it's not hard to understand why people were drawn to it in the past. If you make a sustained effort to unpack the meaning of everyday statements about ordinary physical things, phenomenalism is a very natural place to end up.

When we talk about a physical thing, like a mountain, what do we mean to be talking about? Well, when I talk about a mountain, I take it that I'm talking about a bunch of atoms arranged in a certain way. So, in some sense of "mean", what I mean by "Mauna Kea" (for example) is just some such arrangement of atoms. But there's another sense in which that isn't what I mean. I don't think my beliefs about Mauna Kea would be false if it turned out that mountains weren't made of atoms. If it emerged that mountains were actually made of Aristotelian Prime Matter, I'd be amazed, but I wouldn't conclude that I'd been wrong to think that there were such things as mountains. I'd conclude that I had been mistaken about the nature of Mauna Kea, but not that I'd been mistaken about its existence. This shows that I don't use "Mauna Kea" as a synonym for "such-and-such atoms arranged mountainwise", even though I do take myself to be speaking of atoms arranged mountainwise when I speak of Mauna Kea.[8]

Let's distinguish between (1) what I *take myself to refer to* by "Mauna Kea", and (2) what I *have in mind* by "Mauna Kea". By "Mauna Kea", I take myself to refer to a bunch of atoms arranged mountainwise, but a bunch of atoms arranged mountainwise isn't what I have in mind. What do I have in mind? Is it: something that is *either* a bunch of atoms arranged mountainwise *or* a mass of Prime Matter enformed mountainwise? No. If it turns out that both Aristotle and modern physics have gotten it completely wrong, so that Mauna Kea consists of neither atoms nor Prime Matter, that will undermine my faith in modern physics (and Aristotle), but it won't make me doubt the existence of Mauna Kea. This suggests a test for isolating what I have in mind by "Mauna Kea". By "Mauna Kea", I have in mind x, only if learning that there were no such thing as x would compel me to doubt that Mauna Kea existed. This test rules out atoms arranged mountainwise and Prime Matter enformed mountainwise as candidates for what I have in mind when I speak of Mauna Kea. What doesn't the test rule out?

Here's one thing it might seem not to rule out: *something that tends to give me conscious experiences as of a mountain with such-and-such qualities*. Maybe there's no such thing as a bunch of atoms arranged mountainwise; maybe there's no such thing as a hunk of Prime Matter enformed mountainwise. I might accept all that and more, without relinquishing my belief that Mauna Kea exists. But if you convince me that there is nothing that tends to give me experiences like those I have when I perceive Mauna Kea, won't that compel me to doubt that Mauna Kea exists?

But wait: if what I have in mind when I think of a mountain isn't some nature that the mountain has independent of any potential for conscious experience, why suppose that the mountain is anything more than such a potential? Why think that there is anything "behind" the experiences I have when I perceive Mauna Kea – anything that gives me the experiences, or serves as their source? Instead, we can think of the mountain as a *pure potential* for conscious experience, which may be realized, as it is when I perceive the mountain, but can also exist in the absence of any actual experience.

This is the basic idea behind phenomenalism, a theory first championed by J. S. Mill (1979 [1865]). According to Mill, the physical world is a tendency for conscious experiences to occur in certain patterns. For there to exist some physical object, or occur some physical event, is for it to be the case that conscious experiences with certain phenomenal properties or "qualia" would occur, if certain other conscious experiences (characterized by their own qualia) were to occur.[9]

Define a *sensation-conditional* as a counterfactual conditional whose antecedent and consequent have purely phenomenological import. (A statement has purely phenomenological import just in case it does nothing besides (1) predicate some quale or qualia of some experience or experiences, or (2) predicate some abstract, e.g. logical or mathematical – property or relation of one or more qualia or experiences.) According to Mill, the obtainment of any physical state of affairs is equivalent to the truth of some conjunction of sensation conditionals.[10]

The main source of resistance to phenomenalism is the feeling that in order for physical things to exist, there must be something that *explains why* our world has the phenomenological potential that it does – that, without some such explanation, the "world" is merely a dream.

To overcome this resistance, we can start by drawing a distinction between skeptical hypotheses and metaphysical hypotheses. A hypothesis is skeptical if accepting it would rationally require us to abandon most of our everyday beliefs about the world; a hypothesis that we couldn't rationally accept without abandoning the belief that there are physical objects would be a skeptical hypothesis. A hypothesis is metaphysical if it proposes an account of the ultimate nature of physical reality that is consistent with most of our everyday beliefs and, in particular, with the belief that there are physical objects.[11]

Consider a world that contains the same phenomenological potential as the actual world, and nothing else; call it Mill World. (Two worlds have the same phenomenological potential if the same sensation conditionals are true in both.) The fundamental disagreement between Mill and his opponents is that his opponents think the hypothesis that our world is Mill World is a skeptical hypothesis, whereas Mill thinks it is a (true) metaphysical hypothesis.

I agree with Mill. Discovering that Mill World was our world would have little impact on our beliefs, and no impact at all outside a narrow band of metaphysical theorizing. In particular, it wouldn't require us to revise any of our everyday beliefs about what there is.

For example, I believe that there is coffee. In so believing, I believe, or am disposed to believe, that people who have experiences as of certain plants tend to have experiences as of a certain kind of berry, that people who have experiences as of roasting and grinding such berries tend to have certain olfactory sensations, that people who have experiences as of drinking hot water that has been filtered through the result of such grinding tend to have certain flavour sensations, that people who have experiences as of subjecting such filtrate to various chemical tests tend to have certain visual experiences, etc. But my belief that coffee exists does not come with a belief, or a disposition to believe, that these phenomenological propensities have some deeper, non-phenomenological grounding. My everyday thinking about coffee is completely neutral on the grounding question.

I submit that a world that tends to reward experiences as of the plants with experiences as of the berries, experiences as of the roasting with experiences as of the aroma, experiences as of the hot filtrate with experiences as of the flavour, etc. gives us everything any of us ever wanted from coffee. Whether the reward system is metaphysically fundamental or grounded in something more basic doesn't matter to us, which is why phenomenalism poses no threat to the Guatemalan economy.

As Mill puts it, "these various possibilities" – what I'm calling phenomenological potentials – "are the important thing to me in the world". His point is that whatever must be true in order for us to be justified in caring as we do about whether there are physical phenomena, *is* true in Mill World. So, to whatever extent physical objects are the sort of thing whose existence we should care about, physical objects exist in Mill World. (If physical objects aren't the sort of thing we should care about, phenomenalism can hardly be faulted if it fails to deliver them.)

Unlike traditional idealist theories, phenomenalism allows that most physical entities exist unperceived: a sensation-conditional can be true even if there are no minds or experiences.

Phenomenalism also distinguishes between veridical and non-veridical experiences. A veridical experience is one that fits into the total pattern of experiences (or potential experiences) in a certain way; a non-veridical experience is one that doesn't. When Dorothy dreams of an emerald city towering over a field of poppies, she has an experience intrinsically indistinguishable from some possible veridical perception. Dorothy's dream-experience is non-veridical, because the sensation-conditional, "there would be an experience as of Dorothy looking toward an emerald city if there were an experience as of Dorothy looking across a poppy field" is false.

This isn't the place to mount a detailed defence of phenomenalism. My goal here is just to show that a natural extension of Mill's position creates conceptual space for a satisfactory analysis of time.

For Mill, the fact that a tree has a certain shape and colour reduces to the fact that if experiences with certain qualia were to occur, there would also occur experiences with certain phenomenal shapes and colours. These phenomenal shapes and colours are not physical shapes or colours. A phenomenally green, phenomenally tree-shaped experience isn't (or at least need not be) literally green or tree-shaped – green or tree-shaped in the same sense as a tree. A phenomenally green experience could occur in a world in which nothing *physically* green ever existed. For Mill, the fact that there exist various visible, audible, tangible, odourful, flavourful things reduces to the truth of various counterfactual conditionals concerning invisible, inaudible, intangible, odourless and flavourless experiences.[12]

In Mill's system, all features of the physical world get phenomenalized, *except* for temporal features. The objective roundness of a soap bubble reduces to the *phenomenal* roundness of certain potential experiences – experiences that have no location in objective space. But, according to Mill, the bubble's objective duration just is the *objective* duration of a sequence of potential experiences – experiences that do have location in objective time (or would have such location, if they actually occurred).

Why doesn't Mill try to phenomenalize time? It's because he thinks that consciousness is essentially temporal:

> Sensations exist before and after one another. This is as much a primordial fact as sensation itself; it is a feature always present in sensation, and we have the strongest ground that can ever be had for regarding it as ultimate, because every genesis we assign to any other fact of perception or thought, includes it as a condition.[13]

Mill is far from unique in taking this view. To most people, it seems beyond obvious that experience occurs in time. Their certainty on this point has, I think, three sources, corresponding to three levels of phenomenological reality.

First, there is *phenomenal temporality*, which we find at the level of the individual experience. It consists of the instantiation, by individual conscious experiences, of qualia that we tend to describe in temporal terms: phenomenal duration, phenomenal succession, phenomenal change, etc. When I hear a rising tone, for example, I have an auditory experience that instantiates phenomenal duration and phenomenal change.

Second, there is *phenomenological continuity*, which we find at the level of the stream of consciousness. This is a relationship between the individual conscious experiences that constitute a typical extended conscious episode. When I listen to a song, there is a continuity to my auditory experiences that is missing between the last experience I have when I fall asleep at night and the first experience I have when I wake up the next morning.

Third, there is *experiential memory*. We find this at the level of the stream of consciousness, but it's a relationship that can also span different streams, provided that they belong to the same conscious mental life. Experiential memory includes memories (conscious or not) of one's own conscious experiences, as well as *conscious* memories of anything at all.

I believe that none of these phenomena gives us a compelling reason to locate consciousness in time.

Consider phenomenal temporality. This is a pervasive feature of human experience. For example, when you see the full Moon, you have a visual experience that it's natural to describe in terms of duration, in addition to colour, shape and size. When we describe the experience as "bright" or "round", however, we don't mean that it is literally bright or round, like the Moon itself. Your experience is *phenomenally* bright and *phenomenally* round, but not (as I've put it) *objectively* bright or round.

But, if we can't infer that an experience of the Moon is objectively round from the fact that it's phenomenally round, how can we infer that the experience has objective duration from the fact that it has phenomenal duration? We can't. *Phenomenal duration does not entail objective duration* any more than phenomenal roundness entails objective roundness. The same goes for other aspects of phenomenal temporality (phenomenal succession, phenomenal change, etc.).

If someone says that phenomenal temporality *is* evidence of objective temporality, the burden is on him to substantiate that claim, since he's claiming, in effect, that phenomenal temporality differs from all other phenomenal properties.

I know of only one argument for regarding phenomenal temporality as exceptional in this respect. It goes like this:

If, upon introspective reflection, one of your experiences seems to you to possess some objective temporal feature, then the experience has that feature; many of your experiences *do* seem to you to possess objective temporal features, upon introspective reflection; therefore, many of your experiences have objective temporal features.[14]

The argument fails at step one. Compare: "If, upon introspective reflection, one of your experiences seems to you to possess some spatial feature, then the experience has that feature". But the pain of a stomach cramp isn't located in your stomach, even if it seems to you (upon introspection) that it occurs there. So, the first premise of the argument works only if phenomenal temporality is fundamentally unlike phenomenal spatiality. But that is exactly what the argument was supposed to show.

Furthermore, if introspection seems to reveal anything about the temporal features of experience, it seems to reveal that our experiences have absolute durations. Introspection of the experience you have when you see the second-hand of a clock sweep through a 3° angle suggests that your experience is correctly describable as having a duration of about half a second and not, say, a year. But if the experience has any objective duration, it *is* correctly describable as having a duration of a year, since if it has an objective duration, it occurs in relativistic space-time, in which anything that can be correctly described as having a duration of half a second can also be correctly described as having a duration of a year (or any other non-zero magnitude).

Those looking for a reason to locate consciousness in time must look beyond the individual experience. So let's move up one level in the phenomenological hierarchy, to the stream of consciousness.

Suppose you're watching a car drive down the road, from position P_1 to position P_3 via position P_2. If the car is moving at the right speed (neither too fast nor too slow), you have an experience of the car moving from P_1 to P_2, and an experience of the car moving from P_2 to P_3, but no experience of the car moving from P_1 to P_3 via P_2. Yet, you have only one experience of the car being at P_2. (So it's not like the situation that would have transpired if you had watched the car drive from P_1 to P_2, then lost consciousness, then revived to see the car proceed from P_2 to P_3.)

According to Barry Dainton, "each of the brief phases of your visual experience during this interval is experienced as flowing into its successor".[15] For Dainton, it is this experienced flow of one experience into another that is the distinguishing feature of the stream of consciousness: "these experienced transitions . . . are a crucial component of the continuity of consciousness; if our streams were not continuous this way, they would not have the character they in fact do".[16]

I have two problems with this. First, we don't usually experience our experiences. Usually, we experience our environment. We *experience* our environment by *having* experiences. If we can be said to experience our experiences, it is only when we introspect them. But your experiences stream along even when you're not introspecting.

Second, if you experience, i.e. introspect one experience *A* flowing into another experience *B*, then *A* and *B* are parts of the same (complex) experience; otherwise, you couldn't bring them into the scope of a single act of introspection. This complex *AB* experience may occur in a stream of consciousness before a further experience, *C*. In Dainton's view, you introspect the transition from *AB* to *C*. By the same reasoning as before, it follows that *AB* and *C* belong to a complex experience, *ABC*. And so we are driven to the conclusion that a stream of consciousness is just one big experience – a conclusion that Dainton himself would be the first to reject.[17]

Dainton's talk of experienced flow may miss the mark, but elsewhere he does pinpoint the really distinctive thing about a stream of consciousness. What is really distinctive about a stream of consciousness is the fact that in it, experiences like the P_1 to P_2 experience and the P_2 to P_3 experience can co-exist without multiple occurrences of a P_2 experience – without any "repeated phenomenal contents", as Dainton puts it.[18]

What makes this possible, according to Dainton, is that the P_2 phase of the P_1 to P_2 experience is numerically identical with the P_2 phase of the P_2 to P_3 experience. The P_1 to P_2 and P_2 to P_3 experiences are temporally extended experiences that have a temporal part in common. That's how they can belong to the same stream of consciousness without that stream's involving any repetition of the P_2 experience.[19]

Dainton calls this the "overlap theory" of the stream of consciousness. It's an attractive theory, but if we accept it, we have to give up on the idea of a phenomenological analysis of time, since only experiences that exist in time can overlap temporally.

The crux of the overlap theory is the idea that two experiences can have an experiential part in common. Dainton takes this to be a *temporal* part because he assumes that experiences occur in time. But if experiences can have parts without existing in time, and if some of those parts can be shared by different experiences, then the overlap theory is compatible with a timeless view of experience.

Two experiences can instantiate the same quale without having a part in common; when we look at the sky, our experiences might instantiate the same colour quale without having any common part. But if one experience's instantiation of a quale Q is the same as another experience's instantiation of Q – if the experiences share not just a quale, but a quale-instantiation – then they do have a part in common.

This is just a corollary of the principle that if two things have a property instantiation in common, they share a part. For example, if each of two rooms instantiates the property of having a brick wall, and if the first room's instantiation of the property is the same as the second room's instantiation of it, i.e. if the pair of rooms instantiates the property just once – then the rooms share a wall. There is no requirement that the things instantiating the property exist in time. If the rooms exist in one of Barbour's timeless configurations, they still share a part.[20]

In the stream of consciousness discussed above, you have an experience, E, of the car moving from P_1 to P_2, and an experience, E', of the car moving from P_2 to P_3. E instantiates a quale by virtue of instantiating which E is (among other things) an experience as of a car at position P_2. E' instantiates the same quale. The overlap theory accounts for the stream, provided that E's instantiation of the quale is one and the same instantiation of the quale as E''s instantiation of the quale.

So, instead of thinking of a stream of consciousness as a temporal sequence of partially coinciding phenomenal processes, we can think of it as an atemporal sequence of partially coinciding co-instantiations of qualia. Our experiences can exhibit phenomenological continuity without existing in time.

Thus far, neither individual experiences nor streams of consciousness have compelled us to locate conscious experience in time. This brings us to the third level of phenomenological reality – the conscious mental life – and experiential memory.

On the usual view, the relationship between a memory and that of which it is a memory is temporal, with the memory occurring after the event remembered. This view is incompatible with a timeless conception of experience, since memory is often conscious and sometimes represents conscious episodes from one's own life.

But the usual view isn't compulsory. To see why not, let's start by looking at an epiphenomenalist account of memory. By this account, a memory of an event x is a brain state that is a suitably reliable indicator of the past occurrence of x. In some cases, the indicated event is a past state of the same brain as that to which the indicating state belongs. That past brain state may have caused a conscious experience. If it did, then the present brain state (the memory) is as reliable an indicator of the past occurrence of that conscious experience as it is of the brain state that caused the experience, and therefore counts as a memory of the experience. A conscious memory of an event is just a memory that has some appropriate memorial phenomenology.

To get an account of memory that is compatible with a timeless view of experience, we need only replace the epiphenomenalist's appeals to causation with appeals to timeless neural correlation. By this account, a memory of a conscious experience, E, is a brain state that indicates the occurrence of a past brain state that E has as its neural correlate. (Note that it is only the brain state and not the experience that is past; unlike its neural correlate, E doesn't occur in time.) A conscious memory of an event – any event – is a brain state that (1) indicates the occurrence of that event, and (2) is the neural correlate of some memorial experience.

By this account, brains and brain-states are assumed to be phenomenalistic constructions (just like all other physical phenomena), and neural correlation is assumed to be a relation that isn't essentially temporal. The former assumption goes with the phenomenalist territory. The latter shouldn't be very controversial. There are various ways to understand neural correlation, but the following characterization captures the basic idea. The neural correlate of an instantiation $I(Q)$ of a quale Q is the instantiation $I(P)$ of a physical feature P, such that $I(P)$ naturally necessitates $I(Q)$. (The neural correlate of a quale Q is a physical property P, such that for each instantiation of P, $I(P)$, there is an instantiation of Q that $I(P)$ naturally necessitates.)[21]

One way to interpret natural necessitation is in terms of synchronic or diachronic causality. But that's not the only way. Natural necessitation is simply a form of necessitation weaker than logical or metaphysical necessitation, and there's no obvious reason why such a relation couldn't hold between a temporally located brain state and a non-temporally located phenomenal state. For example, if we understand natural necessitation in terms of entailment by natural law, we can say that it is a natural law, or a consequence of natural laws, that if a certain physical brain state occurs (in time), then a certain phenomenal state exists (not in time).

We use temporal language to describe various aspects of phenomenological reality. I've argued that this usage is strictly optional. "Phenomenal duration", "phenomenal change", "earlier experiences", "later experiences", etc. are terms by which we pick out various features of consciousness, but consciousness doesn't have to exist in time to have those features. We can use the concept of duration to fix the reference of "phenomenal duration", even though the existence of phenomenal duration doesn't entail the existence of objective duration, just as we can fix the reference of "fool's gold" by saying that fool's gold is a worthless mineral that resembles gold, even though the existence of fool's gold doesn't entail the existence of gold. Likewise for all other aspects of consciousness that we use temporal vocabulary to describe.

Mill's reluctance to extend his phenomenalism to the temporal dimension arose from a mistake. He didn't realize that he could phenomenalize the temporal features of the world just as well as he could phenomenalize its spatial features; that when it comes to amenability to phenomenalist reduction, time is in the same boat as shape or colour. Instead of equating the objective duration of a soap bubble with facts about the objective durations of various possible experiences (or sequences of experiences), he could have reduced it to facts about the *phenomenal* durations of various possible experiences. More generally, he could have equated time with the tendency for phenomenological reality to include veridical instances of phenomenal temporality.[22]

We can put this more precisely in terms of scenarios that maximize the quantity of conscious experience, within the constraints imposed by the true sensation conditionals. Call the phenomenological state of affairs expressed by the antecedent of a true sensation-conditional an *antecedent state*. For each antecedent state, there is a *phenomenological set*, S, that contains just that state and anything that is entailed by a member of S via a true sensation–conditional.

Two phenomenological sets are *compatible* if every member of each can co-exist with each member of the other.

Take all the phenomenological sets that are compatible with a given phenomenological set; call the union of these sets a *complete phenomenological set*. A *complete realization of phenomenological potential* is a global state of affairs including all and only the phenomenological states of affairs in a complete phenomenological set.

This terminology in hand, we can say that *time is that which exists if there must be veridical instances of phenomenal temporality, in order for there to be a complete realization of phenomenological potential.*

Here, we understand veridicality as above, in terms of coherence with the overall pattern of potential experience. Just as the difference between a veridical experience as of an emerald city and Dorothy's non-veridical experience is a matter of how the experiences fit into the overall pattern of potential experiences, so the difference between a veridical and a non-veridical experience as of duration, succession, simultaneity or change is a matter of how the experiences fit into the overall pattern of potential experience.

A main weakness of the analyses of time considered earlier (Tooley's and Barbour's) was the existence of possible worlds in which the analyses broke down. It's an advantage of the phenomenalist analysis that it resists this kind of modal counterexample.

We can't conceive of a timeless world that harbours potential for veridical instances of phenomenal temporality any more than we can conceive of a coffeeless world that harbours potential for veridical instances of phenomenal caffeity. Just as a world that features a suitable phenomenological reward system for caffeic experience gives us everything we ever wanted from coffee, a world that features a suitable phenomenological reward system for temporal experience gives us everything we ever wanted from (or feared about) time.

But what about imperceptible things? Isn't there a possible world that has the same phenomenological potential as ours, but in which there fail to occur some (or all) of the imperceptible events and processes that occur in our world?

No. A world that differs from ours at the imperceptible level also differs from ours at the level of phenomenological potential. Maybe it's logically impossible to perceive an individual helium atom. In that case, there's no true sensation-conditional of the form "If there were such-and-such conscious experiences, then there would be an experience as of an enduring helium atom". Still, a world that contains an enduring helium atom is a world in which there would be detections of that atom, if there were a suitably-utilized quantum-gas microscope. In such a world, there is a true sensation-conditional of the form: "If there were experiences as of a certain kind of apparatus being used a certain way, then there would be experiences as of the apparatus doing certain things" – where the latter experiences are the sort that actual scientists have when they detect actual atoms using actual scientific instruments. Any reason to doubt that a world contains the sort of phenomenological potential represented by such a sensation-conditional is equally a reason to doubt that it contains a helium atom. So, if a possible world differs from ours by containing one less helium atom than our world, it also differs from our world by containing one less bit of corresponding phenomenological potential.

Conclusion

I've argued that an analysis of time is possible, given a world-view in which physical facts reduce to facts about experience. Actually carrying out such a reduction would require developing the phenomenalist position much farther than I've developed it here. The goal of the present discussion has only been to show that in our current state of knowledge, a phenomenological analysis of time is an epistemic possibility worth exploring. When it comes to the metaphysics of time, consciousness might not be our biggest problem after all. It might be our best solution.

Notes

1 For Chalmers' distinction, see (Chalmers 1996: xi–xvii).
2 See (Barbour 1999), (Earman 2002) and (Rovelli 2009).
3 Tim Maudlin makes a similar point in (Maudlin 2002: 7–11).
4. A-facts logically supervene on B-facts if logically possible worlds identical with respect to B-facts are identical with respect to A-facts.
5 See (Tooley 1997).
6 Tooley suggests that a world in which all causation takes the form of backward causation is logically impossible (Tooley 1997: 64), but he doesn't consider the possibility of a world, like *W*, in which all causation is simultaneous.
7 (Barbour 2009).
8 As I'm using the phrase "atoms arranged mountainwise", the claim that mountains are atoms arranged mountainwise is compatible with the claim that there are mountains.
9 See Chapter 11 of (Mill 1979 [1865]).
10 The phrase "sensation-conditional" is from (Skorupski 1994: 114).
11 The skeptical/metaphysical distinction comes from (Chalmers 2010).
12 By "phenomenal shapes", "phenomenal colours", etc. I mean the qualia that characterize experiences that we typically describe using the vocabulary of shape, colour, etc., as when we describe a visual experience of a tomato as red and round (or reddish and roundish). I don't take a stand here on whether an experience must represent the world as containing a red or round object, in order to instantiate phenomenal redness or phenomenal roundness.
13 (Mill 1979 [1865]: 198–199).
14 See (Phillips 2010: 183), (Soteriou 2010: 227) and (Rashbrook 2013: 588–609).
15 (Dainton 2012: 177).
16 Ibid.
17 And rightly so, as argued in (Dainton 2006: 113); see also (Pelczar 2015: 85).
18 (Dainton 2006: 141–142).
19 (Dainton 2006: 162–182). As Dainton notes, the overlap theory originates with John Foster; see (Foster 1982: 259–260).
20 Maybe we should limit the principle to non-abstract entities; it doesn't matter for our purposes, since conscious experiences aren't abstract.
21 We could replace "$I(P)$ naturally necessitates $I(Q)$" with "$I(P)$ naturally necessitates $I(Q)$ under conditions C", where C might require the brain to be functioning normally or embedded in a normal environment; for the details, see (Chalmers 2000).
22 Mill isn't the only phenomenalist to lose his nerve in the face of time. The primitive relation of Carnap's *Aufbau*, Recollection of Similarity, is explicitly temporal, precluding any analysis of time in Carnap's system; see (Carnap 1967: 127–128).

References

Barbour, J. (1999) *The End of Time: The Next Revolution in Physics*, Oxford, UK: Oxford University Press.

Barbour, J. (2009) "The nature of time", available at http://arxiv.org/abs/0903.3489, accessed 13 August 2014.

Carnap, R. (1967) *The Logical Structure of the World and Pseudoproblems in Philosophy*, Berkeley, CA: University of California Press.

Chalmers, D. (1996) *The Conscious Mind: In Search of a Fundamental Theory*, Oxford, UK: Oxford University Press.

Chalmers, D. (2000) "What is a neural correlated of consciousness?" in T. Metzinger (ed), *Neural Correlates of Consciousness: Empirical and Conceptual Questions*, Cambridge, MA: MIT Press, pp. 17–39.

Chalmers, D. (2010) "The matrix as metaphysics", in D. Chalmers (ed.), *The Character of Consciousness*, Oxford, UK: Oxford University Press, pp. 455–494.

Dainton, B. (2006) *Stream of Consciousness: Unity and Continuity in Conscious Experience*, New York: Routledge.

Dainton, B. (2012) "Selfhood and the flow of experience", *Grazier Philosophische Studien* 84(1): 161–199.

Earman, J. (2002) "Thoroughly modern McTaggart", *Philosopher's Imprint* 2(3): 1–28.

Foster, J. (1982) *The Case for Idealism*, London: Routledge and Kegan Paul.

Maudlin, T. (2002) "Thoroughly muddled McTaggart: Or, how to abuse gauge freedom to create metaphysical monstrosities", *Philosopher's Imprint* 2(4): 1–23.

Mill, J. S. (1865/1979) *An Examination of Sir William Hamilton's Philosophy, and of the Principal Philosophical Questions Discussed in His Writings*, Toronto, ON: University of Toronto Press.

Pelczar, M. (2015) *Sensorama: A Phenomenalist Analysis of Spacetime and Its Contents*, Oxford, UK: Oxford University Press.

Phillips, I. (2010) "Perceiving temporal properties", *European Journal of Philosophy* 18(2): 176–202.

Rashbrook, O. (2013) "An appearance of succession requires a succession of appearances", *Philosophy and Phenomenological Research* 87: 584–610.

Rovelli, C. (2009) "Forget time", available at http://arxiv.org/abs/0903.3832, accessed 13 August 2014.

Skorupski, J. (1994) "J. S. Mill: Logic and metaphysics", in C. L. Ten (ed.), *The Nineteenth Century*, London: Routledge, pp. 98–121.

Soteriou, M. (2010) "Perceiving events", *Philosophical Explorations: An International Journal for the Philosophy of Mind and Action* 13(3): 223–241.

Tooley, M. (1997) *Time, Tense, and Causation*, Oxford, UK: Oxford University Press.

18

TEMPORAL EXPERIENCE AND THE A VERSUS B DEBATE

Natalja Deng

This chapter discusses some aspects of the relation between temporal experience and the A versus B debate. To begin with, I provide an overview of the A versus B debate and, following Baron *et al.* (2015), distinguish between two B-theoretic responses to the A-theoretic argument from experience, veridicalism and illusionism. I then argue for veridicalism over illusionism, by examining our (putative) experiences as of presentness and as of time passing. I close with some remarks on the relation between veridicalism and a deflationary view of the A versus B debate. I suggest that the deflationary view can provide further support for veridicalism.

Introduction

The metaphysics of time has been characterized by the opposition between the A-theory and the B-theory (or block universe view).

It's an interesting question exactly how to understand "complete", but this is beyond the scope of this chapter. It's likely that the notion of completeness in play will make reference to something like fundamentality or joint-carving. So let's think of the second component of the B-theory as the claim that there is a tenseless description of temporal reality that is more fundamental than any tensed description.

Why might one disagree with the B-theory? One prominent motivation is the conviction that time passes. In John Norton's words: "Time passes. Nothing fancy is meant by that. It is just the mundane fact known to us all that future events will become present and then drift off into the past" (2010: 24). Time's passing seems to involve the transfer of some kind of metaphysical privilege from one time to another. Hence it requires that one time be metaphysically privileged, as captured in a (fundamental) tensed fact like it's 12:27.

The metaphysical privilege consists in different things according to different versions of the A-theory. It might be being the only time that exists (presentism), being the latest time that exists (growing block view), being the time at which possibilities are actualized (dynamic branching views), or simply being the one time that is present in an absolute, non-perspectival sense (moving spotlight view). "Non-perspectival" means not just relative to itself (even B-theorists allow that each time is present in that sense, like each spatial location is here relative to itself), but in an absolute, non-time-relative sense.

So we seem to have a debate about whether time passes (or whether, fundamentally, time passes). However, lately some have asked why B-theorists should feel pressured to uphold something as outlandish as the claim that time doesn't pass. Why shouldn't they instead say that time's passing just consists in there being a succession of times?[1] Let's call this the tenseless passage move. I'll suggest in the final section that this move can be motivated by a substantial thesis, namely a deflationary view of the debate. But for now what matters is the stock reply (see Skow 2015: 2). Sure, we'll give you the label "passage". But the kind of passage the B-theory includes is anemic (i.e. bloodless, lifeless, not the real thing). The debate is about whether there is passage of a robust kind. That's the kind that requires metaphysical privilege to be transferred from time to time. The B-theory excludes *that*. (As mentioned, I re-consider the tenseless passage move in the final section.)

As a final preliminary, note that all these views make use of notions like "times", which are out of place in relativistic physics. That can seem odd, especially if one thinks that much of the interest in this debate ultimately derives from its relation to modern physics. But the B-theory can be straightforwardly adapted to a relativistic context. Its first component, for example, becomes the view that all spatiotemporal regions exist, independently of their extent in spatial, null and temporal directions. A-theoretic views, on the other hand, are notoriously hard to reconcile with relativity. Insofar as they rely on a metaphysically privileged global present, they require structure that is conspicuously absent from Minkowski spacetime, the spacetime of special relativity.[2] For that reason, what follows can be seen as one aspect of the broader project of relating the findings of modern physics to everyday experience.

The argument from experience

A-theorists have long pointed to the nature of experience in support of their view. Nowadays, they often offer the following inference to the best explanation (Baron *et al.* 2015):

1 We have experiences as of time (robustly) passing.[3]
2 If we have experiences as of time (robustly) passing, then any reasonable explanation of this relies on the (robust) passage of time being an objective feature of reality.
3 Hence, the (robust) passage of time is an objective feature of reality.

The thought is that if A-theorists provide the only explanation of our experiences as of time (robustly) passing, then *a fortiori* they provide the best such explanation. Suppose one accepts the assumption that A-theorists can provide a reasonable passage-based explanation of these putative experiences. What should be said about the argument?

Let's call those B-theorists who reject 1, veridicalists.[4] The most salient B-theoretic alternative to veridicalism, and the position that is presented by Baron *et al.* (2015) as the most widespread among B-theorists, is illusionism. Illusionists accept 1, but reject 2, because they think that there are reasonable explanations of our experiences as of time (robustly) passing that don't rely on there being (robust) passage.

Illusionism may be less widespread than Baron *et al.* present it as being. For example, they classify Hugh Mellor (1998), Huw Price (1996) and Craig Callender (2008) as illusionists. But as we'll see, Mellor argues against the claim that we perceive A-properties. Similarly, Callender (2008) argues against the claim that there is an "'experience of the present' as contemporary metaphysicians conceive it" (2008: 2). Moreover, arguably, there are both illusionist and veridi-calist interpretations of Price (1996: 14–15).

I'll offer support for veridicalism over illusionism. That is, I'll argue against premise 1. I'll sometimes speak loosely and say I'm defending veridicalism, but without a defence of the B-theory, it's only a conditional defence of veridicalism. Moreover, since A-theorists can in principle also reject 1, it's a defence of a position about temporal experience (namely the nega-tion of 1) that is compatible with the A-theory, though rarely combined with it.

The first thing to ask about the argument is what is meant by "experience" here. Let's distinguish between two things that could be meant. The distinction is well illustrated by the following quotation from Robin Le Poidevin:

> We are indirectly aware of the passage of time when we reflect on our memories, which present the world as it was, and so a contrast with how things are now. But much more immediate than this is seeing the second hand move around the clock, or hearing a succession of notes in a piece of music, or feeling a raindrop run down your neck. There is nothing inferential, it seems, about the perception of change and motion: it is simply given in experience.
>
> *(2007: 87)*

It's this latter direct, perceptual awareness I take the argument to be about (and that I'll take "experience" to denote). But it will also be useful to have a term for the first, more indirect kind of awareness. Let's call it temporal EXPERIENCE.

The term "temporal experience" in the first sense, i.e. in the sense of time perception, can seem a little puzzling. Time is not an ordinary object, so we don't perceive it in the way that we perceive ordinary objects. But we do seem to perceive temporal features of events (or so I'll assume here). For example, we perceive things happening after one another.

Now, both the veridicalist and the illusionist can allow this. They can agree that we perceive succession, simultaneity and duration. But the illusionist is likely to think we only perceive those things *because* we perceive (robust) passage, or *by* perceiving (robust) passage. In seeing a move-ment, you see the object's being in one place at one time and in another place at another time. But you only see this by seeing the object's being in one place becoming present and then past, while the object's being in another place becomes present. You have an experience as of a change that involves (robust) passage. Some illusionists call this "animated" or "flowing change".

A sense of presentness?

If we have experiences as of time (robustly) passing, then presumably we have experiences as of metaphysical privilege. Do we?

We certainly have a temporally limited perceptual horizon. Most of the time, we perceive events that are roughly simultaneous with our perceptions (Le Poidevin 2007: 85–86). We don't perceive the future because perception is a causal process, and causes, typically at least, precede their effects. And we mostly don't perceive the distant past because there is no action at a spatial and temporal distance. Events can't directly cause perceptual states in us – they must do so via a series of intermediate causes. Moreover, in most circumstances, signals degrade with spatial and temporal distance, so they only reach us if our spatial separation from them is not too large (the obvious exception being the night sky).

Hugh Mellor argues against the claim that we perceive (non-perspectival) presentness by pointing out that when one learns that some celestial event occurred long ago, its perceptible appearance does not change. Hence, events don't look present (1998: 16).

Unfortunately for the veridicalist, this doesn't follow. Indeed, the phenomenon in question might be taken to show that this feature of perception is conspicuously resilient and independent of our tensed beliefs about the event's occurrence. What we should keep in mind, though, is that the veridicalist can allow that we perceive events and indeed that we perceive them as happening presently in a perspectival sense. The question is just whether we also perceive events as happening presently in the absolute, non-perspectival sense.

Uriah Kriegel speaks of a *felt temporal orientation* here: in perceiving rain, one perceives it *as* present, just like in episodically remembering rain, one remembers it *as* past (2015). The veridicalist can say two things about this. The first is that what Kriegel describes as a felt temporal orientation, even if it exists, may simply be due to our present-tensed beliefs that things are happening. It may simply be that while perceiving the rain, we also believe it to be present. And of course, these beliefs can be true. B-theorists needn't deny that tensed beliefs can be true if had at the right times, nor that they are essential for timely action. (And even if there are further unsolved problems about indexicality, these are not specific to time.)

The second thing to say is that even if there is a felt temporal orientation over and above this, the veridicalist may be able to accommodate it using Kriegel's own suggestion. Kriegel says that we needn't think of felt temporal orientation as part of what is perceived, i.e. of perceptual contents. Instead we can think of it as a matter of how we perceive. Call this the attitudinal view.

He finds this idea in Brentano and argues that it describes quite a widespread phenomenon in our mental life. For example, in fearing a snake, there is a sense in which we experience it as dangerous. But what we fear isn't that the snake is dangerous – it's just the snake. The danger is part of the very attitude of fearing, not of its content; it's not attributed to the snake. Similarly, in perceiving, we don't attribute presentness to things in the world, we don't perceive things as present. Rather, we perceive as present the things in the world.

Admittedly, further questions could be raised about this distinction, and it remains to be seen how promising the attitudinal view is. The point is just that if there is felt temporal orientation over and above present-tensed beliefs, and if this is how to think of it, then it actually fits well into the veridicalist's story.[5]

There is another argument from experience in the vicinity. According to this argument, we don't have experiences as of presentness, or a feeling of presentness more easily explicable by A-theorists. But experience nonetheless supports the A-theory, because it singles out the present in another way: only one time's experiences are presented to one, or are available to one, or are occurring *simpliciter* (Balashov 2005; Skow 2015). There is a lack of parity between one's experiences from different times. Callender has articulated understandable dissatisfaction with such claims: "what is occurring *simpliciter*? The answer is more Latin – the experience, [Balashov] says, is '*sui generis*' – but we never get more *lumen*" (2008: 6). And even Skow, one of the two proponents of the argument, concedes that denying the intelligibility of the notion may be a reasonable B-theoretic response (2015: 221).

Suppose the veridicalist is right that we don't have experiences as of one time's being metaphysical privileged. Why then do we tend to *think* of the time we're at as metaphysically privileged and as global? Call this the presentness intuition. Callender suggests that:

> [t]he strength of such an intuition is evinced by the existence of philosophy of time itself, with so many philosophers arguing for presentism, as well as the reaction one finds in students when teaching the relativity of simultaneity. Part of the shock of relativity is its conflict with the idea of a special common now.

(2008: 7)

Jeremy Butterfield (1984) offers an explanation for something in the vicinity of the presentness intuition. Butterfield considers the typical time scales on which objects around us change their observable properties and compares these to how long it takes for perceptual signals to reach us and be processed. At least in the case of sight, sound and touch, we can usually take our perceptual beliefs to still be accurate by the time we form them. This makes sense from the perspective of evolution: it would be a grave disadvantage to take so long to process perceptual signals that one's perceptual beliefs were typically no longer accurate by the time we formed them.

What does this show? Butterfield takes it to explain why observation reports, i.e. perceptual judgments or beliefs tend to have a temporally local but spatially dispersed subject matter. Presumably, the facts about our perceptual horizon rehearsed above are in the background here. The point is that what our senses typically inform us about is the time at which they inform us, rather than some earlier time. So we can proceed as if our perceptual horizon was even more temporally narrow than it is. But we can't proceed as if it's spatially narrow, because it's not. And, says Butterfield, the fact that perceptual judgments typically have this temporally but not spatially limited subject matter means that it's useful to recognize a present-tensed but not a spatially tensed sense of existence. That's close to the explanandum constituted by the presentness intuition. And the explanation carries over.

Butterfield also points to the related fact that verbal communication or communication by signing is usually such that the time-lags involved are negligible. We can usually take the tensed reports we give to each other to be accurate when we receive them, but we can't do the same with reports that incorporate a spatial perspective:

> Each person can usually take a token of "now" which they hear to refer to the time of reception, as well as the time of utterance, without misinterpreting the speaker, [when] they cannot analogously take a token of "here" to refer to where they themselves are.
>
> *(1984: 173)*

Inter-subjective agreement on what's happening now reinforces the impression of objectivity. It gives us the sense of sharing a common now, and this in turn encourages the tendency to think that the now is metaphysically significant.

A sense of passage?

If the veridicalist is right, then we don't have experiences as of time (robustly) passing. Hearing a printer hum, seeing a movement, noticing that five minutes have passed – none of these involve perceiving something's being first present and then past.

That can seem hard to believe. One way to see that it's nonetheless plausible is to take a closer look at typical illusionist explanations. Recall that the illusionist wants to offer a reasonable (robust) passage-free explanation for how the brain creates these experiences in a B-theoretic, (robust) passage-free world. Their explanations have often been based on experimental results from cognitive science concerning certain kinds of perceptual illusions.

For example, according to Laurie Paul, both veridical perception of change and illusory perception of change involve an illusion of (robust) passage (2010). They're both experiences as of animated or flowing change. So the latter is doubly illusory, the former only singly so. And now the idea is that B-theorists can take the explanation appropriate to cases of illusory motion perception and apply it, with very few changes, to the pervasive illusion of passage. The key is to think of the static images involved in perceptual illusions, or of films or flipbooks, as analogous to the B-theorist's static tenseless facts underlying change.

Take, for example, the "color-phi" experiment, in which a subject is presented with a rapid succession of flashes of a static dot of different colors on opposite sides of a screen. If the flashes are timed and spaced appropriately, the subject can have an illusion of a dot moving back and forth, and abruptly changing its color somewhere along the trajectory. Now think of the static inputs (red flash left), (green flash right) as analogous to the static B-theoretic facts underlying any change, such as (O has property P_1 at t_1), (O has property P_2 at t_2). In both cases, the brain "responds to closely spaced inputs that have sufficient similarity (yet have qualitative contrasts of some sort) by accommodating and organizing the inputs", thereby creating a sense of animated change (Paul 2010: 22). In a nutshell, the recommendation is: if you're a B-theorist, think of life as a whole as a kind of film. There are only static images, one after the other, but because of our limited powers of discrimination, we experience animation instead.

The problem with this is that the analogy between film and life is strained, even on the B-theory. Whether there is a continuity of times or not is a question that's entirely orthogonal to the A versus B debate. The block universe needn't have any gaps. And even if it did necessarily involve gaps, they wouldn't be gaps in time. That is, there are in the block universe no static inputs for our brain in the way that there are such static images in films, or in the color-phi experiment. We don't first experience one tenseless fact, O's being P at t_1, and then after a little while, the next tenseless fact, O's being Q at t_2. As Christoph Hoerl says, the argument trades on an equivocation in the word "static". If there's anything static about the block universe, it's in a very different sense of the word from the one applicable to perceptual illusions (2014a, 2014b).

One might object that the point is that the analogy is close enough. But close enough would here mean close enough for the empirically well-documented mechanism to shed light on the putative mechanism responsible for the pervasive illusion of (robust) passage. And it's hard to see how it has done that. (I argue for this in more detail in my (2013b).)

The important thing to note is that if this is right, it doesn't just pose a problem for this particular way of executing the illusionist's explanatory project. Rather, it throws doubt on the project's starting point. The explanation, as mentioned, trades on an ambiguity in the word "static". In order for it to work, there should be, on the B-theory, discreteness or rather a gappiness of the kind that's found in the color-phi phenomenon. If there were, the explanation would work. But plausibly, what it would then explain would be an illusion of continuity – of continuous motion and persistence. In a gappy block universe, the mechanism would produce experiences as of non-gappiness. And if that's all that needs explaining, veridicalists are right.

This isn't knock-down: an illusionist could insist that in this gappy block universe, there would then be two separate illusions produced, one of continuous motion and one of flow, and somehow one mechanism would produce both. But this claim of a second illusion looks contrived in the context of this explanation. Effectively, we've had to *misconstrue* the B-theory in order to offer an explanation for the alleged experience as of (robust) passage. That should give the illusionist some pause.

If veridicalism is correct, then as we've seen already for presentness, the question arises as to why it is we tend to think of time in A-theoretic ways. It's a good question exactly who is meant by "we" here. "The folk" may not have views, let alone uniform views, about this metaphysical issue. But as Callender's remarks suggest (2008: 7), the philosophy of time is some evidence for the following claim: as soon as one reflects on the metaphysics of time and its passing (whether as a metaphysician or not), A-theoretic ideas are likely to surface and be felt to have a certain intuitive appeal, even if they are not ultimately endorsed.

One important part of the story is surely the asymmetry in our epistemic access to the past and the future. Eric Olson imagines a similar spatial asymmetry. Think about how things would seem if light waves only propagated towards the north. Everything to the south would appear bright, while everything to the north would appear dark. You'd feel as if you were at the boundary between the dark and bright parts of the Earth, and as if the dawn followed you around: as you moved north, "the darkness would seem to recede, so that more of the earth became bright" (Olson 2009: 446).

I like this thought experiment, but I think it's significant that it involves movement. One way to think of Olson's point would be that we tend to think that time (robustly) passes because, given the epistemic temporal asymmetry, as we move through time, the boundary of our knowledge shifts. That is, given that at each time we remember only earlier ones, then as we move through time, we (find out and then) remember more. But of course it's precisely this movement through time that's at issue and is so hard to make sense of. On the one hand, we can't move through time, in the way we move through space, at least not when we're not time travelling. On the other, it's precisely a kind of enforced movement through time, or of time past us, that we're prone to imagining.

There seem to be two additional relevant disanalogies between time and space. The first is that time, unlike space, is one-dimensional (Le Poidevin and Mellor 1987). Given that our spacetime route is continuous, we can't leave out any time between two others, while we can leave out any given spatial location between two others. There is no second temporal dimension to move into. In that sense, we have a greater freedom as to which spatial locations to include in our life story than which times to include in it.

The other is that in a causally ordered sequence of pairs of spatial and temporal locations (supposing now that space were one-dimensional too), the temporal coordinate of the elements monotonically increases, but the spatial one need not. This is significant because it helps explain why we feel a certain passivity with respect to time that we don't feel with respect to space (Deng 2013c). Recall the presentness intuition. At each time, that time seems special to the point that we are sometimes inclined to attribute metaphysical significance to it. And we remember all the previous times seeming special in just the same way. So we wonder how this time got to be "it", and how we got "taken to" the later time. After all, we didn't take ourselves there. Of course, by looking after ourselves we contribute to our continued existence; but that the later time figures in our life story isn't the result of any of our actions.

However, we can see now that there's nothing mysterious about this. It's just a reflection of the fact that human action is a causal process, and causes (typically) precede their effects. So whatever we decide to attempt or not to attempt, the result will be an aspect of what happens *at a later time*.

Re-thinking passage

A veridicalist could stop here. They could say that the above provides reasons to reject premise 1 in the argument from experience and an explanation for why we nevertheless sometimes think of time in A-theoretic ways.

Note that on this veridicalist's story, while experience doesn't involve A-theoretic content, EXPERIENCE does. Recall that temporal EXPERIENCE is an indirect kind of temporal awareness that arises when we reflect on how things used to be and compare them to how they are now. One example of this is noticing that the hour-hand of a clock has moved on; another is reflecting on how one has changed over the years. In saying that the content of temporal EXPERIENCE is partly A-theoretic, the veridicalist would be claiming that our indirect awareness of time over longer time scales (than the short time scales most relevant to time perception) is characterized by a tendency towards a false belief in (robust) passage. And prima facie, that seems to be suggested by the previous sections.

So on this veridicalist view, there would be no perceptual illusion involving (robust) passage; but there would be a cognitive illusion coloring our longer term cognitive and emotional relationship to time. In this final section, I want to sketch a different interpretation and development of the veridicalist's story.

Recall the tenseless passage move mentioned at the beginning. Why not say that time's passing consists in there being a succession of times? The stock reply was to agree to the re-labelling, but insist that that kind of passage is anemic, not robust. The reply reiterates a presupposition of the debate, namely that there are theories of time that better capture its dynamicity than others.

But the tenseless passage move can be motivated by a deflationary view of the debate that rejects this presupposition. On that view, there is less at stake in the debate than meets the eye, because the idea of "robust passage" is misguided. There are no robust theories of time's passing.

One immediate worry is this. How can there be no robust theories of passage? If by that we just mean, theories of robust passage, then aren't these just A-theoretic accounts of passage, of which there clearly are some?

Let's concede that there may be a thin reading of "robust" on which that's right. On that thin reading, a robust account of passage is just any A-theoretic account according to which time passes. As long as the view attributes metaphysical privilege to one time, for example sole existence or absolute presentness, and as long as it affirms that time passes, it's a robust account of passage.

This would be an all or nothing sense of "robustness". However, there clearly is also a thick sense of "robustness" on which robustness comes in degrees. And it's the search for robustness in this thick sense that drives the debate. Skow's *Objective Becoming* (2015) is a representative example. Though not without misgivings, he there embarks on the project of finding out *how* robust various versions of the A-theory are, i.e. how robust the passage is that they can deliver. For example, he suggests that presentism contains passage that is *less* robust than that contained in some versions of the moving spotlight view.

The deflationary view rejects the presupposition that some theories are more robust than others. That is, it declines the use of the term "robust" (in this thick sense), and with it the use of the term "anemic". This can provide motivation for the tenseless passage move. The contention is that succession is as good as it gets, passage-wise.

A defence of this view is beyond the scope of this chapter, but I'll close with a few remarks about its relation to veridicalism. None of the above depends on the deflationary view. But veridicalism is compatible with, and can gain further support from, the deflationary view.

There are two related avenues of support. Note first that it's part of the deflationary view that premise 1 is about robust passage in the thick sense in which robustness comes in degrees, i.e. the sense in which, according to the deflationary view, the search for robust theories is misguided. The disagreement about temporal experience concerns whether or not we perceive robust passage in the sense that someone like Skow is trying to capture. The deflationary view rejects this project and maintains that robust theories can't ultimately be made sense of. If that is right, then that is all the more reason to deny that we perceive robust passage.

The second avenue of support for veridicalism is this. The anemia metaphor is apt, precisely because of the contrast with (thickly) robust theories. It derives its legitimacy from that contrast. Without that contrast, B-theoretic succession is left a kind of passage that is free from any anemia-related blemish. We don't perceive the becoming present of events, but we do perceive succession, simultaneity and duration. These latter notions now appear in a different light. There is no sense in which they are static notions, not just because time is included in the block universe but because thereby time's passing is too in a fully adequate sense. The negation of premise 1, and thus veridicalism, gains further plausibility from this.

The deflationary view makes it easier to believe that all temporal experience presents us with is succession, simultaneity and duration.

On this development of the veridicalist's story, there isn't even a cognitive illusion (involving a false belief) coloring our temporal EXPERIENCE. At most, there is an unhelpful cognitive habit.

Of course, all this depends on a good case for the deflationary view. But, as mentioned, the preceding sections stand on their own: even when taking the debate at face-value, B-theorists need not agree with premise 1 of the argument from experience.

Conclusion

The role of temporal experience (and temporal EXPERIENCE) in contemporary metaphysics of time is a complex and interesting one. Veridicalism is a viable B-theoretic response to the A-theoretic argument from experience. It gains further support from a deflationary view of the A versus B debate.

Notes

1 See for example Savitt 2002; Dieks 2006; Dorato 2006; Oaklander 2012; Deng 2013a; Leininger 2013; Mozersky 2015.
2 See for example Saunders 2002; Pooley 2013.
3 The "as of" locution is meant to signal that the experience in question needn't be veridical, i.e. one can have an experience as of x without there being any x.
4 See, for example, Braddon-Mitchell 2013; Deng 2013c; Frischhut 2013; Hoerl 2014a, 2014b.
5 One could perhaps read Kriegel as saying this himself, and thus as intending merely to show that veridicalism is a lot less counterintuitive than it's generally taken to be. However, he does present his proposal as a novel response to the argument from experience, distinct from both veridicalism and illusionism.

References

Balashov, Y. (2005) "Times of our lives: Negotiating the presence of experience", *American Philosophical Quarterly* 42(4): 295–309.

Baron, S., Cusbert, J., Farr, M., Kon, M. and Miller, K. (2015) "Temporal experience, temporal passage, and the cognitive sciences", *Philosophy Compass* 10(8): 560–571.

Braddon-Mitchell, D. (2013) "Against the illusion theory of temporal phenomenology", Proceedings of the CAPE International Workshops, T. Sato, S. Sugimoto and T. Sakon (eds), *CAPE Studies in Applied Philosophy and Ethics Series*, vol. 2, Kyoto University, Japan: CAPE Publications, pp. 211–222.

Butterfield, J. (1984) "Seeing the present", *Mind* 93(370): 161–176.

Callender, C. (2008) "The common now", *Philosophical Issues* 18(1): 339–361.

Deng, N. (2013a) "Fine's McTaggart, temporal passage, and the A versus B-debate", *Ratio* 26(1): 19–34.

Deng, N. (2013b) "On explaining why time seems to pass", *Southern Journal of Philosophy* 51(3): 367–382.

Deng, N. (2013c) "Our experience of passage on the B-theory", *Erkenntnis* 78(4): 713–726.

Dieks, D. (2006) "Becoming, relativity and locality", in D. Dieks (ed.), *The Ontology of Spacetime*, Amsterdam: Elsevier, pp. 157–176.

Dorato, M. (2006) "Absolute becoming, relational becoming and the arrow of time: Some non-conventional remarks on the relationship between physics and metaphysics", *Studies in History and Philosophy of Modern Physics* 37: 559–576.

Frischhut, A. M. (2013) "What experience cannot teach us about time", *Topoi* 34(1): 143–155.

Hoerl, C. (2014a) "Do we (seem to) perceive passage?" *Philosophical Explorations* 17(2): 188–202.

Hoerl, C. (2014b) "Time and the domain of consciousness", *Annals of the New York Academy of Sciences* 1326: 90–96.

Kriegel, U. (2015) "Experiencing the present", *Analysis* 75(3): 407–413.

Le Poidevin, R. (2007) *The Images of Time: An Essay on Temporal Representation*, Oxford, UK: Oxford University Press.

Le Poidevin, R. and Mellor, D. H. (1987) "Time, change, and the 'indexical fallacy'", *Mind* 96(384): 534–538.

Leininger, L. (2013) "On Mellor and the future direction of time", *Analysis* 74(1): 1–9.

Mellor, H. (1998) *Real Time II*, London: Routledge.

Mozersky, M. J. (2015) *Time, Language, and Ontology: The World from the B-Theoretic Perspective*, Oxford, UK: Oxford University Press.

Norton, J. D. (2010) "Time really passes", *Humana Mente: Journal of Philosophical Studies* 13: 23–34.

Oaklander, L. N. (2012) "A-, B-, and R-theories of time: A debate", in A. Bardon (ed.), *The Future of the Philosophy of Time*, London: Routledge, pp. 1–24.

Olson, E. T. (2009) "The passage of time", in R. Le Poidevin, A. Bardon, A. McGonigal and R. P. Cameron (eds), *The Routledge Companion to Metaphysics*, London: Routledge.

Paul, L. A. (2010) "Temporal experience", *Journal of Philosophy* 107(7): 333–359.

Pooley, O. (2013) "Relativity, the open future, and the passage of time", *Proceedings of the Aristotelian Society* 113(3/3): 321–363.

Price, H. (1996) *Time's Arrow and Archimedes' Point: New Directions for the Physics of Time*, Oxford, UK: Oxford University Press.

Saunders, S. (2002) "How relativity contradicts presentism", *Royal Institute of Philosophy Supplement* 50: 277–292.

Savitt, S. (2002) "On absolute becoming and the myth of passage", *Royal Institute of Philosophy Supplement* 50: 153–167.

Skow, B. (2015) *Objective Becoming*, Oxford, UK: Oxford University Press.

Further reading

Bardon, A. (2010) "Time-awareness and projection in Mellor and Kant", *Kant-Studien* 101(1): 59–74.

Benovsky, J. (2013) "From experience to metaphysics: On experience-based intuitions and their role in metaphysics", *Noûs* 49(3): 684–697.

Callender, C. (forthcoming) *What Makes Time Special*, Oxford, UK: Oxford University Press.

Dorato, M. (2015) "Presentism and the experience of time", *Topoi* 34(1): 265–275.

Forbes, G. (2015) "Accounting for experiences as of passage: Why topology isn't enough", *Topoi* 34(1): 187–194.

Ismael, J. (2011) "Temporal experience", in C. Callender (ed.), *The Oxford Handbook of Philosophy of Time*, Oxford, UK: Oxford University Press.

Ludlow, P. (2015) "Tense, the dynamic lexicon, and the flow of time", *Topoi* 34(1): 137–142.

Prosser, S. (2007) "Could we experience the passage of time?" *Ratio* 20(1): 75–90.

Prosser, S. (2012) "Why does time seem to pass?" *Philosophy and Phenomenological Research* 85(1): 92–116.

Prosser, S. (2013) "Passage and perception", *Noûs* 47(1): 69–84.

Prosser, S. (2016) *Experiencing Time*, Oxford, UK: Oxford University Press.

Suhler, C. and Callender, C. (2012) "Thank goodness that argument is over: Explaining the temporal value asymmetry", *Philosophers' Imprint* 12(15): 1–16.

19

PRESENTISM AND TEMPORAL EXPERIENCE

Akiko M. Frischhut

Introduction

When thinking about time, we can distinguish two subjects: the nature of time and our experience of time. A theory of time should be able to accommodate the way we experience temporality. A viable account of temporal consciousness should be compatible with our best theory of time. This chapter investigates how presentism accounts for our experience of time. According to presentism, all and only present things exist.[1] Presentists argue that their view is the most intuitive, capturing best what most people (pre-philosophically) think about time: you and I exist, but the Roman Empire does not exist anymore, whereas the Olympic Games 2020 do not exist yet.[2] Time passes: what is future will be present, what is present will be past and what is past was once present. Presentists not only claim to capture what most people think about time but also how we experience time. In particular, they claim that we all experience time as passing and that this is best explained by the fact that time really does pass.[3] This gives presentism an intuitive advantage over other theories of time. Or so presentists say.

This might puzzle some. After all, change is the having of incompatible properties at different times, but since presentism only ever allows one time, the present time, one might wonder if and how presentists can account for change and change experiences. I will concentrate on the latter and focus on two *central questions*:

- CQ1: Can presentism, given theory X of temporal perception, account for experiences of change and duration?
- CQ2: Can presentism, given theory X of temporal perception, account for experiences of time as passing?

Before we consider these questions, however, we will have to look at a more general problem that arises for presentism and perceptual experience in the first section. Since we only ever perceive what is already past, presentists owe us an explanation of how to make sense of perceptual experience at all. Whether they succeed depends on the theory of perception adopted. From there, I will move on to temporal perception, providing a very brief overview of the debate on temporal perception in the next section. Thereafter, I aim to answer the central questions. Three accounts will be considered: anti-realism, retentionalism and extensionalism. Regarding CQ1,

I argue that the combination of presentism, an indirect theory of perception and retentionalism is most likely able to account for experiences of change, depending on a viable presentist account of causal relations. As for CQ2, it turns out that none of the combinations considered can accommodate experiences of temporal passage in the sense relevant for presentists. The last section concludes with a short summary of the results of my investigation.

Presentism and the time-lag argument

Before starting with the problems that arise for presentism in the context of temporal experience, we need to address a concern about presentism and perceptual experience in general. Of course, if the problem proves serious, it affects all cases of experience, synchronic and diachronic. The problem is the time-lag argument against direct realism. Direct realism is the thesis that we can be directly aware of mind-independent physical objects, where a subject S is directly aware of some object *o* if S is aware of *o*, yet not aware of *o* by virtue of being aware of something else.[4] For the presentists among the direct realists, this argument proves serious. It shows that the combination of the two views is untenable or, at the very least, highly counter-intuitive.

The time lag in experience, in particular visual experience, refers to the fact that the visual information we get from the environment is delayed because of the time it takes for light to travel from the (external) object of experience to the visual system of the perceiving subject. The structure of the time-lag argument is simple:[5]

1   We experience stars that do not exist anymore.
2   When it *seems* to us that we are directly aware of something, then there must *be* something we are directly aware of.
3   We cannot be directly aware of something that does not exist anymore.
4   Therefore, when we see a star that does not exist anymore, what we are directly aware of cannot be the star itself.
5   Since perception *always* involves a time lag, the direct objects of experience can *never* be external objects.[6]

For those direct realists who are also presentists, the time-lag argument is a serious reason for concern. A common response for direct realists is to bite the bullet. Sometimes we have direct veridical experiences of past objects, even if they do not exist anymore. Thus Ayer, for example, asks:

> Why should it not be admitted that our eyes can range into the past, if all that is meant by this is that the time at which we see things may be later than the time when they are in the states in which we see them? And having admitted this, why then should we not also admit it is possible to see things which no longer exist?
>
> *(Ayer 1982: 94–95)[7]*

This sounds like a perfectly sensible response. All the worse for presentist direct realists, since it is not available to them. The problem is that "exists" could be either understood as "local existence" or as "existence *simpliciter*".[8] In the local sense, to say that a star ceased to exist ten years ago, say, just means that it is located ten years and more prior to our time. In contrast, if it has ceased to exist *simpliciter*, then it has ceased to be part of reality. For presentists, wholly non-present things do not exist in the same sense as Sherlock Holmes does not exist: they are not part of reality. Seeing some x requires one to stand in a relation to x. As it is commonly agreed that non-existing things cannot instantiate relations, presentists, it seems, have to reject direct realism about temporal perception.[9]

Since the time–lag problem for presentists is but one instance of the much wider problem concerning presentism and cross-temporal relations, presentist direct realists might be able to help themselves to some of the presentist strategies developed to cope with cross-temporal relations in general. They could, for example, deny that relations are existence entailing. Most people would hesitate to do so, for good reasons.[10]

Other alternatives include adopting Hinchcliff's (1996) "unrestricted presentism", according to which non-present things can instantiate properties and relations. Most presentists are unwilling to accept this, since this sort of Meinongianism about the past only undermines their claim to intuitiveness.[11]

Brogaard (2006) argues for tensed as opposed to tenseless relations, where the former need not be existence entailing. One way to understand this is in terms of presently instantiated, irreducibly tensed, primitive relational properties, as in *having been caused by x*, instantiated by the perception. This seems undesirable since it cuts the explanatory tie between object of perception and perception. My having a particular perception is no longer explained by the external object perceived, but by the fact that my perception instantiates some relational property.[12]

Markosian's (2004) and Sider's (1999) strategy consists in admitting that truths involving cross-temporal relations are not *literally* true. Instead, there are sufficiently similar truths "in the ball park" (Markosian) or "quasi-truths" (Sider) which justify us treating the relevant claims as true. Since direct realists think that perceptual experience can give us immediate and straightforward access to the objects of experience, such solutions do not seem compatible.

But even if a viable solution to the problem of cross-temporal relations can be found, presentist direct realists face another, even more serious problem. Direct realists conceive of veridical experiences as partly constituted by their object(s).[13] Due to the time lag, any object we are perceptually aware of is past when perceived.[14] Thus for the presentist direct realist, veridical experiences themselves must be partly constituted by something that does not exist anymore. If objects of experience are constitutive of experiences, then they must be essentially so, since the idea of a veridical experience (in the direct realist sense) without an object as proper part makes no sense. The result is that presentism, combined with direct realism, renders veridical perceptual experience impossible, independently of how successful the problem of cross-temporal relations can be solved.

Presentists, it seems, have no choice but to reject direct realism. How does the view fare with other theories of perception? According to the sense-data theory of perception, what we are directly aware of in experience is not some past external object but some present internal object that merely mediates the past. Alternatively, representationalists hold that when we perceive some external object like the star, the star causes us (in the right way) to be in a certain representational state which allows us to be aware of it. In both cases, the external object is not constitutive of the perception itself. But in both cases, a veridical perceptual experience requires a causal relation obtaining between a present thing (the sense-datum, the mental state) and something past (the object of experience). Since relations are existence entailing, and past things do not exist for presentists, not much, it seems, has been gained by moving from direct to indirect realism.

One important difference, however, is that presentism + direct realism cannot account for (veridical) perceptual experiences *at all*, whereas presentism + an indirect theory of perception cannot account for the *origin* of these experiences. This is because the objects of experience are constitutive of veridical experiences for direct realists, while they are only their causes on the opponent views. Of course, presentists who choose an indirect theory of perception still need to say something about the causal relations involved.

Presentists have developed various well-known strategies to account for causal relations. One is to treat presentist causation in the way Lewis (2004) treats absence causation, by giving a counterfactual account of causal dependence.[15] Various authors have pointed out though that such an account still requires some genuine relation to supervene on.[16]

Bigelow (1996) and McDaniel (2009) have suggested that presentists invoke relations between "Lucretian properties", i.e. presently instantiated tensed properties as causal relations. The hope is that relations between tensed properties are sufficiently similar to the kind of relation that would satisfy our concept of causation. One might think that instantiations of tensed properties are themselves caused by prior events though, which leads to worries about a threatening infinite regress, involving infinitely many tensed properties to account for each causal relation.[17]

This is by no means exhaustive, and discussing the proposals in detail would bring us too far off focus. What is important is that presentist indirect realist theories of perceptual experience stand and fall with the presentist treatment of causal relations. In so far as the challenge for presentists posed by the time lag in perceptual experience is just a variation of the challenge posed by cross-temporal relations in general, it is not new.

To summarize, whereas presentism and direct realism seem incompatible, the viability of presentism and indirect theories of temporal perception depends on more general problems presentism has with causal relations. Since this chapter focuses on a different problem, we will simply note here that the latter views are at least less obviously troubled by the time lag problem than the former. Keeping this in mind, we can move on to temporal experience. Before turning to our central questions, I will briefly introduce the debate about temporal perception in the following section.

The paradox of temporal awareness

Leaving the metaphysics of time aside, let us concentrate on our experience only for a moment. The debate about temporal perception can be characterized by what Dainton (2000) has called the "paradox of temporal awareness". It can be outlined in three plausible, though incompatible claims:

(A1) We seem to experience change and duration just as we experience colours and shapes.
(A2) In perceptual experience, all we seem to be aware of is what is (was) momentarily present.
(A3) We can only be aware of change as occurring over time.

Of the three claims, (A3) is the safest to hold. Even if some or all changes were instantaneous, we must experience change as occurring over time, for otherwise to experience change would mean to experience an object being F and not F at the same time.[18] This leaves temporal perception theorists with (A1) and (A2): either they abandon the idea that we can experience change or they deny that our experience is bound to what occurs at an instant.

Of course, no one doubts that we are in *some* way aware of change. The dispute is whether one can *strictly speaking experience* change, i.e. be aware of change solely by virtue of one's current perceptual experience, rather than to infer that change has occurred from a combination of memory (or imagination or judgement) and experience.[19]

The consensus appears to be that in order to maintain (A1), we have to abandon (A2). Most people agree that in order to experience change as change, we have to be, in some way or other, aware of more than what occurs at a moment. The big question is whether we should maintain (A1) at this price and, if so, how we are aware of things that do not presently occur. Consequently, the first major divide in the debate is between those who reject (A1) and those who reject (A2).[20] Following Dainton, I shall call the former "anti-realists about temporal perception", and the latter "realists about temporal perception".[21]

Next, I will briefly present three prominent views of temporal perception. The goal, in each case, is not to evaluate the theory but to evaluate how each fares with regard to presentism and our two central questions.

Anti-realism about temporal perception and presentism

Anti-realists about temporal perception think that if change were experienced, it would have to be experienced as taking time (A3), but that our perceptual awareness is confined to what happens at a time (A2). Consequently, they deny (A1), i.e. deny that we can *strictly speaking* experience change. Let us consider anti-realism with regards to our two central questions:

- CQ1: Can presentism, given anti-realism, account for experiences of change and duration?
- CQ2: Can presentism, given anti-realism, account for experiences of time as passing?

On the face of it, anti-realism matches well with the presentist doctrine. Experiencing change requires a perceptual awareness of something past as past, for example of *the chameleon having been yellow*, which is precisely what the anti-realist and the presentist deny is possible. However, due to the time lag in experience, it also requires an awareness of something past as present, for example of *the chameleon currently being green*. This is acceptable for anti-realists but problematic for presentists. In so far as presentism and direct realism are incompatible, so is their combination with anti-realism. Coupled with an indirect theory, the core problem is not related to temporal perception but to the previously discussed problem presentists have with the time lag in perceptual experience. Presentism + an indirect theory of perception + anti-realism (PIA) simply inherits the same problems.

With regards to CQ2, PIA is more problematic. According to its adherents, presentism best captures the way we experience time. Coupled with anti-realism about perception, however, this advantage is lost. The thought is as follows. It is almost universally accepted, by presentists and non-presentists alike, that we experience time as passing.[22] Consider these representative quotes:

> Let me begin this inquiry with the simple but fundamental fact that the flow of time, or passage, as it is known, is given in experience, that it is as indubitable an aspect of our perception of the world as the sights and sounds that come in upon us.
>
> *(Schuster 1986: 695)*

> Above and beyond and before all these considerations, of course, is the manifest fact that the world is given to us as changing, and time as passing.
>
> *(Maudlin 2007: 135)*

Presentism can account for these experiences in a straightforward way: we experience time as passing because time does objectively, i.e. mind-independently pass.[23] The argument that presentists are implicitly relying on here can be summarized with what I call, following Le Poidevin (2007), the Argument from Experience (AFE)[24]:

1 We all experience time as passing.
2 The best explanation for these experiences is that time objectively passes.
3 Therefore time passes.

Anti-realism is incompatible with 1. Since temporal passage is a form of change (the change from future to present to past), and anti-realism is incompatible with experiences of change in general, anti-realism is likewise incompatible with experiences of temporal passage. Thus, if anti-realism about temporal perception is true, then we cannot have experiences of temporal passage, at least not in the sense relevant for presentists.

The relevant sense here is to experience temporal passage *in the strict sense*. Why is that? In order for AFE to go through, our experience needs to be *best explained* by the fact that time passes. Only perceptual experiences are best explained by what they are experiences of. (Non-hallucinatory) perceptual experiences are caused (or even partly constituted) by their objects, and it is an essential function of perceptual experience to give the subject an accurate account of what the world is like. If we simply inferred, believed or imagined that time passes, if our experience was somehow altered by other cognitive states, or if we were just "hard wired" to think that time passes, then these "experiences" in the broad sense would not justify us inferring that time passes. Rather than being best explained by the fact that time passes, these experiences would be just as well or better explained by facts about ourselves – the way we think or the way our brains work, for example. Given anti-realism, we cannot have experience of time as passing in the required, strict sense.

While PIA does not create any new problems, it also undermines presentism by depriving it of its intuitive advantage. Since many would consider this as a (or the) major motivation for the view, presentists should better not be anti-realists.[25]

Presentism and retentionalism

Retentionalism is one of two realist theories of temporal perception I shall discuss. Realists deny (A2): that experience is bound to a durationless instant. We can experience what occurs over short intervals and we experience what happens during these intervals *as present*. Since James (1890), such intervals are referred to as "specious presents".[26] Retentionalism is the view that to experience change, we need to be aware of all parts of the temporally extended structure together, at the present moment. According to the retentionalist, we are *at any instant* aware of what occurs *over an interval* of time.

Let us start with CQ1: Can presentism, given retentionalism, account for experiences of change? Since temporally extended events are experienced at the present moment, the combination of the two theories poses no new problems, i.e. no problems other than those presentism has due to the time lag in experience anyway. So much is true at least for presentism + an indirect theory of perception + retentionalism (PIR).

In contrast, PDR (presentism + direct realism + retentionalism) is not tenable. Direct realists conceive of veridical experiences as partly constituted by their object(s). Ignoring the time lag, an experience of change, as a temporally extended phenomenon, must be an experience of something that is at least partially past. So an experience of change would, even without a time lag, be an experience that is partly constituted by something that does not exist. Since only the present temporal part of change exists, only that part could be constitutive of the experience. But an experience of only the present part of change is indistinguishable from an experience of no change at all. In other words, even if there were no time lag in experience, PDR could not account for experiences of change.

Let us now move on to CQ2: Can presentism, given retentionalism, account for experiences of time as passing? Remember that for presentists, a *relevant* experience of temporal passage is one which is *best explained* by the fact that time passes. If the experience is better or equally well explained by a fact which is compatible with time not passing, then we could not infer from it that time actually passes. What would be the content of such an experience? Can retentionalism accommodate it? Once we have determined the answer to the first question, we will see that the answer to the second must be negative.

Consider some object o that changes from being F at t_1 to G at t_2. Now, if time passes (in the way presentists conceive of it), then o's change is "dynamic" in that it is constituted by temporal passage: o changes from F to G, by virtue of the fact that the state of affairs $(F(o)$ at $t_1)$ ceases to exist and $(G(o)$ at $t_2)$ comes into existence. In contrast, if time does not pass, then o is *always F* at t_1 and *always G* at t_2. Let us call the former change A-change, and the latter B-change. A-change is *brought about* by temporal passage, whereas B-change is qualitative variation over time and does not require time to pass. A relevant experience, in the sense specified, would be an experience of A-change *as* A-change, that is, *as opposed to* as B-change. Since A- and B-change both involve variation over time, we could not infer from an experience of mere variation over time that time passes. For that, a subject would have to experience change as change in what exists rather than as variation over time.

If PIR (presentism + an indirect theory of perception + retentionalism) is correct, then our experience is silent on whether time passes or not. Put in terms of visual experience, PIR cannot account for experiences of A-change *as* A-change, because all changes would look like B-change. Let me explain.

Recall the distinction between "local existence", hence "existence$_L$", and "existence *simpliciter*", hence "existence$_S$". To say that some object o has come into existence$_L$ (or ceased to exist$_L$) is to say that o is not located at any time prior to (or after) the time of reference, whereas to say that o has come into existence$_S$ (or ceased to exist$_S$), is to say that o has become (or ceased to be) part of reality. Note that an object might exist$_S$ after it has ceased to exist$_L$, or before it came into existence$_L$. On the other hand, an object that does not exist$_S$, cannot exist$_L$. A-change involves a change in what exists$_S$, whereas B-change only involves a change in what exists$_L$.

There is no problem in representing B-change in experience, since there is no problem in representing that $F(o)$ is located at t_1 but not after, and that $G(o)$ is located at t_2 but not before. In contrast, A-change involves a change in what is real. The problem with representing A-change is that, what A-change is, and how we are supposed to experience change according to retentionalism, is not compatible. To have an experience of change, retentionalism requires us to represent an interval, whereas A-change is an ontological change from one time to the other. On the one hand, we are supposed to perceptually represent things as coming into and going out of existence *simpliciter*. On the other, we are supposed to perceptually represent the interval over which the change occurs. If time passes, then intervals do not exist, for it is precisely the *replacement* of one present time with the next that constitutes temporal passage. So how could *that* be represented by representing an interval? Retentionalism explains the perceptual experience of change in a manner very much akin to experiences of spatial variation: as instantaneous perceptual representations of qualitatively heterogeneous extensions (of time or of space). Such a heterogeneous "spread" is in itself static. It is not surprising that retentionalists cannot represent a dynamic change by representing a static spread.

One way PIR adherents might respond is by introducing phenomenal A-properties. On this proposal, a subject S represents o as *is G now* and *was F* (a moment ago). For illustration, consider Figure 19.1 below.

The problem with this suggestion is that such an experience could be accurate if time passed, but also if time did not pass. The difference lies only in the veridicality conditions: if time is static, then the experience is veridical if $G(o)$ obtains (more or less) simultaneous with my experience and $F(o)$ obtains at an earlier time. If time passes, the experience is veridical if $G(o)$ exist$_S$ and $F(o)$ has ceased to exist$_S$.[27] In other words, the difference between A-change and B-change is not reflected by experiences that feature A-properties in the perceptual content.

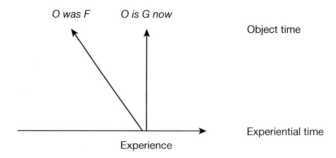

Figure 19.1 Subject *S* represents *o* as *is G now* and *was F* (a moment ago)

Presentism and extensionalism

Just like retentionalism, our second realist theory, extensionalism, holds that we can, strictly speaking, experience change.[28] Consider two successive tones, *Do* and *Re*. Extensionalism holds that one can experience the succession of (*Do-Re*) on the basis of one's current perceptual experience alone. Contrary to retentionalism, extensionalists argue that the experience is concurrent with what is experienced: if the succession (*Do-Re*) seems to last two seconds, then the experiential act will also take two seconds.[29] During this short period we are perceptually aware of (*Do-Re*) – both tones seem (phenomenally) present to us, although as occurring in succession.[30]

Presentism + extensionalism (PEX) is incoherent, on both versions, direct and indirect. If presentism is true, then only what is present exists. But if reality is confined to a moment, then our perceptual experiences (the experiential acts) cannot extend through time. Note that retentional theories do not have this problem: since they hold that our experiences of change take no time, they are, at least in this sense, perfectly compatible with presentism.

This requires some clarification. Although presentists standardly think that (concrete) objects exist wholly in the present, few would insist that events exist entirely in the present. Traditionally, presentists reject quantification over events (cf. Prior 1968). There is no event that is my experience of x, only a process of experien*cing* x. I am experiencing a temporally extended x by having experienced x and currently experiencing x (and, perhaps, going to experience x).[31] But given that the experiential act is concurrent with what is experienced, and my present experiencing is all that ever exists, we can only ever experience what happens now.

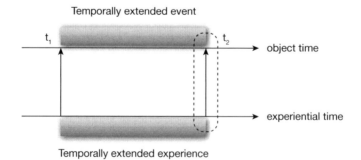

t_2 is present. The perforated oval marks the (only existing) instantaneous present time slice.

Figure 19.2 Change as occurring over time (A3); presentism and extensionalism are incompatible

(See Figure 19.2 for illustration.) An experiencing that is no more can no more represent something than a pillar that does not exist anymore can carry a bridge.[32] Since we can only be aware of change as occurring over time (A3), presentism and extensionalism are incompatible.

Motivated presentists might consider a non-standard form of presentism according to which the objective present has a short non-zero duration, long enough to house an experience which is itself temporally extended but wholly present.[33] Ultimately, this proves a dead-end. *Prima facie*, a problem with any durational present account is that it seems to undermine the way presentists understand tenseless relations of temporal order. A-theorists define B-relations like *earlier than* and *later than* in terms of A-relations such as *n time units past/future*, and it is not obvious how this explanatory priority can be maintained during the extended present.[34] Then it is difficult to see how one might coherently spell out a temporally extended objective present during which change occurs. It seems that the temporal parts of any change must be successive, and yet, by virtue of being all present, simultaneous.[35] Others worry how to avoid an infinitely long durational present and thus a collapse of presentism into the tenseless theory of time.[36] The view is even less plausible when we consider that the duration of the objective present would have to *exactly match* the duration of the temporally extended experience. If the present was longer, then it would be a mystery why the specious present and the concurrent experiential act would not match the duration of the objective present; if it was shorter, then it would be too short to accommodate a temporally extended experience.[37]

Finally, even if we ignored all these difficulties, non-standard-PEX could not accommodate experiences of temporal passage. Consider again object *o* changing between t_1 and t_2 from *F* to *G*: on a presentist account this is analysed as *F(o)* at t_1 ceasing to exist$_S$ and *G(o)* at t_2 coming into existence$_S$, independent of whether or not t_1 and t_2 are (each) temporally extended or not. Now suppose t_1 is an interval, I_1, constituted by temporal parts tp_1 and tp_2. And suppose, given presentism, I_1 is present, so only I_1 exists. Then *o*'s change *during* I_1 could not be analysed in terms of A-change, since time does not pass during the interval that is the present. Instead, during I_1, *o* changes by being *F* at tp_1 and *G* at tp_2. Thus, any change that occurs *over* time (i.e. over two distinct times) would be analysed as A-change, but any change that occurs *during* a time (the interval that is present) would have to be analysed as B-change, as mere qualitative variation over temporal parts of the present time. Since, according to PEX, any change that is experienced has to occur and be experienced during the present time (since only what is present exists and the experience must be concurrent with its object), we could never experience the change that constitutes passage, which is a change *from one present time to the other*, rather than a change that occurs *during* a present time. Thus, even on non-standard-PEX, it would be impossible to experiencing time as passing.

Conclusion

Intuitively, we all believe that we experience change and the passage of time. Presentism prides itself as the most intuitive theory of time. However, a closer look at how we would experience temporality if presentism were true reveals that this is far from obvious. For if presentism were really so intuitive, then it would do justice to these intuitions. In the course of this chapter, I have examined how presentism fares when combined with various leading theories of perception and temporal perception. I focused on two central questions. CQ1: Can presentism, given theory X, account for experiences of change and duration? And CQ2: Can presentism, given theory X, account for experiences of time as passing? The results of my inquiry are set out in Figure 19.3 below.

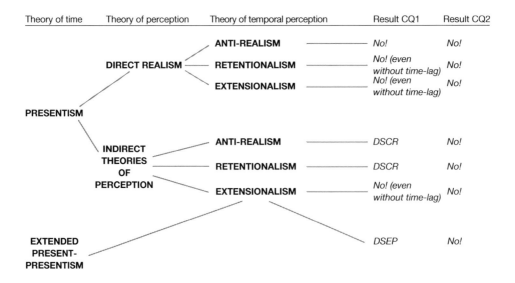

DSCR= Depends on Solution(s) to the presentist problem with Cross-temporal Relations.
DSEP= Depends on Solution(s) to problems related to the temporally Extended objective Present.

Figure 19.3   Results of inquiry

As Figure 19.3 illustrates, there is no possible combination which allows for an experience of time as passing. This result alone undermines the alleged intuitive advantage of presentism and with it the motivation for the view. As for CQ1, presentism and direct realism are incompatible due to the time lag in perception and the fact that direct realism conceives of experiences as partly constituted by its objects.[38] Consequently, any combination of presentism + direct realism + temporal perception theory fails too. Moreover, this would even be the case if there were no time lag in perception. Whether presentism is compatible with indirect theories of perception depends on the presentist's solution for the problem of cross-temporal relations. The very same problem is inherited by combinations of presentism + an indirect theory + anti-realism, and by presentism + an indirect theory + retentionalism. Neither of these combinations adds any more or unique problems. Presentism + an indirect theory/direct realism + extensionalism is not viable, even if there were no time lag. Finally, whether a non-standard presentism featuring a temporally extended objective present is compatible with extensionalism depends on whether presentists can overcome problems that come with the extended present. Presentism, it remains safe to say, is not as intuitive a theory as its adherents like to portray it.[39]

Notes

1 Presentism has been expressed differently. A-theoretic presentism holds that things which exist instantiate an irreducible property of presentness (cf. Bigelow 1996; Hinchliff 1996; Markosian 2004). For tense realists to be present *just is* to exist (cf. Tallant 2010), to be the case (cf. Prior 1968), to be actual (cf. Bigelow 1991) or to belong to a set of propositions that is true (Crisp 2005). I will formulate the discussion A-theoretically and assume a substantivalist framework. Nothing here hangs on these choices though.
2 That presentism is the most intuitive view of time has been claimed, amongst others, by Bigelow (1996: 35), Markosian (2004: 49) and Merricks (2007: 140).
3 Although few have explicitly argued for that view, many take it as an intuitive start. See Schuster 1986, Williams 1951 and Maudlin 2007 among others.

4 It is enough for my purposes if this is a necessary condition.

5 The structure of the argument roughly follows Rashbrook-Cooper's version. For a detailed analysis see Rashbrook-Cooper (ms).

6 I will sometimes omit "perceptual" when I refer to perceptual experience. I will specify whenever I refer to experiences that are not perceptual.

7 This is also noted by Rashbrook-Cooper (ms) and Power (2013).

8 See also Lowe (2006: 284).

9 See also Power (2013) for an argument along these lines.

10 For a detailed discussion of problems with this strategy see for example Keller (2004).

11 See, for example, Baron (2013), Brogaard (2006: 195) and Markosian (2004: 52).

12 A similar problem has been pointed out by Kaplan and Sanson (2011) about presently instantiated past-tensed properties as truthmakers for past-tensed propositions.

13 The disjunctivists among the direct realists hold that all perceptual experience is factive. Whether this holds for all direct realists need not concern us here.

14 More precisely, any state of an object instantiating some property is past when perceived.

15 For an attempt to apply Lewis's account to the presentist's problem with causal relations, see McDaniel (2009), and for discussion, see Baron (2012).

16 See McDaniel (2009) and Baron (2012).

17 See Baron (2012). Baron himself accounts for causal relations by introducing an extended metaphysical present, during which objects can instantiate causal relations. For problems with the extended present, see the section "Presentism and extensionalism" above.

18 Such an experience of some object being F and not F at the same time would not amount to an experience of change *as* change. Having said this, Le Poidevin (2007), in discussing the "waterfall illusion", suggests that there might be two neural mechanisms to detect change. Although we are only perceptually aware of what is momentarily present, we are also (strictly) perceptually aware of motion without a sense of location change ("pure motion").

19 Most of what I say is also valid for the experience of duration.

20 Le Poidevin's account of pure motion may be an exception. The account does not extend to experiences of duration though. For these experiences, Le Poidevin is plausibly interpreted as arguing that we need memory faculties to be aware of temporally extended episodes.

21 Realism is defended among others by Foster (1982), Dainton (2000), Le Poidevin (2007), Phillips (2010); antirealism among others by Chuard (2011) and Dennett (1991).

22 Exceptions are Prosser (2007), Frischhut (2013) and Hoerl (2014), who have argued against this assumption.

23 A static form of presentism is, though deeply implausible, not incoherent. Fine's (2006) "fragmentalism", for example, might be interpreted as a form of static presentism (though not by Fine).

24 My version differs from Le Poidevin's (2007). For a more detailed discussion of my version of this argument, see Frischhut (2013).

25 There are various flaws one might find with AFE, independently of anti-realism. First, it is not at all obvious that we actually have experiences of temporal passage (see note 23). For more discussion on this point, see Prosser (2007), Deng (2013a), Frischhut (2013) and Hoerl (2014). Second, one might wonder whether presentism has the tools to account for any form of objective temporal passage. See, for example, Fine (2005) and Deng (2013b) for discussion.

26 The term "specious" points to the fact that the experienced or phenomenal present deviates from the objective present by having temporal depth, whereas the latter is standardly taken to be durationless.

27 A strange consequence of this view is that, to veridically experience A-change, we have to perceptually represent something that does not exist$_s$ anymore.

28 Extensional accounts of temporal perception have been supported by Stern (2005 [1897]), Mundle (1954, 1966), Foster (1982) and Dainton (2000, 2008).

29 Dainton actually rejects the act/object distinction for experiences. This will play no important role here though.

30 As with retentionalism, I shall use representationalist vocabulary to present the theory. Dainton is not a representationalist. That said, his account is largely independent of these commitments (cf. Zahavi 2007: 454), and compatible with a representationalist view, although certain details of the view are more vulnerable to criticism if expressed in representationalist terms. This is not relevant for the arguments presented here.

31 Presentists who allow for events usually conceive them as having multiple temporal parts. There is thus a sense in which a temporally extended experience (*qua* event) exists for the presentist – by virtue of a constitutive present part that exists. But an analogous worry applies.

32 See Dainton (2000) for a similar example.

33 Standardly, the objective present is taken to be instantaneous, an idea that can be traced back to St. Augustine. See Le Poidevin (2007) for a clear version of St. Augustine's argument.

34 See McKinnon (2009) for one suggestion of how this could be done.

35 See, for example, Benovsky (2013) for this point. McKinnon (2003) makes a similar point. Note, however, that the non-standard presentist is likely to deny that presentness implies simultaneity (cf. Dainton 2000).

36 See McKinnon (2009).

37 See also Benovsky (2013) for a similar worry.

38 Unless, as I said in the section "Presentism and the time-lag argument", one accepts some extremely counter-intuitive views about non-existing objects or relations.

39 Many thanks for comments and discussion to Ian Phillips, Graham Peebles, Emiliano Boccardi and Giuliano Torrengo.

References

Ayer, A. J. (1982) *The Problem of Knowledge*, Harmonsworth: Pelican.

Baron, S. (2012) "Presentism and causation revisited", *Philosophical Papers* 41(1): 1–21.

Baron, S. (2013) "Tensed supervenience: A no go for presentism", *Southern Journal of Philosophy* 51(3): 383–401.

Benovsky, J. (2013) "The present vs. the specious present", *Review of Philosophy and Psychology* 4(2): 193–203.

Bigelow, J. (1991) "Worlds enough for time", *Noûs* 25(1): 1–19.

Bigelow, J. (1996) "Presentism and properties", *Philosophical Perspectives* 10(Metaphysics): 35–52.

Brogaard, B. (2000) "Presentist four-dimensionalism", *The Monist* 83(3): 341–356.

Brogaard, B. (2006) "Tensed relations", *Analysis* 66(3): 194–202.

Caplan, B. and Sanson, D. (2011) "Presentism and truthmaking", *Philosophy Compass* 6(3): 196–208.

Chuard, P. (2011) "Temporal experiences and their parts", *Philosopher's Imprint* 11(11): 1–28.

Crisp, T. (2005) "Presentism and 'cross-time' relations", *American Philosophical Quarterly* 42(1): 5–17.

Dainton, B. (2000) *Stream of Consciousness: Unity and Continuity in Conscious Experience*, London: Routledge.

Deng, N. (2013a) "On explaining why time seems to pass", *Southern Journal of Philosophy* 51(3): 367–382.

Deng, N. (2013b) "Fine's McTaggart, temporal passage, and the A versus B debate", *Ratio* 26(1): 19–34.

Dennett, D. (1991) *Consciousness Explained*, Harmondsworth, UK: Penguin.

Fine, K. (2006) "The reality of tense", *Synthese* 150(3): 399–414.

Foster, J. (1982) *The Case for Idealism*, London: Routledge.

Frischhut, A. M. (2013) "What experience cannot teach us about time", *Topoi* 34(1): 143–155.

Hinchcliff, M. (1996) "The puzzle of change", *Philosophical Perspectives* 10: 119–136

Hoerl, C. (2014) "Do we perceive passage?" *Philosophical Explorations* 17(2): 188–202.

James, W. (1890) *The Principles of Psychology*, New York: Dover.

Keller, S. (2004) "A problem for presentism", *Oxford Studies in Metaphysics* 1: 83–106.

Kiverstein, J. (2010) "Making sense of phenomenal unity: An intentionalist account of temporal experience", *Royal Institute of Philosophy Supplement* 85(67): 155–181.

Le Poidevin, R. (2004) "A puzzle concerning time perception", *Synthese* 142(1): 109–142.

Le Poidevin, R. (2007) *The Images of Time: An Essay on Temporal Representation*, Oxford, UK: Oxford University Press.

Lewis, D. (2004) "Void and object", in J. Collins, N. Hall and L. A. Paul (eds), *Causation and Counterfactuals*, Cambridge, MA: MIT, pp. 277–290.

Lowe, E. J. (2006) "How real is substantial change?" *The Monist* 89(3): 275–293.

Markosian, N. (2004) "A defence of presentism", in D. Zimmerman (ed.), *Oxford Studies in Metaphysics*, Oxford, UK: Oxford University Press.

Maudlin, T. (2007) *The Metaphysics Within Physics*, Oxford, UK: Oxford University Press.

McDaniel, B. (2010) "Presentism and absence causation: An exercise in mimicry", *Australasian Journal of Philosophy* 88(2): 323–332.

McKinnon, N. (2003) "Presentism and consciousness", *Australian Journal of Philosophy* 81(3): 305–323.

Merricks, T. (2007) *Truth and Ontology*, Oxford, UK: Oxford University Press.

Mundle, C. W. K. (1954) "How specious is the 'specious present'?" *Mind* 63(249): 26–48.

Phillips, I. (2010) "Perceiving temporal properties", *European Journal of Philosophy* 18(2): 176–202.

Power, S. (2013) "Perceiving external things and the time-lag argument", *European Journal of Philosophy* 21(1): 94–117.

Prior, A. N. (1968a) "Now", *Noûs* 2(2): 101–119.

Prior, A. N. (1968b) *Changes in Events and Changes in Things: In Papers on Time and Tense*, Oxford, UK: Clarendon Press.

Prosser, S. (2007) "Could we experience the passage of time?" *Ratio* 20(1): 75–90.

Rashbrook-Cooper, O. (manuscript) *Temporal Presence and Time-Lags*, available at http://www.philosophy. ox.ac.uk/__data/assets/pdf_file/0010/30889/Time_Lag_II.pdf. Accessed 1 January 2017.

Schuster, M. M. (1986) "Is the flow of time subjective?" *The Review of Metaphysics* 39(4): 695–714.

Sider, T. (1999) "Presentism and ontological commitment", *Journal of Philosophy* 96(7): 325–347.

Stern, W. L. (1897/2005) "Mental presence-time", in C. Wolfe (ed.), *The New Yearbook for Phenomenology and Phenomenological Research*, London: College Publications.

Tallant, J. (2010) "Time for presence?" *Philosophia* 38(2): 271–280.

Tye, M. (2003) *Consciousness and Persons: Unity and Identity*, Cambridge, MA: MIT Press.

Williams, D. C. (1951) "The myth of passage", *Journal of Philosophy* 48(15): 457–472.

Zahavi, D. (2007) "Perception of duration presupposes duration of perception – or does it? Husserl and Dainton on time", *International Journal of Philosophical Studies* 15(3): 453–471.

Further reading

D. Zimmerman, "The A-theory of time, the B-theory of time, and 'taking tense seriously'", *Dialectica* 59(4) (2005): 401–457, and C. Bourne, *A Future for Presentism* (Oxford, UK: Oxford University Press, 2006), provide a comprehensive defence of presentism.

S. Prosser, *Experiencing Time* (Oxford, UK: Oxford University Press, 2016), relates metaphysical issues of time with temporal experience. For an overview over temporal perception debates, see B. Dainton, "The experience of time and change", *Philosophy Compass* 3(4) (2008): 619–638.

T. Gendler's and J. Hawthorne's *Perceptual Experience* (Oxford, UK: Oxford University Press, 2006) offers a good collection on perceptual experience.

On the extended metaphysical present, see M. S. Hestevold, "Presentism through think and thin", *Philosophical Quarterly* 89(3) (2008), 325–347, and J. Spencer, "A tale of two simples", *Philosophical Studies* 148(2) (2010), 167–181.

20

THE SUBJECTIVELY ENDURING SELF

L. A. Paul

The self can be understood in objective metaphysical terms as a bundle of properties, as a substance, or as some other kind of entity on our metaphysical list of what there is. Such an approach explores the metaphysical nature of the self when regarded from a suitably impersonal, ontological perspective. It explores the nature and structure of the self in objective reality, that is, the nature and structure of the self from without. This is the objective self.[1]

I am taking a different approach. In addition to objective reality, which is usually understood and explored from an impersonal, quasi-observational and metaphysically realist perspective, we can also explore the nature and structure of subjective reality. The nature and structure of subjective reality is defined by the nature and structure of first-personal, conscious experience. Subjective reality is as real as objective reality, and a metaphysical realist such as myself can endorse the existence of both kinds of ontology. The mental states that, as experienced from the first-personal or subjective perspective, capture the nature and structure of subjective reality, are included in objective reality.[2] The questions to explore in a subjective ontology of the self concern the nature and structure of the self from the first-personal or subjective perspective, that is, the nature and structure of the self from within. This is the subjective self.[3]

In this chapter, I will explore the ontology of the subjectively enduring self, an ontology that is structured by one's subjective temporal experience and imaginative identity with one's first-personal, conscious perspective in the present, the (near) past and the (near) future. My thesis is that the subjective self endures, at least for short (but still relatively substantial and extended) stretches. Implicitly, I will assume that an enduring subjective self is consistent with a perduring, four-dimensional objective self. (An enduring self persists through time such that the very same, wholly present self exists at different times. A perduring self persists through time by being a sum of appropriately related but different temporal parts at different times. Subjective endurance is consistent with objective perdurance.)

A first-personal perspective on oneself

Intuitively, the distinction between the subjective perspective of the self and the objective perspective of the self mirrors a distinction between perceptual perspectives I can have.[4] An example will help to bring out the point.

Some contemporary computer games are "first-person shooter" games where you, the agent, have some sort of task to perform. When you play the game, you play as though you were looking out of the eyes of your character. Your line of sight is the one the character you are playing has. You are presented as seeming to hold a weapon, you "turn your head" to gain a line of sight, etc. In general, you know where you are from the first-personal perspective of your character, the character whose "boots" you are occupying as you play the game. You are given an artificial simulation of the first-personal perspective of your character using a visual line of sight, as a first-personal, subjective way for you to know who you are and where you are in the game.[5] In this way, you are immersed in the game. This game perspective is analogous to the subjective perspective.

However, as you play, you have additional information: a different way in which you know which character you are and where you are on the terrain. This information comes from an inset in the frame, where you can see yourself "from above", more or less like you can see yourself represented by a moving dot when you locate yourself using a map application on your phone. The inset simulates a third-personal visual perspective, from above, on your game character, and by watching it you also know who you are and where you are. Your information about yourself from this perspective is merely observational, in that it comes from positional and other descriptive information that anyone could access in order to locate you in the gameworld. This game perspective is analogous to the objective perspective.

Another way to illustrate the distinction comes from Google Maps. If you use Google Maps under the "map view" setting, you'll see where you are from above, with your location represented as a blue dot moving along the map. If you switch to the "street view" setting you drop down to street level. Once you are in the street view mode, you see where you are by occupying a perspective you'd have by being on the street at that location. The view from above, using map view, intuitively corresponds to the (abstract) perspective we take when we explore objective ontology. It's an observer's view of the mapworld with a centre (you).

With this idea in hand, the ontological perspective on the self can be defined as the *observational perspective*. It is analogous to the perspective you take when you are looking at the centred map of reality from above. The subjective perspective from the self, on the other hand, corresponds to the view from *within* the centred mapworld. That can be defined as the *agential perspective*, which is the perspective we need to explore in order to limn the nature of subjective reality. It is an exploration of reality from within, as an experiencer, rather than an exploration of reality from without, as a detached observer.

Temporal prospection

We understand ourselves as persisting selves by understanding ourselves as temporally extended entities existing at different points of time (Paul 2014a). Prospective assessment using a kind of perspectival reasoning plays a role in reasoning about ourselves (as well as about others).

> [These] combined observations suggest that the core network that supports remembering, prospection, theory of mind and related tasks is not shared by all tasks that require complex problem solving or imagination. Rather, the network seems to be specialized for, and actively engaged by, mental acts that require the projection of oneself into another time, place or perspective . . . by projecting our own mental states into different vantage points, in an analogous manner to how one projects oneself into the past and future.
>
> *(Buckner and Carroll 2006: 53)*[6]

When we mentally project ourselves into the past and future, how do we represent ourselves? The question arises because when we understand ourselves to exist at different points in time, there are different ways to mentally project the self into the future or the past. Is the mental projection framed from an observational perspective, where I model the mind of my future or past self more or less in the same way I'd model the mind of another person? Or do I model my past or future self empathetically, that is, from the inside or agentially, attempting to occupy my point of view at that time *as my point of view*? We seem to use both types of representation. You can represent yourself in the past and in the future from an observational perspective, that is, from an external or more impersonal perspective analogous to a perspective that observes your game character from above, as an icon on the game map. Or you can represent yourself in the past and in the future from an agential or "through the eyes of the agent" perspective, that is, from the internal agential perspective analogous to your perspective as a character immersed in the game.

The window of the self

One factor that can influence the nature of how we represent ourselves at different times is the temporal distance of my past and future selves from my current self. When I, at a time, represent my future self in the distant future, I am more likely to represent myself using the observational stance. When I represent a distant past self, I am also more likely to represent myself using the observational stance.

This can be overcome. Sometimes it takes imaginative effort, but sometimes not. If I have an experience that triggers an episodic memory, for example, taking a bite of a cookie whose taste transports me back to my childhood, I can easily represent my past self from my agential perspective, as though I were eating the cookie at my aunt's knee and looking up at her.[7] (I can also represent myself observationally in episodic memory, where I seem to observe myself as a child having the cookie at my aunt's knee, but I don't represent this as looking out from my childlike perspective.)

We do, however, take the agential perspective very naturally under certain circumstances. My representation of myself in my immediate future, as well as in my immediate past, is much more likely to be agential. As Pronin and Ross (2006) show, we tend to represent ourselves agentially in the immediate past, but even a temporal distance of a day can increase the degree of observational representation.[8] Similarly, when we think of ourselves in our immediate future, we tend to represent ourselves agentially, but as we imaginatively increase the temporal distance to a future self, we shift towards an observational representation. Your imaginative representation of yourself and what you'll be doing 30 seconds from now is much more likely to represent the world and yourself as though you are, metaphorically, looking out from your own eyes. That is, at this temporal distance, you can naturally and easily represent yourself from your agential, first-personal perspective. Your episodic memory of yourself in your immediate past, say 30 seconds ago, is also much more likely to be a representation of yourself from your agential, first-personal perspective.

We can think of the structure of this feature of subjective reality as a window to the past and to the future framed from the agential, first-personal perspective. The window is typically small. As I'll explore below, it also requires an implicit assumption that there isn't too much change in the nature of your first-personal experience over its temporal extent. Thinking about yourself persisting through time within this temporal window involves understanding yourself first-personally at the times within. It's also important that this is a default way to understand yourself as persisting in these nearby, short, temporal stretches. You don't need to make any special effort to adopt the agential perspective here. It's just a natural way to represent your near temporal selves.

When we think of our future selves first-personally in this way, we prospectively represent the first-personal perspective of our future self at that time. When we think of our past selves first-personally, we retrospectively represent the first-personal perspective of our past self at that time. This involves thinking about or recalling our past first-personal agential perspectives as well as reflecting on our future agential point of view. In the short term, how I represent myself and my agential perspective stays relatively constant as I project myself forward within the agential temporal window. And the way I represent being me will also stay largely constant as I retrospectively project myself backward and recall my experiences within my agential temporal window.

Temporal empathy

Temporally forward projection of one's first-personal point of view is an anticipatory and imaginative act of prospective representation. Temporally backward projection of one's first-personal point of view is a memory-like and imaginative act of retrospective representation.

As I define them, both types of representation are assessments "from the inside". Prospective representation involves taking the agential perspective on one's future self. When you prospectively assess, you try to grasp your future first-personal perspective at time t from your current first-personal perspective. You try to represent salient features of how you'll actually experience who you'll be. So, ideally, what you want to represent is the subjective, first-personal, experiential character of what it will be like to be you at t.[9] You want to represent what it will be like to be you "from the inside" at t, that is, you want to represent what it will be like to be you then, just as you know what it is like to be you now.

One way to put the point is that you want to project your current first-personal perspective, your perspective as it is now, into your future self (but adjusted given any relevant changes in circumstances and mental states). If you can project in this way, at least along some relevant experiential dimension, you can have the capacity to empathize with your future self. The kind of empathy you want is the rich, cognitive sort, not mere affective empathy where you simply know how you'll feel. You want the sort of empathy that you can use to generate a cognitively rich representation of your future agential perspective. This isn't merely an affective response to who you'd be. With a cognitive type of empathy, you can imagine your future agential perspective in all its cognitive richness, as understood through the lens of your current agential perspective, adjusted for changes in circumstances.[10]

Above, I described the nature of prospective assessment as anticipatory and imaginative. The anticipatory element comes from your anticipation of changes and future events. The imaginative element comes from a distinctive feature of prospective representation: when we prospectively represent our future selves, we imaginatively occupy our future agential points of view. This can be described metaphorically, where we think of ourselves as "stepping into the shoes" of our future self, by imagining being that future self from that future self's agential standpoint. We imaginatively take on that self's point of view as our own.[11] We can take this to be a kind of cognitive empathy for a future self, because we take our current agential point of view and attempt to use it to represent our future agential point of view. In this sense, we prospectively empathize with our future selves in order to understand them. I understand enough about my future self, using my current first-personal conscious perspective, to imaginatively represent myself as sharing an agential point of view with that self. In this sense, I can imagine myself as occupying or embodying this future self. One reason this can be valuable is that by performing the imaginative simulation, I can discover or understand more about my future properties.

My prospective representation thus involves a kind of capture of the first-personal or subjective point of view of my future self. Part of the empathetic act involves representing the nature and character of my future lived experience as I will experience it. That is, I imaginatively experience myself engaging in near future events from my first-personal agential perspective, where the first-personal perspective I have now is qualitatively continuous with the agential perspective I occupy in my imagined future experience.[12]

Retrospective representation also captures my agential perspective. When I retrospect, I imaginatively move my present first-personal perspective back to my past first-personal perspective, adjusting for any changes in circumstance. This imaginative act draws on my memory of the nature and character of my past lived experience, that is, what it was like to be me then. I cognitively empathize with my past self, representing my past self's first-personal or agential perspective on that situation. In this sense, I "occupy the shoes" of my past self. Again, when I retrospect, I imaginatively represent myself as I experienced that past event, where my current agential perspective is effectively continuous with the agential perspective I took in the past when engaging in that activity. I recall engaging in the event via remembering my experience, and I empathetically represent my first-personal agential perspective.

In each kind of temporally empathetic representation of myself, I represent myself from my agential perspective in the near past or near future. My first-personal, agential simulation is constant (at least in essentials) and experienced as shared through the past and future times within my agential temporal window.

The enduring self

My representation of the point of view of my future self (and *mutatis mutandis* of my past self) through my agential window gives me a distinctive kind of understanding of myself as an enduring self in the near future and near past.[13] How?

Start by making some simplifying assumptions about objectively persisting conscious individuals. Assume that the basic objective ontological structure of such individuals is grounded by a series of temporal stages related by appropriate genidentity relations. (Genidentity relations are (usually successive) causal or qualitative relations between temporal stages of a persisting object.) Objective perdurance comes from summing the stages. Objective (qualitative) endurance comes from any partial objective qualitative overlap of these stages.[14]

The structure of subjective endurance for an individual, on the other hand, is grounded by the nature of her first-personal experience. Take the subjective temporal unit of agential experience for a self to be defined by her specious present (Phillips 2010). At subjectively near times, I naturally represent my first-personal perspective as a continuously enduring agential perspective from the near past, through the specious present, into the near future. The nature and character of my experience is as of being the very same enduring self, that is, as of qualitative continuity (with respect to sameness of agential perspective), from the inside, through my temporal window.

The representation relies on the empathetic ability of my current self to (imaginatively) see the world through the eyes of my near past and near future selves, where I represent myself as experiencing the qualitatively same agential perspective throughout my temporal window. This structures my experience as a subjectively enduring point of view, or as a subjectively enduring self.[15] In other words, this is the subjective ontological foundation for the subjective endurance of the self.[16] An important feature of what matters here is that taking the agential perspective, within this window, is the *default* perspective. This is why endurance of my agential perspective seems like such an intuitive and natural way to understand persistence. It's my default mode for the continuous experience of my point of view as I persist through short periods of time.

As time passes, my current self and its temporal endurance window advance.[17] As the nature and character of my first-personal perspective gradually evolves, at some point I can no longer seamlessly represent past agential perspectives as continuous with my own, current agential perspective. Once this happens, it is natural to shift to an observer's perspective on those earlier selves.

Gradual change in the nature of my near temporal experience is consistent with my having the qualitatively same agential perspective throughout a short subjective temporal extent. (For example, I retain my first-personal perspective and identify as the same subjective self from moment to moment as I move around or experience other inessential changes.) However, over time, gradual change can accumulate such that I no longer stand in the same-self relation to a past self. (More radical change can also cause this.) The same-objective-self relation in objective reality is intransitive, and this intransitivity can be manifested when selves (composed of temporal stages) that compose a person objectively change in some significant way over time. The transitivity of the same-subjective-self relation in subjective reality fails when I can no longer subjectively represent my past self or my future self as the same self I am now. It occurs when the subjective character of the agential perspective of that past self or that future self is too qualitatively or phenomenally different from my current agential perspective.

Future-blocked

I have argued elsewhere (Paul 2014b, 2015a) that you can lack the imaginative capacity to first-personally represent possibilities for your future self in contexts of transformative change. If you face an experience that will transform you both epistemically and personally, defined as a "transformative experience", before you actually have that experience you may not have epistemic access to your future self's agential perspective. You can't imaginatively model or simulate the way you will first-personally respond to the experience and the resulting future circumstances. The thesis is explicitly Lewisian: an experience of that kind is needed to give the experiencer the ability to imagine, recognize and cognitively model her possible future selves (Lewis 1990).

The deep issue with respect to subjective selves is that we need the right sort of understanding, in terms of prospective assessment, in order to imaginatively project ourselves forward as enduring selves into the future. We also want to retain an understanding of our past selves that allows us to retrospectively assess ourselves as enduring through change. My ability to empathetically grasp my other selves in a way that represents my agential point of view as enduring is what makes those other selves cognitively mine. That is, I intuitively understand, given the shared character of my agential perspectives, these past and future selves *as me*. The kind of psychological access I want to my future self and past self, where I can empathetically occupy my first-personal perspective, is nicely captured by David Velleman:

> The future "me" whose existence matters [to me] is picked out precisely by his owning a point of view into which I am attempting to project my representations of the future, just as a past "me" can be picked out by his having owned the point of view from which I have recovered representations of the past.
>
> *(2006: 76)*

The problem is that transformative experience can disrupt this first-personal agential access to our past, future and even merely possible selves.

The central examples are those that scale: an experience that is so dramatically epistemically transformative that it carries with it significant first-personal change, making it personally transformative. Examples include a case where you could choose to become a cyborg by getting a neural chip that will give you an unknown, new sense capacity but take away your sense of taste. Another case concerns a congenitally blind adult choosing to have a retinal operation to become sighted. Another much-discussed example involves a person choosing to have her first child (Paul 2015a, 2015b). The idea is that, in such cases, you can't know what it will be like to have the experience before you have it, and if you choose to have it, it will change the nature of your first-personal or agential perspective.

While the claims about transformation are more controversial in some cases than in others, the basic idea is this: experience, especially intense experience, can affect a person's representational capacities and her first-personal preferences. Experience can transform us in a rich, psychologically representational way. What happens to us can affect and control our point of view, because it can affect our preferences and how we model and represent the world and ourselves. On this view, preferences are psychologically real mental states that structure an agent's phenomenology, intentional states and first-personal perspective on the world. An epistemic transformation can transform an agent's abilities and inclinations, and by extension, her preferences and the nature of her agential perspective.

As a result, if we are facing the possibility of significant epistemic transformation, we are facing the possibility of significant self-change. If, because we lack the requisite experiential knowledge, we cannot prospectively assess the nature of the epistemically transformative experience before we undergo it, we cannot prospectively simulate our response from our current first-personal perspective to having an experience like this, and by extension, cannot prospectively model who we'll become.[18] If you can't first-personally model the nature of the experience you'll have, you can't first-personally assess your response to the experience.[19] You can't model your responses in a way that will allow you to "see" your future agential perspectives, the perspectives that could result from your experiences.[20] When the experiences are high-stakes, life-defining experiences, the problem extends past merely being unable to assess the immediate future outcomes of your choice to being unable to assess who you'll become.

To explore this idea a bit more, let's discuss the case of a congenitally blind adult who wants to have retinal surgery in order to be able to see. Imagine that he is a saxophone player, and has built his life around his blindness, choosing a career and a way of living and understanding the world through touch and sound. His soulful music reflects the rich detail that his highly trained auditory capacities give to his lived experience. His dominant sense modality is audition, and thus his way of living in the world is deeply influenced by his blindness. Like all of us, his lived experience is structured by his way of experiencing the world through his senses, especially his dominant sense modality. This affects the details of his life and lived experience, from the way he organizes his day to the way he navigates his environment and understands the world around him.

In our example, the saxophonist doesn't know what it is like to be sighted, and so he can't simulate his possible future (sighted) self after the operation. He thinks he'd be happier if he were sighted, but he knows he will change along many dimensions. Since he can't know what it will be like to be sighted, he cannot use imaginative projection to determine the nature of his future as a sighted person from his agential perspective.

The problem for the saxophonist is that there is an epistemic wall created by the transformative nature of the experience involved in the choice, one that blocks a role for his first-personal perspective in evaluating and assessing his future self from the agential perspective. Experience of a certain sort is required for him to be able to imagine his future point of view.

It's of course possible for him to be informed, via testimony and description, of the value (or utility) for him of possible ways he'll experience the future. The trouble is that this will not help him to imagine the nature of his future lived experience from the agential perspective.

We can see this if we think of the kind of experiential content he must be able to represent in order to prospectively represent his future agential point of view. As I argued above, for a person to imaginatively represent himself as enduring into the future, he must be able to prospectively assess his future point of view. Here, knowing the relevant testimony about his future lived experiences isn't enough for him to be able to imagine his future agential perspective. To grasp the subjective, first-personal perspective of his future (sighted) self, he needs to have the experience of being sighted.

What it's like to be the saxophonist (before the operation) defines his current first-personal subjective self, and what it *will* be like to be him will define his future subjective self. The blind saxophonist's inability to simulate his future lived experience as a sighted individual arises from the fact that he cannot accurately determine, via simulation or imaginative representation, what it will be like for him to see. For this reason, he cannot accurately determine, via simulation, how he'd respond to the experience of seeing. As a result, before the operation, he cannot accurately imagine the nature of his future lived experience from his agential perspective.

The first problem he faces arises from the epistemic transformation that gaining visual information would involve. The second problem the saxophonist faces is that the dramatic nature of the new experience, becoming sighted, scales up into a change in self-defining experience. Once he becomes sighted, he will no longer have hearing as his dominant sense modality. Once he stops relying on auditory cues the way he did before having visual information inform his experiences, his knowledge of the world and his relation to it will change in dramatic ways. This suggests that the nature and character of his agential perspective will also change. If so, he cannot project himself forward as an enduring self through the change.[21]

Because of the massive epistemic change in his future, the blind saxophonist, before the operation, lacks the ability to mentally look forward and prospectively imagine his future, sighted agential perspective. The source of his epistemic failure is the transformative nature of the experience: changing his dominant sense modality *also* changes his psychological capacities and states.[22] Before he becomes sighted, empathetic identification of his current agential perspective with the first-personal perspective of his future, sighted, self is impossible, because he lacks the abilities and information he needs to be able to perform the empathetic task. Without the ability to empathetically model his future self along the dimension that is central to the self-change involved, the blind saxophonist cannot prospectively assess his future lived experience as a sighted person. In this sense, he cannot project himself into the future. In the most personal sense possible, he cannot prefigure his future self.

We can all find ourselves in the position like that of the saxophonist. If you face a transformative experience, it is as if you face a blank concrete wall. You can't see what lies beyond. Perhaps you know that whatever happens in the future, past the wall, will involve you somehow. You know you'll be there, in that future moment, living that future experience. But you don't know what it will be like to be that self. Your enduring self is lost in the vast emptiness of the ungraspable future.[23]

Notes

1 For example, Benovsky 2009.
2 We might model the subjective-objective distinction on Brian Loar's distinction between the phenomenal mode of presentation and the scientific mode of presentation (Loar 1990).

3 We can think of the subjective self as an entity that is subjectively real and numerically distinct from the objective self that is objectively real, or we can think in terms of a subjective ontological perspective on the self (the self from the inside) and the same self as explored from an objective ontological perspective (the self from the outside). I'm inclined to think of the self in terms of the latter conception, but I won't distinguish between these two conceptions here.

4 The locus classicus for discussion of this issue in the philosophy of mind is Nagel's *View from Nowhere* (Nagel 1986). But Nagel's point concerns physicalism, which is not at issue here. Subjective reality does not concern primitive mental states: from the objective ontological perspective, the mental states that represent an individual's subjective reality are fully realized by more fundamental physical states.

5 Which, of course, you grasp from your own first-personal perspective.

6 I am not inclined to interpret prospective and retrospective simulation or imagination in an overly strong way. For discussion, see Saxe 2005; De Brigard *et al.* 2015.

7 This is, of course, the famous Proustian moment with the madeleine, now immortalized in American culture by Starbucks and various other companies. For classic treatments of episodic memory and self-projection, see Tulving 1972, 1983.

8 See especially Pronin and Ross 2006: 203, Study 4 and Figure 4. Also, see Makati *et al.* 2016.

9 There is a clear parallel to the discovery that Mary makes when she leaves her black and white room and discovers what seeing red is like (Jackson 1982).

10 There's a bit of hedging I'm doing here. The core features of my first personal perspective have to remain enough the same over the temporal window for my agential perspective at each time to count, in terms of my experience, as being the same (or representing the same) agential perspective. Inessential changes are OK. But which features are core? How much change is too much change? It's not clear. In any case, when we believe we are prospecting accurately, so we believe we are actually imagining what it will be like to be our future self, we are preserving the relevant core features in the imaginative act. There's more to say here (see Paul 2002 for related discussion), but it's for another paper.

11 I will use the term "imagine" in a broad sense that is consistent with the way many contemporary psychologists would use the term. So while visual imagination is covered by my use of the term, I am taking "imagining" to be an act that involves cognitive modelling of possible situations, which would include modelling without explicit visual imagery. Imagination may or may not involve sensory imagery, and any simulation involved is likely to occur only with the level of detail needed to make the intended projective assessment (Saxe 2005).

12 Of course, "perspective" and "point of view" need not be understood visually. The projection of my current perspective into my future perspective does not need to involve the representation of sensory images, although it might. And the projection does not have to be at a particularly fine level of detail.

13 This is a kind of understanding that I value and use to structure my life and to interpret my lived experience over time. See Paul forthcoming.

14 For my preferred account of objective endurance and perdurance, see Paul 2002: 585–589, where I develop and defend the notion of partial qualitative overlap for persisting objects.

15 Also, see Phillips 2014; Dainton 2000; Watzl 2013.

16 This kind of representation extends to my merely possible selves at near possible worlds. From my agential perspective, I imaginatively represent the perspectives and lived experiences of transworld identical merely possible selves, that is, I simulate who I could become or who I might have been under different circumstances in a non-counterpart theoretical way.

17 The agential perspective is not confined to this temporal window. We can use empathetic memory and anticipation to retrospectively leap to a more distant past or prospectively leap to a more distant future. The window just defines the temporal extent of our ordinary, effortlessly agential subjective perspective.

18 For some representative research on how the inability to model one's future self can lead to poor decisions, see (Mitchell *et al.* 2011).

19 Also, see Carr 2015.

20 As I noted above, the more remote your future or past self is from who you are now, the more likely you are to model your self from the third-personal, or "detached" perspective. Normally, this remoteness is temporal: you are more likely to think of yourself in the third person when you think of yourself in the distant future or in the distant past, as opposed to the immediate past or future (or the present). But temporal distance is only contingently related to the possibility of the first-personal inaccessibility of our selves. Instances of episodic memory (think of Proust's example of the madeleine, which transports him into his first-personal perspective as a child) or holding fixed key internal representational features can help us to imaginatively occupy the first-personal perspectives of temporally distant selves.

And dramatic change, even over the short term, can make a temporally immanent self seem remote. (The same distinction can hold with respect to modality, that is, with respect to possible selves.) The inaccessibility of one's future first-personal perspective across large temporal or modal distances is part of what can make those decisions hard (at least if one wants to choose prospectively, rather than just "picking" or effectively flipping a coin).

21 See Hoerl and McCormack 2016 for a very interesting discussion of episodic memory, mental time-travel and the anticipation of regret in the context of transformative experience and transformative decision-making.

22 In Paul 2014, I argue that this creates a problem for a model of rational choice based on maximizing one's expected utility when making life-changing choices. An agent facing transformative change cannot model the preferences and utilities of her epistemically inaccessible possible future selves. Thus, she cannot represent expected utilities for the acts that would bring about these selves, and so she cannot represent the possibilities in a way that will allow her to make a rational choice between outcomes involving significant self-change.

23 Thanks to Ross Cameron, Trenton Merricks and Ian Phillips for comments and discussion.

References

Benovsky, J. (2009) "The self: A Humean bundle and/or a Cartesian substance?" *European Journal of Analytic Philosophy* 5(1): 7–19.

Buckner, R. L. and Carroll, D. C. (2006) "Self-projection and the brain", *Trends in Cognitive Sciences* 11(2): 49–57.

Carr, J. (2015) "Epistemic expansions", *Res Philosophica* 92(2): 217–236.

Dainton, B. (2000) *Stream of Consciousness: Unity and Continuity in Conscious Experience*, London: Routledge.

De Brigard, F., Spreng, R. N., Mitchell, J. P. and Schachter, D. L. (2015) "Neural activity associated with self, other, and object-based counterfactual thinking", *Neuroimage* 109: 12–26.

Hoerl, C. and McCormack, T. (2016) "Making decisions about the future: Regret and the cognitive function of episodic memory", in K. Michaelian, S. B. Klein and K. Szpunar (eds), *Seeing the Future: Theoretical Perspectives on Future-Oriented Mental Time Travel*, Oxford, UK: Oxford University Press.

Jackson, F. (1982) "Epiphenomenal qualia", *Philosophical Quarterly* 32(127): 127–136.

Lewis, D. (1990) "What experience teaches", in W. G. Lycan (ed.), *Mind and Cognition*, Oxford, UK: Blackwell.

Loar, B. (1990) "Phenomenal states", *Philosophical Perspectives* 4: 81–108.

Makati, R., Tamir, D. and Morelli, S. (2016) "Lay beliefs about the effects of perspective-taking on the self", unpublished poster presentation at *Association for Psychological Science*, 26–29 May 2016, Chicago, IL.

Mitchell, J. P., Schirmer, J., Ames, D. L. and Gilbert, D. T. (2011) "Medial prefrontal cortex predicts intertemporal choice", *Journal of Cognitive Neuroscience* 23(4): 1–10.

Nagel, T. (1986) *The View from Nowhere*, Oxford, UK: Oxford University Press.

Paul, L. A. (2002) "Logical parts", *Noûs* 36(4): 578–596.

Paul, L. A. (2014a) "Experience and the arrow", in A. Wilson (ed.), *Chance and Temporal Asymmetry*, Oxford, UK: Oxford University Press.

Paul, L. A. (2014b) *Transformative Experience*, Oxford, UK: Oxford University Press.

Paul, L. A. (2015a) "What you can't expect when you're expecting", *Res Philosophica* 92(2): 149–170.

Paul, L. A. (2015b) "Transformative choice: Discussion and replies", *Res Philosophica* 92(2): 473–545.

Paul, L. A. (forthcoming 2017). "De se preferences and empathy for future selves", in J. Hawthorne (ed.), *Philosophical Perspectives: Metaphysics*.

Phillips, I. B. (2010) "Perceiving temporal properties", *European Journal of Philosophy* 18(2): 176–202.

Phillips, I. B. (2014) "The temporal structure of experience", in D. Lloyd and V. Arstila (eds), *Subjective Time: The Philosophy, Psychology, and Neuroscience of Temporality*, Cambridge, MA: MIT Press, pp. 139–158.

Pronin, E. and Ross, L. (2006) "Temporal differences in trait self-ascription: When the self is seen as an other", *Journal of Personality and Social Psychology* 90(2): 197–209.

Saxe, R. (2005) "Against simulation: The argument from error", *Trends in Cognitive Sciences* 9(4): 174–179.

Tulving, E. (1972) "Episodic and semantic memory", in E. Tulving and W. Donaldson (eds), *Organization of Memory*, New York: Academic Press.

Tulving, E. (1983) *Elements of Episodic Memory*, Oxford, UK: Oxford University Press.

Velleman, D. (2006) *Self to Self: Selected Essays*, Cambridge, UK: Cambridge University Press.

Watzl, S. (2013) "Silencing the experience of change", *Philosophical Studies* 165(3): 1009–1032.

PART VI

Empirical perspectives

21

PERCEIVING VISUAL TIME

Alan Johnston

Introduction

How does the brain measure time and how does thinking about the biological constraints on mechanism influence our thinking about our experience of time in general? Physical clocks mark the objectively measurable passage of time. The timing of brain events can be assessed in relation to these clocks; however, we need to consider the encoding of temporal information by the brain, not the time course of neural activity in the brain, to relate neural processing and the perceived time course of external events (Johnston and Nishida 2001). Here we make a distinction between event time – the time of events in the physical world, brain time – the time of events in the brain, and perceived time – the perceptual experience and judgement of the time of events in the external world.

It is tempting to think that the time at which events appear to occur simply reflects the time of neural activation of the representations that unambiguously signal the presence of some external feature. However, the flow of neural events, even if it matched the time course of events in the external world, carries only implicit information about temporal relationships, such as whether one event occurs before another or what the duration of an event might be. To encode the time of external events, information about temporal relationships would need to be made explicit, which in this context means encoded as neural activity, whilst also resolving any ambiguity in the signals, so that the relations can be perceived and decisions can be made.

There are a number of problems with the perceived time from brain time perspective. The first is that the time at which brain events occur is only loosely related to the time of occurrence of those events in the external world that trigger them. The latency differences between cortical areas and between neurones within areas (Bullier 2001), and the dependence of neural latencies on stimulus strength (Lee *et al.* 2007), mean that brain events cannot be relied upon to accurately reflect the time of events in the physical world. The second is that it is not clear that the brain can sense its own physical states in this way. Müller's Doctrine of Specific Nerve Energies refers to the fact that neural responses reflect their natural causes, for example, the response of the retina is perceived as light whether caused by light, a blow or electrical stimulation. Similarly, a recipient neurone does not sense an action potential as an action potential per se, it changes its informational state as a consequence. There would need to be dedicated, essentially propriceptive mechanisms, specialised for latency encoding in the service of time perception. However, as indicated above, neural latency information, even if brain mechanisms could access and encode this, is just too numerous and noisy to be useful.

Temporal mechanisms

Although the timing of neural processes are unreliable indicators of the timing of external events, brain time cannot be ignored in thinking about the relationship between neural processing and experience. In human vision, the sensitivity to temporal pattern has been the subject of extensive experimental research. It is well known from everyday observation that the experience of a bright instantaneous flash lasts for an extended period of time and that a bright light seen moving on a dark night will appear to leave a trace in its wake. This "visual persistence" is due to the fact that the visual system sums light presented at the eye over a period of around 150 ms. The precise time window depends upon the illumination level and the adaptive state of the eye. The trace from a moving light source arises because the instantaneous stimulus at the retina still contributes to the sum 150 ms after the stimulus has travelled on. The effect of this temporally extended process is understood through the characterisation of temporal channels in the human visual system.

One of the successes of visual psychophysics is the experimental discovery of visual channels. Adaptation to a visual stimulus has been shown to affect the detection of that adapting stimulus and similar stimuli along some perceptual dimension, like line orientation, for example, but have no effect on stimuli that differ markedly on that dimension (Frisby 1980). This indicates that any stimulus activates a small set of neurones that are said to be tuned to that stimulus but not others, and these neurones together are referred to as a "channel". The term is also used to refer to neurones that are differentially sensitive with respect to some sensory dimension. There are thought to be three temporal frequency channels in the human visual system – channels that respond differentially to different rates of flicker or image motion. In addition to a temporal channel that summates light over time and therefore preferentially enhances static and slowly changing pattern, there are two other channels which are preferentially sensitive to flicker (Watson and Robson 1981; Mandler and Makous 1984; Hess and Plant 1985; Cass and Alais 2006). Hess and Snowden (1992), using a masking paradigm, described three temporal channels or temporal filters, one low-pass (higher gain at low temporal frequencies), one band-pass filter peaking in sensitivity at around 10 cycles per second (Hz) and a third temporal channel peaking at around 16Hz (Figure 21.1). The same temporal filters can be characterised in the frequency domain and the time domain, via the Fourier transform. The Fourier transform expresses a time-windowed signal as a sum of sine and cosine functions of different magnitudes and frequency. The signal can be synthesised through the inverse Fourier transform. It is useful because the effect of a filter expressed in terms of its frequency response can be assessed by multiplying the frequency representation of the signal by the filter, then synthesising using the inverse transform.

Temporal filters modify the response of the visual system to temporal pattern. However, the functional role of these filters may go beyond this characterisation of their action. Figure 21.1C shows the temporal frequency response of the three filters in human vision, which describes their relative sensitivities to different rates of flicker. These are the data used to fit the functions. The time dependent functions are shown in Figure 21.1B. These are calculated as the Fourier transforms of the functions in Figure 21.1C and are referred to as impulse responses. They show the time dependent response of the visual system to a flash of light. The response to a more complex visual stimulus can be calculated by the point by point multiplication and subsequent addition of the impulse response and the time dependent stimulus over the scope of

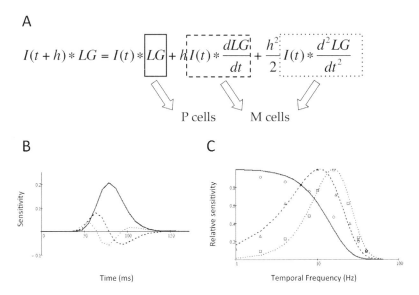

A

$$I(t + h) * LG = I(t) * \boxed{LG} + h\,I(t) * \frac{dLG}{dt} + \frac{h^2}{2} I(t) * \frac{d^2 LG}{dt^2}$$

P cells   M cells

B

C

Sensitivity

Time (ms)

Relative sensitivity

Temporal Frequency (Hz)

Figure 21.1   Three temporal channels using a masking paradigm (Hess and Snowden 1992)

Figure 21.1A. Taylor's series can be used to predict the value of a function (the image brightness, $I(t)$), in the neighbourhood around a point, in time, t. Temporal derivatives of the image brightness are calculated at a point, t, by convolving ($*$) the image brightness with the derivatives of Gaussians in log time. Throughout the figures, continuous lines indicate the temporal blur kernel (the log Gaussian, LG), dashed lines indicate the first derivative and dotted lines indicate the second derivative of the log Gaussian. The excursion parameter, h, indicates the point ($t+h$) at which the value of the function is to be predicted. The parameter, h, can take on a range of values.

Figure 21.1B. The impulse responses for the filters, calculated as the inverse Fourier transform of the corresponding (matching pattern) frequency sensitivity curves in 21.1C.

Figure 21.1C. The temporal tuning functions for human vision. The data are from Hess and Snowden (1992) and the fitted functions, the Gaussian in log time (continuous) and its first (dashed) and second (dotted) derivatives, are from Johnston and Clifford (1995). All data for each of the three functions are fitted by adjusting just one parameter (see Johnston and Clifford 1995 for details). The band-pass filters (dashed and dotted) correspond to the tuning curves of magnocellular (M) neurones and the low-pass temporal filter (continuous) is representative of parvocellular (P) neurone's temporal tuning curves.

the filter. The stimulus steps forward and the calculations are repeated at the next time step – a process called convolution. Johnston and Clifford (1995) showed that a Gaussian in log time and its first and second derivatives provided an excellent fit to the temporal filters measured by Hess and Snowden (1992). A mathematical identity allows us to say that the convolution of a signal with the derivative of the log Gaussian is the same as blurring (convolving) the signal with the log Gaussian and then taking its derivative. This means in essence that the early visual system blurs and differentiates the visual input. We will return to this characterisation later.

One consequence of the action of a temporal filter in integrating information over a period of past time is that the neural representation or neural image of the external world is delayed by around 80 ms relative to external events. We do not therefore have direct access to the present in the external world, although we might be able to predict the retinal image 80 ms ahead of its neuronal impact.

The form of the filters is not fixed. Adapting a localised region of the retina to flicker or a drifting pattern with a local temporal frequency of 20Hz can alter the shape of the temporal filters.

The effect of adaptation is to sharpen and advance the time domain temporal weighting function – the temporal impulse response (Benardete and Kaplan 1999). This aggregates visual signals over a shorter time window in the recent past. This has the effect of advancing the signals in time in the adapted region compared to locations that have not been adapted in which visual information is averaged over a longer time period, thereby locally time shifting the perceptual stream. Hogendoorn *et al.* (2010) introduced a display which provided psychophysical evidence of the effect of this operation on human perception. Observers made judgements about the relative position of the hands on running clocks after motion adaptation. On a given trial, eight clocks located at regular intervals around a circle centred on fixation, were set running. At some point, six clocks were removed and observers had to report which of the two remaining clocks was showing a later time. On each trial prior to the presentation of the clocks, four of the stations were adapted to a bullseye grating pattern whose motion drifted at either 5Hz or 20Hz and oscillated between expansion and contraction. The motion of the adaptor was orthogonal to the motion of the clock hands. The clock hands spun at one full cycle of rotation per second. After 20Hz adaptation, the clock in the adapted region appeared to be around 10 ms ahead of the clock in the unadapted region even though the clocks were physically aligned. This corresponds to an angular difference of around 3.6 degrees. Note that this was not because the 20Hz adapted clock appeared to move faster, as paradoxically it appeared to move more slowly than the unadapted clock. There was also no difference in choice reaction time between an adapted and unadapted region, indicating that the adaptation paradigm did not alter neural latencies in a measurable way. There may be some scepticism about whether Hogendoorn *et al.* measured a temporal shift or a spatial advance. However, more recently, Bruno *et al.* (2015) showed that, after adapting one spatial location using oscillating drifting gratings at 20Hz, simultaneously presented Gaussian luminance patches induced a perception of apparent motion from the adapted to an unadapted location, indicating stimuli in the adapted region were processed as if they arrived first at the retina. Casting a time delay in terms of an apparent motion allows for a very sensitive perceptual measure of time shifts. In both the Hogendoorn *et al.* and Bruno *et al.* experiments the time shift was around 10 ms, which is consistent with a spatially localised shift in the perceptual stream induced by the sharpening of a temporal filter. In this case, a change in neural processing leads to a change in perceptual experience by virtue of a local time shift in the neural stimulus as delivered to perceptual mechanisms.

Time shifts in perceptual experience might also be accomplished by reconstructing the signal at a different time point. This flexible encoding could be achieved using the differentiating temporal filters we introduced above (Figure 21.1). Taylor's series, attributed to the Scottish mathematician James Gregory, is a representation of a function around a point derived from a series of derivatives taken at that point. So the temporal differentiating filters in the human visual system introduced above can provide information about image brightness in the near past and the near future. A time shifted representation of a signal can be generated from a weighted sum of the differentiating filter outputs with the weights determining the degree of shift (Johnston 2010, 2013). A consequence of this view is that measures computed at an instant can provide information about the recent past, present and the future, within limits determined by the effectiveness of the approximation of the Taylor series to the true function. This illuminates the debate about the experience of the specious present in that from an information perspective, the present contains information about the past and future. It is worth noting that one successful model of motion sensing, in its simplest form, is that speed is calculated at a single point in space and time as the ratio of the outputs of a temporal derivative filter and a spatial derivative filter (Johnston *et al.* 1992, 1999). In this model, motion is represented at a point and at an instant from a calculation made over a spatial region and an extended period of time. Motion encoding in this case does not involve a spatial displacement or an experience of succession as such – it only requires the system to sense brightening or darkening at a point and relate that rate to the spatial brightness gradient at that point.

Perceptual fluctuation

The critical flicker frequency (CFF) threshold is the temporal frequency above which visual flicker can no longer be detected. For signals sampled at rates above the CFF it is impossible to distinguish between a sampled and a continuous signal, because the separation of the samples is undetectable. Explicit temporal sampling of continuous motion leads to the classical wagon wheel effect seen in the cinema in which stagecoach wheels appear to rotate in a direction opposite to their true direction. This is simply a reflection of the fact that in the sampled version of the stimulus, the shortest path between the spokes of the wheel is physically in the reversed direction. Cinema projectors update the image at a rate of 24 frames per second. If we saw reversed rotation in the unmediated viewing of a rotating wagon wheel, this would be evidence of temporal sampling in the human visual system. Real wagon wheels do not typically appear to reverse at a particular rate of rotation, so it is unlikely that the retinal image is temporally sampled in any direct sense (Kline *et al.* 2004). However, rotating patterns can appear to reverse their direction of rotation in some conditions (Schouten 1967; Purves *et al.* 1996; VanRullen *et al.* 2005). These reversals are not sustained but rather alternate with periods of forward motion. VanRullen *et al.* (2005) proposed that sampling may arise at a more cognitive level through attentional snapshots. More recently, Busch and VanRullen (2010) have shown that the effects of attention on target detection fluctuates with the phase of a 7Hz periodic EEG component. These results indicate a temporal variation in visual performance linked to a physiological response, which Busch and VanRullen attribute to attention-driven periodic sampling, even in conditions of sustained attention.

Arnold and Johnston (2003) reported an example of a motion display that introduced time-varying perceptual fluctuations where none exist in the physical stimulus. A pattern that differs only in colour and not luminance, and so would be uniformly grey in a black and white photograph, is referred to as isoluminant. Isoluminant chromatic stimuli appear to move more slowly than stimuli defined by luminance contrast (Cavanagh *et al.* 1984). Arnold and Johnston drifted a red-green isoluminant bullseye pattern over a dark background. The red-green border appeared to jitter when isoluminant, even though the bullseye was moving rigidly. The rate of jitter was around 22Hz when measured by matching to a flickering LED. The match frequency remained constant under a change in velocity by a factor of two, but the exact frequency varied between observers, suggesting the perceptual fluctuation was not determined by the stimulus motion as such, but was rather internally generated. We obtained an estimate of around 10Hz when the jitter was measured by matching to a physically jittering display (Amano *et al.* 2008). This was roughly half the frequency measured in the previous studies, suggesting subjects matched each apparent change in position to the bright phase of LED flicker. MEG recordings (Amano *et al.* 2008) showed an enhanced peak around 10Hz for an isoluminant condition which generated illusory jitter compared to real jitter, luminance difference and isoluminant colour on an isoluminant background condition.

Arnold and Johnston (2003) attributed the jitter to a motion induced spatial conflict. They proposed that the velocity signals at the boundary were used to shift forward the spatial pattern (Roach *et al.* 2011). The benefit of this was considered to be that a predicted signal could be used to calibrate the motion analysis system. This process might also be considered an example of the use of predictive coding (Rao and Ballard 1999) in the early visual system. Predictive coding proposes that rather than process a visual stimulus anew through the processing hier-archy, a prediction is formed of the stimulus expected at an early level and only a difference signal or an error signal need be propagated through the hierarchy – a more efficient scheme. In general, isoluminant boundaries appear to move more slowly than luminance-defined bounda-ries (Cavanagh *et al.* 1984). Thus predictions based on motion at luminance and isoluminant boundaries moving together will be discrepant and the prediction at the isoluminant boundaries will subsequently fail leading to a reliance on new data. The persistence of this systems-level visual illusion results from the fact that the velocity difference between isoluminant and lumi-nance boundaries cannot easily be calibrated away. This is because the two types of border are only transiently present at any visual location and there is no opportunity for neurones at each location to adjust to compensate. Note this illusion also highlights the role of prediction, error checking and calibration in linking neural signals to the external world. In this way, perception can come to accurately reflect the external stimulus. We also have to propose that motion shifts spatial pattern location and that we experience both the erroneous prediction of spatial location and the resolution in favour of new data to explain the illusory experience of jitter.

These findings illuminate the question of whether perceptual experience is continuous or sampled. The idea that our visual experience is made up of a series of instants is not supported, otherwise the experience of the wagon wheel effect would be just as salient and persistent for wheels in the real world as it is for moving wheels seen in the cinema. Rather the experience of periodicity in perception may arise from cyclic perceptual routines implementing sophisticated processes like predictive coding, predictive vision or error checking that have a characteristic latency built into their operations through the need to loop though different cortical regions and different representations, as is likely in the case of motion induced spatial displacements.

Temporal synchrony

If we could inspect the brain, we may observe a flow of events within which temporal rela-tionships are implicit. However, since temporal relationships are not encoded in the flow, the registration of a temporal relationship needs something more. Communication delays between different brain areas complicate things and makes brain time relativistic. Suppose we want to encode a temporal relationship such as, for example, simultaneity, with a brain time strategy. Consider simultaneous events in connected but distant areas A and B with the inevitable com-munication delays. From the perspective of A, B will occur later and from the perspective of B, A will occur later. The relative timing might be assessed by another neurone C linked to both A and B. However, this strategy, requiring the linkage of all possible pairs, leads to a combinatoric wiring problem that quickly makes the strategy implausible for a physical biological network, even for binary relationships. This perspective provides another reason why it would be unwise to use the timing of brain events as a proxy for the time course of world events.

The implicit coding of information can be valuable. The utility of a map over an itinerary is that all routes and distances between landmarks are represented. If you only have access to an itinerary and find yourself in an uncharted location, you have no information about how to reach your destination. If you have a map, all information is potentially available and you can discover a new route by inspection. This flexibility in encoding relationships may be the fundamental reason for the ubiquity of topographic and feature maps in the brain. Shifting to the temporal domain, if we were to consider a history of brain states then the state corresponding to watching the titles of a film will occur before the state corresponding to watching the credits; however, the temporal relationship is only implicit, nothing has been made explicit through neural encoding, and to make matters worse, unlike locations on a map, the sequence of brain states is not simultaneously available for inspection. In order to make a relational judgement about the timing of external events, the relation has to be coded explicitly in the activation of some specialised neural circuit implementing some perceptual routine (Ullman 1984; Johnston and Nishida 2001), just as the distance between two points on a map is not made available until you measure it.

The limitations imposed on the perceptual system by requiring it to orchestrate a bespoke neural routine to perform a particularly difficult combinatorial task can lead to profound apparent asynchronies for physically synchronous events. Moutoussis and Zeki (1997) discovered that observers judged changes in motion direction and colour to be synchronous when the colour change preceded the motion direction change by around 100 ms. They used a binding task (e.g. what is the colour when the pattern moves up), but similar apparent temporal shifts can be demonstrated in a synchrony task, such as asking whether motion and colour changes are synchronous or not (Nishida and Johnston 2002). Moutoussis and Zeki (1997) attributed this effect to differences in the time at which the motion and colour changes were represented in the brain, but this interpretation could not account for subsequent manipulations. Nishida and Johnston (2002) showed that the timing of neural processing was not the key factor. They reversed the temporal properties of the position and colour signals. When participants were asked to compare the timing of a reversal in the direction of change of a colour temporal gradient from red to green and back again with a transient jump in position, they reported synchrony when the colour gradient direction change led by around 100 ms indicating that the temporal patterning was the key factor not the sub-modality. Nishida and Johnston proposed that when under time pressure, such that there was insufficient time for some perceptual routine to operate effectively, observers tend to link events with similar properties (Nishida and Johnston 2002, 2010). In the case of colour-motion asynchrony, first-order colour changes are linked to first-order changes in position, which we can think of as motion segments, rather than to motion direction changes which are second-order features that are difficult to individuate and match to first-order features at alternation rates above about 2–3Hz. More recently, it has been shown that when an attentional cue is presented with the change in colour or motion direction for an array of eight stimuli alternating in colour and direction within an annulus around fixation, or when an attentional window is guided around the array, motion asynchrony can be reduced or abolished (Cavanagh *et al.* 2008; Holcombe and Cavanagh 2008). This provides further evidence that colour-motion asynchrony is not a reflection of processing latency.

Motion-colour synchrony provides a nice example of a breakdown in perception that occurs when relative information needs to be extracted from the flow of implicit visual information over time. It also highlights the fact that relative temporal information is not directly accessible from the conscious appreciation of the constantly updating flow of information about visual features.

Duration perception

Judging duration is different from judging other properties of a visual stimulus such as its colour or orientation in that it is not specified until the end of the interval (Morgan *et al.* 2008). In perceptual psychology, the aim is to propose a mechanism by which duration can be measured and to test whether that mechanism corresponds to that used by the brain. The classical model of time perception proposes that duration is encoded by an amodal cognitive clock (Creelman 1962; Treisman 1963). A clock requires a signal generated at an approximately constant rate, e.g. a pacemaker, and a means of integrating the output of the pacemaker over the duration. Typically, the output of the pacemaker is gated into an accumulator and the value in the accumulator reflects the elapsed time between the gate opening and closing. This mechanism could apply generally to all events and temporal scales and is independent of the content of the interval that is being timed. Of course, all cognitive judgements are subject to noise. The precision of duration judgements is approximately proportional to the length of the interval. This is an example of Weber's law for sensory signals and in the time domain is referred to as the scalar property (Gibbon 1977; Wearden 1999). Note that this property is not explained by noise at the level of the clock rate within a single interval, as this would average out as the interval increases in length, rather it reflects variability in estimates across observations for that interval.

Since the mid 2000s, the idea of a universal clock for perceiving the duration of an interval has been challenged. Johnston *et al.* (2006) introduced an adaptation-based approach to time perception. They adapted a region of the near visual periphery on one side of fixation to drifting sine gratings or Gaussian blobs whose luminance varied sinusoidally over time. After a 15 second adaptation period, a subsecond interval of 10Hz drift (motion) or luminance modulation (flicker) was presented sequentially to the adapted and non-adapted sides of the visual field. Observers were asked to report which interval lasted longer. The duration of the interval on the non-adapted side was varied from trial to trial to generate a psychometric function. The point of subjective equality provided a measure of relative duration. They found that apparent duration of a 10Hz motion stimulus on the adapted side was reduced by around 20 per cent after adaptation to a 20Hz drift, but only slightly reduced or unaffected after a 5Hz adaptation. A similar result was found for the flicker stimulus. Note, adapting to motion or flicker may have non-specific effects, such as a change in alertness or arousal, but any non-specific effect will not contribute to the comparison between adapted vs. non-adapted regions of the visual field.

The change in perceived duration of identical intervals after adaptation of a localised region of the visual field cannot be explained by reference to a generic central clock or state changes, such as changes in arousal or attention on the clock rate. This does not of course mean that changes in arousal or other state variables do not affect perceived duration. For example, New and Scholl (2009) find a peripherally placed odd-ball can induce apparent duration expansion in a central target, which they attribute to a general effect on arousal. There are many stimulus or state manipulations that can alter perceived duration. However, an adaptation paradigm provides for local modality specific and spatially specific interventions that allow experimenters to tease apart timing mechanisms.

Evidence that adaptation-based apparent duration compression is not mediated by a change in exogenous attention comes from the observation that time compression occurs even in the case of invisible (60Hz) flicker (Johnston *et al.* 2008). In this paradigm, since the adapter is invisible, it is not possible for observers to tell which side of the visual field is being adapted and willingly attend more to the adapted side. Adaptation may alter the perception of the onset and offset of the interval. For example, the onset might appear to be delayed after adapting to high temporal frequencies with little effect on offset. However, apparent compression was found to be proportional to the length of the interval (Johnston *et al.* 2006), rather than being a subtraction from the length of the interval, which is what would be expected if adaptation introduced some processing delay at onset. Also, apparent onset and offset times measured relative to an auditory tone are little affected by adaptation (Johnston *et al.* 2006). This experiment undermines the idea of a universal clock and directs attention to a timing mechanism whose operations might be altered locally by visual adaptation, but what type of clock mechanism would be consistent with a manipulation that alters the processing of a visual stimulus after adaptation?

Visual mechanisms have been shown to operate over a limited range of some stimulus dimensions such as orientation or spatial frequency. These mechanisms are considered to function relatively independently and are referred to as spatial frequency and orientation channels. Does this design principle also structure the temporal domain? A classic signature of orientation channels is the tilt after effect (Gibson and Radner 1937). In this experiment, after looking at a line that is slightly off vertical, a subsequently viewed vertical line looks tilted in the opposite direction.

This is typically explained as a shift in the distribution of activity of a population of overlapping orientation tuned channels brought about by a reduction in responsivity of the adapted channel. In the time domain, we might expect adapting to a particular interval, say 500 ms, would shift the perceived duration of slightly longer or shorter intervals. Although duration channels have been proposed and empirically supported (Heron *et al.* 2012), the correspondence between spatial and temporal channels breaks down in a number of places. The main difficulty is that duration is only properly defined at the end of an interval. Whereas a clock can provide a running update from the onset of a stimulus to be timed, a number of questions arise about how duration channels would operate in this case. Whereas an orientation tuned channel is active from stimulus onset to offset at a level of activation determined by the match of the stimulus and the channel characteristics, a duration channel would only become active at offset, reducing the scope for adaptation. If duration channels become active at stimulus offset, it is not clear whether they would reset or remain active, since the effective stimulus has not changed state. One would also need to specify how duration channels would carry information about the onset of the interval. The concept is far from simple and recent empirical work in which adaptation to repetition of short intervals introduces duration compression of a longer interval (Curran *et al.* 2016) challenges the empirical support for this view. In any case, the encoding of duration has more in common with how we might encode the length of a line or the width of an object rather than a local visual property such as the orientation of a contour. Duration perception would appear to require a different approach.

A content-dependent clock

The duration channel proposal does not offer an explanation for temporal frequency adaptation-based apparent temporal compression as the observers are not adapted to temporal intervals per se. And a content-independent timer as exemplified by the standard stopwatch model cannot explain the fact that the effects of temporal frequency adaptation on apparent duration are spatially localised. Adaptation to high temporal frequencies alters the properties of temporal filters in the visual system. However, changes to linear filters can only alter the phase and contrast of drifting sine gratings, not their durations. Changes in perceived temporal frequency can be explained by changes in filter sensitivity (Johnston 2010, 2013), but a different approach is necessary to explain changes in apparent duration.

We have characterised the action of temporal filters as blurring and differentiating the temporal image. Temporal differentiation can be accomplished by passing the temporally extended signal through the temporal differentiating filters (Figures 21.1B and 21.1C). Mathematically, the signal and filter are aligned in time and the product at each overlapping time point are summed. This gives a single value for a single time point and the process is repeated for the next time point. The zero-order blur kernel has the low-pass temporal property characteristic of parvocellular neurones (Johnston 2010, 2013). This filter just introduces temporal blur. The derivative filters have the band-pass (tuned) property associated with magnocellular neurones (Johnston 2010, 2013). Parvocellular and magnocellular neurones form the major division in response properties in the lateral geniculate nucleus of the thalamus (Nassi and Callaway 2009). They are distinguished by their response to temporal change, amongst other things. But the temporal properties are most relevant here. Parvocells respond best to static and slow moving pattern, whereas magnocells respond best to moving pattern. The temporal impulse response (the response to a flash of light) and the frequency response of the filters (the response to temporal flicker) are shown in Figures 21.1B and 21.1C. These are different characterisations of the same filter and this relationship is formalised by the Fourier transform.

The characterisation of a filter can provide clues as to how it might function in a neural computation. One can exploit the derivative properties of the temporal filters to construct a Taylor-series approximation (Figure 21.1A) of the image brightness. The Taylor series allows the reconstruction of a function from a sum of terms based on the derivatives of the function at a point. As discussed earlier, the visual system can also use a Taylor series as a simple way of predicting forward (or backward) in time. The parameter, h, in the Taylor series determines the direction and amount of predicted displacement. We can substitute a range for h, instead of an instantaneous value, to predict a displaced temporal sequence. This construction would allow a forward or reverse prediction of the image brightness through time. Note that the prediction is just the weighted sum of parvocellular and magnocellular neuronal outputs.

We can now build a content-sensitive clock in the following way. First, predict the current image brightness sequence forward for, let's say, 30 ms using the magnocellular signal and store it in a temporal buffer. Next, cross-correlate the current parvocellular-based sequence with the stored sequence. The new input has to be filtered by the zero-order kernel, otherwise the phase of the signal will be quite different from the stored signal. After 30 ms of comparing prediction and input, the correlation should peak and, at that point, we determine that 30 ms has passed and reset the prediction. The number of 30 ms resettings (clock ticks) are then accumulated, as in the standard stopwatch model, until the stimulus has completed, at which point the stimulus duration is read out. Note that the parameter that determines the time shift is "h", which only multiplies the magnocellular outputs. The magnocellular pathway controls the temporal prediction. Adaptation advances the phase of signals carried by magnocellular neurons (Benardete and Kaplan 1999). This phase shift is seen in magnocellular but not parvocellular neurones (Benardete and Kaplan 1999). The phase shift will shift the predicted sine-wave forward in time, which is equivalent to having a larger h parameter. This should lead to resetting after a longer delay, leading to fewer ticks, and therefore time compression.

This model, although quite detailed, is like many models in visual perception specific to the visual domain, and should be seen as an exemplar of how one might build a timing mechanism based on the visual input rather than a universal timer. Since publication of the model, there has been evidence that the effects of motion-based adaptation on duration can have a directional component, which may be cortical in genesis, in addition to a non-directional component (Curran and Benton 2012; Bruno *et al.* 2013). The dynamic "predict and compare" strategy, however, can be generalised to any situation where sensory signals are predictable enough that their state can be forecast at some future time.

The fact that we do not have a universal clock for timing perceptual events opens up the possibility that the brain has multiple ways of measuring the duration of events, which are task and modality specific. The predict and compare strategy requires predictable content. Another strategy might be to use knowledge of the time course in the increase in variance associated with image differences over time, calculated by multiple stochastic processes (Ahrens and Sahani 2011). In the end, a timing mechanism just needs a signal that increases at a constant rate and some way of integrating and scaling the signal. From a psychological point of view, whatever the domain, the key problem remains: how do we extract information about temporal properties of external events from time-varying images?

Summary and conclusions

The characterisation of visual temporal filters as differential operators points to a role for early visual processes in prediction as well as shaping contrast sensitivity. Prediction allows a more flexible view of temporal representation and leads us to consider mechanisms by which information may be shifted forward and backward in time to deal with the time delays inherent in neural processing. Although the visual stream does not appear to be sampled like a movie, complex perceptual routines may require synchronous neural processing giving rise to temporal fluctuations in perceptual representations. Prediction also has a role to play in duration encoding through a "predict and compare" content-dependent clock. Temporal prediction just requires a measure of the current value of some representation and its rate of change, making the ideas developed here generalisable to many domains and levels of visual processing. However, there may be many distributed domain-specific timing circuits yet to be discovered.

References

Ahrens, M. B. and Sahani, M. (2011) "Observers exploit stochastic models of sensory change to help judge the passage of time", *Current Biology* 21(3): 200–206.

Amano, K., Arnold, D. H., Takeda, T. and Johnston, A. (2008) "Alpha band amplification during illusory jitter perception", *Journal of Vision* 8(10): 1–8.

Arnold, D. H. and Johnston, A. (2003) "Motion-induced spatial conflict", *Nature* 425(6954): 181–184.

Benardete, E. A. and Kaplan, E. (1999) "The dynamics of primate M retinal ganglion cells", *Visual Neuroscience* 16(2): 355–368.

Bruno, A., Ayhan, I. and Johnston, A. (2015) "Changes in apparent duration follow shifts in perceptual timing", *Journal of Vision* 15(6): 2, 1–18.

Bruno, A., Ng, E. and Johnston, A. (2013) "Motion-direction specificity for adaptation-induced duration compression depends on temporal frequency", *Journal of Vision* 13(12): 19, 1–11.

Bullier, J. (2001) "Integrated model of visual processing", *Brain Research Reviews* 36(2–3): 96–107.

Busch, N. A. and VanRullen, R. (2010) "Spontaneous EEG oscillations reveal periodic sampling of visual attention", *Proceedings of the National Academy of Sciences* 107(37): 16048–16053.

Cass, J. and Alais, D. (2006) "Evidence for two interacting temporal channels in human visual processing", *Vision Research* 46(18): 2859–2868.

Cavanagh, P., Holcombe, A. O. and Chou, W. (2008) "Mobile computation: Spatiotemporal integration of the properties of objects in motion", *Journal of Vision* 8(12): 11–23.

Cavanagh, P., Tyler, C. W. and Favreau, O. E. (1984) "Perceived velocity of moving chromatic gratings", *Journal of the Optical Society of America* 1(8): 893–899.

Creelman, C. (1962) "Human discrimination of auditory duration", *Journal of the Acoustical Society of America* 34(5): 582–593.

Curran, W. and Benton, C. P. (2012) "The many directions of time", *Cognition* 122(2): 252–257.

Curran, W., Benton, C. P., Harris, J. M., Hibbard, P. B. and Beattie, L. (2016) "Adapting to time: Duration channels do not mediate human time perception", *Journal of Vision* 16(5): 1–10.

Frisby, J. P. (1980) *Seeing: Illusion, Brain, and Mind*, Oxford, UK: Oxford University Press.

Gibbon, J. (1977) "Scalar expectancy-theory and Webers law in animal timing", *Psychological Review* 84(3): 279–325.

Gibson, J. J. and Radner, M. (1937) "Adaptation, aftereffect and contrast in the perception of tilted lines: I. Quantitative studies", *Journal of Experimental Psychology* 20(5): 453–467.

Heron, J., Aaen-Stockdale, C., Hotchkiss, J., Roach, N. W., McGraw, P. V. and Whitaker, D. (2012) "Duration channels mediate human time perception", *Proceedings of the Royal Society B: Biological Sciences* 279(1729): 690–698.

Hess, R. F. and Plant, G. T. (1985) "Temporal frequency discrimination in human vision: Evidence for an additional mechanism in the low spatial and high temporal frequency region", *Vision Research* 25(18): 1495–1500.

Hess, R. F. and Snowden, R. J. (1992) "Temporal properties of human visual filters: Number, shapes and spatial covariation", *Vision Research* 32(1): 47–60.

Hogendoorn, H., Verstraten, F. and Johnston, A. (2010) "Spatially localised time shifts of the perceptual stream", *Frontiers in Psychology* 1(181): 1–8.

Holcombe, A. O. and Cavanagh, P. (2008) "Independent, synchronous access to color and motion features", *Cognition* 107(2): 552–580.

Johnston, A. (2010) "Modulation of time perception by visual adaptation", in A. C. Nobre and J. T. Coull (eds), *Attention and Time*, Oxford, UK: Oxford University Press, pp. 187–200.

Johnston, A. (2013) "Visual time perception", in J. S. Werner and L. M. Chalupa (eds), *The New Visual Neurosciences*, Cambridge, MA: MIT Press, pp. 749–762.

Johnston, A. and Clifford, C. W. (1995) "A unified account of three apparent motion illusions", *Vision Research* 35(8): 1109–1123.

Johnston, A. and Nishida, S. (2001) "Time perception: Brain time or event time?" *Current Biology* 11(11): R427–R430.

Johnston, A., Arnold, D. and Nishida, S. (2006) "Spatially localized distortions of event time", *Current Biology* 16(5): 472–479.

Johnston, A., Bruno, A., Watanabe, J., Quansah, B., Patel, N., Dakin, S. and Nishida, S. (2008) "Visually-based temporal distortion in dyslexia", *Vision Research* 48(17): 1852–1858.

Johnston, A., McOwan, P. W. and Benton, C. P. (1999) "Robust velocity computation from a biologically motivated model of motion perception", *Proceedings of the Royal Society of London B: Biological Sciences* 266(1418): 509–518.

Johnston, A., McOwan, P. W. and Buxton, H. (1992) "A computational model of the analysis of some first-order and second-order motion patterns by simple and complex cells", *Proceedings of the Royal Society of London B: Biological Sciences* 250(1329): 297–306.

Kline, K., Holcombe, A. O. and Eagleman, D. M. (2004) "Illusory motion reversal is caused by rivalry, not by perceptual snapshots of the visual field", *Vision Research* 44(23): 2653–2658.

Lee, J., Williford, T. and Maunsell, J. H. (2007) "Spatial attention and the latency of neuronal responses in macaque area V4", *Journal of Neuroscience* 27(36): 9632–9637.

Mandler, M. B. and Makous, W. (1984) "A three channel model of temporal frequency perception", *Vision Research* 24(12): 1881–1887.

Morgan, M. J., Giora, E. and Solomon, J. A. (2008) "A single 'stopwatch' for duration estimation, a single 'ruler' for size", *Journal of Vision* 8(2): 14, 11–18.

Moutoussis, K. and Zeki, S. (1997) "Functional segregation and temporal hierarchy of the visual perceptive systems", *Proceedings of the Royal Society of London B: Biological Sciences* 264(1387): 1407–1414.

Nassi, J. J. and Callaway, E. M. (2009) "Parallel processing strategies of the primate visual system", *Nature Reviews Neuroscience* 10(5): 360–372.

New, J. J. and Scholl, B. J. (2009) "Subjective time dilation: Spatially local, object-based, or a global visual experience?" *Journal of Vision* 9(2): 4, 1–11.

Nishida, S. and Johnston, A. (2002) "Marker correspondence, not processing latency, determines temporal binding of visual attributes", *Current Biology* 12(5): 359–368.

Nishida, S. and Johnston, A. (2010) "Time marker theory of cross-channel temporal binding" in R. Nijhawan and B. Khurana (eds), *Problems of Space and Time in Perception and Action*, Cambridge, UK: Cambridge University Press.

Purves, D., Paydarfar, J. A. and Andrews, T. J. (1996) "The wagon wheel illusion in movies and reality", *Proceedings of the National Academy of Sciences* 93(8): 3693–3697.

Rao, R. P. and Ballard, D. H. (1999) "Predictive coding in the visual cortex: A functional interpretation of some extra-classical receptive-field effects", *Nature Neuroscience* 2(1): 79–87.

Roach, N. W., McGraw, P. V. and Johnston, A. (2011) "Visual motion induces a forward prediction of spatial pattern", *Current Biology* 21(9): 740–745.

Schouten, J. F. (1967) "Subjective stroboscopy and a model of visual movement detectors", in W. Wathen-Dunn (ed.), *Models for the Perception of Speech and Visual Form*, Cambridge, MA: MIT Press, pp. 44–55.

Treisman, M. (1963) "Temporal discrimination and the indifference interval: Implications for a model of the 'internal clock'", *Psychological Monographs* 77(13): 1–31.

Ullman, S. (1984) "Visual routines", *Cognition* 18(1–3): 97–159.

VanRullen, R., Reddy, L. and Koch, C. (2005) "Attention-driven discrete sampling of motion perception", *Proceedings of the National Academy of Sciences* 102(14): 5291–5296.

Watson, A. B. and Robson, J. G. (1981) "Discrimination at threshold: Labelled detectors in human vision", *Vision Research* 21(7): 1115–1122.

Wearden, J. H. (1999) "'Beyond the fields we know . . .': Exploring and developing scalar timing theory", *Behavioural Processes* 45(1–3): 3–21.

22

HOW WE "USE" TIME

Mari Riess Jones

Most of us do not monitor time units of our daily activities. Rarely are we aware of the durations of phonemes or syllables in words uttered by a passing friend who says: "Hi, how are you?" Although we quickly grasp this greeting, it is fair to say we don't calibrate elapsed times of its phonemes or words. Yet, if an experimental psychologist slightly fiddled with the timing of these speech components, this would drastically affect one's comprehension of such a phrase. Nevertheless, we generally take for granted the timing of events such as syllables or words. So much so that, when pointedly asked to "perceive" the duration of an arbitrary stimulus, retrospectively, we can be rather poor at this (Grondin 2010; Matthews and Meck 2016).

J. J. Gibson (1975) famously claimed "we don't perceive time, we perceive events". Yet, as this chapter reveals, evidence is emerging which indicates interesting ways in which the time structure of an event actually influences how we perceive it. Consequently, in departing from Gibson's position, I have suggested that people unwittingly "use" the timing of an event to perceive it. Perceiving time, qua time, then becomes secondary to perceiving an event as a whole. Specifically, the primary function of timing is to ensure synchrony between event and perceiver. This chapter sketches a theoretical approach that not only departs from Gibson's position, but it also differentiates the abstract concept of time as a dimension, gauged by clocks, from its real manifestation in everyday events that we (and other species) use for communication. Thus, the events of interest are ones we live by. Although here, these events are largely acoustical in nature, involving human music and speech, the basic ideas extend to visual events.

So, what is an event? For the present, let an event be an external happening (acoustic or visual) that unfolds in time with a beginning, a middle, and an end (McAuley *et al.* 2006). Perhaps it is the "hoot, hoot, hoot" of an owl, the low frequency purr of a cat, the babbling of a four-month-old infant, or the utterance of a passing friend. Of course, many events also have inanimate origins as with the sound of falling tree, an oncoming train, and so on. The unifying feature is that all events have structure in time.

Consider the above phrase of a passing friend. It is an event consisting of measurable time spans at several nested time scales of speech (Tilsen and Johnson 2008; Tilsen and Arvaniti 2013). For instance, one time scale embedded within this phrase corresponds to a succession of time spans of syllables marked by onsets of prominent vowels (termed *P-centers*). In this phrase (i.e., "Hi, how . . . etc.".) these time spans form a roughly regular rhythm of a speaker's talking rate. Successive P-centers mark out a speaker's articulation rate that unfolds at a time scale slower than phonemes. P-centers are captivating because they unveil a relatively simple time pattern based on relationships among similar time intervals; that is, a P-center rhythm is approximately *isochronous* (Morton *et al.* 1976). A similar analysis applies to nested time scales of rhythms in musical phrases, such as "Old MacDonald has a . . ." (Martin 1972).

More formally, all events convey time structure via rates and rhythms at different time scales. In theory, we can say that such events afford people external (stimulus) rhythms which they *use* to engage with that event. This engagement relies on synchrony. The idea is that the rate and rhythm of an acoustic event at given scale leads to resonance with a corresponding internal cortical oscillation in a listener's brain. That is, listeners are equipped with tunable brains: Cortex and brainstem are populated with active neural oscillations over a wide range of time scales, all with malleable periods capable of synchronization. Thus, neural oscillations come to synchronize with external event rhythms. Simply put, an individual's neural rhythms have a dynamic potential for synchronizing, i.e., "tuning into", corresponding external periodicities embedded in everyday events (e.g., Tilsen and Arvaniti 2013).

Synchrony is the core principle of a universal activity known as *entrainment*. Through synchrony, people "use" event timing to guide internal neural responses that can "track" an unfolding event. This proposal has implications for distinguishing between perceiving time and perceiving events.

The remainder of this chapter unpacks this distinction. It is divided into two sections: the first section contemplates issues surrounding *perceiving time* and provides a background of contrasting psychological approaches to this controversial topic. The second section tackles questions about *using* time to perceive events, which invites discussion of a major construct in psychology, namely attention.

Background: perceiving time?

The concept of time continues to pose unresolved puzzles for contemporary psychology. Some theorists embrace Gibson's skepticism about time whereas others reject his claim altogether, arguing that people *do perceive time*. One influential approach to time perception emphasizes encoding of *time intervals*. The percept of a single time interval becomes an abstract construct involving an internal clock. The core idea is that an internal clock, a *pace-maker*, fills the void of a to-be-perceived time interval with ticks. Thus, time spans filled with many random ticks are judged as longer than time spans with few ticks. This dominant view offers a meaningful backdrop for understanding a contrasting perspective on time perception, based on dynamic attending, which shares a dash of Gibson's skepticism about direct perception of time.

A laboratory paradigm commonly used to study time perception presents people with two discrete time intervals on each of a series of occasions, i.e., *trials*. Typically, a prospective time task is employed which requires people to explicitly focus on time intervals and report whether the second time interval (a comparison) differs from the first (standard). Thus, in judging a standard/comparison pair, one reports the comparison is the "same", "longer", or "shorter" than the standard.

An influential clock model, the Scalar Expectancy Theory (SET), proposed by Gibbon (1977), can explain time perception observed in such tasks. It is schematized in Figure 22.1 (Church *et al.* 1994). Generally, clock theories hold that a perceiver forms time codes of standard and comparison intervals based upon the accumulated number of ticks per interval (Treisman 1963). A just noticeable time difference, expressed in counts, determines time discrimination that follows Weber's Law. That is, this threshold time difference (between comparison and standard) increases proportionally with the scale of a standard's duration. Statistical formulations to tackle

Scalar Expectancy Theory (SET)
and *the Perceptual Clock*

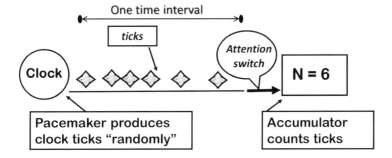

A count code is an N value for a standard interval.
This code is stored in memory for later comparisons.

Figure 22.1   The pace-maker clock of SET produces ticks that are admitted, via an on/off attention switch, to a counter that accumulates ticks, then encodes/compares numbers to explain time perception. From Church, Meck and Gibbon 1994.

Weber's Law typically appeal to distribution properties of ticks filling an interval (e.g., the coefficient of variation). Matthews and Meck (2016) provide a thorough review of this topic.

Despite its widespread popularity, the internal clock concept raises pragmatic and ecological questions. In particular, a clock/pace-maker is assumed to reset with successive time spans (e.g., standard then comparison), meaning that people *independently* encode and store successive time intervals. But, it is not clear that this assumption captures people's real reactions to such intervals.

In fact, Dynamic Attending Theory (DAT) directly challenges the notion that people treat successive time intervals as independent as unrealistic. It also disputes the assumption that individual time intervals are encoded as accumulated clock ticks. Instead, DAT assumes successive time spans, either in a laboratory setting or in real life, are automatically treated as *if they are related*. We are wired to orient to the rhythm formed by successive time spans. With DAT, this rhythm presumably awakens in listeners a resonant periodicity which carries a temporal expectancy about future time spans (Jones *et al.* 1993; McAuley and Kidd 1998; Barnes and Jones 2000).

A time perception task: an example

Figure 22.2 outlines a modified experimental paradigm for studying time perception, one that highlights distinctions between SET and DAT. In this task, on each trial a pair of to-be-perceived time intervals follows a series of similar time spans which form a temporal context. Context intervals are marked by onsets of successive sounds (inter-onset-time intervals). Using a prospective time judgment procedure, participants are told to *ignore the context* and judge only the time difference between standard and comparison intervals.

McAuley and Jones (2003) used this task to test the independence hypothesis. They varied the duration of the standard interval, while retaining an above threshold difference between the standard and comparison. This means that scalar expectancies, based on SET, generate a null hypothesis

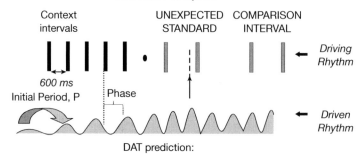

**Dynamic Attending Theory
and Time Perception**

Figure 22.2 Induction of DAT temporal expectancy given a rhythmic context. Recurring driving and driven time intervals synchronize to align with time-markers of intervals. Adapted from Barnes and Jones 2000; Large and Jones 1999; McAuley and Jones 2003.

with respect to variations of standard durations. Hence, SET predicts uniformly good percepts of time differences between comparisons and standards for all standards, regardless of the preceding temporal context. Alternatively, if the rhythm of this context induces temporal expectancies, then DAT predicts that performance will be best for standards that end as expected given the context rhythm. People should accurately anticipate a standard's ending based on the ongoing period of a contextually activated oscillation whereas this was not the case with unexpected standards.

Four studies evaluated SET and DAT predictions, and all confirmed DAT predictions. The reason is simple: Clock resets with unexpected standards do not depend on the context rhythm. Consequently, pace-maker clock models incorrectly predict performance with unexpected standards that is *too good*. By contrast, DAT correctly predicts poorer performance with unexpected standards because people automatically attempt to correct their incorrect temporal expectancy by fleetingly shortening or expanding the period of the entraining oscillation. However, this correction is usually incomplete thereby leading to perceptual distortions of unexpected durations.

Admittedly, laboratory tasks requiring people to explicitly compare two discrete time intervals are artefactual. They fail to capture everyday activities. Tasks requiring us to judge the precise time difference between two arbitrary time intervals are rare in everyday life. How often during daily life do we compare two isolated time intervals, one lasting ½ s and the other perhaps ¾ s? Not often. In fact, it seems implausible that evolution favored wiring in creatures that entails precision comparisons of one or two isolated time intervals, just as it is implausible that people independently encode durations of successive phonemes in a friend's utterance. Often the laboratory tasks psychologists are fondest of turn out to be ecologically remote from timing as we realistically experience it in daily events.

From the perspective of DAT, any rhythmic context is closer to capturing real world events than are arbitrary pairs of isolated time intervals. A rhythmic context can induce in listeners temporal expectancies that lead, rightly or wrongly, to anticipations of the "when" of a future (to-be-judged) time interval. Hence we are quite good at perceiving times of expected durations, but we are less adept in perceiving unexpected (deviant) time intervals. Of course, if a temporal context is rhythmically complex, then temporal expectancies are more likely to be violated leading to correspondingly poorer time perception. In short, because the rhythms buried in environmental events are rarely precisely regular, routine judgments of such time intervals, while possibly acceptable, are often fuzzy estimates of these durations.

Synchrony and time

Synchrony, as developed in DAT, has a special flavor. It refers to a coming together of an individual's internal oscillations with corresponding (resonant) stimulus periodicities. This involves automatic phase/frequency alignments of a listener's internal, i.e., cortical, oscillations with an ongoing series of time spans of an event. More formally, in entrainment terms, successive stimulus time spans form a rhythm termed a *driving rhythm*. A driving rhythm is capable of engaging a similar internal rhythm in a listener. This internal correlate is a cortical oscillation termed a *driven rhythm*. *Entrainment* is the process by which these two rhythms find stable synchrony. Synchrony depends on the adaptability of flexible neural oscillations termed *limit cycle oscillators*.

Generally, synchrony relies on a phase-locking of one periodicity with another periodicity. A basic premise is that synchrony is a goal state; it is attractive in that our bodies gravitate to synchronous states. Synchrony is most evident with, but not limited to, driving rhythms with isochronous rhythms, where successive time intervals are similar. Not surprisingly, it is fairly easy for a limit cycle oscillation to phase adapt to, i.e., synchronize with, isochronous driving rhythms. Assuming different oscillations have specific intrinsic periods (i.e., rates), synchrony is based upon a "driving:driven" ratio of periods. Thus, if two rhythms have a rational rate ratio (e.g., 1:1, 1:2, 1:3, etc.), entrainment is more rapid than with ratios that are not commensurate.

Entrainment is inherently adaptive. Limit cycle oscillations are sufficiently flexible that they can automatically adapt to certain non-isochronous driving rhythms. For instance, if an otherwise regular rhythm contains a deviant time interval, this irregularity automatically triggers an adaptive change in the period of driven rhythm that briefly draws the driven periodicity closer to the unexpected time span. However, such corrective acts are brief, often incomplete, hence resulting in time distortions of the deviant interval. Nevertheless, an ever flexible driven limit cycle oscillation quickly bounces back to its latent period to soldier on.

Oscillations versus clocks

It is tempting to dismiss neural oscillations as clocks in disguise. After all, a pace-maker clock generates ticks, which might be regularly distributed. Certainly the iconic demonstration of synchronization that gave birth to entrainment theory featured two clocks mounted on the same wall. So, isn't enlisting a neural oscillation just a fancy way of using a clock metaphor?

Although entrainment is a universal process, it is a mistake to confuse the mechanical pace-maker clocks of psychological time theories with the more flexible biological oscillations evident in neural recordings (e.g., EEGs, among others). Pace-makers are rigid devices. They have no potential for synchronizing via adaptive changes in phase and/or period. A pace-maker resembles the average wall clock that does not change its ticking rate when a nearby individual begins to clap at a faster rate. One might argue that a perceiver's internal clock rate can change as a perceiver regulates an attentional gate, as suggested in Figure 22.1. But this does not involve synchrony. Internal clock ticks do not speed up to match a faster external driving rhythm. Instead, this pace-maker's clock must reset with each successive interval providing an accurate estimate of individual time spans. This accounts for their inappropriately good performance with unexpected time intervals. Bluntly, internal clocks are *not* limit cycle oscillations. Indeed, as just noted, the flexible limit cycle oscillations of DAT provide less reliable estimates of elapsed time intervals than pace-maker clocks of SET, but they are more realistic estimates.

Finally, scalar timing and Weber's Law, which are at the heart of time discrimination, can be tackled from an entrainment perspective. In particular, DAT predicts that time discrimination depends on a just noticeable phase difference between an expected standard and a comparison, for a rhythm of a given rate (scale). And, when rates change, this threshold phase difference changes proportionately, i.e., relative to the period of the driven oscillation (locked to the new driving rhythm rate). In other words, Weber's Law of temporal acuity naturally falls out of an entrainment framework. Moreover, McAuley *et al.* (2006) show that well-known limits of Weber's Law also flow from DAT.

Summary

The fluidity of biological rhythms, over millennia, probably motivated humankind to develop reliable clocks, ones impervious to event rhythms that spark oscillator activity. Mechanical clocks meet a societal need for indifferent time precision. In fact, our reliance on clocks is tacit cultural acknowledgment of our handicaps in time perception. We often lose track of time.

Humans are unreliable estimators of elapsed time because our internal oscillations are busy responding to more important things like tracking a baby's cry, following a news bulletin, or listening to an enchanting song, and so on. Such communicative time patterns grab our attention. And, their inherent rhythmicity provides a context that elicits dynamic expectancies favoring percepts of expected time intervals while also distorting percepts of unexpected ones. Pacemaker models, which do not accommodate temporal context, cannot explain listeners' inherent tendency to generate temporal expectancies based on driving rhythms nestled within natural events. Neither can such internal clocks handle findings that time estimates are less reliable with unexpected time intervals. We make mistakes, even when told to focus on time. In the dynamics of everyday life, we do not perform as well as clock-timed theories propose. Instead, we behave like the fallible humans we are.

Perceiving events: using time

Gibson was right in suggesting that perceiving events is fundamental to getting around in the world. Yet, in spite of his famous acknowledgment that events are "happenings in time", Gibson ironically overlooked the possibility that perceiving events depends intimately on the timing of such events. In this section, I maintain that perceiving an event depends on attending at the "right" times as this event unfolds. This requires that we somehow follow an event in real time. How does this happen? The engine that drives event perception is the same engine that drives time perception: entrainment. As in time perception, event perception requires synchrony between recurring external periods of the event's driving rhythm and the corresponding internal periodicities of a perceiver's driven rhythm. However, in perceiving events such as melodies or speech utterances, we must also consider that perception depends on one's ability to allocate attending to such unfolding events in a timely fashion.

According to DAT, the time structure of an event influences our perception of it. Often, we are unaware of this. In fact, unless specifically instructed, we usually don't focus on event timing; instead, we spontaneously tend to orient to the non-temporal features of an event, features found in stimuli tagged here as time-markers. While event timing is ever-present, its influence is subtle. Yet, we may suddenly become aware of timing when, for instance, a compelling rock song pops up on a car radio. It has a steady beat and we find ourselves involuntarily tapping in synchrony to the underlying beat period. Even in the absence of overt motor tapping, schools of non-motor neural oscillations remain active as one's brain involuntarily continues silently "humming" in synchrony with a rock beat. Recruitment of such driven oscillations ultimately leads to entrainment, hence synchrony between driving and driven rhythms. Much of this happens involuntarily, i.e., "under our radar".

Entrainment is automatic process. It does not necessarily require significant energy or effort. Synchrony emerges involuntarily to "hook-up" a regular driving rhythm with its correlate, a related neural period. More pointedly, entrainment implicates a new theoretical unit: a *driving/driven dyad*. An asymptotic state of stable synchrony is characterized by the consistency of a phase relationship as the driving and driven members become hooked into a dyad. The idea is that entrainment of cortical oscillations optimizes event listening (Henry and Obleser 2012).

Synchrony states and attractors

The goal of synchrony motivates entrainment. In dynamical systems terminology, synchrony is an *attractor state*. It represents a special time relationship to which we are inexplicably drawn. Synchrony is most familiar when driving and driven rhythms have identical periods, hence one period (**n** = 1) of the driving rhythm equals one driven rhythm period (**m** = 1); together, this dyad yields an **n:m** = 1:1 state of synchrony. This attractor is implicated whenever two (or more) simple, i.e., isochronous, rhythms share the same rate (e.g., see context sequence of Figure 22.2).

Yet, synchrony assumes many **n:m** forms. For instance, another powerful attractor features a driving rhythm with a period twice that of its driven rhythm (**n:m** = 2:1). This pleasing attractor explains our fondness for octaves in melodies, duple musical meters, and the two-step in dancing. More generally, a wide range of synchronous modes form different attractor *states* that describe how a particular driving rhythm phase-locks with a related driven rhythm in a commensurate **n:m** relationship. Attractors can reflect "simple" or "complex" time relations. Thus, attractors, such as **n:m** = 1:1 or, 2:1, are simpler than those of **n:m** = 5:4 or 8:5, etc. Typically, in novel settings, people's expectancies automatically revert to simpler attractors.

In addition to attractors, two other factors contribute to the effectiveness of driving rhythms that synchronize with driven rhythms. One concerns the regularity of a driving rhythm's time-marker and the other is driving rhythm strength, conveyed by marker salience. According to classic entrainment theories, dyadic synchrony is most likely with simple attractor states involving strong and regular driving rhythms.

Dynamics of attending

Although event perception builds on the synchronous states of entraining dyads, a full explanation of perception turns on the behavior of driven rhythms. Specifically, attending energy increases with the amplitude of an entraining oscillation and, in turn, this heightening of attending energy enhances event perception.

To pursue this idea, imagine a melodic event manifest as a sequence of tones. Onsets of successive tones are deemed salient, i.e., noticeable, thereby providing a strong driving rhythm. Let tone onsets mark inter-tone time intervals that outline a roughly regular periodicity (i.e., with similar, not identical, time intervals). When such a driving rhythm is presented to a listener, it should automatically engage a related driven cortical oscillation with a variable amplitude. Importantly in a dynamic account, this entraining oscillation assumes an amplitude that specifies a fleeting level of attending energy. That is, the level of attending energy delivered by a driven oscillation is raised or lowered depending on its momentary amplitude.

Amplitude changes of driven oscillations assume two forms. One involves heightened energy within a sensitive phase region creating a localized *expectancy pulse* (Large and Jones 1999). If these pulses appear at phase points that regularly anticipate tone onsets in a melody, then entrainment generates anticipatory attending in a listener which contributes to optimizing perception of the melodic event. A second form of amplitude modulation involves heightening energy uniformly over the period of a driven rhythm; here, attending is boosted uniformly over the driven *period's amplitude*. Theoretically, in the latter case, listeners selectively "tune into" one or another time scale of an event comprising several time scales (Jones and Boltz 1989). Energy is either finely focused, with an expectancy pulse, or broadly focused over a whole period of an entraining oscillation. In both, attending is a correlate of a driven oscillation's activity level, i.e., its amplitude. In this view, if an auditory event affords a driving rhythm for an entraining limit cycle oscillation, then the efficacy of attending depends on both the amount of attending energy allocated to that event and "when" it is allocated. The main point is that the amplitude of an entraining oscillation is a vehicle for modulating attending and, hence, event perception.

This discussion introduces a central construct in psychology: *Attention*. According to DAT, time and attending are intimately linked. Time, specifically event time structure, becomes a conduit of attending. This portrait of attending dynamics explains how timing functions as an ever-present tool, something we naturally use to explore our environment. For animate creatures, time is the foundation of attending. Whether voluntarily or involuntarily, attending energy is raised or lowered at specific times.

Attending versus attention

In psychology, attention is one of those topics that commands much lively discussion. Not surprisingly, it is a topic about which theorists differ profoundly. Beginning with William James' early observations on the many properties of attention, from its heightened clarity and vividness to its selectivity in focused concentration, psychologists have struggled with a range of fascinating metaphorical explanations of attention.

Historically, the most successful attention theories concentrated on explaining selectivity. Selectivity refers to an individual's ability to focus on one thing while ignoring other, co-occurring, things. Theoretically, attentional selectivity has been addressed metaphorically using mechanisms of constraint such as attention filters, switches, resource pools, spotlights, perceptual load, and even an agency that prioritizes entries into memory to explain one's reliance on one of many sources of stimulation.

The most famous illustration of *selective attention* is the "Cocktail party effect" (Cherry 1953). At a party, a listener often confronts the dilemma of listening to one speaker when surrounded by other competing voices. A central problem involves identifying situational features that allow a listener to selectively attend to a particular speaker. Mechanisms such as filters, limited resource pools, and perceptual load limits are exploited to explain constraints that putatively determine selective attention. They implicate variables such as number of competing speakers, their spatial arrangements, degree of voice overlaps, a listener's goals, and so on. And all do levy some impact on one's ability to selectively "tune into" a single speaker. However, few experiments and fewer theories have considered the role of competing time structure(s) in multiple speakers' driving rhythms.

Neglect of time as an influence on attention is common. Scientific recognition of event time structure in experimental settings and/or in theories of attention, if present at all, is modest. In part, this neglect can be attributed to the fact that time structure does not fit into the prevailing theoretical formulation of time as *processing time*. Processing time is conceived as an empty vessel to be filled with encoding activity. This precludes a role for the *structured time* of a driving rhythm. Rather, fast events allow little time for processing relative to slower events. Event time structure is irrelevant.

A disregard of event timing also makes sense if attention is conceived of as a static, not a dynamic, mechanism which limits processing, using mechanisms such as gates, switches, filters, or spotlights. For instance, internal clock models, as in Figure 22.1 reduce attention to a gate or switch that regulates tick counts at a single point in time. But, if attending is an activity that changes over time, then *attention* becomes an ongoing dynamic undertaking, namely *attending*. And the role of event timing becomes relevant to guiding this activity. I argue that attending involves the energetic activity of a driven rhythm as it entrains to an external driving rhythm. Time and attending are intimately connected; attending, as heightened driven rhythm energy, is time-bound (e.g., Jones and Boltz 1989; Large and Jones 1999).

Attending in time versus time perception

The idea that attending and timing are inter-linked disputes a great divide in psychology between scholars invested in time perception and those concerned with understanding attention. These two research areas are driven by different theories and have typically trodden different paths. This divide reflects a shared belief that attending has a limited role in time perception (e.g., the attention switch in Figure 22.1). Conversely, time as event structure plays no explanatory role in major attention theories. DAT rejects both these positions because it grounds attending in the temporal structure of events. This weakens the theoretical divide between time perception and attention. It speaks to how we *use* time.

What does "using time" mean?

At last we return to the central question posed in this chapter. DAT implies that people *use* time to guide attending *in the moment*. The term "used" is fleshed out by periods of driving and driven rhythms that create entrainment dyads. As these rhythms synchronize during entrainment, amplitude fluctuations of the driven rhythm supply attending energy aimed at future time points in a driving event rhythm. In Gibson's terms, perceiving an event is revealed when an individual identifies its characteristic, invariant properties. In a DAT framework, such perceiving is only possible when an individual allocates sufficient attending energy in synchrony with an unfolding event.

Perceiving an event uses the rate and rhythm of that event, possibly at several time scales, to accomplish this. In melodic events, these temporal relations are outlined by more or less salient tone onsets. In speech, various effective driving rhythms are outlined by different salient time-markers also across several time scales (Ding and Simon 2012, 2014; Giraud and Poeppel 2012; Ding *et al.* 2014). It is the selective coincidence of heightened attending energy with occurrences of certain time-markers in these events that promotes event perception. In this way, time is used to synchronize a driven rhythm with a driving one. And because synchrony itself assumes many forms, some synchronous states take longer to achieve than others (McAuley and Jones 2003).

Psychologists conventionally distinguish voluntary from involuntary attending. With voluntary attending, one consciously intends to focus upon certain features of an event; this happens, for instance, when told to "pay attention to pitch" in a tone sequence. On the other hand, involuntary attending occurs when a strong stimulus automatically commands a certain amount of attention. For example, a perturbing louder sound injected into an otherwise lulling sequence will inevitably grab (capture) attending. But entrainment realizes other involuntary attending activities which are more routine. Listeners automatically synchronize at some level with a variety of environmental events, albeit with driven oscillations of modest to low amplitudes. Involuntary entrainment also supports voluntary attending; it is a critical platform for engaging in timely planned attending. Thus, voluntary attending "rides" on the automaticity of involuntary attending, because the latter effortlessly provides the time schedule of an unfolding event. Involuntary attending tacitly enables consciously scheduled boosts of attending energy in a driven rhythm at special times. In this fashion, both involuntary and voluntary attending *use* event timing because the rate and rhythm of an event determine "when" important event features may occur.

Consider, for instance, a simple melodic event. The ability of a listener to follow a sequence of tones of different pitches depends on the automatic entrainment of a listener's driven rhythm. This rhythm may carry modest levels of attending energy (as low oscillator amplitudes) which critically instantiates automatic temporal expectancies. These expectancies allow a listener to effortlessly "track" successive melodic tones. As well, voluntary attending exploits this entraining activity in scheduling certain boosts in amplitude of the ongoing driven rhythm at certain relevant time points.

Two examples of event perception

Let's consider two examples that clarify the impact of event timing on event perception, given this dynamic perspective. The aim is to illustrate the role of two forms of selective attending, just identified, in event perception.

Example 1: Localized focal attending. This example illustrates focal attending with phase-specific expectancy pulses. A listener encounters several melodies, each consisting of nine tones with different pitches. Each melody occurs three times; on the third presentation, sometimes a pitch target tone (the eighth tone) is changed. Listeners had to identify the pitch of this target tone.

The aim was to discover how well listeners perceive these melodies when event time structure is varied (Jones *et al.* 2006). Each melody was characterized by a regular series of inter-tone-intervals strongly marked by tone onsets, suggesting a strong driving rhythm. However, experimentally, the event timing in the third presentation was varied so that, equally often, the target tone appeared on time, early or late, given preceding event time structure. (Note, the surrounding event time structure implicates a simple prevailing attractor state of **n:m** = 1:1; both driving rhythm and driven rhythms were roughly isochronous and the same rate.)

In theory, DAT maintains that the context driving rhythm will automatically engage involuntary attending in this task. That is, some involuntary attending energy is effortlessly carried along in the driven rhythm's amplitude during entrainment. Furthermore, given task demands, listeners will also voluntarily add energy to optimize focal attending near the eighth tone.

Importantly, when perceiving such events, people do not judge time intervals. Instead, they use these intervals to selectively attend in time to certain melodic features, including the pitch of a target tone. In this regard, DAT conceives of time as relevant to attending dynamics, although many psychologists will disagree with this view. This is because "relevance" usually refers to explicitly cued material, here pitch. In short, conventionally the relevant dimension in this task is deemed to be the pitch dimension, with the time dimension considered irrelevant.

So how irrelevant is the time dimension in event perception? Figure 22.3 presents data that answers this question. For a melodic event, this plot shows a measure of listeners' average accuracy in identifying target pitches in different melodies (d' scores) as a function of target time (early, on time, late). Clearly, perception is best for expected, on time, target tones. This implies

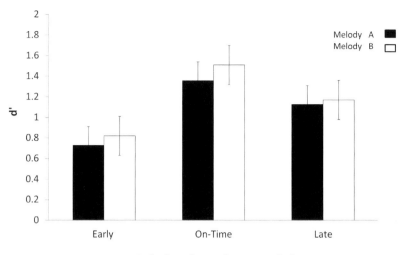

Perceiving Melodic Events

Figure 22.3   Performance in an event perception. Listeners identify the pitch of single target different melodies. High d' reflect best performance for on-time targets

that listeners use event time structure to guide focal attending to the "right" points in time to pick up target pitch information. Generalizing, a temporal expectancy, carried by expectancy pulses, delivers more attending energy to expected than to unexpected points in time. Such findings not only confirm DAT's predictions, they suggest that people use the time of both the driving and driven rhythm to perceive a musical event.

This first example sheds light on one form of attentional selectivity. Specifically, it illustrates that localized focal attending is selective, favoring phase-specific expected targets over unexpected ones. Selectivity here depends on specific heightening of driven rhythm expectancy pulses at regular time points in a melody, especially near the event's ending.

Example 2: General focal attending. This second example illustrates selective attending that is period-specific in heightening the amplitude of driven rhythm (relative to other oscillations). This applies to the cocktail party paradigm where a listener engages in blanket selective attending that systematically "tunes out" all irrelevant talkers. According to DAT, this entails a relative heightening of the overall amplitude of the driven rhythm at a particular time scale. For instance, a listener boosts the amplitude of the oscillation entraining to a certain talker's speaking rate and/or lowers the amplitudes of speaking rates of other talkers.

A musical parallel to the cocktail party paradigm also exists. It presents listeners with different interleaved melodies; two different melodies are interwoven in a piece of music. One melodic line consists of high pitched tones (H) that alternate with pitches of a second melody involving only low pitched tones (L), as in HLHLHL . . . It is possible to simultaneously direct attending to tones in both melodic lines, especially if overall timing is regular (this is *divided attending*). However, more pertinent is *selective attending*, as characterized in the cocktail party paradigm, which entails attending to only one musical line.

A study of a musical analog of the cocktail party scenario involved interleaving high with low pitched melodic lines. Listeners had to selectively attend to only one of the two melodies (Klein and Jones 1996). They were best at perceiving a target melody when this melody was temporally regular and a competing (to-be-ignored) melody was temporally irregular. In short, selective attending depends on the overall rhythmic context in which an event appears.

What are these driven rhythms?

A dynamic attending framework views driven rhythms as cortical oscillations capable of entrainment. These hypothesized driven rhythms are neither fictional, nor epiphenomenal; nor are they metaphors for attention. Instead, driven rhythms are biological components in the basic theoretical unit, a driving/driven dyad. The idea that cortical oscillations may entrain to external driving rhythms was originally proposed in 1976; it is fair to say this met with skepticism at that time (Jones 1976).

Historically, psychology has had an ambivalent stance with respect to brain oscillations. First discovered by Berger in 1929 (the alpha rhythm), brain rhythms were initially treated as curiosities. Yet, as the array of recorded (EEGs) cortical rhythms of different time scales (frequencies) accumulated over the century, neural oscillations became more difficult to ignore. Nevertheless, psychologists were slow to figure out a function for these cortical oscillations. Particularly with theories of attention and memory, wedded to mechanical filtering or encoding/storage metaphors (respectively), discoveries of cortical oscillations were greeted with reserve or dismissed as epiphenomena, i.e., as curious side-effects of real processing activity with no explanatory power.

Contemporary theorizing is more receptive to discoveries of neuroscience. However, few psychological theories explicitly incorporate a role for neural oscillations as driven rhythms in an entrainment process. The groundbreaking research of Charles Schroeder, Peter Lakatos, and colleagues is a notable exception (Lakatos *et al.* 2008; Schroeder and Lakatos 2009; Canolty and Knight 2010; Ding and Simon 2012, 2014; Zion Golumbic *et al.* 2013). Notably, in 2008, Lakatos and Schroeder studied selective attending in a paradigm resembling the interleaved melody experiment just described (Klein and Jones 1996). They presented two different interleaved driving rhythms to participants (humans, monkeys). Instead of high and low pitched melodic tones, one driving rhythm was marked by onsets of brief lights, the other by onsets of beeps. Each driving rhythm had a period that fluctuated around 650 ms (delta range for driven correlates).

Intriguingly, these scientists discovered that brains of both humans and monkeys were tunable, i.e., capable of entrainment. They recorded momentary cortical activities of driven rhythms as these neural rhythms synchronized to external driving rhythms and discovered that both species could effortlessly "keep time" with each of the interleaved driving rhythms. Moreover, participants could voluntarily delegate greater attending energy to one of the interleaved rhythms when it was cued in advance, i.e., they voluntarily attended selectively to either the auditory or the visual sequence.

These findings confirm a prominent role for the driven rhythm amplitude as a source of selective attending with cortical oscillations. Moreover, timing was a critical platform for this. Synchrony between driven and driving rhythms was observed in oscillations tracking both auditory and visual sequences. Thus, selective attending to an initially cued sequence (auditory or visual) was realized by more stable phase-locking between the entraining neural oscillation and its cued (relevant) driving rhythm than for the un-cued (irrelevant) driving rhythm.

Summary

Behavioral and neuroscience studies find compelling evidence for entrainment of cortical oscillations in attending to events. Indeed, the recent explosion of neuroscience research strengthens the case for neural oscillations capable of entraining to external events, whether musical or speech events. It seems clear that despite lingering tendencies in psychology to treat event time structure as irrelevant to event perception, evidence is emerging to suggest that event perception depends on well-timed allocations of attending energy. All of this leads us to revisit Gibson's claim that *we don't perceive time, we perceive events*. A less eloquent version of this phrase may be closer to the truth:

We don't perceive time well, because we use time to perceive events.

References

Barnes, R. and Jones, M. R. (2000) "Expectancy, attention, and time", *Cognitive Psychology* 41(3): 254–311.

Canolty, R. T. and Knight, R. T. (2010) "The functional role of cross-frequency coupling", *Trends in Cognitive Sciences* 14(11): 506–515.

Cherry, E. C. (1953) "Some experiments on the recognition of speech, with one and with two ears", *The Journal of the Acoustical Society of America* 25(5): 974–979.

Church, R. M., Meck, W. H. and Gibbon, J. (1994) "Application of scalar timing theory to individual trials", *Journal of Experimental Psychology: Animal Behavior Processes* 20(2): 135–155.

Ding, N. and Simon, J. Z. (2012) "Emergence of neural encoding of auditory objects while listening to competing speakers", *Proceedings of the National Academy of Sciences* 109(29): 11854–11859.

Ding, N. and Simon, J. Z. (2014) "Cortical entrainment to continuous speech: Functional roles and interpretations", *Frontiers in Human Neuroscience* 8(311): 1–7.

Ding, N., Chatterjee, M. and Simon, J. Z. (2014) "Robust cortical entrainment to the speech envelope relies on the spectro-temporal fine structure", *NeuroImage*, 88: 41–46.

Gibbon, J. (1977) "Scalar expectancy theory and Weber's Law in animal timing", *Psychological Review* 84(3): 279–325.

Gibson, J. J. (1975) "Events are perceivable but time is not", in J. T. Fraser and N. Lawrence (eds), *The Study of Time II*, Berlin: Springer, pp. 295–301.

Giraud, A.-L. and Poeppel, D. (2012) "Cortical oscillations and speech processing: Emerging computational principles and operations", *Nature Neuroscience* 15(4): 511–517.

Grondin, S. (2010) "Timing and time perception: A review of recent behavioral and neuroscience findings theoretical directions", *Attention, Perception and Psychophysics* 17(4): 561–582.

Henry, M. J. and Obleser, J. (2012) "Frequency modulation entrains slow oscillations and optimizes human listening behavior", *Proceedings of the National Academy of Sciences* 109(49): 20095–20100.

Jones, M. R. (1976) "Time, our lost dimension: Toward a new theory of perception, attention, and memory", *Psychological Review* 83(5): 323–355.

Jones, M. R. and Boltz, M. (1989) "Dynamic attending and responses to time", *Psychological Review* 96(3): 459–491.

Jones, M. R., Boltz, M. G. and Klein, J. M. (1993) "Expected endings and judged duration", *Memory & Cognition* 21(5): 646–665.

Jones, M. R., Johnston, H. M. and Puente, J. (2006) "Effects of auditory pattern structure on anticipatory and reactive attending", *Cognitive Psychology* 53: 59–96.

Klein, J. M. and Jones, M. R. (1996) "Effects of attentional set and rhythmic complexity on attending", *Perception & Psychophysics* 58(1): 34–46.

Lakatos, P., Karmos, G., Mehta, A. D., Ulbert, I. and Schroeder, C. E. (2008) "Entrainment of neuronal oscillations as a mechanism of attentional selection", *Science* 320(5872): 110–113.

Large, E. W. and Jones, M. R. (1999) "The dynamics of attending: How people track time-varying events", *Psychological Review* 106(1): 119–159.

Martin, J. G. (1972) "Rhythmic (hierarchical) versus serial structure in speech and other behavior", *Psychological Review* 79(6): 487–509.

Matthews, W. J. and Meck, W. H. (2016) "Temporal cognition: Connecting subjective time to perception, attention, and memory", *Psychological Bulletin* 142(8): 865–907.

McAuley, J. D. and Jones, M. R. (2003) "Modeling effects of rhythmic context on perceived duration: A comparison of interval and entrainment approaches to short-interval timing", *Journal of Experimental Psychology: Human Perception and Performance* 29(6): 1102–1125.

McAuley, J. D. and Kidd, G. R. (1998) "Effect of deviations from temporal expectations on tempo discrimination of isochronous tone sequences", *Journal of Experimental Psychology: Human Perception and Performance* 24(6): 1786–1800.

McAuley, J. D., Jones, M. R., Holub, S., Johnston, H. M. and Miller, N. S. (2006) "The time of our lives: Life span development of timing and event tracking", *Journal of Experimental Psychology: General* 135(3): 348–367.

Morton, J. Marcus, S. Frankish, C. (1976) "Perceptual centers (P-centers)", *Psychological Review* 83(5): 405–408.

Schroeder, C. E. and Lakatos, P. (2009) "Low-frequency neuronal oscillations as instruments of sensory selection", *Trends in Neurosciences* 32(1): 9–18.

Tilsen, S. and Arvaniti, A. (2013) "Speech rhythm analysis with decomposition of the amplitude envelope: Characterizing rhythmic patterns within and across languages", *The Journal of the Acoustical Society of America* 134(1): 628–639.

Tilsen, S. and Johnson, K. (2008) "Low-frequency Fourier analysis of speech rhythm", *The Journal of the Acoustical Society of America* 124(2): EL34–EL39.

Treisman, M. (1963) "Temporal discrimination and the indifference interval: Implications for a model of the 'internal clock'", *Psychological Monographs: General and Applied* 77(13): 1–31.

Zion Golumbic, E. M., Ding, N., Bickel, S., Lakatos, P., Schevon, C. A., McKhann, G. M., . . . Schroeder, C. E. (2013) "Mechanisms underlying selective neuronal tracking of attended speech at a 'cocktail party'", *Neuron* 77(5): 980–991.

23

ATTENTIONAL RESOURCES AND THE SHAPING OF TEMPORAL EXPERIENCE

Scott W. Brown

The experimental study of time perception has a long history in psychology, and researchers have approached the problem from many different viewpoints. Stimulus factors, biological mechanisms, and cognitive processes have all been shown to contribute to our experience of time. Cognitively oriented researchers have increasingly shifted the focus toward the role of attention in time perception. Everyday experience shows that paying attention to time, as in conditions of anticipation or boredom, lengthens perceived duration (creating the impression that time drags by slowly), whereas being distracted from time produces a shortening of perceived duration (causing time to speed by quickly). These fundamental experiences form the basis for many of the experimental paradigms devised by time psychologists, who seek to study the phenomena under controlled laboratory conditions. The purpose of this chapter is to provide a brief survey of some of the main methods, findings, and theoretical formulations derived from this work.

Attention, temporal awareness, and the experience of time

The adage "a watched pot never boils" implies that expectancy is an important factor in perceived duration, and in fact some experimental evidence indicates that waiting for a pot of water to boil does indeed lengthen temporal experience (Cahoon and Edmonds 1980). Expectation of an upcoming event leads to a heightened temporal awareness as attention is increasingly drawn to the passage of time (Brown 2008b). There are two particularly noteworthy techniques developed by researchers to examine the role of expectancy on time perception. One method involves the manipulation of musical structure. Rhythmical patterns, changes in pitch, and accent structure allow listeners to predict when a melody should end. These features may be altered to create the impression that a melody ends sooner or later than expected. A series of experiments showed that melodies ending early are perceived to be short, whereas melodies ending late are perceived to be long (Boltz 1989; Jones and Boltz 1989; Jones *et al.* 1993). This phenomenon extends to non-musical situations as well. In one experiment (Boltz 1993), subjects judged the amount of time they spent waiting for an event to occur. Those waiting for a longer-than-expected time overestimated the interval, while those who waited for a shorter-than-expected time underestimated the same interval. A second method is known as the break expectancy procedure, devised by Fortin and Massé (2000). In a typical experiment, subjects judge the duration of a target interval that is defined by a tone. Part way through, the tone is interrupted by a gap of silence before resuming again to complete the interval. The subjects are instructed to combine the prebreak and postbreak tone intervals, and to not include the duration of the break in making their time judgments. The results show a strong effect for the break location, in that later break locations are associated with a shortening of perceived time relative to earlier breaks. This basic finding has been replicated with different time judgment methods, break locations, break intervals, and target durations (Tremblay and Fortin 2003; Fortin *et al.* 2005, 2009). Fortin and Massé (2000) explain the effect in terms of a pacemaker-accumulator model of time perception. Pacemaker-accumulator models are based on the idea that neural pulses constitute a biological substrate for temporal experience. A continuous stream of neural pulses generated by a hypothetical pacemaker mechanism enters an accumulator (or cognitive counter) mechanism, which determines subjective time (Treisman 1963; Wearden 1991). In the context of break expectancy, the growing expectation of a later-occurring break shifts attention toward monitoring for the break and away from timing, which disrupts the pulse accumulation process. Fewer accumulated pulses result in a shortening of perceived time.

One straightforward way to manipulate temporal awareness is to explicitly direct subjects' attention to the passage of time. Mattes and Ulrich (1998) and Enns *et al.* (1999) have reported systematic investigations on this topic. Collectively, these researchers present data from nine separate experiments in which subjects were provided with cues to attend to certain stimuli for time judgments. Attention was directed to particular stimuli (auditory or visual), or to different locations in a visual display in which stimuli appear. The various studies employed different time judgment methods, performance measures, and stimulus durations. Despite these variations, all the experiments produced the same basic result: directed attention to time lengthens perceived duration.

Another important method for studying attention and time is the oddball paradigm, introduced by Tse *et al.* (2004). A stream of identical stimuli (e.g., black disks) is presented in succession on a screen. At random points within the sequence, a different stimulus of variable duration (an oddball) appears. The oddball may be of a different color, shape, or size, and subjects judge the duration of the oddball relative to the standards. The typical finding is that the oddball is perceived to last longer than the standards, even when they are of equal duration. Tse *et al.* (2004) termed this effect "time's subjective expansion", and argued that it occurs because the oddball captures attention so that more information concerning the stimulus (including temporal information) is processed per unit time. The degree of temporal distortion is quite strong; based on several studies, Seifried and Ulrich (2010) concluded that an oddball produces a 10 to 30 percent lengthening of perceived time. Some investigators have probed the boundary conditions of the oddball effect. Pariyadath and Eagleman (2007) presented an auditory tone or a visual flicker in conjunction with standard and oddball stimuli, and subjects judged whether the pitch or flicker frequency was higher or lower with the oddball compared with the standards. The subjects were accurate in making these judgments, despite the fact that these conditions reliably lengthen the perceived duration of the oddball. Pariyadath and Eagleman (2007) concluded that perceived time in general was not affected, but rather that the temporal distortion applied to the oddball itself. In other work, however, New and Scholl (2009) demonstrated that oddballs are able to lengthen time for other stimuli within the visual display. A series of constant-duration colored squares appeared in the center of a screen, each associated with a peripheral gray disk. Infrequently, a green target square of variable duration appeared, and subjects judged whether the target was longer or shorter than the standards. Some green squares were accompanied by an oddball peripheral disk that either expanded in size or rotated in place. Targets with peripheral oddballs were perceived to last longer. The researchers found that the effect was not diminished by locating the oddballs farther away from the targets, leading them to conclude that the lengthening of perceived time applied to the entire visual display.

A number of studies have focused on the nature of the oddball stimulus. Schindel *et al.* (2011) showed that the more deviant the oddball is from the standard stimuli, the stronger the lengthening effect. This view reinforces the notion that attention is drawn to the oddball because of its oddness. Along the same lines, Kim and McAuley (2013) investigated auditory oddballs, and discovered that oddballs that deviated more in pitch from standard tones were perceived as lasting longer than oddballs that were nearer in pitch to the standards. Ulrich *et al.* (2006) manipulated the frequency with which oddballs occurred within a stimulus stream, and found that infrequent oddballs were perceived as lasting longer than frequent ones. Research by Van Wassenhove *et al.* (2008) indicated that the salience of the oddball, whether it is expected or not, is a critical factor in the temporal distortion. The standard stimuli were constant-duration steady visual disks or pure tones; the variable-duration target stimuli to be judged always occupied position four in a five-item sequence. These targets were either steady disks or tones (control condition), or expanding disks, or increasing-frequency tones (oddball condition). These oddballs are known as looming stimuli because they create the impression that an object is approaching. The results showed that the looming targets were perceived to be longer than the steady targets (see also New and Scholl 2009). However, when the targets were receding (shrinking disks or decreasing-frequency tones), there were no effects on perceived duration. The authors argued that the results reflect ecological relevance. Looming objects are highly salient because they signal approach and potential threat, and so they capture attention more than receding stimuli.

Attentional resources in timing

The distraction of attention away from the passage of time has been the focus of a large amount of research. The most consistent finding in the timing literature is a result known as the "interference effect". The interference effect refers to a disruption in timing performance when subjects must attend to the passage of time and simultaneously perform a demanding distractor task (Brown 1997). Typically, such dual-task situations cause time judgments to become shorter, more variable, and/or more inaccurate compared with timing-only, single-task conditions (see Brown 1997, 2008b, 2010; Block *et al.* 2010 for reviews of this work). Virtually any type of distractor task (e.g., mental arithmetic, manual tracking, visual search, target detection, etc.) will reliably interfere with timing performance. In one variation of this paradigm, the multiple timing procedure, subjects are required to attend to two or more overlapping intervals for a subsequent judgment of one of those intervals selected at random (Brown and West 1990; Brown *et al.* 1992; Ambro and Czigler 1998; Vanneste and Pouthas 1999). One study (Brown and West 1990) showed that time judgments displayed a linear increase in error as subjects attended to one, two, three, or four simultaneous intervals. In other research, experimenters have sought to vary systematically the difficulty of the concurrent distractor task. Reviews of this literature (Brown 1997, 2008b) indicate that in the majority of these studies, increased distractor task demands lead to progressively greater error in time judgment performance.

The interference effect may be explained by reference to an attentional allocation model (Hicks *et al.* 1977; Brown 1985; Zakay 1989; Brown and West 1990). The argument is that attentiveness to time is a capacity-consuming task. As more attention is directed to time, more temporal cues are processed, which produces a lengthening of perceived duration. Dual-task conditions, however, divert attentional resources away from time. The diversion of attention from time reduces the number and/or saliency of temporal cues. This reduction of temporal information creates a more fragmentary temporal record, leading to shortened or less accurate temporal judgments. The attentional-gate model (Block and Zakay 1996; Zakay and Block

1996, 1998) describes this process in terms of a pacemaker-accumulator system. The attentional-gate model postulates the existence of a variable-sized channel or gateway situated between the pacemaker and the accumulator. As more attention is directed to time, the gate becomes wider, allowing more impulses to pass through to the accumulator, which leads to a lengthening of perceived time. Less attention to time (as in dual-task situations) narrows the gate, reducing the number of impulses that are accumulated, thereby producing a shortening of perceived time.

A different approach to manipulating attention in dual-task timing situations is to employ the attentional sharing procedure in which subjects are instructed to devote specified amounts of attention to concurrent tasks. For example, subjects may be asked to devote 25 percent of their attention to one task and 75 percent to the other task. This method was originally devised by researchers studying visual discrimination (Sperling and Melchner 1978; Kinchla 1980), who found that subjects were remarkably accurate at dividing varying proportions of attention between two different spatial locations. Time psychologists studying the interference effect have applied the procedure to concurrent timing and distractor tasks (e.g., Casini et al. 1992; Grondin and Macar 1992; Coull et al. 2004). The usual finding is that as attention is progressively withdrawn from the timing task, temporal judgments become correspondingly shorter or less accurate. That is, less and less attention to time leads to a stronger and stronger interference effect, as predicted by the attentional allocation model.

According to attentional resource theorists, dual-task performance is usually quite difficult because the resource demands of the concurrent tasks exceed available capacity. Due to resource competition, performance on one or both tasks suffers. One way to mitigate this problem is through automaticity. Automaticity refers to a reduction in the resources needed to perform a task as a consequence of extensive practice (Moors and De Houwer 2006). With practice, the task becomes routine and predictable, various cognitive components of the task such as memory and decision making drop out of conscious awareness, and the task is easier to perform in an automatic fashion requiring less effort than before (Laberge and Samuels 1974; Logan 1988). Automaticity training has been shown to lessen dual-task interference. The standard technique is to practice one task sufficiently to achieve automaticity, then pair it with some concurrent task. Because the automatized task uses fewer resources than normal, dual-task interference is minimized (e.g., Ruthruff et al. 2001). Brown (1998a; Brown and Bennett 2002) sought to use automaticity training to reduce the interference effect in timing. Subjects in these experiments received practice on either manual tracking or mirror-reversed reading tasks. Prior to practice, these distractor tasks produced the expected interference effect on concurrent time judgments. After practice, however, interference was sharply reduced, a result termed the "attenuation effect". In later research, Brown (2008a) tested the hypothesis that practice on a timing task would also attenuate the interference effect. In a practice phase, subjects reproduced a series of intervals either with or without feedback regarding reproduction accuracy. In a test phase, subjects reproduced the intervals while simultaneously performing a digit memory task. The results showed that time judgment training reduced the interference effect in timing. All this work supports the idea that keeping track of time is an attentional task that is essentially similar in nature to other resource-demanding cognitive tasks.

Relation between timing and executive functions

Resource theorists contend that attentional resources are always limited, and that dual-task situations necessitate that those resources be shared between the multiple tasks. Brown (2006) reasoned that the same principle should apply to concurrent timing and distractor tasks. Ample evidence demonstrates an interference effect in timing responses, and so a parallel effect should also occur for performance on the concurrent distractor task. That is, the temporal and distractor tasks would be expected to produce a pattern of bidirectional interference, with each task interfering with the other due to resource competition. Unfortunately, most time researchers have concentrated exclusively on timing performance and have disregarded distractor task performance. In a survey of this literature, Brown (2006) found only 33 studies that reported timing and distractor task performance under both single-task and dual-task conditions. Approximately half the studies showed the predicted pattern of bidirectional interference, whereas the other half showed interference with timing only. Those experiments demonstrating bidirectional interference tended to involve distractor tasks that emphasized attention, working memory, and other higher-level cognitive processes; in contrast, experiments reporting interference with timing only tended to include tasks requiring lower-level processing such as visual search, pattern detection, and perceptual judgment. These results may be understood in the context of multiple resource theory (Wickens 1980, 1991; Gopher *et al.* 1982; Cocchini *et al.* 2002), which proposes that rather than a single pool of undifferentiated attentional resources, there exist a number of specialized resource pools dedicated to specific processing demands (e.g., visual, auditory, motor, etc.). Brown (2006) argued that the common feature associated with the distractor tasks producing bidirectional interference with timing is that those tasks invoked executive cognitive resources. The implication is that timing processes depend upon the same attentional resources devoted to executive functions.

Executive functions are those cognitive processes that serve to control thought and regulate behavior (Royall and Mahurin 1996; Stuss and Alexander 2000; Banich 2009). These functions include basic control processes such as inhibiting distractions, switching or shifting attention between different tasks, planning future actions, updating memory, reasoning, and decision making (Burgess 1997; Miyake *et al.* 2000; Jurado and Rosselli 2007). Many of these functions involve coordination, scheduling, and sequencing, processes that are essentially temporal in nature. According to the executive resource theory of timing, tasks such as attending to time, tracking temporal relations between events, and estimating interval durations all require the involvement of executive attentional resources (Brown 1997, 2008b; Brown *et al.* 2013). Bidirectional interference occurs between concurrent timing and executive tasks because of competition for the same set of specialized executive resources. These ideas have led to an increasing research interest in issues related to the nature of the distractor tasks used in timing experiments, distractor task performance, and the role of executive cognitive functions in time perception.

Distractor tasks associated with the executive functions of memory updating, sequencing, and attentional switching have been the focus of a number of recent timing studies. Memory updating involves replacing obsolete information in working memory with newer information. Research entailing various types of updating tasks has demonstrated a reliable pattern of findings. Tasks requiring subjects to report the last few items of a serial list of unpredictable length (Brown and Frieh 2000), to track the changing status of multiple events (Brown *et al.* 2013), to remember the identity of the item two places back in an ongoing series (Krampe *et al.* 2010), and to continuously count backwards by sevens from a three-digit starting number (Ogden *et al.* 2011) have all shown bidirectional interference with concurrent timing tasks. Researchers have also examined the effects of distractor tasks that emphasize another basic executive function, the sequencing or ordering of events. Experiments involving sequence monitoring (Brown and Merchant 2007), sequence reasoning (Brown 2014), and temporal order memory (Brown and Smith-Petersen 2014) have all produced strong evidence of bidirectional interference with concurrent timing. However, studies involving randomization tasks in which subjects are required to generate a sequence of random numbers or letters are less consistent. Whereas Brown (2006) found bidirectional interference between concurrent timing and randomization tasks, Ogden *et al.* (2011) reported interference with the timing task only. Ogden *et al.* (2011) noted that one possible explanation for these discrepant findings is that Brown's (2006) randomization task may have been more demanding of executive resources than that of their own. Findings pertaining to another executive function, attentional switching, are uneven. There are four main studies in this area. Brown *et al.* (2013) had subjects respond to either the local (smaller) or global (larger) elements of visual displays based on an unpredictable cue while they performed a concurrent time judgment task, and found a strong pattern of bidirectional interference in task performance. In contrast, Ogden *et al.* (2011) employed an alternating addition and subtraction task and reported interference with the concurrent timing task only. Fortin *et al.* (2010) and Viau-Quesnel and Fortin (2014) had subjects make differential responses to letter or digit stimuli while judging short intervals. Switching between stimulus types interfered with letter/digit performance, but had no effect on concurrent timing performance. It is unclear as to whether the switching tasks used in these experiments are equivalent, or whether their demand on executive attentional resources is comparable.

Inhibition is a fundamental executive function that was the focus of a recent multi-experiment project that was designed to overcome this issue of the comparability of various executive cognitive tasks. Brown *et al.* (2015) conducted four dual-task timing experiments, with each experiment involving a well-established task emphasizing inhibitory control. There is agreement among theorists that inhibition is not a unified construct, but rather consists of several related processes (e.g., Friedman and Miyake 2004; Hasher *et al.* 2007). Nigg (2000) identified four separate inhibitory functions: interference control (preventing interference due to resource competition), cognitive inhibition (suppressing irrelevant information from working memory), behavioral inhibition (suppressing automatic responses), and oculomotor inhibition (suppressing reflexive eye movements toward a sudden stimulus). Brown *et al.* (2015) selected an inhibition task representing each of these functions to serve as a distractor task in conjunction with a concurrent temporal judgment task. The goal was to determine whether some or all of these inhibition tasks would produce a pattern of bidirectional interference with timing. The results showed that, relative to single-task control conditions, each inhibition task interfered with timing performance and timing interfered with inhibition performance. Moreover, weaker versions of the inhibition tasks requiring a lesser degree of inhibitory control produced weaker interference effects. One additional aspect of the research involves cognitive aging, in that subjects belonged to two age groups (either age 30 years or younger or age 60 years or older). A great deal of research indicates that executive functioning, and especially inhibitory control, declines with age (see Hasher and Zacks 1988; Stoltzfus *et al.* 1996). Because older individuals presumably have diminished executive resource capacity, it was expected that older subjects would exhibit a stronger pattern of bidirectional interference compared with younger subjects. This predicted outcome did in fact occur in three of the four experiments. Overall, the research substantiates the idea that timing is supported by executive attentional resources.

Brown *et al.* (2013) approached the issue of executive functioning and timing from a broader perspective. Miyake *et al.* (2000) conducted an extensive psychometric investigation of executive functions, and concluded that a wide range of executive tasks ultimately represented a core set of just three separable executive functions, namely shifting, updating, and inhibition. Brown *et al.* (2013) devised three dual-task timing experiments, each involving a distractor task associated with one of these three functions, in an effort to determine whether timing was related to a greater or lesser degree to any particular function. The main feature of the research is that resource allocation was manipulated with the attentional sharing procedure. Subjects were instructed to devote attention to the concurrent timing and executive tasks in specific proportions: 25 percent–75 percent, 50 percent–50 percent, and 75 percent–25 percent. The findings demonstrated a reciprocity effect involving performance tradeoffs between the timing and executive tasks. As more attention was directed to the timing task, timing performance improved and executive performance declined; as more attention was directed to the executive task, the opposite pattern occurred. The same basic pattern applied to all three executive functions. The results imply that the timing and executive tasks shared the same set of resources, and that the three basic executive functions are all related to temporal processing.

Unanswered questions and future directions

Since the 1990s, there has been a substantial increase in research on the role of attentional processes in time perception. New paradigms, theoretical models, and empirical findings have helped establish time perception within the larger field of cognitive psychology and cognitive neuroscience. These advances have inevitably also opened up a series of additional questions and uncertainties which point to future research directions.

Some issues pertain to the relation between timing and executive functions. One concern is the "task impurity problem", which refers to the idea that executive tasks typically consist of multiple executive and non-executive components (e.g., Burgess 1997). Tasks that purportedly represent the same executive function typically produce low correlations, presumably because each task possesses its own unique mix of executive and non-executive elements (Van der Sluis *et al.* 2007; Miyake and Friedman 2012). Task impurity creates a serious challenge in interpreting the outcomes of dual-task interference timing studies. If one experiment finds evidence of bidirectional interference with some task related to a particular executive function, but another experiment fails to obtain this result when using a different task that supposedly measures the same executive function, then it is unclear as to which component features of the tasks are critical for the different findings. A related issue involves what is known as the "unity versus diversity" of executive functions. Psychometric investigations of executive tasks (Miyake *et al.* 2000; Miyake and Friedman 2012) show that such tasks are statistically related (unity), but are also statistically separable (diversity). Unity implies the existence of a common, general-purpose set of executive attentional resources, whereas diversity implicates special-purpose resources dedicated to specific executive functions. Time perception studies showing bidirectional interference across different executive functions supports the view that timing relies on generalized executive resources; studies demonstrating bidirectional interference with only some executive functions but not with others is consistent with the idea that timing is related to a subset of specialized executive resources. Firm conclusions must await further research involving a wider assortment of executive tasks than employed in the studies that currently exist.

Another relevant yet largely unexplored issue concerns individual differences in timing ability. Identifying individual differences would not only strengthen the statistical power of experiments by reducing response variability, but would also provide a different avenue for the study of attention and time. In an early paper, Brown *et al.* (1995) developed a duration discrimination task to classify subjects into high and low temporal sensitivity groups. They showed that high sensitivity subjects were also more accurate on a temporal reproduction task and benefitted more from informational feedback on a temporal production task, relative to low sensitivity subjects. In subsequent research (Brown 1998b), high and low temporal sensitivity groups performed timing and digit memory tasks under dual-task conditions. Increases in memory task difficulty led to greater time judgment error for both groups, but the low sensitivity subjects averaged 4.5 to 5.0 percent more timing error under all conditions compared with the high sensitivity subjects. The low sensitivity subjects were also more variable on a serial temporal production task. Other research has examined the role of individual differences in working memory as a mediator in temporal processing. Working memory refers to a cognitive system that controls attention, and that maintains and manipulates information being actively held in memory. Working memory capacity (WMC) varies between individuals and has been shown to relate to numerous cognitive processes, including a variety of executive functions. Broadway and Engle (2011a) compared high and low WMC groups on a temporal discrimination task, and found that the high WMC subjects were more sensitive at discriminating intervals across a range of durations and duration differences. The authors suggested that the low WMC subjects had lapses of attention to presented intervals, and experienced greater confusion between the memory representations of previous intervals. In another study, Broadway and Engle (2011b) reported that low WMC subjects made more variable responses on a temporal reproduction task compared with high WMC subjects. Relative to high WMC subjects, the low WMC subjects also showed a stronger effect related to Vierordt's law, which refers to a tendency to overestimate the short intervals in a series and underestimate the longer intervals. Woehrle and Magliano (2012) had high and low WMC groups perform concurrent temporal production and arithmetic tasks in which the arithmetic task was primary (higher priority) and the timing task was secondary (lower priority). The results revealed that the low WMC subjects tended to be less accurate at arithmetic but more accurate at timing, whereas the high WMC subjects showed the opposite pattern. The authors argued that the high WMC subjects lost track of time because they prioritized the arithmetic task over the timing task; the low WMC subjects were more distracted by time's passage.

One final approach to the role of individual differences in timing was offered by Ogden *et al.* (2014), who sought to determine whether different executive functions are differentially involved in different timing tasks. Based on their performance on representative executive tasks, the subjects were divided into high and low scorers for memory updating, attentional switching, inhibition, and access to semantic memory (i.e., verbal fluency). The results showed that access influenced performance on temporal generalization, reproduction, and verbal estimation timing tasks; updating was also related to the generalization and reproduction tasks. None of the timing tasks was influenced by inhibition, which suggested to the authors that these resources are not involved in timing. However, it is important to note that these findings are based on single executive tasks chosen to represent particular executive functions, and so are constrained by the task impurity problem. But this basic approach in considering variations in executive function, along with those emphasizing temporal sensitivity and WMC, has great potential to lead to a more detailed understanding of the role of individual differences in attentional processes and time perception.

More than any other single cognitive process, attention exerts a powerful influence on one's perception of time. Attentional focus, attentional allocation, and resource specialization all act to shape our temporal experience and the perceived duration of events.

References

Ambro, A. and Czigler, I. (1998) "Parallel estimation of short durations in humans", in V. DeKeyser, G. d'Ydewalle and A. Vandierendonck (eds), *Time and the Dynamic Control of Behavior*, Seattle, WA: Hogrefe and Huber, pp. 143–156.

Banich, M. T. (2009) "Executive function: The search for an integrated account", *Current Directions in Psychological Science* 18(2): 89–94.

Block, R. A. and Zakay, D. (1996) "Models of psychological time revisited", in H. Helfrich (ed.), *Time and Mind*, Seattle, WA: Hogrefe and Huber, pp. 171–195.

Block, R. A., Hancock, P. A. and Zakay, D. (2010) "How cognitive load affects duration judgments: A meta-analytic review", *Acta Psychologica* 134: 330–343.

Boltz, M. G. (1989) "Time judgments of musical endings: Effects of expectancies on the 'filled interval effect'", *Perception and Psychophysics* 46(5): 409–418.

Boltz, M. G. (1993) "Time estimation and expectancies", *Memory and Cognition* 21(6): 853–863.

Broadway, J. M. and Engle, R. W. (2011a) "Individual differences in working memory capacity and temporal discrimination", *PLoS ONE* 6: e25422.

Broadway, J. M. and Engle, R. W. (2011b) "Lapsed attention to elapsed time? Individual differences in working memory capacity and temporal reproduction", *Acta Psychologica* 137(1): 115–126.

Brown, S. W. (1985) "Time perception and attention: The effects of prospective versus retrospective paradigms and task demands on perceived duration", *Perception and Psychophysics* 38(2): 115–124.

Brown, S. W. (1997) "Attentional resources in timing: Interference effects in concurrent temporal and nontemporal working memory tasks", *Perception and Psychophysics* 59(7): 1118–1140.

Brown, S. W. (1998a) "Automaticity versus timesharing in timing and tracking dual-task performance", *Psychological Research* 61(1): 71–81.

Brown, S. W. (1998b) "Influence of individual differences in temporal sensitivity on timing performance", *Perception* 27(5): 609–625.

Brown, S. W. (2006) "Timing and executive function: Bidirectional interference between concurrent temporal production and randomization tasks", *Memory and Cognition* 34(7): 1464–1471.

Brown, S. W. (2008a) "The attenuation effect in timing: Counteracting dual-task interference with time judgment skill training", *Perception* 37(5): 712–724.

Brown, S. W. (2008b) "Time and attention: Review of the literature", in S. Grondin (ed.), *Psychology of Time*, Bingley, UK: Emerald, pp. 111–138.

Brown, S. W. (2010) "Timing, resources, and interference: Attentional modulation of time perception", in K. C. Nobre and J. T. Coull (eds), *Attention and Time*, New York: Oxford University Press, pp. 107–121.

Brown, S. W. (2014) "Involvement of shared resources in time judgment and sequence reasoning tasks", *Acta Psychologica* 147: 92–96.

Brown, S. W. and Bennett, E. D. (2002) "The role of practice and automaticity in temporal and nontemporal dual-task performance", *Psychological Research* 66(1): 80–89.

Brown, S. W. and Frieh, C. T. (2000) "Information processing in the central executive: Effects of concurrent temporal production and memory updating tasks", in P. Desain and L. Windsor (eds), *Rhythm Perception and Production*, Lisse, The Netherlands: Swets & Zeitlinger, pp. 193–196.

Brown, S. W. and Merchant, S. M. (2007) "Processing resources in timing and sequencing tasks", *Perception and Psychophysics* 69(3): 439–449.

Brown, S. W. and Smith-Petersen, G. A. (2014) "Time perception and temporal order memory", *Acta Psychologica* 148: 173–180.

Brown, S. W. and West, A. N. (1990) "Multiple timing and the allocation of attention", *Acta Psychologica* 75(2): 103–121.

Brown, S. W., Collier, S. A. and Night, J. C. (2013) "Timing and executive resources: Dual-task interference patterns between temporal production and shifting, updating, and inhibition tasks", *Journal of Experimental Psychology: Human Perception and Performance* 39: 947–963.

Brown, S. W., Johnson, T. M., Sohl, M. E. and Dumas, M. K. (2015) "Executive attentional resources in timing: Effects of inhibitory control and cognitive aging", *Journal of Experimental Psychology: Human Perception and Performance* 41: 1063–1083.

Brown, S. W., Newcomb, D. C. and Kahrl, K. G. (1995) "Temporal-signal detection and individual differences in timing", *Perception* 24: 525–538.

Brown, S. W., Stubbs, D. A. and West, A. N. (1992) "Attention, multiple timing, and psychophysical scaling of temporal judgments", in F. Macar, V. Pouthas and W. J. Friedman (eds), *Time, Action, and Cognition: Towards Bridging the Gap*, Dordrecht, The Netherlands: Kluwer Academic Publishers, pp. 129–140.

Burgess, P. W. (1997) "Theory and methodology in executive function research", in P. Rabbit (ed.), *Methodology of Frontal and Executive Function*, Hove, UK: Psychology Press, pp. 81–116.

Cahoon, D. and Edmonds, E. M. (1980) "The watched pot still won't boil: Expectancy as a variable in estimating the passage of time", *Bulletin of the Psychonomic Society* 16(2): 115–116.

Casini, L., Macar, F. and Grondin, S. (1992) "Time estimation and attentional sharing", in F. Macar, V. Pouthas and W. J. Friedman (eds), *Time, Action, and Cognition: Towards Bridging the Gap*, Dordrecht, The Netherlands: Kluwer Academic Publishers, pp. 177–180.

Cocchini, G., Logie, R. H., Della Sala, S., MacPherson, S. E. and Baddeley, A. D. (2002) "Concurrent performance of two memory tasks: Evidence for domain-specific working memory systems", *Memory and Cognition* 30(7): 1086–1095.

Coull, J. T., Vidal, F., Nazarian, B. and Macar, F. (2004) "Functional anatomy of the attentional modulation of time estimation", *Science* 303(5663): 1506–1508.

Enns, J. T., Brehaut, J. C. and Shore, D. I. (1999) "The duration of a brief event in the mind's eye", *Journal of General Psychology* 126(4): 355–372.

Fortin, C. and Massé, N. (2000) "Expecting a break in time estimation: Attentional time-sharing without concurrent processing", *Journal of Experimental Psychology: Human Perception and Performance* 26(6): 1788–1796.

Fortin, C., Bédard, M-C. and Champagne, J. (2005) "Timing during interruptions in timing", *Journal of Experimental Psychology: Human Perception and Performance* 31(2): 276–288.

Fortin, C., Fairhurst, S., Malapani, C., Morin, C., Towey, J. and Meck, W. H. (2009) "Expectancy in humans in multisecond peak-interval timing with gaps", *Attention, Perception, and Psychophysics* 71(2): 789–802.

Fortin, C., Schweickert, R., Gaudreault, R. and Viau-Quesnel, C. (2010) "Timing is affected by demands in memory search but not by task switching", *Journal of Experimental Psychology: Human Perception and Performance* 36(3): 580–595.

Friedman, N. P. and Miyake, A. (2004) "The relations among inhibition and interference control functions: A latent-variable analysis", *Journal of Experimental Psychology: General* 133(1): 101–135.

Gopher, D., Brickner, M. and Navon, D. (1982) "Different difficulty manipulations interact differently with task emphasis: Evidence for multiple resources", *Journal of Experimental Psychology: Human Perception and Performance* 8(1): 146–157.

Grondin, S. and Macar, F. (1992) "Dividing attention between temporal and nontemporal tasks: A performance operating characteristic—POC—analysis", in F. Macar, V. Pouthas and W. J. Friedman (eds), *Time, Action, and Cognition: Towards Bridging the Gap*, Dordrecht, The Netherlands: Kluwer Academic Publishers, pp. 119–128.

Hasher, L. and Zacks, R. T. (1988) "Working memory, comprehension, and aging: A review and a new view", in G. H. Bower (ed.), *The Psychology of Learning and Motivation: Advances in Research and Theory*, San Diego, CA: Academic Press, pp. 193–225.

Hasher, L., Lustig, C. and Zacks, R. (2007) "Inhibitory mechanisms and the control of attention", in A. R. A. Conway, C. Jerrold, M. Kane, A. Miyake and J. N. Towse (eds), *Variations in Working Memory*, New York: Oxford University Press, pp. 227–249.

Hicks, R. E., Miller, G. W., Gaes, G. and Bierman, K. (1977) "Concurrent processing demands and the experience of time-in-passing", *American Journal of Psychology* 90(3): 431–446.

Jones, M. R. and Boltz, M. (1989) "Dynamic attending and responses to time", *Psychological Review* 96(3): 459–491.

Jones, M. R., Boltz, M. G. and Klein, J. M. (1993) "Expected endings and judged duration", *Memory and Cognition* 21(5): 646–665.

Jurado, M. B. and Rosselli, M. (2007) "The elusive nature of executive functions: A review of our current understanding", *Neuropsychology Review* 17(3): 213–233.

Kim, E. and McAuley, J. D. (2013) "Effects of pitch distance and likelihood on the perceived duration of deviant auditory events", *Attention, Perception, and Psychophysics* 75: 1547–1558.

Kinchla, R. A. (1980) "The measurement of attention", in R. S. Nickerson (ed.), *Attention and Performance VIII*, Hillsdale, NJ: Erlbaum, pp. 213–238.

Krampe, R. T., Doumas, M., Lavrysen, A. and Rapp, M. (2010) "The costs of taking it slowly: Fast and slow movement timing in older age", *Psychology and Aging* 25: 980–990.

Laberge, D. and Samuels, S. J. (1974) "Toward a theory of automatic information processing in reading", *Cognitive Psychology* 6: 293–323.

Logan, G. D. (1988) "Automaticity, resources, and memory: Theoretical controversies and practical implications", *Human Factors* 30(6): 583–598.

Mattes, S. and Ulrich, R. (1998) "Directed attention prolongs the perceived duration of a brief stimulus", *Perception and Psychophysics* 60(8): 1305–1317.

Miyake, A. and Friedman, N. P. (2012) "The nature and organization of individual differences in executive functions: Four general conclusions", *Current Directions in Psychological Science* 21: 8–14.

Miyake, A., Friedman, N. P., Emerson, M. J., Witzki, A. H., Howerter, A. and Wager, T. (2000) "The unity and diversity of executive functions and their contributions to complex 'frontal lobe' tasks: A latent variable analysis", *Cognitive Psychology* 41(1): 49–100.

Moors, A. and De Houwer, J. (2006) "Automaticity: A theoretical and conceptual analysis", *Psychological Bulletin* 132(2): 297–326.

New, J. J. and Scholl, B. J. (2009) "Subjective time dilation: Spatially local, object-based, or global visual experience?" *Journal of Vision* 9(4): 1–11.

Nigg, J. T. (2000) "On inhibition/disinhibition in developmental psychopathology: Views from cognitive and personality psychology and a working inhibition taxonomy", *Psychological Bulletin* 126(2): 220–246.

Ogden, R. S., Salominaite, E., Jones, L. A., Fisk, J. E. and Montgomery, C. (2011) "The role of executive functions in human prospective interval timing", *Acta Psychologica* 137(3): 352–358.

Ogden, R. S., Wearden, J. H. and Montgomery, C. (2014) "The differential contribution of executive functions to temporal generalization, reproduction and verbal estimation", *Acta Psychologica* 152: 84–94.

Pariyadath, V. and Eagleman, D. (2007) "The effect of predictability on subjective duration", *PLoS ONE* 2: e1264.

Royall, D. R. and Mahurin, R. K. (1996) "Neuroanatomy, measurement, and clinical significance of the executive cognitive functions", in L. J. Dickstein, M. B. Riba and J. M. Oldham (eds), *American Psychiatric Press Review of Psychiatry*, vol. 15, Washington, DC: American Psychiatric Press, pp. 175–204.

Ruthruff, E., Johnston, J. C. and Van Selst, M. (2001) "Why practice reduces dual-task interference", *Journal of Experimental Psychology: Human Perception and Performance* 27(1): 3–21.

Schindel, R., Rowlands, J. and Arnold, D. H. (2011) "The oddball effect: Perceived duration and predictive coding", *Journal of Vision* 11(2): 1–9.

Seifried, T. and Ulrich, R. (2010) "Does the asymmetry effect inflate the temporal expansion of oddball stimuli?" *Psychological Research* 74(1): 90–98.

Sperling, G. and Melchner, M. J. (1978) "The attention operating characteristic: Examples from visual search", *Science* 202(4365): 315–318.

Stoltzfus, E. R., Hasher, L. and Zacks, R. T. (1996) "Working memory and aging: Current status of the inhibitory view", in J. T. E. Richardson, R. W. Engle, L. Hasher, R. H. Logie, E. R. Stoltzfus and R. T. Zacks (eds), *Working Memory and Human Cognition*, New York: Oxford University Press, pp. 66–88.

Stuss, D. T. and Alexander, M. P. (2000) "Executive functions and the frontal lobes: A conceptual view", *Psychological Research* 63(3/4): 289–298.

Treisman, M. (1963) "Temporal discrimination and the indifference interval: Implications for a model of the 'internal clock'", *Psychological Monographs* 77(13): 1–31.

Tremblay, S. and Fortin, C. (2003) "Break expectancy in duration discrimination", *Journal of Experimental Psychology: Human Perception and Performance* 29(4): 823–831.

Tse, P. U., Intriligator, J., Rivest, J. and Cavanagh, P. (2004) "Attention and the subjective expansion of time", *Perception and Psychophysics* 66(7): 1171–1189.

Ulrich, R., Nitschke, J. and Rammsayer, T. (2006) "Perceived duration of expected and unexpected stimuli", *Psychological Research* 70(2): 77–87.

Van der Sluis, S., de Jong, P. F. and van der Leij, A. (2007) "Executive functioning in children, and its relations with reasoning, reading, and arithmetic", *Intelligence* 35(5): 427–449.

Van Wassenhove, V., Buonomano, D. V., Shimojo, S. and Shams, L. (2008) "Distortions of subjective time perception within and across senses", *PLoS ONE* 3: e1437.

Vanneste, S. and Pouthas, V. (1999) "Timing in aging: The role of attention", *Experimental Aging Research* 25(1): 49–67.

Viau-Quesnel, C. and Fortin, C. (2014) "Bivalent task switching and memory load: Similar costs on reaction times, different costs on concurrent timing", *Canadian Journal of Experimental Psychology* 68: 194–203.

Wearden, J. H. (1991) "Do humans possess an internal clock with scalar timing properties?" *Learning and Motivation* 22(1): 59–83.

Wickens, C. D. (1980) "The structure of attentional resources", in R. S. Nickerson (ed.), *Attention and Performance VIII*, Hillsdale, NJ: Lawrence Erlbaum, pp. 239–257.

Wickens, C. D. (1991) "Processing resources and attention", D. L. Damos (ed.), *Multiple-Task Performance*, London: Taylor and Francis, pp. 3–34.

Woehrle, J. L. and Magliano, J. P. (2012) "Time flies faster if a person has a high working-memory capacity", *Acta Psychologica* 139(2): 314–319.

Zakay, D. (1989) "Subjective time and attentional resource allocation: An integrated model of time estimation", in I. Levin and D. Zakay (eds), *Time and Human Cognition: A Life-Span Perspective*, Amsterdam: Elsevier, pp. 365–397.

Zakay, D. and Block, R. A. (1996) "The role of attention in time estimation processes", in M. A. Pastor and J. Artieda (eds), *Time, Internal Clocks and Movement*, Amsterdam: Elsevier, pp. 143–164.

Zakay, D. and Block, R. A. (1998) "New perspective on prospective time estimation", in V. DeKeyser, G. d'Ydewalle and A. Vandierendonck (eds), *Time and the Dynamic Control of Behavior*, Seattle, WA: Hogrefe and Huber, pp. 129–141.

PART VII

Temporal experience and aesthetics

24

MOTION AND THE FUTURISTS

Capturing the dynamic sensation

Robin Le Poidevin

The Italian Futurist painters who were active in the early years of the twentieth century sought to capture in a single image the experience of motion. Could such a project succeed? It might be thought that, insofar as the aim is to depict motion, it is doomed to fail, for (with the possible exception of optical illusions) no static image evokes the experience of movement. But we can discern a number of possible aesthetic projects here, and their chances of success will, in some cases, depend on our favoured account of motion and motion experience. Does Futurism simply reduce the experience of motion to a series of psychological "snapshots", for example? Futurist paintings also provide an intriguing and revelatory case study in which we can examine the nature of depiction and its connection to artistic realism. We need to supplement accounts of conventional depiction if we are to reconcile the evident non-realist nature of Futurist imagery with the thought that Futurism is somehow true to temporal experience.

The goal of Futurist painting

We affirm that the world's magnificence has been enriched by a new beauty: the beauty of speed. A racing car whose hood is adorned with great pipes, like serpents of explosive breath – a roaring car that seems to ride on grapeshot is more beautiful than the Victory of Samothrace.

(Apollonio 1973: 21)

With this controversial aesthetic announcement, together with other more alarming ones glorifying war and violence and calling for the destruction of libraries and museums (as repositories of defunct past values), the Italian Futurist movement was officially inaugurated, in the *Manifesto of Futurism* by Filippo Tommaso Marinetti (1876–1944). It first appeared in the Italian periodical, *Gazzetta dell'Emilia*, on 5 February 1909, and then later that month, in *Le Figaro*. This inflammatory and intemperate piece was followed a year later by a somewhat more considered aesthetic programme, in *Futurist Painting: Technical Manifesto*, by the core members of the movement: Giacomo Balla (1871–1958), Umberto Boccioni (1882–1916), Carlo Carrà (1881–1966), Luigi Russolo (1885–1947) and Gino Severini (1883–1966). This set out an ambitious aim, with an accompanying vision of reality:

The gesture which we would reproduce on canvas shall no longer be a fixed *moment* in universal dynamism. It shall simply be the *dynamic sensation* itself.

Indeed, all things move, all things run, all things are rapidly changing. A profile is never motionless before our eyes, but it constantly appears and disappears. On account of the persistency of an image upon the retina, moving objects constantly multiply themselves; their form changes like rapid vibrations, in their mad career. Thus a running horse has not four legs, but twenty, and their movements are triangular . . .

To paint a human figure you must not paint it; you must render the whole of its surrounding atmosphere.

Space no longer exists: the street pavement, soaked by rain beneath the glare of electric lamps, becomes immensely deep and gapes to the very centre of the earth. Thousands of miles divide us from the sun; yet the house in front of us fits into the solar disk . . .

The sixteen people around you in a rolling motor bus are in turn and at the same time one, ten, four, three; they are motionless and they change places; they come and go, bound into the street, are suddenly swallowed up by the sunshine, then come back and sit before you, like persistent symbols of universal vibration . . .

The motor bus rushes into the houses which it passes, and in their turn the houses throw themselves upon the motor bus and are blended with it.

(*Apollonio 1973: 27–28*)

The key idea is that of *motion* and its representation. What the Futurists objected to was the static nature of conventional painting and sculpture. What in contrast informs the new programme is, apparently, a vision of reality as *Heraclitean*, as being in constant flux, and it is this – or at least, the Heraclitean nature of perceptual experience – which is to be represented on canvas. The words of the *Manifesto* do not make a careful distinction between reality and appearance, but it will be convenient for the purposes of this discussion to distinguish between two aims: to represent motion (as it is), and to represent the experience of motion. There is more to Futurism than these two, but they are ambitious enough, and the central question of this chapter is whether the Futurists did or could succeed in meeting them. Within each of these aims, however, we can discern further aesthetic projects. Although I shall have something to say about what the Futurists may have intended, I am largely concerned with a conceptual inquiry: in what senses is the attempt to depict motion by static, non-changing images a feasible one? To answer this, we will need to begin by considering the structure of motion and of the experience of motion.

Motion and the instant

To get a sense of the range of positions on the nature of motion, it will be helpful to consider these questions concerning the structure of time and its relation to motion:

1 Is there such a thing as an instant – that is, a temporal location that cannot be divided into shorter parts?
2 If so, is the difference between motion and rest intrinsic to the instant?
3 If intrinsic, how?

To answer *yes* to the first question is not necessarily to view time as a series of discrete, indivisible but extended temporal intervals. Neither is it necessarily to think of the relation between instants and intervals as one of parts to whole. In Aristotle's conception, for example, the "now" is the dimensionless boundary between past and future, but time is not composed of nows (*Physics* VI.9). To deny the existence of instants in the fairly minimal sense defined by 1 would be to deny that time has any structure at all.

Supposing, then, that there are instants, we can intelligibly talk of what is *intrinsic to an instant*, that is, of those states of affairs obtaining at that instant which do not logically depend on what obtains at any other time. Now consider two objects, A and B, during a certain non-zero period of time. A moves continuously during that period, while B is at rest for the entire period. Apart from that, the objects are indistinguishable. Now consider some instant *i* during that period. With respect only to states intrinsic to *i*, is there anything to distinguish A from B, which reveals A, but not B, to be in motion? Can one, that is, talk of A's motion as intrinsic to *i*? Suppose that the answer to that question is *no*: nothing at *i* distinguishes A from B. Then the difference between an object in motion and one at rest emerges only *over* time. At any given instant, any object, whether in motion or not, simply occupies a position. To be in motion is to occupy different positions at other moments. As this is mirrored by cinema, where a series of stills are presented in quick succession, giving rise to the impression of movement, we can call it the *cinematic* account of motion:[1]

> *The cinematic account of motion*: *x* moves during an interval if and only if *x* occupies different positions at different instants during that interval.

Motion, on this account, is simply *displacement*. We can continue to talk of motion "at" an instant as long as this is understood in a purely derivative sense: *x* moves at instant *i* if and only if *x* is in different positions immediately before or after *i*. Motion is not intrinsic to the instant. This was Russell's account of motion, and he proposed that not only was this an adequate answer to Zeno's Arrow paradox (the arrow does not move during a period, since it cannot move at any instant of that period), but that it also involved an important concession to Zeno: that insofar as we suppose motion to be intrinsic to the instant, we are mistaken (Russell 1937: 347–348, 350, 469–473).

One worry one might have about the cinematic account is that if we combine it with a certain form of *presentism*, the view that only what is present is real, it seems to follow that motion is, after all, unreal, for motion as the cinematic account conceives of it is never intrinsic to the present (assuming the present to be instantaneous). The form of presentism in question is one which both concedes the need for truth-makers for past-tense statements and locates these truth-makers in the present (thus guaranteeing their reality).[2] Presentists of this stripe thus have some motivation to think of motion as being intrinsic to an instant – the view that Russell supposes is the intuitive one. This kind of presentist will be reluctant to allow that there is motion in an instant only in a purely derivative sense, for this alludes to other, unreal, times, and this would conflict with the proposal that what is true of other times can only have present truth-makers. From these reflections emerges a very different conception of motion, one which we might dub the *instant-intrinsic* account. On the instant-intrinsic account, there is such a thing as instantaneous motion, where this is understood as motion which is intrinsic to an instant and not something merely derivative. (The cinematic theorist will allow instantaneous motion in the purely derivative sense of an instantaneous state that is part of a temporal extended displacement.) Motion, on such an account, is not to be identified with displacement, but is perhaps what *explains* displacement. (See, e.g., Bigelow and Pargetter 1989.)

A variant on this theme – though a rather controversial one – is to identify instantaneous motion with displacement in the instant. The result, of course, is that the moving object is, at any given instant of its motion, both at, and not at, a given position. This, in fact, is the basis of another of Zeno's paradoxes of motion. We could accept, as Zeno perhaps intended, that such a view of motion leads to self-contradiction. Or, like Hegel, we could embrace the contradiction and take this to be precisely what distinguishes, at any given instant, the moving object from the one at rest. This Hegelian view of motion has in modern times received support from Graham Priest (1987), who defends a dialetheist view both of truth – that is, one which allows true contradictions – and of reality: incompatible states of affairs may co-exist.

There are, then, a range of metaphysical theories concerning the nature of motion. They are concerned with motion as it is in itself. But what of motion as it is experienced?

The experience of motion

Corresponding to the questions we asked above about the structure of time and motion are questions about the temporal structure of experience:

1   Is there such a thing as a psychological instant – that is, an experience which cannot be decomposed into shorter items which themselves count as experiences?
2   If so, is the experience of motion contained in that instant?
3   If so, how?

To answer *yes* to the first question is to adopt an atomistic account of temporal experience. It is as if we take perceptual snapshots and build up extended experience from these experiential atoms. Granting for a moment that this is indeed the structure of our experience, how, to tackle the second question, might this accommodate the experience of motion? One account is the experiential analogue of the cinematic account of motion:

> *The cinematic account of motion experience*: we perceive the motion of *x* by virtue of having a sequence of experiences of *x* at different positions, which are presented in different psychological instants.[3]

The cinematic answer to question 2, then, is *no*: the content of each psychological instant does not convey motion, but merely position. It might seem that, if this were the true account of motion experience, we would experience motion as a sequence of discrete jumps. This is (normally) not how we experience it. But then one might wonder how much phenomenological introspection can reveal the structure of experience. Indeed, the cinematic analogy suggests that it does not. For at the cinema, we are presented with a series of stills, in rapid succession. The simplest account of how this translates into experience is in terms of a series of experiences of those stills. Yet the motion we seem to perceive on the screen is smooth and continuous. That experience has a certain structure need not imply that we can discern that structure.

A closer link between structure and phenomenology would be provided by what we could call (again exploiting analogies with the analysis of motion) the *instant-intrinsic account of motion experience*, according to which each psychological instant could be an experience of (or as-of) motion. Can this be identified with displacement? That would imply that motion experience would consist of perceptions of an object as being both in, and displaced from, a given position. When motion is sufficiently rapid and consists of an oscillation between two positions, this is arguably exactly what we perceive. Hold a pencil in the middle between thumb and forefinger and wiggle it back and forth. The pencil is a blur, but the two positions between which it oscillates are discernible. The pencil thus seems to occupy different positions simultaneously. If we hesitate to ascribe self-contradictoriness to reality, no such scruples need apply to experience. The perception of the oscillating pencil is, as we might put it, "Hegelian" (again, by analogy with the corresponding account of motion). But this will plainly not be true of motion experience in general. To see a bus moving down the street is not to see it as occupying different positions simultaneously. The instant-intrinsic account of motion experience would therefore have to make room for the thought that it is possible to experience motion in the psychological instant without an accompanying sense of displacement. The sense of displacement has to be built up from successive instants.

Returning to a point made above, that the phenomenology of motion experience does not imply a particular structure, we might nevertheless be suspicious of a model which posited experiential "atoms" which we could not discern. What sense can be made of the idea of something which cannot be discerned as an individual experience amid the experiential flow, but which is nevertheless an experience in its own right, and one of the building blocks of which extended experience is composed?

Consider, as a test case, the *phi phenomenon* (Wertheimer 1912), the illusory sense of movement produced by two alternating dots or lights (as at a railway crossing). Despite the unmistakable sense of movement, it is hard to isolate an experience as-of the dot/light being at an intermediate position. Yet this is suggested by the experience of motion as a whole. So perhaps we have a series of psychological states which do not quite count as experiences in their own right, but which contribute to the overall experience. The structure of experience itself may be indeterminate, in that we struggle to decompose it into parts which are themselves isolatable experiences. A negative answer to question 1 above may be rather more tempting than a negative answer to the corresponding question about motion itself.

Perhaps, however, the reason we struggle to determine the character and content of psychological instants is that we are trying to isolate them from their experiential surroundings. The cinematic account builds extended experiences from their components: the content of the extended experience is determined by the content of its parts. But suppose we reverse this conception, as Phillips (2011) suggests, and conceive of the content of the parts as derived from the content of the whole? That would allow us to say, of the experience of constant (not jerky) motion, that (i) there was no moment at which the object appeared not to be moving, while conceding that (ii) there are temporal limits to our powers of discrimination, and that our experience will contain sub-intervals during which the movement of the object is too small to be detected. If the experience of motion over an interval were built up from temporally minimal experience, Phillips argues, (i) and (ii) would be in conflict. Phillips does not offer a name for this account, but we might call it the *holistic account*.

With these various accounts of motion and motion experience in mind, let us return to the Futurist aim to "capture the dynamic sensation", and how the Futurists went about realizing that aim.

Futurist techniques

The Futurist painters' *Technical Manifesto* offered not just an aim but a suggestion as to how it was to be accomplished:

> On account of the persistency of an image upon the retina, moving objects constantly multiply themselves; their form changes like rapid vibrations, in their mad career. Thus a running horse has not four legs, but twenty, and their movements are triangular.
>
> *(Apollonio 1973: 28)*

The suggestion, then, is to present successive positions of a moving object on the canvas, partially superimposed on each other. And that precisely captures two of the best-known of the early Futurist paintings: Balla's *Dynamism of a Dog on a Leash*, and *Little Girl Running on a Balcony*, both from 1912. The first of these is almost photographic in character, especially the rendering of the leash, as it sways back and forth. The connection with the multiple-exposure "chronophotographs" of E. J. Marey, which predate the Futurist paintings by almost 20 years, is unmistakable. *Little Girl Running on a Balcony* is more impressionistic, but here too, the successive positions of the subject are individually represented. The same technique is evident in Balla's *The Violinist's Hands*, also from 1912, and *Swifts: Paths of Movement and Dynamic Sequences* from 1913. The second of these is an explicit reference to Marey's photographic studies of birds in flight.[4]

To what extent do these images succeed in representing motion? Let us put this in the context of the metaphysical theories of motion outlined above. The cinematic account treats motion as displacement over time: the successive occupancy of different positions. And if Balla had intended his paintings as an analysis of motion in this sense, then they clearly succeed. (It might be suggested, indeed, that the chronophotographs which inspired Balla's paintings establish the truth of the cinematic account, for do they not precisely show what is happening at each instant of the movement? Unfortunately not. The photographic exposure cannot be confined to an instant in the technical sense of an indivisible moment, but must take up a minimal amount of time. The photograph is the causal result of what is happening over that interval, and so there is no instant such that the photograph represents precisely what is happening at that instant, but not what is happening at any other instant.) If, in contrast, the instant-intrinsic account is correct, then the paintings represent motion less directly, by depicting the effects of motion. These two approaches presuppose that the painting is intended as representing motion over time. If, instead, we (less plausibly) take it as presenting a snapshot, then the incompatible positions of the objects represented entail a Hegelian account.

But that it was not the intention, at least of some of Futurist practitioners, to present an artistic analysis of motion is evident in Anton Giulio Bragaglia's *Futurist Photodynamism* of 1911:

> We are certainly not concerned with the aims and characteristics of cinematography and chronophotography. We are not interested in the precise reconstruction of movement, which has already been broken up and analysed. We are involved only in the area of movement which produces sensation, the memory of which still palpitates in our awareness.
>
> *(Apollonio 1973: 38)*

There is even the suggestion that cinematography, and by extension, chronophotography, mispresents motion, at least as it is experienced:

> Cinematography does not trace the shape of movement. It subdivides it, without rules, with mechanical arbitrariness, disintegrating and shattering it without any kind of aesthetic concern for rhythm.
>
> *(Ibid.: 39)*[5]

Could Bragaglia's criticism be applied to Balla's paintings mentioned above? *Dynamism of a Dog* is perhaps the most cinematic, but the others are certainly not mere mechanical representations of different stages of motion. Although to some extent individual positions can be discerned, the images are fused in such a way that at points the moving object seems almost to dissolve.

Bragaglia's 1912 photograph of Balla has him standing with *Dynamism of a Dog*, evidently having recently completed it. The picture is blurred, as if either Balla or (more likely) Bragaglia shifted during the exposure. The painting too is blurred, thus perhaps transforming it into something more like Bragaglia's conception of what the depiction of movement should be. The precise representation of individual positions is gone, to be replaced by an indeterminacy of location. Closer to *The Violinist's Hands* is Bragaglia's *The Guitarist* of 1912, in which the right hand is caught several times in mid-flight.

The depiction of moving objects as almost dissolving in the motion is perhaps more evident in Boccioni's studies, such as *Dynamism of a Cyclist* (1913), *Dynamism of a Human Body* (1913) and *Charge of the Lancers* (1915), where the objects become a series of abstract shapes. This abstraction is taken to a further level in Balla's *Abstract Speed – The Car has Passed* (1913), *Speeding Car* (1913) and *Dynamic Expansion + Speed* (1913). In Boccioni's *States of Mind* studies, the boundaries between different objects are dissolved, and even what is presumably empty space takes on a texture, also fused with the occupying bodies.

A further technique exploits the effects of juxtaposing small strokes of vividly contrasting colours. Balla's *Street Light* (1911) has a sphere of light composed of tiny white, yellow, red and green chevrons, forming concentric circles around the central lamp, creating, almost, an illusion of movement similar to those achieved in Bridget Riley's paintings in the 1960s. Boccioni's *The City Rises* (1910–11), while not creating quite the same illusion, nevertheless exploits colour contrasts, with its central figure of a straining horse seemingly composed of flame.[6]

These images are certainly aesthetically successful: they are visually exhilarating pieces, they offer novel methods of representation, and in the case of *States of Mind*, they clearly convey distinctive moods. But to relate them back to the Futurists' professed aim of reproducing "the dynamic sensation", can they succeed in this respect? The notion of reproducing a sensation on canvas is not an immediately transparent one, and we need to interpret it further before answering that question.

Interpreting "reproducing the dynamic sensation"

By "the dynamic sensation" we can, I think, safely assume that what is referred to is an experience as-of motion or change in general. What would it be to reproduce this experience?

It will be helpful, first, to distinguish between *depictive* and *non-depictive* representation. We might non-depictively represent the passage of time, for example, in a series of cartoon pictures. Of course, the experience of such a sequence, laid out before our eyes simultaneously, is not like the experience of the passage of time, but the sequence nevertheless conveys temporal content. In contrast, a film, unfolding on screen, manages to depict the passage of time by inducing in us the same kind of experience as we would have were we to witness the events represented in reality. So, at a first attempt, we might characterise depiction as a form of visual representation that represents by evoking the same kind of experience as would the object represented. A suitably realistic painting of a horse induces an experience that is relevantly like the visual experience of an actual horse, and it is the capacity of the painting to do this which is part of the representational mechanism.

So, do, or can, Futurist paintings depict motion? As noted above, if the cinematic account of motion is correct, then the chronophotograph-inspired paintings of Balla succeed in representing motion, by depicting the successive positions of a moving object. But this does not give rise to the experience as-of-motion. The painting, that is, is not experienced as itself moving! (Balla's *Street Light*, mentioned above, is perhaps the closest case where something like a sensation of movement is induced, but optical illusion is not generally a characteristic of Futurist painting, and illusions do not in general represent what they evoke.) So, at best, the paintings could be described as non-depictive representations of motion.

This uncompromising conclusion should be qualified. In the case of very rapid, oscillatory movement, the object is experienced in part as a blur, with perhaps the terminal positions picked out in experience. And this plausibly is captured by, e.g., the representation of the leash (and perhaps also the dog's legs) in *Dynamism of a Dog on a Leash*. So it is, arguably, possible to depict this kind of movement. But then, it might be said, we do not in these cases experience the motion itself, precisely because the different positions of the oscillating object are presented all at once. A truly dynamic sensation is not captured like this.

Before we conclude that Futurist images cannot depict motion, however, we need to refine the rather rough characterisation of depiction offered above. A picture of a horse, it might be said, evokes an experience that is significantly *unlike* the experience of an actual horse, since we are never fooled by the picture into thinking that there is a horse here, as opposed to merely a picture of a horse. This is accommodated by Flint Schier's (1986) account of depiction: a picture depicts an *F* by triggering our *F*-recognition capacities. In order for the picture to do this, admittedly, we will need already to have grasped certain conventions of artistic representation. Once we have, however, we can go on more or less immediately to recognise novel images as visual representations of their objects. This is the sense in which the experience of the picture is relevantly like the experience of the actual object: both trigger our visual recognition capacities. Some pictures will do this more readily than others. Currie (1995) proposes that there are two mechanisms that may be called into play in object recognition. One is more primitive, direct and instinctive, requiring little, if anything, in the way of reasoning and reflection. The second does require such reasoning and reflection. A depiction of a horse triggers the first mechanism; but the second mechanism prevents us from being fooled into thinking that we really are seeing a horse rather than a picture of a horse (Currie 1995: 85). Currie also argues that there is a connection between depiction (thus understood) on the one hand, and artistic realism on the other (1995: 90–91). Thus, a painting represents a feature realistically to the extent that it triggers our more primitive recognition capacities. But Futurist paintings are not realist paintings, and do not set out to be. Our recognising the representation of motion in them is less immediate and more the result of reflection.

If depiction of motion is off the table (for the time being), there is another way of interpreting the idea of reproducing the dynamic sensation, and that is to represent an *analysis* of that experience. On this interpretation, what Futurists paintings do is to represent the different components of the experience of motion. What are these components? On one account, it is the successive perceptions of an object at its different locations. This is the controversial cinematic account of motion experience, which takes that experience simply to be a series of different perceptual snapshots of an object's position. Even granting that an experience built up in such a way might give one the sensation of continuous motion, rather than motion as a series of jumps, such a perceptual mechanism would arguably make huge demands on the visual processing system. The position of the object would have to be registered (even if at some sub-conscious level), and then somehow retained, thus colouring the next perceptual snapshot. How many of these would be required to build up the experience of even a short burst of motion? Quite apart from these difficulties, we may wonder how much the Futurists would have wanted to commit themselves to any particular theory of motion experience. Still, the idea is not completely implausible: the remark quoted above from the *Technical Manifesto* concerning "the persistency of an image upon the retina" does suggest that they were prepared to speculate about precisely this issue. And Bragaglia's mention of memory "palpitating" in our sensory awareness is similarly suggestive of a view on the mechanism of motion experience.

If we are inclined to read into Futurist paintings, or the Futurist's own comments, views about the psychological mechanism behind motion perception, the cinematic account is not the only one we might suppose is represented. If the two remarks just mentioned suggest any of the models of motion experience we have canvassed, they perhaps fit better with the instant-intrinsic account than with the cinematic account. The persistence of the image colours the psychological instant so as to provide an instantaneous experience of motion. Or consider the Hegelian account, on which the moving object is represented, at one and the same time, as being both in a certain position and as not being in that position. Is that not also conveyed by some of those images? Different Futurist techniques, indeed, appear to correspond to different models of perception. Boccioni's *States of Mind* series is less suggestive of either the cinematic or Hegelian accounts, as in the indeterminacy of motion of perception, where we struggle to pinpoint the position, or boundaries, of the moving object. And what of the holistic account? In presenting different positions of an object as simultaneous aspects of an image, apprehended in an instant, the message could be that the content of a psychological instant is derived from experience over a period.

I want to conclude this brief discussion by pursuing a different approach, one which re-opens the question of whether static images can depict motion. Perhaps we need a different account of depiction for Futurist paintings.

Depiction and non-realism

The Futurists clearly felt that their artistic efforts were truer to experience than the static productions of the past – or, at least, that it was an achievable aim to be true to that experience. This is, however, somewhat at odds with the conventional wisdom concerning depiction and its relation to pictorial realism. We may set out the propositions which are in tension with each other, as follows:

1   The degree of realism in a picture is determined by the extent to which the features it represents are represented depictively rather than non-depictively.
2   Futurist pictures are, to a large extent, non-realist representations.
3   If a picture depicts *F*s, then the experience of the picture is closer to visual experience of actual *F*s than that of non-depictive representations of *F*s.
4   Futurist pictures are closer to experience than conventional (realist) representational pictures.

Propositions 1 and 2 imply that Futurist pictures are non-depictive representations. Propositions 3 and 4 imply that they are depictive representations. They cannot be both! So what should go here?

The simplest move at this point would be to give up on the Futurist dream and reject 4, leaving the theoretical framework intact. But there is a more interesting response, and that is to offer an alternative view of depiction, one suitable for non-realist representation. This need not be in tension with the feature-recognition-triggering account, which can remain in place as a way of distinguishing realist from non-realist pictures. But we also want a sense of depiction that allows a non-realist painting to be a depiction of its object in a way in which a linguistic description of that object plainly is not.

The Futurists were by no means the first to aim at a truer representation of experience than that provided by traditional realist artworks. The Impressionists also aimed at this. Take, for example, Van Gogh's *Starry Night*. With its enormous yellow moon, stars represented as concentric circles of light and the great swirling mass at the centre of the painting, this is, in terms of its effect upon the retina, less like a photograph of the night sky than, say, the seventeenth-century Dutch painter Aers Van der Neer's *River Scene with a Bonfire, Moonlight*. Yet we might feel that Van Gogh's painting conveys the experience of a night sky more intensely than the Van der Neer (beautiful and atmospheric though the realist painting is).

So here is a proposal: non-realist paintings depict, in part, by taking an *aspect* of our ordinary visual experience and making it the *object* of a visual experience. In Van Gogh's case, it is the salience of the heavenly objects in the night sky, despite the smallness of the corresponding retinal images, which is made the object of experience when we look at the painting. It offers us a visual representation of that salience. In the case of the Futurists, the aspect is the way in which the perception of a shifting scene is influenced by past perceptions, which are present in the picture. The picture thus confronts us with a temporally extended vision of the scene. This is not a depiction of motion in the recognition-capacity-triggering sense, since the picture does not, at least directly, trigger our visual recognition capacities for motion. But what makes it appropriate to talk of depiction here is that the experience nevertheless has something in common with the visual experience of motion, namely awareness of the multiple or indeterminate locations of the depicted object. We need this second kind of depiction to accommodate the depiction of features of our own experience, as opposed to depiction of external objects.

Propositions 1 and 3 connect closeness to experience with realism. But insofar as Futurism is a non-realist technique which nevertheless delivers something that is closer to experience, we need to break this link: or at least, allow that there is more than one way of being true to experience. Not all depiction is realist. It is a specific kind of depiction, namely that defined by Schier and Currie, in terms of which realism can be understood. It is a rather different kind of depiction according to which Futurist pictures capture an aspect of experience. Once we recognise these two kinds of depiction, the contradiction disappears.

Now we are back with an earlier worry: does the depictive status of Futurist paintings depend on a particular model of motion experience, viz. the cinematic account? If so, then it faces the objections that might be raised against that account. No, I think our account of depiction can be neutral on that point. True, it presupposes that part of the experience of motion is awareness of multiple location, but it is not further presupposed that we experience motion *by* perceiving multiple occupancy, as the cinematic account suggests: the direction of causation could run the other way.

What this discussion has attempted to do is to tease out different aesthetic projects concerning the pictorial representation of motion, using the Futurists as a case study. Some of these projects look more promising than others, and some leave hostages to theoretical fortune insofar as they depend on controversial theories of motion and motion experience. But we can, I think, begin to see that the Futurist aim of reproducing on canvas the "dynamic sensation" characteristic of temporal experience was not necessarily a vain one.[7]

Notes

1 Since this defines motion in terms of being *at* different positions *at* different times, it has also been called the "at-at" account of motion. And since being at a position is a *state*, rather than an event, another name for it is the "static" account. As this is a chapter on art, however, it seems appropriate to name it after an artistic analogy.

2 See, for example, Bigelow (1996) and Ludlow (1999). Not all presentists concede the need for presently-existing truth-makers, however. Bourne (2006), for example, develops an "ersatzer presentism", based on abstract objects (he also surveys a variety of presentist positions). And Tallant and Ingram (2015) recommend a "nefarious" presentism, according to which there *were* truth-makers for propositions about the past, in virtue of which those propositions are presently true.

3 In calling this the "cinematic" account of motion experience (Phillips (2011), in similar vein, calls it the "zoëtrope conception", applying it to change experience generally), I mean only to draw attention to the structural similarity between the accounts of motion and of motion experience. I do not mean to imply that the cinematic account of motion is committed to this particular account of motion experience, or vice versa. And a "psychological instant" is not an instant in the sense of lacking temporal parts: it is just that any temporal parts it does have will not themselves be experiences.

4 Selections of Futurist works can be found in Carrieri (1961), Apollonio (1973), Lista (2001) and Greene (2014).

5 Ironically, Boccioni urged Futurist painters to distance themselves from experiments such as Bragaglia's: "We have always rejected with disgust and scorn even a distant relationship with photography, because it is outside art"; "These purely photographic researches have absolutely nothing to do with the plastic dynamism invented by us" (translated and quoted in Braun 2014: 97).

6 See Fraquelli (2014) for a discussion of the use of colour in Futurist paintings.

7 I am very grateful to Ian Phillips for numerous detailed and constructive suggestions on a previous version of this chapter.

References

Apollonio, U. (ed.) (1973) *Futurist Manifestos*, London: Thames and Hudson.

Bigelow, J. (1996) "Presentism and properties", in J. E. Tomberlin (ed.), *Philosophical Perspectives 10: Metaphysics*, Oxford, UK: Blackwell.

Bigelow, J. and Pargetter, R. (1989) "Vectors and change", *British Journal for the Philosophy of Science* 40(3): 289–306.

Bourne, C. (2006) *A Future for Presentism*, Oxford, UK: Oxford University Press.

Braun, M. (2014) "Giacomo Balla, Anton Giulio Bragaglia, and Etienne-Jules Marey", in V. Greene (ed.), *Italian Futurism 1909–1944*, New York: Guggenheim Museum Publications, pp. 95–8.

Carrieri, R. (1961) *Il Futurismo*, Milan, Italy: Edizioni del Milione.

Currie, G. (1995) *Image and Mind: Film, Philosophy and Cognitive Science*, Cambridge, UK: Cambridge University Press.

Fraquelli, S. (2014) "Modified divisionism: Futurist painting in 1910", in V. Greene (ed.), *Italian Futurism 1909–1944*, New York: Guggenheim Museum Publications, pp. 79–82.

Greene, V. (2014) *Italian Futurism 1909–1944*, New York: Guggenheim Museum Publications.

Lista, G. (2001) *Futurism and Photography*, London: Merrell Publishers Ltd.

Ludlow, P. (1999) *Semantics, Tense, and Time*, Cambridge, MA: MIT Press.

Phillips, I. (2011) "Indiscriminability and experience of change", *Philosophical Quarterly* 61(245): 808–827.

Priest, G. (1987) *In Contradiction: A Study of the Transconsistent*, Dordrecht, The Netherlands: Nijhoff.

Russell, B. (1937) *The Principles of Mathematics*, 2nd ed., Cambridge, UK: Cambridge University Press.

Schier, F. (1986) *Deeper into Pictures: An Essay on Pictorial Representation*, Cambridge, UK: Cambridge University Press.

Tallant, J. and Ingram, D. (2015) "Nefarious presentism", *Philosophical Quarterly* 65(260): 355–371.

Wertheimer, M. (1912) "Experimentelle Studien uber Sehen von Bewegung", *Zeitschrift für Psychologie* 61(1): 161–265.

25

ON TIME IN CINEMA

Enrico Terrone

Cinema as an art of time passing

In a seminal paper on the definition of cinema, Noël Carroll (1996) pointed out five basic features an entity x must satisfy in order to qualify as a moving image:

1   "x is a detached display" (1996: 70). More specifically, the moving image is a "display" since it is constituted by a visual array; and it is "detached" since it induces the spectator to visually experience a space which, unlike her ordinary space, is not centered in and connected to her body (namely, it is not an "egocentric space").
2   "x belongs to the class of things from which the impression of movement is technically possible" (1996: 70). That is, the cinematic display is produced in such a way that it can induce the spectator to visually experience things moving.
3   "Performance tokens of x are generated by a template that is a token" (1996: 70). Here, Carroll treats the moving image as a type and calls "templates" the particular objects (e.g., film prints, videotapes, DVDs, computer files) that instantiate the type by storing it, while he calls "performance tokens" the particular events (namely, screenings) that instantiate the type by showing it.
4   "Performance tokens of x are not artworks in their own right" (1996: 70). That is, the screening of a movie, unlike the execution of a symphony or the staging of a play, cannot be artistically assessed in its own right.
5   "x is . . . two-dimensional" (1996: 70). That is, the visual array constituting the cinematic display is a flat surface.

Interestingly, Carroll never mentions time in his five conditions. Conditions 1 and 5 concern spatial features, while conditions 3 and 4 concern the process through which a film is instantiated, and condition 2 concerns movement. Nevertheless, in condition 2, time seems to play a crucial role, albeit unnoticed – a more fundamental role than movement.

In fact, Carroll does not require that the moving image elicits the impression of movement from the spectator, but only that it has the possibility of eliciting such an impression. He does so because he wants to take into account "static films" such as *La Jetée* (C. Marker, 1962), *One Second in Montreal* (M. Snow, 1969), and *Poetic Justice* (H. Frampton, 1972), which are made, partly or wholly, by still images (for a thorough account of static films, see Remes 2015). Although in such works there is no movement, in principle there might have been movement, and for Carroll this is enough to count them as cinematic works; the possibility of eliciting the impression of movement distinguishes such works from fully-fledged static images like paintings or photographs.

Still, one might wonder why static films have the possibility of eliciting the impression of movement whereas paintings and photographs lack this possibility. The most basic reason seems to be that static films, unlike paintings and photographs, have *a duration*. Although static films do not in fact elicit the impression of movement, their duration in principle gives them the possibility, albeit in fact unexploited, of eliciting the impression of movement (cf. Ponech 2006; Terrone 2014; Remes 2015). Conversely, static pictures such as paintings and photographs *cannot* elicit the impression of movement *even in principle*.

The point is that any film, as such, has a fixed duration, namely its runtime, which is a *normative* feature of the film as a type. That is to say, every *correct* screening of a film that has a duration D_f^* *ought* to last D_f^*. Because of that, the duration of the spectator's experience is in turn *normatively* set by D_f^*: a proper experience of a film the duration of which is D_f^* *ought* to last D_f^*. As Craig Bourne and Emily Caddick Bourne point out:

> [t]here is an important sense in which a film has duration and static images lack duration. You can sensibly say "The film lasted ninety minutes", but not "The painting lasted ninety minutes". The moving nature of the film determines a particular viewing time in a way static images do not.
>
> *(2016: 136)*

Such a feature distinguishes cinema not only from static images but also from literature and theater. Indeed, neither literary works nor theatrical works have a fixed duration. Theatrical works have a fixed duration, which sets the duration of the spectator's experience, only at the performance level, not at the work level; a certain performance of *Hamlet* may last four hours, but *Hamlet* as a work does not have a fixed duration. And literary works lack duration even at the performance level, since any reader can take all the time she wants to read a certain book (even a book made of pictures, such as a comic book). The only form of art that functions like cinema with respect to duration is recorded music; from an ontological point of view, indeed, one might conceive of a piece of recorded music as a film pared down to its soundtrack (cf. Kania 2006).

If this is right, Carroll's condition 2, i.e., the possibility of eliciting the impression of movement, is rooted in a more basic feature of the moving image, namely the possession of a duration. A film can lack movement, as in the case of static films, but it cannot lack a duration. As Justin Remes puts is:

> Whether one is considering Gérard Courant's 187-hour *Cinématon* (1978–2014) or Thomas Edison's five-second *Fred Ott's Sneeze* (1894), all films have a running time . . . the more fundamental distinction between cinema and photography (as well as other traditional visual arts) is not movement but duration.
>
> *(2015: 12)*

Notoriously, cinema is the abbreviation of "cinematography", a term coming from the two Greek terms "kinema", which means movements, and "graphein", which means writing. Yet, if we agree to treat static films as works of cinema, then a more appropriate name for this medium would be "chronography", that is, the writing of time. In the domain of continental philosophy, such a priority of time over movement in cinema has been emphasized by Gilles Deleuze (1983, 1985). Deleuze splits up films into two kinds, namely, the "movement-image" and the "time-image". Films of the former kind focus on the movements and changes of the characters that liven up the narrative, whereas films of the latter kind focus on the passage of time as such and treat the movements and changes of the characters as nothing but accidental ways in which the passage of time can show up. Deleuze suggests that the latter films get closer than the former to what is fundamental in cinema, inasmuch as they show that cinema is more than merely an art of depicting movement.

Film as depiction of time

In order to investigate how cinema "writes" time, I shall focus on the notions of representation and depiction. First, by *representation*, I mean an entity that elicits thoughts or experiences about some other entities from a *suitable recipient*. That is to say, a representation is an entity that *prescribes* thoughts or experiences concerning other entities. The content of a representation is what this representation mandates us to think or experience. As Recanati puts it:

> Representations have two aspects: they are objects like tables and chairs, and as such they belong to the real world; but they also have a content by virtue of which they *represent* the world as being a certain way, possibly distinct from the way it actually is.
>
> *(1996: §6)*

To sum up, I conceive of a representation as a normative notion inasmuch as it requires a *correct* attitude, namely the attitude of a suitable recipient who entertains the thoughts or enjoys the experiences prescribed by the representation itself.

Second, by *depiction*, I mean a representation that shares some relevant features with the entity it represents thereby prescribing and supporting a perceptual experience that shares some relevant features with a possible experience of the entity represented. Moreover, the sharing of features between the representation and the entity represented cannot be accidental; the representation must represent an entity as possessing certain features *in virtue of* the representation's possessing some identical or, at least, relevantly similar features (cf. Currie 1995: 91; Yaffe 2003: 118; Le Poidevin 2007: 133). For instance, a painting can represent the sky as being blue in virtue of being itself blue, whereas the inscription "black" does not represent the color black in virtue of being black; it does so in virtue of a convention. That is why the inscription is just a representation, whereas the painting is a depiction.

In cinematic depiction, the relevant features shared by the representation and what is represented are not only spatial but also temporal. In Catharine Abell's terms, "cinematic representation is a distinctive form of depiction, unique in its capacity to depict temporal properties" (2010: 278). In Gregory Currie's terms, "What is distinctively temporal about film is not its portrayal of time, but the manner of its portrayal: its portrayal of time by means of time" (1995: 96). For instance, a film can depict an event that lasts three minutes by means of its own duration of three minutes. In this case, the property of the event of "lasting three minutes" is depicted by the property of the representation of the event of "lasting three minutes", namely by the *same* property. Thus, experience prescribed by a cinematic depiction lasts exactly the *same* time as a possible direct experience of the event represented.

Still, the fact that cinema *can* represent a three-minute event by means of a three-minute representation does not entail that any film necessarily does so. Indeed, in cinema, we often find representations that last less time than the events represented; for instance, *American Graffiti* (G. Lucas, 1973) represents an event lasting one night (namely, the adventures of a group of teenagers) in less than two hours, as do *Into the Night* (J. Landis, 1985) and *After Hours* (M. Scorsese, 1985). Though less frequently, we can also find cinematic representations that last longer than the events represented, namely "expansions" (cf. Bordwell 1985: 83–88). For instance, a film can implement an expansion by resorting to slow-motion, or by showing multiple points of view on the same event – for example, the three points of view on the money exchange in *Jackie Brown* (Q. Tarantino, 1997).

In order to take such possibilities into account, we should distinguish three kinds of cinematic duration, namely, the duration D_f of the film itself; the duration D_s of the spectator's experience; and the duration D_e of the events portrayed (cf. Levinson and Alperson 1991: 446; Currie 1995: 92). By "event portrayed" I mean an event that the film represents by prescribing a *continuous* experience that enables the suitable spectator to *perceive* either the event in its entirety or at least the highlights of it. In the former case, the cinematic depiction is more complete than in the latter, just as a portrait of a person that shows her body in its entirety is more complete than one that shows only her face. Yet, many cinematic representations are of the latter kind. For instance, *American Graffiti* portrays an event lasting one night by prescribing a *continuous* experience lasting about 100 minutes, and this experience enables the suitable spectator to *perceive* the highlights of this event.

David Bordwell and Kristin Thompson (2001) call the duration of the events portrayed the "plot duration", and distinguish it from the "story duration", which encompasses the events portrayed as well as other events related to them. In Bordwell and Thompson's example, "The *plot* of *North by Northwest* (A. Hitchcock, 1959) presents four crowded days and nights in the life of Roger Thornhill. But the *story* stretches back far before that, since information about the past is revealed in the course of the plot" (2001: 75, my italics for emphasis). In fact, films can also represent events without depicting them at all. For instance, when a film shows a character telling a past episode – say, when Alexandre in *La Maman et la Putain* (J. Eustache, 1973) tells the episode of the people crying in a café – the episode is represented but not depicted; what is depicted is just the event of telling, namely Alexandre's speech act.

To sum up, among the distinct kinds of duration that are relevant for cinema, the duration D_f of the film is the ontologically fundamental one, in virtue of its grounding the possibility of the impression of movement, which Carroll treats as an essential feature of the moving image. D_f normatively sets not only the duration of any correct screening of the work but also the duration D_s of any correct experience of the work. Yet, such a normative requirement does not hold for the duration D_e of the events represented. A film lasting D_f^* *can* portray an event lasting D_f^*, but it might also portray an event lasting more than D_f^* or even less than D_f^*.

If a film that lasts D_f^* actually depicts an event that lasts D_f^*, then, following Alaina Schempp (2012), I shall call it a "real-time film". Examples of real-time films are *Rope* (A. Hitchcock, 1948) and *Timecode* (M. Figgis, 2000), as well as *12 Angry Men* (S. Lumet, 1957) and *Buried* (R. Cortés, 2010) – and arguably even the experimental film lasting 24 hours *The Clock* (C. Marclay, 2010). *Rope* notoriously achieves the real-time effect by means of a unique long take (with ten hidden cuts) while *Timecode* is a four-panel split screen display that was filmed with four cameras running simultaneously. In general, the property of being constituted by a unique long take is neither necessary nor sufficient for a film to be a real-time film. It is not necessary since a film lasting D_f^* *can* depict an event lasting D_f^* even if it exploits editing, as in *Twelve Angry Men* or in *Buried* – let alone *The Clock*. And it is not sufficient since a film lasting D_f^* *can* portray an event that lasts more than D_f^* even if it is constituted by a unique long take. For instance, *Birdman* (or *The Unexpected Virtue of Ignorance*) (A. González Inarritu, 2014) portrays several days in the life of the hero by means of a long take lasting about two hours; *Imagine* (Z. Rybczyński, 1987) portrays an entire life by means of a long take lasting three minutes and fifteen seconds; and *Russian Ark* (A. Sokurov, 2002) portrays centuries of the history of Russia by means of a unique long take lasting about 90 minutes.

In fact, most movies are not real-time films. A film usually portrays a story that lasts longer – sometimes much longer – than the film itself. Yet, if we focus on a single shot of a movie, we find that the real-time principle normally holds. A shot seems to infringe the real-time principle only in special cases such as fast-motion or slow-motion (for subtler violations, see Bordwell 1985: 81–82; and Smith 1995: 42–44). I will discuss such cases later in the chapter. Alleged exceptions like these aside, the real-time principle seems to be standard for single shots. Bourne and Caddick Bourne characterize what I have called the "real-time principle" as a "norm of duration" according to which "the fictional duration of an episode and the amount of viewing time over which it is represented are *identical*" (2016: 137). Likewise, Currie observes that:

> [i]n the filmic case, at least within the confines of a single shot (and frequently across the class of shots that constitute a scene), there is no violation of the time of the film – neither with respect to order nor with respect to duration.
>
> *(1995: 220)*

As suggested by Currie, most movies are inclined to abide by the real-time principle not only for single shots, but also for bigger temporal units that depict unitary events that are relevant for the progression of the story. Following Christian Metz (1966), I shall call the latter units "scenes". A scene is a real-time portion of a film even if it can be – and in fact often is – constituted by the editing of several shots; the temporal continuity in such cases is often warranted by sound. The special case in which a scene is constituted by a unique shot, without any cut, is called "sequence shot" (cf. Metz 1966: 122).

Ultimately, with respect to duration, the spectator's experience exhibits analogies but also differences in comparison with ordinary perception. Both at the shot level and at the scene level, the spectator's experience normally has the same duration as the event it is about, just as ordinary perception does. Conversely, at the level of the whole film, the spectator's experience normally lasts much less time than the event it is about, and, in this sense, it significantly differs from ordinary experience. In watching *American Graffiti*, we experience an event lasting one night by means of a continuous perceptual experience lasting two hours, whereas in ordinary perception we could never do so. That is why real-time films are correctly said to be more realistic than the other films with respect to duration; the former, unlike the latter, provide us with the same temporal relation between experience and experienced events that we enjoy in ordinary perception.

Film experience as a temporal experience

Let us initially focus on the case of real-time films, which is the one that exhibits the strongest analogy with ordinary perception. Is the experience of a real-time film a temporal experience of the same kind as ordinary perception? In order to address this question, it is worth noting that, even in the case of a real-time film, film experience remains a pictorial experience, that is, an experience of entities depicted.

Richard Wollheim (1998) characterizes the pictorial experience as a peculiar perceptual state, namely "seeing-in", constituted by two folds; in the "configurational fold" we experience the marks on the picture's surface as content-fixing features, while in the "recognitional fold" we experience the depicted scene as the picture's content. In cinema, the configurational fold is harder to characterize than, say, in painting, since the film's spectator does not normally pay attention to the light spots projected on the screen. Nevertheless, the film's spectator is aware at least of the shape and the size of the screen, and this seems enough to have a configurational fold also in the case of cinema. As Robert Hopkins puts it:

> Perhaps cinema images differ in that we find it hard to see the content-fixing features. We are frequently aware of them only by seeing in them the content they fix, and see what is before us as a picture only by seeing other features, such as the shape and size of the screen.
>
> *(2009: 69)*

Interestingly, Francis Sparshott foreshadows cinematic twofoldness when he writes:

> [m]ost of the time one is simultaneously aware of a film (as one is of a painting) both as a two-dimensional arrangement on the screen and as a three-dimensional scene, so that neither aspect dominates the mind except in moments of excitement or disaffection.
>
> *(1971: 18)*

And so does Alexander Sesonske:

> We experience a film as a two-dimensional design on a flat surface and a three-dimensional space within which the action of the film occurs. Cinema shares this duality of its space with painting.
>
> *(1974: 54)*

Such a twofoldness – or, as Sesonske calls it, "duality" – is related to the basic feature of the moving image that Carroll calls "detached display". On the one hand, the spectator experiences the screen as having its place in her egocentric space (i.e., the space centered in and connected to her body); the screen is at a certain distance from the spectator who can orient herself with respect to it and even move towards it. On the other hand, the spectator does not experience the entities depicted as having their place in her egocentric space (cf. Matthen 2005). Thus, the space depicted "is discontinuous with the space of our normal world" (Sesonske 1974: 55); "we observe from a viewpoint at which we are not situated" (Sparshott 1971: 19). This is what Carroll calls "detached display".[1]

That being the case, one might wonder whether what holds for space also holds for time. Given that the spectator does not experience the events depicted as happening here, in front of her, in her environment, can we conclude that she also does not experience those events as happening now, in her own present? The inference seems to be hasty. Indeed, there is at least one case in which the spectator experiences the events depicted in the moving image as happening now. This is the case of live television, in which the spatial detachment of the pictorial experience does not prevent the spectator from experiencing the events depicted in the moving image as temporally present. In short, the spectator of live television does not experience the events depicted as happening here, but nevertheless she experiences those very events as happening now.[2]

Is live television a paradigmatic case for all the other kinds of cinematic experience, including the experience of fiction movies? Currie calls the positive answer to this question "the Claim of Presentness" (1995: 200). I am focusing here on the Claim of Presentness understood as the *phenomenological* claim that the spectator experiences the events depicted in a film as being present, as going on right now. As pointed out by Gideon Yaffe (2003), Robin Le Poidevin (2007), and Bourne and Caddick-Bourne (2016), we may also interpret the Claim of Presentness as the metaphysical claim that a film ascribes the property of being present to the events depicted, so that the fictional events represented in a film constitute what McTaggart (1908) calls an "A-series".

From Currie's perspective, the Claim of Presentness is wrong both as a phenomenological claim and as a metaphysical claim. The point is that cinema cannot depict tensed properties (or "A-series" features) of pastness, presentness, and futurity; it only depicts tenseless relations (or "B-series" features) of precedence or simultaneity (cf. Currie 1995: 218). Therefore, cinema can neither elicit a sense of presentness from the spectator (phenomenological claim) nor ascribe the property of presentness to the events depicted (metaphysical claim). The metaphysical interpretation of the Claim of Presentness lies beyond the scope of this chapter, which concerns temporal experience. In what follows, I focus on the Claim of Presentness as a phenomenological claim.

Accounts of film experience like those proposed by George Wilson (1997, 2011) or Hopkins (2008, 2010) make room for the Claim of Presentness inasmuch as they treat the experience of a fiction movie as having the same phenomenology as the experience of moving pictures of real events – for instance, live television pictures. Yet, according to Currie, the Claim of Presentness is flawed since it cannot take such "anachronies" as flashbacks into account (1995: 201).

A film exhibits an anachrony when the temporal order of the depiction of the events does not comply with the temporal order of the events depicted. In the paradigmatic case of a flashback, a film *depicts* an event X_1 *after* another event X_2 even though, in the objective order of the events in the fictional world, X_1 *occurs before* X_2. Currie argues that if the spectator's ordinary phenomenology involves a sense of presentness, then the experience of a flashback should exhibit a distinctive phenomenology, which either suspends the sense of presentness or preserves it by supplementing it with a sense of time traveling. According to Currie, no phenomenological changes of these sorts show up in the experience of flashbacks. Although the spectator *knows* that the event X_1 that she is seeing in a flashback objectively precedes the event X_2 that she saw before, at the experiential level she *perceives* X_1 in the same way as she perceived X_2 (instead of *perceiving* X_1 as past, or as the experiential result of a time travel of her own). For these reasons, Currie finally rejects the Claim of Presentness.

In the first instance, one might defend the Claim of Presentness against Currie's argument by observing that when an exciting scene of a movie is suddenly interrupted by a flashback, the phenomenology slightly changes. The flashback seems to modify the spectators' phenomenology just as a commercial break would modify the phenomenology of the experience of a live broadcast of a football match.

More generally, the Claim of Presentness can be defended by arguing that film experience, as a *perceptual* experience, should conform to a principle that Le Poidevin (2015: §1) expresses in the following terms, "what we perceive, we perceive as present – as going on right now". If one combines Le Poidevin's principle, which states that the *perceptual* experience is an experience of events as happening now, with the premise that film experience is a *perceptual* experience of depicted events, one can conclude that film experience is an experience of depicted events as happening now. As Yaffe puts it, "if ordinary visual experiences represent A-series properties, why should films be any different?" (2003: 125).

Still, this conclusion is debatable if we go back to the consideration that film experience, as a *pictorial experience*, is a *peculiar* perceptual experience. It might be that the peculiarity of film experience as a pictorial experience also involves the possibility of an infraction of Le Poidevin's principle. Since pictorial experience has two folds – one might argue – Le Poidevin's principle only holds for the configurational fold, not for the recognitional fold. The spectator experiences the projection of light on the screen as going on right now, but not the events depicted as going on right now.

However, the perceptual experience of the spectators normally focuses on the events depicted, not on the light projected. If the perceptual experience that is more relevant for the spectator is that in the recognitional fold, why should Le Poidevin's principle not apply to this experience? We can try to address this issue by relating the peculiar temporality of film experience to its peculiar spatiality. Film experience, as pictorial experience, involves two spaces, namely the egocentric space in the configurational fold and the pictorial space in the recognitional fold; the spectator experiences the screen as being located in her egocentric space and the depicted events as taking place in the pictorial space. In Sesonske's terms, we can draw a distinction between "screen space, the two-dimensional rectangle on the surface of the screen" and "action-space, the three dimensional space within which characters live and die, horses run, lovers sigh, and we can encounter almost any imaginable kind of event" (1980: 420).

That being the case, one might wonder whether film experience involves not only two spaces, but also two temporal dimensions. Henry Wallon (1953) answers this question affirmatively. He argues that film experience involves two temporal series. The first one, which I shall call the "egocentric series", is based on the spectator's proprioception of her own body, which is at the center of her *egocentric* space, but may also involve a visual component (for instance, noticing a moviegoer who checks her smartphone) and an auditory component (for instance, hearing a moviegoer who munches popcorn). The second one, which I shall call the "pictorial series", is based on the visual and auditory experience of the events that occur in the *pictorial* space. In short, the egocentric series is an experiential route through egocentric space whereas the pictorial series is an experiential route through pictorial space.

In the experience of live television, the suitable spectator treats the events experienced as present in the pictorial series *as simultaneous with* what is felt as present in the egocentric series. In contrast, in the experience of a recording of a real event, the suitable spectator treats the events experienced as present in the pictorial series *as prior to* what is felt as present in the egocentric series. Finally, in the experience of a fiction movie, the suitable spectator treats the events experienced as present in the pictorial series *as completely disconnected from* what is felt as present in the egocentric series; the two temporal series run parallel and never converge. Although in all three cases (live TV, recording, fiction) the events in the pictorial series are *experienced* as present at the perceptual level according to Le Poidevin's principle, nevertheless they are *treated* differently at the cognitive level. Therefore, the experiences in the pictorial series, depending on their different relationships to the egocentric series, have different inferential roles and lead to the creation of different beliefs.

The spectator as a time explorer

In an insightful book on time in literature, Marcel Vuillaume (1990) argues that the recipient of a work of fiction can play the role of an unnoticed observer who enjoys special perceptual capacities not available in ordinary perception – first of all, the capacity to observe events without any spatial connection to them. If one combines this hypothesis by Vuillaume with Wallon's (1953) hypothesis that film experience consists of two temporal series, one might conclude that the film spectator can enjoy the privilege described by Vuillaume, i.e., observing events without any spatial connection to them, in the pictorial series described by Wallon. I shall call this "the Wallon-Vuillaume hypothesis".

This hypothesis provides us with a way of facing another objection that Currie raises against the Claim of Presentness, namely that the spectator cannot experience the fictional events as happening now since she has no place in the fictional world. According to the Wallon-Vuillaume hypothesis, the pictorial series provides the unnoticed observer, whose role can be played by the spectator, with the capacity to observe events in the fictional world without having a place in that world (for similar arguments against Currie's point, see also Wilson 1997, 2011; and Walton 1997).

If all of this is right, cinema is capable of supplementing our ordinary temporal experience with a peculiar temporal experience, which unfolds in the pictorial series. In ordinary temporal experience, experiencing an event as happening now involves a strong inclination to believe (unless one has independent reasons for not doing so) that this event is actually happening now. This can occasionally lead us to undergo some temporal illusions, as when we instinctively treat a distant star displaying long past states as present. Conversely, in the peculiar temporal experience that fiction films provide us with, experiencing an event as happening now in the pictorial series does not involve a strong inclination to believe that this event is really happening now inasmuch as such a putative inclination to believe also requires a correspondence between the pictorial series and the egocentric series (as in the case of live television). Thus, in experience of fiction films, the sense of presentness comes down to our way of experiencing the portion of fictional time that we are currently exploring.

Furthermore, the pictorial series makes room for additional experiential privileges that specifically concern the temporal dimension, viz. jumps (flashback, ellipsis, flashforward) and phenomena of acceleration (fast-motion) and deceleration (slow-motion, freeze-frame). Currie characterizes such cases as "a violation of a cinematic norm", namely "the violation of real time" (1995: 119–220). According to the Wallon-Vuillaume hypothesis, the violation is carried out by the pictorial series, which violates the constraints of standard temporal experience which the egocentric series abides by. In particular, as suggested by Currie, in such cases the pictorial series violates the real-time principle, which is a core feature of ordinary perception. Yaffe nicely expresses this point when he writes:

> [f]ilms . . . freely transform the location of the present, and thus give to viewers the sense that the spotlight of the present – the spotlight that, in life, moves so doggedly to the right across the timeline – can be shined on any time.
>
> *(2003: 138)*

The first kind of temporal experiential privilege I shall consider is that of jumps. In the pictorial series, indeed, the spectator can jump from experiencing an event X to experiencing another event that is not temporally contiguous to X. If the spectator jumps to an event W that is successive but not contiguous to X, we have an *ellipsis*. If the spectator jumps to an event U that is prior to X we have a *flashback*. As suggested by Yaffe (2003: 136) the *flashforward* can be conceived of as a strong ellipsis, which produces a narrative gap that is then filled – or, at least, it should be – by a flashback (or a series thereof). In this sense, the flashforward "lets us glimpse the outcome before we have grasped all the causal chains that lead up to it" (Bordwell 1985: 79). In other words, the spectator jumps from an event X to an event W successive to and apparently disconnected from X (here is the strong ellipsis), and then she jumps back from W either to X itself or to an event Y located between X and W (here is the flashback).

In sum, the pictorial series allows the spectator to jump both towards the future and towards the past. In the pictorial series, time can be explored by moving back and forth, as we normally explore space, and nevertheless the Claim of Presentness remains in force. Indeed, if we acknowledge the distinction between egocentric series and pictorial series, we can interpret Currie's criticism of the Claim of Presentness as stating that the suitable spectator of a fiction movie, unlike the suitable spectator of live television, does not treat the pictorial series as coinciding with the egocentric series. So far, we can agree with Currie. Nevertheless, the Claim of Presentness still holds in the pictorial series: the spectator can jump from an event to another, as in the case of a flashback, but once she has jumped to a certain event, she starts experiencing this event as present, in accordance with Le Poidevin's principle. To borrow Yaffe's expression, "The cut resets the location of the present within the fiction" (2003: 134–135).

Cases of acceleration and deceleration also can be treated as a peculiarity of perceptual experience in the pictorial series. In such cases, the spectator experiences an event in its entirety through an experience lasting less (fast-motion) or more (slow-motion) time than the event's actual duration. It is worth noting that what accelerates or decelerates here is not the event itself, but the spectator's perceptual experience of it. A slow-motion shot does not normally ascribe the property of slowness to the things depicted, just as a wide-lens shot does not normally ascribe the property of being warped (and a black and white shot does not normally ascribe the property of being black and white) to them. In other words, the pictorial series allows the spectator to enjoy a peculiar perceptual experience that, instead of sharing the duration of the event perceived, speeds through it (fast-motion) or lingers on it (slow-motion) or even stops at a certain moment of it (freeze-frame).[3]

Such an account of slow/fast-motion and freeze-frame works well when their primary function consists in modifying the *phenomenology* of the spectator's temporal experience. It seems to me that the uses of the fast-motion in grotesque films such as *The Ballad of Cable Hogue* (S. Peckinpah, 1970) or *A Clockwork Orange* (S. Kubrick, 1972) are of this kind, as well as the slow-motion in dramatic films such as *Zabriskie Point* (M. Antonioni, 1970), *The Killer* (J. Woo, 1989), *2046* (Wong Kar-wai, 2004), and *Closer* (M. Nichols, 2004); the freeze-frame in such films as *Les 400 Coups* (F. Truffaut, 1959) or *Goodfellas* (M. Scorsese, 1990) also seems to be of this kind (for a thorough account of slow-motion in cinema, see Rogers 2013).

However, cinema makes room for at least two other uses (or interpretations) of these techniques. First, they can be used to represent peculiar ontological singularities of the fictional world, namely, temporal acceleration or deceleration: consider for instance the fast-motion in *Click* (F. Coraci, 2006) or the slow-motion and the freeze-frame in *The Matrix* (A. and L. Wachowski, 1999). Second, these techniques can be used to represent *psychological* states of characters, that is, as Bourne and Caddick-Bourne put it, to "convey fictional truths about time as it is experienced by characters in the fictional situation" (2016: 148). For instance, "A slow-motion representation of a car accident may communicate fictional truths about how the fictional driver experiences his world, fictional truths which we know in the form: *That* is what it was like for him" (Bourne and Caddick-Bourne 2016: 148). In sum, the slow/fast-motion and the freeze-frame function *phenomenologically* inasmuch as such techniques shape the spectator's temporal experience, but they can also function *ontologically* inasmuch as they depict the temporal singularities of the fictional world, and even *psychologically* inasmuch as they represent a peculiar temporal experience of some character.

Conclusions

La Sortie de l'Usine Lumière à Lyon (A. and L. Lumière, 1895), traditionally considered the first film in the history of cinema, is a real-time film. That is, an event lasting 46 seconds is depicted as lasting 46 seconds by a film lasting 46 seconds. However, the real-time principle not only lies at the origin of the history of cinema, but also constitutes a core principle of the moving image as a medium. The spectator normally experiences the events depicted in a shot or in a scene as having the same duration as the shot itself or as the scene itself. The Claim of Presentness adds that the spectator experiences these events as present, as going on right now. This claim is highly debatable, and yet a weaker and maybe more acceptable version of it can be formulated by means of what I have called the Wallon-Vuillaume hypothesis. The idea is that the spectator's experience of the depicted events as present occurs in a peculiar temporal series, namely the pictorial series. First of all, the spectator does not treat the pictorial series as coinciding with the temporal series she experiences through the proprioceptive feedback of her body, unless she is watching such moving images as those of live television. Furthermore, the pictorial series makes room for temporal experiences that are not possible in ordinary temporal experience, namely flashbacks, ellipses, flashforwards, fast-motion, slow-motion, and freeze-frames. Such special experiences violate the real-time principle, thereby allowing the spectator to experience an event through a continuous experience that lasts less or more time than that event. While ordinary perceptual experience is forced to obey the real-time principle, the pictorial series normally abides by it but can sometimes violate it.

On the one hand, when the pictorial series abides by the real-time principle, film experience emulates ordinary perception. Such an emulation allows films to elicit intense emotions of fear, hope, suspense, disappointment, surprise, exultation, which seem to require a sense of presentness inasmuch as they depend on the *imminent* resolution of a certain uncertainty in what we are perceptually experiencing. As Yaffe puts it, "The point is that in whatever sense sensory experiences represent A-series properties, films do also, and this is a large part of the reason that films have the particular emotional effects that they have" (2003: 128). On the other hand, when the pictorial series violates the real-time principle, the film experience overcomes ordinary perception thereby turning the spectator into a sort of time explorer, who can do in time what we normally can do only in space, namely slowing down, stopping, lingering on, speeding through, or jumping. Both the emulation of ordinary temporal experience and its overcoming, when skillfully exploited by filmmakers, can elicit valuable aesthetic experiences from spectators. As a matter of fact, some films favor the former and others the latter. Yet, in principle, cinema consists of them both.[4]

Notes

1 3D films can reduce such a detachment but cannot completely suppress it, since the events depicted are relegated into a parallelepiped which intersects the spectator's egocentric space but remains distinct from it. Instead, in the case of virtual reality, the space depicted wholly replaces the spectator's egocentric space.

2 One might wonder whether a screen on a wall providing a depiction of just what was going on behind the wall would count as both live and "here" TV (I owe this suggestion to Ian Phillips; Currie (1995: 64) considers a similar case involving a window instead of a wall). I think that there remains an asymmetry between time and space in this respect since live television is live at the type level (all the broadcast tokens of that moving image are live) whereas Phillips's wall or Currie's window are "here" only at the token level (only one special token of that moving image has the privilege of being "here").

3 If one conceives of depiction in terms of the sharing of features between the representation and the represented, then, strictly speaking, a slow motion shot *depicts* things slowed just as a wide-lens shot depicts things as warped, and a black and white shot depicts things as black and white (cf. Phillips 2009, §3.4). Yet, a slow motion shot, as a representation, does not prescribe an experience of things slowed, but rather a slowed experience of things moving at their normal speed (likewise, a wide-lens shot prescribes a warped experience of things having their normal shape, and a black and white shot prescribes a black and white experience of things having their normal shape). That is to say that, in such cases, what matters is not depiction strictly understood but the way in which depiction is exploited in order to prescribe a certain experience. I believe that this holds also in the case of the backwards shots that we can find in films such as *Je T'Aime, Je T'Aime* (A. Resnais, 1968) or *The Rules of Attraction* (R. Avary, 2002).

4 Thanks to Alaina Schempp, Filippo Contesi, Anna Giustina, Luca Bandirali, and Ian Phillips for their helpful comments on earlier versions of this chapter.

References

Abell, C. (2010) "Cinema as a representational art", *British Journal of Aesthetics* 50(3): 273–286.

Bordwell, D. (1985) *Narration in the Fiction Film*, Madison, WI: University of Wisconsin Press.

Bordwell, D. and Thompson, K. (2001) *Film Art: An Introduction*, New York: McGraw Hill.

Bourne, C. and Caddick-Bourne, E. (2016) *Time in Fiction*, Oxford, UK: Oxford University Press.

Carroll, N. (1996) "Defining the moving image", in N. Carroll (ed.), *Theorizing the Moving Image*, Cambridge, UK: Cambridge University Press, pp. 49–74.

Currie, G. (1995) *Image and Mind: Film, Philosophy, and Cognitive Science*, Cambridge, UK: Cambridge University Press.

Deleuze, G. (1983) *Cinéma 1. L'Image-mouvement*, Paris: Minuit; English translation by H. Tomlinson and B. Habberjam (1986) *Cinema 1: The Movement-Image*, London: Athlone.

Deleuze, G. (1985) *Cinéma 2. L'Image-temps*, Paris: Minuit; English translation by H. Tomlinson and R. Galeta (1989) *Cinema 2: The Time-Image*, Minneapolis, MN: University of Minnesota Press.

Hopkins, R. (2008) "What do we see in film?" *The Journal of Aesthetics and Art Criticism* 66(2): 149–159.

Hopkins, R. (2009) "Depiction", in P. Livingston and C. Plantinga (eds), *The Routledge Companion to Philosophy and Film*, London: Routledge, pp. 64–74.

Hopkins, R. (2010) "Moving because pictures? Illusion and the emotional power of film", *Midwest Studies in Philosophy* 34(1): 200–218.

Kania, A. (2006) "Making tracks: The ontology of rock music", *The Journal of Aesthetics and Art Criticism* 64(4): 401–414.

Le Poidevin, R. (2007) *The Images of Time: An Essay on Temporal Representation*, Oxford, UK: Oxford University Press.

Le Poidevin, R. (2015) "The experience and perception of time", *The Stanford Encyclopedia of Philosophy* (Summer 2015 Edition), E. N. Zalta (ed.), available at http://plato.stanford.edu/entries/time-experience/. Accessed 23 December 2016.

Levinson, J. and Alperson, P. (1991) "What is a temporal art?" *Midwest Studies In Philosophy* 16(1): 439–450.

Matthen, M. (2005) *Seeing, Doing, and Knowing: A Philosophical Theory of Sense Perception*, Oxford, UK: Oxford University Press.

McTaggart, J. M. E. (1908) "The unreality of time", *Mind* 17(68): 457–484.

Metz, C. (1966) "La grande syntagmatique du film narratif", *Communications* 8(1): 120–124.

Phillips, I. (2009) *Experience and Time*, PhD Thesis, University College London.

Ponech, T. (2006) "The substance of cinema", *The Journal of Aesthetics and Art Criticism* 64(1): 187–198.

Recanati, F. (1996) "Domains of discourse", *Linguistics and Philosophy* 19(5): 445–475.

Remes, J. (2015) *Motion(less) Pictures: The Cinema of Stasis*, New York: Columbia University Press.

Rogers, S. (2013) "Truth, lies, and the meaning of slow motion images", in A. P. Shimamura (ed.), *Psychocinematics: Exploring Cognition at the Movies*, Oxford, UK: Oxford University Press, pp. 149–164.

Schempp, A. (2012) *Fiction in Real-Time: Aesthetics, Perception, and Cognition of Real-Time Narrative Cinema*, Research Master in Media Studies Thesis, Universiteit van Amsterdam.

Sesonske, A. (1974) "Aesthetics of film, or a funny thing happened on the way to the movies", *The Journal of Aesthetics and Art Criticism* 33(1): 51–57.

Sesonske, A. (1980) "Time and tense in cinema", *The Journal of Aesthetics and Art Criticism* 38(4): 419–426.

Smith, M. (1995), *Engaging Characters*, Oxford, UK: Oxford University Press.

Sparshott, F. E. (1971) "Basic film aesthetics", *Journal of Aesthetic Education* 5(2): 11–34.

Terrone, E. (2014) "The digital secret of the moving image", *Estetika: The Central European Journal of Aesthetics* LI/VII(1): 21–41.

Vuillaume, M. (1990) *Grammaire temporelle des récits*, Paris: Les Éditions de Minuit.

Wallon, H. (1953) "L'acte perceptif et le cinéma", *Revue internationale de filmologie* 13: 100–110.

Walton, K. (1997) "On pictures and photographs: Objections answered", in R. Allen and M. Smith (eds), *Film Theory and Philosophy*, Oxford, UK: Oxford University Press, pp. 60–75.

Wilson, G. M. (1997) "Le grand imagier steps out: The primitive basis of film narration", *Philosophical Topics* 25: 295–318.

Wilson, G. M. (2011) *Seeing Fictions in Film: The Epistemology of Movies*, Oxford, UK: Oxford University Press.

Wollheim, R. (1998) "On pictorial representation", *The Journal of Aesthetics and Art Criticism* 56(3): 217–226.

Yaffe, G. (2003) "Time in the movies", *Midwest Studies in Philosophy* 27(1): 115–138.

Further reading

J. Leirens, *Le cinéma et le temps* [Cinema and time] (Paris: Éditions du Cerf, 1954) and F. Bettetini, *Tempo del senso. La logica temporale dei testi audiovisivi* [*Time and meaning. The temporal logic of audiovisual works*] (Milan, Italy: Bompiani, 1979) are two seminal books on time in cinema.

T. Grodal, *Moving Pictures – A New Theory of Film Genres, Feelings, and Cognition* (Oxford, UK: Oxford University Press, 1997) explains the distinction between objective and subjective time in terms of temporal schemata and modalities.

S. L. Feagin, "Time and timing", (in C. Plantinga and G. M. Smith. (eds.), *Passionate Views: Film, Cognition, and Emotion*, Baltimore, MD: Johns Hopkins University Press, 1999) investigates how timing in film affects both spectators' cognition and emotions.

26

DANCING IN TIME

Aili Bresnahan

This chapter will analyze the experience and, in particular the conscious experience, of dancing in time from the perspective of the trained dancer *while performing*. The focus is thus on the experience and consciousness of a dancer who is moving her body in time rather than on the experience of a seated audience member or dance appreciator who is watching a dancer move. The question of how temporality is experienced in dance by the appreciator will therefore not be addressed here. The primary kind of "experience" that will be the focus of my discussion of temporal experience comes from classical pragmatists William James, Charles Sanders Peirce, and John Dewey, for whom experience is "a series of purposive bodily activities immersed in the ongoing flow of organism-environment interactions" (Johnson 2006: 48). The mind-body engaged in this experience, according to the pragmatists, is one that is sensate to its environmental stimuli and interactions while acting within it. Both Peirce and Dewey, for example, view the person as a "psycho-physical" organism – one that is conscious of both qualitative experiences such as feelings towards the environment (attraction, repulsion, and the like) as well as physical sensations (see Peirce 1998 [1892]: 263 and Dewey 2008 [1925]: 229). James acknowledges that we are aware of qualitative aspects of our experience such as sensations of difference or change (see James 1950 [1890a]: 495). My account of the experience of dancing in time will also include conscious aspects of this experience (what-it-feels-like-to-the-dancer herself) as well as any sensorimotor pre-conscious or non-conscious processes of which she is not aware by virtue of her bodily engagement with the world (cf. Maurice Merleau-Ponty 2008 [1945]: 235–239).

In short, the experience of dancing to be addressed here takes place in both the dancer's consciousness of it and in the temporal and spatial parameters that have been set for the dancing. It is thus not strictly analogous to the sort of consciousness involved in other sorts of bodily experiences where there are no such explicit parameters (e.g., taking a walk without a clear destination or route in mind and without any time limitations). In addition, dancing is a thinking-while-doing process that involves the sort of temporal consciousness that is itself either both thoroughly embodied and spatial in an integrated way or in which embodied and spatial experiences occur concurrently. The hope here is that analyzing the experience and consciousness of temporality while dancing will be useful for those who are interested in understanding the full range of temporal experience, including the sort of experience that thinkers engage in while active and moving in a structured way.

To what extent temporal experience while dancing is inextricably bound up with, accompanies, depends on, supervenes on, or forms the base or floor of physical and spatial experience will be left to specialists in philosophy of mind, psychology, neuroscience, and cognitive science to articulate. The sections that follow will just take the first step of explaining how the temporal experience of dancing arises with spatial and bodily movement experience, and then progress towards analyzing how it appears in and in relation to the dancer's subjective consciousness.

How dancers' training to dance in time affects their temporal consciousness

When a dancer steps into a ballet class and takes a position at the barre, his experience of dance is already spatially located. When he begins to move through space, this spatiality is explored in a more particularly embodied way, through his toe's movement across the floor or through his leg's extension from one place to another. This takes place within a duration of time that is set for the movement and that the dancer must comply with in order to meet the requirements of the classroom exercise. Both temporal and spatial factors are focused on during this movement, as there is a duration and area that is set for it. Sondra Horton Fraleigh points out that for the dancer, "movement, space, and time are only abstractions until they are embodied" (1987: 182). Thus the dancer's consciousness of time and space arises with and is influenced by his dynamic and embodied experience, and this is one of interacting with the world outside of himself.

Most dance classes involve dancing on the beat of either melodic or percussive music, which is either played by a live musical accompanist or on a sound system from a recording. Dancers are typically trained to count the beats of music in sets of eight. To begin, a dance instructor may start with "And . . ." or "5–6–7–8 . . ." with the dancers beginning their exercises on the downbeat right after that. This starting point shows how integral the temporality of music is to the dancer's process of learning to move in time. A dancer's movement limits, at least at first and for a large portion of her training, thus have thoroughly temporal parameters. If the dancers are struggling with completing the steps in musical time, if they are unable to accent each beat with the appropriate movement, the music or beat may be slowed down until the dancers can accomplish the movements with the requisite speed. In any event, dancers learn where the beats and limits of the musical phrases are, and how to stay within (or to violate, whether intentionally or not) those parameters.

Dances made for performance are usually not quite this conventional in aligning movements to the temporal parameters of music. Here a dancer may accent a beat or arrive early or late for a musical cue for certain artistic and stylistic effects. Doing this intentionally and skillfully, however, still requires a dancer to know where and what the temporal parameters of the music are. A dancer's physical movement training, then, and any accompanying consciousness that arises as a result of this training, is often inherently connected to musical tempo, a certain kind of temporality.

Some dancers, particularly in contemporary dance, may train without music (using breath, foot, or body impacts for the beat, for example) or to less beat-driven music, but even here there is usually some sort of time parameter that emerges. In addition, timing of movements and rests may be set by the choreographer for performance, or left open or more variable (as in improvisational dance). Dancers may also experience the temporal parameters of moving in synchronization with or in conjunction with other dancers. Dancers rehearsing and training together for extended periods of time will also experience "a palpable sense of anticipation, synchrony, or 'felt time'" (Stevens *et al.* 2009: 451).

In general, fast tempos require what dancers call "attack" and energy in the movements. For a movement to be quicker in tempo, a dancer might need either a smaller movement or a greater amount of force behind the movement (so that a bigger jump or leg movement, for example, can span a larger amount of space more quickly). In all cases a dancer's movements occur in space, and what is needed to traverse the available or designated space is essential for a dancer to know in order to be in time.

Once a dancer has trained to do certain movements in a certain tempo his body and brain become accustomed to that tempo and the movements become easier to perform. Performing repeated longer-duration movements that allow for greater extension, for example, make it easier and easier for the dancer to perform those movements. In general, thorough dance training will include both lento or adagio (slower), and andante or allegro (faster) movements so that a dancer will end up with a body that can perform both fast and slow movements well. Some dancers, however, have a greater capacity for faster or slower physical motion by virtue of their training, their individual body type, and genetic makeup, or all three. (Some people are better suited for long-distance running and some fare better with sprinting for similar reasons.)

What happens as a result of this training is that a dancer often learns to *feel* (physically and often consciously) what it would be like to perform the same movement in variable time durations, such as performing a sequence of turns in either a three-second or one-second duration. If the music's tempo changes mid-dance, the trained dancer can usually adjust accordingly and still be "on the music" as long as the movement to the new tempo is within her physical repertoire. A dancer who wishes to dance with music, then, needs to be able to hear (among other things) the temporality in music. She also needs to be able to navigate the available space in accordance with the musical and other temporal parameters. (For more on how this is done in contemporary dance, see Stevens *et al.* 2009.)

Thus dancing in time requires the dancer to both focus on, and to have a deep understanding of, how her own body can move physically in both time and space. The dancer's experience of time is therefore either inherently spatial or occurs in close congruence with her experience of space. (For a theory that movement thoroughly integrates time and space together, see Fraleigh 1987, particularly chapter 10.) As mentioned earlier, this physical-spatial awareness is a precondition for fitting within a prescribed temporality. A dancer may need to shorten the height of a jump if it needs to fit within a quick time period – or she may allow it to soar but then have to adjust the rest of the phrase to catch up. This is true whenever there is a particular beat or note or part of the music on which the sequence must stop. If a conductor of a live orchestra is asked to follow the dancer's timing lead, then the dancer needs to know this (and usually does) ahead of time. In either case, though, the temporal-spatiality of the movement must be fully understood by the dancer or her movements will be "off", which means that they are out of sync with the spatio-temporal parameters of the choreography and performance space. Thus in the initial stages of creating or performing a particular dance, a dancer needs to be conscious of what Fraleigh calls the moving "time-space" of a dance (1987: 179, 183–184). Once she has performed the same dance numerous times, however, she can move within the correct parameters in a faster way and need not be as reflectively conscious of particular temporal and spatial markers.

Bettina Bläsing *et al.* confirm the account provided above, noting that the dancer's ability to synchronize her movements with others' or to the music is an essential part of dance performance (2012: 302). They point to a study by Honisch *et al.* (2009), focused on temporal accuracy in ballet movement. Here the results showed that expert ballet dancers (as opposed to novices) had greater accuracy synchronizing the dynamics of their movements to both temporal markers and to others' movements. A trained dancer, for example, is better able to either perform a movement at a particular temporal point in the music, or after, before, or with the movement of one or more other dancers (which itself may or may not be temporally guided by the parameters of the dance). This demonstrates that a dancer's timing skills are affected by motor experience and training with particular movements. "In addition", Bläsing *et al.* point out, expert "dancers' anticipation of target positions may enable faster detection and rapid adjustment to errors that may be performed by other dancers" (2012: 303; see further, Washburn *et al.* 2014). What this shows is that expert dancers are better able to synchronize both their movements with temporal and other parameters in the present moment, and are better able to use their ability to make on-the-fly adjustments during performance based on knowing which position in the dance will arrive next.

For the dancer, this understanding feels bodily, or what Maxine Sheets-Johnstone would call part of a "kinesthetic consciousness" that is highly subjective and in which "the streaming present is a dynamic flux that we experience *qualitatively*", by which she means with an awareness of features such as grace, tension, energy, or beauty as perceived by the dancer both consciously and through bodily feelings and sensorimotor responses (2011: 131). It is within this qualitative experience that Sheets-Johnstone says that temporality arises for dancers (Ibid.). Dancers move first, and through movement come to be conscious of time and space – through how it feels to us as our bodies move through it (see Sheets-Johnstone, 2011: 139).[1] In addition, this kinesthetic, bodily, motor awareness includes what dancers, musicians, athletes, and others often term "muscle memory" – over time, it can occur without the sort of conscious direction or thought that involves planning first and movement second, the way one can physically manipulate a combination lock or drive to a particular destination without knowing at which numbers one should stop or how to map the trip (see Sudnow 1979, 2002; Bläsing 2010: 82–83; and Bresnahan 2014 for more on how this entrained mind-body capacity is at the heart of improvisation and live performance of many kinds).

To sum up our conclusions thus far, the dancer's consciousness and experience of dancing in time includes qualitative conscious and kinesthetic awareness. It is also embodied in a sensate, physical vehicle that is simultaneously moving through and inhabiting space. Temporal consciousness and experience do not arise for dancers in isolation from their embodied and spatial experience. This chapter will now connect this idea of dancers' moving, embodied, and temporal-spatial consciousness to one line of thinking in the philosophy of temporal consciousness, which can be traced from William James to Antonio Damasio and Marc Wittmann, in order to see what fits and what still remains to be explored.

Dancing within (and beyond) the specious present

William James provides an account of consciousness in which thought, among other things, is personal, sensibly continuous, and appears to deal with objects independent of itself (1950 [1890a]: 225). He also notes that when we are engaged in thinking, we are not always aware of the fact that we are thinking (1950 [1890a]: 275–276). Thus thought itself need not be self-conscious even though it is a self that is doing the thinking.

Further, James considers consciousness to be something that occurs in a stream in which the future and present move into the past so continuously that we are aware that the present is something that "*must* exist, but that it *does* exist can never be a fact in our immediate experience" (1950 [1890a]: 608–609). He uses the term "specious present", which he says he has borrowed from E. R. Clay, to characterize this phenomenon, quoting him at length:

> The present to which the datum refers is really a part of the past – a recent past – delusively given as being a time that intervenes between the past and the future. Let it be named the specious present, and let the past, that is given as being the past, be

known as the obvious past. All the notes of a bar of a song seem to the listener to be contained in the present. All the changes of place of a meteor seem to the beholder to be contained in the present. At the instant of the termination of such series, no part of the time measured by them seems to be a past.

(1950 [1890a]: 609; see also Andersen 2014: 290, who observes that E. R. Clay is a mistaken attribution and that the actual author is E. Robert Kelly)

James later characterizes the specious present as a "duration-block" that makes us aware of a succession lasting from a few seconds to not more than a minute in which one part is perceived as earlier and one as later (1950 [1890a]: 642). This does not, however, mean that we are not also aware of moments as they pass. James says that we perceive time through our awareness of change, that "we tell it off in pulses. We say 'now! now! now!' or we count 'more! more! more!' as we feel it bud" (1950 [1890a]: 620). In addition, when the experience is over, we can remember and keep in mind the successions of "nows" and use them to inform our current conscious awareness, as when a trained and practiced musical performer plays a piece from memory with ease (see James 1950 [1890a]: 117 on habit). This squares well with the consciousness and experience of the dancer while dancing in performance.

The expert dancer who is moving in time has both the memory of the past and the imagination of the future. She experiences in consciousness the step she has just taken and anticipates the one she will take next. As noted earlier, this is part of her ability to synchronize her movements with the temporal and spatial parameters of the dance as well as with the other dancers. (See Bläsing 2010 on memory in trained dancers, and Bläsing *et al.* 2012 for how expertise in dance allows for heightened imagination of future movement. See also Stevens *et al.* 2009, 2011 for how contextual factors such as music affect dancers' long-term memory.) This is similar to the phenomenon that James noticed with trained musicians, where he describes the "acquired aptitudes" that he says are due both to memory and to "the guiding sensations derived from the muscles themselves" (1950 [1890a]: 117, quoting Carpenter 1874: 217). Thus James has set the stage for the later studies in entrained motor abilities that are informally called "muscle memory".

It is true both that a dancer's memory and consciousness can contain a whole dance, while dancing, and that the dancer is extremely and excruciatingly aware of passing from one step or movement to the next in both time and in space. The moment she is in *at the moment* is made vivid by the physical sensations of dance – the twinge of a toe in a pointe shoe or the feel of a thigh muscle as the dancer calibrates the landing from a jump. It is this physicality, among other things, that marks the temporal moments as significant for the dancer, and they come forward in her consciousness *as* moments and she feels them as part of a whole dance. In addition, thinking-while-dancing takes place in an ever-changing present of which she is aware even while it is constantly changing, even if this is specious rather than the precise dividing line between future and past. This is particularly true during dance improvisations or in improvisational moments of a set dance. Sheets-Johnstone points out, for example, that thinking-while-dancing takes place "within the experience of an ongoing present" rather than as a pre-danced plan that the dancer then executes (1981: 401). (For more on this point see Merritt 2015: 106–107.)

Of course, the dancer's moving through time and space together makes it difficult to determine what is coming forwards into the dancer's consciousness as the experience of time and what as the experience of space. James thinks that time, for example, is necessarily ordered (and, indeed, that this is what music is about), but that space need not have any order in it at all (1950 [1890b]: 145 and footnote). For a dancer moving in time from point A to point B on the stage, however, space has marks that are ordered in time (he will try to hit point A at temporal musical marker X, for example, and point B at temporal music marker Y). This makes the dancer's experience of space an ordered one even if what orders it is temporality. It also makes the dancer's experience of time feel and seem spatial.

James does acknowledge that movement helps perception of space. "A fly is sitting unnoticed", he points out, "we feel it the moment it crawls. A shadow may be too faint to be perceived. As soon as it moves, however, we see it" (1950 [1890b]: 174). Indeed, James says with emphasis that "*in the education of spatial discrimination the motions of impressions across sensory surfaces must have been the principle agent* in breaking up our consciousness of the surfaces into a consciousness of their parts" (1950 [1890b]: 175). He also acknowledges that perception of space occurs in a sensory, bodily way that includes not just vision but tactile perception via the muscles, the skin, and the joints (1950 [1890b]: 176, 268). Again, though, for the dancer who experiences space and time together while moving to music, the movement through space feels as if he is simultaneously moving through the music as well. It may be the case that the feeling of moving in music (while hearing it and feeling its rhythmic vibrations through the body) is thus an experience of time and space that is so integrated that it seems artificial to say that the experience of dancing to music is *either* temporal *or* spatial *or* even that two separate things are happening together. What this means is that to the dancer they arise in consciousness as one singular and fused process. Therefore, it is not clear what to make of the fact that James treats "the perception of time" and "the perception of space" in two separate and so-named chapters in *The Principles of Psychology* (chapters XV and XX, respectively). Perhaps he would acknowledge that felt and lived experience does fuse processes together in consciousness that can be treated discretely for the purposes of philosophical analysis even though they are not discrete in experience. This would be one broadly pragmatist way of handling this apparent disjunction between the dancer's experience and subjective consciousness, and James' treatment of the consciousness of time and space as separate. Indeed, there are other instances of temporal-spatial fusing in experience of which James was probably aware. For example, a deaf person may feel music's temporality through the floor (some deaf dancers have reported feeling the beat through their bare feet) rather than perceiving it via their ears in sound in a way that seems not all that different from how James says that a blind person perceives space through a sort of "locomotor feeling" (1950 [1890b]: 207). Thus there is a bodily aspect of the experience of perceiving both time and space that adds to the analysis of how time shows up for the dancer in consciousness that seems at least consistent with James' philosophy of the consciousness and experience of space, even though James did not connect time and space together explicitly.

In *The Feeling of What Happens: Body and Emotion in the Making of Consciousness* (1999) Antonio Damasio provides a theory of how emotion is bodily, and how much of what occurs at this bodily level happens before we are conscious of it. He does not address dance, specifically, or temporal experience, but this section will now mine his idea of how consciousness works in order to show how his account is consistent with James'. In short, his view affirms that it is possible for a dancer to be both conscious of the experience of dancing in time in the present (even if it is of a specious rather than actual present), and contain the consciousness of the dance in all its physical, spatial, and temporal aspects, as a whole.

Damasio uses the example of a performer stepping into the light after a door to the stage opens as a metaphor for consciousness (1999: 3). What he is trying to capture with this metaphor is "the sense of a self in the act of knowing" (1999: 11). A person dancing in time is precisely that – a conscious, embodied agent who is acting in time and space (see Ibid: 145 and 148 for his account of consciousness as part of agency; see Montero 2016, chapter 2, for an account of expert cognition-in-action; see Bresnahan 2014 and Merritt 2015 for more on conscious agency in dance). Dancing in time involves the sort of consciousness that is a self in the act of knowing what he has been trained to know – how to move so that he meets the temporal, spatial, and other parameters of the dance. A dancer thus follows the rules of dancing the dance "as it comes into being at this particular moment at this particular place" (Sheets-Johnstone 1981: 399).

Damasio attributes the elements that occur automatically in the present (and the moment just before) to what he calls the "core consciousness", a biological function of human beings that includes no memory, reasoning, or language, and that remains stable throughout a person's lifetime (1999: 16, 195). The core consciousness is the basic biological substrate upon which other forms of more complex consciousness operate (Ibid.). This level of consciousness is shared with animals, according to Damasio – it is not trained, culturally influenced, or part of any expertise or acquired aptitudes. For trained expertise, a developed cultural understanding and knowledge, and for language, memory, imagination, and everything else that makes human expert action and creativity possible, Damasio says that one needs to make recourse to the "extended consciousness", an awareness that extends forwards and backwards over a longer duration of time, that has multiple levels of complexity, and that changes and grows across a person's lifetime (1999: 16–17).

Although the time duration of what the core consciousness can apprehend is similar to James' consciousness of the specious present, the two are not identical. James did not, for example, divide consciousness into the biologically base (core) and culturally developed (extended) forms that Damasio does. In general, though, Damasio claims that the properties of James' view of consciousness – being selective, continuous, personal, and related to objects other than itself – are evident in both core and extended forms of consciousness (1999: 126 and endnote 4 at 346).

A more significant difference between the two views arises when we consider the trained aptitude of performing dance at issue in this chapter. Damasio, like James, uses a musical performance reference that we can adopt for dance purposes. "It may be helpful to think of the behavior of an organism as the performance of an orchestral piece whose score is being invented as it goes along", Damasio says, where "the behavior of an organism is the result of several biological systems performing concurrently" (1999: 87). Here it seems clear that Damasio would agree that *both* core and extended consciousnesses are at work simultaneously – the core consciousness is noting basics such as "the concurrent stacking of musical parts" and the extended consciousness is evaluating "mental streams of images" that connect these to "an orchestral score in the private mind" (1999: 88). In James, there is similar multi-layering. We are aware of both the specious present (in James it is not clear if this is culturally rich or biologically basic because he does not make that distinction) and can use memory, past training, and imagination to inform the ease and quality of the performance.

We can now add Damasio to our list of implicit supporters for our claim that a dancer can be aware of the moment while dancing, as well as have a consciousness of what has just taken place and what is to come. The dancer maintains the whole dance in his mind's eye and sensorimotor system, and develops a skilled and bodily consciousness as a dancer that may last for the entire duration of his dance life. The reason these core and extended forms of consciousness are possible is that they are tied to the repository of a self that has what Damasio would call genomic components (biological attributes) and cultural ones that are developed over time as the human self encounters and learns from his environment (see Damasio 1999: 228–229; see also the distinction between natural and artistic style in Bresnahan 2014). There is more than one "self" for Damasio – a core, an autobiographic, and a proto-self, but this chapter holds that there is just one self with various aspects and capacities (see Damasio 1999: 174 for more on this).

Thus dancing in time involves at least two aspects of a self from which consciousness springs, and these two can exist together without contradiction. Dancing in time involves an acting self who is both a biological person who is dancing and a trained *dancer* who can encompass the entirety of a dance in her consciousness and alter her planned movements to fit the contingencies of what may be a changing temporal flow – the tempo of music played by a live orchestra let us say. In conclusion, then, both forms of consciousness (core and extended) are derived from the experience of dancing in time. It involves the dancer's ability to both think and move on-the-fly, to use her memory of previous experiences of dancing in time, and to use her imagination of what to do in the future.

In an essay entitled, "Embodied time: The experience of time, the body, and the self", Marc Wittmann has a view that fits with both James' and Damasio's above. He claims that "the bodily self, the continuous visceral and proprioceptive input from the body, which is a basis for our mental self, is the functional anchor of phenomenal experience" (2014: 512; see also Damasio 1999: 153). Curiously, Wittmann does not believe that time is a property of the external world but is instead part of a "mental construct" (2014: 512–513). Despite this, he claims that "subjective time emerges through (or is bound to) the existence of self across time as an enduring and embodied entity" (Ibid.). Wittmann uses the example of tapping one's finger to a regular beat as an example of the capacity that we have to integrate bodily movement in a way that "defines the present moment in experience" but notes that we can only do this with short intervals of time between beats (2014: 514). And yet he acknowledges that we can learn to match "the duration of external events with interoceptive afferent activity" (our internal neuronal processes), which begs the question of what this "duration of external events" is if there is not a sort of temporality that exists in the world outside of ourselves (see 2014: 516).

We turn now to where the account of dancing in time developed thus far fits within the standard terminology used in the temporal consciousness literature.

A broadly retentional model of subjective consciousness

James, Damasio, and Wittmann all have views that fit to some extent with what is known as "the retentional model" of temporal consciousness in the sense that they treat experience that represents extended intervals of time as showing up for us in at least some cases in moments of consciousness that are not themselves extended (see Dainton 2014: section 1 and Wittmann 2011: 1). In *The Principles of Psychology*, for example, James acknowledges that even the feeling of past time is a present feeling (1950 [1890a]: 627–631). This evidences a focus on the sort of consciousness that is separable from the initial event (the past time) that has taken place, which he likens to "a sort of *perspective projection* of past objects upon present consciousness, similar to that of wide landscapes upon a camera screen" (1950 [1890a]: 630). James also says, however, that we can register *actual* duration-blocks in our consciousness, which seems to suggest that the content of our consciousness has some sort of matching relationship with duration-blocks as they occur in the world outside of consciousness, or that it can match them or make room for them at times. If by "actual" he means that the outside world can and does match our phenomenological consciousness of it in some ways, then it suggests that his view of consciousness is one that might be friendly to an *inheritance* view in which our subjective consciousness can sometimes inherit temporal properties of experience itself, but that it need not do so in all cases or for all experiential objects (see Phillips 2014 for more on the inheritance view).

Damasio declares his view to be consistent with James', as well as with the views of Locke, Brentano, Kant, and Freud, who he says "believed as I do that consciousness is 'an inner sense'" (1999: 126). He clarifies in an extended endnote that by this he means that "consciousness pertains to objects other than itself. There is an object, on the one hand, and there is consciousness of the object, on the other, separable from it although clearly related to it" (1999: 346). Damasio's example of the musician complying with the temporality of an orchestral score and

Wittmann's finger-tapping example demonstrate that this relationship can be adjusted and fine-tuned – that our consciousness can adapt to certain kinds of external parameters. Remember too that on Damasio's view, core and extended consciousnesses can operate in a multi-layered way at the same time. In that same endnote, he says that as complex organisms we can engage perceptually with the outside world, produce "internally recalled images", or do both at once (Ibid.). This sounds very much like a contemporary analogue of James' past feeling recalled in the present moment.

As we have seen, the dancer while dancing is often aware of the "now!" of experience in a way that appears to extend beyond the non-experienced and mathematically precise instant in which "now!" actually occurs. This fits with the retentionalist approach. The performing dancer is also engaged in matching her movements to temporal and spatial parameters as they take place, with an unfolding of consciousness that has to adjust in order to do this accurately. Here, some sort of inheritance from the world outside of her own consciousness may also be taking place, but this suggestion is offered merely as a speculative possibility that would require further work to articulate and to support.

Conclusion

In conclusion, the trained dancer's consciousness and experience of dancing in time in performance has sensorimotor, kinesthetic, and spatial aspects. The dancer's body, with all its sensory awarenesses and neuromuscular sensations of moving, is a large component of her experience of time either in conjunction with or combined with her experience of space. While dancing, certain moments are marked in her conscious awareness by both the perception of change and by the feeling of hitting a mark in a temporal parameter that is linked to a physical movement and a spatial location. This is conscious in the sense that she is aware of this "now", in at least a specious present and a core consciousness way, even if she is not conscious of the mathematical present as experiential. In addition, her extended consciousness remembers, anticipates, and imagines where she has just been, where she is now, and where she is going. She can thus incorporate the entire dance in her self-aware consciousness. The performing dancer's trained ability to synchronize her movements with external temporal, spatial, and other parameters as a performing dancer seems to also suggest that the dancer's consciousness can be trained to match extended and external events. Indeed, it is only after numerous attempts to synchronize her movements with external temporal parameters, failing, and noticing the failure of congruence that the dancer becomes better able through practice and trial and error to dance in time. Thus dancing in time in performance introduces a kind of thinking-while-doing that involves acquired and developed aptitudes, sensorimotor skills, kinesthetic awareness, and coordination with external temporal and spatial parameters and persons. It also provides evidence of a phenomenon that might make use of more than one aspect of consciousness.

Note

1 Here Sheets-Johnstone is developing a dance-centered account of consciousness based on the body-first theory of consciousness put forth by Merleau-Ponty 2008 [1945].

References

Andersen, H. (2014) "The development of the 'specious present' and James's views on temporal experience", in V. Arstila and D. Lloyd (eds), *Subjective Time: The Philosophy, Psychology, and Neuroscience of Temporality*, Cambridge, MA: MIT Press, pp. 25–42.

Bläsing, B. (2010) "The dancer's memory", in B. Bläsing, M. Puttke, and T. Schack (eds), *The Neurocognition of Dance: Mind, Movement and Motor Skills*, Hove, UK and New York: Psychology Press, pp. 75–98.

Bläsing, B., Calvino-Merino, B., Cross, E. S., Jola, C., Honisch, J. and Stevens, C. J. (2012) "Neurocognitive control in dance perception and performance", *Acta Psychologica* 139(2): 300–308.

Bresnahan, A. (2014) "Improvisational artistry in live dance performance as embodied and extended agency", *Dance Research Journal* 46(1): 85–94.

Carpenter, W. B. (1874) *Principles of Mental Physiology: With Their Applications to The Training and Discipline of the Mind, and the Study of Its Morbid Conditions*, New York: Appleton.

Dainton, B. (2014) "Temporal consciousness", in *The Stanford Encyclopedia of Philosophy* (Spring Edition), E. N. Zalta (ed.), available at http://plato.stanford.edu/archives/spr2014/entries/consciousness-temporal/. Accessed 1 August 2016.

Damasio, A. (1999) *The Feeling of What Happens: Body and Emotion in the Making of Consciousness*, San Diego, CA: Harcourt, Inc.

Dewey, J. (2008/1925) "Existence, ideas and consciousness", in J. Boydston (ed.), *John Dewey: The Later Works, 1925–1953, Vol. 1: 1925, Experience and Nature*, Carbondale, IL: Southern Illinois University Press, pp. 226–265.

Fraleigh, S. H. (1987) *Dance and the Lived Body: A Descriptive Aesthetics*, Pittsburgh, PA: University of Pittsburgh Press.

Honisch, J. J., Roach, N. and Wing, A. M. (2009) "Movement synchronization in a virtual dancer: How do expert dancers adjust to perceived temporal and spatial changes whilst performing ballet versus abstract dance sequences?" *Paper presented at the ISSP 12th World Congress of Sport Psychology.*

James, W. (1950 [1890a]) *The Principles of Psychology, Vol. I, Authorized Edition*, New York: Dover Publications.

James, W. (1950 [1890b]) *The Principles of Psychology, Vol. II, Authorized Edition*, New York: Dover Publications.

Johnson, M. (2006) "Mind incarnate: From Dewey to Damasio", *Daedalus* 135(3): 46–54.

Merleau-Ponty, M. (2008/1945) *The Phenomenology of Perception*, London and New York: Routledge.

Merritt, M. (2015) "Thinking-*is*-moving: Dance, agency, and a radically enactive mind", *Phenomenology and Cognitive Science* 14(1): 95–110.

Montero, B. (2016) *Thought In Action: Expertise and the Conscious Mind*, Oxford, UK: Oxford University Press.

Peirce, C. S. (1998/1892) "Man's glassy essence", in M. R. Cohen (ed.), *Chance, Love and Logic: Philosophical Essays*, Lincoln, NE: University of Nebraska Press, pp. 238–266.

Phillips, I. (2014) "Experience of and in time", *Philosophy Compass* 9(2): 131–144.

Sheets-Johnstone, M. (1981) "Thinking in movement", *The Journal of Aesthetics and Art Criticism* 39(4): 399–407. (A substantively expanded version of this paper also appears in chapter 12 of Sheets-Johnstone, 2011.)

Sheets-Johnstone, M. (2011) *The Primacy of Movement, Expanded Second Edition*, Amsterdam: Johns Benjamin Publishing Company.

Stevens, C., Ginsborg, J. and Lester, G. (2011) "Backwards and forwards in space and time: Recalling dance movement from long-term memory", *Memory Studies* 4(2): 234–250.

Stevens, C., Schubert, E., Wang, S., Kroos, C. and Halovic, S. (2009) "Moving with and without music: Scaling and lapsing in time in the performance of contemporary dance", *Music Perception* 26(5): 451–464.

Sudnow, D. (1979) *Talk's Body: A Meditation Between Two Keyboards*, New York: Alfred A. Knopf.

Sudnow, D. (2002) *Ways of the Hand: A Re-written Account*, Cambridge, MA: MIT Press.

Washburn, A., DeMarco, M., De Vries, S., Ariyabuddhiphongs, K., Schmidt, R. C., Richardson, M. J. and Riley, M. A. (2014) "Dancers entrain more effectively than non-dancers to another actor's movements", *Frontiers in Human Neuroscience* 8(800): 1–14.

Wittmann, M. (2011) "Moments in time", *Frontiers in Integrative Neuroscience* 5(66): 1–8, available at http://www.ncbi.nlm.nih.gov/pmc/articles/PMC3196211/. Accessed 6 August 2016.

Wittmann, M. (2014) "Embodied time: The experience of time, the body, and the self", in V. Arstila and D. Lloyd (eds), *Subjective Time: The Philosophy, Psychology, and Neuroscience of Temporality*, Cambridge, MA: MIT Press, pp. 507–524.

27

MUSIC AND TIME

Andrew Kania

In a survey of discussions of the idea, Philip Alperson (1980) compellingly argues that there is no coherent account of a metaphysically distinctive *musical time*. Music takes place in "ordinary" time, and our experience of it is ordinary temporal experience. Alperson argues that music is nonetheless distinctively an "art of time" in that it exploits and thereby draws attention to certain aspects of (ordinary) temporal experience. It is no coincidence then, Alperson suggests, that philosophers have often drawn on musical experience in order to make points about the nature of temporal experience in general. In this chapter, I survey some temporal features of music and the debates about the nature and value of musical experience that they have engendered. I restrict myself to consideration of Western music because it is the music with which I am most familiar and on which most of the literature I discuss is focused.

The definition of music

In the course of constructing a definition of music, Jerrold Levinson claims that "music as we conceive it seems as essentially an art of time as it is an art of sound" (1990: 273). His aim is to exclude from the realm of music, on grounds of intuitive adequacy, "colorful instantaneous combinations of sounds – i.e., chords of vanishingly brief duration" (1990: 273). Given Levinson's own gloss here, together with the reasonable assumption that the notion of a literally instantaneous sound is incoherent, it seems charitable to take the sonic events in question as extremely short, though not of any particular duration. Such sounds are surely far from being paradigms of music for anyone. Yet there are actual candidates for the status of music that arguably violate the necessary condition that Levinson proposes on the basis of such considerations, namely that for sounds to count as music they must be "temporally organized" or developed (1990: 273). And these candidates vary significantly in length. One is La Monte Young's *Composition 1960 #7*, which consists of a single open fifth "to be held for a long time" on the piano. It might be argued that there is temporal development in this piece, since one point of interest is how the inevitably "impure" sound changes over time, as a result of the decay of, and interference between, the sound waves produced by the various strings of the piano responsible for producing the two tones. But there are other pieces where such development is minimized, whether through the use of electronic sound sources or ensemble effects. For instance,

Yves Klein's *Monotone-Silence Symphony* (*c.*1957) consists of a D-major chord played by a chamber instrumental and vocal ensemble for 5 to 7 minutes (followed by 44 seconds of silence).

A different way to try to bring such pieces into the fold of music might begin with the fact that they are not even close to instantaneous, unlike the examples of near-music Levinson gives. Perhaps their mere duration – a significant feature of such minimalist works – could be argued to meet the temporal-organization condition. However, this would put the defender of the condition in an awkward position. If a chord held for five minutes counts as music, but a "vanishingly brief" chord does not, what is the minimum duration of a piece of music? Any answer specifying a particular length will be unacceptably arbitrary. One could appeal to audibility as the criterion, but only at the expense of classifying as music the examples that motivate Levinson in the first place. Besides, finally, there are extremely brief candidate musical performances. On 16 July 2007, for instance, the White Stripes played a show in St. John's, Newfoundland, comprising a single note on the guitar and a cymbal crash (both stopped short). The band ostensibly took this to be a musical performance, since guitarist Jack White immediately announced that they had now performed in every province and territory in Canada.

A more likely strategy for anyone convinced of the necessity of temporal organization for music would surely be to *reject* these candidates for musical status on the grounds that they fail to meet the condition. Presumably what Levinson had in mind by "temporal organization" or "development" was, at the very least, two temporally distinct musical events, such as two notes or chords, constituting temporal parts of a larger musical whole. (If this is right, then the length of the events in question turns out to be a red herring.) Levinson is surely right that pieces violating this condition are non-paradigmatic at best, and perhaps borderline cases of music. This might suggest, however, that an adequate definition of music should not definitively rule them out, but rather explain why they are borderline cases (McKeown-Green 2014). One way to do so would be to give a definition (or other kind of account) of music that appeals to "basic musical features" (Kania 2011a) or "salient features" of paradigmatic instances of music (Hamilton 2007: 46–59), without making any individual such feature necessary. Both Andrew Kania and Andy Hamilton give a prominent place to *rhythm*, the most obviously temporal such feature, in their respective accounts, in addition to other candidates such as melody, harmony, and tonality. Kania suggests that music is: "(1) any event intentionally produced or organized (2) to be heard, and (3) *either* (a) to have some basic musical feature, such as pitch or rhythm, *or* (b) to be listened to for such features" (2011a: 12).

As the phrasing of the definition suggests, Kania does not commit himself to a particular set of basic musical features, but he clearly takes pitch and rhythm to be promising candidates. Unfortunately, he says very little about the nature of rhythm, doing little more than gesturing towards a distinction between the rhythms of language and musical rhythm, characterizing the latter in terms of "division into stricter units of time, such as . . . measures of two or three beats" (2011a: 8). Stephen Davies points out that this will not do in the context of Kania's definition, since, on the one hand, Morse code will now count as music and, on the other, music "in free rhythm" may fail to qualify (2012: 538). At the very least, it is clear that more would have to be said about the nature of musical rhythm to defend Kania's approach. Anyway, although rhythm is not a necessary condition of music for Kania, the disjunctive nature of his definition fails to account for the borderline nature of the kinds of cases that concern Levinson. If a vanishingly brief sonic event is pitched (and meets all of Kania's other proposed necessary conditions), it will be as fully fledged an example of music as a Beethoven symphony.

Hamilton's approach, by contrast, is less vulnerable to the kinds of criticisms McKeown-Green and Davies raise against Kania's definition, since Hamilton denies that concepts of cultural products, such as music, can be defined in terms of necessary and sufficient conditions.

He argues that the best we can hope for is a list of salient features of paradigms of music. However, the list he defends does not include rhythm, but only sound, intentionality, the disposition to elicit aesthetic experience, and tonal organization. Since Hamilton makes a distinction between music and non-musical sound art, *tonal organization* is clearly the distinctively musical feature on this list. (All other arts are intentionally designed to elicit aesthetic experiences, according to Hamilton.) But Hamilton also claims that "rhythm is essential" to music as well as poetry and dance (2007: 119), "the one indispensable element of all music" (2007: 122), and that "music could be defined as *the rhythmicization of sound*" (2007: 121). The most charitable way to understand this, it seems to me, is to consider rhythm, broadly construed, not a necessary feature of all music, as Hamilton claims here, but rather one of the "salient features" of paradigm instances of music, on a par with tonal organization in his account. On this account, the cases Levinson is concerned about are on the border of the concept of music because although they possess many of the salient features of paradigm instances of music, they lack one, namely rhythm.

Rhythm

So what is musical rhythm? We can begin with the idea that, in a broad sense, rhythm is the temporal organization of music – the timing and duration of musical events. But we will immediately want to distinguish between objective and subjective, or descriptive and phenomenological, construals of this idea. Consider, for instance, this musical "duck–rabbit" effect: One can hear the opening of the second movement of Saint-Saëns's Organ Symphony in two different ways, as beginning on an upbeat (as notated by the composer) or on a downbeat (see Figure 27.1). These are two quite different rhythmic experiences of one and the same musical passage (cf. Scruton 1983: 88–89). We can say that this music is rhythmically ambiguous, but there will be no way of explaining what that means without appealing to the phenomenology of our experiences of it. Thus, the concept of rhythm central to musical experience is essentially phenomenological or response-dependent. (It is also worth noting that there are at least two objective or descriptive concepts of rhythm. We can describe the music as conceived or notated (e.g., four sixteenth notes followed by an eighth note, etc.) or in all its sonic detail, which will not have the clean precision of its notation.)

This example illustrates a further notable feature of rhythm: though it seems right to think of rhythm as primarily a *temporal* feature, the perceived *organization* essential to rhythm is not exclusively a matter of purely temporal features. For to hear the theme in one of the two ways is not to hear any of the notes as occurring at different points in time or as longer or shorter than in the other way of hearing it, nor to hear a different periodicity in the temporal organization; it is to hear the notes as *grouped* differently, to hear the "period" or group as beginning at one point or another in the musical manifold. And such grouping is often heavily influenced, if not determined, by non-temporal features. Perhaps most obviously, merely by *accenting* every third note (e.g., playing it more loudly), we can "group" a string of otherwise identical notes into threes beginning with the accented note. But tonal (harmonic or melodic) features also give rise to such grouping phenomena, as when the harmony begins to change at a rate at odds with the

Figure 27.1　Saint-Saëns, Symphony No. 3, second movement, mm. 1–3: (a) as written, (b) an alternative way of hearing the passage

Figure 27.2   Bach, "Jesu, Joy of Man's Desiring." A well-established meter of three groups of three notes is disrupted (in the second measure of this excerpt) by a repeated melodic shape with a periodicity of two groups of three notes (indicated by the square brackets), reinforced by harmonic change with the same periodicity. The original meter is restored with the return of the main theme (in the last measure of this excerpt)

meter established up to that point (see Figure 27.2). Our sensitivity to such cues for grouping musical events is somewhat ironically illustrated by our tendency to group temporal stimuli even in the absence of any differentiating features. That is, when played an identical series of tones at identical temporal (isochronous) intervals, people will hear them as grouped into twos or threes (see the references at London 2004: 14–15).

Most theorists have found a distinction between *rhythm* and *meter* to be essential for investigating such temporal musical phenomena (London n.d.: §I.1). Rhythm, in this narrower sense, is the temporal structure and patterning of the musical surface – the perceptible temporal properties of and relationships between various musical events – while meter is a more abstract hierarchical structure that emerges in our perception of the musical surface, allowing us to make sense of the rhythm (and other musical features) by, say, anticipating when certain musical events will occur. For instance, in the Saint-Saëns example given above, the rhythmic "feel" of the passage is quite different when heard in the two different ways (meters) mentioned. If the repeated tonic Cs are heard as falling on the downbeat (the first beat of the perceived measure), the melody has a heavier, more foursquare character, while if the Ds and G – elements of the dominant harmony – are heard as falling on the downbeat, the melody is more forward-driven and less stable. We might speculate that the accents marked by Saint-Saëns are intended in part to promote hearing the melody in this second way.

It is not possible to have music with meter but no rhythm; the generation of meter requires *some* temporally distributed musical events, even if those events boringly occur with metronomic regularity on metrical beats. But it is possible to have music with rhythm but no meter, since the temporal intervals between the musical events may be such that no pulse can be heard in them. Justin London (2004: 24) gives an example from the opening of Milton Babbitt's *Composition for 12 Instruments* where, even though the music is *notated* with metrical precision, the meter that is notated cannot be heard by a listener unfamiliar with the score (even if very familiar with avant-garde Western music). One might ask whether this is the relevant listener, however. London acknowledges that the performers must keep track of a consistent quarter-note pulse and the changing time signatures in the score in order to perform the work accurately. Couldn't such a performer hear the meter in another group's performance of the piece? This question raises a fundamental issue about musical understanding, which I consider briefly below. But the point of the example for London is that metrical notation does not necessarily imply the existence of meter. A simpler example of music with rhythm but no meter would be an avant-garde work consisting entirely of a few notes spread so far apart in time that they are beyond the human capacity for perceiving a pulse.

Philosophers of music have disagreed about what is minimally required to account for our experience of rhythm and meter. Roger Scruton has argued that the experience of rhythm, like the experience of melody and harmony, is necessarily a form of *imaginative* perception. In earlier work, he describes the experience as "metaphorical" in that it involves the application to the sounds we hear of concepts that we know do not literally apply to them. In the case of rhythm, these concepts are concepts of *action*, particularly dance:

> In hearing rhythm we hear the music as *active*; it seems to be doing something (namely, dancing) which no sounds can do. . . . We hear sounds joining to and diverging from each other. . . . At the same time, we do not believe that any such thing is happening in the realm of sound.
>
> *(1983: 90)*

Malcolm Budd takes issue with this account for three reasons (1985: 239–245). First, it is circular, since the relevant metaphorical concept of *dancing* cannot be understood without the concept of rhythm (or meter). Second, the crucial notion of an experience itself, as opposed to a description of it, being *metaphorical* stands in need of explanation. (For a summary of recent moves in this debate, see Kania 2015: 158–161.) Third, Budd claims that an account of rhythm can be given without appeal to any concepts that fail to apply literally to the musical sounds:

> [t]he experience of rhythm in a sequence of sounds and rests . . . (i) . . . does not require that the sounds should be heard as differing in pitch, timbre, duration or loudness, and (ii) the sequence must be heard as grouped into units in which one element is heard as accented (prominent, salient) relative to the others.
>
> *(1985: 243)*

Andy Hamilton agrees with Budd that Scruton's appeal to metaphorical experience is obscure, but he agrees with Scruton that reference to movement is ineliminable from an account of rhythm. Hamilton argues that physical spatial movement is not the only paradigm of motion; other temporal processes, such as the rise and fall of the price of fish, are literally described in terms of motion (2007: 142–148). (Stephen Davies makes a similar argument about pitch space and melodic motion (2011: 27–30).) But Hamilton makes the stronger claim that the movement essential to rhythm is *bodily* movement in some sense; where Scruton sees spatial concepts applied to non-spatial sonic phenomena, Hamilton sees bodily movement manifested in different ways – in musical sounds, dancing, marching, and some physical work. (He gives the example of the rhythmic pounding of rice in Bali.) Hamilton's point that rhythm and meter are not exclusive to musical experience is plausible. But it is not clear what the "manifestation" of bodily motion in music amounts to. One possibility is the strong view espoused by Tiger Roholt in a recent book on musical *grooves* (Roholt 2014). A groove (or at least its "objective" aspect) is a repeated rhythmic nuance, such as playing the third ("back") beat of a 4/4 rock drum pattern slightly early or late. Following the work of Diana Raffman (1993), Roholt argues that though we can perceive these temporal nuances, we cannot develop distinct concepts for all the nuances we can perceive, any more than we can develop concepts for every color difference we can perceive. Hence we appeal to metaphors, among other resources, to refer to these nuances, describing the groove with an early backbeat as "driving" and the one with a late backbeat as "laid back". But, drawing on Merleau-Ponty's theory of perception (1962, among other work), Roholt argues that one can only successfully employ such metaphors, since one can only perceive the groove, if one moves one's body in sympathy with the temporal nuances. In short, "the feel of a groove is the affective dimension of the relevant motor-intentional movements" (Roholt 2014: 105, italics removed). There seems to be no reason why we could not extend Roholt's theory to other rhythmic aspects of music.

Ordinary experience and empirical research suggest that this view is implausibly strong, however. Though actual bodily movement may be essential for acquiring the ability to perceive grooves (and other rhythmic features), once that ability is established we are able to perceive a groove while engaging in bodily activities that preclude moving in sympathy with it (e.g., operating machinery or sitting in a concert hall) or while unable to move at all (e.g., while being restrained or undergoing some form of paralysis). Justin London points to research that suggests motor representations, if not actual bodily movements, are essential to the perception of such rhythmic features (2016: 102–103). This may be the most plausible way for theorists such as Hamilton to argue that bodily movement is essential to rhythm.

Musical works, performances and recordings

I have thus far discussed ways in which temporal experience is fundamental to music considered as an artistic medium or material. But when we experience this medium or material, it is usually parceled out in the form of works, performances, or recordings. I now turn to ways in which our temporal experience of these items gives rise to philosophical questions.

Jerrold Levinson and Philip Alperson (1991) discuss 14 distinct senses in which an art could be considered a "temporal" art, which they classify into object-, experience-, and content-based senses. For instance, novels are not temporal in one object-based sense, while dance performances are, since an entire novel is present simultaneously, while a dance performance, being an event, is stretched out over a period of time, with only one temporal slice available at any given moment. Both novels and dance performances, however, are temporal in the experience-based sense that their elements must be appreciated in a particular order over a period of time. As for the content-based senses, there is at least one according to which different novels will be more or less *about* time or temporal experience; Proust's *À la recherche du temps perdu* (*In Search of Lost Time*) is an obvious example at one end of the spectrum, while at the other are the many novels that do not take time as a theme at all. Levinson and Alperson point out, however, that certain features of some media automatically make time or temporal experience part of the content of works in those media. For instance, the temporal distinction between the process of narration and the events narrated makes time part of the content of all narrative works, albeit in a recessive way in many cases. To the extent that music is essentially temporal due to the centrality of rhythm, it too will be a temporal art in this content-based sense.

When Levinson and Alperson discuss music, they typically discuss musical *performances*. They point out that, like other artistic performances, musical performances must be presented over a period of time (as opposed to, say, paintings), and their temporal parts must be appreciated over that same time period, in the order in which they are presented. But often when one attends a musical performance, one apparently hears not just that performance, but a musical work which the performance is a performance *of*. There has been much discussion of the ontology of musical works. For instance, one popular theory has been that musical works are abstract objects, with performances their instantiations. (Levinson 1980 is the *locus classicus*.) But if Beethoven's First Symphony is an abstract object, how can it be true that it begins with a slow introduction? Abstracta are traditionally taken to exist "outside time", and nothing outside time can have a temporal property such as slowness (let alone begin or end). Serious consideration of such matters would take us too far afield. (For an introduction to the issues and literature, see Matheson and Caplan 2011 and D. Davies 2011: 23–70.) But whatever view we take of the fundamental ontology of musical works and their relationships to performance, there are "higher-order" questions about these things that seem to be independent of those answers. For instance, though any given performance will have completely determinate temporal properties, is a particular tempo – the pace at which a performance proceeds – an essential part of a musical work?

Considering typical works of classical music, there seem to be sensible "yes" and "no" answers to this question. No *precise* tempo is essential to a given work; part of the value of works for performance is their potential for performative interpretation. One cellist may take the Prelude to Bach's first unaccompanied cello suite to be a melancholy meditation while another plays it as a dance. On the other hand, not just anything goes. To choose a tempo that would make the Prelude last for two hours would seem to be to engage in a conceptual- or performance-art event, rather than a performance of Bach's work. However, some have questioned these sensible answers.

On the one hand, Nelson Goodman argues that a musical score "has as a primary function the authoritative identification of a work from performance to performance" (1976: 128). This implies, according to Goodman, that a score must be a "character in a notational system", a technical notion with very strict requirements. Because verbal tempo indications such as "allegro" or "slow" do not meet these requirements (in short, they are not precise enough), they cannot be part of a score nor thus constitutive of a work: "No departure from the indicated tempo disqualifies a performance as an instance – however wretched – of the work defined by the score" (1976: 185). Goodman does allow that metronome markings could count as work-determinative, but this would require conditions that would strike the typical musician or listener as bizarre. (For instance, some deviation from an indication of 100 quarter-notes per minute would be allowed, but only if the range of deviation did not admit an overlap with that of another potential tempo marking, e.g., 96 quarter-notes per minute.) Goodman is explicit about his reasons for positing such an unintuitive theory: "I [am not] quibbling about the proper use of such words as 'notation,' 'score,' and 'work.' That matters little more than the proper use of a fork. What does matter is that [a score should provide a] means of identifying a work from performance to performance" (1976: 189). However, most philosophers of music have rejected his theory nonetheless, for reasons similar to what David Davies calls the "pragmatic constraint" on the ontology of art: "Artworks must be entities that can bear the sorts of properties rightly ascribed to what are termed 'works' in our reflective critical and appreciative practice" (2004: 18). There will, of course, be debate about what sorts of properties are *rightly* ascribed to works *upon reflection* on our musical practices, but Goodman's theory seems so clearly to violate the pragmatic constraint that it could be said "to change the subject, rather than answer the questions that motivate philosophical aesthetics" (D. Davies 2004: 21).

On the other hand, some proponents and opponents of "authentic performance practice" have taken the notion of an authentic performance of a musical work to amount to the replication of a particular (actual or ideal) performance of the work. (For a recent survey of the debate, see Thom 2011.) If this were the case, musical works, like performances, would have wholly determinate tempi (along with many other properties such as timbre, rhythm, dynamics, etc.). There would still be various performances of the work that differed with respect to tempo and other features, but to the extent that these performances departed from the ideal, they would be defective instances of the work. Though the value of authentic performance is still debated (e.g. Dodd 2015 and S. Davies 2013), the notion of authenticity as replication of a single, wholly determinate, ideal performance has been widely rejected in favor of the view that the work comprises those properties mandated by the composer. There is still some disagreement about which properties these include, but not about the fact that in many cases what is mandated admits to a range of possibilities, nor about the idea that such mandates can be implicit, as, for example, with tempi of baroque works. The essential argument for the inclusion of tempo as a constitutive property of musical works is that the perception of many other features of the work depends upon it (S. Davies 2001: 59). If an absurdly glacial tempo is adopted, audiences will be unable to perceive rhythmic, melodic, expressive, and even harmonic and structural features that are essential to the work. In many cases, even timbral properties will be affected, due to physical limitations on the production of sound (e.g., the lung capacity of wind players or the length of a violin bow).

There are two quite common kinds of music-making that do not seem to fit the "classical paradigm" (D. Davies 2011: 23 *et passim*), in that they do not obviously result in instances of works for performance, and thereby offer no distinction between the particular, specific temporal properties of the musical event one experiences directly and the "determinable" temporal properties of the work the performance is of. One is musical improvisation, the other the creation of a musical "work for playback" (S. Davies 2001: 25). Improvisation is commonly understood to be the spontaneous creation of music as it is being performed. This gloss requires some clarification since, in one reasonable sense, even a very mechanical performer of a piano sonata, say, is creating the musical event of his performance *as he performs*, i.e., spontaneously. The difference between his case and that of the improviser is that the work-performer has made all the decisions about what he will (attempt to) do in his performance before the performance begins – perhaps far in advance of it. This is a simplification of actual musical practice, however. On the one hand, the work-performer may make interpretive decisions on the spot, without thereby ceasing to perform the work. These will range in significance, from the decision to emphasize one note a little more, through ornamenting a baroque melody in different ways, to an ensemble of various such choices amounting to a radically different interpretation from performance to performance. As long as the performer delivers everything essential to the work, he can improvise everything else. On the other hand, the instrumental jazz performer, widely taken to be the paradigmatic improviser by philosophers of music, almost invariably takes a preexisting musical structure (often a "standard") as the basis or framework for her performance. This has led some to argue that the primary concept here is that of improvis*ing*, or improvisation in the mass-noun sense, and that there is no clear criterion for an entire performance, or section thereof, being *an* improvisation, as opposed to a work-performance (Kania 2011b: 396). But others have argued that such a criterion can be found in the overarching attitude the musician takes to the preexisting materials she draws on in her performance (e.g. S. Davies 2001: 16–17). Even if this correct, it is not obvious that we should think of the categories of improvisation and work-performance as mutually exclusive, since some works (e.g. jazz "heads") are composed explicitly for use as the basis of improvisations (D. Davies 2011: 157).

Many have argued that much of the value of an improvisation depends on our appreciation of its being a creative musical action (Alperson 1984; Brown 1996; Hamilton 2000). When we attend to an improvisation, we perceive musical decisions being made, rather than simply the results of those decisions. These theorists have thus seen improvisation as resisting a general deep-seated tendency in artistic practice and art theory to valorize persisting entities as opposed to ephemeral events – what Lee B. Brown calls the "principle of continuity" (1996) – which we might see as an instance of the ancient dispute between Parmenidean theorists of being and Hericlitean theorists of becoming. Andy Hamilton (2000), for instance, argues that the classical practice of creating musical works for performance and then stable, repeatable interpretations of them, reflect an "aesthetics of perfection", while most jazz practice, with its emphasis on improvisation, reflects an "aesthetics of imperfection" – the missteps and stumbles in a jazz solo signifying in part the authentic spontaneity of the music-making. (Hamilton acknowledges that things are not as simple as this suggests, no practice being a pure instance of either aesthetic.)

It may be true that improvisations collapse the temporal properties of work and performance, but the way that most improvisations – indeed most *music* – is now experienced introduces a further temporal distinction, that between (i) the time at (and during) which the musical sounds are made and (ii) the time at (and during) which they are experienced. Since most people around the world now listen to music primarily as recordings, they do not experience the music as it is being created, whether they are listening to a free improvisation or a meticulously rehearsed work-performance. One might resist this claim by arguing that there is one important sense in which we *do* hear recorded music as it is being created: Since recordings are mechanical, in the sense that what we hear is unmediated by anyone's beliefs or other intentional states, they are *transparent*, in the sense in which Kendall Walton argues that photographs are transparent. We literally, if indirectly, hear the musicians performing when we listen to a recording, just as we literally, if indirectly, see someone through a photograph (Walton 1984; Kania 2009). This is not to deny the temporal difference between the creation and the experience of the music, but it might be thought to transform it from a shortcoming to a benefit. Recording technology temporally shears the experience of the music from its creation, but in doing so, it enables a much wider audience to hear that music (Gracyk 1997). If recordings are transparent in this sense, they allow us to "hear into" the past, just as photographs allow us to see into the past on Walton's view. It is worth noting that this sense of transparency is independent of notions of accuracy or clarity, with which some may have confused it (e.g., Hamilton 2003; Glasgow 2007). One hears Pablo Casals on recordings, if the transparency thesis is true, in the same way that one sees a friend in a fun-house mirror: One has an auditory experience as of Casals playing the cello (the recording must bear some minimal sonic resemblance to its source) that is mechanically counterfactually dependent on the sounds he produced when the recording was made, even if no one would confuse the experience of hearing the recording with the experience of hearing Casals play live. M. G. F. Martin (2012) has recently defended a variation on this claim. He argues that sounds are abstract particulars and thus that when we hear a Casals recording, we hear the very sounds Casals made; they are quite literally reproduced when the recording is played back. However, though this puts us in causal contact with Casals's original production of these sounds, Martin does not think that in hearing the reproduced sounds we thus hear Casals playing his cello.

I noted above that improvisation is one kind of music-making that collapses the distinction between the specific temporal properties of the musical event one experiences directly and the determinable temporal properties of a work for performance. The other is the creation of works for playback, that is, works the instances of which are generated mechanically from some sort of template (S. Davies 2001: 25). Recordings are by far the most common kind of such template, though there are many others, e.g., player-piano rolls. Defenders of the notion of works for playback do not claim that all musical recordings (or other musical templates) are works for playback. Rather, they argue that not all musical recordings are the same kind of artistic entity. In particular, not all recordings are works in their own right. Such claims depend on a conception of a work of art as something like a primary focus of critical attention in an artistic practice (e.g., Gracyk 1996; S. Davies 2001; D. Davies 2004). "Live recordings" of classical works for performance, for instance, are certainly targets of critical attention in the classical music world, but they are of interest mostly as vehicles for delivering instances of those works; they are not works in their own right. Then there is the messy middle ground of recordings that largely comprise chunks of recorded performance, but edited in ways that give people pause when considering their status. Aron Edidin suggests that in the world of classical music, at least, many of these recordings belong to a new category he calls "recordings of compositions" (Edidin 1999: 30–36). Works for playback are unlike either of these kinds of recording in that they are not presented as proxies for live performances in any way; their soundscapes are to be appreciated in their own right. The clearest examples are works of "electronic music" in the classical tradition.

Works for playback may be constructed entirely electronically, rather than by "recording" any actual sounds. But this is not essential; works for playback may incorporate recorded sounds. Theodore Gracyk (1996) has influentially argued that rock music, broadly construed, is a tradition of works for playback in this sense. Thus, when one hears a rock recording one does not hear a recording of a performance of a song, in the sense in which one hears a performance of a Schubert song when listening to a classical recording. While singing and the playing of musical instruments often contribute to the construction of a rock track, and a song, in the sense of a "thin" musical structure, is manifested in the result, that result is an ontologically "thick" work for playback, replete with sonic properties. ("Thinness" and "thickness" in this sense are matters of the relative number of properties necessary for a proper instance of something (S. Davies 2001).) One cannot hear a different performance of such a rock work, since it is for playback rather than performance, though there could be a different such work that manifests the same song (i.e., a cover version), just as one cannot experience a different performance of a film, though one might see a remake, i.e., a different film that shares significant features with the "original" (Kania 2006: 408–409). If Gracyk is right, then when you listen to a rock track, you experience the same detailed temporal (and other) properties of the work as anyone else who listens to that work, unlike the case of the audience member for a live performance of a work of classical music, say.

Musical understanding

Formalism – the view that understanding a musical work is primarily a matter of grasping relations between its far-flung parts – has dominated the study of "pure" musical works in the Western tradition for over a century. One puzzle the view raises is that, since performances of such works take place over an extended period of time, it is not obvious that we can *hear* such relations, as opposed to a succession of relata – whatever constituent chords and melodies, say, can be grasped in the "specious present". An extreme formalist might respond that this is only a puzzle if one assumes that music is not only a sonic but also an aural art; perhaps music is properly appreciated not by being listened to, but rather by being thought about. No one seems to have actually defended such a position, however, since, at the very least, everyone agrees that the character of the elements of a musical work – the melodies, rhythms, etc. – must be appreciated at least in part on the basis of their aural appearance (Hamilton 2007: 66–94). But Jerrold Levinson has argued that large-scale formal properties of musical works have been grossly over-valued by music theorists, and that the lion's share of musical understanding, and thereby of the enjoyment and value of music, resides in our experience of "apprehending individual bits of music and immediate progressions from bit to bit" (Levinson 1997: 13). The upshot of the debate over Levinson's theory seems to have been what he intended: a corrective to philosophers' (and perhaps some musicologists') overemphasis on the importance of formalism in theories of musical experience and value (Kania 2007: §4; Huovinen 2011). Since even Levinson does not deny the relevance of large-scale structural relationships to a *complete* understanding of many musical works, any stance on this issue requires some explanation of what it is to "perceive" such relationships. Pursuing this question would involve grappling with quite general issues in the philosophy of temporal experience; I thus direct readers to other chapters in this volume. However, it is worth noting that a theory of *any* art will face a similar problem. Understanding any complex artwork requires not simply perception of its appearance but also reflection on the nature of that experience – reflection informed by "background" knowledge of the work. Though a painting is atemporal in the sense that it is entirely before one as one appreciates it, for any complex painting, one cannot appreciate all of its artistically and aesthetically relevant features at once. Temporal arts such as music and film, and even those temporal only in their experience, such as novels, merely throw this issue into sharper relief.

The value of music

In what ways does the temporal experience of music contribute to its value? Levinson and Alperson provide an argument schema they find fleshed out in different ways by a succession of philosophers from Hegel to Susanne Langer:

> (1) Identify some temporal aspect of music as the core of musical experience or significance. (2) Argue that no other art exhibits this temporal feature as purely or prominently as music. (3) Argue that this aspect of temporality is intimately associated with consciousness. (4) Argue that music, the most temporal of the arts, is therefore best suited to the expression of consciousness. (5) Advance an expression theory of art. (6) Conclude that music, in virtue of its being the most temporal of the arts, is the purest or highest form of art.
>
> *(Levinson and Alperson 1991: 448)*

It would be fair to characterize each of these premises as highly controversial and thus the prospects of defending the conclusion dim. In the end, it may be that the best we can hope for is a kind of piecemeal theory in which we account for the various values of metrical complexity, improvisation, and so on. And while some of these aspects of music may foreground the temporality of musical experience, it is likely that others will not.

References

Alperson, P. (1980) "'Musical time' and music as an 'art of time'", *Journal of Aesthetics and Art Criticism* 38: 407–418.

Alperson, P. (1984) "On musical improvisation", *Journal of Aesthetics and Art Criticism* 43: 17–29.

Brown, L. B. (1996) "Musical works, improvisation, and the principle of continuity", *Journal of Aesthetics and Art Criticism* 54(4): 353–369.

Budd, M. (1985) "Understanding music", *Proceedings of the Aristotelian Society*, supp. vol. 59: 233–248.

Davies, D. (2004) *Art as Performance*, Malden, MA: Blackwell.

Davies, D. (2011) *Philosophy of the Performing Arts*, Malden, MA: Wiley-Blackwell.

Davies, S. (2001) *Musical Works and Performances: A Philosophical Exploration*, Oxford, UK: Clarendon Press.

Davies, S. (2011) "Music and metaphor", in S. Davies (ed.), *Musical Understandings*, Oxford, UK: Oxford University Press), pp. 21–33.

Davies, S. (2012) "On defining music", *The Monist* 95(4): 535–555.

Davies, S. (2013) "Performing musical works authentically: A response to Dodd", *British Journal of Aesthetics* 53(1): 71–75.

Dodd, J. (2015) "Performing works of music authentically", *European Journal of Philosophy* 23(3): 485–508.

Edidin, A. (1999) "Three kinds of recording and the metaphysics of music", *British Journal of Aesthetics* 39(1): 24–39.

Glasgow, J. (2007) "Hi-fi aesthetics", *Journal of Aesthetics and Art Criticism* 65(2): 163–174.

Goodman, N. (1976) *Languages of Art: An Approach to a Theory of Symbols*, 2nd ed., Indianapolis, IN: Hackett.

Gracyk, T. (1996) *Rhythm and Noise: An Aesthetics of Rock*, Durham, NC: Duke University Press.

Gracyk, T. (1997) "Listening to music: Performances and recordings", *Journal of Aesthetics and Art Criticism* 55: 139–150.

Hamilton, A. (2000) "The art of improvisation and the aesthetics of imperfection", *British Journal of Aesthetics* 40(1): 168–185.

Hamilton, A. (2003) "The art of recording and the aesthetics of perfection", *British Journal of Aesthetics* 43(4): 345–362.

Hamilton, A. (2007) *Aesthetics and Music*, New York: Continuum.

Huovinen, E. (2011) "Understanding music", in T. Gracyk and A. Kania (eds), *The Routledge Companion to Philosophy and Music*, New York: Routledge, pp. 123–133.

Kania, A. (2006) "Making tracks: The ontology of rock music", *Journal of Aesthetics and Art Criticism* 64(4): 401–14.

Kania, A. (2007) "The philosophy of music", in E. N. Zalta (ed.), *The Stanford Encyclopedia of Philosophy*, winter 2007 edition, available at http://plato.stanford.edu/archives/win2007/entries/music/ (accessed 5 July 2016).

Kania, A. (2009) "Musical recordings", *Philosophy Compass* 4(1): 22–38.

Kania, A. (2011a) "Definition", in T. Gracyk and A. Kania (eds), *The Routledge Companion to Philosophy and Music*, New York: Routledge, pp. 3–13.

Kania, A. (2011b) "All play and no work: An ontology of jazz", *Journal of Aesthetics and Art Criticism* 69(4): 391–403.

Kania, A. (2015) "An imaginative theory of musical space and movement", *British Journal of Aesthetics* 55(2): 157–172.

Levinson, J. (1980) "What a musical work is", *Journal of Philosophy* 77(1): 5–28.

Levinson, J. (1990) "The concept of music", in J. Levinson (ed.) *Music, Art, and Metaphysics*, Ithaca, NY: Cornell University Press, pp. 267–278.

Levinson, J. (1997) *Music in the Moment*, Ithaca, NY: Cornell University Press.

Levinson, J. and Alperson, P. (1991) "What is a temporal art?" *Midwest Studies in Philosophy* 16(1): 439–450.

London, J. (n.d.) "Rhythm", in *Grove Music Online*, Oxford University Press, available at http://www.oxfordmusiconline.com/subscriber/article/grove/music/45963 (accessed 5 July 2016).

London, J. (2004) *Hearing in Time: Psychological Aspects of Musical Meter*, Oxford, UK: Oxford University Press.

London, J. (2016) "Review of *Groove* by Tiger Roholt", *Journal of Aesthetics and Art Criticism* 74(1): 101–104.

Martin, M. G. F. (2012) "Sounds and images", *British Journal of Aesthetics* 52(4): 331–351.

Matheson, C. and Caplan, B. (2011) "Ontology", in T. Gracyk and A. Kania (eds), *The Routledge Companion to Philosophy and Music*, New York: Routledge, pp. 38–47.

McKeown-Green, J. (2014) "What is music? Is there a definitive answer?" *Journal of Aesthetics and Art Criticism* 72(4): 393–403.

Merleau-Ponty, M. (1962) *Phenomenology of Perception*, trans. C. Smith, London: Routledge & Kegan Paul.

Raffman, D. (1993) *Language, Music, and Mind*, Cambridge, MA: MIT Press.

Roholt, T. (2014) *Groove: A Phenomenology of Rhythmic Nuance*, New York: Bloomsbury.

Scruton, R. (1983) "Understanding music", in R. Scruton (ed.), *The Aesthetic Understanding: Essays in the Philosophy of Art and Culture*, Manchester: Carcanet Press, pp. 77–100.

Thom, P. (2011) "Authentic performance practice", in T. Gracyk and A. Kania (eds), *The Routledge Companion to Philosophy and Music*, New York: Routledge, pp. 91–100.

Walton, K. L. (1984) "Transparent pictures: On the nature of photographic realism", *Critical Inquiry* 11(2): 246–276.

INDEX